Reading STREET

Grade 2, Unit 1

Exploration

PEARSON
Scott
Foresman

scottforesman.com

Editorial Offices: Glenview, Illinois • Parsippany, New Jersey • New York, New York
Sales Offices: Boston, Massachusetts • Duluth, Georgia • Glenview, Illinois
Coppell, Texas • Sacramento, California • Mesa, Arizon

T59186

We dedicate Reading Street to
Peter Jovanovich.

His wisdom, courage,
and passion for education
are an inspiration to us all.

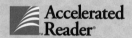

Cover Scott Gustafson

About the Cover Artist
When Scott Gustafson was in grade school, he spent most of his spare time drawing pictures. Now he gets to make pictures for a living. Before he starts a painting, he photographs his family, pets, or friends posing as characters that will appear in the illustration. He then uses the photos to inspire the finished picture.

ISBN-13:   978-0-328-24367-9

ISBN-10:   0-328-24367-1

Copyright © 2008 Pearson Education, Inc.

All Rights Reserved. Printed in the United States of America. This publication is protected by Copyright, and permission should be obtained from the publisher prior to any prohibited reproduction, storage in a retrieval system, or transmission in any form by any means, electronic, mechanical, photocopying, recording, or likewise. For information regarding permission(s), write to: Permissions Department, Scott Foresman, 1900 East Lake Avenue, Glenview, Illinois 60025.

Many of the designations used by manufacturers and sellers to distinguish their products are claimed as trademarks. Where those designations appear in this book, and Scott Foresman was aware of a trademark claim, the designations have been printed with initial capitals and in cases of multiple usage have also been marked with either ® or ™ where they first appear.

8 9 10 V064 16 15 14 13 12 11 10 09

CC: N1

Reading STREET

Where the Love of Reading Begins

There's a moose on the loose.

Where can I go to find just what I need?

You don't have to go far to find the big, lovable, moose-spectacular reading program you crave. You're on *Reading Street,* where the love of reading begins. *Reading Street* provides research-based reading instruction that meets the needs of teachers, students, and administrators. It works perfectly with *Scott Foresman My Sidewalks* and *Reading Street for the Guided Reading Teacher* to answer all your reading needs.

Reading STREET

Where the Love of Reading Begins

Literature for Learning and Thinking

Deepen students' understanding with literature that's organized around themes.

Priority Skills and Success Predictors

Teach the right skills at the right time and monitor students' progress.

Differentiated Instruction for Group Time

Ensure success for students of varying ability levels and experiences.

More Reading Support

Reinforce instruction with intensive reading intervention and leveled text.

When I was little, I'd curl up in bed and wait for a sssssssssssstory.

In ancient Greece, there was a golden fleece.

How do I help every child love to read?

It all starts with a "golden" collection of literature. *Reading Street* has funny stories, scary stories, real-life adventures! One story perfectly leads to the next—one concept is explored from many sides. Children have enough time to think about a big idea, learn, and enjoy.

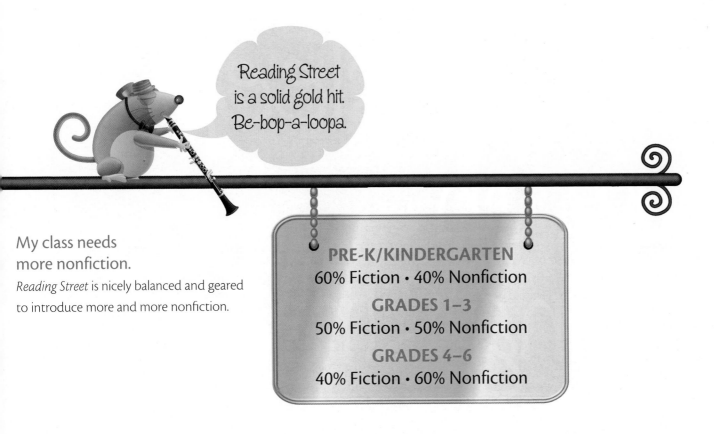

My class needs
more nonfiction.

Reading Street is nicely balanced and geared
to introduce more and more nonfiction.

PRE-K/KINDERGARTEN
60% Fiction • 40% Nonfiction

GRADES 1–3
50% Fiction • 50% Nonfiction

GRADES 4–6
40% Fiction • 60% Nonfiction

How do I get children to
think about what they read?

The literature in *Reading Street* is organized
around unit themes. Each selection
connects and expands the concept
to build deeper understanding.

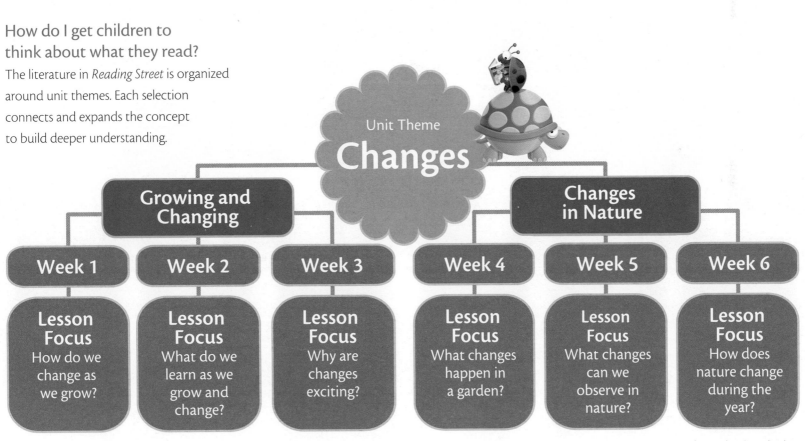

Unit Theme
Changes

Growing and Changing

Changes in Nature

Week 1 — **Week 2** — **Week 3** — **Week 4** — **Week 5** — **Week 6**

Lesson Focus
How do we change as we grow?

Lesson Focus
What do we learn as we grow and change?

Lesson Focus
Why are changes exciting?

Lesson Focus
What changes happen in a garden?

Lesson Focus
What changes can we observe in nature?

Lesson Focus
How does nature change during the year?

Grade 1, Unit 3 Organization

There's never enough time
to cover content areas.

Every selection in *Reading Street* emphasizes
a science or social studies concept.
Your reading lessons become the tools
to meet content-area standards.

Don't lose sleep! You're on Reading Street.

Am I teaching the right skills at the right time?

You'll never have to worry about this question again. *Reading Street* prioritizes skills instruction so you place the correct emphasis on the most important skills at your grade. Built-in progress monitoring helps you zoom ahead or slow down, depending on your students' needs.

Help me prioritize my day!

Reading Street prioritizes the five core areas of reading instruction across the grades, so you know where to place your instructional emphasis. By assessing key predictors, you can ensure student success. (See below.)

PRIORITY SKILL	SUCCESS PREDICTOR
PHONEMIC AWARENESS	Blending and Segmenting
PHONICS	Word Reading
FLUENCY	Words Correct per Minute
VOCABULARY	Word Knowledge
COMPREHENSION	Retelling

Can I predict reading success?

The research says "YES!" Only *Reading Street* helps you monitor students' progress by assessing the research-based predictors of reading success.

Monitor Progress

Check Retelling `Rubric 4 3 2 1`

If... students have difficulty retelling the story,

then... use the Scoring Rubric for Retelling below to help move them toward fluent retelling.

SUCCESS PREDICTOR

I need a data management system.

Success Tracker is an online assessment and data management system that prescribes remediation, helps with grouping, and disaggregates and aggregates data.

Learn more at www.scottforesman.com/tours.

One size never fits all.

How can I make sure every child reads?

One of the most important lessons our teachers taught us was that everyone is unique *and* the same. *Reading Street* provides a daily plan for whole-group teaching and for meeting with small groups to attend to specific needs. Don't you just love it?

We got style, we got class, we got fancy yellow pants.

Reading
STREET

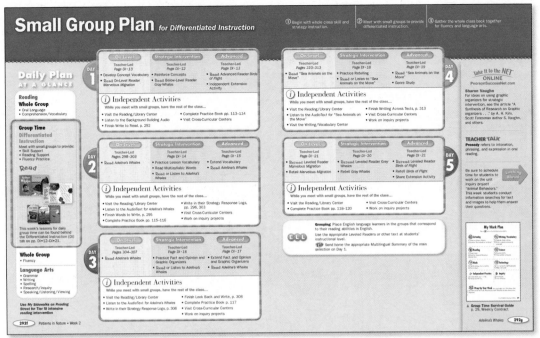

Teacher's Edition Grade 4 Unit 3

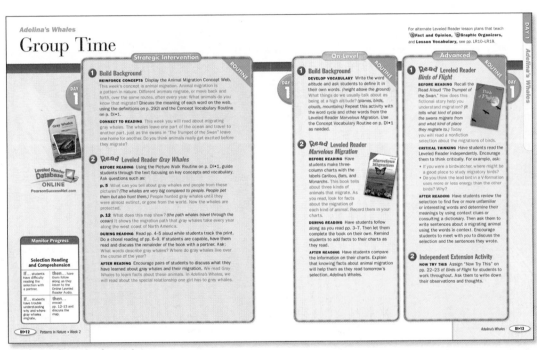

Teacher's Edition Grade 4 Unit 3

Give me a plan for group time.

Reading Street provides a daily plan for whole-group and small-group instruction. Assign the Independent Activities to the rest of the class when you meet with your small groups.

Help me teach my struggling and advanced readers.

Reading Street has daily instructional routines for both your Strategic Intervention and Advanced groups. See the Differentiated Instruction section at the back of the Teacher's Edition.

ELL

How can I support my English language learners?

Look for ELL instructional strategies, alternate comprehension lessons, and grade-level readers to build vocabulary and key concepts each week.

Q: Why did the chicken cross the road?
A: To get to the sidewalk!

What do I do when *Reading Street* isn't enough?

Every teacher knows that some students need more support. For those children, Scott Foresman provides *My Sidewalks*—an intensive reading intervention program that aligns perfectly with *Reading Street*. *My Sidewalks* accelerates reading development for children at risk.

B-A-W-K! It's so good it works with any core program.

What is Tier III Instruction?

Tier III instruction is for students with low reading skills and a lack of adequate progress. *My Sidewalks* provides sustained instruction, intensive language and concept development, and more focus on critical comprehension skills and strategies for Tier III students.

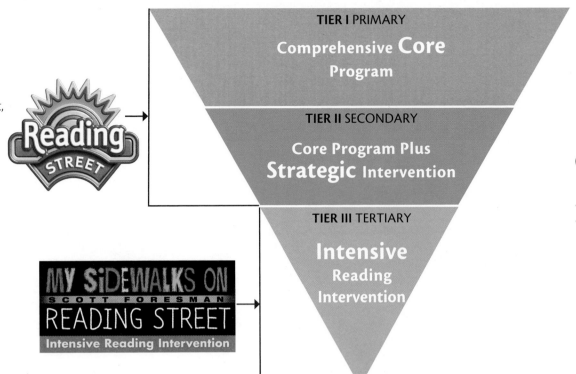

How does *My Sidewalks* support *Reading Street*?

My Sidewalks provides daily lessons for 30 weeks—for a minimum of 30 minutes a day. The oral language, vocabulary, and concepts developed in *My Sidewalks* parallel those in *Reading Street*.

My Sidewalks Student Reader

Reading Street Student Edition

When do I teach *My Sidewalks*?

Use *My Sidewalks* during group time, as a pull-out intervention program, or as a before- or after-school program. The *My Sidewalks* acceleration plan prioritizes skills so you teach less, more thoroughly.

Are you an adventurous reading teacher?

Do you love teaching with leveled text?

Reading Street for the Guided Reading Teacher will support you in organizing research-based reading instruction. It features the *Guide on the Side* to implement instruction around leveled text. All the resources are derived from *Reading Street* and its proven teaching methods.

LEARN

PLAN

TEACH

GUIDED READING LEVELS

DRA

LEXILE

I want to match my students to leveled text.

Reading Street for the Guided Reading Teacher organizes instruction around leveled text and helps you differentiate instruction. It's a complete guided reading program with leveled readers, lessons plans, practice, and assessment.

Does the program support *Reading Street*?

The scope and sequence, instructional routines, and teacher resources all align with *Reading Street*. Use the *Guide on the Side* as your main Teacher's Edition or to supplement your *Reading Street* Teacher's Edition.

Will I teach the skills my students need?

Reading Street for the Guided Reading Teacher provides a comprehensive scope and sequence that helps you pace instruction and prepare students for your state test.

READING

Pace Yourself

How do I know I am covering all the skills before the test?
This chart shows the instructional sequence from Scott Foresman Reading Street. You can use this pacing guide as is to ensure you're following a comprehensive scope and sequence, or you can adjust it to match your school/district focus calendar, curriculum map, or testing schedule.

BACK TO SCHOOL!

	WEEK 1	WEEK 2	WEEK 3	WEEK 4	WEEK 5	WEEK 6	WEEK 7	WEEK 8	WEEK 9	WEEK 10	WEEK 11	WEEK 12	WEEK 13	WEEK 14	WEEK 15
	UNIT 1					**UNIT 2**					**UNIT 3**				
Comprehension Skill	Realism and Fantasy	Sequence of Events	Sequence of Events	Realism and Fantasy	Character and Setting	Main Idea and Details	Character	Main Idea and Details	Author's Purpose	Draw Conclusions	Cause and Effect	Author's Purpose	Draw Conclusions	Generalize	Compare/Contrast
Comprehension Strategy	Activate/Use Prior Knowledge	Summarize	Visualize	Monitor and Fix Up	Story Structure	Graphic Organizers	Visualize	Monitor and Fix Up	Predict	Ask Questions	Story Structure	Summarize	Ask Questions	Answer Questions	Monitor and Fix Up
Vocabulary Strategy/Skill	Context Clues/Homonyms	Word Structure/Compound Words	Reference Sources/Unfamiliar Words	Context Clues/Multiple-Meaning Words	Word Structure/Prefixes and Suffixes	Context Clues/Synonyms	Context Clues/Unfamiliar Words	Dictionary/Unfamiliar Words	Context Clues/Antonyms	Context Clues/Unfamiliar Words	Word Structure/Endings	Glossary/Unfamiliar Words	Word Structure/Compound Words	Context Clues/Unfamiliar Words	Dictionary/Unfamiliar Words
Fluency	Accuracy	Appropriate Pace/Rate	Express Character-ization	Expression/Intonation	Appropriate Phrasing	Accuracy and Appropriate Pace/Rate	Expression/Intonation	Expression/Intonation	Appropriate Phrasing	Read Silently with Fluency	Expression/Intonation	Express Character-ization	Appropriate Phrasing	Accuracy and Appropriate Pace/Rate	Read Silently with Fluency and Accuracy
Spelling/Word Work	Short Vowels VCCV	Plurals -s, -es	Adding -ed, -ing, -er, -est	Long Vowel Digraphs	Vowel Sounds in out and toy	Syllable Patterns V/CV, VC/V	Words Ending in -le	Compound Words	Words with spl, thr, squ, str	Digraphs sh, th, ph, ch, tch	Contractions	Prefixes un-, re-, mis-, dis-	Consonant Sounds /j/ and /k/	Suffixes -ly, -ful, -ness, -less	Words with wr, kn, mb, gn

	WEEK 16	WEEK 17	WEEK 18	WEEK 19	WEEK 20	WEEK 21	WEEK 22	WEEK 23	WEEK 24	WEEK 25	WEEK 26	WEEK 27	WEEK 28	WEEK 29	WEEK 30
	UNIT 4					**UNIT 5**					**UNIT 6**				
Comprehension Skill	Cause and Effect	Compare and Contrast	Generalize	Fact and Opinion	Plot and Theme	Compare and Contrast	Fact and Opinion	Sequence	Draw Conclusions	Author's Purpose	Main Idea	Cause and Effect	Fact and Opinion	Plot and Theme	Generalize
Comprehension Strategy	Answer Questions	Ask Questions	Activate and Use Prior Knowledge	Monitor and Fix Up	Graphic Organizers	Predict	Text Structure	Monitor and Fix Up	Summarize	Prior Knowledge	Text Structure	Graphic Organizers	Answer Questions	Visualize	Predict
Vocabulary Strategy/Skill	Word Structure/Endings	Word Structure/Compound Words	Context Clues/Multiple-Meaning Words	Context Clues/Multiple-Meaning Words	Word Structure/Endings	Context Clues/Synonyms	Context Clues/Antonyms	Word Structure/Compound Words	Context Clues/Unfamiliar Words	Context Clues/Homonyms	Word Structure/Prefixes	Context Clues/Antonyms	Glossary/Unfamiliar Words	Word Structure/Prefixes and Suffixes	Context Clues/Synonyms
Fluency	Accuracy and Appropriate Pace/Rate	Read Silently with Fluency and Accuracy	Character-ization	Appropriate Phrasing	Expression/Intonation	Accuracy and Appropriate Pace/Rate	Read Silently with Fluency and Accuracy	Expression/Intonation	Express Character-izations	Appropriate Phrasing	Accuracy and Appropriate Pace/Rate	Appropriate Phrasing	Read Silently with Fluency and Accuracy	Accuracy and Appropriate Pace/Rate	Express Character-ization
Spelling/Word Work	Plurals	Vowels with r	Prefixes pre-, mid-, over-, out-	Suffixes -er, -or, -ess, -ist	Syllable Pattern VCCCV	Syllable Patterns CVVC, CVV	Homo-phones	Vowel Sound in ball	More Vowel Sound in ball	Suffixes -y, -ish, -hood, -ment	Vowels in tooth, cook	Schwa	Words with -tion, -sion, -ture	Multisyllabic Words	Related Words

4   IT'S TEST TIME!   WHEN IS YOUR STATE TEST?   5

Guide on the Side Grade 3

Welcome to Reading Street!

PRE-KINDERGARTEN

Hip, hip, hooray! We're on the way.

KINDERGARTEN

GRADE 1

Student Edition (Unit 1)

Student Edition (Unit 2)

Student Edition (Unit 3)

Student Edition (Unit 4)

Student Edition (Unit 5)

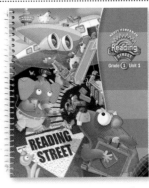
5 Teacher's Editions
(1 per unit)

GRADE 2

Student Edition
(Units 1–3)

Student Edition
(Units 4–6)

6 Teacher's Editions
(1 per unit)

GRADE 3

Student Edition
(Units 1–3)

Student Edition
(Units 4–6)

6 Teacher's Editions
(1 per unit)

GRADE 4

Student Edition

6 Teacher's Editions
(1 per unit)

GRADE 5

Student Edition

6 Teacher's Editions
(1 per unit)

GRADE 6

Student Edition

6 Teacher's Editions
(1 per unit)

MORE READING SUPPORT

My Sidewalks Intensive
Reading Intervention (Levels A–E)

Reading Street for the Guided
Reading Teacher (Grades 1–6)

Ready, Teddy?

(On Reading Street, you're ready for everything and anything!)

Student Editions (1–6)

Teacher's Editions (PreK–6)

Assessment
Assessment Handbook (K–6)
Baseline Group Tests (K–6)
DIBELS™ Assessments (K–6)
Examview® Test Generator CD-ROM (2–6)
Fresh Reads for Differentiated
Test Practice (1–6)
Online Success Tracker™ (K–6)*
Selection Tests Teacher's Manual (1–6)
Unit and End-of-Year
Benchmark Tests (K–6)

Leveled Readers
Concept Literacy Leveled Readers (K–1)
Independent Leveled Readers (K)
Kindergarten Student Readers (K)
Leveled Reader Teaching Guides (K–6)
Leveled Readers (1–6)
Listen to Me Readers (K)
Online Leveled Readers Database (K–6)*
Take-Home Leveled Readers (K–6)

Trade Books and Big Books
Big Books (PreK–2)
Read Aloud Trade Books (PreK–K)
Sing with Me Big Book (1–2)
Trade Book Library (1–6)

Decodable Readers

Decodable Readers (K–3)

Strategic Intervention
Decodable Readers (1–2)

Take-Home Decodable Readers (K–3)

Phonics and Word Study

Alphabet Cards in English and Spanish
(PreK–K)

Alphabet Chart in English and Spanish
(PreK–K)

Animal ABCs Activity Guide (K)

Finger Tracing Cards (PreK–K)

Patterns Books (PreK–K)

Phonics Activities CD-ROM (PreK–2)*

Phonics Activities Mats (K)

Phonics and Spelling Practice Book (1–3)

Phonics and Word-Building Board and Letters
(PreK–3)

Phonics Songs and Rhymes Audio CD (K–2)

Phonics Songs and Rhymes Flip Chart (K–2)

Picture Word Cards (PreK–K)

Plastic Letter Tiles (K)

Sound-Spelling Cards and Wall Charts (1–2)

Strategies for Word Analysis (4–6)

Word Study and Spelling Practice Book (4–6)

Language Arts

Daily Fix-It Transparencies (K–6)

Grammar & Writing Book and
Teacher's Annotated Edition, The (1–6)

Grammar and Writing Practice Book
and Teacher's Manual (1–6)

Grammar Transparencies (1–6)

Six-Trait Writing Posters (1–6)

Writing Kit (1–6)

Writing Rubrics and Anchor Papers (1–6)

Writing Transparencies (1–6)

Practice and Additional Resources

AlphaBuddy Bear Puppet (K)

Alphasaurus Annie Puppet (PreK)

Amazing Words Posters (K–2)

Centers Survival Kit (PreK–6)

Graphic Organizer Book (2–6)

Graphic Organizer Flip Chart (K–1)

High-Frequency Word Cards (K)

Kindergarten Review (1)

Practice Book and Teacher's Manual (K–6)

Read Aloud Anthology (PreK–2)

Readers' Theater Anthology (K–6)

Research into Practice (K–6)

Retelling Cards (K–6)

Scott Foresman Research Base (K–6)

Skill Transparencies (2–6)

Songs and Rhymes Flip Chart (PreK)

Talk with Me, Sing with Me Chart (PreK–K)

Tested Vocabulary Cards (1–6)

Vocabulary Transparencies (1–2)

Welcome to Reading Street (PreK–1)

ELL

ELL and Transition Handbook (PreK–6)

ELL Comprehensive Kit (1–6)

ELL Posters (K–6)

ELL Readers (1–6)

ELL Teaching Guides (1–6)

Ten Important Sentences (1–6)

Digital Components

AudioText CDs (PreK–6)

Background Building Audio CDs (3–6)

ExamView® Test Generator
CD-ROM (2–6)

Online Lesson Planner (K–6)

Online New Literacies Activities (1–6)*

Online Professional Development (1–6)

Online Story Sort (K–6)*

Online Student Editions (1–6)*

Online Success Tracker™ (K–6)*

Online Teacher's Editions (PreK–6)

Phonics Activities CD-ROM (PreK–2)*

Phonics Songs and Rhymes
Audio CD (K–2)

Sing with Me/Background Building
Audio CDs (PreK–2)

Songs and Rhymes Audio CD (PreK)

My Sidewalks Early Reading Intervention (K)

My Sidewalks Intensive Reading Intervention (Levels A–E)

Reading Street for the Guided Reading Teacher (1–6)

We told you a moose was on the loose.

Reading Street Program Authors

Peter Afflerbach, Ph.D.
Professor, Department of
Curriculum and Instruction
University of Maryland at
College Park

Camille L.Z. Blachowicz, Ph.D.
Professor of Education
National-Louis University

Candy Dawson Boyd, Ph.D.
Professor, School of Education
Saint Mary's College of California

Wendy Cheyney, Ed.D.
Professor of Special Education
and Literacy, Florida
International University

Connie Juel, Ph.D.
Professor of Education, School of
Education, Stanford University

Edward J. Kame'enui, Ph.D.
Professor and Director, Institute for
the Development of Educational
Achievement, University of Oregon

Donald J. Leu, Ph.D.
John and Maria Neag Endowed
Chair in Literacy and Technology
University of Connecticut

Marvin D. Moose, Ph.D.
Reading Street University
(Hee-hee)

Jeanne R. Paratore, Ed.D.
Associate Professor of Education
Department of Literacy
and Language Development
Boston University

P. David Pearson, Ph.D.
Professor and Dean,
Graduate School of Education
University of California, Berkeley

Sam L. Sebesta, Ed.D.
Professor Emeritus,
College of Education,
University of Washington, Seattle

Deborah Simmons, Ph.D.
Professor, College of Education
and Human Development
Texas A&M University
(Not pictured)

Sharon Vaughn, Ph.D.
H.E. Hartfelder/Southland Corporation
Regents Professor
University of Texas

Susan Watts-Taffe, Ph.D.
Independent Literacy Researcher
Cincinnati, Ohio

Karen Kring Wixson, Ph.D.
Professor of Education
University of Michigan

Consulting Authors

Jim Cummins, Ph.D.
Professor
Department of Curriculum, Teaching and Learning, University of Toronto
Toronto, Ontario, Canada
English Language Learners

Lily Wong Fillmore, Ph.D.
Professor Emerita
Graduate School of Education
University of California, Berkeley
English Language Learners

Barbara Kay Foots, M.Ed.
Science Education Consultant
Houston, Texas
Science Integration

Georgia Earnest García, Ph.D.
Professor
Language and Literacy Division,
University of Illinois at Urbana-Champaign
English Language Learners

George González, Ph.D.
Professor (Retired)
School of Education, University of Texas
Pan-American, Edinburg
*English Language Learners,
Bilingual Education*

Valerie Ooka Pang, Ph.D.
Professor
School of Teacher Education
San Diego State University
Social Studies Integration

Sally M. Reis, Ph.D.
Professor and Department Head
Educational Psychology
University of Connecticut
Gifted and Talented

Consultants

V. Karen Hatfield, Ed.D.
Harrodsburg, Kentucky
Assessment

Lynn F. Howard, M.Ed.
Huntersville, North Carolina
Assessment

Student Edition Reviewers

Lahna Anhalt
Reading Coordinator
DeForest Area School District
DeForest, Wisconsin

Teresa M. Beard
Cary Elementary School
Cary, North Carolina

Ebony Cross
Glassmanor Elementary School
Oxon Hill, Maryland

Melisa G. Figurelli
Fourth and Fifth Grade Teacher
Hans Herr Elementary School
Lampeter, Pennsylvania

Jennifer Flynn
Second Grade Teacher
Weatherstone Elementary School
Cary, North Carolina

Linda Halbert
Centennial Elementary School
Springfield, Oregon

Angela Hartman
Hutto Elementary School
Hutto, Texas

Judy Holiday
Program Coordinator for
Special Education
Woodmen Center, Academy SD #20
Colorado Springs, Colorado

Victoria Holman
Third Grade Teacher
Mount Pleasant Elementary School
San Jose, California

Harriett Horton
Barnwell Elementary School
Alpharetta, Georgia

Mary Beth Huber
Elementary Curriculum Specialist
Calcasieu Parish School System
Lake Charles, Louisiana

Jeff James
Fay Wright Elementary School
Salem, Oregon

Debbie Jessen
Learning Strategist
Clifford J. Lawrence Jr. High School
Las Vegas, Nevada

Sherry Johnston
Literacy Coach
Bruce Elementary School
Milwaukee, Wisconsin

Carol Kelly
Hudson School
Union City, New Jersey

Linda Lindley
Fort Hall Elementary School
Pocatello, Idaho

Karen McCarthy
Goddard School
Brockton, Massachusetts

Patsy Mogush
Educational Coordinator
Central Kindergarten Center
Eden Prairie, Minnesota

Stacie Moncrief
Ventura Park Elementary School
Portland, Oregon

Nancy Novickis
Support Services
Douglass Valley Elementary School
United States Air Force Academy,
Colorado

Betty Parsons
Past President
Santa Clara Reading Council
San Jose, California

Greta Peay
Clark County School District
North Las Vegas, Nevada

Leslie Potter
Blackwood Elementary School
Blackwood, New Jersey

Cyndy Reynolds
Williams Elementary School
Georgetown, Texas

Sharyle Shaffer
Fourth Grade Teacher
Summit Elementary School
Smithfield, Utah

Barbara Smith
Goddard School
Brockton, Massachusetts

Jane Stewart
Lakeshore Elementary School
Monroe, Louisiana

Nancey Volenstine
Chinle Elementary School
Chinle, Arizona

Teacher's Edition Reviewers

Alyssa E. Agoston
First Grade Teacher
Elms Elementary School
Jackson, New Jersey

Laura Beltchenko
Wauconda CUSD #118
Wauconda, Illinois

Lisa Bostick
NSU Elementary Lab School
Natchitoches, Louisiana

Debra O. Brown
First Grade Teacher
McFadden School
Murfreesboro, Tennessee

Cheri S. DeLaune
Paulina Elementary School
Paulina, Louisiana

Dr. Susan B. Dold
Elementary English/Language Arts Staff
Development Coordinator
Memphis City Schools
Memphis, Tennessee

Amy Francis
Montview Elementary School
Aurora, Colorado

Dawn Julian
First Grade Teacher
Elms Elementary School
Jackson, New Jersey

Suzette Kelly
Woodmen-Roberts
Elementary School
Colorado Springs, Colorado

Suzanne Lank
Primary Teacher
Maury Elementary School
Alexandria, Virginia

Sharon Loos
Foothills Elementary School
Colorado Springs, Colorado

R. Franklin Mace
Title I Teacher
Bridgeview Elementary Center
South Charleston, West Virginia

Carol Masur
Second Grade Teacher
Elms Elementary School
Jackson, New Jersey

Jennifer D. Montgomery
Houston, Texas

Diana B. Nicholson
Cynthia Mann Elementary School
Boise, Idaho

Richard Potts
Memphis, Tennessee

Antonia Rogers
Richardson Independent
School District
Richardson, Texas

Audrey Sander
Brooklyn, New York

Dr. Johnny Warrick
Gaston County Schools
Gastonia, North Carolina

Diane Weatherstone
Second Grade Teacher
Elms Elementary School
Jackson, New Jersey

Becky Worlds
Charlotte, North Carolina

Later, Gator!

xxi

Grade 2
Priority Skills

Priority skills are the critical elements of reading—phonemic awareness, phonics, fluency, vocabulary, and text comprehension—as they are developed across and within grades to assure that instructional emphasis is placed on the right skills at the right time and to maintain a systematic sequence of skill instruction.

Key
● = Taught/Unit priority
◐ = Reviewed and practiced
○ = Integrated practice

	UNIT 1 Weeks 1–2	UNIT 1 Weeks 3–5	UNIT 2 Weeks 1–2	UNIT 2 Weeks 3–5
Phonemic Awareness	Appears in Strategic Intervention lessons (pp. DI•14–DI•64)			
Phonics				
Know letter-sound relationships	●	●	●	●
Blend sounds of letters to decode				
Consonants	●	◐	○	◐
Consonant blends and digraphs	●	●	◐	◐
Short Vowels	●	◐	◐	◐
Long Vowels	●	◐	◐	◐
r-Controlled Vowels			●	●
Vowel Digraphs				●
Diphthongs				
Other vowel patterns	●	◐	◐	○
Phonograms/word families	●	●	○	○
Decode words with common word parts				
Base words and inflected endings		●	◐	●
Contractions			●	◐
Compounds				
Suffixes and prefixes				
Blend syllables to decode multisyllabic words	◐	◐	●	●
Fluency				
Read aloud with accuracy, comprehension, and appropriate rate	●	●	●	○
Read aloud with expression		●	●	●
Attend to punctuation and use appropriate phrasing		●	●	●
Practice fluency in a variety of ways, including choral reading, paired reading, and repeated oral reading	●	●	●	●
Work toward appropriate fluency goals	50–60 WCPM	50–60 WCPM	58–68 WCPM	58–68 WCPM
Vocabulary				
Read high-frequency words and lesson vocabulary automatically	●	●	●	●
Develop vocabulary through direct instruction, concrete experiences, reading, and listening to text read aloud	●	●	●	●
Use word structure to figure out word meaning				
Use context clues to determine word meaning of unfamiliar words, multiple-meaning words, homonyms, homographs				●
Use grade-appropriate references sources to learn word meanings			●	○
Use new words in a variety of contexts	○	○	○	○
Use graphic organizers to group, study, and retain vocabulary	●	●	●	●
Classify and categorize words				
Understand antonyms and synonyms		●		
Examine word usage and effectiveness	●	●	●	●

UNIT 3		UNIT 4		UNIT 5		UNIT 6	
Weeks		**Weeks**		**Weeks**		**Weeks**	
1–2	3–5	1–2	3–5	1–2	3–5	1–2	3–5

66–76 WCPM	66–76 WCPM	74–84 WCPM	74–84 WCPM	82–92 WCPM	82–92 WCPM	90–100 WCPM	90–100 WCPM

Grade 2
Priority Skills

Key
- ● = Taught/Unit priority
- ◐ = Reviewed and practiced
- ○ = Integrated practice

	UNIT 1		UNIT 2	
	Weeks		Weeks	
	1–2	3–5	1–2	3–5
Text Comprehension				
Strategies				
Preview the text	○	○	○	○
Set and monitor purpose for reading	○	○	○	○
Activate and use prior knowledge			●	○
Make and confirm predictions	●	○	●	○
Monitor comprehension and use fix-up strategies		●	○	○
Use graphic organizers to focus on text structure, to represent relationships in text, or to summarize text	○	○	○	○
Answer questions	○	○	○	○
Generate questions				
Recognize text structure: story and informational	●	●	○	●
Summarize text by retelling stories or identifying main ideas	○	○	○	●
Visualize; use mental imagery				●
Make connections: text to self, text to text, text to world	○	○	○	○
Use parts of a book to locate information		●	●	○
Skills				
Author's purpose	◐	○	○	●
Cause and effect				
Compare and contrast		◐	○	○
Draw conclusions				●
Fact and opinion				
Graphic sources (charts, diagrams, graphs, maps, tables)			●	○
Main idea and supporting details	●	●	○	○
Realism/fantasy		●	●	◐
Sequence of events			●	●
Literary Elements				
Character (Recognize characters' traits, actions, feelings, and motives)	●	●	◐	○
Plot and plot structure				
Setting	●	●	◐	○
Theme				

UNIT 3		UNIT 4		UNIT 5		UNIT 6	
Weeks		Weeks		Weeks		Weeks	
1–2	3–5	1–2	3–5	1–2	3–5	1–2	3–5

You Are Here

Unit 1
Exploration

Unit 2
Working Together

Unit 3
Creative Ideas

Unit 4
Our Changing World

Exploration

What can we learn from exploring new places and things?

Unit 1
Skills Overview

		WEEK 1	WEEK 2
		16–39 **Iris and Walter/ Morning Song/ My Travel Tree** — REALISTIC FICTION	46–65 **Exploring Space with an Astronaut/ A Trip to Space Camp** — EXPOSITORY NONFICTION
Oral Language		*What might we discover in a new neighborhood?*	*Why would anyone want to explore space?*
Word Work	Phonics	T ⊙ Short Vowels T REVIEW Syllable Patterns VC/CV and VCC/V	T ⊙ Long Vowels CVCe T REVIEW Short Vowels
	Spelling	T Words with Short Vowels	T Words with Long Vowels CVCe
	High-Frequency Words	T *someone, somewhere, friend, country, beautiful, front*	T *everywhere, live, work, woman, machines, move, world*
Reading	Comprehension	T ⊙ Character and Setting ⊙ **Strategy** Predict REVIEW **Skill** Main Idea and Details	T ⊙ **Skill** Main Idea and Details ⊙ **Strategy** Text Structure REVIEW **Skill** Author's Purpose
	Vocabulary	Figurative Language/Simile	Position Words
	Fluency	Read with Appropriate Pace and Rate	Read with Accuracy
Language Arts	Writing	**Weekly Writing** A Story About Me **Unit Process Writing**	**Weekly Writing** A Story About Me **Unit Process Writing**
	Grammar	T Sentences	T Subjects
	Speaking, Listening, Viewing	Why We Speak	Why We Listen
	Research/Study Skills	Media Center/Library	Alphabetical Order: First Letter
Integrate Science and Social Studies Standards		*Time for SOCIAL STUDIES* Comparing Communities, Geography, Exploration, Friendship	*Time for SCIENCE* Space Exploration and Travel, Astronauts, Solar System, Technology, Space Research

10c Exploration

⊙ Target Skill   T Tested Skill

WEEK 3	WEEK 4	WEEK 5
72–93	100–125	132–155
Henry and Mudge and the Starry Night/ Star Pictures in the Sky REALISTIC FICTION	**A Walk in the Desert/ Rain Forests** EXPOSITORY NONFICTION	**The Strongest One/ Anteaters** PLAY
What can we discover by exploring nature?	*What can we learn by exploring the desert?*	*When we are searching for answers, whom can we ask?*
T 🔊 Consonant Blends T REVIEW Long Vowels CVCe	T 🔊 Inflected Endings T REVIEW Consonant Blends	T 🔊 Consonant Digraphs T REVIEW Inflected Endings
T Words with Consonant Blends	T Words with Inflected Endings	T Words with Consonant Digraphs
T *couldn't, love, build, mother, bear, father, straight*	T *water, eyes, early, animals, full, warm*	T *together, very, learn, often, though, gone, pieces*
T 🔊 **Skill** Character and Setting 🔊 **Strategy** Monitor and Fix Up: Read On REVIEW **Skill** Realism and Fantasy	T 🔊 **Skill** Main Idea and Details 🔊 **Strategy** Text Structure REVIEW **Skill** Compare and Contrast	T 🔊 **Skill** Realism and Fantasy 🔊 **Strategy** Monitor and Fix Up: Text Features REVIEW **Skill** Character and Setting
Synonyms	Descriptive Words	Synonyms
Read with Accuracy and Appropriate Pace/Rate	Attend to Punctuation	Read with Expression/Intonation
Weekly Writing A Story About Me **Unit Process Writing**	**Weekly Writing** A Story About Me **Unit Process Writing**	**Weekly Writing** A Story About Me **Unit Process Writing**
T Predicates	Statements and Questions	Commands and Exclamations
Be a Good Speaker	Be a Polite Listener	Ask and Answer Questions
Parts of a Book	Technology: Using Online Reference Sources	Maps
Science Living and Nonliving Things, Day and Night Sky, Habitats, Solar System and Stars, Senses	**Science** Desert, Energy, Interdependence, Climate, Habitats, Adaptation	**SOCIAL STUDIES** Native American Cultures, Exploration, Geography, Concept of Place, Oral Tradition

Unit 1
Monitor Progress

Predictors of Reading Success	WEEK 1	WEEK 2	WEEK 3	WEEK 4
Word Reading / **Phonics**	Short Vowels	Long Vowels CVCe	Consonant Blends	Inflected Endings
WCPM / **Fluency**	Read with Appropriate Pace/Rate 50–60 WCPM	Read with Accuracy 50–60 WCPM	Read with Accuracy and Appropriate Pace/Rate 50–60 WCPM	Attend to Punctuation 50–60 WCPM
High-Frequency Words / **High Frequency Words/ Vocabulary**	beautiful country friend front someone somewhere	everywhere live machines move woman work world	bear build couldn't father love mother straight	animals early eyes full warm water
Oral Vocabulary / **Vocabulary/ Concept Development** (assessed informally)	brittle creature dart decision investigate rural underground urban	ascend descend enormous journey launch meteorite orbit universe	detective fascinating galaxy identify slimy tranquil underneath wildlife	arid discovery dunes forbidding haven landform ledge precipitation
Retelling / **Text Comprehension**	**Skill** Character and Setting **Strategy** Predict	**Skill** Main Idea and Details **Strategy** Text Structure	**Skill** Character and Setting **Strategy** Monitor and Fix Up	**Skill** Main Idea and Details **Strategy** Text Structure

Target Skill   SuccessTracker/Unit 1 Benchmark Tested Skills

Make Data-Driven Decisions

Data Management
- Assess
- Diagnose
- Prescribe
- Disaggregate

Classroom Management
- Monitor Progress
- Group
- Differentiate Instruction
- Inform Parents

Success Tracker™

ONLINE CLASSROOM

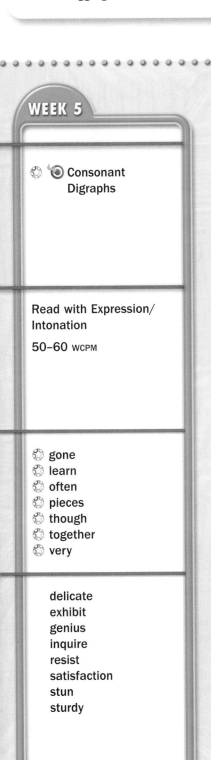

Consonant Digraphs

Read with Expression/ Intonation

50–60 WCPM

- gone
- learn
- often
- pieces
- though
- together
- very

delicate
exhibit
genius
inquire
resist
satisfaction
stun
sturdy

Skill Realism and Fantasy

Strategy Monitor and Fix Up

Manage Data

- Assign the Unit 1 Benchmark Test for students to take online.
- SuccessTracker records results and generates reports by school, grade, classroom, or student.
- Use reports to disaggregate and aggregate Unit 1 skills and standards data to monitor progress.
- Based on class lists created to support the categories important for adequate yearly progress (AYP, i.e., gender, ethnicity, migrant education, English proficiency, disabilities, economic status), reports let you track AYP every six weeks.

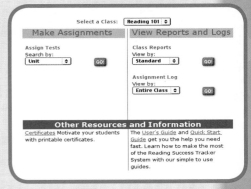

Group

- Use results from Unit 1 Benchmark Tests taken online through SuccessTracker to regroup students.
- Reports in SuccessTracker suggest appropriate groups for students based on test results.

On-Level

Strategic Intervention

Advanced

Individualize Instruction

- Tests are correlated to Unit 1 tested skills and standards so that prescriptions for individual teaching and learning plans can be created.
- Individualized prescriptions target instruction and accelerate student progress toward learning outcome goals.
- Prescriptions include resources to reteach Unit 1 skills and standards.

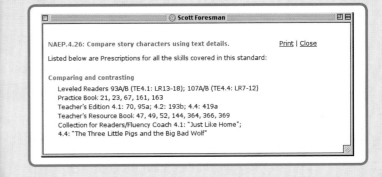

NAEP.4.26: Compare story characters using text details.   Print | Close

Listed below are Prescriptions for all the skills covered in this standard:

Comparing and contrasting
Leveled Readers 93A/B (TE4.1: LR13-18); 107A/B (TE4.4: LR7-12)
Practice Book: 21, 23, 67, 161, 163
Teacher's Edition 4.1: 70, 95a; 4.2: 193b; 4.4: 419a
Teacher's Resource Book: 47, 49, 52, 144, 364, 366, 369
Collection for Readers/Fluency Coach 4.1: "Just Like Home";
4.4: "The Three Little Pigs and the Big Bad Wolf"

Unit 1
Grouping for AYP

Diagnose and Differentiate

Diagnose
To make initial grouping decisions, use the Baseline Group Test or another initial placement test. Depending on children's ability levels, you may have more than one of each group.

Differentiate

If... a child's performance is **Below-Level** **then...** use the regular instruction and the daily Strategic Intervention, pp. DI·14–DI·62.

If... a child's performance is **On-Level** **then...** use the regular instruction for On-Level learners throughout each week.

If... a child's performance is **Advanced** **then...** use the regular instruction and the daily instruction for Advanced learners, pp. DI·9–DI·63.

Group Time

On-Level	Strategic Intervention	Advanced
• Explicit instructional routines teach core skills and strategies.	• Daily Strategic Intervention provides more intensive instruction, more scaffolding, more practice with critical skills, and more opportunities to respond.	• Daily Advanced lessons provide compacted instruction for accelerated learning, options for independent investigative work, and challenging reading content.
• Ample practice for core skills.		
• Independent activities provide practice for core skills.	• Decodable readers practice word reading skills.	• Leveled readers (LR1–48) provide additional reading tied to lesson concepts.
• Leveled readers (LR1–48) and decodable readers provide additional reading and practice with core skills and vocabulary.	• Reteach lessons (DI·64–DI·68) provide additional instructional opportunities with target skills.	
	• Leveled readers (LR1–48) build background for the selections and practice target skills and vocabulary.	

Additional opportunities to differentiate instruction:
- Reteach Lessons, pp. DI·64–DI·68
- Leveled Reader Instruction and Leveled Practice, LR1–LR48
- My Sidewalks on Scott Foresman Reading Street Intensive Reading Intervention Program

4-Step Plan for Assessment

1. Diagnose and Differentiate
2. Monitor Progress
3. Assess and Regroup
4. Summative Assessment

Monitor Progress

STEP 2

- **Monitor Progress boxes** to check word reading, high-frequency words, retelling, and fluency
- **Weekly Assessments** on Day 5 for phonics, high-frequency words, comprehension, fluency, and retelling
- **Guiding comprehension questions** and skill and strategy instruction during reading
- **Practice Book** pages at point of use
- **Weekly Selection Tests** or **Fresh Reads for Differentiated Test Practice**

Assess and Regroup

STEP 3

- **Day 5 Assessments** Record results of weekly Day 5 assessments for phonics, high-frequency words, and fluency (pp. WA18–WA19) to track children's progress.
- **Unit 1 Benchmark Test** Administer this test to check mastery of unit skills.
- The first opportunity for regrouping occurs at the end of Unit 2. Use weekly assessment information, Unit Benchmark Test performance, and the Unit 1 Assess and Regroup (p. WA20) to inform regrouping decisions at the end of Unit 2. See the time line below.

YOU ARE HERE
Begin Unit 1

SCOTT FORESMAN ASSESSMENT

Group Baseline Group Test

→ Regroup Units 1 and 2 → Regroup Unit 3 → Regroup Unit 4 → Regroup Unit 5 → END OF YEAR

| Week | 1 | | 5 | | 10 | | 15 | | 20 | | 25 | | 30 |

OUTSIDE ASSESSMENT

Initial placement — Outside assessment for regrouping — Outside assessment for regrouping

Outside assessments (e.g., **DIBELS**) may recommend regrouping at other times during the year.

Summative Assessment

STEP 4

- **Benchmark Assessment** Use to measure a child's mastery of each unit's skills.
- **End-of-Year Benchmark Assessment** Use to measure a child's mastery of program skills covered in all six units.

Unit 1
Theme Launch

Discuss the Big Idea

As children begin the school year, remind them to handle this Student Book, and all books, carefully and with respect.

Read and discuss the theme question. Explain

- you can find many new things at school or in your neighborhood (new friends, new things to learn, new places to go)

- there are many places to explore (outer space, outdoors, desert, forest)

- there are many new things to learn when you explore (learn about others, find how to be friends, learn about new places)

Have children use the pictures along the side of the page to preview the stories in this unit. Read the titles and captions together. Ask children how each selection might tell about "exploration."

Read Aloud

Read the big book *In the Forest.*

- What things can you discover when you explore a forest?

- How can looking closely at something help you explore?

- How can you find out more about things that live and grow in the forest?

- What would you like to explore more in the forest?

For more read alouds related to the theme, see the *Read Aloud Anthology.*

UNIT 1

Read I
Onlin
PearsonSuccessNet.

Exploration
What can we learn from exploring new places and things?

10

CONNECTING CULTURES

You can use the following selection to help children learn about their own and other cultures and explore common elements of culture.

Iris and Walter Children can reflect on the friends they have made who are from their neighborhood or from other cultures. They can share how friends are the same, no matter where they are from or where they live.

Iris and Walter

Iris goes exploring and finds a friend.
REALISTIC FICTION

connect to
SOCIAL STUDIES

Paired Selection
"Morning Song" and "My Travel Tree"
POETRY

Exploring Space with an Astronaut

Astronauts explore space.
EXPOSITORY NONFICTION

connect to
SCIENCE

Paired Selection
A Trip to Space Camp
EXPOSITORY NONFICTION

Henry and Mudge and the Starry Night

Henry and Mudge explore the outdoors.
REALISTIC FICTION

connect to
SCIENCE

Paired Selection
Star Pictures in the Sky
EXPOSITORY NONFICTION

A Walk in the Desert

The desert is an interesting place to explore.
EXPOSITORY NONFICTION

connect to
SCIENCE

Paired Selection
Rain Forests
ONLINE REFERENCE SOURCE

The Strongest One

Little Ant explores the answer to an important question.
PLAY

connect to
SOCIAL STUDIES

Paired Selection
Anteaters
EXPOSITORY NONFICTION

11

Unit Inquiry Project
Research Places to Explore

Children can work individually, in pairs, or in groups to plan a trip to explore a place where they would learn new and exciting things.

PROJECT TIMETABLE

WEEK	ACTIVITY/SKILL CONNECTION
1	**BRAINSTORM** Children work in a group and list places they would like to explore. Encourage them to list places both practical, such as the neighborhood zoo, and impractical, like the international space station.
2	**GATHER INFORMATION** Children choose one place to explore and research it. They gather information from a variety of sources about what they would like to explore and what they might find.
3	**PREPARE FOR THE TRIP** Children can draw a map that shows how they would travel to the place they are exploring. They can also make a list of things they would need to take.
4	**MAKE PREDICTIONS** Children make predictions about what they think they will find or accomplish on their exploration.
5	**PRESENT** Children present their exploration plans to the class.

An assessment rubric can be found on p. 158a. Rubric 4 3 2 1

Unit 1
Exploration

CONCEPT QUESTION

What can we learn from exploring new places and things?

Week 1

Expand the Concept
What might we discover in a new neighborhood?

Connect the Concept

Literature

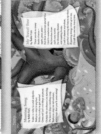

Develop Language
brittle, creature, dart, decision, investigate, rural, underground, urban

Teach Content
Comparing Communities
Geography: Urban, Suburban, Rural
Exploration
Friendship

Writing
A Plan

Week 2

Expand the Concept
Why would anyone want to explore space?

Connect the Concept

Literature

Develop Language
ascend, descend, enormous, journey, launch, meteorite, orbit, universe

Teach Content
Space Exploration
Astronauts (Careers in Space)
Space Travel
Technology
Space Research
Solar System

Writing
A List

Week 3

Expand the Concept
What can we discover by exploring nature?

Connect the Concept

Literature

Develop Language
detective, fascinating, galaxy, identify, slimy, tranquil, underneath, wildlife

Teach Content
Living and Nonliving Things
Habitats
Day/Night Sky
Solar System/Stars
Senses

Writing
A Story

Week 4

Expand the Concept
What can we learn by exploring the desert?

Connect the Concept

Literature

Develop Language
arid, discovery, dunes, forbidding, haven, landform, ledge, precipitation

Teach Content
Earth Science: Desert
Energy: Light, Heat
Climate
Adaptation
Habitats
Interdependence

Writing
A Report

Week 5

Expand the Concept
When we are searching for answers, whom can we ask?

Connect the Concept

Literature

Develop Language
delicate, exhibit, genius, inquire, resist, satisfaction, stun, sturdy

Teach Content
Native American Cultures/Beliefs
Exploration
Concept of Place
Oral Tradition
Geography

Writing
A News Report

RESOURCES FOR THE WEEK

- Practice Book 2.1, *pp. 1–10*
- Phonics and Spelling Practice Book, *pp. 1–4*
- Grammar and Writing Practice Book, *pp. 1–4*
- Selection Test, *pp. 1–4*

- Fresh Reads for Differentiated Test Practice, *pp. 1–6*
- Phonics Songs and Rhymes Chart 1
- The Grammar and Writing Book, *pp. 50–55*

Grouping Options for Differentiated Instruction

Turn the page for the small group lesson plan.

DAY 3 PAGES 36a–37b

Oral Language

QUESTION OF THE DAY, 36a
What plants could we investigate in the forest?

Oral Vocabulary/Share Literature, 36b
Big Book *In the Forest*
Amazing Word *underground*

Word Work

Phonics, 36c
REVIEW Syllable Patterns VC/CV and VCC/V **T**

High-Frequency Words, 36d
Practice *beautiful, country, friend, front, someone, somewhere* **T**

Spelling, 36d
Practice

Comprehension/Vocabulary/Fluency

Vocabulary, 36e
Figurative Language: Similes

Read *Iris and Walter,* 16–37

Grouping Options
12f–12g

Fluency, 36f
Read with Appropriate Pace and Rate

Think and Share, 36g

Trait of the Week, 37a
Introduce Voice

Grammar, 37b
Write with Sentences **T**

Day 3 Use the word *as* to write a comparison about Iris and Walter.

Day 3 Urban/Rural Concept Chart, 37b

DAY 4 PAGES 38a–39d

Oral Language

QUESTION OF THE DAY, 38a
What makes a poem different from a story?

Oral Vocabulary/Share Literature, 38b
Read Aloud Anthology "The Mystery Eggs"
Amazing Words *brittle, dart, decision*

Word Work

Phonics, 38c
REVIEW Sentence Reading **T**

Spelling, 38d
Partner Review

Comprehension/Vocabulary/Fluency

Read "Morning Song," "My Travel Tree,"
38–39
Leveled Readers

Grouping Options
12f–12g

Figurative Language: Similes
Reading Across Texts

Fluency, 39a
Read with Appropriate Pace and Rate

Writing Across the Curriculum, 39b
Two-Column Chart

Grammar, 39c
Review Sentences **T**

Speaking and Listening, 39d
Why We Speak

Day 4 List topics you would like to investigate.

Day 4 Urban/Rural Concept Chart, 39d

DAY 5 PAGES 40a–41b

Oral Language

QUESTION OF THE DAY, 40a
What did Iris investigate?

Oral Vocabulary/Share Literature, 40b
Read Aloud Anthology "The Mystery Eggs"
Amazing Words Review

Word Work

Phonics, 40c
REVIEW Short Vowels; *ea*/e/ **T**

High-Frequency Words, 342c
Review *beautiful, country, friend, front, someone, somewhere* **T**

Spelling, 40d
Test

Comprehension/Vocabulary/Fluency

Read Leveled Readers

Grouping Options 12f–12g

Monitor Progress, 40e–40g
Read the Sentences
Read the Story

Writing and Grammar, 40–41
Develop Voice
Use Sentences **T**

Research/Study Skills, 41a
Media Center/Library

Day 5 Write about a family that moves.

Day 5 Revisit the Urban/Rural Concept Chart, 41b

KEY 🎯 = Target Skill **T** = Tested Skill

Comprehension
Check Retelling, *36g*

Fluency
Check Fluency WCPM, *39a*
Spiral REVIEW Phonics,
High-Frequency Words

Oral Vocabulary
Check Oral Vocabulary, *40b*
Assess Phonics,
High-Frequency Words, Fluency,
Comprehension, *40e*

SUCCESS PREDICTOR

Small Group Plan *for Differentiated Instruction*

Daily Plan
AT A GLANCE

Reading
Whole Group
- Oral Language
- Word Work
- Comprehension/Vocabulary

Group Time

Meet with small groups to provide:
- Skill Support
- Reading Support
- Fluency Practice

Read

This week's lessons for daily group time can be found behind the Differentiated Instruction (DI) tab on pp. DI·14–DI·23.

Whole Group
- Comprehension/Vocabulary
- Fluency

Language Arts
- Writing
- Grammar
- Speaking/Listening/Viewing
- Research/Study Skills

Use *My Sidewalks on Reading Street* for Tier III intensive reading intervention.

DAY 1

On-Level
Teacher-Led
Page 12q
- **Read** Decodable Reader 1
- **Reread** for Fluency

Strategic Intervention
Teacher-Led
Page DI·14
- Blend Words with Short Vowels
- **Read** Decodable Reader 1
- **Reread** for Fluency

Advanced
Teacher-Led
Page DI·15
- Extend Word Reading
- **Read** Advanced Selection 1
- Introduce Concept Inquiry

i **Independent Activities**

While you meet with small groups, have the rest of the class...

- Reread for fluency
- Write in their journals
- Read self-selected reading
- Visit the Word Work Center
- Complete Practice Book 2.1, pp. 3–4

DAY 2

On-Level
Teacher-Led
Pages 16–35
- **Read** *Iris and Walter*
- **Reread** for Fluency

Strategic Intervention
Teacher-Led
Page DI·16
- Blend Words with Short Vowels
- **Read** SI Decodable Reader 1
- **Read** or Listen to *Iris and Walter*

Advanced
Teacher-Led
Page DI·17
- **Read** *Iris and Walter*
- Continue Concept Inquiry

i **Independent Activities**

While you meet with small groups, have the rest of the class...

- Read self-selected reading
- Write in their journals
- Visit the Listening Center
- Complete Practice Book 2.1, pp. 5–7

DAY 3

On-Level
Teacher-Led
Pages 16–37
- **Reread** *Iris and Walter*

Strategic Intervention
Teacher-Led
Page DI·18
- **Reread** *Iris and Walter*
- Read Words and Sentences
- Review Character and Setting and Predict
- **Reread** for Fluency

Advanced
Teacher-Led
Page DI·19
- Self-Selected Reading
- Continue Concept Inquiry

i **Independent Activities**

While you meet with small groups, have the rest of the class...

- Read self-selected reading
- Write in their journals
- Visit the Writing Center
- Complete Practice Book 2.1, pp. 8–9

---

① Begin with whole class skill and strategy instruction.

② Meet with small groups to provide differentiated instruction.

③ Gather the whole class back together for fluency and language arts.

On-Level
Teacher-Led
Pages 38–39, LR4–LR6
- **Read** "Morning Song"/"My Travel Tree"
- Practice with On-Level Reader *The New Kid*

Strategic Intervention
Teacher-Led
Pages DI · 20, LR1–LR3
- **Read** or Listen to "Morning Song"/"My Travel Tree"
- **Reread** for Fluency
- Build Concepts
- Practice with Below-Level Reader *City Mouse and Country Mouse*

Advanced
Teacher-Led
Pages DI · 21, LR7–LR9
- **Read** "Morning Song"/"My Travel Tree"
- Extend Vocabulary
- Continue Concept Inquiry
- Practice with Advanced Reader *City Friends, Country Friends*

DAY 4

ⓘ Independent Activities

While you meet with small groups, have the rest of the class...

- Reread for fluency
- Write in their journals
- Read self-selected reading
- Review spelling words with a partner
- Visit the Listening and Social Studies Centers

On-Level
Teacher-Led
Pages 40e–40g, LR4–LR6
- Sentence Reading, Set B
- Monitor Comprehension
- Practice with On-Level Reader *The New Kid*

Strategic Intervention
Teacher-Led
Pages DI · 22, LR1–LR3
- Practice Word Reading
- Sentence Reading, Set A
- Monitor Comprehension
- Practice with Below-Level Reader *City Mouse and Country Mouse*

Advanced
Teacher-Led
Pages DI · 23, LR7–LR9
- Sentence Reading, Set C
- Share Concept Inquiry
- Monitor Fluency and Comprehension
- Practice with Advanced Reader *City Friends, Country Friends*

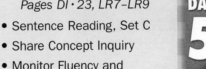
DAY 5

ⓘ Independent Activities

While you meet with small groups, have the rest of the class...

- Reread for fluency
- Write in their journals
- Read self-selected reading
- Visit the Technology Center
- Complete Practice Book 2.1, p. 10

ELL

Grouping Place English language learners in the groups that correspond to their reading abilities in English.

Use the appropriate Leveled Reader or other text at children's instructional level.

TiP Send home the appropriate Multilingual Summary of the main selection on Day 1.

Take It to the NET™ ONLINE
PearsonSuccessNet.com

Connie Juel
For research on the importance of phonemic awareness for early reading success, see the article "Learning to Read and Write" by Scott Foresman author Connie Juel.

TEACHER TALK

Phonics is instruction in the relationships between letters and sounds.

Looking Ahead

Be sure to schedule time for children to work on the unit inquiry project "Take a Trip." This week children should work in a group and list places they would like to explore.

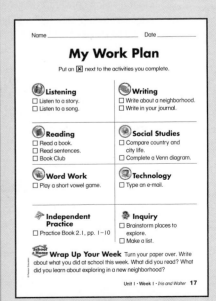

Name _____ Date _____

My Work Plan
Put an ☒ next to the activities you complete.

Listening
☐ Listen to a story.
☐ Listen to a song.

Writing
☐ Write about a neighborhood.
☐ Write in your journal.

Reading
☐ Read a book.
☐ Read sentences.
☐ Book Club

Social Studies
☐ Compare country and city life.
☐ Complete a Venn diagram.

Word Work
☐ Play a short vowel game.

Technology
☐ Type an e-mail.

Independent Practice
☐ Practice Book 2.1, pp. 1–10

Inquiry
☐ Brainstorm places to explore.
☐ Make a list.

Wrap Up Your Week Turn your paper over. Write about what you did at school this week. What did you read? What did you learn about exploring in a new neighborhood?

Unit 1 · Week 1 · *Iris and Walter* 17

▲ **Group-Time Survival Guide**
p. 17, Weekly Contract

Customize Your Plan *by Strand*

ORAL LANGUAGE

Concept Development

What might we discover in a new neighborhood?

 *to build oral vocabulary*

brittle   creature   dart
decision   investigate   rural
underground   urban

BUILD

❑ **Question of the Week** Use the Morning Warm-Up! to introduce and discuss the question of the week. This week children will talk, sing, read, and write about what we might find in a new neighborhood. **DAY 1** *12l*

❑ **Sing with Me Big Book** Sing a song about investigating rural and urban places. Ask children to listen for the concept-related Amazing Words *investigate, rural, urban.* **DAY 1** *12m*

Sing with Me Big Book

❑ **Let's Talk About Exploration** Use the Let's Talk About It lesson in the Student Edition to build background, vocabulary, and concepts. Then create a concept chart for children to add to throughout the week. **DAY 1** *12r–13*

Let's Talk About It

DEVELOP

❑ **Question of the Day** Use the questions in the Morning Warm-Ups! to discuss lesson concepts and how they relate to the unit theme, Exploration. **DAY 2** *14a*, **DAY 3** *36a*, **DAY 4** *38a*, **DAY 5** *40a*

❑ **Share Literature** Read big books and read aloud selections that develop concepts, language, and vocabulary related to the lesson concept and the unit theme. Continue to develop this week's Amazing Words. **DAY 2** *14b*, **DAY 3** *36b*, **DAY 4** *38b*, **DAY 5** *40b*

CONNECT

❑ **Wrap Up Your Week!** Revisit the Question of the Week. Then connect concepts and vocabulary to next week's lesson. **DAY 5** *41b*

CHECK

❑ **Check Oral Vocabulary** To informally assess children's oral vocabulary, ask individuals to use some of this week's Amazing Words to tell you about the illustration and photographs on Student Edition pp. 12–13. **DAY 5** *40b*

PHONICS

 SHORT VOWELS EA/E/ When there is only one vowel at the beginning or in the middle of a word or syllable, it usually stands for its short sound. The letters *ea* can stand for short *e* or long *e*. Context provides the clue to pronunciation.

TEACH

❑ **Short Vowels** Introduce the blending strategy for words with short vowels and *ea/e/*. Then have children blend and build words with short vowel sounds using letter tiles. **DAY 1** *12n–12o*

❑ **Fluent Word Reading** Use the Fluent Word Reading Routine to develop children's word reading fluency. Use the Phonics Songs and Rhymes Chart for additional word reading practice. **DAY 2** *14c–14d*

Phonics Songs and Rhymes Chart 1

PRACTICE/APPLY

❑ **Decodable Reader 1** Practice reading words with short vowels in context. **DAY 1** *12q*

❑ *Iris and Walter* Practice decoding words in context. **DAY 2** *16–35*

Decodable Reader 1

❑ **Homework** Practice Book 2.1 p. 3. **DAY 1** *12o*

❑ **Word Work Center** Practice short vowels. **ANY DAY** *12j*

Main Selection—Fiction

RETEACH/REVIEW

❑ **Review** Review words with this week's phonics skills. **DAY 5** *40c*

❑ **Reteach Lessons** If necessary, reteach short vowels. **DAY 5** *DI·64*

❑ **Spiral REVIEW** Review previously taught phonics skills. **DAY 1** *12o*, **DAY 3** *36c*, **DAY 4** *38c*

ASSESS

❑ **Sentence Reading** Assess children's ability to read words with short vowels. **DAY 5** *40e–40f*

① Use assessment data to determine your instructional focus.

② Preview this week's instruction by strand.

③ Choose instructional activities that meet the needs of your classroom.

SPELLING

SHORT VOWELS When there is only one vowel at the beginning or in the middle of a word or syllable, it usually stands for its short sound.

TEACH

☐ **Pretest** Before administering the pretest, model how to segment short vowel words to spell them. Dictate the spelling words, segmenting them if necessary. Then have children check their pretests and correct misspelled words. DAY 1 12p

PRACTICE/APPLY

☐ **Dictation** Have children write dictation sentences to practice spelling words. DAY 2 14d

☐ **Write Words** Have children practice writing the spelling words by writing down and finishing sentence starters with spelling words. DAY 3 36d

☐ **Homework** Phonics and Spelling Practice Book pp. 1–4. DAY 1 12p, DAY 2 14d, DAY 3 36d, DAY 4 38d

RETEACH/REVIEW

☐ **Partner Review** Have pairs work together to read and write the spelling words. DAY 4 38d

ASSESS

☐ **Posttest** Use dictation sentences to give the posttest for words with short vowels. DAY 5 40d

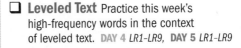

Spelling Words

Short Vowels

1. drum
2. rock
3. list
4. desk
5. job
6. sad*
7. chop
8. sack
9. tag
10. rib
11. mess
12. dust

Challenge Words

11. pocket
12. lettuce
13. engine

* **Words from the Selection**

HIGH-FREQUENCY WORDS

WORDS TO READ

beautiful   country   friend   front
someone   somewhere

TEACH

☐ **Words to Read** Introduce this week's high-frequency words and add them to the Word Wall. DAY 2 14-15a

High-Frequency Words

PRACTICE/APPLY

☐ **Words in Context** Read high-frequency words in the context of *Iris and Walter*. DAY 2 16-35

☐ **Word Wall** Use the Word Wall to review and practice high-frequency words throughout the week. DAY 3 36d, DAY 5 40c

Main Selection—Fiction

☐ **Leveled Text** Practice this week's high-frequency words in the context of leveled text. DAY 4 LR1-LR9, DAY 5 LR1-LR9

☐ **Homework** Practice Book 2.1 pp. 6, 9. DAY 2 15a, DAY 3 36d

Leveled Readers

RETEACH/REVIEW

☐ **Spiral REVIEW** Review previously taught high-frequency words. DAY 2 15a, DAY 4 38c

ASSESS

☐ **Sentence Reading** Assess children's ability to read this week's high-frequency words. DAY 5 40e-40f

VOCABULARY

TEACH

☐ **Vocabulary Transparency 1** Use Vocabulary Transparency 1 to introduce the selection words from *Iris and Walter*. Children will read these words but will not be tested on them. DAY 2 16a

☐ **Figurative Language: Similes** Discuss similes using *like* and *as*. DAY 3 36e

COMPREHENSION

🎯 **SKILL CHARACTER AND SETTING** Characters are the people or animals in a story. The setting is when and where the story takes place.

🎯 **STRATEGY PREDICT** Predict means you try to figure out what will happen next in a story.

TEACH

☐ **Listening Comprehension** Read "A New Neighborhood" and model how to identify *character and setting*. DAY 1 *13a-13b*

☐ **Skill/Strategy Lesson** Review how to identify *character and setting*. Then introduce this week's strategy, *predict*. DAY 2 *14e*

PRACTICE/APPLY

☐ **Skills and Strategies in Context** Read *Iris and Walter*, using the Guiding Comprehension questions to apply *character and setting* and *predict*. DAY 2 *16–35a*

Main Selection—Fiction

☐ **Think and Share** Use the questions on Student Edition p. 36 to discuss the selection. DAY 3 *36g-37*

☐ **Skills and Strategies in Context** Read the poems, guiding children as they apply skills and strategies. After reading have children make connections across texts. DAY 4 *38e-39*

Paired Selection— Poetry

☐ **Leveled Text** Apply *character and setting* and *predict* to read leveled text. DAY 4 *LR1-LR9*, DAY 5 *LR1-LR9*

Leveled Readers

☐ **Homework** Practice Book 2.1 pp. 4–5. DAY 1 *13a*, DAY 2 *14e*

ASSESS

☐ **Selection Test** Determine children's understanding of the main selection and assess their ability to identify *character and setting*. DAY 3

☐ **Story Reading** Have children read the passage " The New Friend." Ask what the *character and setting* of the story is and have them retell. DAY 5 *40e-40g*

RETEACH/REVIEW

☐ **Reteach Lesson** If necessary, reteach *character and setting*. DAY 5 *DI-64*

FLUENCY

SKILL READ WTH APPROPRIATE PACE AND RATE When you read, try to read all the words in a sentence at a speed that sounds as if you are speaking.

REREAD FOR FLUENCY

☐ **Oral Rereading** Have children reread orally from Decodable Reader 1 or another text at their independent reading level. Listen as children read and provide corrective feedback regarding their oral reading and their use of the blending strategy. DAY 1 *12q*

☐ **Paired Reading** Have pairs of children read orally from the main selection or another text at their independent reading level. Listen as children read and provide corrective feedback regarding their oral reading and their use of the blending strategy. DAY 2 *35a*

TEACH

☐ **Model** Use passages from *Iris and Walter*, "Morning Song," and "My Travel Tree" to model reading with appropriate pace and rate. DAY 3 *36f*, DAY 4 *39a*

PRACTICE/APPLY

☐ **Choral Reading** Choral read passages from *Iris and Walter* and "Morning Songs." Monitor progress and provide feedback regarding children's pace and rate. DAY 3 *36f*, DAY 4 *39a*

☐ **Listening Center** Have children follow along with the AudioText for this week's selections. ANY DAY *12j*

☐ **Reading/Library Center** Have children build fluency by rereading Leveled Readers, Decodable Readers, or other text at their independent level. ANY DAY *12j*

☐ **Fluency Coach** Have children use Fluency Coach to listen to fluent reading or to practice reading on their own. ANY DAY

ASSESS

☐ **Story Reading** Take a one-minute timed sample of children's oral reading. Use the passage "The New Friend." DAY 5 *40e-40g*

Use assessment data to determine your instructional focus.

Preview this week's instruction by strand.

Choose instructional activities that meet the needs of your classroom.

WRITING

Trait of the Week

VOICE Voice is the way a writer feels about a topic.

TEACH

- **Write Together** Engage children in writing activities that develop language, grammar, and writing skills. Include independent writing as an extension of group writing activities.

  Shared Writing DAY 1 *13c*
  Interactive Writing DAY 2 *35b*
  Writing Across the Curriculum DAY 4 *39b*

- **Trait of the Week** Introduce and model the Trait of the Week, *voice.* DAY 3 *37a*

PRACTICE/APPLY

- **Write Now** Examine the model on Student Edition pp. 40–41. Then have children write plans. DAY 5 *40-41*

  Prompt In *Iris and Walter,* Iris visits a treehouse and makes a friend. Think about a place you would like to visit. Now write a plan that tells what you will see and do there.

Write Now

- **Daily Journal Writing** Have children write about concepts and literature in their journals. **EVERY DAY** *12d-12e*

- **Writing Center** Write a story about one thing they might find in a new neighborhood. **ANY DAY** *12k*

ASSESS

- **Scoring Rubric** Use a rubric to evaluate children's plans. DAY 5 *40-41*

RETEACH/REVIEW

- **The Grammar and Writing Book** Use pp. 50–55 of The Grammar and Writing Book to extend instruction. **ANY DAY**

The Grammar and Writing Book

SPEAKING AND LISTENING

TEACH

- **Why We Speak** Demonstrate different reasons why we speak. Then have children answer a question to demonstrate speaking. DAY 4 *39d*

GRAMMAR

SKILL SENTENCES A sentence is a group of words that tells a complete idea. The words are in an order that makes sense. A sentence begins with a capital letter. Many sentences end with a period.

TEACH

- **Grammar Transparency 1** Use Grammar Transparency 1 to teach *sentences.* DAY 1 *13d*

Grammar Transparency 1

PRACTICE/APPLY

- **Develop the Concept** Review the concept of *sentences* and provide guided practice. DAY 2 *35c*

- **Apply to Writing** Have children use sentences in writing. DAY 3 *37b*

- **Define/Practice** Review the definition of *sentences.* Then have children identify complete sentences. DAY 4 *39c*

- **Write Now** Discuss the grammar lesson on Student Edition p. 41. Have children use sentences in their own plans about a place they would like to visit. DAY 5 *40-41*

Write Now

- **Daily Fix-It** Have children find and correct errors in grammar, spelling, and punctuation. DAY 1 *13c*, DAY 2 *35c*, DAY 3 *37a*, DAY 4 *39c*, DAY 5 *40-41*

- **Homework** The Grammar and Writing Practice Book pp. 1–4. DAY 2 *35c*, DAY 3 *37b*, DAY 4 *39c*, DAY 5 *40-41*

RETEACH/REVIEW

- **The Grammar and Writing Book** Use pp. 50–53 of The Grammar and Writing Book to extend instruction. **ANY DAY**

The Grammar and Writing Book

RESEARCH/INQUIRY

TEACH

- **Media Center/Library** Model using a media center/library. Then have children find a fiction or nonfiction book about something that interests them. DAY 5 *41a*

- **Unit Inquiry Project** Allow time for children to work in a group and list places they would like to explore. **ANY DAY** *11*

Resources for Differentiated Instruction

LEVELED READERS

▶ **Comprehension**
- ↻ **Skill** Character/Setting
- ↻ **Strategy** Predict

▶ **Lesson Vocabulary**

High-Frequency Words

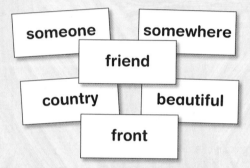

someone   somewhere
friend
country   beautiful
front

▶ **Social Studies Standards**
- Comparing Communities
- Geography: Urban, Suburban, Rural
- Exploration
- Friendship

Leveled Reader Database ONLINE

PearsonSuccessNet.com

Use the Online Database of over 600 books to
- Download and print additional copies of this week's leveled readers
- Listen to the readers being read online
- Search for more titles focused on this week's skills, topic, and content

---

On-Level

Social Studies
The New Kid
by Eve Beck
illustrated by Nicole Wong

On-Level Reader

Character and Setting

Read the paragraphs.
Look for words that tell you about the setting. Write these words under Setting.
Then, look for words that tell you about the character, Denny. Write these words under Character.

> When Dad got the job I was glad. I like traveling with my family to see new places. I like the adventure of going to different places, even if I have to be the new kid there.
> Dad helps out on small farms around the world. This summer we went to the island country of Bali. Kids speak Indonesian there. They eat meals with their fingers. And best of all, they love soccer, just like at home!

Setting	Character
small farms	glad
Bali	new kid
island	adventurous
summer	likes soccer

On-Level Practice TE p. LR5

Vocabulary

Synonyms are words that have the same meaning. Draw lines to match the synonyms.

1. beautiful — a. playmate—a child that plays with other children
2. country — b. pretty—pleasing to look at
3. friend — c. nation—a large group of people that share the same government

4. Write a sentence with the word *someone*.

Mom says someone from school can come along.

5. Write a sentence with the word *somewhere*.

I know my key is somewhere in my room.

On-Level Practice TE p. LR6

Strategic Intervention

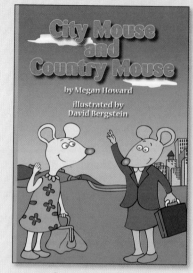

City Mouse and Country Mouse
by Megan Howard
illustrated by David Bergstein

Below-Level Reader

Character and Setting

Read the following paragraph from the story.
Write what you know about the setting.

> The very next day Country Mouse went to see her friend in the city. The mice went roller-skating on the sidewalk. They ate bread at a bakery. They heard someone sing at a club.

Setting:

city   sidewalk
bakery   club

Character:
Think about what you know about Country Mouse and City Mouse after reading the story. Match the characters to what each character likes.

Characters	What Characters Like
1. Country Mouse	a. the country best
	b. the city best
	c. peace and quiet
2. City Mouse	d. to do many things
	e. to visit other places

Below-Level Practice TE p. LR2

Vocabulary

Synonyms are words that have the same meaning. Draw a line to match the synonyms.

1. beautiful — a. nation—a large group of people that share the same government
2. country — b. playmate—a child that plays with other children
3. friend — c. pretty—pleasing to look at

4. Write a sentence with the word *someone*.

On my birthday I feel like someone special.

5. Write a sentence with the word *somewhere*.

Each winter, we take a trip somewhere warm.

Below-Level Practice TE p. LR3

Advanced

City Friends, Country Friends
by Christine Wolf

illustrated by C.D. Hullinger

Advanced Reader

Character and Setting
Read this chart from the story. Think about what the chart tells you about the story's characters and settings. Then fill in the diagram below.

5 Senses	Henry's Favorite	Tasha's Favorite
Sight	Green fields, pigs	View from apartment
Sound	Crickets, tractors	People shouting "Taxi"
Smell	Grass, mud, Mom's pie	Mom's perfume
Touch	Soft skin on piglets	Elevator buttons
Taste	Water from our well	Fresh bagels, Mom's pie

Tasha/urban setting — Both — Henry/rural setting

apartment · taxis · elevator | Mom's pie · bagels · grass · perfume | pigs · mud · well water · tractors

Advanced Practice TE p. LR8

Vocabulary
Choose the word from the box that best completes each sentence.

Words to Know		
investigate	rural	urban

1. In ___urban___ places many people live in apartment buildings.

2. The teacher asked us to ___investigate___ the trees around the school.

3. My friend from a ___rural___ town likes to ride the tractor with his father.

Antonyms are two words that mean the opposite of each other.

4. Which two words from the word box are antonyms?
___rural___ ___urban___

Advanced Practice TE p. LR9

ELL

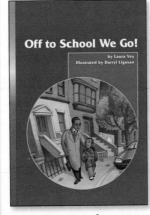

ELL Reader

ELL Poster 1

Teacher's Edition Notes
ELL notes throughout this lesson support instruction and reference additional resources at point of use.

ELL Teaching Guide pp. 1–7, 212–213

- Multilingual summaries of the main selection
- Comprehension lesson
- Vocabulary strategies and word cards
- ELL Reader 1 lesson

ELL and Transition Handbook

Ten Important Sentences

- Key ideas from every selection in the Student Edition
- Activities to build sentence power

More Reading

Readers' Theater Anthology
- Fluency practice
- Five scripts to build fluency
- Poetry for oral interpretation

Leveled Trade Books

- Extend reading tied to the unit concept
- Lessons in Trade Book Library Teaching Guide

School + Home

Homework
- Family Times Newsletter
- ELL Multilingual Selection Summaries

Take-Home Books
- Decodable Readers
- Leveled Readers

Iris and Walter

Literacy Centers

 Listening

Let's Read
Along

MATERIALS `SINGLES`
CD player, headphones, print copies of recorded pieces

LISTEN TO LITERATURE As children listen to the following recordings, have them follow along or read along in the print version.

AudioText
Iris and Walter
"Morning Song"/"My Travel Tree"

Sing with Me/Background Building Audio
"Let's Go Investigate"

Phonics Songs and Rhymes Audio
"Let's Go Explore"

Let's Go Explore!

I grab my sweater and get my cap.
I want to go explore.
Mom said we can go see the town
On our way to the store.

We saw a clock tower in the park,
A bank, and my new school.
The school bell rang; kids waved at me.
This place just might be cool.

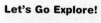 **Audio CD** **Phonics Songs and Rhymes Chart 1**

 Reading/Library

Read It
Again!

MATERIALS `SINGLES` `PAIRS` `GROUPS`
collection of books for self-selected reading, reading logs

REREAD BOOKS Have children select previously read books from the appropriate book box and record titles of books they read in their logs. Use these previously read books:

- Decodable Readers
- Leveled Readers
- ELL Readers
- Stories written by classmates
- Books from the library

TEN IMPORTANT SENTENCES Have children read the Ten Important Sentences for *Iris and Walter* and locate the sentences in the Student Edition.

BOOK CLUB Other Iris and Walter books are listed on p. 37 of the Student Edition. Encourage interested children to read one and tell everyone about it.

 Word Work

Bread
Basket

MATERIALS `PAIRS`
15 cut-out paper slices of bread, 5 cardboard bread baskets

SHORT VOWELS Pairs fill vowel bread baskets.

1. Write each of this week's spelling words on a paper bread slice.
2. Label each basket with a short vowel.
3. Pairs take turns reading the words on the bread slices and placing them in the appropriate basket.
4. Continue until all words have been read.

 Phonics Activities CD This interactive CD provides additional practice.

Scott Foresman Reading Street Centers Survival Kit
Use the *Iris and Walter* materials from the Reading Street
Centers Survival Kit to organize this week's centers.

 Writing

 Social Studies

 Technology

Make a Discovery

MATERIALS **PAIRS**
paper, pencils, crayons, markers

WRITE A STORY Review what Iris discovered when she explored her new neighborhood.

1. Pairs discuss what they might find in a new neighborhood.
2. Have them write about one thing they discover.
3. Then have them draw a picture to illustrate what they wrote.

LEVELED WRITING Encourage children to write at their own ability level. Some may have difficulty focusing on the topic. Others may stray from the topic. Your best writers will be well-focused on the topic.

I found a new friend. We play soccer together.

City or COUNTRY?

MATERIALS **PAIRS**
copies of Venn diagram or Graphic Organizer 17 labeled *City, Country, Both*; pencils

MAKE A VENN DIAGRAM Review *Iris and Walter*. Discuss the similarities and differences between living in the country and living in the city.

1. Give each pair of children a copy of the Venn diagram.
2. Have pairs work together to complete the diagram about country life and city life.

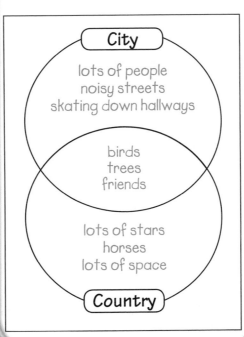

City
lots of people
noisy streets
skating down hallways

birds
trees
friends

lots of stars
horses
lots of space

Country

Easy E-Mails

MATERIALS **SINGLES** **PAIRS**
computer with Internet access

WRITE AN E-MAIL Have children practice sending an e-mail to a friend.

1. Have children turn on the computer and open an e-mail program.
2. They should address an e-mail to a friend.
3. Have each child write a one- or two-sentence e-mail to a friend in the class. Remind them to use correct punctuation.
4. Children can print out their e-mails.

To: Kathy
From: Jill
Subject: Hi!

Hi, Kathy! Let's play today.
Jill

ALL CENTERS

Day 1
AT A GLANCE

Oral Vocabulary
"Let's Go Investigate" 1

Phonics and Spelling
 Short Vowels
Spelling Pretest:
Words with Short Vowels

Read Apply Phonics Word Wall

Group Time < Differentiated Instruction

Build Background
Let's Talk About Exploration

Listening Comprehension
 Character and Setting

Shared Writing
Plan

Grammar
Sentences

Materials

- *Sing with Me Big Book*
- Sound-Spelling Cards 1, 9, 15, 23, 35
- Letter Tiles
- Decodable Reader 1
- Student Edition 12–13
- Graphic Organizer 17
- Writing Transparency 1
- Grammar Transparency 1

Take It to the NET ONLINE

Professional Development
To read excerpts from *Put Reading First,* summarizing findings of the National Reading Panel, go to PearsonSuccessNet.com.

Morning Warm~Up!

People live in urban and rural areas. What might we discover in a new neighborhood?

QUESTION OF THE WEEK Tell children they will talk, sing, read, and write about what we might find in a new neighborhood. Explain that an urban neighborhood is in the city and that a rural neighborhood is in the country. Write and read the message and discuss the question.

CONNECT CONCEPTS Ask questions to connect what children already know about urban and rural neighborhoods.

- Do we live in a rural neighborhood in the country or an urban neighborhood in the city?

- Which kind of neighborhood has lots of open space but not many people?

- Which one has lots of people and buildings but not very much open space?

REVIEW HIGH-FREQUENCY WORDS

- Circle the high-frequency words *people, live, we,* and *new* in the message.

- Have children say and spell each word as they write it in the air.

ELL

Build Background Use the Day 1 instruction on ELL Poster 1 to assess knowledge and develop concepts.

ELL Poster 1

Oral Vocabulary

SHARE LITERATURE Display p. 1 of the *Sing with Me Big Book.* Tell children that the class is going to sing a song about investigating rural and urban places. Read the title. Ask children to listen for the Amazing Words **rural, urban,** and **investigate** as you sing. Then sing the song again and encourage children to sing along with you. Have children demonstrate their understanding of *rural, urban,* and *investigate* by asking:

- What kinds of things would you find in a rural area?
- What kinds of things would you find in an urban area?
- What is the first place you would investigate in a new neighborhood?

**Sing with Me/
Background Building Audio**

Let's Go Investigate!

In the country, it's so peaceful.
Rural places are so great.
We'll see farms and open spaces.
Let's go investigate!

In the city, it's so noisy.
Urban places are so great.
We can walk through friendly neighborhoods.
Let's go investigate!

Sing with Me Big Book

 **to build oral vocabulary**

Amazing Words	MONITOR PROGRESS
investigate rural urban creature underground brittle dart decision	**If...** children lack oral vocabulary experiences about the concept Exploration, **then...** use the Oral Vocabulary Routine below to teach *investigate*.

Oral Vocabulary ROUTINE

1 Introduce the Word Relate the word *investigate* to the song. Supply a child-friendly definition. Have children say the word. Example: When you *investigate* something, you try to find out all about it.

2 Demonstrate Provide an example to show meaning. She couldn't wait to *investigate* her new neighborhood.

3 Apply Have children demonstrate their understanding. Which one of these things would you most likely *investigate*—your friend's new tree house or the dinner dishes?

4 Display the Word/Word Parts Write the word on a card. Display it. Say *in-ves-ti-gate* slowly as you clap with each syllable. See p. DI·3 to teach *rural* and *urban*.

Build Oral Vocabulary Have children use words and actions to demonstrate the meanings of the words *peaceful* and *noisy*.

Iris and Walter **12m**

⟳ Short Vowels; *ea*/e/

TEACH/MODEL

OBJECTIVES

- ⟳ Associate the short vowel sounds with the CVC, CCVC, CVCC spelling patterns.
- Associate the sound /e/ with the letters *ea*.
- Blend, read, and build short vowel words.

Skills Trace

⟳ Short Vowels	
Introduce/Teach	TE: 2.1 12n–o
Practice	TE: 2.1 12q, 14c–d; PB: 2.1 3, 18; DR1
Reteach/Review	TE: 2.1 40c, 60c, DI-64
Assess/Test	TE: 2.1 40e–g; Benchmark Test: Unit 1

Generalization

Short Vowels When there is only one vowel at the beginning or in the middle of a word or syllable, it usually stands for its short sound.

The letters *ea* can stand for short *e* or long *e*. Context provides the clue to pronunciation.

Strategic Intervention

Use **Monitor Progress**, p. 12o, during Group Time after children have practiced with short vowels.

Advanced

Use **Monitor Progress**, p. 12o, as a preassessment to determine whether this group would benefit from instruction on short vowels.

Support Phonics In many languages, short vowel sounds may not exist or may only have approximations. English language learners may have a hard time hearing the differences in these sounds. Provide additional phonemic awareness activities to help children.

See the Phonics Transition Lessons in the ELL and Transition Handbook.

Blending Strategy

ROUTINE

1 **Connect** Write *am, end, it, on, up.* What do you know about the vowel sounds in these words? (They are all short vowel sounds.) Today we'll review short vowel sounds, and we'll learn another spelling for short *e.*

2 **Use Sound-Spelling Cards** Display Card 1. This is *astronaut.* Say the first sound in *astronaut*: /a/. /a/ is the short *a* sound. Say it with me: /a/.

3 **Model** Write *brand.* When a word has just one vowel at the beginning or in the middle, it usually has its short sound. This word has the short *a* sound, /a/. We can blend words by saying the sound for each letter: /b//r//a//n//d/, *brand.* Have children blend *brand* with you. We can also blend bigger chunks of words. I can blend this word by saying the sounds before the vowel together, /br/, and then saying all the rest of the sounds together, /and/. Then I blend the two chunks together: /br//and/, *brand.* Run your hand under the onset and rime as you model. Do it with me: /br//and/, *brand.*

Repeat steps 2 and 3. Use Cards 15 for *i*/i/, 23 for *o*/o/, 35 for *u*/u/, and 9 for *e*/e/. Model blending with *bring, clock, junk, best.* Then write *head.* Sometimes the letters *ea* stand for short *e,* /e/. Model blending: /h//ed/, *head.* Do it with me: /h//ed/, *head.*

4 **Group Practice** Blend these words together. Continue with *sang, desk, shock, wing, bread, drum.*

5 **Review** What do you know about reading these words? One vowel at the beginning or in the middle of a word usually has its short sound. The letters *a, e, i, o, u,* and *ea* can all stand for short vowel sounds.

Sound-Spelling Card 1

BLEND WORDS

INDIVIDUALS BLEND SHORT VOWEL WORDS Call on individuals to blend *bank, held, swing, flock, luck, sick, blink, dust.* Have them tell what they know about each word before reading it. For feedback, refer to step five of the Blending Strategy Routine.

KEYBOARD ROUTINE Use the Routine on the back of the Keyboard Card to show where the letters *a, e, i, o,* and *u* are located on a keyboard.

BUILD WORDS

INDIVIDUALS MAKE SHORT VOWEL WORDS Write *desk* and have the class blend it. Have children spell *desk* with letter tiles. Monitor work and provide feedback.

- Change the *s* to *c*.
  What is the new word?

- Change the *e* to *o*.
  What is the new word?

- Change the *o* to *u*.
  What is the new word?

- Change the *c* to *n*.
  What is the new word?

- Change the *du* to *si*.
  What is the new word?

- Change the *i* to *a*.
  What is the new word?

- Change the *k* to *g*.
  What is the new word?

d e c k

d o c k

d u c k

d u n k

s i n k

s a n k

s a n g

Vocabulary TiP

You may wish to explain the meanings of these words.

dock a platform built on the shore
dread fear of something that may happen
speck a small spot or stain
tank a large container to hold liquid, such as gasoline

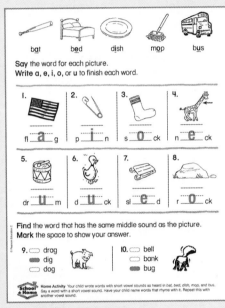

▲ **Practice Book 2.1** p. 3, Short Vowels

Monitor Progress | Check Word Reading Short Vowels

Write the following words and have individuals read them.

hum	bed	rip	van	jag
bread	lump	slim	pond	dread
tank	speck	swing	hung	dock

If... children cannot blend words with short vowels at this point,

then... have them isolate difficult parts of words in order to correct a mispronunciation. Continue to monitor their progress as they decode unfamiliar words using other instructional opportunities during the week so that they can be successful with the Day 5 Assessment. See the Skills Trace on p. 12n.

SUCCESS PREDICTOR

Spiral REVIEW

- Row 2 reviews initial and final consonant blends.
- Row 3 reviews final *ck*, *ng*, and *nk*.

▶ **Day 1 Check** Word Reading • **Day 2 Check** High-Frequency Words • **Day 3 Check** Retelling • **Day 4 Check** Fluency • **Day 5 Assess** Progress

Word Reading SUCCESS PREDICTOR

Spelling Words

Short Vowels

1.	drum	7.	chop
2.	rock	8.	sack
3.	list	9.	tag
4.	desk	10.	rib
5.	job	11.	mess
6.	sad*	12.	dust

Challenge Words

13.	pocket	15.	engine
14.	lettuce		

* Words from the Selection

Spelling

PRETEST Short Vowels

MODEL WRITING FOR SOUNDS Each spelling word has a short vowel sound. Before administering the spelling pretest, model how to segment short vowel words to spell them.

- What sounds do you hear in *lock?* (/l/ /o/ /k/)
- What is the letter for /l/? Write *l.* Continue with the *o*/o/ and *ck*/k/.
- What letter stands for /o/? *(o)*
- Repeat with *mask, less, pick,* and *must.*

PRETEST Dictate the spelling words. Segment the words for children if necessary. Have children check their pretests and correct misspelled words.

HOMEWORK Spelling Practice Book, p. 1

Short Vowels CVC, CVCC, CCVC

Generalization Short vowels are often spelled a: sad, e: desk, i: rib, o: job, u: drum.

Sort the list words by the short vowel.

a
1. sad
2. sack
3. tag

e
4. desk
5. mess

i
11. list

o
6. rock
7. job
8. chop

u
9. drum
10. dust

i
12. rib

Challenge Words
e
13. lettuce
15. engine

o
14. pocket

Spelling Words
1. drum
2. rock
3. list
4. desk
5. job
6. sad
7. chop
8. sack
9. tag
10. rib
11. mess
12. dust
Challenge Words
13. pocket
14. lettuce
15. engine

Home Activity Your child is learning to spell words with short vowels and these consonant/vowel patterns: CVC, CVCC, CCVC. To practice at home, have your child look at the word, pronounce it, and then write it.

▲ **Spelling Practice Book** p. 1

New to the City

Joan woke to a loud thud as a garbage truck collected the trash outside her family's new apartment. She heard bottles breaking and the truck's motor as it roared down the block. She got up to fix herself a bowl of cereal and saw that her mother was already sitting at the table. "Did the garbage truck wake you up too?" Mom asked.

"I liked it better when the rooster would wake me up with his cock-a-doodle-do," Joan said, nodding. She and her family had lived on a farm in a rural area, but they moved to a large city so that Joan's father could take a new job. "I really miss the animals," Joan said sadly. "There are no animals in the city."

"I have an idea," said Mom. "Let's go to the park today. We'll take this bread with us."

Decodable Reader 1
Gus

Group Time

On-Level	Strategic Intervention	Advanced
Read Decodable Reader 1.	**Read** Decodable Reader 1.	**Read** Advanced Selection 1.
• Use p. 12q.	• Use the **Routine** on p. DI·14.	• Use the **Routine** on p. DI·15.

ELL Place English language learners in the groups that correspond to their reading abilities in English.

ⓘ Independent Activities

Fluency Reading Pair children to reread Leveled Readers or the ELL Reader from the previous week or other text at children's independent level.

Journal Writing Write about whether your neighborhood is urban or rural. Share writing.

Independent Reading See p. 12j for Reading/Library activities and suggestions.

Literacy Centers To practice short vowels, you may use Word Work, p. 12j.

Practice Book 2.1 Short Vowels, p. 3; Character and Setting, p. 4

ELL

Support Spelling Before giving the spelling pretest, clarify the meaning of each spelling word with examples, such as pretending to cry for *sad* and pointing to a desk to illustrate *desk.*

Break into small groups after Spelling and before Build Background.

Apply Phonics

⟳ PRACTICE Short Vowels

HIGH-FREQUENCY WORDS Review *does*, *together*, and *under* from grade 1.

READ DECODABLE READER 1

- Pages 2–3 Read aloud quietly with the group.
- Pages 4–5 Have the group read aloud without you.
- Pages 6–8 Select individuals to read aloud. Encourage children to use onset and rime blending.

CHECK COMPREHENSION AND DECODING Ask children the following questions:

- Who are the characters in the story? (Ken, Gus)
- What happens when Gus tugs on his bell? (Ken lets Gus out.)

Then have children locate short vowel words in the story. Review short vowel spelling patterns. Sort words according to their vowel sounds.

a	*e*	*i*	*o*	*u*
back	bed	big	fond	bunk
can	bell	did	got	fun
fast	Ken	lick	job	Gus
hand	let	his	long	hug
mat	pet	six	lot	jump
nap	red	quick	not	pup
pat	tell	ring	on	run
rang	well	will		tug
has				

HOMEWORK Take-Home Decodable Reader 1

REREAD FOR FLUENCY

Oral Rereading

ROUTINE

1 **Read** Have children read the entire story orally.

2 **Reread** To achieve optimal fluency, children should reread the text three or four times.

3 **Provide Feedback** Listen as children read and provide feedback regarding their oral reading and their use of the blending strategy.

Monitor Progress

Decoding

If... children have difficulty decoding a word,	then... prompt them to blend the word.
	• What is the new word?
	• Is the new word a word you know?
	• Does it make sense in the story?

Access Content

Beginning Lead children on a picture walk through *Gus*, identifying verbs, such as *run*, *jump*, and *tug*, in the pictures and print.

Intermediate Preview *Gus*, pointing out short vowel words, such as *Ken*, *Gus*, *mess*, and *bunk*.

Advanced After reading *Gus*, have partners take turns retelling the first few pages of the story.

Build Background

LET'S TALK ABOUT Exploration

DEVELOP ORAL LANGUAGE Read the title and have children view the photographs. Ask them to tell you what they see. Allow ample time for children to respond. Remind children to phrase their ideas in complete sentences and to speak loudly enough to be heard. Use open-ended prompts to model language use and to encourage discussion. For example:

Tell me what you see on these pages. That's right, everybody is looking at something. Some of the people look like they are in the city, or an urban area, and some of them look as if they are in the country, or a rural area. Can you tell me what kind of area you live in?

BUILD ORAL VOCABULARY As you continue the discussion, have children use today's Amazing Words: *investigate, rural, urban*.

- Use the word *urban* to tell about the background picture.
- What is the boy in the topmost picture investigating?
- How are the urban and rural areas different?

DEVELOP CONCEPTS

CONCEPT CHART Remind children of the question of the week.

- What might we discover in a new neighborhood?

Display Graphic Organizer 17 or draw a Venn diagram. Label the circles *Urban* and *Rural*. Using what they already know and the pictures in the Student Edition, help children write in each circle words to describe each kind of area and, in the center overlap section, words that describe both. Display the diagram for use throughout the week.

- Are the people looking at the buildings in the city or the country? (city)
- Is the boy looking at the frog in an urban or rural area? (rural)

CONNECT TO READING Point out the illustration at the bottom of p. 13 in the Student Edition. Ask children whether this illustration shows an urban area or rural area. (rural) Explain that this week children will read a story about the girl in the picture and what she discovers when she and her grandfather investigate her new neighborhood.

Strategic Intervention

Invite children to find pictures in old magazines of urban and rural areas or to look up *urban* and *rural* in a picture dictionary. Remind them as necessary that *urban* refers to a city and that *rural* refers to the country. Ask them to label each picture *urban* or *rural*.

Advanced

Suggest that children use dictionaries and encyclopedias, in the library or on the Web, for comparisons of urban and rural areas. Encourage them to find other ways in which they are similar and different.

Activate Prior Knowledge
Invite children who have lived in rural or urban areas to describe them. You may want to encourage children to use some words from their home language as they do so.

Let's Talk About
EXPLORATION

12
13

Urban   Rural

big buildings

lots of people

many cars,
buses, and
trucks

houses
cars

not many
buildings

lots of open space

many flowers,
trees, and birds

▲ **Graphic Organizer 17**

Take It to the NET™
ONLINE

For a Web site that tells you more about living in the country like Iris and Walter, do an Internet search using the keywords *farm life*.

Access Content To prepare children for reading *Iris and Walter*, send home the story summary in English and/or the home language. See the ELL Teaching Guide, pp. 5–7.

OBJECTIVE

⊙ Identify character and setting.

Skills Trace

⊙ **Character and Setting**

Introduce/Teach	TE: 2.1 13a–b, 14e, 69a–b, 70e; 2.6 408r, 408–409
Practice	TE: 2.1 18–19, 82–83; 2.6 422–423; PB: 2.1 4–5, 24–25; 2.2 144–145
Reteach/Review	TE: 2.1 140–141, DI·64, DI·66; 2.6 DI·68; PB: 2.1 47, 57; 2.2 7
Test	TE: 2.1 40e–g, 95e–g; 2.6 432e–g; Selection Tests: 2.1 1–4, 9–12; 2.6 117–120; Benchmark Test: Units 1, 2, 4, 5

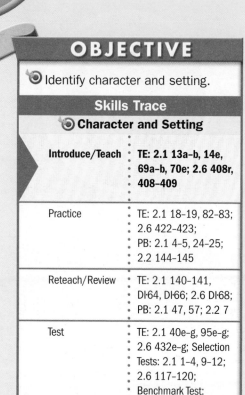

Read the story and look at the picture to find out about the character Mr. James.

Mr. James has a shop on my corner. He sells bread and milk. He has a kind word for everyone who comes in his store. When it is hot, Mr. James makes ice cream cones. He gives them away to kids for a treat. Mr. James likes people, and people like him.

Circle the word that answers each question.

1. Which word describes Mr. James?
   younger (older)

2. Which word describes what Mr. James sells?
   signs (bread)

Write your answer to each question.

3. Why do you think people like Mr. James?

   Possible responses: Mr. James is kind or Mr. James gives away
   ice cream cones.

4. What is the setting of the story?

   a neighborhood grocery store

 **Home Activity** Your child described the character and setting of a story. Work with your child to write about an interesting person in your neighborhood. Make sure your child describes what makes that person likeable or interesting.

▲ **Practice Book 2.1** p. 4, Character and Setting

ELL

Access Content For a Picture It! lesson on character and setting, see the ELL Teaching Guide, pp. 1–2.

Listening Comprehension

⊙ TEACH/MODEL Character and Setting

DEFINE CHARACTER AND SETTING

- Characters are the people or animals in a story.

- Authors describe characters' traits. They tell what characters are like, what they think, and what they say and do.

- The setting is the time and place of a story. A setting can be a real place or an imaginary one.

- Good readers look for clues that tell about characters and setting.

READ ALOUD Read "A New Neighborhood" and model how to identify character traits and setting.

 MODEL To figure out who the characters are, I ask myself who the story is mostly about. The story is mostly about Jamal and Christine. To find the setting, I look for clues about where and when the story takes place. The story says Jamal moved to the city from the country, so the story takes place in the city. To figure out character traits, I look to see what the author tells about what the characters are like. The author says that Jamal is too shy to go meet new people and that he is miserable and lonely when he first moves to the city.

PRACTICE

CLUES TO CHARACTER AND SETTING Ask children to identify some character traits for Christine. (Christine is friendly and knows many people in the neighborhood.) How are Christine and Jamal alike and different? (Jamal is shy while Christine isn't afraid to introduce herself to him. Christine likes the city and knows lots of people while Jamal is still getting used to living there. They both like playing basketball.) Have children identify other clues that tell the story setting is the city. (Jamal lives in an apartment building. Jamal's neighborhood has a park and a library.)

IDENTIFY CHARACTER AND SETTING Have children recall characters from previously read stories.

- Who was a character in a story you have read?

- What are some things the author told you about what that character was like and what he or she felt and did?

- What was the setting of the story?

CONNECT TO READING Tell children that when they read any story, they should identify the characters and setting of the story.

A New Neighborhood

Read ALOUD

Jamal and his family moved into a new city apartment in June. Jamal missed his friends and all the things he used to do in the country. Even though he was in a large urban area with many kids his age, he knew no one and he was too shy to go places to meet other kids.

When he looked out the window he saw plenty of boys his age, but they were always going somewhere else—running down the street together or getting on buses. He felt miserable and lonely. When would he ever meet anyone?

Then one morning in early July, Jamal was sitting on his front stairs and feeling sad when a girl his age came up to him holding a basketball.

"I'm Christine," she said. "I haven't seen you around before. What's your name?"

"I'm Jamal," he answered. "My family just moved here from the country, and I can't find anything to do."

"Are you kidding?" Christine said. "There's tons of things to do in the city. Do you want to shoot some hoops in the park?"

"Sure!" he said.

Christine had grown up in the neighborhood and knew many people who lived in it. As she showed Jamal the way to their neighborhood park, she stopped several times to say hello to people and ask them how they were doing. Jamal shyly said hello to them too, once Christine introduced him. He was glad she was there to help him meet people and investigate his new neighborhood.

At the park, they took turns shooting baskets until they were tired.

"Now let's get something to drink," Christine said. She showed Jamal the way to a corner where a woman with a cart was selling glasses of lemonade.

"It'll be too hot to be outside this afternoon," Christine said as they walked back to Jamal's apartment building. "I was going to go to the library. The librarian reads stories at 3:00. Would you like to come with me?"

"Yes!" Jamal said. "That would be great. And thanks for showing me around. I never realized there were so many things to do in this neighborhood!"

DAILY FIX-IT

1. We will lits what we might see
We will <u>list</u> what we might see<u>.</u>

2. iris wanted a friend
<u>I</u>ris wanted a friend<u>.</u>

This week's practice sentences appear on Daily Fix-It Transparency 1.

Strategic Intervention

Help children who have difficulty writing or spelling the words they want to use by writing models for them.

Advanced

Have children include in their plan some ideas about the people they might meet when they visit their new place.

ELL

Support Writing Pair each student with a more proficient English speaker. Let partners brainstorm where they want to plan to visit. You may want to allow partners to work together to complete the Independent Writing task.

▲ **The Grammar and Writing Book**
For more instruction and practice, use pp. 50–55.

Shared Writing

WRITE Plan

GENERATE IDEAS Ask children to think of a new place they would like to visit. Ask them what they think they might see and do there.

WRITE A PLAN Explain that the class will write a plan that tells what children think they might see and do in a new place they visit.

 COMPREHENSION SKILL Have children think of a setting—a time and a place—for their visit to a new place. Ask them also to think of people they might meet there.

- Display Writing Transparency 1 and read the title.

- Have children brainstorm a new place they all want to visit.

- Read the first sentence and record the new place they chose.

- Read the remaining titles and incomplete sentences. As children discuss their ideas, record endings to the sentences in the blanks.

HANDWRITING While writing, model the letter forms as shown on pp. TR14–17.

READ THE PLAN Have children read the completed plan aloud as you track the print.

A New Place

Possible answers:

Let's go to <u>**the Grand Canyon**</u>

Things We Might See There

We might see **colorful rocks**

We might see **great views**

Things We Might Do There

We might **hike on a trail**

We might **take pictures**

Unit 1 Iris and Walter   Writing Model **1**

▲ **Writing Transparency 1**

INDEPENDENT WRITING

WRITE SENTENCES Have children write their own plan for a visit to a new place. Encourage them to use words from the Word Wall and the Amazing Words board. Let children illustrate their writing. You may gather children's work to display on a bulletin board.

ADDITIONAL PRACTICE For additional practice, use pp. 50–55 in the Grammar and Writing Book.

Grammar

TEACH/MODEL Sentences

IDENTIFY SENTENCES Display Grammar Transparency 1. Read the definition aloud.

- The phrase "The sand" does not make a complete sentence. It is a fragment.
- If we add "felt hot," we will have a complete sentence. Remember that we must end the sentence with a period.

Continue modeling with items 2–5.

PRACTICE

ADD SENTENCES Have children add one or two other sentences to the story about the beach. Write the sentences.

- Let's think about the people who went to the beach.
- What else did they do there?

objective

OBJECTIVE

● Identify sentences.

Sentences

A **sentence** is a group of words that tells a complete idea. The words are in an order that makes sense. A sentence begins with a capital letter. Many sentences end with a **period** (.).

We went to the beach. ← This is a complete sentence.

the beach ← This is not a complete sentence.

Make each group of words a sentence.
Write a group of words from the box.

| packed a picnic. | felt hot. | |
| was cool and blue. | dived in the waves. | was fun. |

1. The sand **felt hot.**

2. The water **was cool and blue.**

3. My brother and I **dived in the waves.**

4. Mom **packed a picnic.**

5. Our first trip to the beach **was fun.**

Unit 1 Iris and Walter   Grammar **1**

▲ **Grammar Transparency 1**

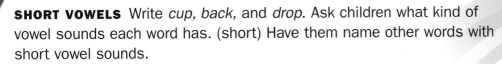

Wrap Up Your Day!

✓ **SHORT VOWELS** Write *cup, back,* and *drop.* Ask children what kind of vowel sounds each word has. (short) Have them name other words with short vowel sounds.

✓ **SPELLING SHORT VOWEL WORDS** Have children name the letters for each sound in *rug.* Write the letters as children write them in the air. Continue with *flat* and *gift.*

✓ **CHARACTER AND SETTING** To help children recognize character and setting, ask: Does every story have to have characters? Why or why not? Could every story happen at any time or place? Why or why not? Use examples from stories familiar to children to help them answer.

LET'S TALK ABOUT IT Review the Venn diagram or Graphic Organizer 17 and children's comparisons of urban and rural places. Add to the diagram children's answers to: What else might we find out if we visited an urban place and a rural place?

School + Home **HOMEWORK** Send home this week's Family Times newsletter.

PREVIEW Day 2

Tell children that tomorrow the class will read about a girl who moves from the city to the country, and what she finds in her new neighborhood.

13d

Day 2
AT A GLANCE

Share Literature
In the Forest

Phonics and Spelling
Short Vowels
Spelling: Words with Short Vowels

Comprehension
Skill Character and Setting
Strategy Predict

Build Background
Discuss City and Country Life

High-Frequency Words

someone	somewhere	**Word Wall**
friend	country	
beautiful	front	

Vocabulary
Selection Words

amazing	roller-skate
ladder	meadow

Read Apply Phonics **Word Wall**

Group Time < Differentiated Instruction

Iris and Walter

Interactive Writing
Paragraph

Grammar
Sentences

Materials

- *Sing with Me Big Book*
- Big Book *In the Forest*
- Phonics Songs and Rhymes Chart 1
- Background Building Audio
- Vocabulary Transparency 1
- Graphic Organizer 25
- Letter Tiles
- Student Edition 14–35
- Tested Word Cards

Morning Warm-Up!

Today we will read about Iris.
Iris moves to a new neighborhood, but
she is lonely. What could she discover
that might help her?

QUESTION OF THE DAY Encourage children to sing "Let's Go Investigate!" from the *Sing with Me Big Book* as you gather. Write and read the message and discuss the question.

REVIEW SHORT VOWEL CCVC

- Read the last sentence of the message.

- Have children raise their hands when they hear a word with a short *a* sound. *(that)* Point out the consonant digraph *th*, which has two consonant letters standing for a single sound.

ELL

Build Background Use the Day 2 instruction on ELL Poster 1 to preview high-frequency words.

ELL Poster 1

Share Literature

BUILD CONCEPTS

NONFICTION Have children read the title. Identify the author. Explain that books about real people, animals, or things doing real things are nonfiction. Nonfiction books often have photographs as this book does.

Big Book

BUILD ORAL VOCABULARY Invite children to discuss kinds of animals and plants they have seen and looked at closely. Tell children that a forest is home to many different plants and animals. One **creature,** or animal, you might see is a chipmunk. Suggest that as you read, children listen to find out about other creatures in the forest.

- What type or rural area do these animals and plants live in? (the forest)

- How is investigating something very close up different from looking at it from farther away? (Possible answer: Sometimes something close up looks very different, and you can't really tell what it is.)

MONITOR LISTENING COMPREHENSION

- Why does a chipmunk look different from other creatures? (It has a bright white streak on its back.)

- What is another creature you read about? (box turtle, bull moose, ermine)

- What do you think you might find if you investigated a rural area near where you live? What if you investigated an urban area? (Possible response: We might find a big cactus in the desert near us. We could find tall palm trees in the city near us.)

Amazing Words to build oral vocabulary

	MONITOR PROGRESS
investigate **rural** **urban** **creature** **underground** **brittle** **dart** **decision**	**If…** children lack oral vocabulary experiences about the concept Exploration, **then…** use the Oral Vocabulary Routine. See p. DI·3 to teach *creature*.

Build Concepts Moving from an urban area to a rural one is a major concept in this week's selection *Iris and Walter*. Discuss with children the differences between living in the country and living in a city.

OBJECTIVES

 Review short vowels.
● Sort and read words with short vowels.
● Preview words before reading them.
● Spell words with short vowels.

Strategic Intervention

Use **Strategic Intervention Decodable Reader 1** for more practice with short vowels.

ELL

Support Phonics Have children point to and name the people, places, and things pictured in the art for "Let's Go Explore!" as you replay the Phonics Songs and Rhymes Audio CD.

Short Vowels

TEACH/MODEL

ROUTINE

Fluent Word Reading

1 **Connect** Write *stock.* You can read this word because you know how to read words with short vowel sounds. What sound does the letter *o* stand for in this word? (/o/) What's the word? (*stock*) Do the same with *track, dead, peck, trunk, sing.*

2 **Model** When you come to a new word, look at the letters from left to right and think about the vowel sounds. Say the sounds in the word to yourself and then read the word. **Model** reading *stack, head, step, bring, lock, jump.* When you come to a new word, what are you going to do?

3 **Group Practice** Write *dress, bread, back, rust, fist.* Read these words. Look at the letters, think about the vowel sounds, say the sounds to yourself, and then read the word aloud together. **Allow 2–3 seconds previewing time.**

WORD READING

PHONICS SONGS AND RHYMES CHART 1 Frame each of the following words on Phonics Songs and Rhymes Chart 1. Call on individuals to read them. Guide children in previewing. Review with children the unique spelling pattern of *ea* as in *bread.* Have a volunteer find the word that has the short *e* sound spelled *ea.*

can	**grab**	**clock**	**get**
bank	**cap**	**rang**	**sweater**

Sing "Let's Go Explore!" to the tune of "Over the River and Through the Woods," or play the CD. Have children follow along on the chart as they sing. Then have individuals take turns underlining and reading short words on the chart.

Let's Go Explore!

I grab my sweater and get my cap.
I want to go explore.
Mom said we can go see the town
On our way to the store.

We saw a clock tower in the park,
A bank, and my new school.
The school bell rang; kids waved at me.
This place just might be cool.

 **Phonics Songs and Rhymes Audio**

Phonics Songs and Rhymes Chart 1

BUILD WORDS

INDIVIDUALS MAKE SHORT VOWEL WORDS Write *neck* and have the class blend it. Have children spell *neck* with letter tiles. Monitor work and provide feedback.

- Change the *n* to *s*, and the *e* to *a*. What is the new word?

  s a c k

- Change the *a* to *i*, and the *c* to *n*. What is the new word?

  s i n k

- Change the *i* to *a*. What is the new word?

  s a n k

- Change the *k* to *g*. What is the new word?

  s a n g

- Change the *a* to *u*. What is the new word?

  s u n g

- Change the *g* to *k*. What is the new word?

  s u n k

Spelling

⟳ PRACTICE Short Vowels

WRITE DICTATION SENTENCES Have children write these sentences. Repeat words slowly, allowing children to hear each sound. Children may use the Word Wall to help with spelling high-frequency words. [Word Wall]

The list is on my desk.

It is sad to see the mess and dust!

My job is to chop the apple.

HOMEWORK Spelling Practice Book, p. 2

Spelling Words

Short Vowels

1.	drum	7.	chop
2.	rock	8.	sack
3.	list	9.	tag
4.	desk	10.	rib
5.	job	11.	mess
6.	sad*	12.	dust

Challenge Words

13.	pocket	15.	engine
14.	lettuce		

* **Words from the Selection**

Short Vowels CVC, CVCC, CCVC

Write a list word to finish the rhyme.

Spelling Words	
drum	chop
rock	sack
list	tag
desk	rib
job	mess
sad	dust

1. gum on a **drum**   2. Zack in a **sack**   3. bag with a **tag**

4. lock on a **rock**   5. Tess is a **mess**   6. fist with a **list**

Write a list word to finish the sentence.

dust
job
sad
chop
rib
desk

7. Tom's **job** was to set the table.

8. My teacher sits at a **desk**.

9. Will you **chop** this apple?

10. Get a rag and **dust** the bench.

11. Sara was **sad** when her dog got lost.

12. Andy fell and hurt his **rib**.

School + Home **Home Activity** Your child wrote words with short vowels and these consonant/vowel patterns: CVC, CVCC, CCVC. Give clues about a word. Say, for example, "You play it in a band. It has a short u." Have your child guess and spell the word (drum).

▲ **Spelling Practice Book** p. 2

Look at each picture.
Pick a word from the box that tells about each person.
Write the word on the line.

| bus | horses | stairs | walks |

1. Gina **walks** to school.

2. After school, Gina climbs **stairs** to get home.

3. Ben takes the **bus** to school.

4. After school, Ben and his brother ride **horses**

Write the answers on the lines.

5. Where does Gina live? Answer should include a city, a town, or a neighborhood.

Where does Ben live? Answer should include a farm, a ranch, or the country.

School + Home Home Activity Your child compared characters in different settings. Ask your child to describe a family member or friend who lives in a place that is different from your family's home. Encourage your child to describe what makes the place different from home.

▲ **Practice Book 2.1** p. 5, Character and Setting

Comprehension

◉ SKILL Character and Setting

RECOGNIZE CHARACTER AND SETTING Review with children that characters are the people or animals in a story. Authors describe characters' traits by telling what characters are like, what they think, and what they say and do. Setting is when and where the story takes place. A setting can be a real or imaginary place. Invite children to name the characters and describe the setting in several stories they have recently read.

CONNECT TO READING

- As you read, ask yourself who the people in the story are and where and when it takes place.

- Pay attention to clues in the illustrations that help you figure out where and when the story takes place.

◉ STRATEGY Predict

INTRODUCE THE STRATEGY Tell children that it can be fun to try to figure out what will happen next in a story or what a character will probably do. Predicting can help you be a better reader because you learn to use clues in the story.

 MODEL When I read a story, I like to try to figure out what will happen next. Lots of times the words and the pictures give me clues. When I'm right and my prediction matches what actually happens, I know I understood the clues. But sometimes I'm surprised!

CONNECT TO READING Encourage children to ask themselves these questions as they read *Iris and Walter.*

- Can I guess who the people in the story are?
- Can I guess where and when the story takes place?

Build Background

DISCUSS CITY AND COUNTRY LIFE Display a picture of an urban residential area with large apartment buildings along with a picture of a farmhouse surrounded by open fields. Invite children to tell what they know about living in the city or country.

- Which kind of place do we live in?
- How might living in the country (or city) be different from living here?
- What do children do for play in the city? in the country?

BACKGROUND BUILDING AUDIO Have children listen to the audio and share the new information they learned about city life and country life.

 **Sing with Me/ Background Building Audio**

COMPLETE A T-CHART Draw a T-chart or display Graphic Organizer 25. Write *City* and *Country* as column headings. Work with children to list ideas about living in the city and the country in each column. Have them include ways children might play in each place.

City	Country
crowded	lots of space
lots of noise	room to run
roller-skate on sidewalks	climb trees
play in parks	build tree houses
go to the zoo	ride horses

▲ Graphic Organizer 25

CONNECT TO SELECTION Connect background information to *Iris and Walter*.

Sometimes when people move to a different kind of place, it is hard to figure out what to do there. In the story we are about to read, Iris moves from the city to the country to live with her grandpa. She is lonely because there aren't many people around, especially kids to play with. We'll find out what happens when she meets someone who lives in her new place.

Iris and Walter
by Elissa Haden Guest
illustrated by Christine Davenier

What new things does Iris learn when she moves to the country?

 **ELL**

Activate Prior Knowledge Ask children whether they have ever lived in or visited a big city or a place in the country. Have them tell what they can about their experiences.

Words to Read

country
beautiful
front
someone
somewhere
friend

Read the Words

Iris and her family have moved to the country. It is a beautiful place. Iris looked at the long road in front of her house. She hopes that someone out there somewhere is waiting to be her friend.

Genre: Realistic Fiction
Realistic fiction is a made-up story that could happen in real life. Now read about Iris, a girl who moves to the country and finds a new friend.

High-Frequency Words

Nondecodable Words

ROUTINE

1 **Say and Spell** Look at the words on page 14. You cannot blend the sounds in these words. We will spell the words and use letter-sounds we know to learn them. Point to the first word. This word is *country, c-o-u-n-t-r-y, country.* What is this word? What are the letters in this word?

2 **Identify Familiar Letter-Sounds** Point to the first letter in *country.* What is this letter? What is the sound for this letter? (*c*/k/)

3 **Demonstrate Meaning** Tell me a sentence using this word.

Repeat the routine with the other Words to Read. Have children identify these familiar letter-sounds: *beautiful* (*b*/b/ and */l/), *front* (*t*/t/), *someone* (*s*/s/), *somewhere* (*s*/s/), *friend* (*d*/d/).

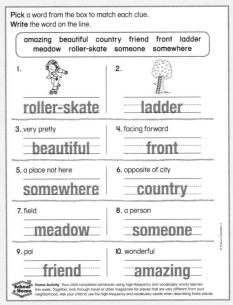

Pick a word from the box to match each clue. **Write** the word on the line.

amazing beautiful country friend front ladder meadow roller-skate someone somewhere

I.	2.
roller-skate	ladder
3. very pretty	4. facing forward
beautiful	front
5. a place not here	6. opposite of city
somewhere	country
7. field	8. a person
meadow	someone
9. pal	10. wonderful
friend	amazing

Home Activity Your child completed sentences using high-frequency and vocabulary words learned this week. Together, look through travel or other magazines for places that are very different from your neighborhood. Ask your child to use the high-frequency and vocabulary words when describing these places.

▲ **Practice Book 2.1** p. 6, High-Frequency Words and Selection Words

Have children read aloud the sentences on p. 15 and point to the Words to Read. Add the words to the Word Wall. **Word Wall**

Use Vocabulary Transparency 1 to review this week's words.

- Point to a word. Say and spell it.
- Have children say and spell the word.
- Ask children to identify familiar letter-sounds.

Monitor Progress | **Check High-Frequency Words**

Point to the following words on the Word Wall and have individuals read them.

country	beautiful	front	friend	someone	somewhere
door	about	wild	house	opened	across

If . . . children cannot read these words,

then . . . have them practice in pairs with word cards before reading the selection. Monitor their fluency with these words during reading, and provide additional practice opportunities before the Day 5 Assessment.

SUCCESS PREDICTOR

Spiral REVIEW

- Reviews previously taught high-frequency words.

Day 1 Check Word Reading

▶**Day 2 Check High-Frequency Words**

Day 3 Check Retelling

Day 4 Check Fluency

Day 5 Assess Progress

High-Frequency Words

SUCCESS PREDICTOR

Going to the Meadow

1. Iris learned to <u>roller-skate</u> when she was little.

2. "You're <u>amazing</u>," Grandpa said when she told him that.

3. Walter climbed down his <u>ladder</u> to meet them.

4. They all went to the <u>meadow</u> to see the horses.

Words to Read

beautiful	country	friend	front
someone	somewhere		

Unit 1 Iris and Walter   Vocabulary **1**

▲ **Vocabulary Transparency 1**

Vocabulary

SELECTION WORDS

Use Vocabulary Transparency 1 to introduce the selection words.

- Read each sentence as you track the print.

- Frame each underlined word. Explain the word's meaning.

  ladder set of steps with two side pieces and rungs for climbing
  amazing wonderful or surprising
  roller-skate to move on roller skates, which are skates with wheels
  meadow piece of grassy land

- Ask children to identify familiar letter-sounds and word parts: *amazing* (m/m/, z/z/), *roller-skate* (r/r/), *ladder* (two syllables with a double consonant in the middle), *meadow* (ea/e/).

- Have children read each sentence aloud with you.

- To encourage discussion using the selection words, ask children to tell something they have seen that is amazing. How does it feel to roller-skate the first time? What might it be like to climb a rope ladder? What might you do in a meadow?

- Introduce these nondecodable names that appear in the selection: *Iris, Walter.*

Group Time

On-Level	Strategic Intervention	Advanced
Read *Iris and Walter.*	**Read** SI Decodable Reader 1.	**Read** *Iris and Walter.*
• Use pp. 16–35.	• Read or listen to *Iris and Walter.*	• Use the **Routine** on p. DI·17.
	• Use the **Routine** on p. DI·16.	

 Place English language learners in the groups that correspond to their reading abilities in English.

i Independent Activities

Independent Reading See p. 12j for Reading/Library activities and suggestions.

Journal Writing Write about a time you explored or investigated a rural place or an urban place. Share your writing.

Literacy Centers To provide experiences with *Iris and Walter,* you may use the Listening Center on p. 12j.

Practice Book 2.1 Character and Setting, p. 5; High-Frequency Words and Selection Words, p. 6; Main Idea and Details, p. 7

Access Content Use the vocabulary strategies and word cards in the ELL Teaching Guide, pp. 3–4.

Break into small groups after Vocabulary and before Writing.

Iris and Walter

by Elissa Haden Guest
illustrated by Christine Davenier

What new things does Iris learn
when she moves to the country?

16   17

read
Prereading Strategies

PREVIEW AND PREDICT Have children read the title of the story. Identify Iris and
Walter as the children in the picture. Identify the author and illustrator. Do a
picture walk of pp. 16–23. Ask children what they think this story will be about.

DISCUSS REALISTIC FICTION Read the definition of realistic fiction on p. 15 of
the Student Edition. Explain that fiction is a made-up story and that realistic fiction could happen in real life. Ask if Iris is a real girl. Make sure children understand that Iris is a made-up girl who does things a real girl can do.

SET PURPOSE Read the question on p. 16. Ask children what they would like to
find out as they read this story.

AudioText

Access Content Before reading,
review the story summary in English
and/or the home language. See the ELL
Teaching Guide, pp. 5–7.

A Walk and a Talk

Iris and Grandpa went for a walk.

"Can I tell you something?" Iris asked.

"You can tell me anything," said Grandpa.

"I hate the country," said Iris.

"Why?" asked Grandpa.

"Because there are no children here,"

said Iris. "The country is as lonely as Mars."

18   19

▲ **Pages 18–19**
Have children read and look at the pictures to find out who the people in the story are and where and when it takes place.

Skills in Context

↻ CHARACTER AND SETTING

- **Who are the people in this story? Does the story take place in an urban or rural setting? What time of the year is it?**
Iris and Grandpa are the people so far. The story takes place in the country. It seems to be a cool spring or summer day.

Monitor Progress	Character and Setting
If... children are unable to answer the questions,	**then...** model how to determine the characters and setting.

Think Aloud · **MODEL** The story says that Iris and Grandpa are taking a walk. Iris says that she does not like the country. I can see in the picture that Grandpa and Iris are on a country road. They are both wearing jackets, but there are leaves on the trees, so I think it is spring or summer.

ASSESS Ask children how Iris describes the setting. (She thinks it's lonely and feels like Mars.)

EXTEND SKILLS

Text Features/Chapters

For instruction in chapters, discuss the following:

- Chapter titles break a story up into different parts. Some tell you exactly what a chapter will be about. Others give you information that you can use to predict what will happen next.

- Read the chapter title on this page. What does it tell you about what might happen next?

Assess Have children see whether their prediction matches what really happens as they read the chapter.

___ Short Vowels   ⬜ high-frequency/tested vocabulary

"Iris, my girl, there must be some children somewhere," said Grandpa.
"Do you think so?" asked Iris.
"I know so. We shall have to find them, Iris. We shall be explorers!"

Iris and Grandpa walked down the road. The birds were singing. The roses were blooming. And around the bend, someone was waiting.

20

21

Guiding Comprehension

◉ Character • Inferential
- **How does Grandpa try to make Iris feel better?**
  He says that they will find children for her to play with.

◉ Setting • Inferential
- **What is the day like?**
  Birds are singing, and flowers are blooming. It seems to be a beautiful day.

Draw Conclusions • Inferential
- **Where do you think Iris usually lives? Why do you think so?**
  Possible response: I think she lives in a place with more people. She doesn't like the country because she doesn't see any other children.

▲ **Pages 20–21**
Have children read to find out what Iris and Grandpa plan to do.

Monitor Progress
High-Frequency Words

If... children have a problem reading a new high-frequency word,	**then...** use the High-Frequency Routine on p. 15a to reteach the problematic word.

Iris and Grandpa walked around the bend. They saw a great big green tree.

"What a tree!" said Grandpa.

"So green!" said Iris.

"So beautiful," said Grandpa.

"I want to climb it," said Iris.

Down came a ladder.

22   23

▲ **Pages 22–23**
Have children read to decide what Iris will do next.

Time for SOCIAL STUDIES

Cities, Suburbs, Country

A city is a huge place where lots of people live and work. Sometimes smaller towns are close to cities and around them. They are called suburbs. There is usually more room between houses in suburbs than there is in cities. The country is sometimes called a rural area. It is outside of cities and towns. There aren't as many people in the country as in cities or suburbs. Have children discuss whether they live in a city, in a suburb, or in the country.

Strategies in Context

⊙ PREDICT

- **What do you think will happen next? Why do you think so?**
  Possible response: Maybe Iris will find a person in the tree house. That might happen because we know that Iris wants someone to play with.

Monitor Progress	Predict
If... children have difficulty predicting what might happen next,	**then...** model how to use the text and pictures to confirm understanding.

 Think Aloud **MODEL** I know Iris is lonely and thinks there are no children in the country. She and Grandpa said they would be explorers to find someone. I also know the name of the story is *Iris and Walter*, and we haven't met anyone named Walter yet. So I think this might be Walter in the tree.

ASSESS Work with children to write their predictions. Tell them they will see whether their predictions match what really happens in the story.

___ Short Vowels   ☐ high-frequency/tested vocabulary

"Amazing! I wonder what's <u>up</u> there?" said Grandpa.

"I'll go see," said Iris. Iris began to climb.

"How <u>is</u> <u>it</u> <u>up</u> there?" called Grandpa.

"<u>It</u>'s very green!" <u>y</u>elled Iris.

Iris climbed higher and higher until she was almost <u>at</u> the <u>top</u> of the great <u>big</u> green tree.

24

"Grandpa?!" called Iris. "There's a house <u>up</u> here." "Amazing!" said Grandpa.

25

Guiding Comprehension

Draw Conclusions • Critical
- **Why do you think there is a house in the tree?**
Possible response: A child might have a playhouse in the tree.

Summarize • Inferential
- **What has happened in the story so far?**
Iris is with her Grandpa in the country, and she complains that she is lonely because there are no children there. Then she sees a ladder in a tree and climbs it to find a house.

◎ Character • Inferential
- **What kind of a person is Iris? Why do you think so?**
Possible response: I think she is friendly because she wants to meet other kids. She's curious because she climbs the ladder to investigate what's in the tree.

▲ **Pages 24–25**
Have children read to find out what Iris does next.

Strategy Self-Check

Have children ask themselves these questions to check their reading.

Decoding Words
- Do I blend all the sounds in a new word to read it?
- Does the new word make sense in the story?

Predict
- Can I guess who the people in the story are?
- Can I guess where and when the story takes place?

Iris knocked <u>on</u> the door.

"Come <u>in</u>," said a voice.

Iris opened the door.

"Hi, I'm Walter," said Walter.

"I'm Iris," said Iris.

Iris <u>and</u> Walter shook <u>hands</u>.

"Hey, Grandpa, there's a <u>kid</u> <u>up</u> here named Walter!" yelled Iris.

"How wonderful," said Grandpa.

<u>And</u> <u>it</u> was.

26

27

▲ **Pages 26–27**
Have children read to find out whether the story matches what they've predicted.

Monitor Progress	
Decoding	
If… children come to a word they don't know,	**then…** remind them to: 1. Blend the word. 2. Decide if the word makes sense. 3. Look in a dictionary for more help.

Guiding Comprehension

Predict • Inferential

- **Did the story match your prediction? Explain.**
  Possible response: I thought that Iris would find a person in the tree house, and she did. So my prediction matched what happened.

Author's Purpose • Critical

- *Question the Author* **Why did the author write this story—to entertain or to inform? How can you tell?**
  Possible response: The author wrote this story to entertain. It is interesting to read about how Iris feels about the country and who was in the tree house.

Character • Critical

- *Text to Self* **How would you feel if you were Iris and had found Walter?**
  Possible response: I would feel very glad and happy to have a friend.

___ Short Vowels   high-frequency/tested vocabulary

A New Life

Iris and Walter played every day. They climbed trees. They rolled down hills. They played hide-and-seek.

28

When it rained, Walter showed Iris his hat collection. And Iris showed Walter how to roller-skate–indoors.

Some days they rode Walter's sweet pony, Sal. Other days they sat on a fence and watched a horse named Rain running wild.

29

Guiding Comprehension

▲ **Pages 28–29**
Have children read to find out what "A New Life" means for Iris and Walter.

Plot • Inferential
- **What do Iris and Walter do together?**
They climb trees, roll down hills, play hide-and-seek, play with hats, roller-skate, and ride a pony.

Compare and Contrast • Inferential
- **How is Iris's life different since she met Walter?**
Possible response: She has a friend and someone to do things with, which she didn't have before.

Compare and Contrast • Critical
- **How are Iris and Walter alike and different?**
Possible response: They are alike because they both like to climb trees, roll down hills, and play hide-and-seek. They are different because at first Iris knows how to roller-skate and Walter doesn't, and because Walter has a pony and Iris doesn't.

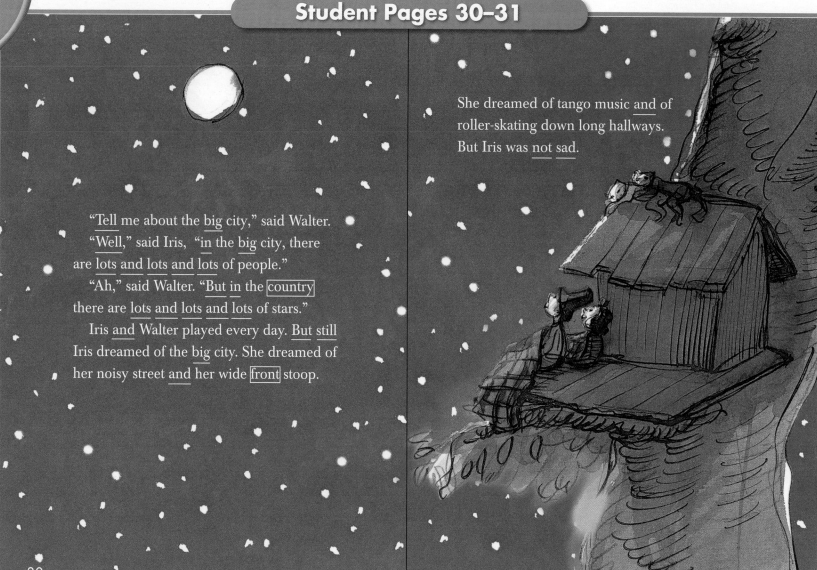

"Tell me about the big city," said Walter.

"Well," said Iris, "in the big city, there are lots and lots and lots of people."

"Ah," said Walter. "But in the country there are lots and lots and lots of stars."

Iris and Walter played every day. But still Iris dreamed of the big city. She dreamed of her noisy street and her wide front stoop.

She dreamed of tango music and of roller-skating down long hallways. But Iris was not sad.

30

31

▲ **Pages 30–31**
Have children read to find out how the country is different from the city where Iris has lived.

EXTEND SKILLS

Categorize/Classify

For instruction in categorizing and classifying, discuss the following:

• Sometimes it helps us understand a group of things better if we put together the things that are alike or belong together.

• Tell me which of the following things belong in a group called *City Things* and which belong in a group called *Country Things:* pony, bus, noisy streets, lots of people, lots of stars, meadow, stream, big buildings.

Assess Have children add other things to the groups from their own experience.

Guiding Comprehension

Compare and Contrast • Inferential

• **How is the country where Walter lives different from the city where Iris has lived?**

The city has lots of people, a noisy street, and Iris's wide front stoop. But the country has lots of stars and Walter.

◉ Character • Inferential

• **Do you think Iris misses the city? Why or why not?**

Possible response: She misses some of the things about the city, but she is not sad because she is with Walter in the country.

Compare and Contrast • Critical

• *Text to World* **Do you think you can really see lots of stars when you're out in the country that you can't see when you're in an urban area? Why or why not?**

Possible response: Yes. I saw lots of stars when I was in the country once. It's darker in the country, so the stars are easier to see.

____ Short Vowels   high-frequency/tested vocabulary

There were pale roses. And there was cool grass beneath her feet. There was a wild horse named Rain and a sweet pony named Sal.

For in the country, there were red-tailed hawks and starry skies.

32

33

Skills in Context

REVIEW MAIN IDEA AND DETAILS

- **What is this story all about? Is it about Walter and Iris riding a pony or is that just one little piece of the story?**
The story is all about Iris finding a friend to have fun with in the country.

Monitor Progress	Main Idea and Details
If… children are unable to identify the main idea and details of the story,	**then…** model how to use the text to determine the main idea and separate it from details.

 Think Aloud

MODEL I know the title of a story can tell what it is about. Since the title of this story is *Iris and Walter*, I think the story is really about Iris finding a friend named Walter. There are lots of little pieces of the story that tell what they do together, but I don't think that's what the story is really about.

ASSESS Have children tell what pp. 32–33 are all about. (Some of the things Iris and Walter see and do together in the country.)

▲ **Pages 32–33**
Have children read to decide what the story is all about.

Read the story.
Answer the questions.

Every day I feed the chickens and clean the horse stalls. I do my chores as quickly as I can. Then I sit and dream. I plan to move far away when I grow up. I will live in a place with tall buildings and many cabs. I will become an artist and paint. I like my farm, but my dream is to live in a city.

1. cabs (chickens)
Which word tells about where the girl lives?
2. (buildings) stalls
Which word tells about where the girl would like to live?
3. Write the sentence that tells the main idea.

I like my farm, but my dream is to live in a city.

4. Which is a chore?
○ painting pictures
○ dreaming
● cleaning the stalls

5. Which is a dream?
● moving far away
○ living on the farm
○ feeding the chickens

Home Activity Your child described the main idea and supporting details in a story. Select a favorite or familiar story. As you read together, ask your child to identify details and sentences that tell the main idea of the story.

▲ **Practice Book 2.1** p. 7, Main Idea and Details

And across the <u>meadow</u>,
over the stream, high in a tree,
was a little house. <u>And</u> inside
there was a new <u>friend</u>. . . Walter.

34

35

▲ **Pages 34–35**
Have children read to find out how
the story ends.

Big Cities

Time for **SOCIAL STUDIES**

About the time your
grandparents were born, about half
the people in the United States
lived in cities. Now most people
do. Fewer people live out in the
country than ever before.

_____ Short Vowels   high-frequency/tested vocabulary

Guiding Comprehension

Character • Inferential

• **How do you think Iris feels at the end of the story? How about Walter?**
Possible response: They're probably both happy to have a friend to do things with in the country.

Plot • Inferential

• **How did the story begin? How did it end?**
The story began with Iris in the country wishing there were children to play with. It ended with Iris having a new friend, Walter.

Analyze • Critical

• *Text to Self* **Based on the descriptions in this story and what you know about the country and cities, where do you think it would be more fun to live—in a city or in the country?**
Possible response: It would be more fun to live in the country because you could ride ponies and watch horses run wild.

Fluency

REREAD FOR FLUENCY

Paired Reading

ROUTINE

Reader 1 Begins Children read the entire book, switching readers at the end of each page.

Reader 2 Begins Have partners reread; now the other partner begins.

Reread For optimal fluency, children should reread three or four times.

Provide Feedback Listen to children read and provide corrective feedback regarding their oral reading and their use of the blending strategy.

OBJECTIVES

- Write a paragraph.
- Identify sentences.
- Capitalize the first word of a sentence and end it with a period.

Strategic Intervention

Show children how to form margins around their writing and to indent their paragraph by drawing vertical dotted lines on their papers for them to follow.

Advanced

Have children expand what they wrote about Iris and Walter by writing a paragraph telling something else Iris showed Walter how to do in the city.

Support Writing Before writing, children might share ideas in their home languages.

Beginning Provide a written framework of a paragraph about Iris and Walter, leaving out several words that children know. Have them copy the paragraph and fill in the missing words.

Intermediate Discuss with children what they want to write. Restate one of their key ideas in conventional English to get them started.

Advanced Have children work with a partner to brainstorm what they plan to write.

Support Grammar Ask children if they know how to write the beginning and ending of sentences in their own language. See the Grammar Transition lessons in the ELL and Transition Handbook.

Interactive Writing

WRITE Paragraph

BRAINSTORM Use the story *Iris and Walter* to encourage a discussion about problems people have when they move from the city to the country. Then invite children to think what might have happened if Walter had moved to the city and found Iris as a friend.

SHARE THE PEN Have children work together to write a paragraph about Walter moving to the city. Begin by asking children what to say in the first sentence. Write their first sentence, inviting children to write the first word, capitalizing the first letter, and the period that ends the sentence. Ask questions such as:

- How do we show the beginning of a paragraph? (We indent it, or start the first sentence a little bit in from the margin.)
- What is the margin? (the space we leave on both sides of our writing on the paper)
- How do we write a title? (We capitalize the important words.)

Continue to have individuals make contributions. Frequently reread what has been written while tracking the print.

READ THE PARAGRAPH Read the completed paragraph aloud, having children echo you.

Walter Moves to the City

Walter liked living in the country. But his family moved to the city. He was lonely there. Then he met Iris. Iris showed him how to skate in the hall. They were friends. Walter wasn't lonely anymore.

INDEPENDENT WRITING

WRITE A PARAGRAPH Have children write their own paragraph about Walter and Iris. Let children illustrate their writing.

Grammar

DEVELOP THE CONCEPT Sentences

IDENTIFY SENTENCES Write *roller-skated in the hallway* and *Iris and Walter* on the board. Point to each word as you read the phrases aloud. Ask children whether these phrases are sentences or fragments.

A sentence is a group of words that tells a complete idea. The words are in an order that makes sense. A sentence always begins with a capital letter, and most sentences end with a period. How can we make these two groups of words into a sentence? (Iris and Walter roller-skated in the hallway.)

PRACTICE

WRITE SENTENCES Display a picture of children playing together. Model writing a sentence about the picture.

Think Aloud **MODEL** If I want to write a sentence about this picture, first I would give the children names. Write *Iris and Walter.* Then I would tell what they are doing in the picture. Write *Iris and Walter rode their bikes.* The name Iris already begins with a capital letter, so that's a good way to start the sentence. And I have to remember to put a period at the end.

Have children suggest and write other sentences about the picture.

DAILY FIX-IT

3. played tag Iris and Walter
   Iris and Walter played tag.

4. Then rode a pony they
   Then they rode a pony.

Sentences

A **sentence** is a group of words that tells a complete idea. The words are in an order that makes sense. A sentence begins with a capital letter. Many sentences end with a **period** (.).

I have many friends. ← This is a complete sentence.
many friends ← This is not a complete sentence.

Find the sentence. **Write** the sentence.

1. a friend   I have a friend.
   I have a friend.

2. We climbed a tree.   climbed a tree
   We climbed a tree.

3. Walter is my friend.   is my friend
   Walter is my friend.

4. my grandpa   I love my grandpa.
   I love my grandpa.

5. Walter has a pony.   has a pony
   Walter has a pony.

Home Activity Your child learned about sentences. Read a story together. Have your child point out a sentence and tell what capital letter it begins with and what punctuation mark is at the end.

▲ **Grammar and Writing Practice Book** p. 1

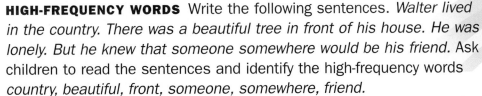

✓ **HIGH-FREQUENCY WORDS** Write the following sentences. *Walter lived in the country. There was a beautiful tree in front of his house. He was lonely. But he knew that someone somewhere would be his friend.* Ask children to read the sentences and identify the high-frequency words *country, beautiful, front, someone, somewhere, friend.*

✓ **PREDICT** Ask children whether they think Iris and Walter will continue to be friends after the story ends. Encourage discussion.

LET'S TALK ABOUT IT Discuss what Iris discovered when she moved to a new neighborhood. Encourage children to add to their Venn diagrams what they learned about urban and rural life from the story.

PREVIEW Day 3

Tell children that tomorrow they will read about forest animals.

Day 3
AT A GLANCE

Share Literature
In the Forest

Phonics and Spelling
REVIEW Syllable Patterns VC/CV and VCC/V

Spelling: Words with Short Vowels

High-Frequency Words
someone somewhere **Word Wall**
friend country
beautiful front

Vocabulary
Figurative Language: Simile

Fluency
Read with Appropriate Pace/Rate

Writing Trait
Voice

Grammar
Sentences

Materials
• *Sing with Me Big Book*
• Big Book *In the Forest*
• Student Edition 36–37

Morning Warm~Up!
Today we will read more about the forest.
What plants could we investigate in the forest?

QUESTION OF THE DAY Encourage children to sing "Let's Go Investigate!" from the *Sing with Me Big Book* as you gather. Write and read the message and discuss the question.

REVIEW SENTENCES

• Read the first sentence aloud again, indicating the words as you do so. Ask children whether it is a sentence. (yes) Why does the word *Today* begin with a capital letter? (Sentences always begin with a capital letter.)

Build Background Use the Day 3 instruction on ELL Poster 1 to support children's use of English to communicate about lesson concepts.

ELL Poster 1

Share Literature

LISTEN AND RESPOND

GLOSSARY Recall what *In the Forest* is about. Ask if the book is fiction or nonfiction. Point out the glossary. Explain that a glossary is an alphabetical collection of special terms and their meanings used in a nonfiction book.

Big Book

BUILD ORAL VOCABULARY Review that yesterday the class read the book to find out about some plants and creatures they might investigate in a forest. Tell children that they learned about the chipmunk's den, which is **underground,** or beneath the surface. Ask that children listen today to find out more about animals and plants in the forest and how they live.

MONITOR LISTENING COMPREHENSION

- Why is a chipmunk's den underground? (An underground den is a place to safely store food for the winter; it is also a place for the chipmunk to sleep.)

- Is a forest a rural place or an urban place? How do you know? (It is a rural place because it is in the country away from people.)

- What does a box turtle do if another creature scares it? (It pulls itself into its shell for protection.)

OBJECTIVES

- Identify features of nonfiction.
- Set purpose for listening.
- Build oral vocabulary.

Amazing Words to build oral vocabulary

	MONITOR PROGRESS
investigate rural urban creature **underground** brittle dart decision	**If...** children lack oral vocabulary experiences about the concept of Exploration, **then...** use the Oral Vocabulary Routine. See p. DI·3 to teach *underground*.

Listen and Respond Help children describe and demonstrate the actions conveyed by the words *gather, bury, disappear,* and *travel* in *In the Forest*.

- Review VC/CV and VCC/V words with short vowels.
- Sort, blend, and read VC/CV and VCC/V words.
- Recognize high-frequency words.
- Spell short vowel words.

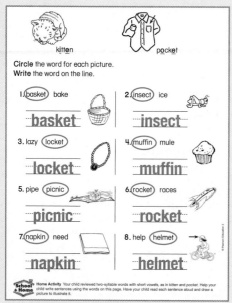

▲ **Practice Book 2.1** p. 8,
Syllable Patterns VC/CV and VCC/V

Review Phonics

REVIEW Syllable Patterns VC/CV and VCC/V

READ VC/CV AND VCC/V WORDS Write *kitten* and *pocket*. You can read these words because you know how to divide words into smaller parts. If a word has two consonants together in the middle, you know that usually we divide between them. Remember that some consonants are not divided, such as *ck*, *ch*, and *sh*. The vowel in each syllable usually makes a short vowel sound. How do you divide *kitten* and *pocket*? (*kit/ten; pock/et*) What vowel sound do you hear in each syllable? (**short vowel sounds**) What are these words?

SORT WORDS Write *VC/CV* and *VCC/V* as headings. Have individuals write words with VC/CV and VCC/V spelling patterns under the appropriate headings, divide the words, and circle the letters that stand for the short vowel sounds. Have all children complete the activity on paper. Ask individuals to read the words. Provide feedback as necessary.

VC/CV	VCC/V
mit/ten	lock/et
pup/pet	pack/age
in/sect	jack/et
prob/lem	rock/et
can/not	pack/et

High-Frequency Words

PRACTICE

STORY CLUES Read the following story to children. Have children find the word on the Word Wall that fills each blank in the story. **Word Wall**

Long ago in a faraway _____, (country) there lived a young prince. He had all the gold and riches in the world, but he was not happy. The prince spent all day in the castle. He never had a chance to make a single _____. (friend) Late one afternoon he went for a walk. "I wish I had _____ (someone) to talk to," he said. The prince sat down in _____ (front) of a pond and stared at the _____ (beautiful) sunset. "There must be a boy or girl _____ (somewhere) who will run and play with me. Just then several children approached. They were happy to see that the prince finally came out of the castle. Ever since, the young prince ran, jumped, played, and had fun with lots of new friends.

Spelling

◎ PRACTICE Short Vowels

FINISH THE SENTENCE Have children practice spelling words by writing down and finishing these sentence starters that use spelling words.

- The *drum* was…
- The big *rock* was…
- Make a *list* so…
- My *desk* is…
- Do your *job* because…
- He was *sad* when…
- Did you *chop* the…
- The big *sack* had…
- I put the *tag* on the…
- My *rib* felt…
- Do not *mess* up my…
- There is *dust* under…

HOMEWORK Spelling Practice Book, p. 3

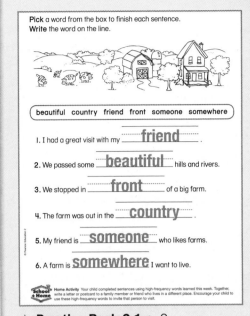

Pick a word from the box to finish each sentence. Write the word on the line.

beautiful country friend front someone somewhere

1. I had a great visit with my **friend**.
2. We passed some **beautiful** hills and rivers.
3. We stopped in **front** of a big farm.
4. The farm was out in the **country**.
5. My friend is **someone** who likes farms.
6. A farm is **somewhere** I want to live.

Home Activity Your child completed sentences using high-frequency words learned this week. Together, write a letter or postcard to a family member or friend who lives in a different place. Encourage your child to use these high-frequency words to invite that person to visit.

▲ **Practice Book 2.1** p. 9, High-Frequency Words

Spelling Words

Short Vowels

1.	drum	7.	chop
2.	rock	8.	sack
3.	list	9.	tag
4.	desk	10.	rib
5.	job	11.	mess
6.	sad*	12.	dust

Challenge Words

13.	pocket	15.	engine
14.	lettuce		

* Word from the Selection

Short Vowels CVC, CVCC, CCVC
Read the report Jenny wrote. Circle two spelling mistakes. Write the words correctly. Then write Jenny's last sentence correctly.

Spelling Words	
drum	chop
rock	sack
list	tag
desk	rib
job	mess
sad	dust

The artist took som clay out of a sack. It looked like a rock. He put it on the desk. He made it into a bird. The desk was a mess. The bird very pretty.

1. **some** 2. **sack**
3. **The bird was very pretty.**

Circle the word that is spelled correctly. Write it.

4.	dus	(dust)	**dust**
5.	(drum)	drun	**drum**
6.	chopp	(chop)	**chop**
7.	(job)	jub	**job**
8.	(list)	lis	**list**

Frequently Misspelled Words
with
have
them
some

Home Activity Your child has identified and corrected misspelled words with short vowels and these consonant/vowel patterns: CVC, CVCC, CCVC. Have your child spell one of the words and then change a vowel to make another word. For example, the word rib could become rob or rub.

▲ **Spelling Practice Book** p. 3

Strategic Intervention

Invite children to discuss other comparisons that can be similes. Make sure they realize that similes compare things that are not basically alike. For example, "My brother runs as fast as I do" is a simple comparison; "My brother runs as fast as the wind" is a simile.

Advanced

Encourage children to make up other similes using the words *like* or *as*, comparing things that are basically unlike.

Extend Language Hold up two things that are not alike except in one way, such as a red apple and a red scarf. Explain to children that you can compare the two things by using the words *like* or *as*. You might say, for example, "This scarf is as red as an apple." Help children develop several other simple similes.

Vocabulary

FIGURATIVE LANGUAGE: SIMILES

DISCUSS SIMILES Recall with children that on p. 19, Iris said, "The country is as lonely as Mars." She compared the country to Mars because Mars has no people living on it. Point out to children that the comparison includes the word *as* twice. Explain that a simile is a statement that uses *like* or *as* to compare one thing to another.

EXPAND VOCABULARY Discuss with children ways to use the selection words *amazing, ladder,* and *meadow* in comparisons. Provide an example for each word. Have children work with partners to write other comparisons, using each word. Ask them to share their comparisons.

amazing Joey's long jump was as amazing as the one in the Olympics.

ladder The tree branches are as easy to climb as a ladder.

meadow The lake is as smooth and calm as a meadow.

Group Time

On-Level	Strategic Intervention	Advanced
Read *Iris and Walter.*	**Read** or listen to *Iris and Walter.*	**Read** Self-Selected Reading
• Use pp. 16–35.	• Use the **Routine** on p. DI·18.	• Use the **Routine** on p. DI·19.

DAY 3

 Place English language learners in the groups that correspond to their reading abilities in English.

(i) Independent Activities

Independent Reading See p. 12j for Reading/Library activities and suggestions.

Journal Writing Use the word *as* to write a comparison about Iris and Walter. Share your writing.

Literacy Centers To provide experiences with *Iris and Walter,* you may use the Writing Center on p. 12k.

Practice Book 2.1 Syllable Pattern VC/CV and VCC/V, p. 8; High-Frequency Words, p. 9

Break into small groups after Vocabulary and before Writing.

Fluency

READ WITH APPROPRIATE PACE AND RATE

MODEL READING WITH APPROPRIATE PACE AND RATE Use *Iris and Walter.*

- Have children turn to p. 19. You should change how fast or slow you read depending on what is comfortable and how easy the selection is to understand. For stories, you might read pretty quickly because you don't have to stop to figure out information.

- Ask children to follow along as you read the page aloud.

- Have children read the page after you. Encourage them to read smoothly and at a steady pace. Continue in the same way with pp. 20–21.

REREAD FOR FLUENCY

Choral Reading

ROUTINE

1 **Select a Passage** For *Iris and Walter,* use pp. 28–34.

2 **Divide into Groups** Assign each group a part to read. For this story, use these parts: the narrator, Iris, Walter.

3 **Model** Have children track the print as you read.

4 **Read Together** Have children read along with you.

5 **Independent Readings** Have the groups read aloud without you. Monitor progress and provide feedback. For optimal fluency, children should reread three to four times.

Monitor Progress	Fluency
If... children have difficulty reading with an appropriate rate or pace,	**then...** read aloud with them to model the rate.
If... the class cannot read fluently without you,	**then...** continue to have them read along with you.

OBJECTIVE
- Read aloud with appropriate pace and rate.

Options for Oral Reading
Use *Iris and Walter* or one of the following Leveled Readers.

On-Level

The New Kid

Strategic Intervention

City Mouse and Country Mouse

Advanced

City Friends, Country Friends

ELL

Use *Off to School We Go!* or *Iris and Walter.* Model reading p. 21 of *Iris and Walter* at an appropriate rate of speed. Have ELL children reread the paragraph several times at the same rate of speed. As needed, help children read the dialogue on pp. 19–20, making sure they follow the quotation marks and can tell the difference between the speakers.

Fluency Coach CD To develop fluent readers, use Fluency Coach.

Look Back and Write For test practice, assign a 10–15 minute time limit. For informal or formal assessment, see the Scoring Rubric below.

Think and Share

TALK ABOUT IT Model a response. I think Iris and Walter will be good friends. Iris won't think the country is lonely anymore.

1. RETELL Have children use the retelling strip in the Student Edition to retell the story.

Monitor Progress | **Check Retelling**

If... children have difficulty retelling the story,

then... use the Retelling Cards and the Scoring Rubric for Retelling on p. 36–37 to help them move toward fluent retelling.

 SUCCESS PREDICTOR

Day 1 Check Word Reading ⋮ **Day 2** Check High-Frequency Words ⋮ ▶**Day 3 Check Retelling** ⋮ **Day 4** Check Fluency ⋮ **Day 5** Assess Progress

---

2. ◉ **CHARACTER AND SETTING** Model a response. It takes place in the country. If Iris and Walter met in the city, they would do city things like ride buses and skate in hallways. They might have other friends around.

3. ◉ **PREDICT** Model a response. I predicted that Iris would find a person. I was right. I also predicted that they would be friends.

 LOOK BACK AND WRITE Read the writing prompt on p. 36 and model your thinking. I'll look back at page 19 and read that part of the story again. I'll look for two things: the problem Iris had and how that problem changed. Then I'll write my response. **Have children write their responses.**

Scoring Rubric | **Look Back and Write**

Top-Score Response A top-score response will use details from p. 19 and other parts of the selection to describe Iris's problem and explain how it changed.

Example of a Top-Score Response Iris's problem was that she hated the country because there were no children there. That changed when she met Walter. He became her new friend and taught her how to have fun in the country.

For additional rubrics, see p. WA10.

Think and Share

Talk About It Stories can go on and on. What do you think Iris and Walter do next?

1. Use the pictures below to retell the story. **Retell**

2. Where does *Iris and Walter* take place? How might the story be different if Iris and Walter had met in the city? **Character/Setting**

3. What did you predict Iris would find in the tree? Were you right? What other predictions did you make? **Predict**

Look Back and Write Look back at page 19. What problem did Iris have? How did that change? Use details from the story to help you.

Meet the Author and the Illustrator

Elissa Haden Guest

Elissa Haden Guest likes big cities. She says, "New York was a very exciting place to grow up. You can walk for miles there without getting tired or bored because there's so much to see. Many of the streets are crowded with people and there's this terrific energy in the air."

Christine Davenier

Christine Davenier lives in France, where she grew up. She taught kindergarten for four years before attending art school. She has illustrated many children's books.

Read more books about Iris and Walter.

Retelling Strip

36

37

Scoring Rubric — Narrative Retelling

Rubric 4 3 2 1	4	3	2	1
Connections	Makes connections and generalizes beyond the text	Makes connections to other events, stories, or experiences	Makes a limited connection to another event, story, or experience	Makes no connection to another event, story, or experience
Author's Purpose	Elaborates on author's purpose	Tells author's purpose with some clarity	Makes some connection to author's purpose	Makes no connection to author's purpose
Characters	Describes the main character(s) and any character development	Identifies the main character(s) and gives some information about them	Inaccurately identifies some characters or gives little information about them	Inaccurately identifies the characters or gives no information about them
Setting	Describes the time and location	Identifies the time and location	Omits details of time or location	Is unable to identify time or location
Plot	Describes the events in sequence, using rich detail	Tells the plot with some errors in sequence that do not affect meaning	Tells parts of plot with gaps that affect meaning	Retelling has no sense of story

Use the Retelling Chart on p. TR20 to record retelling.

Selection Test To assess with *Iris and Walter*, use Selection Tests, pp. 1–4.
Fresh Reads for Differentiated Test Practice For weekly leveled practice, use pp. 1–6.

Retelling

SUCCESS PREDICTOR

OBJECTIVE

● Recognize and use voice in writing.

DAILY FIX-IT

5. Iris was sd and lonely
   Iris was <u>sad</u> and lonely<u>.</u>

6. wanted she a friend
   <u>She</u> wanted a friend<u>.</u>

Connect to Unit Writing

Writing Trait

Have children use strategies for developing **voice** when they write a personal narrative in the Unit Writing Workshop, pp. WA2–WA9.

Voice Show pictures that convey people's feelings, such as being happy, excited, or scared. Model discussion of these feelings: *The boy is excited about his story.* Explain that *excited* tells about a feeling. Remind language learners to show their feelings when they write.

Writing Trait of the Week

INTRODUCE Voice

TALK ABOUT VOICE Explain to children that voice shows how a writer feels and thinks about a topic. A writer's voice shows that the writer knows and cares about the topic. Ask children how they think Iris feels after she meets Walter. Then model your thinking.

MODEL Iris did not like the country at first. When I reread pages 32 and 33, though, I think Iris likes the country better. Let me read these sentences Iris might have written.

I played with Walter in the country. We played hide-and-seek. We rode Walter's pony.

These sentences don't tell me how Iris feels about the country now. How could Iris show her feelings in her sentences? Let's think of words Iris might use to show how she feels about the country. (Children might suggest words such as these: *interesting, fun, peaceful, beautiful, good friend, colorful,* and *amazing.*)

Let me read some sentences that show Iris's voice.

Read the sentences below and talk about how they show voice.

The country is peaceful, but it is also amazing. There are beautiful stars, colorful flowers, and interesting birds. It is fun playing with my good friend Walter.

STRATEGY FOR DEVELOPING VOICE On the board, write topics such as those below. Ask children to write a sentence about each topic to tell how they feel about it.

a food you don't like *(Squash tastes mushy and boring.)*

an animal you like *(I love this soft, furry hamster.)*

a noise that scared you *(Glass breaking made my heart pound.)*

PRACTICE

APPLY THE STRATEGY Ask children to think of something they would like to do in the country. Have them list words that show how they feel about this experience. Now have them write a paragraph that shows their feelings about doing an activity in the country.

Grammar

APPLY TO WRITING Sentences

IMPROVE WRITING WITH SENTENCES Explain to children that writing sentences correctly makes them clear for readers. Remind children that a sentence must always make sense. Also recall with them that when they write a sentence they should always begin the first word with a capital letter and end the sentence with a punctuation mark such as a period. Remind children to use sentences correctly in their own writing.

Suggest that children write two or three sentences about a good friend of theirs. Remind them to write their sentences correctly.

> **My best friend is Tony.**
> **He and I like to play ball together.**
> **We have fun.**

PRACTICE

WRITE WITH SENTENCES Have children add more sentences about their best friend and what they like to do together.

Sentences
Write the name of your friend.
Possible answer:
Alicia

Write sentences about what you and your friend do.
Possible answer:
We ride our bikes. We play games. We tell stories. We have fun together.

Draw a picture of you and your friend doing something together.

Home Activity Your child learned how to use sentences in writing. Have your child write two sentences about what he or she likes to do with a friend. Make sure each sentence begins with a capital letter and ends with a period.

▲ **Grammar and Writing Practice Book** p. 2

Wrap Up Your Day!

 CHARACTER AND SETTING Have children recall where and when *Iris and Walter* takes place. (in the country on a nice spring day) Who are the characters in the story? (Iris, Walter, and Iris's grandpa)

 FLUENCY SKILL Recall with children that they need to change the speed with which they read depending on how easy the material is. Call on individuals to read pp. 29–30 aloud to show how they adjust their rate.

LET'S TALK ABOUT IT Display the Venn diagram from Day 1. Now that we have read the story about Iris and Walter, what can we add to our Venn diagram about rural and urban places?

PREVIEW Day 4

Tell children that tomorrow they will read two poems about the promise of a new day and a special "travel" tree.

Day 4
AT A GLANCE

Share Literature
The Mystery Egg

Phonics and Spelling

Short Vowels
Spelling: Words with Short Vowels

Read
Group Time < Differentiated Instruction

"Morning Song"/"My Travel Tree"

Fluency
Read with Appropriate Pace/Rate

Writing Across the Curriculum
Two-Column Chart

Grammar
Sentences

Speaking and Listening
Why We Speak

Materials
- *Sing with Me Big Book*
- Read Aloud Anthology
- Student Edition 38–39

Morning Warm-Up!

Today we will read two poems.
What makes a poem
different from a story?
Can a poem be as warm as a bath?

QUESTION OF THE DAY Encourage children to sing "Let's Go Investigate" from the *Sing with Me Big Book* as you gather. Write and read the message and discuss the question.

REVIEW FIGURATIVE LANGUAGE/SIMILE

- Ask children what a poem is compared to in the message. (a bath)
- Then have children answer the question. (Possible answer: Yes, a poem could make you feel as warm as a bath does.)

ELL

Extend Language Use the Day 4 instruction on ELL Poster 1 to extend and enrich language.

ELL Poster 1

Share Literature

CONNECT CONCEPTS

ACTIVATE PRIOR KNOWLEDGE Recall with children that Iris explored her new neighborhood with Walter and enjoyed finding new things. Explain that you will read a story about something a girl discovers on the ground.

BUILD ORAL VOCABULARY Explain that **brittle** means very easily broken. Tell children that two girls in the story have a **decision** to make; they must make up their minds about some eggs they find. Ask them if they've ever seen birds hatch. Do they **dart,** or move very quickly, from the egg? Then read "The Mystery Eggs" aloud.

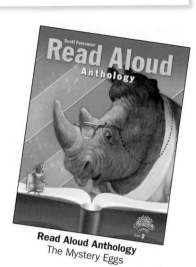

Read Aloud Anthology
The Mystery Eggs

REVIEW ORAL VOCABULARY After reading, review all the Amazing Words for the week. Have children take turns using them in sentences that tell about the concept for the week.

- If you moved to a new neighborhood, what would be the first thing you would want to **investigate?**

- When outside exploring, where have you seen **creatures** go **underground?**

MONITOR LISTENING COMPREHENSION

- How were the eggs Melanie found different from the kind of eggs Clara got from the refrigerator? (The eggs from the refrigerator were hard and brittle, and the ones Melanie found were long and narrow and had little bumps.)

- Why did Melanie want to keep the eggs? (She thought they were birds' eggs.) What decision did Clara make after she thought about the eggs hatching snakes in the bedroom? (She made the decision to take the eggs outside.)

- How do you know snakes move fast? (The baby snakes dart quickly.)

- What could Melanie have done to investigate the kinds of eggs she found? (Possible response: looked in an encyclopedia or on the Internet)

OBJECTIVES

- Set purpose for listening.
- Build oral vocabulary.

 to build oral vocabulary

	MONITOR PROGRESS
investigate rural urban creature underground brittle dart decision	**If...** children lack oral vocabulary experiences about the concept Exploration, **then...** use the Oral Vocabulary Routine. See p. DI·3 to teach *brittle, dart,* and *decision*.

Connect Concepts Explain that Melanie was from the city and didn't know much about life in the country. Clara, on the other hand, liked to hike and explore, so she probably knew more about nature than Melanie did.

Phonics **WORD WORK**

Spiral REVIEW

- Reviews high-frequency words *people, together, nothing, enough, become, stories* and *goodbye.*

Sentence Reading

REVIEW WORDS IN CONTEXT

READ DECODABLE AND HIGH-FREQUENCY WORDS IN CONTEXT Write these sentences. Call on individuals to read a sentence. Then randomly point to words and have them read. To help you monitor word reading, high-frequency words are underlined and decodable words are circled.

Two <u>people</u> (went) <u>together</u> to (pick) (up) the (big) (drum).

There was <u>nothing</u> on (top) of her (head) but a (red) (wig).

Is there <u>enough</u> (mud) in the (pen) for the (pig) to (sink)?

I (drop) my (head) (when) I <u>become</u> (sad) or (mad).

I (dread) <u>stories</u> that have a (bad) (fox) in (them).

(Did) they (ask) (them) to (sing) a <u>goodbye</u>?

Monitor Progress	Word Reading
If... children are unable to read an underlined word,	**then...** read the word for them and spell it, having them echo you.
If... children are unable to read a circled word,	**then...** have them use the blending strategy they have learned for that word type.

Support Phonics For additional review, see the phonics activities in the ELL and Transition Handbook.

Spelling

PARTNER REVIEW Short Vowels

READ AND WRITE Supply pairs of children with index cards on which the spelling words have been written. Have one child read a word while the other writes it. Then have children switch roles. Have them use the cards to check their spelling.

HOMEWORK Spelling Practice Book, p. 4.

Group Time

On-Level	Strategic Intervention	Advanced
Read "Morning Song."	**Read** or listen to "Morning Song."	**Read** "Morning Song."
• Use pp. 38–39.	• Use the **Routine** on p. DI·20.	• Use the **Routine** on p. DI·21.

ELL Place English language learners in the groups that correspond to their reading abilities in English.

ⓘ Independent Activities

Fluency Reading Pair children to reread *Iris and Walter.*

Journal Writing List topics you would like to investigate. Share writing.

Spelling Partner Review

Independent Reading See p. 12j for Reading/Library activities and suggestions.

Literacy Centers To provide listening opportunities, you may use the Listening Center on p. 12j. To extend social studies concepts, you may use the Social Studies Center on p. 12k.

Short Vowels CVC, CVCC, CCVC
Circle the list words in the puzzle. Some words go across. Some go down. **Write** each word.

Spelling Words
drum chop
rock sack
list tag
desk rib
job mess
sad dust

m	r	s	d	t	a	g
e	i	g	s	i	r	b
s	b	o	c	h	o	p
s	s	a	d	s	u	j
d	u	s	t	m	d	o
e	l	i	s	t	o	b

chop
list
sad
tag
mess
dust
job
rib

1. mess   2. rib
3. tag   4. chop
5. sad   6. job
7. dust   8. list

 Home Activity Your child has been learning to spell words with short vowels and these consonant/vowel patterns: CVC, CVCC, CCVC. Suggest that your child illustrate some of the words on the list. Then have your child label the sketches.

▲ **Spelling Practice Book** p. 4

OBJECTIVES

- Respond to poems read aloud.
- Recognize rhyme in poetry.

Audio CD **AudioText**

Trees

Apple and pear trees are deciduous—they drop their leaves in the fall. Pine trees have needles as leaves. They keep their needles year round. All three kinds of trees thrive in areas with cold winters. The seeds of apple and pear trees are inside their fruit. The cones of pine trees contain their seeds.

Read Poetry

PREVIEW AND PREDICT Read the titles and author's name of both poems. Point out that the same person wrote both poems. Have children preview the illustrations and note the format of the poems. Ask them to tell what they think the poems are about. Suggest that children read the poems to discover something else about exploring.

POETRY Recall with children that poems usually have short lines that often end in rhyming words. Review that most poems have rhythm that is most evident when they are read aloud.

ALLITERATION Discuss the poet's use of alliteration. Point out that alliteration is using words that have repeating consonant sounds. Read the title and ask children to identify the alliteration. *(travel, tree)* Then have children find other examples in the poem.

VOCABULARY/RHYMING WORDS Remind children that rhyming words have the same ending vowel and consonant sounds and that many poems have rhyming words at the ends of some lines. Have children locate the rhyming words in "Morning Song" at the ends of lines 2 and 4 *(explore, anymore)* and 6 and 8 *(song, along).* Ask: Which words in "My Travel Tree" rhyme? (lines 3 and 5: *pine, mine;* lines 7 and 9: *nooks, books;* lines 10 and 11: *anywhere, there;* lines 12 and 13: *me, tree)*

Poetry

Morning Song
by Bobbi Katz

Today is a day to catch tadpoles.
Today is a day to explore.
Today is a day to get started.
Come on! Let's not sleep anymore.

Outside the sunbeams are dancing.
The leaves sing a rustling song.
Today is a day for adventures,
and I hope that you'll come along!

38

My Travel Tree
by Bobbi Katz

There are oh-so-many
kinds of trees—
apple, pear, pine—
but there is just one special tree
I feel is somehow mine.
Its branches form
such cozy nooks
for dreaming dreams
and reading books.
I sail to almost anywhere,
perched among the leaves up there.
If naming things were up to me,
I'd call this one my travel tree.

39

BUILD CONCEPTS

Categorize and Classify • Critical

- **Do you think that the child saying the poem "Morning Song" lives in a rural or urban area? What makes you think so?**
Possible response: The child probably lives in a rural area because he wants to catch tadpoles, which are most often found in the country.

Draw Conclusions • Literal

- **Why does the child saying the poem "My Travel Tree" call his special tree a travel tree? What else might the tree be called? Why?**
It's a travel tree because when the child sits in it and reads, the stories allow him to travel anywhere. The tree might be called a reading tree.

CONNECT TEXT TO TEXT

Do you think that Iris and Walter might say "Morning Song" to each other? Why or why not? Do you suppose that Walter might have said the poem "My Travel Tree" when he was in his tree house all alone? Why or why not?

Have children discuss how Iris and Walter might like the two poems.

Fluency Have children do a choral reading of the poems with you so that they can understand the rhythm and intonation.

Iris and Walter **38–39**

- Read aloud with an appropriate pace and rate.

Options for Oral Reading

Use *Iris and Walter* or one of the following Leveled Readers.

On-Level

The New Kid

Strategic Intervention

City Mouse and Country Mouse

Advanced

City Friends, Country Friends

Use *Off to School We Go!*, "Morning Song," or "My Travel Tree." Encourage children to repeatedly read aloud texts that they already understand. This extra practice reinforces and improves fluency.

Fluency

READ WITH APPROPRIATE PACE AND RATE

MODEL READING WITH APPROPRIATE PACE AND RATE Use "Morning Song."

- Have children turn to p. 38. You should read different kinds of stories at different speeds that are comfortable and allow you to understand what you are reading. Poems often have a rhythm that help you as you read.

- Ask children to follow along as you read the poem on p. 38 at a rate similar to children's comfort level.

- Have children read the poem after you. Encourage them to read at a comfortable rate. Continue in the same way with "My Travel Tree" on p. 39.

REREAD FOR FLUENCY

Choral Reading   ROUTINE

1 **Select a Passage** Use "Morning Song" on p. 38.

2 **Divide into Groups** Assign each group a part to read. For this poem, have each group read two lines.

3 **Model** Have children track the print as you read.

4 **Read Together** Have children read along with you.

5 **Independent Readings** Have the groups read aloud without you. Monitor progress and provide feedback. For optimal fluency, children should reread three to four times.

Monitor Progress | Check Fluency WCPM

As children reread, monitor their progress toward their individual fluency goals. Current Goal: 50–60 words correct per minute. End-of-Year Goal: 90 words correct per minute.

If... children cannot read fluently at a rate of 50–60 correct words per minute,

then... make sure children practice with text at their independent level. Provide additional fluency practice, pairing nonfluent readers with fluent readers.

If... children already read at 90 words correct per minute,

then... they do not need to reread three to four times.

SUCCESS PREDICTOR

Day 1 Check Word Reading | **Day 2** Check High-Frequency Words | **Day 3** Check Retelling | ▶ **Day 4 Check Fluency** | **Day 5** Assess Progress

Writing Across the Curriculum

WRITE Two-Column Chart

BRAINSTORM Discuss with children what they have learned about rural and urban places. Encourage them to use oral language such as *investigate, urban,* and *rural.* Ask those who have lived in each kind of place to tell what they know about it.

SHARE THE PEN Invite children to help create a two-column chart. Draw such a chart on the board or chart paper, writing *Urban* at the head of one column and *Rural* at the head of the other column. Tell children that making a chart like this is one way to compare things. Discuss whether the area where you live is urban or rural. Encourage children to tell what about their area makes it urban or rural. Ask children to take turns coming up to write their names in the column *Urban* or *Rural* to identify where they live now. As children write their names, ask them whether they have ever lived in a different rural or urban place. Have them write their names in the other column as appropriate. As children write their names, ask questions like these:

- What is the first sound you hear in the name *Charles?* (/ch/)
- What letters stand for that sound? *(ch)* Have a volunteer write *ch.*
- Since *Charles* is a name, how should we write the first letter? (as a capital *C*)

Continue having individuals contribute to the chart. Frequently reread children's names aloud. Finally have children count the number of children who have lived in urban areas and the number who have lived in rural areas. Ask them to write a sentence that compares the two numbers.

Urban	Rural
Amanda	Amanda
Paul	Tina
José	LaToya
Tina	
Charles	

More children have lived in urban areas than have lived in rural areas.

DAILY FIX-IT

7. will go on a field trip
<u>We</u> will go on a field trip<u>.</u>

8. will go with us Mrs. Brody
<u>Mrs. Brody</u> will go with us<u>.</u>

Sentences

Mark the words that complete each sentence.

1. The children ____
   ⊗ A rode a pony.
   ○ B corn.
   ○ C ice cream.
2. Iris and Walter ____
   ○ A grass.
   ○ B beautiful day.
   ⊗ C are friends.
3. I ____
   ○ A cold day.
   ⊗ B play with friends.
   ○ C blue chair.
4. Grandpa ____
   ○ A snowy winter.
   ⊗ B lives in the country.
   ○ C telephone.
5. The city ____
   ⊗ A has many people.
   ○ B fire.
   ○ C day off.
6. The boy ____
   ○ A lettuce patch.
   ○ B movie star.
   ⊗ C makes a tree house.

Home Activity Your child prepared for taking tests on sentences. Have your child tell you three sentences about his or her day.

▲ **Grammar and Writing Practice Book** p. 3

Grammar

REVIEW Sentences

DEFINE SENTENCES

● When is a group of words a sentence? (when it tells a complete idea and the words are in an order that makes sense)
● How does a sentence begin and end? (It always begins with a capital letter, and many sentences end with a period.)

PRACTICE

IDENTIFY SENTENCES Write the following. Have children identify the sentences. Then have them add words to make each of the remaining phrases into sentences. Remind them to begin each one with a capital letter and end it with a period.

live in a city

our second-grade class

Tom used to live in a small town.

we took

a trip to see a farm

Juanita is moving to the country.

Speaking and Listening

WHY WE SPEAK

OBJECTIVES
- Speak to share ideas.
- Listen to hear others' ideas.

DEMONSTRATE SPEAKING Explain to children that people speak for several different reasons.

- We speak to share ideas.
- We speak to ask and answer questions.
- We speak to express our needs, wants, and feelings.
- We speak to entertain.

Discuss with children which of these reasons you have for speaking now. (to share ideas) Then ask children to consider which of these reasons Iris had for speaking to Grandpa at the beginning of the story.

Speaker	Reason
Iris talking to Grandpa	wants to share feelings

ANSWER A QUESTION Ask children to answer a question: What did you discover in a new neighborhood? Allow each child to respond in several oral sentences. Point out that they are speaking to answer a question and also to share ideas.

Wrap Up Your Day!

✓ **MAKING CONNECTIONS: TEXT TO TEXT** Recall *Iris and Walter* and the two poems that followed it. Invite children to discuss why they think these two poems were chosen to go with the story about Iris and Walter. Do you think the poems could have been said by Iris or Walter? Which one reminds you especially of Walter? Why?

LET'S TALK ABOUT IT Ask children what they discovered about Walter's neighborhood as they read the poems. Display the Urban/Rural Venn diagram. Discuss with children what they might add to the diagram.

PREVIEW Day 5

Tell children that tomorrow they will read about an exciting discovery.

Day 5

AT A GLANCE

Share Literature
"The Mystery Eggs"

Phonics and Spelling
 Review Short Vowels

High-Frequency Words

someone	somewhere	**Word Wall**
friend	country	
beautiful	front	

Monitor Progress
Spelling Test: Words with Short Vowels

Group Time < Differentiated Assessment

Writing and Grammar
Trait: Voice
Sentences

Research and Study Skills
Media Center/Library

Materials

- *Sing with Me Big Book*
- *Read Aloud Anthology*
- Reproducible Pages TE 40f–40g
- Student Edition 40–41

Morning Warm-Up!

This week we read about what we might find in a new neighborhood. Iris moved from an urban neighborhood to a rural one. What did she investigate?

QUESTION OF THE DAY Encourage children to sing "Let's Go Investigate!" from the *Sing with Me Big Book* as you gather. Write and read the message and discuss the question.

REVIEW ORAL VOCABULARY Have children describe the rural neighborhood where Iris found Walter and tell what they did there.

- What did you discover about the urban neighborhood that Iris moved from? (Possible answer: There were lots and lots of people. Iris lived on a noisy street and had a wide front stoop. She used to roller-skate in the halls and hear tango music.)

- If you moved to a new neighborhood, what would you want to investigate? Why? (Answers will vary.)

Assess Vocabulary Use the Day 5 instruction on ELL Poster 1 to monitor children's progress with oral vocabulary.

ELL Poster 1

Share Literature

LISTEN AND RESPOND

USE PRIOR KNOWLEDGE Review that yesterday the class listened to find out what the odd eggs Melanie found were and what decision she made about them. Suggest that as you reread the story today, children listen to find out what Melanie discovered in the new neighborhood of the vacation cabin.

MONITOR LISTENING COMPREHENSION

- What did Melanie discover about the neighborhood of the vacation cabin and the creatures in the eggs? (She found out that she was not always right and didn't know everything about things like eggs on the ground because she expected the creatures to be birds, not snakes.)

- Could this story have taken place in an urban setting? Why or why not? (No, because the snake eggs wouldn't appear in the city.)

- What did the snakes do when they came out of the eggs? (They darted quickly out of sight.)

- Do you think that Clara made the right decision to put the eggs outside? Why or why not? (Yes, because they did turn out to be snakes that would have darted all around the bedroom.)

Read Aloud Anthology
The Mystery Eggs

BUILD ORAL VOCABULARY

GENERATE DISCUSSION Recall how Clara made a decision about the eggs that did not please Melanie. In the end, however, Clara knew she had done the right thing. Invite children to discuss a time when they were exploring their neighborhood and saw something that didn't seem right. What did they do about it? Have them use some of this week's Amazing Words as they share their stories.

Monitor Progress | Check Oral Vocabulary

Display pp. 12–13 in the Student Edition and remind children of the unit concept—Exploration. Ask them to tell you about the photographs using some of this week's Amazing Words: *investigate, rural urban, creature, underground, brittle, dart,* and *decision.*

If…children have difficulty using the Amazing Words,

then… ask questions about the photographs using the Amazing Words. Note which questions children can respond to. Reteach unknown words using the Oral Vocabulary Routine on p. DI·1.

SUCCESS PREDICTOR

Day 1 Check Word Reading

Day 2 Check High-Frequency Words

Day 3 Check Retelling

Day 4 Check Fluency

▶ **Day 5** Check Oral Vocabulary/ Assess Progress

OBJECTIVES

- Set purpose for listening.
- Build oral vocabulary.

Amazing Words to build oral vocabulary

investigate	underground
rural	brittle
urban	dart
creature	decision

Extend Language Recall that the baby snakes darted quickly out of sight when they hatched. Use and discuss figurative language to compare the snakes' movements. For example, The tiny snake darted as quickly as a shooting star. Invite children to tell some figurative language comparisons in their own language, asking them to translate as much as they can into English.

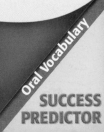

Oral Vocabulary

SUCCESS PREDICTOR

OBJECTIVES
- ◉ Review short vowels.
- ● Review high-frequency words.

◉ Short Vowels

REVIEW

IDENTIFY SHORT VOWEL WORDS Write these sentences. Have children read each one aloud. Call on individuals to name and underline the short vowel words and identify the vowel sounds.

> I left my sack at the bank.
>
> That black duck has a red head.
>
> Did I thank you for my ring?
>
> Ling has a spot on her sock.

High-Frequency Words

REVIEW

COMPLETE THE RHYME Read the following rhyme aloud. Have children write one of the Words to Read from p. 14 for each blank. Then read the completed rhyme as children check their answers.

> Everyone needs a _____ . (friend)
>
> _____ who is true. (Someone)
>
> You can find one in the _____ , (country)
>
> Or across the ocean blue.
>
> _____ you will find one. (Somewhere)
>
> He or she may be new,
>
> Or this _____ person, (beautiful)
>
> Might be right in _____ of you! (front)

Access Content For additional practice with the high-frequency words, use the vocabulary strategies and word cards in the ELL Teaching Guide, pp. 3–4.

SPELLING TEST Short Vowels

DICTATION SENTENCES Use these sentences to assess this week's spelling words.

1. Did you see the <u>list</u>?
2. Dad can <u>chop</u> the log.
3. He cut the <u>tag</u> from the pants.
4. I sat at my <u>desk</u>.
5. Look at the big <u>mess</u>!
6. That is my <u>drum</u>.
7. It was in the green <u>sack</u>.
8. The <u>rock</u> is pink.
9. He got a new <u>job</u>.
10. I was <u>sad</u> when I got sick.
11. My brother ate the <u>rib</u>.
12. It is good to get rid of <u>dust</u>!

CHALLENGE WORDS

13. I have the locket in my <u>pocket</u>.
14. The rabbit likes <u>lettuce</u>.
15. Dad will fix the <u>engine</u>.

ASSESS

● Spell words with short vowels.

Spelling Words

Short Vowels

1.	drum	7.	chop
2.	rock	8.	sack
3.	list	9.	tag
4.	desk	10.	rib
5.	job	11.	mess
6.	sad*	12.	dust

Challenge Words

13.	pocket	15.	engine
14.	lettuce		

* Word from the Selection

Group Time

On-Level	Strategic Intervention	Advanced
Read Set B Sentences.	**Read** Set A Sentences.	**Read** Set C Sentences and the Story.
• Use pp. 40e–40g.	• Use pp. 40e–40g.	• Use pp. 40e–40g.
	• Use the **Routine** on p. DI·22.	• Use the **Routine** on p. DI·23.

DAY 5

 Place English language learners in the groups that correspond to their reading abilities in English.

(i) Independent Activities

Fluency Reading Children reread selections at their independent level.

Journal Writing Write a story about an urban family that moves to a rural area. Share writing.

Independent Reading See p. 12j for Reading/Library activities and suggestions.

Literacy Centers Use the Technology Center on p. 12k to support this week's concepts and reading.

Practice Book 2.1 Media Center/Library, p. 10

Break into small groups after Spelling and before Grammar and Writing.

- Decode words with short vowels.
- Read high-frequency words.
- Read aloud with appropriate speed and accuracy.
- Recognize story characters and setting.
- Retell a story.

Differentiated Assessment

On-Level
Set B

Strategic Intervention
Set A

Advanced
Set C

Fluency Assessment Plan

☑ **This week assess Advanced students.**

☐ Week 2 assess Strategic Intervention students.

☐ Week 3 assess On-Level Intervention students.

☐ Week 4 assess Strategic Intervention students.

☐ Week 5 assess any students you have not yet checked during this unit.

Set individual fluency goals for children to enable them to reach the end-of-year goal.

- Current Goal: 50–60 wcpm
- End-of-Year Goal: 90 wcpm
- **ELL** Fluency, particularly for English learners reading texts in English, develops gradually and through much practice. Focus on each child's improvement rather than solely monitoring the number of words correct per minute.

SENTENCE READING

ASSESS SHORT VOWELS AND HIGH-FREQUENCY WORDS Use one of the reproducible lists on p. 40f to assess children's ability to read words with short vowels and high-frequency words. Call on individuals to read two sentences aloud. Have each child in the group read different sentences. Start over with sentence one if necessary.

RECORD SCORES Use the Sentence Reading Chart for this unit on p. WA19.

Monitor Progress	Short Vowels
If... children have trouble reading words with short vowels,	**then...** use the Reteach Lessons on p. DI·64.
High-Frequency Words	
If... children cannot read high-frequency words,	**then...** mark the missed words on a high-frequency word list and send the list home for additional word reading practice, or have the child practice with a fluent reader.

FLUENCY AND COMPREHENSION

ASSESS FLUENCY Take a one-minute sample of children's oral reading. See Monitoring Fluency, p. WA17. Have children read "The New Friend," the on-level fluency passage on p. 40g.

RECORD SCORES Record the number of words read correctly in one minute on the child's Fluency Progress Chart.

ASSESS COMPREHENSION Have the child read to the end of the passage. (If the child had difficulty with the passage, you may read it aloud.) Ask who the characters are and where and when the story takes place. Have the child retell the passage. Use the Retelling Rubric on p. 36–37 to evaluate the child's retelling.

Monitor Progress	Fluency
If... a child does not achieve the fluency goal on the timed reading,	**then...** copy the passage and send it home with the child for additional fluency practice, or have the child practice with a fluent reader.
Character and Setting	
If... a child cannot tell who the characters are or when and where the story takes place,	**then...** use the Reteach Lesson on p. DI·64.

READ THE SENTENCES

Set A

1. Someone did drop a ring.
2. We will pick up bread at a store somewhere.
3. My friend went to the ice rink.
4. The red bird sings out in the country.
5. I spot a rock by the beautiful house.
6. A girl with a pink hat on her head was in front.

Set B

1. My friend Tom got sick last week.
2. Jim steps in front of the big sink.
3. I think the top of the box is here somewhere.
4. On her head was a beautiful pink hat.
5. Someone will bring bread for lunch.
6. We can pick plums out in the country.

Set C

1. My friend Chuck got a cut on his chin when he slipped on the stick.
2. The breakfast milk dripped down the front of her dress.
3. Dead leaves hang from the tree in the country.
4. Meg wanted someone to bring watermelons back.
5. He lives somewhere on that block.
6. The beautiful sunset in the west took Frank's breath away.

Monitor Progress | Short Vowels
High-Frequency Words

SUCCESS PREDICTOR

The New Friend

Jack walked slowly home from school. "Why do   8
we have to live here, anyway?" he grumbled.   16

This had been Jack's third day at his new   25
school. It was the same every day. No one said   35
anything to Jack. Everyone had their own friends.   43
He wished that he had someone to eat lunch with.   53
Jack counted cracks in the sidewalk on his way   62
home. "Watch out!" a girl said. "You almost walked   71
right into me!"   74

She looked at him. "My name is Ming. I saw you   85
in school. Do you live on this block?"   93

Jack was shocked that she talked to him. "Yes,"   102
he said. "My house is around the corner."   110

The girl nodded her head. "I live on the next   120
street. I'm meeting my friend Frank. We're going to   129
play soccer. Want to come?"   134

"Sure!" Jack said. "This place isn't so bad after   143
all."   144

See also Assessment Handbook, p. 302 • REPRODUCIBLE PAGE

Write Now
Writing and Grammar

Plan

Prompt

In *Iris and Walter*, Iris visits a treehouse and makes a friend. Think about a place you would like to visit.
Now write a plan that tells what you will see and do there.

Writing Trait

Voice tells how you feel about your topic.

Student Model

Place is named at beginning.

Writer lists things to do and see.

Voice shows how writer feels.

I plan to visit Chicago.
• I will see many tall buildings.
• I will see busy streets with people.
• I will ride on the train.
• I will go to the zoo.
• It will be an exciting trip.

40

Writer's Checklist

☐ **Focus** Do all sentences tell about one place?
☐ **Organization** Is the place named at the beginning?
☐ **Support** Do details tell about things to see and do?
☐ **Conventions** Do sentences begin with capital letters?

Grammar

Sentences

A **sentence** is a group of words that tells a complete idea. The words are in an order that makes sense. A sentence begins with a capital letter. Many sentences end with a **period (.)**.

Iris and Walter went swimming.

This is a sentence. It tells a complete idea.

Look at the sentences in the plan. How do you know they are sentences?

41

Writing and Grammar

LOOK AT THE PROMPT Read p. 40 aloud. Have children select and discuss key words or phrases in the prompt. *(place you would like to visit, plan, what you will see and do there)*

STRATEGIES TO DEVELOP VOICE Have children

• think about the reason for writing and match the voice to the purpose.

• read their plans aloud to see if the voice sounds natural.

• include their feelings about the topic in their writing.

See Scoring Rubric on p. WA11. **Rubric 4 3 2 1**

HINTS FOR BETTER WRITING Read p. 41 aloud. Use the checklist to help children revise their plans. Discuss the grammar lesson. (Answer: *Each one tells a complete idea, and the words are in an order that makes sense. Each begins with a capital letter and ends with a period.*) Have children write complete sentences with correct capitalization and punctuation in their own plans.

DAILY FIX-IT

9. We helped clean up the mes
We helped clean up the <u>mess.</u>

10. picked up she the pieces
<u>She</u> picked up the pieces<u>.</u>

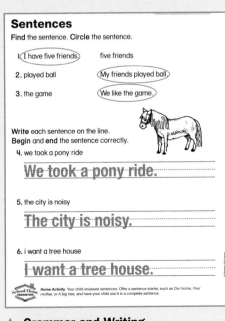

Sentences
Find the sentence. Circle the sentence.

1. (I have five friends.)   five friends

2. played ball   (My friends played ball.)

3. the game   (We like the game.)

Write each sentence on the line.
Begin and **end** the sentence correctly.

4. we took a pony ride
We took a pony ride.

5. the city is noisy
The city is noisy.

6. i want a tree house
I want a tree house.

Home Activity Your child reviewed sentences. Offer a sentence starter, such as *Our home, Your mother,* or *A big tree,* and have your child use it in a complete sentence.

▲ **Grammar and Writing Practice Book** p. 4

Iris and Walter   **40–41**

Research/Study Skills

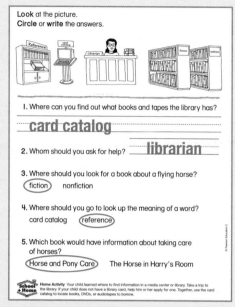

Look at the picture.
Circle or **write** the answers.

1. Where can you find out what books and tapes the library has?

card catalog

2. Whom should you ask for help? **librarian**

3. Where should you look for a book about a flying horse?
(fiction)   nonfiction

4. Where should you go to look up the meaning of a word?
card catalog   (reference)

5. Which book would have information about taking care of horses?
(Horse and Pony Care)   The Horse in Harry's Room

▲ **Practice Book 2.1** p. 10,
Media Center/Library

TEACH/MODEL Media Center/Library

MODEL USING A MEDIA CENTER/LIBRARY Take children to your school media center or library. Explain to them that they can find many things in the library. Introduce them to various resources, such as books, magazines, videos, cassettes, CDs, CD-ROMs, computers, and picture files. Remind children to handle any media they use carefully and with respect. Show them how to find fiction, nonfiction, references, and periodicals. Help them figure out how to use the card catalog or computer catalog and a library card. Introduce them to the librarian and explain that she or he can help them find what they want.

Model how to use the library to find another book like *Iris and Walter*.

 MODEL I liked the story about Iris and Walter so much that I would like to read another one like it. I'll look in the card catalog for the title *Iris and Walter* or for the author's name, Elissa Haden Guest, to see whether she wrote any more stories that are in this library. I'll remember that authors are always listed in alphabetical order by their last name, so I'll look in the *G*'s for *Guest*. If I don't find what I want, I'll ask the librarian for help.

FIND POEMS BY BOBBI KATZ Ask children to use what they know about the library to find more poems by Bobbi Katz like the two they read this week.

PRACTICE

DEMONSTRATE USING A MEDIA CENTER OR LIBRARY Ask children to locate a fiction or nonfiction book or an article in a children's magazine about something that interests them. Encourage them to check the book or magazine out and read it at home. Offer your or the librarian's help in choosing topics if necessary.

Access Content As you or the librarian shows children each element of the media center and library, make sure children understand what it is used for and how they can use it. You may want to personalize the search by suggesting that children look for something about their native country.

Wrap Up Your Week!

LET'S TALK ABOUT Exploration

QUESTION OF THE WEEK Recall this week's question.

• What might we discover in a new neighborhood?

Display the Venn diagram. Recall with children the similarities and differences between urban and rural neighborhoods. Ask children to add other items to the diagram now. Write their ideas in the appropriate part of the diagram.

Urban   Rural

big buildings
lots of people
many cars, buses, and trucks
skating in hallways

houses
cars

not many buildings
lots of open space
many flowers, trees, and birds
ponies in fields

CONNECT Use questions such as these to prompt a discussion:

• Iris lived in two different kinds of neighborhoods. Which one was urban? Which one was rural?

• What kind of creatures might Iris and Walter investigate in the country?

• Some people make a decision to investigate space instead of Earth. Why do you suppose someone would want to do that?

Build Background Use ELL Poster 2 to support the Preview activity.

You've learned	You've learned
008 Amazing Words	**008** Amazing Words
this week!	**so far this year!**

PREVIEW Tell children that next week they will read about another new place people explore—space.

PREVIEW Next Week

Assessment Checkpoints *for the Week*

Selection Assessment

Use pp. 1–4 of Selection Tests to check:

 Selection Understanding

 Comprehension Skill *Character and Setting*

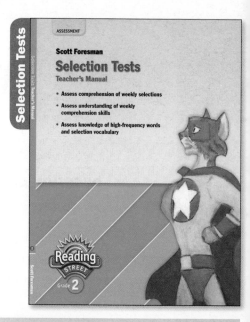 **High–Frequency Words**

beautiful   front
country   someone
friend   somewhere

Leveled Assessment

On-Level

Strategic Intervention

Advanced

Use pp. 1–6 of Fresh Reads for Differentiated Test Practice to check:

 Comprehension Skill *Character and Setting*

 REVIEW Comprehension Skill *Main Idea and Details*

 Fluency *Words Correct Per Minute*

Managing Assessment

Use Assessment Handbook for:

 Weekly Assessment Blackline Masters for Monitoring Progress

 Observation Checklists

 Record-Keeping Forms

 Portfolio Assessment

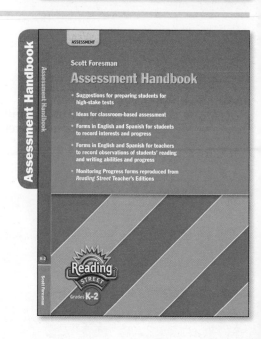

Unit 1
Exploration

CONCEPT QUESTION

What can we learn from exploring new places and things?

Week 1
What might we discover in a new neighborhood?

Week 2
Why would anyone want to explore space?

Week 3
What can we discover by exploring nature?

Week 4
What can we learn by exploring the desert?

Week 5
When we are searching for answers, whom can we ask?

EXPAND THE CONCEPT
Why would anyone want to explore space?

CONNECT THE CONCEPT

▶ **Build Background**

ascend	journey	orbit
descend	launch	universe
enormous	meteorite	

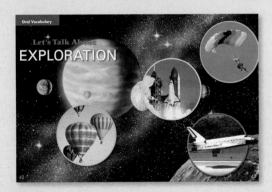

▶ **Science Content**
Space Exploration, Astronauts (Careers in Space), Space Travel, Technology, Space Research, Solar System

▶ **Writing**
A List

Preview Your Week

Why would anyone want to explore space?

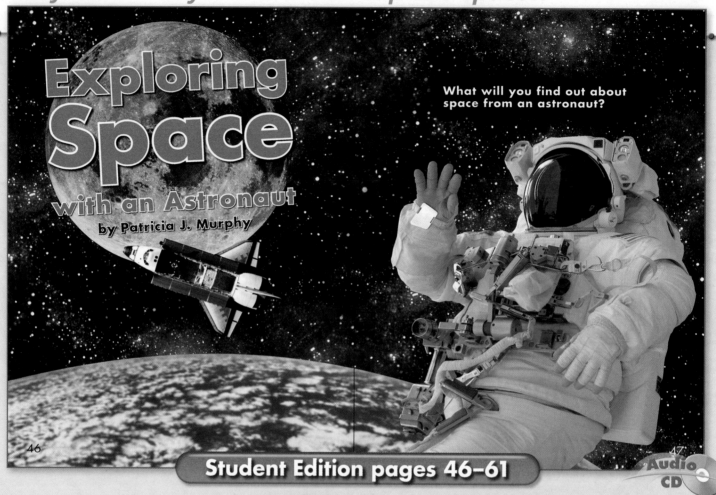

What will you find out about space from an astronaut?

Exploring **Space** with an Astronaut
by Patricia J. Murphy

46

47

Audio CD

Student Edition pages 46–61

Genre Expository Nonfiction

🔄 **Phonics** Long Vowels CVCe

🔄 **Comprehension Skill** Main Idea and Details

🔄 **Comprehension Strategy** Text Structure

Science in Reading

TIME FOR Science

Paired Selection

Reading Across Texts
Learn About Astronauts

Genre
Nonfiction

Text Features
Photographs
Captions

A Trip to **Space Camp**

by Ann Weil

What does it feel like to go into space? Would you like to find out? Then maybe Space Camp is for you!

There are all sorts of space camps that you could try. Some are for adults. Some are for teens. There is even a Space Camp for children as young as 7 years old. It is called Parent-Child Space Camp. Parent-Child Space Camp takes place over a long weekend. Families can go to Space Camp together.

62

Student Edition pages 62–65

Audio CD

Read It ONLINE
PearsonSuccessNet.com

- Student Edition
- Leveled Readers
- Decodable Reader

Leveled Readers

Skill Main Idea and Details

Strategy Text Structure

Lesson Vocabulary

Below-Level

On-Level

Advanced

ELL Reader
- Concept Vocabulary
- Text Support
- Language Enrichment

Decodable Reader

Apply Phonics
- *Ike and Ace*

Integrate Science Standards

- Space Exploration
- Astronauts
- Space Travel
- Technology
- Space Research
- Solar System

✓ **Read**

Exploring Space with an Astronaut pp. 46–61

"A Trip to Space Camp" pp. 62–65

✓ **Read**

Leveled Readers

Below-Level   **On-Level**   **Advanced**

- Support Concepts
- Develop Concepts
- Extend Concepts
- Science Extension Activity

✓ **Read**

ELL Reader

✓ **Build Concept Vocabulary**
Exploration, pp. 42r, 42–43

✓ **Teach Science Concepts**
Space Walk, p. 50–51
Astronauts, p. 62–63

✓ **Explore Science Center**
Ask an Astronaut, p. 42k

Weekly Plan

READING

90–120 minutes

TARGET SKILLS OF THE WEEK

Phonics
Introduce Long Vowels CVCe

Comprehension Skill
Main Idea and Details

Comprehension Strategy
Text Structure

DAY 1 — PAGES 42l–43d

Oral Language

QUESTION OF THE WEEK, 42l
Why would anyone want to explore space?

Oral Vocabulary/Share Literature, 42m
Sing with Me Big Book, Song 2
Amazing Words *ascend, descend, orbit*

Word Work

Phonics, 42n–42o
Introduce Long Vowels CVCe **T**

Spelling, 42p
Pretest

Comprehension/Vocabulary/Fluency

Read Decodable Reader 2

Grouping Options 42f–42g

Review High-Frequency Words
Check Comprehension
Reread for Fluency

Build Background, 42r–43
Exploration

Listening Comprehension, 43a–43b
Main Idea and Details **T**

DAY 2 — PAGES 44a–59b

Oral Language

QUESTION OF THE DAY, 44a
What do you think it feels like to take off into space?

Oral Vocabulary/Share Literature, 44b
Read Aloud Anthology "Gloria Rising"
Amazing Word *universe*

Word Work

Phonics, 44c–44d
Review Long Vowels CVCe **T**

Spelling, 44d
Dictation

Comprehension/Vocabulary/Fluency

Read *Exploring Space with an Astronaut,*
44e–59

Grouping Options
42f–42g

Introduce High-Frequency
Words *everywhere, live,
machines, move, woman,
work, world* **T**

Introduce Selection Words
*astronaut, experiment,
gravity, shuttle, telescope*

Reread for Fluency

Main Idea and
Details **T**
Text Structure **T**
REVIEW Author's
Purpose **T**

LANGUAGE ARTS

20–30 minutes

Trait of the Week

Word Choice

Shared Writing, 43c
List

Grammar, 43d
Introduce Subjects **T**

Interactive Writing, 59a
Questions and Answers

Grammar, 59b
Practice Subjects **T**

DAILY JOURNAL WRITING

Day 1 Write a story about a rocket that goes into orbit.

Day 2 Write about what you would like to see and do in space.

DAILY SCIENCE CONNECTIONS

Day 1 Exploring Space Concept Chart, 42r–43

Day 2 Time for Science: Space Walk, 50–51

DAILY SUCCESS PREDICTORS
for Adequate Yearly Progress

Monitor Progress and Corrective Feedback

Phonics
Check Word Reading, *42o*
Spiral REVIEW Phonics

Fluency
Check High-Frequency Words, *45a*
Spiral REVIEW High-Frequency Words

RESOURCES FOR THE WEEK

- Practice Book 2.1, *pp. 11–20*
- Phonics and Spelling Practice Book, *pp. 5–8*
- Grammar and Writing Practice Book, *pp. 5–8*
- Selection Test, *pp. 5–8*
- Fresh Reads for Differentiated Test Practice, *pp. 7–12*
- Phonics Songs and Rhymes Chart 2
- The Grammar and Writing Book, *pp. 56–61*

Grouping Options for Differentiated Instruction

Turn the page for the small group lesson plan.

DAY 3 — PAGES 60a–61b

Oral Language

QUESTION OF THE DAY, 60a
What will Gloria do when she grows up?

Oral Vocabulary/Share Literature, 60b
Read Aloud Anthology *Gloria Rising*
Amazing Words *enormous, journey*

Word Work

Phonics, 60c
REVIEW Short Vowels **T**

High-Frequency Words, 60d
Practice *everywhere, live, machines, move, woman, work, world* **T**

Spelling, 60d
Practice

Comprehension/Vocabulary/Fluency

Vocabulary, 60e
Position Words

Read *Exploring Space with an Astronaut,* 46–61

Grouping Options
42f–42g

Fluency, 60f
Read with Accuracy

Think and Share, 60g

Trait of the Week, 61a
Introduce Word Choice

Grammar, 61b
Write with Subjects **T**

Day 3 Use position words in sentences about exploring space.

Day 3 Exploring Space Concept Chart, 61b

DAY 4 — PAGES 62a–65d

Oral Language

QUESTION OF THE DAY, 62a
What do you think being in space camp is like?

Oral Vocabulary/Share Literature, 62b
Read Aloud Anthology *Mission to Mars*
Amazing Words *launch, meteorite*

Word Work

Phonics, 62c
REVIEW Sentence Reading **T**

Spelling, 62d
Partner Review

Comprehension/Vocabulary/Fluency

Read "A Trip to Space Camp," 62–65
Leveled Readers

Grouping Options
42f–42g

Position Words
Reading Across Texts

Fluency, 65a
Read with Accuracy

Writing Across the Curriculum, 65b
Three-Column Chart

Grammar, 65c
Review Subjects **T**

Speaking and Listening, 65d
Why We Listen

Day 4 List things that can ascend and descend.

Day 4 Time for Science: Astronauts, 62–63

DAY 5 — PAGES 66a–67b

Oral Language

QUESTION OF THE DAY, 66a
What do real astronauts do in space?

Oral Vocabulary/Share Literature, 66b
Read Aloud Anthology *Mission to Mars*
Amazing Words Review

Word Work

Phonics, 66c
🎯 Review Long Vowels CVCe **T**

High-Frequency Words, 66c
Review *everywhere, live, machines, move, woman, work, world* **T**

Spelling, 66d
Test

Comprehension/Vocabulary/Fluency

Read Leveled Readers

Grouping Options 42f–42g

Monitor Progress, 66e–66g
Read the Sentences
Read the Story

Writing and Grammar, 66–67
Develop Word Choice
Use Subjects **T**

Research/Study Skills, 67a
Alphabetical Order

Day 5 Write about children who ascend into space.

Day 5 Revisit the Exploring Space Concept Chart, 67b

KEY 🎯 = Target Skill **T** = Tested Skill

Comprehension — Check Retelling, *60g*

Fluency — Check Fluency WCPM, *65a*
Spiral **REVIEW** Phonics, High-Frequency Words

Oral Vocabulary — Check Oral Vocabulary, *66b*
Assess Phonics, High-Frequency Words, Fluency, Comprehension, *66e*

SUCCESS PREDICTOR

Small Group Plan *for Differentiated Instruction*

Daily Plan
AT A GLANCE

Reading
Whole Group
- Oral Language
- Word Work
- Comprehension/Vocabulary

Group Time

Meet with small groups to provide:
- Skill Support
- Reading Support
- Fluency Practice

Read

This week's lessons for daily group time can be found behind the Differentiated Instruction (DI) tab on pp. DI·24–DI·33.

Whole Group
- Comprehension/Vocabulary
- Fluency

Language Arts
- Writing
- Grammar
- Speaking/Listening/Viewing
- Research/Study Skills

Use *My Sidewalks on Reading Street* for Tier III intensive reading intervention.

DAY 1

On-Level	Strategic Intervention	Advanced
Teacher-Led *Page 42q*	Teacher-Led *Page DI·24*	Teacher-Led *Page DI·25*
• **Read** Decodable Reader 2 • **Reread** for Fluency	• Blend Words with Long Vowels CVCe • **Read** Decodable Reader 2 • **Reread** for Fluency	• Extend Word Reading • **Read** Advanced Selection 2 • Introduce Concept Inquiry

(i) Independent Activities

While you meet with small groups, have the rest of the class...

- Reread for fluency
- Write in their journals
- Read self-selected reading
- Visit the Word Work Center
- Complete Practice Book 2.1, pp. 13–14

DAY 2

On-Level	Strategic Intervention	Advanced
Teacher-Led *Pages 46–59*	Teacher-Led *Page DI·26*	Teacher-Led *Page DI·27*
• **Read** *Exploring Space with an Astronaut* • **Reread** for Fluency	• Blend Words with Long Vowels CVCe • **Read** SI Decodable Reader 2 • **Read** or Listen to *Exploring Space with an Astronaut*	• **Read** *Exploring Space with an Astronaut* • Continue Concept Inquiry

(i) Independent Activities

While you meet with small groups, have the rest of the class...

- Read self-selected reading
- Write in their journals
- Visit the Listening Center
- Complete Practice Book 2.1, pp. 15–17

DAY 3

On-Level	Strategic Intervention	Advanced
Teacher-Led *Pages 46–61*	Teacher-Led *Page DI·28*	Teacher-Led *Page DI·29*
• **Reread** *Exploring Space with an Astronaut*	• **Reread** *Exploring Space with an Astronaut* • Read Words and Sentences • Review Main Idea and Details and Text Structure • **Reread** for Fluency	• Self-Selected Reading • Continue Concept Inquiry

(i) Independent Activities

While you meet with small groups, have the rest of the class...

- Read self-selected reading
- Write in their journals
- Visit the Writing Center
- Complete Practice Book 2.1, pp. 18–19

① Begin with whole class skill and strategy instruction.

② Meet with small groups to provide differentiated instruction.

③ Gather the whole class back together for fluency and language arts.

On-Level

Teacher-Led

Pages 62–65, LR13–LR15

Read "A Trip to Space Camp"

Practice with On-Level Reader *Space Walk*

Strategic Intervention

Teacher-Led

Pages DI · 30, LR10–LR12

- **Read** or Listen to "A Trip to Space Camp"
- **Reread** for Fluency
- Build Concepts
- Practice with Below-Level Reader *Being an Astronaut*

Advanced

Teacher-Led

Pages DI · 31, LR16–LR18

- **Read** "A Trip to Space Camp"
- Extend Vocabulary
- Continue Concept Inquiry
- Practice with Advanced Reader *Explore the Galaxy*

DAY 4

ⓘ Independent Activities

While you meet with small groups, have the rest of the class...

- Reread for fluency
- Write in their journals
- Read self-selected reading
- Review spelling words with a partner
- Visit the Listening and Science Centers

On-Level

Teacher-Led

Pages 66e–66g, LR13–LR15

- Sentence Reading, Set B
  Monitor Comprehension
- Practice with On-Level Reader *Space Walk*

Strategic Intervention

Teacher-Led

Pages DI · 32, LR10–LR12

- Practice Word Reading
- Sentence Reading, Set A
- Monitor Fluency and Comprehension
- Practice with Below-Level Reader *Being an Astronaut*

Advanced

Teacher-Led

Pages DI · 33, LR16–LR18

- Sentence Reading, Set C
- Monitor Comprehension
- Share Concept Inquiry
- Practice with Advanced Reader *Explore the Galaxy*

DAY 5

ⓘ Independent Activities

While you meet with small groups, have the rest of the class...

- Reread for fluency
- Write in their journals
- Read self-selected reading
- Visit the Technology Center
- Complete Practice Book 2.1, p. 20

Grouping Place English language learners in the groups that correspond to their reading abilities in English.

Use the appropriate Leveled Reader or other text at children's instructional level.

TIP Send home the appropriate Multilingual Summary of the main selection on Day 1.

ELL

Take It to the NET ONLINE
PearsonSuccessNet.com

Peter Afflerbach
For ideas on implementing on-going assessment, see the article "STAIR" by Scott Foresman author Peter Afflerbach.

TEACHER TALK

Establish rules for independent work stations.
Talk with children about the rules, such as sharing materials and taking turns. Discuss what to do if they run out of materials or finish early. Post rules and guidelines.

Be sure to schedule time for children to work on the unit inquiry project "Take a Trip." This week children should choose one place to explore and research it to find information.

Looking Ahead

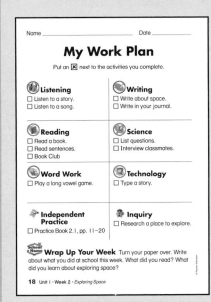

▲ **Group-Time Survival Guide**
p. 18, Weekly Contract

Customize Your Plan *by Stran*

 Science

Concept Development

Why would anyone want to explore space?

 *to build oral vocabulary*

ascend	descend	enormous
journey	launch	meteorite
orbit	universe	

BUILD

☐ **Question of the Week** Use the Morning Warm-Up! to introduce and discuss the question of the week. This week children will talk, sing, read, and write about why anyone would want to explore space. DAY 1 *42l*

☐ **Sing with Me Big Book** Sing a song about astronauts in orbit. Ask children to listen for the concept-related Amazing Words *ascend*, *descend*, and *orbit*. DAY 1 *42m*

Sing with Me Big Book

☐ **Let's Talk About Exploration** Use the Let's Talk About It lesson in the Student Edition to build background, vocabulary, and concepts. Then create a concept chart for children to add to throughout the week. DAY 1 *42r-43*

Let's Talk About It

DEVELOP

☐ **Question of the Day** Use the questions in the Morning Warm-Ups! to discuss lesson concepts and how they relate to the unit theme, Exploration. DAY 2 *44a* DAY 3 *60a*, DAY 4 *62a*, DAY 5 *66a*

☐ **Share Literature** Read big books and read aloud selections that develop concepts, language, and vocabulary related to the lesson concept and the unit theme. Continue to develop this week's Amazing Words. DAY 2 *44b*, DAY 3 *60b*, DAY 4 *62b*, DAY 5 *66b*

CONNECT

☐ **Wrap Up Your Week!** Revisit the Question of the Week. Then connect concepts and vocabulary to next week's lesson. DAY 5 *67b*

CHECK

☐ **Check Oral Vocabulary** To informally assess children's oral vocabulary, ask individuals to use some of this week's Amazing Words to tell you about the photograph on Student Edition pp. 42–43. DAY 5 *66b*

 LONG VOWELS CVCe When a word has a consonant-vowel-consonant-silent *e* pattern, the vowel usually stands for its long sound. The letter *c* usually stands for the sound /s/ when followed by *e, i,* or *y*. The letter *g* usually stands for the sound /j/ when followed by *e* or *i*. The letter *s* can stand for /s/ or /z/.

TEACH

☐ **Long Vowels CVCe** Introduce the blending strategy for words with long vowels CVCe pattern. Then have children blend and build words with the CVCe pattern using letter tiles. DAY 1 *42n-42o*

☐ **Fluent Word Reading** Use the Fluent Word Reading Routine to develop children's word reading fluency. Use the Phonics Songs and Rhymes Chart for additional word reading practice. DAY 2 *44c-44d*

Phonics Songs and Rhymes Chart 2

PRACTICE/APPLY

☐ **Decodable Reader 2** Practice reading words with long vowels CVCe in context. DAY 1 *42q*

☐ *Exploring Space with an Astronaut* Practice decoding words in context. DAY 2 *46-59*

Decodable Reader 2

☐ **Homework** Practice Book 2.1 p. 13. DAY 1 *42o*

☐ **Word Work Center** Practice long vowels CVCe. **ANY DAY** *42j*

Main Selection—Nonfiction

RETEACH/REVIEW

☐ **Review** Review words with this week's phonics skills. DAY 5 *66c*

☐ **Reteach Lessons** If necessary, reteach long vowels CVCe. DAY 5 *DI·65*

☐ **Spiral REVIEW** Review previously taught phonics skills. DAY 1 *42o*, DAY 3 *60c*, DAY 4 *62c*

ASSESS

☐ **Sentence Reading** Assess children's ability to read words with long vowels CVCe. DAY 5 *66e-66f*

❶ Use assessment data to determine your instructional focus.

❷ Preview this week's instruction by strand.

❸ Choose instructional activities that meet the needs of your classroom.

SPELLING

LONG VOWELS CVCe When a word has a consonant-vowel-consonant-silent *e* pattern, the vowel usually stands for its long sound.

TEACH

☐ **Pretest** Before administering the pretest, model how to segment long vowel words to spell them. Dictate the spelling words, segmenting them if necessary. Then have children check their pretests and correct misspelled words. **DAY 1** *42p*

PRACTICE/APPLY

☐ **Dictation** Have children write dictation sentences to practice spelling words. **DAY 2** *44d*

☐ **Write Words** Have children practice writing the spelling words by creating a word orbit. **DAY 3** *60d*

☐ **Homework** Phonics and Spelling Practice Book pp. 5–8.
DAY 1 *42p*, **DAY 2** *44d*, **DAY 3** *60d*, **DAY 4** *62d*

RETEACH/REVIEW

☐ **Partner Review** Have pairs work together to read and write the spelling words. **DAY 4** *62d*

ASSESS

☐ **Posttest** Use dictation sentences to give the posttest for words with long vowels CVCe. **DAY 5** *66d*

Spelling Words

Long Vowels CVCe

1. tune	7. mice
2. page	8. late
3. nose	9. cube
4. space*	10. blaze
5. size	11. home
6. fine	12. vote

Challenge Words

13. erase	15. confuse
14. spice	

* Words from the Selection

HIGH-FREQUENCY WORDS

WORDS TO READ

everywhere	live	machines	move
woman	work	world	

TEACH

☐ **Words to Read** Introduce this week's high-frequency words and add them to the Word Wall. **DAY 2** *44–45a*

High-Frequency Words

PRACTICE/APPLY

☐ **Words in Context** Read high-frequency words in the context of *Exploring Space with an Astronaut.* **DAY 2** *46–59*

☐ **Word Wall** Use the Word Wall to review and practice high-frequency words throughout the week. **DAY 3** *60d*, **DAY 5** *66c*

Main Selection—Nonfiction

☐ **Leveled Text** Practice this week's high-frequency words in the context of leveled text. **DAY 4** *LR10–LR18*, **DAY 5** *LR10–LR18*

☐ **Homework** Practice Book 2.1 pp. 16, 19. **DAY 2** *45a*, **DAY 3** *60d*

Leveled Readers

RETEACH/REVIEW

☐ **SPIRAL REVIEW** Review previously taught high-frequency words. **DAY 2** *45a*, **DAY 4** *62c*

ASSESS

☐ **Sentence Reading** Assess children's ability to read this week's high-frequency words. **DAY 5** *66e–66f*

VOCABULARY

TEACH

☐ **Vocabulary Transparency 2** Use Vocabulary Transparency 2 to introduce the selection words from *Exploring Space with an Astronaut.* Children will read these words but will not be tested on them. **DAY 2** *46a*

☐ **Position Words** Have children brainstorm position words, act out their meaning, and then create an oral sentence using the position word. **DAY 3** *60e*

☑ Customize Your Plan *by Strand*

COMPREHENSION

⊙ **SKILL MAIN IDEA AND DETAILS** The main idea is the most important idea about the topic. Details are the small pieces of information that tell more about the main idea.

⊙ **STRATEGY TEXT STRUCTURE** Text structure is a method an author uses to introduce information. Authors often use headings to help readers know what they are going to read about next.

TEACH

❑ **Listening Comprehension** Read "Eating in Space" and model how to identify the *main idea and details*. **DAY 1** *43a–43b*

❑ **Skill/Strategy Lesson** Review how to identify the *main idea and details*. Then introduce this week's strategy, *text structure*. **DAY 2** *44e*

PRACTICE/APPLY

❑ **Skills and Strategies in Context** Read *Exploring Space with an Astronaut*, using the Guiding Comprehension questions to apply *main idea and details* and *text structure*. **DAY 2** *46-59*

Main Selection—Nonfiction

❑ **Think and Share** Use the questions on Student Edition p. 60 to discuss the selection. **DAY 3** *60g-61*

❑ **Skills and Strategies in Context** Read "A Trip to Space Camp," guiding children as they apply skills and strategies. After reading have children make connections across texts. **DAY 4** *62-65*

Paired Selection—Nonfiction

❑ **Leveled Text** Apply *main idea and details* and *text structure* to read leveled text. **DAY 4** *LR10-LR18*, **DAY 5** *LR10-LR18*

Leveled Readers

❑ **Homework** Practice Book 2.1 p. 14, 15. **DAY 1** *43a*, **DAY 2** *44e*

ASSESS

❑ **Selection Test** Determine children's understanding of the main selection and assess their ability to identify *main idea and details*. **DAY 3**

❑ **Story Reading** Have children read the passage "Going into Space." Ask what the *main idea and details* of the story is and have them retell. **DAY 5** *66e-66g*

RETEACH/REVIEW

❑ **Reteach Lesson** If necessary, reteach *main idea and details*. **DAY 5** *DI·65*

FLUENCY

SKILL MODEL READING WITH ACCURACY Accuracy is identifying words correctly as you read and reading without omitting or substituting any words.

REREAD FOR FLUENCY

❑ **Oral Rereading** Have children read orally from Decodable Reader 2 or another text at their independent reading level. Listen as children read and provide corrective feedback regarding their oral reading and their use of the blending strategy. **DAY 1** *42q*

❑ **Paired Reading** Have pairs of children read orally from the main selection or another text at their independent reading level and apply their knowledge of reading with accuracy. Listen as children read and provide corrective feedback regarding oral reading and their use of the blending strategy. **DAY 2** *58-59*

TEACH

❑ **Model** Use passages from *Exploring Space with an Astronaut* to model reading with accuracy. **DAY 3** *60f*, **DAY 4** *65a*

PRACTICE/APPLY

❑ **Choral Reading** Choral read passages from *Exploring Space with an Astronaut*. Monitor progress and provide feedback regarding children's reading with accuracy. **DAY 3** *60f* **DAY 4** *65a*

❑ **Listening Center** Have children follow along with the AudioText for this week's selections. **ANY DAY** *42j*

❑ **Reading/Library Center** Have children build fluency by rereading Leveled Readers, Decodable Readers, or other text at their independent level. **ANY DAY** *42j*

❑ **Fluency Coach** Have children use Fluency Coach to listen to fluent reading or to practice reading on their own. **ANY DAY**

ASSESS

❑ **Story Reading** Take a one-minute timed sample of children's oral reading. Use the passage "Going into Space." **DAY 5** *66e-66g*

❶ Use assessment data to determine your instructional focus.

❷ Preview this week's instruction by strand.

❸ Choose instructional activities that meet the needs of your classroom.

WRITING

Trait of the Week

WORD CHOICE Good word choice adds style to your writing. Use exact nouns, strong verbs, and exciting adjectives to make your writing interesting, clear, and lively.

TEACH

☐ **Write Together** Engage children in writing activities that develop language, grammar, and writing skills. Include independent writing as an extension of group writing activities.

    Shared Writing DAY 1 *43c*
    Interactive Writing DAY 2 *59a*
    Writing Across the Curriculum DAY 4 *65b*

☐ **Trait of the Week** Introduce and model the Trait of the Week, *word choice*. DAY 3 *61a*

PRACTICE/APPLY

☐ **Write Now** Examine the model on Student Edition pp. 66–67. Then have children write lists. DAY 5 *66-67*

> *Prompt Exploring Space with an Astronaut* tells about astronauts. Think about astronauts' jobs in space. Now write a list of sentences that tell what they do.

Write Now

☐ **Daily Journal Writing** Have children write about concepts and literature in their journals. **EVERY DAY** *42d-42e*

☐ **Writing Center** Have children write a space story. **ANY DAY** *42k*

ASSESS

☐ **Scoring Rubric** Use a rubric to evaluate children's lists. DAY 5 *66-67*

RETEACH/REVIEW

☐ **The Grammar and Writing Book** Use pp. 56–61 of The Grammar and Writing Book to extend instruction. **ANY DAY**

The Grammar and Writing Book

SPEAKING AND LISTENING

TEACH

☐ **Why We Listen** Explain why we listen. Then have children listen to each others' ideas about why they think people want to explore space. DAY 4 *65d*

GRAMMAR

SKILL SUBJECTS The subject of a sentence tells who or what does something.

TEACH

☐ **Grammar Transparency 2** Use Grammar Transparency 2 to teach *subjects*. DAY 1 *43d*

Grammar Transparency 2

PRACTICE/APPLY

☐ **Develop the Concept** Review the concept of *subjects* and provide guided practice. DAY 2 *59b*

☐ **Apply to Writing** Have children use subjects in writing. DAY 3 *61b*

☐ **Define/Practice** Review the definition of *subjects*. Then have children identify subjects. DAY 4 *65c*

☐ **Write Now** Discuss the grammar lesson on Student Edition p. 67. Have children use subjects in their own list of sentences that tell what astronauts do. DAY 5 *66-67*

Write Now

☐ **Daily Fix-It** Have children find and correct errors in grammar, spelling, and punctuation.
DAY 1 *43d*, DAY 2 *59b*, DAY 3 *61b*, DAY 4 *65c*, DAY 5 *66-67*

☐ **Homework** The Grammar and Writing Practice Book pp. 5–8.
DAY 2 *59b*, DAY 3 *61b*, DAY 4 *65c*, DAY 5 *66-67*

RETEACH/REVIEW

☐ **The Grammar and Writing Book** Use pp. 56–59 of The Grammar and Writing Book to extend instruction. **ANY DAY**

The Grammar and Writing Book

RESEARCH/INQUIRY

TEACH

☐ **Alphabetical Order** Model using alphabetical order to the first letter. Then have children demonstrate understanding by looking up topics in a reference book, and then alphabetizing the topics. DAY 5 *67a*

☐ **Unit Inquiry Project** Allow time for children to choose one place to explore and research it to find information. **ANY DAY** *11*

Resources for Differentiated Instruction

LEVELED READERS

▶ **Comprehension**
- 🎯 **Skill** Main Idea/Details
- 🎯 **Strategy** Text Structure

▶ **Lesson Vocabulary**

High-Frequency Words

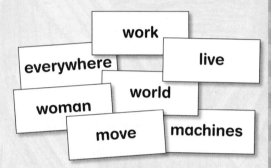

work
everywhere
live
world
woman
move
machines

▶ **Science Standards**
- **Space Exploration**
- **Astronauts**
- **Space Travel**
- **Technology**
- **Space Research**
- **Solar System**

Leveled Reader Database ONLINE

PearsonSuccessNet.com

Use the Online Database of over 600 books to
- Download and print additional copies of this week's leveled readers
- Listen to the readers being read online
- Search for more titles focused on this week's skills, topic, and content

---

On-Level

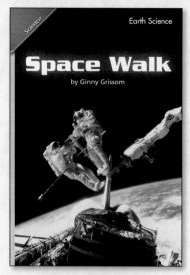

Science — Earth Science

Space Walk
by Ginny Grissom

On-Level Reader

Main Idea and Details
Read the passage below.
Fill in the topic, the main idea, and two supporting details.

> There are problems for an astronaut on a space walk. In space, there is no air to breathe. There is no water to drink. Rocks, ice, and "space junk" can hit you.

Possible responses given.

Topic
space walks

Main Idea
There are problems on a space walk.

Supporting Details

| There is no air in space. | Space junk can hit you. |

🎯 **On-Level Practice** TE p. LR14

Vocabulary
Write a word from the box to answer each riddle.

Words to Know

| everywhere | live | machines | move |
| woman | work | world | |

1. Some people travel around this. **world**
2. Your work will be easier with these to help. **machines**
3. If I am your mother, I must be this. **woman**
4. Food, air, and water will help you do this. **live**
5. Don't do this if you want to hide. **move**
6. We can't be here at the same time. **everywhere**
7. You must do this to do a good job. **work**

🎯 **On-Level Practice** TE p. LR15

Strategic Intervention

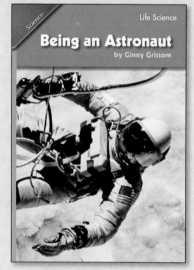

Science — Life Science

Being an Astronaut
by Ginny Grissom

Below-Level Reader

Main Idea and Details
Read the passage below.
Fill in the topic, the main idea, and two supporting details.
Possible responses given.

> Where do astronauts sleep? Some astronauts sleep in sleeping bags. Other astronauts sleep in bunks. Some just find a quiet spot to rest.

Topic
where astronauts sleep

Main Idea
Astronauts sleep in different places.

Supporting Details

| Some use sleeping bags. | Some sleep in bunks. |

🎯 **Below-Level Practice** TE p. LR11

Vocabulary
Draw a line from each word to the word that means the opposite.

1. everywhere   a. man
2. live   b. nowhere
3. move   c. die
4. woman   d. stay

Write the words from the box to best complete the sentence.

Words to Know

| machines | work | world |

5. All around the **world**, people use **machines** to help them do their **work**.

🎯 **Below-Level Practice** TE p. LR12

Advanced

Advanced Reader

Main Idea and Details

Read the paragraph below. Write the topic, the main idea, and three supporting details.

> People called astronauts travel into space. Many astronauts are also scientists. Astronauts train for many years to do their jobs. They need to be healthy. They also need to know how spaceships work.

1. Topic: **astronauts**   Possible responses given.

2. Main Idea: **Astronauts need to be well trained.**

3. Details: **Many are scientists. They need to be healthy. They need to know how spaceships work.**

Advanced Practice TE p. LR17

Vocabulary

Choose a word from the box to finish each sentence.

Words to Know			
ascend	asteroids	descend	gravity
laboratory	orbit	satellites	

1. The astronauts **orbit** around Earth on the space shuttle.

2. The astronauts **descend** back to Earth at the end of their trip.

3. When will the astronauts **ascend** into space again?

4. Astronauts often see rocks, or **asteroids** orbiting the sun.

5. **Satellites** can be used to broadcast television and radio signals.

6. Astronauts float in space, but **gravity** keeps us on Earth.

7. The astronauts use a **laboratory** on the shuttle to do experiments.

Advanced Practice TE p. LR18

ELL Reader

ELL Poster 2

Teacher's Edition Notes

ELL notes throughout this lesson support instruction and reference additional resources at point of use.

ELL Teaching Guide pp. 8–14, 214–215

- Multilingual summaries of the main selection
- Comprehension lesson
- Vocabulary strategies and word cards
- ELL Reader 2 lesson

ELL and Transition Handbook

Ten Important Sentences

- Key ideas from every selection in the Student Edition
- Activities to build sentence power

More Reading

Readers' Theater Anthology

- Fluency practice
- Five scripts to build fluency
- Poetry for oral interpretation

Leveled Trade Books

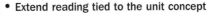

- Extend reading tied to the unit concept
- Lessons in Trade Book Library Teaching Guide

School + Home

Homework

- Family Times Newsletter
- ELL Multilingual Selection Summaries

Take-Home Books

- Decodable Readers
- Leveled Readers

Literacy Centers

Listening

Let's Read
Along

MATERIALS `SINGLES`
CD player, headphones, print copies of recorded pieces

LISTEN TO LITERATURE As children listen to the following recordings, have them follow along or read along in the print version.

AudioText
Exploring Space
"A Trip to Space Camp"

Sing with Me Background Building Audio
"Astronauts in Orbit"

Phonics Songs and Rhymes Audio
"Race into Space"

Race into Space

Chris and Pat, the astronauts,
Are heading into space.
Click! The door did close.
Air rushed through the hose.
Then the spaceship rose
And flew to a new place.

Chris and Pat, the astronauts,
Like living in the Space Age.
They have gone up twice.
They think space is nice,
Though it's cold as ice.
Look for them on the front page.

Audio CD **Phonics Songs and Rhymes Chart 2**

Reading/Library

Read It
Again!

MATERIALS `SINGLES` `PAIRS` `GROUPS`
collection of books for self-selected reading, reading logs

REREAD BOOKS Have children select previously read books from the appropriate book box and record titles of books they read in their logs. Use these previously read books:

- **Decodable Readers**
- **Leveled Readers**
- **ELL Readers**
- **Stories written by classmates**
- **Books from the library**

TEN IMPORTANT SENTENCES Have children read the Ten Important Sentences for *Exploring Space* and locate the sentences in the Student Edition.

BOOK CLUB Provide children with books about space to read. Ask them to compare the information in these books with the information in the selection.

Word Work

Space
MICE

MATERIALS `PAIRS`
15 cut-out paper mice, picture of a rocket ship

LONG VOWELS CVC*e* Have pairs send mice into space.

1. Make 15 cut-out paper mice and provide one large picture of a rocket ship. Write a CVC*e* word with *-ace*, *-age*, *-ice*, or *-ose* on ten of the mice and a short vowel word on the remaining five.
2. Mix up the mice and scatter them facedown on a table. Have children take turns choosing a mouse and reading the word aloud.
3. If the word has a long vowel sound, the mouse is put on the rocket.
4. Continue until all words have been read and all ten CVC*e* mice are ready to blast off into space.

Phonics Activities CD This interactive CD provides additional practice.

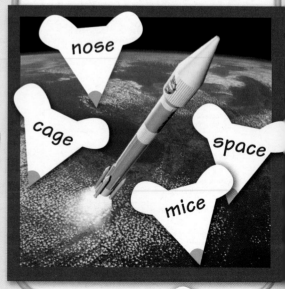

Scott Foresman Reading Street Centers Survival Kit

Use the *Exploring Space* materials from the Reading Street Centers Survival Kit to organize this week's centers.

Writing

Be an Astronaut

MATERIALS SINGLES
paper, pencils, crayons, markers

WRITE A SPACE STORY Invite children to think about being in space. What would it be like?

1. Ask children what they would like to do if they were astronauts.
2. Tell them to write about what being in space would feel like and what they would do when they were there.
3. Children may illustrate their writing.

LEVELED WRITING Encourage children to write at their own ability level. Some will have trouble organizing their writing. Others' writing will have more organization. Your best writers will organize their stories logically.

It would feel strange to float in space. I would walk on the moon. I would look at Earth and try to find where I live.

Science

Ask an Astronaut

MATERIALS PAIRS
pencils, paper

TODAY'S GUEST Briefly review *Exploring Space* with children.

1. In pairs, children list questions they would like to ask an astronaut.
2. Partners take turns pretending to be an interviewer asking questions and an astronaut answering questions.
3. Invite pairs to act out their interviews for others.

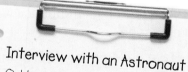

Interview with an Astronaut

Q: How does it feel to float in space?

A: It feels like you don't weigh anything.

Q: Is it hard to become an astronaut?

A: It is not easy. I had to study a lot of math and science.

Technology

Space Story

MATERIALS SINGLES
computer, printer, list of selection words

WRITE A STORY Have individuals use selection words to write a story.

1. Ask children to turn on the computer and open a word processing program.
2. Supply children with a list of selection words: *astronaut, shuttle, telescope, gravity, experiment.*
3. Children use at least three of the words to type a short story about space. They then print out their stories.

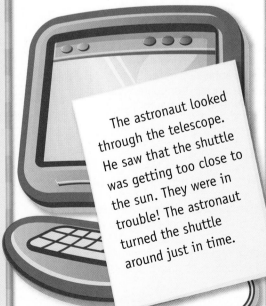

The astronaut looked through the telescope. He saw that the shuttle was getting too close to the sun. They were in trouble! The astronaut turned the shuttle around just in time.

ALL CENTERS

Day 1
AT A GLANCE

Oral Vocabulary
"Astronauts in Orbit" 2

Phonics and Spelling
Long Vowels CVC*e*
Spelling Pretest:
  Words with Long Vowels

Read Apply Phonics Word Wall

Group Time < Differentiated Instruction

Build Background
Let's Talk About Exploration

Listening Comprehension
Skill Main Idea and Details

Shared Writing
List

Grammar
Subjects

Materials
- *Sing with Me Big Book*
- Sound-Spelling Card 2
- Letter Tiles
- Decodable Reader 2
- Student Edition 42–43
- Graphic Organizer 3
- Grammar Transparency 2
- Writing Transparency 2

Take It to the NET™ ONLINE

Professional Development To learn more about phonemic awareness, go to PearsonSuccessNet.com and read "Phonemic Awareness Instruction . . ." by L. Ehri.

Morning Warm-Up!

Astronauts fly somewhere into space.
They can fly around our beautiful Earth.
Why would anyone
want to explore space?

QUESTION OF THE WEEK Tell children they will talk, sing, read, and write about why anyone would want to explore space. Write and read the message and discuss the question.

CONNECT CONCEPTS Ask questions to connect to the previous Unit 1 selections.

- Did Iris and Walter explore where they lived? How do you know?
- What did the author of the poems "Morning Song" and "My Travel Tree" want to explore?

REVIEW HIGH-FREQUENCY WORDS

- Circle the high-frequency words *somewhere* and *beautiful* in the message.
- Have children say and spell each word as they write it in the air.

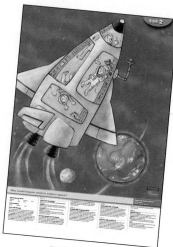

Build Background Use the Day 1 instruction on ELL Poster 2 to assess knowledge and develop concepts.

ELL Poster 2

Oral Vocabulary

SHARE LITERATURE Display p. 2 of the *Sing with Me Big Book.* Tell children that the class is going to sing a song about astronauts in orbit. Read the title. Ask children to listen for the Amazing Words **ascend, orbit,** and **descend** as you sing. Then sing the song again and encourage children to sing and do the motions along with you, demonstrating their understanding of *ascend, descend,* and *orbit.* In discussion, explain that *ascend* means "to go up," *descend* means "to go down," and orbit means "to go around a planet."

Sing with Me/
Background Building Audio

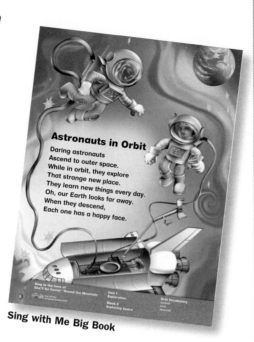

Sing with Me Big Book

OBJECTIVE

● Build oral vocabulary.

Amazing Words to build oral vocabulary

	MONITOR PROGRESS
ascend **descend** **orbit** **universe** **enormous** **journey** **launch** **meteorite**	**If...** children lack oral vocabulary experiences about the concept Exploration, **then...** use the Oral Vocabulary Routine below to teach *ascend.*

Oral Vocabulary ROUTINE

1 Introduce the Word Relate the word *ascend* to the song. Supply a child-friendly definition. Have children say the word. Example: When astronauts *ascend,* they go up.

2 Demonstrate Provide an example to show meaning. You *ascend* to the second floor when you go upstairs.

3 Apply Have children demonstrate their understanding. Which of these things is most likely to *ascend*—a rock, a book, or a balloon?

4 Display the Word/Letter-Sounds Write the word on a card. Display it. Have children identify the sound for *sc/s/.* See p. DI·4 to teach *descend* and *orbit.*

Build Oral Vocabulary Help children recognize the meanings of the English words *daring* and *strange* in "Astronauts in Orbit." Discuss with them that *daring* can mean "bold or courageous" and that *strange* means "very unusual."

Long Vowels CVCe

TEACH/MODEL

OBJECTIVES

- Associate the long vowel sounds with the CVCe spelling patterns.
- Blend, read, and build long vowel words.

Skills Trace

Long Vowels CVCe

Introduce/Teach	TE: 2.1 42n–o
Practice	TE: 2.1 42q, 44c–d; PB: 2.1 13, 28; DR2
Reteach/Review	TE: 2.1 66c, 88c, DI·65; PB: 2.1 28
Assess/Test	TE: 2.1 66e–g; Benchmark Test: Unit 1

Generalization

CVCe When a word has a consonant-vowel-consonant-silent e pattern, the vowel usually stands for its long sound.

The letter *c* usually stands for the sound /s/ when followed by *e, i,* or *y*. The letter *g* usually stands for the sound /j/ when followed by *e* or *i*. The letter *s* can stand for /s/ or /z/.

Strategic Intervention

Use **Monitor Progress,** p. 42o, during Group Time after children have had more practice with long vowels.

Advanced

Use **Monitor Progress,** p. 42o, as a preassessment to determine whether this group of children would benefit from this instruction on long vowels.

Support Phonics Some long vowel sounds in English are similar to the sounds represented by different vowels in Spanish. As a result, Spanish speakers may spell long *a* words with an *e* (*shek* for *shake*), long *e* words with an *i* (*bit* for *beat*), and long *i* words with *ai* (*laik* for *like* or *draive* for *drive*). Help children practice English spelling conventions for long vowels.

See the Phonics Transition Lessons in the ELL and Transition Handbook.

Blending Strategy

ROUTINE

1 **Connect** Write *cap* and *cape*. Read *cap*. What vowel sound do you hear in the word *cap?* (the short *a* sound) Read the word *cape*. What happened to the short *a* sound when an *e* was added to the end of *cap?* (The *a* stands for the long *a* sound. It says its name.) Today we'll learn about long vowel sounds.

2 **Use Sound-Spelling Cards** Display Card 2. This is *apron*. Say the first sound in *apron*: /ā/. /ā/ is the long *a* sound. Say it with me: /ā/.

3 **Model** Write *bake*. When a word has a vowel followed by a consonant and *e*, the vowel usually has its long sound and the *e* is silent. This word has the long *a* sound, /ā/. We can blend the word by saying the sound for each letter: /b//ā/ /k/, *bake*. Have children blend *bake* with you. We can also blend bigger chunks of words. I can blend this word by saying the sound before the vowel /b/, and then saying all the rest of the sounds together, /āk/. Then I blend the two chunks together: /b//āk/, *bake*. Run your hand under the onset and rime as you model. Do it with me: /b//āk/, bake. Repeat steps 2 and 3. Use Cards 16 for *i*/ī/, 24 for *o*/ō/, 36 for *u*/ū/. Model blending with *like*, *poke*, and *fuse*.

4 **Group Practice** Blend these words together. Continue with *tame, pile, hose, plume*.

5 **Review** What do you know about reading these words? A vowel that is followed by a consonant and *e* usually says its name.

a

Sound-Spelling Card 2

b a k e

BLEND WORDS

INDIVIDUALS BLEND LONG VOWEL WORDS Call on individuals to blend *lace, nose, wage, rice, cube, make*. Have them tell what they know about each word before reading it. For feedback, refer to step five of the Blending Strategy Routine.

BUILD WORDS

a c d e f g l n o r s u

INDIVIDUALS MAKE LONG VOWEL WORDS Write *face* and have the class blend it. Have children spell *face* with letter tiles. Monitor work and provide feedback.

• Change the *f* to *r*.
  What is the new word?

r a c e

• Change the *c* to *g*.
  What is the new word?

r a g e

• Change the *ag* to *ud*.
  What is the new word?

r u d e

• Change the *d* to *l*.
  What is the new word?

r u l e

• Change the *u* to *o*.
  What is the new word?

r o l e

• Change the *l* to *s*.
  What is the new word?

r o s e

• Change the *r* to *n*.
  What is the new word?

n o s e

Vocabulary TiP

You may wish to explain the meanings of these words.

lack	the condition of being without
sift	to separate large pieces from small pieces by shaking them through a sieve
wage	the money paid for work done

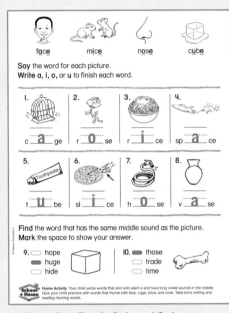

▲ **Practice Book 2.1** p. 13, Long Vowels CVC*e*

Monitor Progress | Check Word Reading Long Vowels CVC*e*

Write the following words and have individuals read them.

those	stage	ice	chose	place
came	wage	cent	game	rose
lack	home	sift	check	ripe

If... children cannot blend words with long vowels at this point,

then... continue to monitor their progress using other instructional opportunities during the week so that they can be successful with the Day 5 Assessment. See the Skills Trace on p. 42n.

SUCCESS PREDICTOR

Spiral REVIEW

● Row 2 contrasts hard and soft *c* and *g*, and *s*/s/ and *s*/z/.
● Row 3 contrasts short and long vowels.

▶ **Day 1 Check Word Reading** | **Day 2 Check** High-Frequency Words | **Day 3 Check** Retelling | **Day 4 Check** Fluency | **Day 5 Assess** Progress

Word Reading

SUCCESS PREDICTOR

Spelling

PRETEST Long Vowels CVCe

Spelling Words

Long Vowels CVCe

1.	**tune**	7.	**mice**
2.	**page**	8.	**late**
3.	**nose**	9.	**cube**
4.	**space***	10.	**blaze**
5.	**size**	11.	**home**
6.	**fine**	12.	**vote**

Challenge Words

13.	**erase**	15.	**confuse**
14.	**spice**		

* **Word from the Selection**

MODEL WRITING FOR SOUNDS Each spelling word has a long vowel sound. Before administering the spelling pretest, model how to segment long vowel words to spell them.

- What sounds do you hear in rose? (/r/ /ō/ /z/)
- What is the letter for /r/? Write *r*. Continue with the o/ō/, s/z/, and silent *e*.
- Repeat with *date, mine,* and *note.*

PRETEST Dictate the spelling words. Segment the words for children if necessary. Have children check their pretests and correct misspelled words.

HOMEWORK Spelling Practice Book, p. 5

Long Vowels CVCe

Generalization Long vowels are often spelled CVCe: page, fine, nose, tune.

Sort the list words by the long vowel spelling.

a		o	
1. **page**	8. **nose**		
2. **space**	9. **home**		
3. **late**	10. **vote**		
4. **blaze**			
i		u	
5. **size**	11. **tune**		
6. **fine**	12. **cube**		
7. **mice**			

Challenge Words

a		i	
13. **erase**	14. **spice**		
u			
15. **confuse**			

Spelling Words
1. tune
2. page
3. nose
4. space
5. size
6. fine
7. mice
8. late
9. cube
10. blaze
11. home
12. vote

Challenge Words
13. erase
14. spice
15. confuse

Home Activity Your child is learning to spell words with long vowel sounds (consonant-vowel-consonant-e.) To practice at home, have your child look at the word, say it, spell it and point to the long vowel sound.

▲ **Spelling Practice Book** p. 5

Mae Jemison

Mae Jemison was the first African American woman astronaut. She studied science in college, and then she went to medical school. Mae worked as a doctor before she became an astronaut.

Mae went on her first space mission in 1992 for the National Aeronautics and Space Administration (NASA). She was part of the crew of the space shuttle Endeavor.

Mae did experiments in space as the space shuttle was in orbit around Earth. Many of the experiments focused on plants and animals. What she learned helped make

Exploring Space

Decodable Reader 2
Ike and Ace

Group Time

DAY 1

On-Level	Strategic Intervention	Advanced
Read Decodable Reader 2. • Use p. 42q.	**Read** Decodable Reader 2. • Use the **Routine** on p. DI·24.	**Read** Advanced Selection 2 • Use the **Routine** on p. DI·25.

ELL Place English language learners in the groups that correspond to their reading abilities in English.

(i) Independent Activities

Fluency Reading Pair children to reread Leveled Readers or the ELL Reader from the previous week or other text at children's independent level.

Journal Writing Write a story about a rocket that goes into orbit. Share writing.

Independent Reading See p. 42j for Reading/ Library activities and suggestions.

Literacy Centers To practice long vowels, you may use Word Work, p. 42j.

Practice Book 2.1 Long Vowels, p. 13; Main Idea and Details, p. 14

ELL

Support Spelling Before giving the spelling pretest, clarify the meaning of each spelling word with examples, such as humming a song for *tune* and turning the page in a book to illustrate *page*.

Break into small groups after Spelling and before the Comprehension lesson.

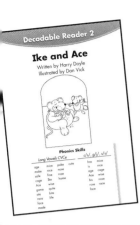

Decodable Reader 2

Ike and Ace
Written by Harry Doyle
Illustrated by Dan Vick

Apply Phonics

⏺ PRACTICE Long Vowels CVCe

HIGH-FREQUENCY WORDS Review *every, have, one, put, their* and *what*. If necessary, have children practice in pairs with word cards.

READ DECODABLE READER 2

Pages 10–11 Read aloud quietly with the group.

Pages 12–13 Have the group read aloud without you.

Pages 14–16 Select individuals to read aloud.

CHECK COMPREHENSION AND DECODING Have children retell the story to include characters, setting, and plot. Then have children locate long vowel words in the story. Review the CVC*e* pattern. Sort words according to their long vowel sounds.

a: Ace, age, ate, cage, face, game, made, make, race, safe
i: bite, fine, Ike, life, mice, nice, quite, wise
o: home, nose, poke, rose
u: cute

HOMEWORK Take-Home Decodable Reader 2

REREAD FOR FLUENCY

Paired Reading

ROUTINE

1 **Reader 1 Begins** Children read the entire story, switching readers at the end of each page.

2 **Reader 2 Begins** Have partners reread; now the other partner begins.

3 **Reread** For optimal fluency, children should reread three or four times.

4 **Provide Feedback** Listen to children read and provide corrective feedback regarding their oral reading and their use of the blending strategy.

OBJECTIVES

- Apply knowledge of letter-sounds and word parts to decode unknown words when reading.
- Use context with letter-sounds and word parts to confirm the identification of unknown words.
- Practice fluency in paired reading.

Monitor Progress

Decoding

If...	then...
children have difficulty decoding a word,	prompt them to blend the word.
	• What is the new word?
	• Is the new word a word you know?
	• Does it make sense in the story?

Access Content

Beginning Page through the story with children and point out the characters Tess, Ike, and Ace in pictures and print.

Intermediate Preview *Ike and Ace,* pointing out verbs, such as *add, see, poke,* and *play.* Have children use each verb in a sentence.

Advanced After reading *Ike and Ace,* build conversational fluency by asking children to name differences between Ike and Ace.

Strategic Intervention

Explain to children that they can help themselves be better readers by thinking of questions about exploring space that they would like to find answers for. Invite them to brainstorm questions to list in the middle column of the chart. Point out that they will list answers and other information they learn in the third column as they read.

Advanced

Provide several children's encyclopedias and books about space travel, NASA, the moon walk, astronauts, or other related topics. Invite children to read one or two of the books and tell the rest of the class what they discovered.

Build Background Explain that we live on a planet called Earth, and that it orbits around the sun. You may want to illustrate with a quick sketch or encyclopedia drawing that shows our solar system. Tell children that people use space shuttles and rockets to explore space.

Build Background

LET'S TALK ABOUT Exploration

DEVELOP ORAL LANGUAGE Read the title and have children view the photographs. Ask them to tell you what they see. Allow ample time for children to respond. Have children ask questions they may have about the pictures. Model how to ask questions using complete sentences and proper inflection. For example, ask:

Tell me about what you see here. Yes, we can see the space shuttle taking off and landing. Where do you suppose the shuttle went after it took off and before it landed? Do you think the balloons or the skydiver can do what the shuttle does? Why or why not?

BUILD ORAL VOCABULARY As you continue the discussion, have children use today's Amazing Words: *ascend, descend, orbit.*

- Use the word *orbit* to tell me about the picture of the planets in outer space.
- Is the skydiver ascending or descending? Why do you think so?
- What do you think it would feel like to orbit Earth in a spacecraft?

DEVELOP CONCEPTS

CONCEPT CHART Remind children of the question of the week.

- Why would anyone want to explore space?

Display Graphic Organizer 3 or draw a K-W-L chart. Write *Exploring Space* on the topic line. Draw children's attention to the first two columns, inviting them to brainstorm answers to the following questions. Write their answers in the appropriate column. Display the K-W-L chart for use during the week.

- What do you already know about exploring space?
- What do you want to know?

Explain to children that they will be able to list what they have learned about exploring space in the third column as they read this week's selection.

CONNECT TO READING Point out the photograph at the bottom of p. 43 in the Student Edition. Explain to children that this is a space shuttle. It takes astronauts into space. Tell children that this week they will read a selection about what astronauts do when they explore space.

Oral Vocabulary

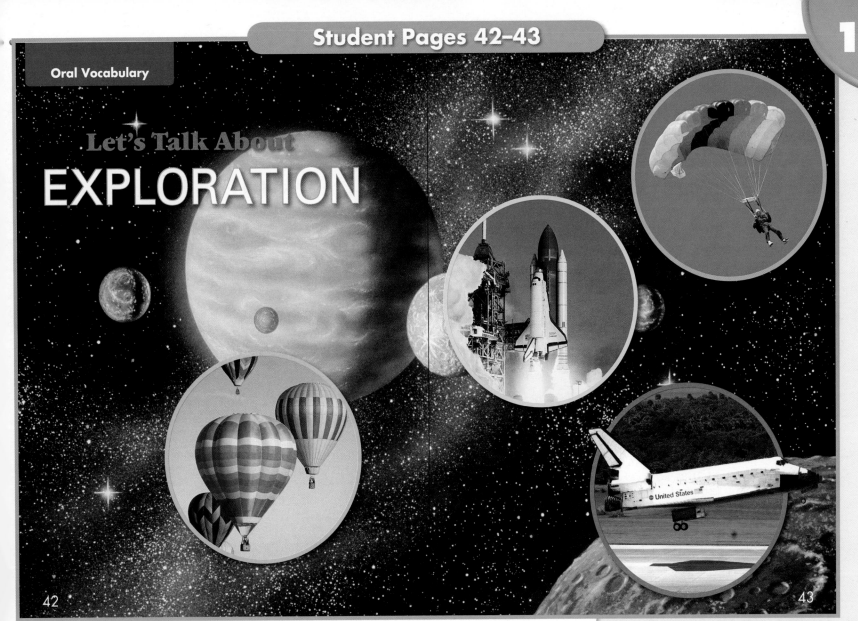

Let's Talk About
EXPLORATION

42

43

Topic Exploring Space

What We Know	What We Want to Know	What We Learned
Astronauts explore space. They go up in big rockets. They wear special suits.	What do astronauts want to find out in space? What is it like inside the shuttle?	

▲ **Graphic Organizer 3**

Take It to the **NET**
ONLINE

For a Web site that tells more about space and astronauts, do an Internet search using the keywords *space camp.*

ELL

Access Content To prepare children for reading *Exploring Space*, send home the story summary in English and/or the home language. See the ELL Teaching Guide, pp. 12–14.

OBJECTIVE

Identify main idea and details.

Skills Trace

Main Idea and Details

Practice/Teach	TE: 2.1 43a–b, 44e, 97a–b, 98e; 2.5 154r, 154–155
Practice	TE: 2.1 102–103; 2.5 160–161; PB: 2.1 14–15, 34–35; 2.2 54–55
Reteach/Review	TE: 2.1 32–33, DI·65, DI·67; 2.4 132–133; 2.5 DI·64; 2.6 338–339; PB: 2.1 7; 2.2 47, 117
Test	TE: 2.1 66e–g, 126e–g; 2.5 178e–g; Selection Tests: 2.1 5–8, 13–16; 2.5 81–84; Benchmark Test: Units 1, 3–6

Read each story. **Answer** the questions.

We know a lot about the moon. It orbits Earth. It reflects the light of the sun. It has craters on its surface. Wouldn't it be fun to hop on a ship and go to the moon?

1. **Write** the sentence that tells the main idea.

We know a lot about the moon.

2. **Write** one detail that tells more about the main idea.

Possible responses: orbits Earth, reflects the light of the sun, has craters

We know that Mars is red. We also know there was once water on the planet. Mars is a place we want to learn more about.

3. **Write** the sentence that tells the main idea.

Mars is a place we want to learn more about.

4. **Write** one detail that tells more about the main idea.

Possible responses: is red, once had water

 Home Activity Your child described the main idea and supporting details in two selections. Tell your child about your childhood. Ask your child to tell you the important parts. Together, brainstorm a good title.

▲ **Practice Book 2.1** p. 14, Main Idea and Details

Access Content For a Picture It! lesson on main idea and details, see the ELL Teaching Guide, pp. 8–9.

Listening Comprehension

TEACH/MODEL Main Idea and Details

DEFINE MAIN IDEA AND DETAILS

• The topic is what a selection is about. The main idea is the most important idea about the topic.

• Small pieces of information in a selection that tell more about the main idea are called details.

• Good readers look for the main idea to help them understand what the whole story is about.

READ ALOUD Read the first paragraph of "Eating in Space" and model how to identify main idea and details.

Think Aloud **MODEL** First I ask myself what the topic of this paragraph is. This paragraph is mainly about eating in space. The most important idea about this topic is that eating in space is more difficult than eating on Earth. A bit of information that tells me more about the main idea is that, without gravity, food floats around.

PRACTICE

CLUES TO MAIN IDEA AND DETAILS Read the rest of the selection. What is the topic of the second paragraph? (how to eat in space) What is the most important idea about this topic? (Food in space has to be held so it doesn't spill.) What are some details that tell more about this idea? (Floating food can damage things; astronauts strap food trays to their legs.) What is the main idea of "Eating in Space"? (Eating in space is different from eating on Earth.) What are some details that tell more about this idea? (Food in space can damage things; food in space is dehydrated.)

IDENTIFY MAIN IDEA AND DETAILS Have children recall the topic, main idea, and details from a previously read selection.

• In a word or two, what was the topic you read about?

• What was the most important idea about this topic?

• What were some details that told more about this main idea?

CONNECT TO READING Tell children that when they read any selection, they should think about the most important, or main, idea.

Eating In Space

Life in space can be very different from life on Earth. For example, once you ascend into space where there is no gravity, eating food is a bit trickier. Without gravity, things float around. Eating in orbit is no picnic.

Food in space has to be held so that it does not spill. If food were floating around in the space shuttle, it could be difficult to clean up. If food got into computers or equipment, it could cause a lot of damage. So when it's dinnertime, astronauts strap a food tray to their leg. That way the food is held in place and there is no mess to clean.

Astronauts have plenty of kinds of food to choose from when they are in space. The best foods are sticky, so they don't crumble. Astronauts enjoy fruit and hot meals like pasta.

On the space shuttle, many foods need to be mixed with water. The foods have been dehydrated, which means the water has been removed. This makes them easier to store and keep safe to eat. Once the astronauts add water, they can enjoy anything from macaroni and cheese to freeze-dried ice cream!

OBJECTIVE

● Write a list.

DAILY FIX-IT

1. we will fly into spac.

   <u>W</u>e will fly into spac<u>e</u>.

2. it will be lots of fun

   <u>I</u>t will be lots of fun<u>.</u>

This week's practice sentences appear on Daily Fix-It Transparency 2.

Strategic Intervention

Brainstorm with children about going to the moon and what they would have to do to get there. Then have them think how to get ready for each step of their trip.

Advanced

Invite children to consider not only what they would have to do to get ready to go to the moon but also what they do on the moon when they are there.

ELL

Support Writing Ask children to work in pairs. Have them do a "think-aloud" with their partners to decide what they should take with them to the moon before they write their own lists.

▲ **The Grammar and Writing Book**
For more instruction and practice, use pp. 56–61.

Shared Writing

WRITE List

GENERATE IDEAS Ask children to imagine they are going to take a trip to the moon. What things would they have to do to get ready for such a trip?

MAKE A LIST Explain that the class will make a list of the things they think they should do before they go on a trip to the moon.

COMPREHENSION SKILL Tell children that the topic—Things to Do to Get Ready—is the main idea of their list, and the things they will have to do are the details.

- Display Writing Transparency 2 and read the title and first item on the list.
- Have children brainstorm other things they would have to do to get ready to go to the moon.
- Record each idea as children agree to add it to the list.

HANDWRITING While writing, model the letter forms as shown on pp. TR14–17.

READ THE LIST Have children read the completed list aloud as you track the print.

> **Trip to the Moon**
>
> Things to Do to Get Ready
>
> • Learn how to fly a spaceship.
> Possible answers:
> • Get a spacesuit, a helmet, and boots.
> • Take enough air, water, and food.
> • Get to know the other astronauts.
> • Pack a toothbrush.
>
> Unit 1 Exploring Space with an Astronaut   Writing Model **2**

▲ **Writing Transparency 2**

INDEPENDENT WRITING

WRITE A LIST Have children write their own list of what to take when they go to the moon. Encourage them to use words from the Word Wall and the Amazing Words board. Let children illustrate their writing. You may want to display children's lists with a copy of their Things to Do to Get Ready list.

ADDITIONAL PRACTICE For additional practice, use pp. 56–61 in the Grammar and Writing Book.

Grammar

- Identify subjects.

TEACH/MODEL Subjects

REVIEW SENTENCES Recall with children that a sentence is a group of words that tells a complete idea. The words are in an order that makes sense. A sentence always begins with a capital letter, and many sentences end with a period.

IDENTIFY SUBJECTS Display Grammar Transparency 2. Read the definition.

- *The girl* tells who does something in the first sentence.
- The word *astronaut* is not a subject because the sentence is not about an astronaut doing something.

Continue modeling with items 2–6.

PRACTICE

UNDERLINE SUBJECTS Write the following sentences on the board and ask children to identify the subjects. Have volunteers underline the subjects.

Tony wants to be a firefighter.

Firefighters put out fires.

Subjects

The **subject** of a sentence tells who or what does something.

Neil Armstrong walked on the moon.

The moon goes around the Earth.

Circle the subject of each sentence.

1. The girl will be an astronaut.

2. Astronauts study space.
3. She dreams about spaceships.

4. My father is a zoologist.
5. Zoologists study animals.

6. My uncle explores the rain forest.

Unit 1 Exploring Space with an Astronaut   Grammar **2**

▲ **Grammar Transparency 2**

Wrap Up Your Day!

✓ **LONG VOWELS** Write *space, nice, cage,* and *nose.* Ask children what kind of vowel sounds each word has. (long) Have them name other words with long vowel sounds.

✓ **SPELLING LONG VOWEL WORDS** Have children name the letters for each sound in *rose.* Write the letters as children write them in the air. Continue with *cube, face, these,* and *bike.*

✓ **MAIN IDEA AND DETAILS** To help children identify main idea and details, ask: Is the main idea of something you read what it is all about or is it one of the small pieces of information? Which are the details? When I say that Iris and Walter became good friends, is that the main idea of the story or a detail?

LET'S TALK ABOUT IT Review with children their discussion of why anyone would want to explore space. Display the K-W-L chart and add to children's lists of what they know and what they want to know about exploring space.

 HOMEWORK Send home this week's Family Times newsletter.

PREVIEW Day 2

Tell children that tomorrow the class will read about how astronauts explore space.

Day 2
AT A GLANCE

Materials
- *Sing with Me Big Book*
- *Read Aloud Anthology*
- Phonics Songs and Rhymes Chart 2
- Graphic Organizer 3
- Student Edition 44–59
- Tested Word Cards
- Vocabulary Transparency 2
- Background Building Audio CD

Morning Warm-Up!

Today we will read about astronauts who explore space. What do you think it feels like to take off into space?

QUESTION OF THE DAY Encourage children to sing "Astronauts in Orbit" from the *Sing with Me Big Book* as you gather. Write and read the message and discuss the question.

REVIEW LONG VOWELS CVC*e*

- Read the message aloud, indicating each word as you do so.
- Have children raise their hands when they hear a word with a long vowel sound spelled with the CVC*e* pattern. *(space, like, take)*

Build Background Use the Day 2 instruction on ELL Poster 2 to preview high-frequency words.

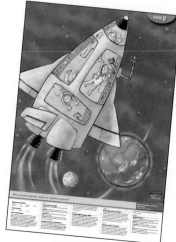

ELL Poster 2

Share Literature

BUILD CONCEPTS

STORY PLOT Read the title aloud and identify the author. Discuss with children that what happens in a story is called the plot. Briefly review the plot of *Iris and Walter*, which children read last week. Explain that the plot of the story they will hear today is a little like the plot of *Iris and Walter*.

BUILD ORAL VOCABULARY Recall with children that Iris and Walter liked to look at the stars in the sky. Explain that those stars, our sun, and our world are all part of our **universe.** Suggest that as you read, children listen to find out what the universe has to do with a girl called Gloria and an onion.

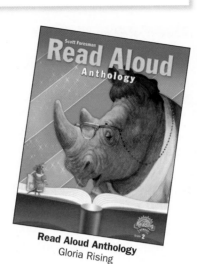

Read Aloud Anthology
Gloria Rising

MONITOR LISTENING COMPREHENSION

- What happened at the beginning of the story that led to Gloria hearing about the universe? (Gloria's mother sent her to the store to buy an onion. At the store, Gloria met a woman who was an astronaut. She and Gloria talked about what the woman had done as an astronaut, including floating outside and staring out at the universe.)

- What did the astronaut tell Gloria that she did when she had to fix things outside of the space station? (She got her job done and floated and stared at the universe.)

- Do you think Gloria will tell her mother about meeting the astronaut? Why or why not? (Possible response: Yes, because it was so exciting and the astronaut told her some important things.)

OBJECTIVES

- Discuss story plot.
- Set purpose for listening.
- Build oral vocabulary.

 **to build oral vocabulary**

Amazing Words	MONITOR PROGRESS
ascend descend orbit **universe** enormous journey launch meteorite	**If...** children lack oral vocabulary experiences about the concept Exploration, **then...** use the Oral Vocabulary Routine. See p. DI·4 to teach *universe*.

Build Concepts Make sure children understand that astronauts are people who go up into space in special rockets that can carry them far away from Earth. Point out that astronauts usually work while they are in space. Sometimes they stay in a space station, which is in orbit in space.

◎ Long Vowels CVC*e*

TEACH/MODEL

Fluent Word Reading

ROUTINE

① Connect Write *twice*. You can read this word because you know how to read words with long vowel sounds. What sound does the letter *i* stand for in this word? (/ī/) What's the word? *(twice)* Do the same with *made*, *code*, and *fuse*.

② Model When you come to a new word, look at the letters from left to right and think about the vowel sounds. Say the sounds in the word to yourself and then read the word. Model reading *cage, slice, pose, trace.* When you come to a new word, what are you going to do?

③ Group Practice Write *face, spice, confuse, mute, close, sage.* Read these words. Look at the letters, think about the vowel sounds, say the sounds to yourself, and then read the word aloud together. Allow 2–3 seconds previewing time.

WORD READING

PHONICS SONGS AND RHYMES CHART 2 Frame each of the following words on Phonics Songs and Rhymes Chart 2. Call on individuals to read them. Guide children in previewing.

race	age	twice	close
rose	space	nice	page
ice	place	hose	spaceship

Sing "Race into Space" to the tune of "B-I-N-G-O," or play the CD. Have children follow along on the chart as they sing. Then have individuals take turns circling long vowel words on the chart.

 Phonics Songs and Rhymes Audio

Race into Space

Chris and Pat, the astronauts,
Are heading into space.
Click! The door did close.
Air rushed through the hose.
Then the spaceship rose
And flew to a new place.

Chris and Pat, the astronauts,
Like living in the Space Age.
They have gone up twice.
They think space is nice,
Though it's cold as ice.
Look for them on the front page.

Phonics Songs and Rhymes Chart 2

SORT WORDS

INDIVIDUALS SORT WORDS WITH LONG VOWELS Write *-ace, -age, -ice,* and *-ose* as headings. Have individuals write *-ace, -age, -ice,* and *-ose* words from the Phonics Chart under the appropriate headings and circle the letters that stand for the long vowel sounds. Have all children complete the activity on paper. Ask individuals to read the completed lists. Provide feedback as necessary.

-ace	*-age*	*-ice*	*-ose*
race	age	twice	close
space	page	nice	hose
place		ice	rose

Spelling

PRACTICE Long Vowels CVCe

WRITE DICTATION SENTENCES Have children write these sentences. Repeat words slowly, allowing children to hear each sound. Children may use the Word Wall to help with spelling high-frequency words. **Word Wall**

> **It was late when we got home.**
> **Look at the size of the mice!**
> **I vote for the fine tune.**

HOMEWORK Spelling Practice Book, p. 6

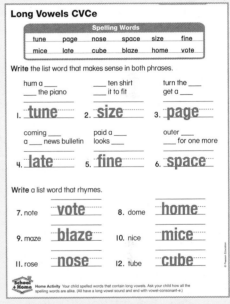

▲ **Spelling Practice Book** p. 6

Spelling Words

Long Vowels CVCe

1. tune	7. mice
2. page	8. late
3. nose	9. cube
4. space*	10. blaze
5. size	11. home
6. fine	12. vote

Challenge Words

13. erase   15. confuse
14. spice

* Word from the Selection

OBJECTIVES

- Recognize main idea and details.
- Understand text structure.
- Build background.

Read the story. **Answer** the questions.

Today our class will take its first field trip. We won't go far. We will get to the moon at noon. We will eat lunch. Then we will play a game of Space Catch. A trip into space will be a lot of fun!

1. **Write** a sentence from the paragraph that tells the main idea.

   Today our class will take its first field trip.

2. **Write** a detail from the paragraph that tells more about the main idea.

   Possible responses: not far, arrive at noon, eat lunch, play Space Catch

3. **Write** a title for the story.

   Title should include the words *Space, Trip,* or *Class.*

4. **Write** a sentence about what you would do in space.

   Answers will vary but should include what the child would do on a trip to space.

School + Home   Home Activity Your child described the main idea and supporting details of a story. Gather materials about outer space and encourage your child to select one planet to read about. Then look for two interesting facts about the planet.

▲ **Practice Book 2.1** p. 15, Main Idea and Details

Comprehension

⊚ SKILL Main Idea and Details

RECOGNIZE MAIN IDEA AND DETAILS Review with children that the main idea is the most important idea in the story. Details are the smaller pieces of information that tell more about the main idea.

CONNECT TO READING

- As you read, ask yourself what the whole story is about.
- Notice details that tell more about the main idea.

⊚ STRATEGY Text Structure

INTRODUCE TEXT STRUCTURE Explain to children that authors often use headings to help readers know what they are going to read about next. Paying attention to headings can help children be better readers.

Think Aloud

MODEL When I read an article, I pay attention to the ways the author helps me know what it is about. Often I see that the author has put headings inside boxes to show me what he or she is going to talk about next. That helps me think about the topic more carefully as I read.

CONNECT TO READING Encourage children to ask themselves these questions as they read *Exploring Space with an Astronaut.*

- Do I pay attention to the headings so I know what I will read about next?
- What are some important details about astronauts and space shuttles?

Build Background

DISCUSS BEING AN ASTRONAUT Display pictures of a space shuttle and an astronaut. Ask children what they know about astronauts going into space.

- What do you think astronauts do when they are in space?
- How do astronauts eat and sleep inside a space shuttle?
- Why do you think astronauts ascend into space?

BACKGROUND BUILDING AUDIO Have children listen to the audio and share the new information they learn about being an astronaut.

 **Sing with Me/
Background Building Audio**

COMPLETE A K-W-L CHART Draw a K-W-L chart or display Graphic Organizer 3. Write *astronauts exploring space* on the topic line. Ask children to suggest things they already know about astronauts and space, and have them write those ideas in the first column of the chart. Ask them to write what they want to know about the topic in the second column. Finally, have them list in the third column what they learned.

Topic <u>astronauts exploring space</u>

What We Know	What We Want to Know	What We Learned
wear a space suit	How do astronauts sleep?	Astronauts sleep in sleeping bags tied to the shuttle's walls.
work on experiments	What kind of experiments do they do?	Experiments might include launching telescopes into space or experiments with plants, exercise, and life without gravity.

▲ **Graphic Organizer 3**

CONNECT TO SELECTION Connect background information to *Exploring Space with an Astronaut.*

Astronauts do exciting things. They put on special suits and fly in space shuttles into space. As we read the story about astronauts, we'll find out what they do in space and what it's like to live inside a space shuttle.

 **ELL**

Build Background Tell children that some people study and work very hard to become astronauts. They want to find out more about space. Invite children to tell what they know about astronauts, rockets, and space shuttles.

Words to Read

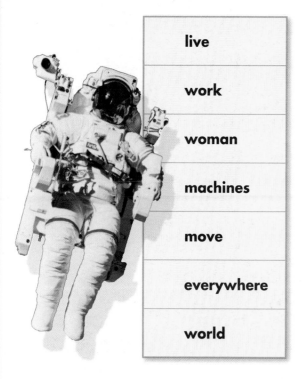

live
work
woman
machines
move
everywhere
world

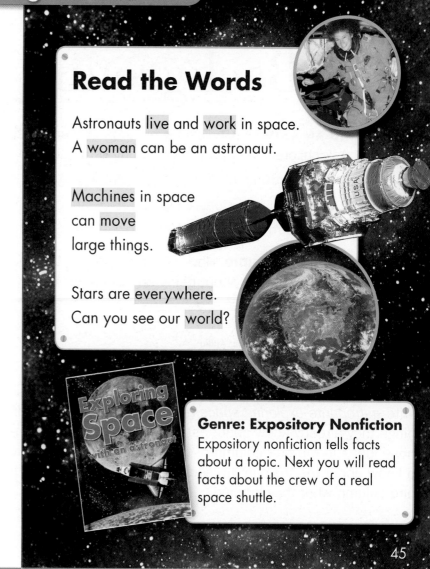

Read the Words

Astronauts live and work in space.
A woman can be an astronaut.

Machines in space
can move
large things.

Stars are everywhere.
Can you see our world?

Genre: Expository Nonfiction
Expository nonfiction tells facts
about a topic. Next you will read
facts about the crew of a real
space shuttle.

44

45

High-Frequency Words

Nondecodable Words

ROUTINE

1 **Say and Spell** Look at the words on p. 44. You cannot blend the sounds in these words. We will spell the words and use letter-sounds we know to learn them. Point to the first word on the Words to Read list. This word is *live, l-i-v-e, live.* What is this word? What are the letters in this word?

2 **Identify Familiar Letter-Sounds** Point to the first letter in *live.* What is this letter? What is the sound for this letter? (/l/)

3 **Demonstrate Meaning** Tell me a sentence using this word.

Repeat the routine with the other Words to Read. Have children identify the two words in *everywhere (every, where)* and these familiar letter-sounds: *work* (w/w/), *woman* (w/w/ and n/n/), *machines* (m/m/), *move* (m/m/), *world* (w/w/).

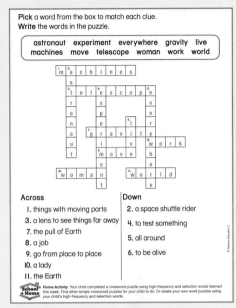

Pick a word from the box to match each clue.
Write the words in the puzzle.

astronaut experiment everywhere gravity live
machines move telescope woman work world

Across
1. things with moving parts
3. a lens to see things far away
7. the pull of Earth
8. a job
9. go from place to place
10. a lady
11. the Earth

Down
2. a space shuttle rider
4. to test something
5. all around
6. to be alive

School + Home Home Activity Your child completed a crossword puzzle using high-frequency and selection words learned this week. Find other simple crossword puzzles for your child to do. Or create your own word puzzles using your child's high-frequency and selection words.

▲ **Practice Book 2.1** p. 16, High-Frequency Words and Selection Words

Have children read aloud the sentences on p. 45 and point to the Words to Read. Add the words to the Word Wall. **Word Wall**

Use Vocabulary Transparency 2 to review this week's words.

• Point to a word. Say and spell it.

• Have children say and spell the word.

• Ask children to identify familiar letter-sounds.

Monitor Progress | **Check High-Frequency Words**

Point to the following words on the Word Wall and have individuals read them.

everywhere	live	machines	move	work	woman	world
about		other	become	many	always	use	into

If . . . children cannot read these words,

then . . . have them practice in pairs with word cards before reading the selection. Monitor their fluency with these words during reading, and provide additional practice opportunities before the Day 5 Assessment.

SUCCESS PREDICTOR

Spiral REVIEW

● Reviews previously taught high-frequency words.

Day 1 Check Word Reading

▶ **Day 2 Check High-Frequency Words**

Day 3 Check Retelling

Day 4 Check Fluency

Day 5 Assess Progress

High-Frequency Words

SUCCESS PREDICTOR

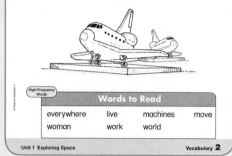

The Space Center

Selection Words

1. At the Space Center we saw an <u>astronaut</u> in her spacesuit.

2. It would be fun to float without <u>gravity</u> like she does.

3. We looked through a <u>telescope</u> to see some stars.

4. We saw pictures of an <u>experiment</u> in space with plants and rocks.

5. There was a huge space <u>shuttle</u> parked there too.

High-Frequency Words

Words to Read			
everywhere	live	machines	move
woman	work	world	

Unit 1 Exploring Space   Vocabulary **2**

▲ **Vocabulary Transparency 2**

Vocabulary

SELECTION WORDS

Use Vocabulary Transparency 2 to introduce the selection words.

- Read each sentence as you track the print.

- Frame each underlined word. Explain the word's meaning.

  astronaut a person who goes into space
  shuttle vehicle that carries astronauts into space
  experiment test to find out something
  telescope an instrument that makes things far away appear to be close
  gravity the natural force that makes everything on Earth move toward it

- Ask children to identify familiar letter-sounds and word parts: *astronaut* (*astro* means "stars," as in *astronomy*), *shuttle* (two syllables with a double consonant in the middle), *telescope* (*tele* means "far" and *scope* means "to see"), *gravity* (blend the syllables: *grav, i, ty*), *experiment* (*ment* shows that the word is a noun).

- Have children read each sentence aloud with you.

- To encourage discussion using the selection words, ask children what they think it would be like to be an astronaut on a space shuttle.

- Introduce these nondecodable names that appear in the selection: *Eileen, Collins, Chandra, Colorado.*

Group Time

DAY 2

On-Level	Strategic Intervention	Advanced
Read *Exploring Space.*	**Read** SI Decodable Reader 2.	**Read** *Exploring Space.*
• Use pp. 46–59.	• Read or listen to *Exploring Space.*	• Use the **Routine** on p. DI·27.
	• Use the **Routine** on p. DI·26.	

 Place English language learners in the groups that correspond to their reading abilities in English.

(i) Independent Activities

Independent Reading See p. 42j for Reading/Library activities and suggestions.

Journal Writing Write about what you would like to see and do in space. Share your writing.

Literacy Centers To provide experiences with *Exploring Space,* you may use the Listening Center on p. 42j.

Practice Book 2.1 Main Idea and Details, p. 15; High-Frequency Words and Selection Words, p. 16; Author's Purpose, p. 17

Access Content Use the vocabulary strategies and word cards in the ELL Teaching Guide, pp. 14–15.

Break into small groups after Vocabulary and before Writing.

Exploring Space
with an Astronaut
by Patricia J. Murphy

What will you find out about space from an astronaut?

46

47

AudioText

read
Prereading Strategies

PREVIEW AND PREDICT Help children read the title of the article, having them decode *exploring, space,* and *astronaut.* Identify the author. Have children preview several pages of the selection, reading the headings and photo captions. Ask them what they think the article is about.

DISCUSS EXPOSITORY NONFICTION Read the definition of expository nonfiction on p. 45 of the Student Edition. Point out that the prefix *non-* means "not," so *nonfiction* is not fiction. It provides information about the world. Have children to discuss things they would like to know about the universe.

SET PURPOSE Read the question on p. 47. Ask children what they think they will find out about space.

ELL

Access Content Before reading, review the story summary in English and/or the home language. See the ELL Teaching Guide, pp. 12–14.

2

Lift-off!

3 . . . 2 . . . 1 . . . Lift-off!
A space shuttle climbs high into the sky. Inside the shuttle, astronauts are on their way to learn more about space.

48

What is an astronaut?

An astronaut is a person who goes into space. Astronauts fly on a space shuttle.

The space shuttle takes off like a rocket. It lands like an airplane.

49

▲ **Pages 48–49**
Have children look at the pictures and read to find out about space shuttles and astronauts.

Monitor Progress

Decoding

If... children come to a word they don't know,	**then...** remind them to:
	1. Blend the word.
	2. Decide if the word makes sense.
	3. Look in a dictionary for more help.

Guiding Comprehension

Details and Facts • Literal

• **What does a space shuttle do?**
It carries astronauts into space. It takes off like a rocket when it ascends into space and lands like an airplane when it descends.

Draw Conclusions • Inferential

• **What do you think astronauts have to do and learn before they can go into space?**
Possible response: They have to learn how to fly a space shuttle. They need information to do their experiments. Since they float everywhere, they probably have to practice how to move around.

_____ Long Vowels CVCe; Consonants c/s/, g/j/, s/z/   high-frequency/tested vocabulary

Meet Eileen Collins.

Eileen Collins is an astronaut. She was the first woman to be a space shuttle pilot. She was also the first woman to be the leader of a space shuttle trip.

She and four other astronauts worked as a team. Some astronauts flew the space shuttle. Others did experiments.

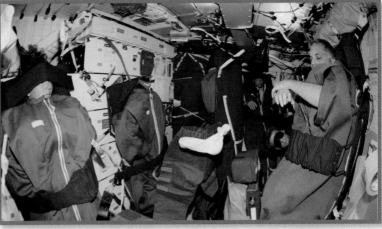

How do astronauts live in space?

In the space shuttle, astronauts float everywhere. Sleeping bags are tied to walls. Toilets have a type of seat belt.

Astronauts exercise to stay strong. They take sponge baths to keep clean.

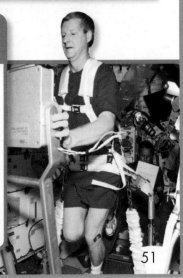

50

51

Strategies in Context

🎯 TEXT STRUCTURE

- **What are the headings at the top of the boxes for?**
  Possible response: To show us what we are going to read about next.

Monitor Progress	🎯 Text Structure
If... children have difficulty identifying headings and their purpose,	**then...** model identifying structural elements.

Think Aloud **MODEL** When we looked through the article, I noticed the author used headings and boxes on each page. The words in the boxes provide information about the subjects in the headings. I think she wants to show us what kind of information she is going to tell us. It helps me understand what I'm reading when I know what to expect.

ASSESS Have children write the title of the selection in the center of a web and the other headings in the circles around the center.

▲ **Pages 50–51**
Have children read to find out what the headings on the boxes tell them.

Monitor Progress	
High-Frequency Words	
If... children have a problem reading a new high-frequency word,	**then...** use the High-Frequency Routine on p. 45a to reteach the problematic word.

TIME FOR Science

Space Walk
On June 3, 1965, Edward H. White became the first United States astronaut to move around in space outside a spacecraft. How do you think he felt while he was out there?

Why do astronauts go into space?

Astronauts test ways to live and work in a world that is very different from Earth. In space, there is no up and down, no air, and the sun always shines.

Astronauts do experiments. They look for problems and fix them. This will make space travel safer.

52

53

▲ **Pages 52–53**
Have children read to find out the answer to the question in the heading.

Strategy Self-Check

Have children ask themselves these questions to check their reading.

Decoding Words
• Do I use what I know about endings and syllables to decode unfamiliar words?
• Does the new word make sense in the sentence and in the article?

Text Structure
• Do I pay attention to the headings so I know what I will read about next?
• What are some important details about astronauts and space shuttles?

Guiding Comprehension

Text Structure • Literal
• **What is the question in the heading? What is the answer?**
Why do astronauts go into space? They test ways to live and work, they do experiments, and they look for problems to fix.

Summarize • Inferential
• **What have we found out in the article so far?**
We have found out what astronauts and space shuttles are, who Eileen Collins is, how astronauts live in space, and why astronauts go into space.

Cause and Effect • Critical
• *Text to World* **If you were in a place with no up and down, how would you sleep? How would you move around?**
Possible response: I'd have to be tied to a bed! I'd move around by floating, I think.

____ Long Vowels CVC*e*; Consonants *c*/s/, *g*/j/, *s*/z/   high-frequency/tested vocabulary

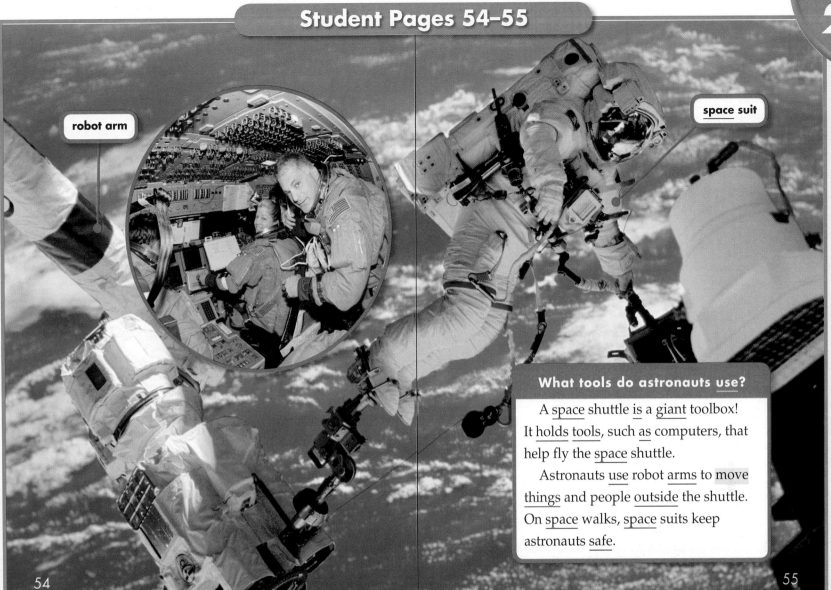

robot arm

space suit

What tools do astronauts use?

A space shuttle is a giant toolbox! It holds tools, such as computers, that help fly the space shuttle.

Astronauts use robot arms to move things and people outside the shuttle. On space walks, space suits keep astronauts safe.

54

55

▲ **Pages 54–55**
Have children read to find out what tools astronauts use in space.

Skills in Context

⊙ MAIN IDEA AND DETAILS

- **Is this article mostly about the tools astronauts use or what life in space is like for astronauts?**
  It is about what life in space is like for astronauts.

Monitor Progress	Main Idea and Details
If... children have difficulty identifying the main idea and details,	**then...** model how to use the text and pictures to confirm understanding.

Think Aloud

MODEL As I read, I learn facts and details about the tools and equipment astronauts use. However, I think these facts and details are there to provide information about the main idea, what life is like for an astronaut. That's what the article is mostly about.

ASSESS Have children recall other details they have read that tell more about this main idea.

EXTEND SKILLS

Text Features: Captions
For instruction in captions, discuss the following:

- The author puts captions or labels on parts of the picture so we know what things are.
- Captions can provide more information when we have trouble understanding the text.
- Read the captions aloud. What does each caption point to?

Assess Have children discuss other captions or labels and connect them to what they read in the text.

Exploring Space **54–55**

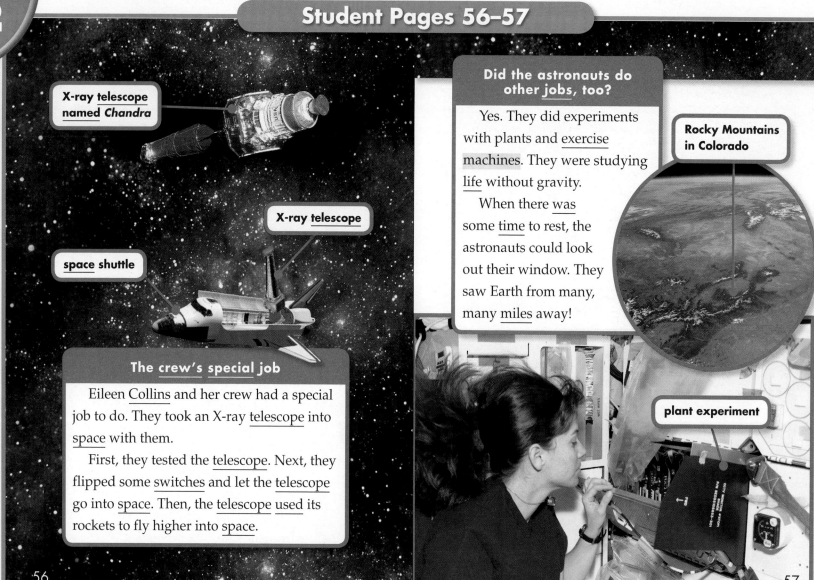

X-ray telescope named *Chandra*

X-ray telescope

space shuttle

The crew's special job

Eileen Collins and her crew had a special job to do. They took an X-ray telescope into space with them.

First, they tested the telescope. Next, they flipped some switches and let the telescope go into space. Then, the telescope used its rockets to fly higher into space.

56

Did the astronauts do other jobs, too?

Yes. They did experiments with plants and exercise machines. They were studying life without gravity.

When there was some time to rest, the astronauts could look out their window. They saw Earth from many, many miles away!

Rocky Mountains in Colorado

plant experiment

57

▲ **Pages 56–57**
Have children read to decide why the author wrote the article.

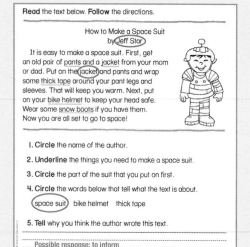

Read the text below. **Follow** the directions.

How to Make a Space Suit
by Jeff Star

It is easy to make a space suit. First, get an old pair of pants and a jacket from your mom or dad. Put on the jacket and pants and wrap some thick tape around your pant legs and sleeves. That will keep you warm. Next, put on your bike helmet to keep your head safe. Wear some snow boots if you have them. Now you are all set to go to space!

1. **Circle** the name of the author.

2. **Underline** the things you need to make a space suit.

3. **Circle** the part of the suit that you put on first.

4. **Circle** the words below that tell what the text is about.
   space suit   bike helmet   thick tape

5. **Tell** why you think the author wrote this text.

_____

Possible response: to inform

School + Home **Home Activity** Your child identified the author's purpose for writing informational text. Work with your child to write directions for an activity he or she is familiar with, such as planting a garden or making a sandwich.

▲ **Practice Book 2.1** p. 17,
Author's Purpose

Skills in Context

REVIEW AUTHOR'S PURPOSE

- **Why do you think Patricia J. Murphy wrote this article?**
  She wanted to tell us some facts about space shuttles and what astronauts do in space.

Monitor Progress	Author's Purpose
If... children have difficulty identifying author's purpose,	**then...** model how to use the text and pictures to confirm understanding.

Think Aloud **MODEL** The author has given us a lot of photographs of astronauts and space shuttles. She has told us a lot of facts about them. I think she must want us to know about life in space for an astronaut.

ASSESS Have children identify other facts and information about astronauts and space shuttles.

58

59

Would you like to fly into space?

Do you like math and science? Do you like to visit new places? Do you like fast roller coasters? Astronauts do, too! Maybe someday you will become an astronaut, just like Eileen Collins.

▲ **Pages 58–59**
Have children read to decide whether they would like to become astronauts.

Guiding Comprehension

Compare and Contrast • Critical

• *Text to World* **How is being an astronaut different from other kinds of jobs? How is it the same?**
No other job has people ascending from Earth and going into outer space to work. But, like other people, astronauts have to work hard. They have to do many things while they're in space.

Author's Purpose • Inferential

• *Question the Author* **Why do you suppose the author asks you whether you might like to fly into space?**
Possible response: She probably wants us to think about whether we would want to do the things we just read about. Maybe she wants to make what she is writing about seem exciting to us.

Draw Conclusions • Critical

• *Text to Self* **Would you like to be an astronaut? Why or why not?**
Possible response: Yes, because I think it would be exciting, and I could learn so much.

Reread For Fluency ROUTINE

1 **Reader 1 Begins** Children read the entire book, switching readers at the end of each page.

2 **Reader 2 Begins** Have partners reread; now the other partner begins.

3 **Reread** For optimal fluency, children should reread three or four times.

4 **Provide Feedback** Listen to children read and provide corrective feedback regarding their oral reading and their use of blending.

OBJECTIVES

● Write questions and answers.
● Identify subjects.

Strategic Intervention

Before carrying out the interactive writing activity, have children work in pairs, with one pretending to be an astronaut and the other asking questions. Have the "astronaut" give answers to the questions.

Advanced

Suggest that children write questions about space travel that were not addressed in the selection. Encourage them to use research sources to find and write answers for their questions.

Support Writing Before writing, list important words that are often used to begin questions, such as *who, what, when, where, why,* and *how.*

Beginning Discuss with children what they want to ask. Restate their ideas in conventional English and, if necessary, provide an answer.

Intermediate Point out the question mark. Invite children to explain how questions and statements are indicated in their own written language.

Advanced Have children brainstorm several questions and answers with a partner before they offer them in the general discussion.

Support Grammar In some languages, the subjects are not routinely at the beginning of sentences as is typical in English. Help children practice by reading sentences from the selection aloud and identifying the subjects. See the Grammar Transition lessons in the ELL and Transition Handbook.

Interactive Writing

WRITE Questions and Answers

DISCUSS Invite children to think about questions they would like to ask an astronaut and some answers they learned when they read *Exploring Space.*

SHARE THE PEN Encourage children to work together to write a question for an astronaut. Invite a volunteer to write the first word, being sure to capitalize the first letter. Ask questions such as:

● What punctuation mark do we write at the end of a question? (a question mark)

Then discuss with children any answer they discovered when they read *Exploring Space.* Write their answer below the question, again having children write the first word with a capital letter.

● What punctuation mark do we write at the end of most sentences? (a period)

Continue to have children brainstorm questions and answers, with individuals making contributions as each one is written. Frequently reread what has been written while tracking the print.

READ QUESTIONS AND ANSWERS Read the completed questions and answers aloud, having children echo you.

What is it like inside the space shuttle?

Astronauts float around.

How do astronauts sleep?

They sleep in sleeping bags tied to the wall.

INDEPENDENT WRITING

WRITE QUESTIONS AND ANSWERS Have children write their own questions for astronauts and the answers to the questions. Let children illustrate their writing.

Grammar

DEVELOP THE CONCEPT Subjects

IDENTIFY SUBJECTS Write on the board: *An astronaut goes into space. A space shuttle goes up like a rocket.* Point to each word as you read the sentences aloud. Discuss with children whether these are sentences.

The subject of a sentence tells who or what does something. What is the subject of the first sentence? (An astronaut) What is the subject of the second sentence? (A space shuttle)

PRACTICE

WRITE SUBJECTS Display two pictures of children playing. Write on the board sentence endings that fit the pictures, such as *plays ball* and *rides a bike.* Model writing a subject to complete each sentence about the picture, for example:

MODEL If I want to write a sentence about the first picture, I would have to add a subject to the words *plays ball.* Write *The boy.* These words give this sentence a subject: *The boy plays ball.* Then I can do the same thing to add a subject to the words *rides a bike.* I think I will write *The girl* so this sentence says *The girl rides a bike.* Now both sentences have subjects.

Have children write other subjects for sentences about the pictures.

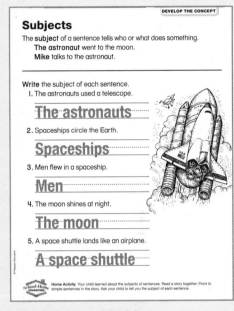

DEVELOP THE CONCEPT

Subjects

The **subject** of a sentence tells who or what does something.
  The astronaut went to the moon.
  Mike talks to the astronaut.

Write the subject of each sentence.
  1. The astronauts used a telescope.
  The astronauts

  2. Spaceships circle the Earth.
  Spaceships

  3. Men flew in a spaceship.
  Men

  4. The moon shines at night.
  The moon

  5. A space shuttle lands like an airplane.
  A space shuttle

Home Activity Your child learned about the subjects of sentences. Read a story together. Point to simple sentences in the story. Ask your child to tell you the subject of each sentence.

▲ **Grammar and Writing Practice Book** p. 5

Wrap Up Your Day!

☑ **HIGH-FREQUENCY WORDS** Write the following sentences. *Astronauts live and work in space. We read about a woman astronaut. Machines can help move things in space. Things are different everywhere in an astronaut's world in space.* Ask children to read the sentences and identify the high-frequency words *live, work, woman, machines, move, everywhere, world.*

☑ **TEXT STRUCTURE** Invite children to discuss how the question-and-answer format of the selection helped them understand what they were reading.

LET'S TALK ABOUT IT Discuss why the astronauts in the selection wanted to explore space. Have children complete the third column of their K-W-L charts.

PREVIEW Day 3

Tell children that tomorrow they will read about a girl who meets someone famous.

Share Literature
Gloria Rising

Phonics and Spelling
REVIEW Short Vowels

Spelling: Words with Long Vowels

High-Frequency Words
everywhere   live   work
woman   machines move
world

Vocabulary
Position Words

Fluency
Read with Accuracy

Writing Trait
Word Choice

Grammar
Subjects

Materials
- *Sing with Me Big Book*
- *Read Aloud Anthology*
- Student Edition 60–61
- Letter Tiles

Morning Warm-Up!

An astronaut helps Gloria think that she can do anything she wants to do. What will Gloria do when she grows up?

QUESTION OF THE DAY Encourage children to sing "Astronauts in Orbit" from the *Sing with Me Big Book* as you gather. Write and read the message and discuss the question.

REVIEW SUBJECTS

- Indicate the first sentence in the message and read it aloud again. What is the subject of this sentence? Who is or what does something? (an astronaut)

Build Background Use the Day 3 instruction on ELL Poster 2 to support children's use of English to communicate about lesson concepts.

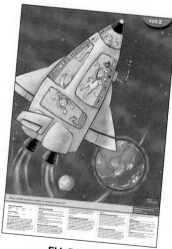

ELL Poster 2

Share Literature

LISTEN AND RESPOND

REVIEW STORY PLOT Recall what *Gloria Rising* is about. What happens at the beginning of the story? (Gloria goes to the store to buy an onion.) What do you think is the most important or exciting thing that happens in the story? (Gloria meets the astronaut, Dr. Street.) How does the story end? (Gloria and Dr. Street say good-by, but the astronaut has given Gloria a lot to think about.)

BUILD ORAL VOCABULARY Review with children that the last time they heard the story, they listened to hear what the universe had to do with Gloria and an onion. Discuss children's ideas about this. Then recall with children that the astronaut had gone on a long trip into space. Explain that another word for a long trip is **journey.** Dr. Street saw huge clouds above Earth. She called them **enormous,** which means very huge. Suggest that children listen this time for details about what Dr. Street tells Gloria.

MONITOR LISTENING COMPREHENSION

What are some things the astronaut saw on her journey into space? (Possible answer: lots of stars, black space, Earth with clouds over it, the ocean)

What word did the astronaut use to tell how big the clouds were? *(enormous)*

Dr. Street talked with Gloria about things like taming her fears. How do you think this made Gloria feel? (Possible answer: Gloria felt she could do anything she wanted to do after Dr. Street talked to her.)

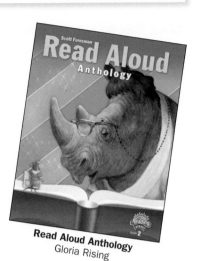

Read Aloud Anthology
Gloria Rising

Amazing Words to build oral vocabulary

	MONITOR PROGRESS
ascend **descend** **orbit** **universe** **enormous** **journey** **launch** **meteorite**	**If...** children lack oral vocabulary experiences about the concept Exploration, **then...** use the Oral Vocabulary Routine. See p. DI·4 to teach *enormous* and *journey*.

Listen and Respond Recall with children that when Gloria thought the onion she threw was going to crash the baby food display, she felt *paralyzed*. Make sure children understand that this means she felt she couldn't move. Help children recall that later Dr. Street says that telling yourself "Probably I couldn't" can be paralyzing—meaning you won't do anything.

Review Phonics

REVIEW SHORT VOWELS

READ SHORT VOWEL WORDS Write *hop, chat,* and *list.* Look at these words. You can read these words because you know that *a, e, i, o, u* can stand for short vowel sounds. What sounds do *hop, chat,* and *list* make? (They make the /o/, /a/, and /i/ sounds.) What are the words?

BUILD WORDS Have children spell *mist* with letter tiles. Monitor work and provide feedback.

- Change the *i* to *u.*
  What is the new word?

  m u s t

- Change the *st* to *g.*
  What is the new word?

  m u g

- Change the *m* to *sl.*
  What is the new word?

  s l u g

- Change the *ug* to *ip.*
  What is the new word?

  s l i p

- Change the *i* to *o.*
  What is the new word?

  s l o p

- Change the *o* to *a.*
  What is the new word?

  s l a p

- Change the *ap* to *ed.*
  What is the new word?

  s l e d

Circle a word to finish each sentence.
Write the word on the line.

1. Al __grabs__ two things. (grabs) grins
2. Al __drips__ milk on the rug. drives (drips)
3. Al __drops__ his plate. drags (drops)
4. What a __mess__ Al makes. (mess) must
5. What will Al have for __lunch__ now? lamp (lunch)

▲ **Practice Book 2.1** p. 18, Short Vowels

High-Frequency Words

PRACTICE

CONTEXT CLUES Provide clues such as the following. Have children find the word on the Word Wall that fits each clue. **Word Wall**

- The word begins with *l* and rhymes with *give*. (live)

- The word begins with *w* and makes sense in this sentence: Uncle Andy tells the funniest jokes in the whole _____! (world)

- The word begins with *m* and makes sense in this sentence: There were "Out of Order" signs posted on all the snack _____. (machines)

- The word begins with *w* and makes sense in this sentence: After he dropped me off at school, Dad drove to _____. (work)

- The word begins with *e* and makes sense in this sentence: Mom said, "These toys are scattered _____!" (everywhere)

- The word begins with *m* and makes sense in this sentence: In two weeks my best friend Jack will _____ to a different town. (move)

- The word begins with *w* and makes sense in this sentence: Mrs. Sage is the _____ in the green dress. (woman)

Spelling

PRACTICE Long Vowels CVCe

MAKE AN ORBIT Have children practice spelling words by creating an orbit of sentences that use spelling words.

- Give each child twelve sheets of paper with the outline of a rocket on each one.

- Have children write sentences that use the spelling words on each rocket. Ask them to underline the spelling words.

- Display the class "orbit" of rockets on a bulletin board or on the wall.

HOMEWORK Spelling Practice Book, p. 7

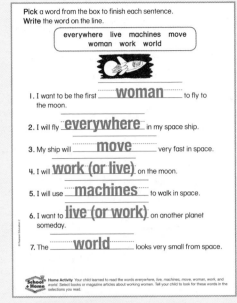

Pick a word from the box to finish each sentence.
Write the word on the line.

> everywhere live machines move
> woman work world

1. I want to be the first **woman** to fly to the moon.

2. I will fly **everywhere** in my space ship.

3. My ship will **move** very fast in space.

4. I will **work (or live)** on the moon.

5. I will use **machines** to walk in space.

6. I want to **live (or work)** on another planet someday.

7. The **world** looks very small from space.

School + Home Home Activity Your child learned to read the words everywhere, live, machines, move, woman, work, and world. Select books or magazine articles about working women. Tell your child to look for these words in the selections you read.

▲ **Practice Book 2.1** p. 19, High-Frequency Words

Spelling Words

Long Vowels CVCe

1. tune	7. mice
2. page	8. late
3. nose	9. cube
4. space*	10. blaze
5. size	11. home
6. fine	12. vote

Challenge Words

13. erase	15. confuse
14. spice	

* Word from the Selection

Long Vowels CVCe

Read the note Jeff wrote about his pets. Circle three spelling mistakes. Write the words correctly. Then write the last sentence and add the missing subject.

Spelling Words	
tune	mice
page	late
nose	cube
space	blaze
size	home
fine	vote

> Some people do not like mice, but I do. I have two pet mice at horm. One has a black nose. knows Think mice make fine pets.

1. **like** 2. **nose** 3. **home**

4. **I think mice make fine pets.**

Frequently Misspelled Words
nice
like
baseball

Circle the word that is spelled correctly. Write it.

5. blaze / blaiz — **blaze**
6. voat / vote — **vote**
7. hom / home — **home**
8. page / paje — **page**
9. qube / cube — **cube**
10. space / spase — **space**

School + Home Home Activity Your child has been learning to spell words with long vowels. Have your child write a paragraph using some of the spelling words.

▲ **Spelling Practice Book** p. 7

Strategic Intervention

Demonstrate to children the meanings of such position words as *in, out, up, down, inside,* and *outside* by using classroom objects. Ask them to use each word in an oral sentence as you demonstrate it.

Advanced

Invite children to use position words and phrases of their own in written sentences. Let them illustrate their sentences and display their work.

Extend Language Tell children that we use many words that tell where something is. Hold a book up over your head and ask, "Where is this book?" As necessary, help children respond that the book is *over* your head. Write several position words such as *under, in, on, inside,* and *outside* on the board. Read the words aloud one at a time and help children act out and use each one in an oral sentence.

Vocabulary

POSITION WORDS

DISCUSS POSITION WORDS Discuss words and groups of words that tell the position of something. Point out examples from the selection, such as the ones shown below.

<u>into</u> the sky (p. 48)

<u>inside</u> the shuttle (p. 48)

<u>on</u> a space shuttle (p. 49)

float <u>everywhere</u> (p. 51)

<u>up</u> and <u>down</u> (p. 52)

<u>outside</u> the shuttle (p. 55)

<u>out</u> their window (p. 57)

Discuss with children how each of these position words tells where something is.

EXPAND VOCABULARY Brainstorm with children to think of other position words or groups of words. Model for children how to act out the meaning of each one, using objects such as a book and a pencil. Have them create an oral sentence using each word or phrase.

over I'm holding the book *over* my head.

beside The red book is *beside* the blue book.

around There are books all *around* the room.

Group Time

<table>
<tr>
<td>**On-Level**</td>
<td>**Strategic Intervention**</td>
<td>**Advanced**</td>
</tr>
<tr>
<td>**Read** *Exploring Space.*
• Use pp. 46–59.</td>
<td>**Read** or listen to *Exploring Space.*
• Use the **Routine** on p. DI·28.</td>
<td>**Read** Self-Selected Reading.
• Use the **Routine** on p. DI·29.</td>
</tr>
</table>

 Place English language learners in the groups that correspond to their reading abilities in English.

(i) Independent Activities

Independent Reading See p. 42j for Reading/Library activities and suggestions.

Journal Writing Use position words in sentences about exploring space. Share your writing.

Literacy Centers To provide experiences with *Exploring Space,* you may use the Writing Center on p. 42k.

Practice Book 2.1 Short Vowels, p. 18; High-Frequency Words, p. 19

Break into small groups after Vocabulary and before Writing.

DAY 3

Fluency

READ WITH ACCURACY

MODEL READING WITH ACCURACY Use *Exploring Space with an Astronaut*.

- Have children turn to p. 48. You need to be careful to pay attention to each word and read with no mistakes.

- Ask children to follow along as you read p. 48 aloud.

- Have children read the page after you. Encourage them to read accurately. Continue similarly with p. 49.

REREAD FOR FLUENCY

Choral Reading

ROUTINE

1 **Select a Passage** For *Exploring Space with an Astronaut,* use pp. 50–53.

2 **Divide into Groups** Assign each group a part to read. For this selection, have each group read a paragraph.

3 **Model** Have children track the print as you read.

4 **Read Together** Have children read along with you.

5 **Independent Readings** Have the groups read aloud without you. Monitor progress and provide feedback. For optimal fluency, children should reread three to four times.

Monitor Progress	Fluency
If... children have difficulty reading with accuracy,	**then...** prompt: • Read more slowly. • Pay close attention to each word.
If... the class cannot read fluently without you,	**then...** continue to have them read along with you.

OBJECTIVE

● Read aloud with accuracy.

Options for Oral Reading

Use *Exploring Space with an Astronaut* or one of the following Leveled Readers.

On-Level

Space Walk

Strategic Intervention

Being an Astronaut

Advanced

Explore the Galaxy

E L L

Use *The First Man on the Moon* or *Exploring Space with an Astronaut*. Read p. 48 aloud of *Exploring Space* and then have children read it with you chorally. Give help with individual words as necessary. Model reading phrases such as "who goes into space" and "on a space shuttle" so that beginning English language learners can practice reading meaningfully.

Fluency Coach CD To develop fluent readers, use Fluency Coach.

Retelling Plan

☑ Week 1 assess Strategic Intervention students.

☑ **This week assess Advanced students.**

☐ Week 3 assess Strategic Intervention students.

☐ Week 4 assess On-Level students.

☐ Week 5 assess any students you have not yet checked during this unit.

Look Back and Write
For test practice, assign a 10–15 minute time limit. For informal or formal assessment, see the Scoring Rubric below.

Think and Share

TALK ABOUT IT Model a response. We can see the world from here. It is beautiful! It is fun to float around without gravity, but it is hard to sleep. I worked today to do an experiment. I used a big telescope.

1. RETELL Have children use the retelling strip in the Student Edition to retell what they read about astronauts.

Monitor Progress | **Check Retelling**

If... children have difficulty retelling the selection,

then... use the Retelling Cards and Scoring Rubric for Retelling on p. 60–61 to help them move toward fluent retelling.

SUCCESS PREDICTOR

Day 1 Check Word Reading   **Day 2** Check High-Frequency Words   ▶**Day 3 Check Retelling**   **Day 4** Check Fluency   **Day 5** Assess Progress

2. ◉ **MAIN IDEA AND DETAILS** Model a response. I think the author wants us to know how different it is in space and what astronauts do while they are there.

3. ◉ **TEXT STRUCTURE** Model a response. The questions and answers helped me know what I was going to read about. They also helped me organize the author's ideas.

LOOK BACK AND WRITE Read the writing prompt on p. 60 and model your thinking. I'll look back at page 59 and read that part of the selection again. I'll think about the things I should like if I really want to be an astronaut. Then I'll write my response. **Have children write their responses.**

Scoring Rubric | **Look Back and Write**

Top-Score Response A top-score response will use details from p. 59 of the selection to name the things that an astronaut should like.

Example of a Top-Score Response To be an astronaut, you should like math and science to do experiments in space. You should like visiting new places. You should also like riding fast roller coasters because space shuttles are also fast.

For additional rubrics, see p. WA10.

E L L

Assessment Work through the photographs with children, making sure they know what is being shown in each one. For more ideas on assessing comprehension, see the ELL and Transition Handbook.

Think and Share

Talk About It You are an astronaut. Send a one-minute message to Earth. Tell about your trip.

1. Use the pictures below to summarize what you read about astronauts. **Retell**

2. What do you think is the most important thing the author wanted you to know? **Main Idea**

3. Most sections of this selection begin with a question. The next part answers the question. How did that format help you as you read? **Text Structure**

Look Back and Write If you really want to be an astronaut, what things should you like? Look back on page 59 to help you answer.

Meet the Author
Patricia J. Murphy

Read more books by Patricia Murphy.

Patricia Murphy likes everything about writing a book. When she starts a new book, she says, it's "fun and scary." When she's in the middle, her days are filled with "unexpected adventure and surprises—and a lot of mess and hard work." In the end, when the book is written, she feels excited and a little sad that it's all over. Then it's on to the next book!

Ms. Murphy is a writer and a photographer. She lives in Illinois.

Retelling Strip

60

61

Scoring Rubric | Expository Retelling

Rubric 4 3 2 1	4	3	2	1
Connections	Makes connections and generalizes beyond the text	Makes connections to other events, texts, or experiences	Makes a limited connection to another event, text, or experience	Makes no connection to another event, text, or experience
Author's Purpose	Elaborates on author's purpose	Tells author's purpose with some clarity	Makes some connection to author's purpose	Makes no connection to author's purpose
Topic	Describes the main topic	Identifies the main topic with some details early in retelling	Identifies the main topic	Retelling has no sense of story
Important Ideas	Gives accurate information about ideas using key vocabulary	Gives accurate information about ideas with some key vocabulary	Gives limited or inaccurate information about ideas	Gives no information about ideas
Conclusions	Draws conclusions and makes inferences to generalize beyond the text	Draws conclusions about the text	Is able to draw some conclusions about the text	Is unable to draw conclusions or make inferences about the text

Use the Retelling Chart on p. TR21 to record retelling.

Selection Test To assess with *Exploring Space*, use Selection Tests, pp. 5–8.

Fresh Reads for Differentiated Test Practice For weekly leveled practice, use pp. 7–12.

Retelling

SUCCESS PREDICTOR

OBJECTIVE

• Recognize and use good word choice in writing.

DAILY FIX-IT

5. it is a fine day to fly into space

<u>It</u> is a fine day to fly into space<u>.</u>

6. are in the sky no clouds

<u>No clouds</u> are in the sky<u>.</u>

Connect to Unit Writing

Writing Trait

Have children use strategies for developing **word choice** when they write a personal narrative in the Unit Writing Workshop, pp. WA2–WA9.

Word Choice Work with children to use vivid words that appeal to readers' senses. A bilingual dictionary, picture dictionary, or thesaurus, as well as other home-language speakers, may help provide words that create pictures for readers.

Writing Trait of the Week

INTRODUCE Word Choice

TALK ABOUT WORD CHOICE Explain to children that they should choose words carefully to add style to their writing. Using exact nouns, strong verbs, and exciting adjectives will make their work interesting, clear, and lively. Ask them to think about words the author used to make *Exploring Space with an Astronaut* clear and lively. Then model your thinking.

MODEL This article has many facts about what astronauts do. I feel the excitement of being an astronaut. I wonder how the author creates excitement. When I reread page 59, I see that strong words make the topic exciting. Here are some sentences that show the author's word choice.

Do you like fast roller coasters? Astronauts do too!

Which words are exact nouns that give readers a clear picture? *(roller coasters, astronauts)*

A space shuttle climbs high into the sky.
In the space shuttle, astronauts float everywhere.
Astronauts exercise to stay strong.

Which words are strong verbs that give readers a clear picture? *(climbs, float, exercise)*

STRATEGY FOR DEVELOPING WORD CHOICE On the board, write sentences with dull words underlined, such as those below. Then ask children to replace these words with more precise, vivid ones.

The sun is <u>nice</u>. *(bright, shiny)*
Spacesuits are <u>big</u>. *(bulky, clumsy)*
The space shuttle <u>went</u> up into the sky. *(climbed, shot)*
Astronauts have <u>good</u> jobs. *(interesting, exciting)*

PRACTICE

APPLY THE STRATEGY Ask children to imagine what they would see if they went up in a space shuttle. Have them write a list of specific nouns, strong verbs, and exciting adjectives to describe the sights. Now have them use their lists to write a paragraph describing what they see.

Grammar

APPLY TO WRITING Subjects

IMPROVE WRITING WITH SUBJECTS Review with children that every sentence must have a subject. Remind children to use subjects correctly in their writing.

Have children write two or three sentences about what they would like to be when they grow up. Tell them to make sure they use subjects correctly.

I want to be a police officer when I grow up.
Police officers drive police cars and make the sirens go.
Police officers keep us safe.

PRACTICE

WRITE WITH SUBJECTS Have children add two or three sentences that tell what they like best about what they want to be when they grow up. Remind them to be sure every sentence has a subject.

Subjects

Write four sentences about the planets or space travel.
Use words from the box or words of your own.
Circle the subject in each sentence.

| Jupiter | sun | rocket ship | astronauts |
| Mars | moon | shuttle | Earth |

Possible answer: Our planet is Earth. Astronauts go into space. The sun is hot. Jupiter is far away.

Home Activity Your child learned how to use the subjects of sentences in writing. Have your child write two sentences about astronauts and underline the subjects of the sentences.

▲ **Grammar and Writing Practice Book** p. 6

Wrap Up Your Day!

✓ **MAIN IDEA AND DETAILS** Have children discuss what the whole selection is all about in order to identify the main idea. (what it is like to be an astronaut and explore space) The selection says that astronauts do experiments in space. Is that a main idea or a detail about the main idea? (a detail)

✓ **FLUENCY SKILL** Reread sentences from *Exploring Space,* modeling how to read with accuracy. Invite children to read with accuracy together.

✓ **READ WITH ACCURACY** Remind children of the importance of reading every word exactly as it is written. Ask a volunteer to read aloud the second paragraph on p. 55 to demonstrate.

LET'S TALK ABOUT IT Discuss with children what they have learned about why astronauts want to explore space. Display the K-W-L chart from Day 1. What did we learn about astronauts by reading this selection? What answers did we get to the questions we asked in the second column? Let's finish the third column to tell what we learned.

PREVIEW Day 4

Tell children that tomorrow they will read about space camps that children can attend to find out if they want to explore space.

Day 4
AT A GLANCE

Materials

- *Sing with Me Big Book*
- *Read Aloud Anthology*
- Student Edition 62–65

Morning Warm-Up!

Today we'll read about kids
going to space camps.
They find out how it feels
to be up in space.
What do you think
being in space camp is like?

QUESTION OF THE DAY Encourage children to sing "Astronauts in Orbit" from the *Sing with Me Big Book* as you gather. Write and read the message and discuss the question.

REVIEW POSITION WORDS

- Ask children to identify the position words they see in the message. *(to, up in, in)*
- Have children read the position words aloud, giving help as necessary.

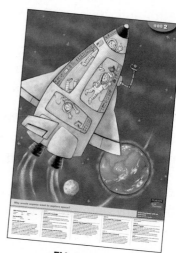

ELL

Extend Language Use the Day 4 instruction on ELL Poster 2 to extend and enrich language.

ELL Poster 2

Share Literature

CONNECT CONCEPTS

ACTIVATE PRIOR KNOWLEDGE Recall with children what they have read and listened to about astronauts and going into space. Explain that they will listen to another story about astronauts ascending into space, but this one is about what it might be like when they grow up to be an astronaut who takes a journey to Mars. Explain that Mars is a planet very, very far away from Earth.

Read Aloud Anthology
Mission to Mars

BUILD ORAL VOCABULARY Read aloud the second paragraph of the selection. Discuss with children that **launch** means "put something out into space with force." **Meteorites,** or large masses of stone and metal that have fallen from outer space to a planet or moon, can change the surface of a planet. Have children listen to the selection to find out what will probably happen after a spaceship to Mars is launched.

REVIEW ORAL VOCABULARY After reading, review all the Amazing Words for the week. Have children take turns using them in sentences that tell about the concept for the week. Then talk about Amazing Words they learned in other weeks and connect them to the concept, as well. For example, ask:

- Where would you be more likely to have a clear view of stars in the night sky—an **urban** or a **rural** area? Why?
- If you were an astronaut, what sorts of things would you want to **investigate?**

MONITOR LISTENING COMPREHENSION

- What will happen when the spaceship is launched? (It will leave the International Space Station and travel for more than six months to Mars.)
- What happened to Mars billions of years ago when meteorites crashed into it? (Huge craters were formed; one is at least 200 miles across.)
- Why do you think that astronauts are not going in spaceships to Mars now? (Possible answer: Some things that will be needed, such as the Mars Station, have not been built or invented yet.)

OBJECTIVES

- Set purpose for listening.
- Build oral vocabulary.

Amazing Words to build oral vocabulary

Amazing Words	MONITOR PROGRESS
ascend **descend** **orbit** **universe** **enormous** **journey** **launch** **meteorite**	**If...** children lack oral vocabulary experiences about the concept Exploration, **then...** use the Oral Vocabulary Routine. See p. DI•4 to teach *launch* and *meteorite*.

ELL

Connect Concepts Explain to children that Mars is a planet that orbits the sun the way Earth does, but that it is much farther away. Make sure children understand that the story *Mission to Mars* tells about what might happen. The information about Mars and future space travel to that planet is based on what scientists know now.

Spiral REVIEW

- Reviews short vowel words.
- Reviews high-frequency words *beautiful, country, friend, front, someone, somewhere.*

Sentence Reading

REVIEW WORDS IN CONTEXT

READ DECODABLE AND HIGH-FREQUENCY WORDS IN CONTEXT Write these sentences. Call on individuals to read a sentence. Then randomly point to words and have them read. To help you monitor word reading, high-frequency words are underlined and decodable words are circled.

My (jacket) is somewhere, but I (cannot) find it.

I know someone who (has) a long (nose) on (his) (face).

My friend (has) (nine) (mice) in a (huge) (cage).

He (can) (drive) (his) (nice) car in the country.

One (cent) in my (pocket) will not get a beautiful (gem) for (Mom).

We (sat) (at) the front of the (rink) to see them (skate) on (ice).

Monitor Progress	Word Reading
If... children are unable to read an underlined word,	**then...** read the word for them and spell it, having them echo you.
If... children are unable to read a circled word,	**then...** have them use the blending strategy they have learned for that word type.

Support Phonics For additional review, see the phonics activities in the ELL and Transition Handbook.

Spelling

PARTNER REVIEW Long Vowels CVCe

READ AND WRITE Supply pairs of children with index cards on which the spelling words have been written. Have one child read a word while the other writes it. Then have children switch roles. Have them use the cards to check their spelling.

HOMEWORK Spelling Practice Book, p. 8

Group Time

On-Level	Strategic Intervention	Advanced
Read "A Trip to Space Camp."	**Read** or listen to "A Trip to Space Camp."	**Read** "A Trip to Space Camp."
• Use pp. 62–65.	• Use the **Routine** on p. DI·30.	• Use the **Routine** on p. DI·31.

 Place English language learners in the groups that correspond to their reading abilities in English.

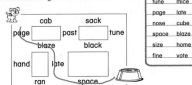

Long Vowels CVCe

Draw a path through the maze. Follow the words with long *a*. Write each word.

Spelling Words	
tune	mice
page	late
nose	cube
space	blaze
size	home
fine	vote

1. page 2. blaze 3. late 4. space

Cross out the letters p and a. Write a list word by copying the letters that are left.

5. home   6. tune
7. vote   8. fine
9. size   10. nose

Home Activity Your child has been learning to spell words with long vowels. Take turns with your child thinking of and spelling similar words with long vowels.

Spelling Practice Book p. 8

DAY 4

(i) Independent Activities

Fluency Reading Pair children to reread *Exploring Space.*

Journal Writing List things that can ascend and descend. Share writing.

Spelling Partner Review

Independent Reading See p. 42j for Reading/Library activities and suggestions.

Literacy Centers To provide listening opportunities, you may use the Listening Center on p. 42j. To extend science concepts, you may use the Science Center on p. 42k.

Break into small groups after Spelling and before Fluency.

Science in Reading

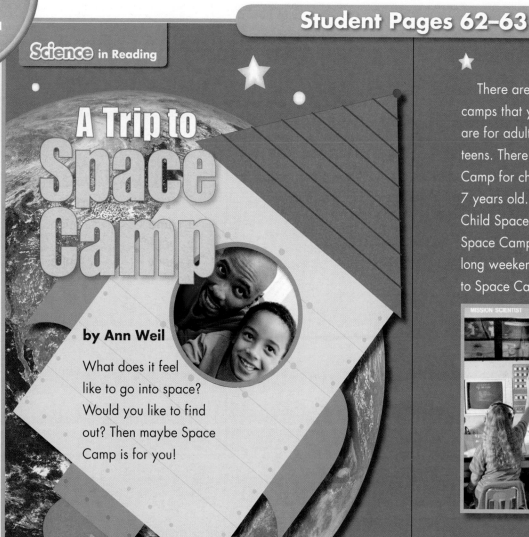

A Trip to Space Camp

by Ann Weil

What does it feel like to go into space? Would you like to find out? Then maybe Space Camp is for you!

62

There are all sorts of space camps that you could try. Some are for adults. Some are for teens. There is even a Space Camp for children as young as 7 years old. It is called Parent-Child Space Camp. Parent-Child Space Camp takes place over a long weekend. Families can go to Space Camp together.

63

AudioText

OBJECTIVE

● Recognize text structure: nonfiction.

Astronauts
TIME FOR Science

All American astronauts train at the Lyndon B. Johnson Space Center in Houston, Texas. They take classes taught by astronauts and other experts, as well as have flight training, survival training, and mission training.

Read Science in Reading

PREVIEW AND PREDICT Read the title, author's name, and the sentences on p. 62. Have children preview the article, looking at the photographs and reading their captions. Provide help as necessary with the captions. Then ask children to predict what they think they might find out when they read the selection. Have children read to learn whether they might want to explore space themselves.

INFORMATIONAL TEXT Recall with children that the article they read about astronauts was expository nonfiction because it told facts about a topic. Explain that the photographs in this article show real things. Invite children to discuss whether they think this article about space camp is also expository nonfiction and why.

VOCABULARY/POSITION WORDS Review with children that position words tell where something is. Have children locate _on the moon_ and _outside their rocket ship_ on p. 64. After reading the selection, ask: What other position words did you read in this article? (_into the air_ and _up_ and _down_, p. 64)

A Multi-Axis Giro

Space Camp uses some of the same machines used to train real astronauts. There's a special chair that makes you feel like you are walking on the moon. Another chair is like the kind that astronauts use when they go outside their rocket ship to fix something. A third kind of chair makes you feel like you're floating in space. Still another machine spins you in circles and flips you head over heels. Then there's the Space Shot. The Space Shot shoots you straight into the air at about 45 to 50 miles per hour. You fall back down just as fast. Then you bump up and down a few times before it's over.

Y6 Gravity Chair

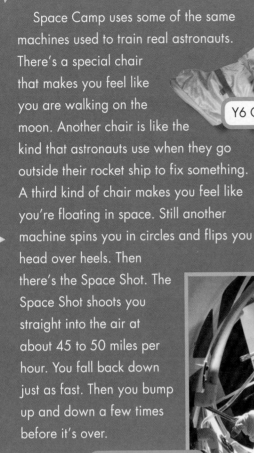

Working in Space

Everyone at space camp works together on special missions. On these missions you'll do work like real astronauts do in space. You might get to fly a rocket ship. It's only pretend, of course. You won't really fly into space. But it looks and feels like the real thing. And that's really fun!

Moon Gravity Chair

64

65

BUILD CONCEPTS

Draw Conclusions • Critical

- **How do you think going to space camp could help you decide whether you really want to become an astronaut?**
  You can find out what it feels like to do some of the things astronauts do by trying them out in space camp.

Details and Facts • Inferential

- **Which activities that astronauts do are ones that kids try out at space camp?**
  They walk on the moon, go outside the rocket ship to fix something, float in space, spin in circles and flip head over heels, ascend straight into the air at 45 to 50 miles per hour and descend just as fast, work on a mission, and fly a rocket ship.

CONNECT TEXT TO TEXT

How is what kids do in space camp like what the real astronauts you read about do? How is it different?

Have children review *Exploring Space* and compare it to *A Trip to Space Camp.*

Access Content Discuss with children what camp is. Explain that some children go away to a camp in the summer where they experience the outdoors and living together with other children, often in tents or cabins. In space camp, children are also away from home in a special place.

Options for Oral Reading

Use *Exploring Space with an Astronaut* or one of the following Leveled Readers.

On-Level

Space Walk

Strategic Intervention

Being an Astronaut

Advanced

Explore the Galaxy

Use *The First Man on the Moon* or "A Trip to Space Camp." English learners benefit from assisted reading, with modeling by the teacher or by a skilled classmate. When the English learner reads the passage aloud, the more proficient reader assists by providing feedback and encouragement.

 To develop fluent readers, use Fluency Coach.

Fluency

READ WITH ACCURACY

MODEL READING WITH ACCURACY Use *Exploring Space with an Astronaut.*

• Have children turn to pp. 54–55. It is important to read each word exactly the way it is written. Notice that p. 54 is mostly a picture, yet there is an important label to read.

• Ask children to follow along as you read pp. 54–55 aloud.

• Have children read the page after you. Encourage them to read every word accurately. Continue in the same way with p. 56.

REREAD FOR FLUENCY

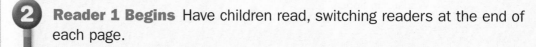

Paired Reading

1 **Select a Passage** For *Exploring Space,* use pp. 57 and 59.

2 **Reader 1 Begins** Have children read, switching readers at the end of each page.

3 **Reader 2 Begins** Have partners reread; now the other partner begins.

4 **Reread** For optimal fluency, children should reread three or four times with attention to accuracy, pace, and expression.

5 **Provide Feedback** Listen as children read and provide corrective feedback regarding their oral reading and their use of the blending strategy.

ROUTINE

Monitor Progress | Check Fluency WCPM

As children reread, monitor their progress toward their individual fluency goals. Current Goal: 50–60 words correct per minute. End-of-Year Goal: 90 words correct per minute.

If... children cannot read fluently at a rate of 50–60 words correct per minute,

then... make sure children practice with text at their independent level. Provide additional fluency practice, pairing nonfluent readers with fluent readers.

If... children already read at 90 words correct per minute,

then... they do not need to reread three to four times.

SUCCESS PREDICTOR

Day 1 Check Word Reading

Day 2 Check High-Frequency Words

Day 3 Check Retelling

▶ **Day 4 Check Fluency**

Day 5 Assess Progress

Writing Across the Curriculum

WRITE Three-Column Chart

BRAINSTORM Recall with children that astronauts live and work in space. Invite children to name people who do other kinds of things and tell where they live and work. For example, a police officer might live in an apartment and work in a police car.

SHARE THE PEN Have children help create a three-column chart. Draw a chart on the board or chart paper, writing *Worker, Lives,* and *Works* as the headings of the columns. Explain that a chart like this is one way to compare information. Begin by having children brainstorm one kind of worker they know about. Write the word, inviting individuals to help spell the word by writing familiar letter-sounds. Follow a similar procedure to fill in the other two columns to tell where each worker lives and works. Ask questions like the following:

- What is the first sound you hear in *police officer?* (/p/)
- What letter stands for that sound? *(p)* Have a volunteer write *p.*

Continue having individuals contribute to writing the names of workers and the places where they live and work. Frequently reread the columns aloud. Then ask each child to write a sentence about one of the workers that tells where that person lives and works.

Worker	Lives	Works
police officer	apartment	police car
firefighter	house	fire engine
teacher	apartment	school

A firefighter lives in a house and works on a fire engine.

OBJECTIVE

• Identify subjects.

DAILY FIX-IT

7. was late for the soccer game
<u>He</u> was late for the soccer game.

8. they missed the first goal
<u>They</u> missed the first goal.

Subjects   TEST PREPARATION

Mark the letter of the subject that completes each sentence.

1. ___ is an astronaut.
   ○ A Seeing
   ⊗ B Paula
   ○ C Fun

2. ___ have hard jobs.
   ⊗ A Astronauts
   ○ B And
   ○ C Watch

3. ___ is a big star.
   ○ A Chair
   ○ B Leaves
   ⊗ C The sun

4. ___ is a planet.
   ○ A Jack
   ⊗ B Mars
   ○ C Play

5. ___ is our home.
   ○ A The chair
   ○ B Tell
   ⊗ C The Earth

6. ___ sees the stars.
   ⊗ A Maya
   ○ B Sit
   ○ C Have

Home Activity Your child prepared for taking tests on the subjects of sentences. Say simple sentences such as *The moon is full. The sun is hot. The Earth is round.* Then ask your child to tell you the subjects of the sentences.

▲ **Grammar and Writing Practice Book** p. 7

Grammar

REVIEW Subjects

DEFINE SUBJECTS

• What is the subject of a sentence? (the part that tells who or what does something)

• What part of a sentence tells who or what does something? (the subject)

PRACTICE

IDENTIFY SUBJECTS Write the following sentences. Have children underline the subject in each one.

We go to a big school.

Many kids are here.

Our teacher's name is Mr. Hunt.

He plays soccer with us during recess.

Mr. Hunt can kick a soccer ball very far.

Speaking and Listening

WHY WE LISTEN

OBJECTIVES
- Speak to share ideas.
- Listen to hear others' ideas.

DEMONSTRATE LISTENING Explain to children that people listen for several different reasons.

- We listen to hear questions.
- We listen to hear other people's ideas.
- We listen for enjoyment and appreciation.
- We listen for information.

Discuss with children which of these reasons they have for listening to you now. (for information)

LISTEN TO OTHERS Have children take turns telling the class why they think people want to explore space. Tell the class to listen carefully to hear each speaker's ideas.

Wrap Up Your Day!

 TEXT TO WORLD Recall with children what they have read about astronauts.

LET'S TALK ABOUT IT Point out that children who go to space camp really want to know what it's like to be an astronaut. Why do you think the kids who go to space camp want to explore space?

PREVIEW Day 5

Tell children that tomorrow they will read about a space mission.

Day 5
AT A GLANCE

Share Literature
Mission to Mars

Phonics and Spelling

Review Long Vowels CVC*e*

High-Frequency Words

everywhere	live	**Word Wall**
work	woman	
machines	move	world

Monitor Progress
Spelling Test: Words with Long
　　Vowels CVC*e*

Group Time < Differentiated
Assessment

Writing and Grammar
Trait: Word Choice

Subjects

Research and Study Skills
Alphabetical Order: First Letter

Materials

- *Sing with Me Big Book*
- *Read Aloud Anthology*
- Reproducible Pages TE 66f–66g
- Student Edition 66–67

Morning Warm-Up!

This week we read about people who want to explore space. What do real astronauts do in space?

QUESTION OF THE DAY Encourage children to sing "Astronauts in Orbit" from the *Sing with Me Big Book* as you gather. Write and read the message and discuss the question.

REVIEW ORAL VOCABULARY Have children tell

- what astronauts do when they ascend into space

- what astronauts do when they descend from space

- what astronauts do when they orbit the Earth

- about the enormous universe that astronauts see on their journey into space

- what happens when a spaceship is launched

ELL

Assess Vocabulary Use the Day 5 instruction on ELL Poster 2 to monitor children's progress with oral vocabulary.

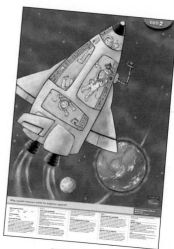

ELL Poster 2

Share Literature

LISTEN AND RESPOND

USE PRIOR KNOWLEDGE Recall with children that they first listened to *Mission to Mars* to find out what might happen after a spaceship to Mars is launched. Discuss what they discovered. Have them listen again to figure out why people would want to explore Mars.

MONITOR LISTENING COMPREHENSION

- Why do people want to explore Mars? (Possible answers: They want to help future astronauts. People want to find things no one could have imagined. Because no one knows what might be discovered, people want to see for themselves what is there.)

- Meteorites are pieces of stone and metal from space that sometimes crash into planets like Mars. What have falling meteorites done on Mars? (They have dug huge craters on Mars.)

- The selection told us about meteorites on Mars. Was this the main idea of the book or was it just a detail? What makes you think so? (That is just a detail. The whole selection is about traveling to Mars in the future.)

Read Aloud Anthology
Mission to Mars

BUILD ORAL VOCABULARY

GENERATE DISCUSSION Recall that *Mission to Mars* predicts how astronauts may travel to and explore Mars in the future. Invite children to discuss areas of the universe they would like to explore if they were astronauts of the future and ways they could do so. Have them use some of this week's Amazing Words as they share their ideas.

Monitor Progress | Check Oral Vocabulary

Display pp. 42–43 in the Student Edition and remind children of the unit photographs—Exploration. Ask them to tell you about the concept using some of this week's Amazing Words: *ascend, descend, orbit, universe, enormous, journey, launch,* and *meteorite.*

If... children have difficulty using the Amazing Words,

then... ask questions about the photographs using the Amazing Words. Note which questions children can respond to. Reteach unknown words using the Oral Vocabulary Routine on p. DI·1.

SUCCESS PREDICTOR

OBJECTIVES
- Set purpose for listening.
- Build oral vocabulary.

 **to build oral vocabulary**

ascend	enormous
descend	journey
orbit	launch
universe	meteorite

 ELL

Extend Language Brainstorm with children a list of common English position words and phrases such as *from, to, in, out, up, down, outside, inside, next to, beside, far from,* and so on. Help children as necessary to use each one in an oral sentence.

 **Oral Vocabulary SUCCESS PREDICTOR**

5

OBJECTIVES
- Review long vowels CVCe.
- Review high-frequency words.

Long Vowels CVCe

REVIEW

IDENTIFY LONG VOWEL WORDS Write these sentences. Have children read each one aloud. Call on individuals to name and underline the long vowel words and identify the vowel sounds.

> The slice of cake is nice.
> Did you erase the note on the page?
> I will make a space in the cage for the mice.
> The mule has a huge white nose.

High-Frequency Words

REVIEW

COMPLETE THE QUESTIONS Read the following questions aloud. Have children write one of the Words to Know from p. 44 for each blank. Then read the completed questions together.

Does he drive his car to _____? (work)

Was this bench made by people or _____? (machines)

Who is that _____? (woman)

Did they _____ to a new home? (move)

Does your family _____ next door to Joe? (live)

How big is our _____? (world)

Have you looked _____ for the lost pup? (everywhere)

ELL

Access Content For additional practice with the high-frequency words, use the vocabulary strategies and word cards in the ELL Teaching Guide, pp. 10–11.

SPELLING TEST Long Vowels CVCe

DICTATION SENTENCES Use these sentences to assess this week's spelling words.

1. I put a <u>cube</u> in my glass.
2. My <u>nose</u> is red.
3. Are you on the last <u>page</u>?
4. The <u>blaze</u> is hot.
5. Dad said it was <u>fine</u> with him.
6. I can hum a <u>tune</u>.
7. Look at the <u>size</u> of that cat!
8. I like to spend time at my <u>home</u>.
9. Sal has two black <u>mice</u>.
10. Mom went to <u>vote</u>.
11. The rocket will go into <u>space</u>.
12. I do not want to be <u>late</u>.

CHALLENGE WORDS

13. Did you <u>erase</u> it?
14. I will mix in the <u>spice</u>.
15. I do not want to <u>confuse</u> you!

ASSESS

● Spell words with long vowels.

Spelling Words

Long Vowels CVCe

1.	tune	7.	mice
2.	page	8.	late
3.	nose	9.	cube
4.	space*	10.	blaze
5.	size	11.	home
6.	fine	12.	vote

Challenge Words

13.	erase	15. confuse
14.	spice	

* Words from the Selection

Group Time

On-Level	Strategic Intervention	Advanced
Read Set B Sentences.	**Read** Set A Sentences and the Story.	**Read** Set C Sentences.
• Use pp. 66e–66g.	• Use pp. 66e–66g.	• Use pp. 66e–66g.
	• Use the **Routine** on p. DI·32.	• Use the **Routine** on p. DI·33.

DAY 5

ELL Place English language learners in the groups that correspond to their reading abilities in English.

(i) Independent Activities

Fluency Reading Children reread selections at their independent level.

Journal Writing Write a story about a group of second graders who will ascend into space on a shuttle. Share writing.

Independent Reading See p. 42j for Reading/ Library activities and suggestions.

Literacy Centers You may use the Technology Center on p. 42k to support this week's concepts and reading.

Practice Book 2.1 Alphabetical Order: First Letter, p. 20

Break into small groups after Spelling and before Grammar and Writing.

ASSESS

- Decode long-vowel (CVCe) and c/s/, g/j/, and s/z/ words.
- Read high-frequency words.
- Read aloud with appropriate speed and accuracy.
- Identify main idea and details.
- Retell a story.

Differentiated Assessment

On-Level

Set B

Strategic Intervention

Set A

Advanced

Set C

Fluency Assessment Plan

☑ Week 1 assess Strategic Intervention students.

☑ **This week assess Advanced students.**

☐ Week 3 assess Strategic Intervention students.

☐ Week 4 assess On-Level students.

☐ Week 5 assess any students you have not yet checked during this unit.

Set individual fluency goals for children to enable them to reach the end-of-year goal.

- Current Goal: 50–60 wcpm
- End-of-Year Goal: 90 wcpm
- **ELL** An informal method of assessing oral reading fluency is to simply listen to a child reading orally and judge how clear the reading is.

SENTENCE READING

ASSESS LONG VOWELS (CVCe); c/s/, g/j/, s/z/; AND HIGH-FREQUENCY WORDS Use one of the reproducible lists on p. 66f to assess children's ability to read words with long vowels (CVCe); c/s/, g/j/, s/z/ and high-frequency words. Call on individuals to read two sentences aloud. Have each child in the group read different sentences. Start over with sentence one if necessary.

RECORD SCORES Use the Sentence Reading Chart for this unit on p. WA19.

Monitor Progress	Long Vowels (CVCe), c/s/, g/j/, s/z/
If... children have trouble reading words with long vowels and c/s/, g/j/, s/z/,	**then...** use the Reteach Lesson on p. DI·65.
High-Frequency Words	
If... children cannot read a high-frequency word,	**then...** mark the missed words on a high-frequency word list and send the list home for additional word reading practice, or have the child practice with a fluent reader.

FLUENCY AND COMPREHENSION

ASSESS FLUENCY Take a one-minute sample of children's oral reading. See Monitoring Fluency, p. WA17. Have children read "Going into Space," the on-level fluency passage on p. 66g.

RECORD SCORES Record the number of words read correctly in one minute on the child's Fluency Progress Chart.

ASSESS COMPREHENSION Have the child read to the end of the passage. (If the child had difficulty with the passage, you may read it aloud.) Ask whether the title of the story tells the main idea or just a detail about the main idea. Have the child retell the passage. Use the Retelling Rubric on p. 36–37 to evaluate the child's retelling.

Monitor Progress	Fluency
If... a child does not achieve the fluency goal on the timed reading,	**then...** copy the passage and send it home with the child for additional fluency practice, or have the child practice with a fluent reader.
Main Idea and Details	
If... a child cannot identify the main idea or supporting details,	**then...** use the Reteach Lesson on p. DI·65.

READ THE SENTENCES

Set A

1. The wise woman had lace on her dress.
2. Those machines move things.
3. That page shows the age of the woman.
4. Nice people live by that gate.
5. Work with a pencil in that space.
6. Roses grow everywhere in the city.

Set B

1. The sun rose as I drove to work.
2. We live by a nice ice rink.
3. My mom works at a place where lace is made.
4. The woman gave me a case of fake gems.
5. There is a huge machine in that place.
6. Those men moved the garbage.

Set C

1. I want to race in places all around the world.
2. Many people like to live in big cities.
3. Some people ride a train to work in the city.
4. The woman ran a fast race through the village.
5. Huge machines move big blocks of stone.
6. The wise woman teaches me how to make fine lace.

Monitor Progress Long Vowels (CVCe); c/s/, g/j/, s/z/
High-Frequency Words

SUCCESS
PREDICTOR

Going into Space

Do you want to go to new places? Do you like fast   12
rides? If you said yes to all these things, then you   23
can go into space. Some people who went into   32
space began planning for it when they were your   41
age. You can too.   45

You will need to go to school for a long time. You   57
will need to know about math. You will need to   67
know about the sun and the stars.   74

Before you go into space, you will find out how   84
machines in space work. You will know what to do if   95
something goes wrong. You might even take along   103
some mice to see how they do in space.   112

Who knows? Maybe one day you will pose in a   122
spacecraft for the news on TV!   128

See also Assessment Handbook, p. 304 • REPRODUCIBLE PAGE

Write Now
Writing and Grammar

List

Prompt

Exploring Space with an Astronaut tells about astronauts. Think about astronauts' jobs in space. Now write a list of sentences that tell what they do.

Writing Trait

Good **word choice** makes your list interesting to read.

Student Model

Bullets separate items on list.

Each item on list is a sentence.

Writer chooses clear words to explain tasks.

- Astronauts exercise to keep fit.
- Some astronauts pilot shuttles.
- Some astronauts do experiments.
- Many astronauts repair things.
- Astronauts walk in space.
- Astronauts enjoy a great view of Earth.

Writer's Checklist

- **Focus** Do all sentences tell about astronauts?
- **Organization** Are sentences written in list form?
- **Support** Does each sentence support the main idea?
- **Conventions** Are all words spelled correctly?

Grammar

Subjects

The **subject** of a sentence tells who or what does something.

An astronaut goes into space.

An astronaut is the subject of this sentence.

. . . .

Look at the sentences in the list. Write the subject of each sentence.

66

67

Writing and Grammar

LOOK AT THE PROMPT Read p. 66 aloud. Have children select and discuss key words or phrases in the prompt. *(astronauts' jobs, list of sentences that tell what they do)*

STRATEGIES TO DEVELOP WORD CHOICE Have children

- list words that can help readers see, hear, and feel what the astronauts are doing.

- look at their verbs and replace weak ones, such as *move,* with stronger verbs, such as *exercise.*

- rewrite any sentences that contain unneeded words.

  See Scoring Rubric on p. WA11. **Rubric** 4 3 2 1

HINTS FOR BETTER WRITING Read p. 67 aloud. Use the checklist to help children revise their lists. Discuss the grammar lesson. (Answers: *Astronauts, Some astronauts, Some astronauts, Many astronauts, Astronauts, Astronauts*) Have children make sure the sentences in their lists have subjects.

DAILY FIX-IT

9. That space suit is not my siz
That space suit is not my <u>size.</u>

10. my friend it will fit
<u>It will fit</u> my friend.

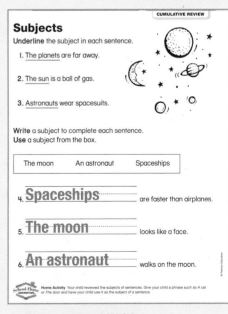

CUMULATIVE REVIEW

Subjects

Underline the subject in each sentence.

1. The planets are far away.

2. The sun is a ball of gas.

3. Astronauts wear spacesuits.

Write a subject to complete each sentence.
Use a subject from the box.

| The moon | An astronaut | Spaceships |

4. **Spaceships** ———— are faster than airplanes.

5. **The moon** ———— looks like a face.

6. **An astronaut** ———— walks on the moon.

Home Activity Your child reviewed the subjects of sentences. Give your child a phrase such as *A cat* or *The door* and have your child use it as the subject of a sentence.

▲ **Grammar and Writing Practice Book** p. 8

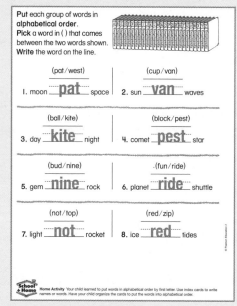

▲ **Practice Book 2.1** p. 20, Alphabetical Order

Research/Study Skills

TEACH/MODEL Alphabetical Order

MODEL USING ALPHABETICAL ORDER Recall with children the alphabet in sequence. You may want to provide children with a strip of paper with the alphabet on it as a reminder. Explain that the alphabet is used to organize many things. Words in a dictionary or glossary are listed in alphabetical, or ABC, order. Topics in an encyclopedia and names in a phone book are also listed in alphabetical order. This makes it easier to find things we need. Even fiction books in a library are organized in alphabetical order according to the last name of the authors.

Model how to use alphabetical order to the first letter to find a word in a dictionary.

 MODEL Let's look up the word *astronaut* in this dictionary. This word begins with the letter *a*, so I know we'll find it near the beginning of the dictionary. Here it is!

PUT WORDS IN ALPHABETICAL ORDER Give children the following word pairs and have them tell which word in each pair would come first in a dictionary.

everywhere	**live**
woman	**someone**
machine	**beautiful**

PRACTICE

DEMONSTRATE USING ALPHABETICAL ORDER Give pairs of children a copy of a children's dictionary or encyclopedia and a slip of paper with two or three topics on it. Have them look up each topic and write next to it the page number on which they found it. You may want to ask them to copy the topics in alphabetical order.

Wrap Up Your Week!

LET'S TALK ABOUT Exploration

QUESTION OF THE WEEK Recall this week's question.

• Why would anyone want to explore space?

Display the K-W-L chart that children began on Day 1. Review what children have already completed of the chart. Invite them to add more ideas to the What We **L**earned column. Suggest that they think of new questions to add to the What We **W**ant to Know column as they read other books about space.

What We **K**now	What We **W**ant to Know	What We **L**earned
Astronauts explore space.	What do astronauts want to find out in space?	Astronauts want to find out ways to live and work in space.
They go up in big rockets.	What is it like inside the shuttle?	Inside the space shuttle, astronauts float around.
They wear special suits.	How can I learn to be an astronaut?	A space shuttle takes off like a rocket, but it lands like an airplane.

CONNECT Use questions such as these to prompt a discussion:

• What happens when a space shuttle ascends and descends?

• Do you think astronauts always orbit Earth as they explore space? Why?

• Why is going into space such an enormous journey? How does it teach us about nature?

Build Background Use ELL Poster 3 to support the Preview activity.

You've learned **008** Amazing Words this week!	You've learned **016** Amazing Words so far this year!

PREVIEW Tell children that next week they will find out more about what people discover by exploring nature.

PREVIEW
Next Week

Assessment Checkpoints *for the Week*

Selection Assessment

Use pp. 5–8 of Selection Tests to check:

 Selection Understanding

 Comprehension Skill *Main Idea and Details*

 High–Frequency Words

everywhere	woman
live	work
machines	world
move	

ASSESSMENT

Scott Foresman
Selection Tests
Teacher's Manual

- Assess comprehension of weekly selections
- Assess understanding of weekly comprehension skills
- Assess knowledge of high-frequency words and selection vocabulary

Selection Tests

Reading STREET Grade 2

Leveled Assessment

- On-Level
- Strategic Intervention
- Advanced

Use pp. 7–12 of Fresh Reads for Differentiated Test Practice to check:

 Comprehension Skill *Main Idea and Details*

 REVIEW Comprehension Skill *Author's Purpose*

 Fluency *Words Correct Per Minute*

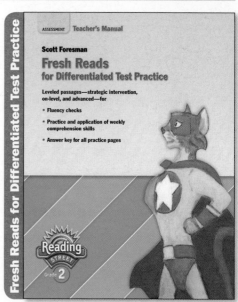

ASSESSMENT   Teacher's Manual

Scott Foresman
Fresh Reads
for Differentiated Test Practice

Leveled passages—strategic intervention, on-level, and advanced—for

- Fluency checks
- Practice and application of weekly comprehension skills
- Answer key for all practice pages

Fresh Reads for Differentiated Test Practice

Reading STREET Grade 2

Managing Assessment

Use Assessment Handbook for:

 Weekly Assessment Blackline Masters for Monitoring Progress

 Observation Checklists

 Record-Keeping Forms

 Portfolio Assessment

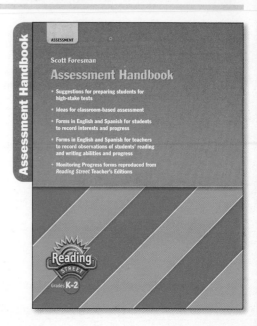

ASSESSMENT

Scott Foresman
Assessment Handbook

- Suggestions for preparing students for high-stake tests
- Ideas for classroom-based assessment
- Forms in English and Spanish for students to record interests and progress
- Forms in English and Spanish for teachers to record observations of students' reading and writing abilities and progress
- Monitoring Progress forms reproduced from *Reading Street* Teacher's Editions

Assessment Handbook

Reading STREET Grades K-2

Unit 1
Exploration

CONCEPT QUESTION

What can we learn from exploring new places and things?

EXPAND THE CONCEPT
What can we discover by exploring nature?

CONNECT THE CONCEPT

▶ **Build Background**

detective	identify	underneath
fascinating	slimy	wildlife
galaxy	tranquil	

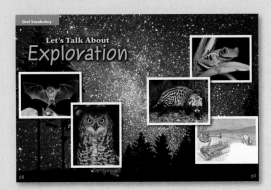

▶ **Science Content**
Living and Nonliving Things, Habitats, Day/Night Sky, Solar System/Stars, Senses

▶ **Writing**
A Story

Preview Your Week

What can we discover by exploring nature?

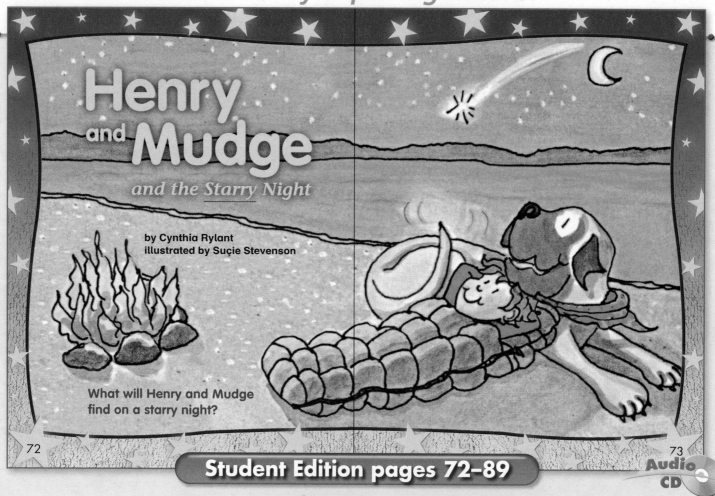

Henry and Mudge and the *Starry Night*

by Cynthia Rylant
illustrated by Suçie Stevenson

What will Henry and Mudge find on a starry night?

72

73

Student Edition pages 72–89

Audio CD

Genre	Realistic Fiction
◉ **Phonics**	Consonant Blends
◉ **Comprehension Skill**	Character and Setting
◉ **Comprehension Strategy**	Monitor and Fix Up

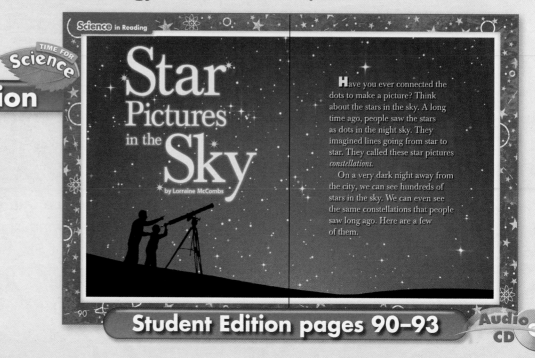

Science in Reading

TIME FOR Science

Paired Selection

Reading Across Texts
Viewing Constellations

Genre
Expository Nonfiction

Text Features
Captions

Star Pictures in the Sky by Lorraine McCombs

Have you ever connected the dots to make a picture? Think about the stars in the sky. A long time ago, people saw the stars as dots in the night sky. They imagined lines going from star to star. They called these star pictures *constellations*.

On a very dark night away from the city, we can see hundreds of stars in the sky. We can even see the same constellations that people saw long ago. Here are a few of them.

90

Student Edition pages 90–93

Audio CD

Read It
ONLINE
PearsonSuccessNet.com

- Student Edition
- Leveled Readers
- Decodable Reader

Leveled Readers

🎯 **Skill** Character and Setting
🎯 **Strategy** Monitor and Fix Up
Lesson Vocabulary

Below-Level

On-Level

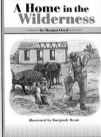

Advanced

ELL Reader

· Concept Vocabulary
· Text Support
· Language Enrichment

Decodable Reader

Apply Phonics

· On Stage

Integrate Science Standards

- Living/Nonliving Things
- Habitats
- Day and Night Sky
- Solar System/Stars
- Senses

✓ **Read**

Henry and Mudge and the Starry Night pp. 72–89

"Star Pictures in the Sky" pp. 90–93

✓ **Read**

Leveled Readers

Below-Level **On-Level** **Advanced**

- Support Concepts
- Develop Concepts
- Extend Concepts
- Science Extension Activity

✓ **Read**

ELL Reader

✓ **Build Concept Vocabulary**
Exploration, pp. 68r, 68–69

✓ **Teach Science Concepts**
Forest Animals, p. 82–83
Stars, p. 90–91

✓ **Explore Science Center**
Draw a Constellation, p. 68k

Weekly Plan

READING

90–120 minutes

TARGET SKILLS OF THE WEEK

- **Phonics**
  Consonant Blends
- **Comprehension Skill**
  Character and Setting
- **Comprehension Strategy**
  Monitor and Fix Up

DAY 1   PAGES 68l–69d

Oral Language

QUESTION OF THE WEEK, 68l
What can we discover by exploring nature?

Oral Vocabulary/Share Literature, 68m
Sing with Me Big Book, Song 3
Amazing Words *galaxy, tranquil, wildlife*

Word Work

Phonics, 68n–68o
   Introduce Consonant Blends **T**

Spelling, 68p
Pretest

Comprehension/Vocabulary/Fluency

Read Decodable Reader 3

Grouping Options 68f–68g

Review High-Frequency Words
Check Comprehension
Reread for Fluency

Build Background, 68r–69
Exploration

Listening Comprehension, 69a–69b
   Character and Setting **T**

DAY 2   PAGES 70a–87c

Oral Language

QUESTION OF THE DAY, 70a
What do people do when they go camping?

Oral Vocabulary/Share Literature, 70b
Big Book *In the Forest*
Amazing Word *underneath*

Word Work

Phonics, 70c–70d
   Review Consonant Blends **T**

Spelling, 70d
Dictation

Comprehension/Vocabulary/Fluency

Read *Henry and Mudge and the Starry Night,*
70e–87a

Grouping Options
68f–68g

Introduce High-Frequency
   Words *bear, build, couldn't,*
   father, love, mother,
   straight **T**
Introduce Selection Words
   drooled, lanterns, shivered,
   snuggled

   Character and
   Setting **T**
   Monitor and Fix Up
REVIEW Realism and
   Fantasy **T**

Reread for Fluency

LANGUAGE ARTS

20–30 minutes

Trait of the Week

Word Choice

Shared Writing, 69c
Story

Grammar, 69d
Introduce Predicates **T**

Interactive Writing, 87b
Letter

Grammar, 87c
Practice Predicates **T**

DAILY JOURNAL WRITING

Day 1 *List activities that make you feel tranquil.*

Day 2 *Write about what you might see and feel while camping outside overnight.*

DAILY SCIENCE CONNECTIONS

Day 1 Exploring Nature Concept Web, 68r–69

Day 2 Time for Science: Forest Animals, 82–83

DAILY SUCCESS PREDICTORS
for Adequate Yearly Progress

Monitor Progress and Corrective Feedback

Phonics
Check Word Reading, *68o*
Spiral REVIEW Phonics

Fluency
Check High-Frequency Words, *71a*
Spiral REVIEW High-Frequency Words

RESOURCES FOR THE WEEK

- Practice Book 2.1, *pp. 21–30*
- Phonics and Spelling Practice Book, *pp. 9–12*
- Grammar and Writing Practice Book, *pp. 9–12*
- Selection Test, *pp. 9–12*

- Fresh Reads for Differentiated Test Practice, *pp. 13–18*
- Phonics Songs and Rhymes Chart 3
- The Grammar and Writing Book, *pp. 62–67*

Grouping Options for Differentiated Instruction

Turn the page for the small group lesson plan.

DAY 3 — PAGES 88a–89b

Oral Language

QUESTION OF THE DAY, 88a
What else can we discover by exploring nature in the forest?

Oral Vocabulary/Share Literature, 88b
Big Book *In the Forest*
Amazing Word *identify*

Word Work

Phonics, 88c
REVIEW Long Vowels CVCe **T**

High-Frequency Words, 88d
Practice *bear, build, couldn't, father, love, mother, straight* **T**

Spelling, 88d
Practice

Comprehension/Vocabulary/Fluency

Vocabulary, 88e
Synonyms

Read *Henry and Mudge and the Starry Night,* 72–89

Grouping Options 68f–68g

Fluency, 88f
Read with Accuracy/Appropriate Pace

Think and Share, 88g

Trait of the Week, 89a
Introduce Word Choice

Grammar, 89b
Write with Predicates **T**

Day 3 *Use synonyms in pairs of sentences about going camping.*

Day 3 *Exploring Nature Concept Web, 89b*

DAY 4 — PAGES 90a–93d

Oral Language

QUESTION OF THE DAY, 90a
How do stars make pictures in the sky?

Oral Vocabulary/Share Literature, 90b
Read Aloud Anthology *Insects Are My Life*
Amazing Words *detective, fascinating, slimy*

Word Work

Phonics, 90c
REVIEW Sentence Reading **T**

Spelling, 90d
Partner Review

Comprehension/Vocabulary/Fluency

Read "Star Pictures in the Sky," 90–93
Leveled Readers

Grouping Options 68f–68g

Synonyms
Reading Across Texts

Fluency, 93a
Read with Accuracy/Appropriate Pace

Writing Across the Curriculum, 93b
Captioned Drawing

Grammar, 93c
Review Predicates **T**

Speaking and Listening, 93d
Be a Good Speaker

Day 4 *List wildlife in a park or your backyard.*

Day 4 *Time for Science: Stars, 90–91*

DAY 5 — PAGES 94a–95b

Oral Language

QUESTION OF THE DAY, 94a
If we looked underneath rocks, could we identify fascinating insects?

Oral Vocabulary/Share Literature, 94b
Read Aloud Anthology *Insects Are My Life*
Amazing Words Review

Word Work

Phonics, 94c
Review Consonant Blends **T**

High-Frequency Words, 94c
Review *bear, build, couldn't, father, love, mother, straight* **T**

Spelling, 94d
Test

Comprehension/Vocabulary/Fluency

Read Leveled Readers

Grouping Options 68f–68g

Monitor Progress, 94e–94g
Read the Sentences
Read the Story

Writing and Grammar, 94–95
Develop Word Choice
Use Predicates **T**

Research/Study Skills, 95a
Parts of a Book

Day 5 *Write about traveling through the galaxy.*

Day 5 *Revisit the Exploring Nature Concept Web, 95b*

KEY 🎯 = Target Skill **T** = Tested Skill

Comprehension — Check Retelling, *88g*

Fluency — Check Fluency WCPM, *93a*
Spiral **REVIEW** Phonics, High-Frequency Words

Oral Vocabulary — Check Oral Vocabulary, *94b*
Assess Phonics, High-Frequency Words, Fluency, Comprehension, *94e*

SUCCESS PREDICTOR

Small Group Plan *for Differentiated Instruction*

Daily Plan
AT A GLANCE

Reading
Whole Group
- Oral Language
- Word Work
- Comprehension/Vocabulary

Group Time

Meet with small groups to provide:
- Skill Support
- Reading Support
- Fluency Practice

Read

This week's lessons for daily group time can be found behind the Differentiated Instruction (DI) tab on pp. DI·34–DI·43.

Whole Group
- Comprehension/Vocabulary
- Fluency

Language Arts
- Writing
- Grammar
- Speaking/Listening/Viewing
- Research/Study Skills

Use *My Sidewalks on Reading Street* for Tier III intensive reading intervention.

DAY 1

On-Level	Strategic Intervention	Advanced
Teacher-Led *Page 68q*	**Teacher-Led** *Page DI·34*	**Teacher-Led** *Page DI·35*
• **Read** Decodable Reader 3 • **Reread** for Fluency	• Blend Words with Consonant Blends • **Read** Decodable Reader 3 • **Reread** for Fluency	• Extend Word Reading • **Read** Advanced Selection 3 • Introduce Concept Inquiry

i Independent Activities

While you meet with small groups, have the rest of the class...

- Reread for fluency
- Write in their journals
- Read self-selected reading
- Visit the Word Work Center
- Complete Practice Book 2.1, pp. 23–24

DAY 2

On-Level	Strategic Intervention	Advanced
Teacher-Led *Pages 72–87*	**Teacher-Led** *Page DI·36*	**Teacher-Led** *Page DI·37*
• **Read** *Henry and Mudge and the Starry Night* • **Reread** for Fluency	• Blend Words with Consonant Blends • **Read** SI Decodable Reader 3 • **Read** or Listen to *Henry and Mudge and the Starry Night*	• **Read** *Henry and Mudge and the Starry Night* • Continue Concept Inquiry

i Independent Activities

While you meet with small groups, have the rest of the class...

- Read self-selected reading
- Write in their journals
- Visit the Listening Center
- Complete Practice Book 2.1, pp. 25–27

DAY 3

On-Level	Strategic Intervention	Advanced
Teacher-Led *Pages 72–87*	**Teacher-Led** *Page DI·38*	**Teacher-Led** *Page DI·39*
• **Read** *Henry and Mudge and the Starry Night*	• **Reread** *Henry and Mudge and the Starry Night* • Read Words and Sentences • Review Character and Setting and Monitor and Fix Up • **Reread** for Fluency	• Self-Selected Reading • Continue Concept Inquiry

i Independent Activities

While you meet with small groups, have the rest of the class...

- Read self-selected reading
- Write in their journals
- Visit the Writing Center
- Complete Practice Book 2.1, pp. 28–29

① Begin with whole class skill and strategy instruction.

② Meet with small groups to provide differentiated instruction.

③ Gather the whole class back together for fluency and language arts.

DAY 4

On-Level
Teacher-Led
Pages 90–93, LR22–LR24
- **Read** "Star Pictures in the Sky"
- Practice with On-Level Reader *Let's Camp at Crescent Lake*

Strategic Intervention
Teacher-Led
Pages DI · 40, LR19–LR21
- **Read** or Listen to "Star Pictures in the Sky"
- **Reread** for Fluency
- Build Concepts
- Practice with Below-Level Reader *Pup Camps Out*

Advanced
Teacher-Led
Pages DI · 41, LR25–LR27
- **Read** "Star Pictures in the Sky"
- Extend Vocabulary
- Continue Concept Inquiry
- Practice with Advanced Reader *A Home in the Wilderness*

ⓘ Independent Activities

While you meet with small groups, have the rest of the class...

- Reread for fluency
- Write in their journals
- Read self-selected reading
- Review spelling words with a partner
- Visit the Listening and Science Centers

DAY 5

On-Level
Teacher-Led
Pages 94e–94g, LR22–LR24
- Sentence Reading, Set B
- Monitor Fluency and Comprehension
- Practice with On-Level Reader *Let's Camp at Crescent Lake*

Strategic Intervention
Teacher-Led
Pages DI · 42, LR19–LR21
- Practice Word Reading
- Sentence Reading, Set A
- Monitor Comprehension
- Practice with Below-Level Reader *Pup Camps Out*

Advanced
Teacher-Led
Pages DI · 43, LR25–LR27
- Sentence Reading, Set C
- Monitor Comprehension
- Share Concept Inquiry
- Practice with Advanced Reader *A Home in the Wilderness*

ⓘ Independent Activities

While you meet with small groups, have the rest of the class...

- Reread for fluency
- Write in their journals
- Read self-selected reading
- Visit the Technology Center
- Complete Practice Book 2.1, p. 30

Grouping Place English language learners in the groups that correspond to their reading abilities in English.

Use the appropriate Leveled Reader or other text at children's instructional level.

TIP Send home the appropriate Multilingual Summary of the main selection on Day 1.

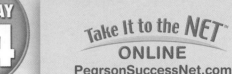
Take It to the NET
ONLINE
PearsonSuccessNet.com

Connie Juel
For ideas and activities on anchored vocabulary instruction, see the article "Making Words Stick" by Scott Foresman authors C. Juel and R. Deffes.

TEACHER TALK

A **consonant blend** is two or more consonants whose sounds are blended together, such as the *tr* in *train*.

Looking Ahead

Be sure to schedule time for children to work on the unit inquiry project "Take a Trip." This week children should draw a map to show how they would travel to the place they are exploring and make a list of things they would need to take.

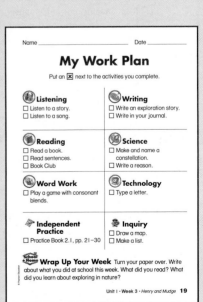
Name _____ Date _____
My Work Plan
Put an ☒ next to the activities you complete.

🎧 Listening
☐ Listen to a story.
☐ Listen to a song.

✏️ Writing
☐ Write an exploration story.
☐ Write in your journal.

📖 Reading
☐ Read a book.
☐ Read sentences.
☐ Book Club

🔬 Science
☐ Make and name a constellation.
☐ Write a reason.

Word Work
☐ Play a game with consonant blends.

💻 Technology
☐ Type a letter.

✍️ Independent Practice
☐ Practice Book 2.1, pp. 21–30

📋 Inquiry
☐ Draw a map.
☐ Make a list.

Wrap Up Your Week Turn your paper over. Write about what you did at school this week. What did you read? What did you learn about exploring in nature?

Unit 1 · Week 3 · *Henry and Mudge* **19**

▲ **Group-Time Survival Guide**
p. 19, Weekly Contract

Henry and Mudge **68g**

Customize Your Plan *by Strand*

ORAL LANGUAGE

 Science

Concept Development

What can we discover by exploring nature?

 *to build oral vocabulary*

detective   fascinating   galaxy
identify   slimy   tranquil
underneath   wildlife

BUILD

☐ **Question of the Week** Use the Morning Warm-Up! to introduce and discuss the question of the week. This week children will talk, sing, read, and write about what else we can discover by exploring nature. DAY 1 *68l*

☐ **Sing with Me Big Book** Sing a song about camping and looking at stars. Ask children to listen for the concept-related Amazing Words *galaxy, tranquil, wildlife.* DAY 1 *68m*

Sing with Me Big Book

☐ **Let's Talk About Exploration** Use the Let's Talk About It lesson in the Student Edition to build background, vocabulary, and concepts. Then create a concept chart for children to add to throughout the week. DAY 1 *68r-69*

Let's Talk About It

DEVELOP

☐ **Question of the Day** Use the questions in the Morning Warm-Ups! to discuss lesson concepts and how they relate to the unit theme, Exploration. DAY 2 *70a*, DAY 3 *88a*, DAY 4 *90a*, DAY 5 *94a*

☐ **Share Literature** Read big books and read aloud selections that develop concepts, language, and vocabulary related to the lesson concept and the unit theme. Continue to develop this week's Amazing Words. DAY 2 *70b*, DAY 3 *88b*, DAY 4 *90b*, DAY 5 *94b*

CONNECT

☐ **Wrap Up Your Week!** Revisit the Question of the Week. Then connect concepts and vocabulary to next week's lesson. DAY 5 *95b*

CHECK

☐ **Check Oral Vocabulary** To informally assess children's oral vocabulary, ask individuals to use some of this week's Amazing Words to tell you about the illustration and photographs on Student Edition pp. 68–69. DAY 5 *94b*

PHONICS

 CONSONANT BLENDS Consonant blends consist of two or more letters whose sounds are blended together when pronouncing a word.

TEACH

☐ **Consonant Blends** Introduce the blending strategy for words with consonant blends. Then have children blend and build words with consonant blends. DAY 1 *68n-68o*

☐ **Fluent Word Reading** Use the Fluent Word Reading Routine to develop children's word reading fluency. Use the Phonics Songs and Rhymes Chart for additional word reading practice. DAY 2 *70c-70d*

Phonics Songs and Rhymes Chart 3

PRACTICE/APPLY

☐ **Decodable Reader 3** Practice reading words with consonant blends in context. DAY 1 *68q*

☐ *Henry and Mudge and the Starry Night* Practice decoding words in context. DAY 2 *72-87*

Decodable Reader 3

☐ **Homework** Practice Book 2.1 p. 23. DAY 1 *68o*

☐ **Word Work Center** Practice consonant blends. **ANY DAY** *68j*

Main Selection—Fiction

RETEACH/REVIEW

☐ **Review** Review words with this week's phonics skills. DAY 5 *94c*

☐ **Reteach Lessons** If necessary, reteach consonant blends. DAY 5 *DI-66*

☐ **Spiral REVIEW** Review previously taught phonics skills. DAY 1 *68o*

ASSESS

☐ **Sentence Reading** Assess children's ability to read words with consonant blends. DAY 5 *94e-94f*

① Use assessment data to determine your instructional focus.

② Preview this week's instruction by strand.

③ Choose instructional activities that meet the needs of your classroom.

SPELLING

CONSONANT BLENDS Consonant blends consist of two or more letters whose sounds are blended together when pronouncing a word.

TEACH

☐ **Pretest** Before administering the pretest, model how to segment words with consonant blends to spell them. Dictate the spelling words, segmenting them if necessary. Then have children check their pretests and correct misspelled words. DAY 1 68p

PRACTICE/APPLY

☐ **Dictation** Have children write dictation sentences to practice spelling words. DAY 2 70d

☐ **Write Words** Have children practice writing the spelling words by using rhyming clues. DAY 3 88d

☐ **Homework** Phonics and Spelling Practice Book pp. 9–12. DAY 1 68p, DAY 2 70d, DAY 3 88d, DAY 4 90d

RETEACH/REVIEW

☐ **Partner Review** Have pairs work together to read and write the spelling words. DAY 4 90d

ASSESS

☐ **Posttest** Use dictation sentences to give the posttest for words with consonant blends. DAY 5 94d

Spelling Words

Consonant Blends

1. stop
2. strap*
3. nest
4. hand*
5. brave
6. ask
7. clip
8. stream*
9. mask
10. twin
11. breeze
12. state

Challenge Words

13. browse
14. straight
15. skeleton

* Words from the Selection

HIGH-FREQUENCY WORDS

WORDS TO READ

bear	build	couldn't	father
love	mother	straight	

TEACH

☐ **Words to Read** Introduce this week's high-frequency words and add them to the Word Wall. DAY 2 70-71a

High-Frequency Words

PRACTICE/APPLY

☐ **Words in Context** Read high-frequency words in the context of *Henry and Mudge and the Starry Night.* DAY 2 72-87

Main Selection—Fiction

☐ **Word Wall** Use the Word Wall to review and practice high-frequency words throughout the week. DAY 3 88d, DAY 5 94c

☐ **Leveled Text** Practice this week's high-frequency words in the context of leveled text. DAY 4 LR19-LR27, DAY 5 LR19-27

Leveled Readers

☐ **Homework** Practice Book 2.1 pp. 26, 29. DAY 2 71a, DAY 3 88d

RETEACH/REVIEW

☐ **Spiral REVIEW** Review previously taught high-frequency words. DAY 2 71a, DAY 4 90c

ASSESS

☐ **Sentence Reading** Assess children's ability to read this week's high-frequency words. DAY 5 94e-94f

VOCABULARY

TEACH

☐ **Vocabulary Transparency 3** Use Vocabulary Transparency 3 to introduce the selection words from *Henry and Mudge and the Starry Night.* Children will read these words but will not be tested on them. DAY 2 72a

☐ **Synonyms** Have children expand selection words by thinking of synonyms for *shivered, lanterns,* and *snuggled.* DAY 3 88e

COMPREHENSION

SKILL CHARACTER AND SETTING Characters are the people or animals in a story. The setting is where and when a story takes place.

STRATEGY MONITOR AND FIX UP To monitor means to stop occasionally and check to be sure you understand what you are reading. Fix up means to do something if you do not understand or are confused about what you are reading. For example, you can reread or read on.

TEACH

☐ **Listening Comprehension** Read "Just a Little Practice" and model how to identify the *character and setting*. DAY 1 69a-69b

☐ **Skill/Strategy Lesson** Review how to identify the *character and setting*. Then introduce this week's strategy, *monitor and fix up*. DAY 2 70e

PRACTICE/APPLY

☐ **Skills and Strategies in Context** Read *Henry and Mudge and the Starry Night*, using the Guiding Comprehension questions to apply *character and setting* and *monitor and fix up*. DAY 2 72-87a

Main Selection—Fiction

☐ **Think and Share** Use the questions on Student Edition p. 88 to discuss the selection. DAY 3 88g-89

Paired Selection—Nonfiction

☐ **Skills and Strategies in Context** Read "Star Pictures in the Sky," guiding children as they apply skills and strategies. After reading have children make connections across texts. DAY 4 90-93

☐ **Leveled Text** Apply *character and setting* and *monitor and fix up* to read leveled text. DAY 4 LR19–LR27, DAY 5 LR19–LR27

Leveled Readers

☐ **Homework** Practice Book 2.1 p. 24. DAY 1 69a

ASSESS

☐ **Selection Test** Determine children's understanding of the main selection and assess their ability to identify *character and setting*. DAY 3

☐ **Story Reading** Have children read the passage "A World in the City." Ask what the *character and setting* of the story are and have them retell. DAY 5 94e-94g

RETEACH/REVIEW

☐ **Reteach Lesson** If necessary, reteach *character and setting*. DAY 5 DI·66

FLUENCY

SKILL READ WITH ACCURACY/APPROPRIATE PACE You adjust your reading pace based on what you are reading. Sometimes you must slow down to read each word accurately.

REREAD FOR FLUENCY

☐ **Oral Rereading** Have children read orally from Decodable Reader 3 or another text at their independent reading level. Listen as children read and provide corrective feedback regarding their oral reading and their use of the blending strategy. DAY 1 68q

☐ **Paired Reading** Have pairs of children read orally from the main selection or another text at their independent reading level and apply their knowledge of reading with accuracy and at an appropriate pace. Listen as children read and provide corrective feedback regarding oral reading and their use of the blending strategy. DAY 2 87a

TEACH

☐ **Model** Use passages from *Henry and Mudge and the Starry Night* to model reading with accuracy/appropriate pace. DAY 3 88f, DAY 4 93a

PRACTICE/APPLY

☐ **Choral Reading** Choral read passages from *Henry and Mudge and the Starry Night*. Monitor progress and provide feedback regarding children's reading with accuracy/appropriate pace. DAY 3 88f

☐ **Paired Reading** Have partners read passages from *Henry and Mudge and the Starry Night*, switching readers at the end of each page. Monitor progress and provide feedback regarding children's reading with accuracy/appropriate pace. DAY 4 93a

☐ **Listening Center** Have children follow along with the AudioText for this week's selections. ANY DAY 68j

☐ **Reading/Library Center** Have children build fluency by rereading Leveled Readers, Decodable Readers, or other text at their independent level. ANY DAY 68j

☐ **Fluency Coach** Have children use Fluency Coach to listen to fluent reading or to practice reading on their own. ANY DAY

ASSESS

☐ **Story Reading** Take a one-minute timed sample of children's oral reading. Use the passage "A World in the City." DAY 5 94e-94g

WRITING

Trait of the Week

WORD CHOICE Good words make your writing more interesting. Use exact nouns, strong verbs, and exciting adjectives to make your writing interesting, clear, and lively.

TEACH

☐ **Write Together** Engage children in writing activities that develop language, grammar, and writing skills. Include independent writing as an extension of group writing activities.

> **Shared Writing** DAY 1 *69c*
> **Interactive Writing** DAY 2 *87b*
> **Writing Across the Curriculum** DAY 4 *93b*

☐ **Trait of the Week** Introduce and model the Trait of the Week, *word choice*. DAY 3 *89a*

PRACTICE/APPLY

☐ **Write Now** Examine the model on Student Edition pp. 94–95. Then have children write stories. DAY 5 *94-95*

> **Prompt** In *Henry and Mudge*, a family camps in the woods. Think about a fun outdoor place. Now write a story that tells about something that happens at this place.

Write Now

☐ **Daily Journal Writing** Have children write about concepts and literature in their journals. **EVERY DAY** *68d-68e*

☐ **Writing Center** Have children write sentences about their discovery on an outdoor adventure. **ANY DAY** *68k*

ASSESS

☐ **Scoring Rubric** Use a rubric to evaluate children's stories. DAY 5 *94-95*

RETEACH/REVIEW

☐ **The Grammar and Writing Book** Use pp. 62–67 of The Grammar and Writing Book to extend instruction. **ANY DAY**

The Grammar and Writing Book

SPEAKING AND LISTENING

TEACH

☐ **Be a Good Speaker** Demonstrate good speaking skills. Then draw a web and have children demonstrate how to be a good speaker as they add information to the web about exploring nature. DAY 4 *93d*

GRAMMAR

SKILL PREDICATES The predicate tells what the subject of a sentence does or is.

TEACH

☐ **Grammar Transparency 3** Use Grammar Transparency 3 to teach *predicates*. DAY 1 *69d*

Grammar Transparency 3

PRACTICE/APPLY

☐ **Develop the Concept** Review the concept of *predicates* and provide guided practice. DAY 2 *87c*

☐ **Apply to Writing** Have children use predicates in writing. DAY 3 *89b*

☐ **Define/Practice** Review the definition of *predicates*. Then have children identify predicates. DAY 4 *93c*

☐ **Write Now** Discuss the grammar lesson on Student Edition p. 95. Have children use predicates in their own stories about something that happens at an outdoor place. DAY 5 *94-95*

Write Now

☐ **Daily Fix-It** Have children find and correct errors in grammar, spelling, and punctuation. DAY 1 *69d*, DAY 2 *87c*, DAY 3 *89b*, DAY 4 *93c*, DAY 5 *94-95*

☐ **Homework** The Grammar and Writing Practice Book pp. 9–12. DAY 2 *87c*, DAY 3 *89b*, DAY 4 *93c*, DAY 5 *94-95*

RETEACH/REVIEW

☐ **The Grammar and Writing Book** Use pp. 62–65 of The Grammar and Writing Book to extend instruction. **ANY DAY**

The Grammar and Writing Book

RESEARCH/INQUIRY

TEACH

☐ **Parts of a Book** Model using parts of a book. Then have partners locate parts of a book and record on to a chart. DAY 5 *95a*

☐ **Unit Inquiry Project** Allow time for children to draw a map to show how they would travel to the place they are exploring and make a list of things they would need to take. **ANY DAY** *11*

Resources for
Differentiated Instruction

LEVELED READERS

▶ **Comprehension**
  - 🎯 **Skill** Character/Setting
  - 🎯 **Strategy** Monitor/Fix Up

▶ **Lesson Vocabulary**

High-Frequency Words

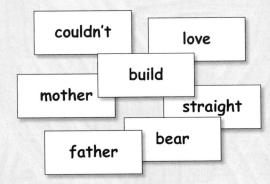

couldn't | love | build | mother | straight | father | bear

▶ **Science Standards**

- **Living and Nonliving Things**
- **Habitats**
- **Day and Night Sky**
- **Solar System/Stars**
- **Senses**

Leveled Reader Database ONLINE

PearsonSuccessNet.com

Use the Online Database of over 600 books to

- Download and print additional copies of this week's leveled readers
- Listen to the readers being read online
- Search for more titles focused on this week's skills, topic, and content

---

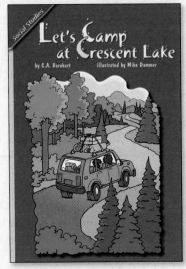

On-Level Reader

Character and Setting

Read each sentence below.
Circle the answer that best completes each sentence.

1. In the beginning of the story, Mother wants to
   a. read the newspaper. (b.) plan a trip. c. go back to bed.

2. The family camped
   a. in the desert. b. near the beach. (c.) in the forest.

3. Father was
   (a.) helpful. b. sad. c. tired.

4. In the story, Mother
   a. drove the car. (b.) read the map. c. saw a bear.

5. Write three things that Jean liked. Possible responses given.

   pancakes, the beach, building
   sand castles

🎯 **On-Level Practice** TE p. LR23

Vocabulary

Draw a line to match each word on the left with the word or words on the right that mean the opposite.

1. build   a. hate
2. couldn't   b. mother
3. father   c. was able to
4. love   d. tear down

Write each word from the box to best complete the sentence.

Words to Know
bear   mother   straight

5. The little **bear** cub walked
   straight up to Jean's
   mother

🎯 **On-Level Practice** TE p. LR24

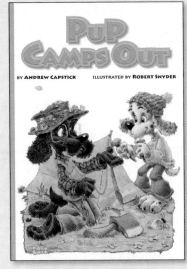

Below-Level Reader

Character and Setting

Read each sentence below. Then circle the answer that best completes each sentence.

1. When Pup asked Father Dog to teach him, he was by the
   a. car. (b.) tent. c. house.

2. The story happened
   a. at night. b. 100 years ago. (c.) in the present day.

3. Mother Dog
   (a.) likes to camp. b. stayed at home. c. is reading a book.

4. Father Dog is
   (a.) wise. b. forgetful. c. angry.

5. Write a sentence about Pup. Possible responses given.

   Pup likes to camp.

🎯 **Below-Level Practice** TE p. LR20

Vocabulary

Draw a line from each word at the left to the word or words at the right that mean the same.

1. build   a. dad
2. father   b. care about
3. love   c. mom
4. mother   d. make

Complete the sentence using the words from the box.

Words to Know
bear   couldn't   straight

5. The big **bear** was strong, but he **couldn't**
   run in a **straight** line.

🎯 **Below-Level Practice** TE p. LR21

Advanced

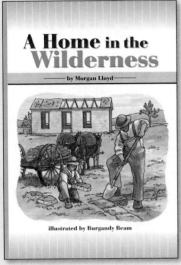

Advanced Reader

Character and Setting

Answer these questions about Jeremiah.

Possible responses given.

1. Where did he live?

in the wilderness; in Nebraska

2. When did he live?

back when people were moving

west in wagons

3. What did he do? What happened to him?

heard a coyote; helped Papa work;

worked in garden; saw a tornado;

found chicken eggs for Ruthie

4. How did he feel about Ruthie?

He cared for her; he helped take

care of her when she was sick.

Advanced Practice TE p. LR26

Vocabulary

Choose the best word from the box to complete each sentence.

Words to Know		
galaxy	tranquil	wildlife

1. Many kinds of **wildlife** , such as prairie chickens, coyotes, and rabbits, lived on the prairie.

2. On summer nights, the prairie was quiet and

tranquil

3. All the stars in the **galaxy** glowed in the night sky.

Write a sentence about life on the prairie. Use a vocabulary word in your sentence.

Responses will vary.

Advanced Practice TE p. LR27

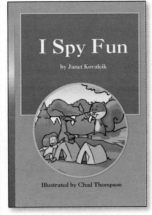

ELL Reader

ELL Poster 3

Teacher's Edition Notes

ELL notes throughout this lesson support instruction and reference additional resources at point of use.

ELL Teaching Guide pp. 15–21, 216–217

- Multilingual summaries of the main selection
- Comprehension lesson
- Vocabulary strategies and word cards
- ELL Reader 3 lesson

ELL and Transition Handbook

Ten Important Sentences

- Key ideas from every selection in the Student Edition
- Activities to build sentence power

More Reading

Readers' Theater Anthology

- Fluency practice
- Five scripts to build fluency
- Poetry for oral interpretation

Leveled Trade Books

- Extend reading tied to the unit concept
- Lessons in Trade Book Library Teaching Guide

School + Home

Homework

- Family Times Newsletter
- ELL Multilingual Selection Summaries

Take-Home Books

- Decodable Readers
- Leveled Readers

Henry and Mudge

Literacy Centers

Listening

Let's Read Along

MATERIALS `SINGLES`
CD player, headphones, print copies of recorded pieces

LISTEN TO LITERATURE As children listen to the following recordings, have them follow along or read along in the print version.

AudioText
Henry and Mudge and the Starry Night
"Star Pictures in the Sky"

Sing with Me/Background Building Audio "Tranquil Nights"

Phonics Songs and Rhymes Audio "Nature's Creatures"

Nature's Creatures

What can we discover outdoors?
What creatures can we see?
A flock of crows, a little black ant—
They interest me.

A bluebird nest, a screeching gray owl,
A pond with croaking frogs.
Snakes that like to sun themselves,
Stretched out on logs.

Audio CD **Phonics Songs and Rhymes Chart 3**

Reading/Library

Read It Again!

MATERIALS `SINGLES` `PAIRS` `GROUPS`
collection of books for self-selected reading, reading logs

REREAD BOOKS Have children select previously read books from the appropriate book box and record titles of books they read in their logs. Use these previously read books:

- Decodable Readers
- Leveled Readers
- ELL Readers
- Stories written by classmates
- Books from the library

TEN IMPORTANT SENTENCES Have children read the Ten Important Sentences for *Henry and Mudge* and locate the sentences in the Student Edition.

BOOK CLUB Ask children to discuss *Henry and Mudge and the Starry Night*. Have them tell what they liked and did not like about the story.

Word Work

Starry Night

MATERIALS `GROUPS`
15 cut-out paper stars, posterboard of night sky

CONSONANT BLENDS Have groups place stars in the sky.

1. Cut out fifteen paper stars and write a word with a consonant blend on each.
2. Place a cut-out moon on a dark-colored posterboard.
3. Scatter the stars facedown. Children take turns choosing a star, reading the word, and placing the star in the sky.
4. Continue until all stars have been placed.

 Phonics Activities CD This interactive CD provides additional practice.

Scott Foresman Reading Street Centers Survival Kit

Use the *Henry and Mudge and the Starry Night* materials from the Reading Street Centers Survival Kit to organize this week's centers.

Writing

What Did You Discover?

MATERIALS [SINGLES]
paper, pencils, crayons, markers, old magazines

WRITE AN EXPLORATION STORY Ask children to recall a time when they explored the outdoors as Henry and Mudge did when they went camping.

1. Have children think about something they discovered.
2. Tell them to write several sentences about their discovery.
3. Encourage children to illustrate their sentences by drawing pictures or using pictures from magazines.

LEVELED WRITING Encourage children to write at their own ability level. Some may have trouble with organization and transitions. Others will organize their writing logically but might need improvement with transitions. Your best writers will write logically with transitions.

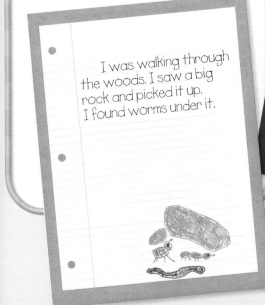

I was walking through the woods. I saw a big rock and picked it up. I found worms under it.

Science

Seeing Stars

MATERIALS [SINGLES]
pencils, paper, crayons

MY CONSTELLATION Briefly review "Star Pictures in the Sky" with children.

1. Have each child draw dots to stand for stars and draw lines to connect some of the dots to make a new constellation.
2. Tell children to name their constellation and write an explanation for their choice.

I named this Buster for my dog.

Technology

Starry Sky

MATERIALS [SINGLES] [PAIRS]
computer, printer, paper

PRINT A LETTER Children discuss what they have learned about constellations.

1. Have children turn on the computer and open a word processing document.
2. Provide a letter format model and have children refer to it as they type a letter to a family member about constellations.
3. If possible, have children print out their letters to take home.

Dear Mom and Dad,
I learned about sky pictures made of stars. One is Big Bear and one is Little Bear.
Love, Mark

(ALL CENTERS)

Oral Vocabulary
"Tranquil Nights" 3

Phonics and Spelling
Consonant Blends
Spelling Pretest:
 Words with Consonant Blends

Read Apply Phonics [Word Wall]
[Group Time] < Differentiated Instruction

Build Background
Let's Talk About Exploration

Listening Comprehension
Skill Character and Setting

Shared Writing
Story

Grammar
Predicates

Materials

• *Sing with Me Big Book*
• Sound-Spelling Cards 5 and 30
• Letter Tiles
• Decodable Reader 3
• Student Edition 68–69
• Graphic Organizer 15
• Writing Transparency 3
• Grammar Transparency 3

Take It to the NET
ONLINE

Professional Development
To learn more about phonics, go to PearsonSuccessNet.com and read "Saying the 'P' Word" by S. Stahl.

Morning Warm-Up!

We can learn about animals everywhere in the world.

We can learn how stars move in the sky.

What else can we discover by exploring nature?

QUESTION OF THE WEEK Tell children they will talk, sing, read, and write about what else we can discover by exploring nature. Write and read the message and discuss the question.

CONNECT CONCEPTS Ask questions to connect to the previous Unit 1 selections.

• Did Iris and Walter explore nature? What do you think they discovered?

• What have astronauts discovered by exploring nature?

REVIEW HIGH-FREQUENCY WORDS

• Circle the high-frequency words *everywhere*, *world,* and *move* in the message.

• Have children say and spell each word as they write it in the air.

Build Background Use the Day 1 instruction on ELL Poster 3 to assess knowledge and develop concepts.

ELL Poster 3

Oral Vocabulary

SHARE LITERATURE Display p. 3 of the *Sing with Me Big Book.* Tell children that the class is going to sing a song about camping and looking at stars. Read the title. Ask children to listen for the Amazing Words **wildlife, galaxy,** and **tranquil** as you sing. Then sing the song again and encourage children to sing along with you. Have children demonstrate their understanding of *wildlife, galaxy,* and *tranquil* by asking:

- What type of wildlife would you find in your neighborhood?

- How would you travel to a galaxy, and what would you see?

- What time of day do you feel the most tranquil?

**Sing with Me/
Background Building Audio**

Tranquil Nights

Camping out is lots of fun.
We love the tranquil nights.
Gaze at a galaxy of stars
Away from city lights.

We might see wildlife like deer,
And hear spring peepers peep.
Curled up inside our sleeping bags,
We'll get a good night's sleep.

*Sing to the tune of
Auld Lang Syne*

Unit 1
Exploration
Week 3
Henry and Mudge

Oral Vocabulary
*tranquil
galaxy
wildlife*

Sing with Me Big Book

Amazing Words **to build oral vocabulary**

MONITOR PROGRESS

galaxy **tranquil** **wildlife** underneath identify detective fascinating slimy	**If...** children lack oral vocabulary experiences about the concept Exploration, **then...** use the Oral Vocabulary Routine below to teach *galaxy*.

Oral Vocabulary ROUTINE

1 **Introduce the Word** Relate the word *galaxy* to the song. Supply a child-friendly definition. Have children say the word. Example: Our entire solar system is a small part of the Milky Way *galaxy.*

2 **Demonstrate** Provide an example to show meaning. On a clear night you can see a *galaxy* of stars.

3 **Apply** Have children demonstrate their understanding. Would a *galaxy* more likely be made up of an enormous group of stars or just a few stars?

4 **Display the Word/Letter-Sounds** Write the word on a card. Display it. Point out *g*/g/, *l*/l/, and *x*/ks/. See p. DI・5 to teach *tranquil* and *wildlife*.

Build Oral Vocabulary Help children recognize the meanings of the English words *gaze* and *spring peepers* in "Tranquil Nights." Discuss with them that *gaze* means "look at or stare" and that *spring peepers* are little frogs that make peeping noises in spring.

Henry and Mudge **68m**

OBJECTIVES

- Associate consonant sounds with consonant blends.
- Blend, read, and build words with consonant blends.

Skills Trace

Consonant Blends

Introduce/Teach	TE: 2.1 68n–o
Practice	TE: 2.1 68q, 70c–d; PB: 2.1 23, 38; DR3
Reteach/Review	TE: 2.1 94c, 120c, DI-66
Test	TE: 2.1 94e–g; Benchmark Test: Unit 2

Generalization

Consonant blends consist of two or more letters whose sounds are blended together when pronouncing a word.

Strategic Intervention

Use **Monitor Progress,** p. 68o, during Group Time after children have had more practice with consonant blends.

Advanced

Use **Monitor Progress,** p. 68o, as a preassessment to determine whether this group would benefit from this instruction.

Support Phonics Initial blends *pl, pr, bl, br, tr, dr, cl, cr, gl, gr, fl,* and *fr* exist in both English and Spanish. Help Spanish-speaking children compare the beginning sounds in cognates such as *planta/plant* and *precio/price.*

Final consonant blends are challenging for speakers of Greek, Italian, Spanish, and other languages. Provide additional practice for these children.

See the Phonics Transition Lessons in the ELL and Transition Handbook.

⟳ Consonant Blends

TEACH/MODEL

Blending Strategy

ROUTINE

1 **Connect** Write *back* and *wing.* What do you know about the consonants at the end of these words? (Both words end with two consonants that stand for one sound.) What are the words? Today we'll learn about consonant letters whose sounds are blended together in words.

2 **Model** Write *trust.* This word begins with two consonants and ends with two consonants. We have to blend two consonant sounds together to read the word. This is how I blend this word: /t/ /r//u//s//t/, *trust.* Have children blend *trust* with you. You can also blend words by saying the sounds before the vowel together, saying the sounds of all the rest of the letters together, and then blending the two chunks. Model blending /tr/ *-ust, trust;* then have children blend *spread* with you, using onset and rime. Write *spread.* This word begins with three consonants. We have to blend the sounds of all three consonants together to read the word. Listen: /s//p//r/, /spr/. Have children blend the consonants with you; then have them blend the whole word using onset and rime.

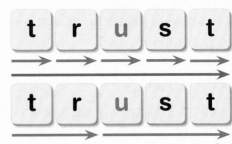

3 **Group Practice** Blend these words together. Continue with *ask, tribe, grand, flute, stamp, place, stripe, scrub.*

4 **Review** What do you know about reading these words? They have two or three consonants whose sounds have to be blended together to read the words.

BLEND WORDS

INDIVIDUALS BLEND WORDS WITH CONSONANT BLENDS Call on individuals to blend *dusk, strap, mask, blame, bride, splat, clamp, frame.* Have them tell what they know about each word before reading it. For feedback, refer to step four of the Blending Strategy Routine.

BUILD WORDS

a b c d f l m n

o p r s t

INDIVIDUALS MAKE CONSONANT BLEND

WORDS Write *raft* and have the class blend it.
Have children spell *raft* with letter tiles. Monitor
work and provide feedback.

r a f t

- Add *c* to the beginning.
  What is the new word?

c r a f t

- Change *ft* to *mp*.
  What is the new word?

c r a m p

- Change *cr* to *st*.
  What is the new word?

s t a m p

- Change *mp* to *nd*.
  What is the new word?

s t a n d

- Change *st* to *br*.
  What is the new word?

b r a n d

- Change *r* to *l* and *a* to *o*.
  What is the new word?

b l o n d

Vocabulary TiP

You may wish to explain the meanings
of these words.

dwell   to live in
scrub   to rub hard
flex   to bend

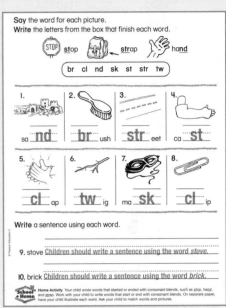

▲ **Practice Book 2.1** p. 23,
Consonant Blends

Monitor Progress | Check Word Reading Consonant Blends

Write the following words and have individuals read them.

dwell	jump	mask	plug	smile
strong	scrub	spring	scrape	split
stink	track	stung	flex	drank

If... children cannot blend words with consonant blends at this point,

then... continue to monitor their progress using other instructional
opportunities during the week so that they can be successful with the
Day 5 Assessment. See the Skills Trace on p. 68n.

SUCCESS
PREDICTOR

Spiral
REVIEW

- Row 3 reviews *-ck, -ng, -nk, -x.*

▶ **Day 1 Check**
Word Reading

Day 2 Check
High-Frequency
Words

Day 3 Check
Retelling

Day 4 Check
Fluency

Day 5 Assess
Progress

Word Reading

SUCCESS
PREDICTOR

OBJECTIVES

- Segment sounds to spell words.
- Spell words with consonant blends.

Spelling Words

Consonant Blends

1.	stop	7.	clip
2.	strap*	8.	stream*
3.	nest	9.	mask
4.	hand*	10.	twin
5.	brave	11.	breeze
6.	ask	12.	state

Challenge Words

13.	browse	15.	skeleton
14.	straight		

* Words from the Selection

Consonant Blends

Generalization Two or three consonants that are said together are called blends: <u>st</u>op, a<u>sk</u>, <u>str</u>ap.

Sort the list words by consonant blends.

sk	st
1. ask	6. stop
2. mask	7. nest
str	8. state
3. strap	cl
4. stream	9. clip
nd	tw
5. hand	10. twin
	br
11. brave	12. breeze

Spelling Words
1. stop
2. strap
3. nest
4. hand
5. brave
6. ask
7. clip
8. stream
9. mask
10. twin
11. breeze
12. state

Challenge Words

br	sk
13. browse	14. skeleton
	str
	15. straight

13. browse
14. straight
15. skeleton

School + Home **Home Activity** Your child is learning to spell words with consonant blends. To practice at home, help your child circle the letters that make up the consonant blend. Then ask your child to say each word.

▲ **Spelling Practice Book** p. 9

Support Spelling Before giving the spelling pretest, clarify the meaning of each spelling word with examples, such as holding up your palm for *stop* and pointing to your hand to illustrate *hand*.

Spelling

PRETEST Consonant Blends

MODEL WRITING FOR SOUNDS Each spelling word has a consonant blend. Before administering the spelling pretest, model how to segment words with consonant blends to spell them.

- What sounds do you hear in *strike?* (/s /t/ /r/ /ī/ /k/)
- What is the letter for /s/? Write *s.* Continue with the *t*/t/, *r*/r/, *i*/ī/, *k*/k/, and silent *e.*
- What letters stand for /str/? *(str)*

PRETEST Dictate the spelling words. Segment the words for children if necessary. Have children check their pretests and correct misspelled words.

HOMEWORK Spelling Practice Book, p. 9

Group Time

The Milky Way

Think about where you live. You live in a community, maybe a town or city, in a state, in America, on planet Earth, in our solar system, in the Milky Way galaxy.

The Milky Way galaxy is shaped like a disk with a bulge in the middle. It is a spiral galaxy and spins around its center. If you could look at it from above, the Milky Way would look like a giant, spinning pinwheel.

Our planet is close to the edge of the Milky Way galaxy. On a clear night, away from city lights, you can see our galaxy in the night sky. It looks like a thick band of light that

On-Level	Strategic Intervention	Advanced
Read Decodable Reader 3.	**Read** Decodable Reader 3.	**Read** Advanced Selection 3.
• Use p. 68q.	• Use the **Routine** on p. DI·34.	• Use the **Routine** on p. DI·35.

ELL Place English language learners in the groups that correspond to their reading abilities in English.

(i) Independent Activities

Fluency Reading Pair children to reread Leveled Readers or the ELL Reader from the previous week or other text at children's independent level.

Journal Writing List activities that make you feel tranquil. Share writing.

Independent Reading See p. 68j for Reading/Library activities and suggestions.

Literacy Centers To practice consonant blends, you may use Word Work, p. 68j.

Practice Book 2.1 Consonant Blends, p. 23; Character and Setting, p. 24

Break into small groups after Spelling and before Build Background.

Apply Phonics

⟳ PRACTICE Consonant Blends

HIGH-FREQUENCY WORDS Review *again*, *front*, and *laugh* on the Word Wall. `Word Wall`

EXCLAMATION MARKS Point out the exclamation mark after the word *day* on p. 18. Explain that exclamation marks are used to show excitement. Model reading a sentence with an exclamation mark. Have children read the sentence with you.

READ DECODABLE READER 3

• Pages 18–19 Read aloud quietly with the group.

• Pages 20–21 Have the group read aloud without you.

• Pages 22–24 Select individuals to read aloud.

CHECK COMPREHENSION AND DECODING Ask children the following questions:

• Who are the characters in the story? (Max, Mel, Mom, Dad)

• What is the problem? (The sun is not out, and it is wet outside.)

• How do Max and Mel solve their problem?

Then have children locate words with consonant blends in the story. List words as they are named. Story words include *act, and, ask, black, glad, mask, next, plan, prop, skit, stage, stop, strap, strong*. Then have individuals circle the initial and final consonant blends in the words.

HOMEWORK Take-Home Decodable Reader 3

REREAD FOR FLUENCY

Oral Rereading   ROUTINE

① **Read** Have children read the entire selection orally.

② **Reread** To achieve optimal fluency, children should reread the text three or four times.

③ **Provide Feedback** Listen as children read and provide corrective feedback regarding their oral reading and their use of the blending strategy.

OBJECTIVES

● Apply knowledge of letter-sounds to decode unknown words when reading.

● Use context with letter-sounds to confirm the identification of unknown words.

● Practice fluency in oral rereading.

Monitor Progress

Decoding	
If... children have difficulty decoding a word,	**then...** prompt them to blend the word. • What is the new word? • Is the new word a word you know? • Does it make sense in the story?

Access Content

Beginning Lead children on a picture walk through *On Stage*, identifying things in the pictures and print.

Intermediate Preview *On Stage* and help children understand the meaning of *prop* by providing examples of props that could be used in a play or performance.

Advanced After reading *On Stage*, have partners take turns retelling the first few pages of the story.

Build Background

LET'S TALK ABOUT Exploration

DEVELOP ORAL LANGUAGE Read the title and have children view the illustration. Ask them to tell you what they see. Allow ample time for children to respond. Remind children that good speakers take turns and speak loudly and clearly so everyone in the room can hear them. If children are reluctant to talk, use open-ended prompts to model language use and to encourage conversation. For example:

Tell me about what you see here. Yes, that's right, a nighttime sky and several different animals. What do you think these animals have in common? That's right, they are all active at night. What about all the stars in the background? Have you ever seen so many stars where you live?

BUILD ORAL VOCABULARY As you continue the discussion, encourage children to use today's Amazing Words: *galaxy, tranquil, wildlife.*

- Describe the background photograph using the word *galaxy*.
- How would you spend a tranquil evening?
- Which pictures show wildlife that live where you live?

DEVELOP CONCEPTS

CONCEPT CHART Remind children of the question of the week.

- What can we discover by exploring nature?

Display Graphic Organizer 15 or draw a web. Write *Exploring Nature* in the center. Brainstorm with children some possible answers to the question, filling in the outside ovals of the web. Display the web for use during the week.

- What have you discovered by exploring nature?
- What other things do you think we can discover by exploring nature?

CONNECT TO READING Point out the illustration at the bottom of p. 69 in the Student Edition. Ask children what the family is doing. (looking at the stars) Explain that this week children will read about a family that gets to explore nature by going on a camping trip.

Oral Vocabulary

Let's Talk About Exploration

68

69

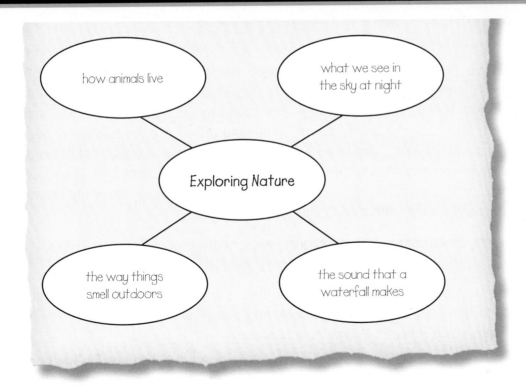

how animals live

what we see in the sky at night

Exploring Nature

the way things smell outdoors

the sound that a waterfall makes

▲ **Graphic Organizer 15**

Take It to the NET™
ONLINE

For Web sites that tell more about exploring nature, do an Internet search using the keywords *animal habitats* and *constellations*.

ELL

Access Content To prepare children for reading *Henry and Mudge*, send home the story summary in English and/or the home language. See the ELL Teaching Guide, pp. 19–21.

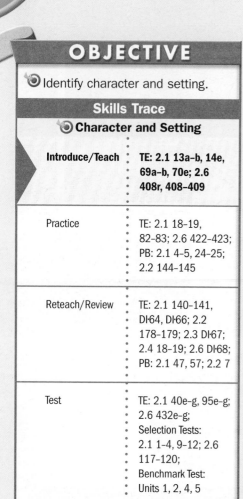

▲ **Practice Book 2.1** p. 24, Character and Setting

Access Content For a Picture It! lesson on character and setting, see the ELL Teaching Guide, pp. 15–16.

Listening Comprehension

◎ TEACH/MODEL Character and Setting

DEFINE CHARACTER AND SETTING

- Characters are the people or animals in stories.
- Authors describe their characters. They tell what the characters look like, how they act, and how they think. They also tell about the setting, or where the story takes place.
- Knowing about characters and setting can help a reader better understand a story.

READ ALOUD Read "Just a Little Patience" and model how to identify characters' points of view and setting.

MODEL Angie is a character in this story. As I read, I look for clues that tell me what she is like. She is excited about seeing animals and impatient when she and her father don't see any right way. I also look for clues about the setting. The characters are hiking in a forest and by the sea, so those places are the setting.

PRACTICE

CLUES TO CHARACTER AND SETTING Ask children to identify and compare Angie's father's point of view. What is Angie's father like? (He knows a lot about animals. He is patient when they don't see any animals at first.) How are Angie and her father alike and different? (They are alike because they both like to see animals in the wild. They are different because Angie is impatient when they don't see any animals at first, and Angie's father is patient.) What are some things that tell you what the setting is? (The author talks about the characters climbing a forest path and hiking by the sea.)

IDENTIFY CHARACTER AND SETTING Have children recall *Iris and Walter*.

- Who are the main characters in this story? (Iris, Grandpa, and Walter)
- What is Iris like? (She is an explorer. She is a good friend and likes to do fun things like play hide-and-go seek and ride a pony. She also is a teacher because she teaches Walter how to skate.)
- What is Walter like? (He likes to play in his tree house and watch his pony. He is a good friend to Iris because he shows her things to do in the country.)
- What is the setting of this story? (the country)

CONNECT TO READING Tell children that when they read any story, they should identify the characters and setting in the story and pay attention to what the characters are like.

Just a Little Patience

"Look, Angie!" her father said. "There's a beaver pond!"

Angie asked, "But where are the beavers? We've been hiking for hours and haven't seen any wildlife except other people's dogs!"

"Just be patient, Angie," her father said. "I'm sure we'll see some animals today."

They kept walking and climbed a forest path. The forest was tranquil and still. They reached the top of a hill, and then they heard a haunting sound, "Whooo—leee—ah!"

"What's that?" Angie asked.

Her father smiled. "That's a loon. A loon is a bird that has a sweet song."

"But where is it? I want to see it," Angie said impatiently.

"Loons stay near the water, " her father said. "Like beavers, they are hard to spot. But just wait and be patient. We're bound to see some kind of animal soon."

Angie and her father ate a quick lunch. Then they returned to their car and drove near the sea to hike. After twenty minutes, they reached the water. The surf crashed on the rocks below. They looked down into the water. That's when they saw it.

A sleek, wet otter lay on the rocks.

"An otter!" Angie cried. "I can't believe it! I'm seeing an otter with my own eyes!"

They watched the otter as it quickly slipped back into the water and swam out into the ocean, diving under the water and out of sight. A large black bird swooped down and landed almost where the otter had been.

"That is so cool!" Angie cried. "We've seen two animals in one minute!"

"All it takes is patience," her father said, "and a little cooperation from nature!"

Henry and Mudge   **69b**

OBJECTIVE

● Write a story.

DAILY FIX-IT

1. we saw a bird's nesst in a tree.
   <u>We</u> saw a bird's <u>nest</u> in a tree.

2. went on a camping trip
   <u>We</u> went on a camping trip<u>.</u>

This week's practice sentences appear on Daily Fix-It Transparency 3.

Strategic Intervention

Give children additional help by providing specific suggestions to complete each sentence, such as "We like to go to <u>the woods.</u>"

Advanced

Suggest that children list what they should take with them when they go to their favorite outdoor place and why.

Support Writing Reread the completed outdoor story that the group wrote. Ask children to brainstorm another outdoor place they like to go or would like to go to explore nature. As necessary, you may want to help children work through the format on the Transparency to write their own outdoor story about a different place.

▲ **The Grammar and Writing Book**
For more instruction and practice, use pp. 62–67.

Shared Writing

WRITE Story

GENERATE IDEAS Ask children to think of a favorite outdoor place. Ask them what they see there and what they like to do there. Focus on the natural features, such as plants and animals.

WRITE A STORY Explain that the class will choose a favorite outdoor place and write a story about what they see and what they like to do when they go to this place.

COMPREHENSION SKILL Tell children that the people they will write about will be the characters of their story, and the place and time will be the setting of their story.

- Display Writing Transparency 3 and read the title and first incomplete sentence.
- Have children brainstorm to complete the sentence by naming a place the class agrees on.
- Have children brainstorm the endings to the remaining sentences to complete their outdoor story.

HANDWRITING While writing, model the letter forms as shown on pp. TR14–17.

READ THE STORY Have children read the completed story aloud as you track the print.

Our Outdoor Story
Possible answers:
We like to go to **Thompson Park**_____.

It has **trees and flowers**_____.

It has **birds and squirrels**_____.

We like to **look at the flowers**_____.

We like to **feed the birds**_____.

The best thing is **playing hide-and-seek**

in the trees_____.

Unit 1 Henry and Mudge   Writing Model **3**

▲ **Writing Transparency 3**

INDEPENDENT WRITING

WRITE A STORY Have children write their own outdoor story about a place they like to go to explore nature. Encourage them to use words from the Word Wall and the Amazing Words board. Let children illustrate their writing. You may want to display children's stories on the bulletin board or let them share their stories by reading them aloud.

ADDITIONAL PRACTICE For additional practice, use pp. 62–67 in the Grammar and Writing Book.

Grammar

TEACH/MODEL Predicates

REVIEW SUBJECTS Recall with children that the subject of a sentence tells who or what does something.

IDENTIFY PREDICATES Display Grammar Transparency 3. Read the definition.

- In the first sentence, the subject is *we*. *We* tells who or what does something.
- The predicate is *hiked up a mountain*. Those words tell what the subject of the sentence—*we*—did.

Continue modeling with items 2–6.

PRACTICE

IDENTIFY PREDICATES Write the following sentences without the underlines on the board and ask children to identify the predicates. Have volunteers underline them.

My dad <u>carried a backpack</u>.

He <u>gave me a snack</u>.

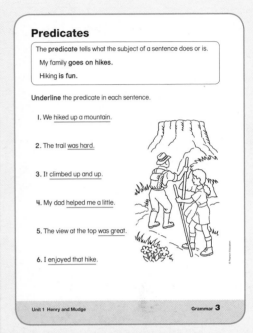

Predicates

The predicate tells what the subject of a sentence does or is.
My family **goes on hikes.**
Hiking **is fun.**

<u>Underline</u> the predicate in each sentence.

1. We <u>hiked up a mountain</u>.
2. The trail <u>was hard</u>.
3. It <u>climbed up and up</u>.
4. My dad <u>helped me a little</u>.
5. The view at the top <u>was great</u>.
6. I <u>enjoyed that hike</u>.

Unit 1 Henry and Mudge   Grammar **3**

▲ **Grammar Transparency 3**

Wrap Up Your Day!

✓ **CONSONANT BLENDS** Write *band, fist, street,* and *clean.* Ask children to read each word aloud together. Have them name other words that begin or end with consonant blends.

✓ **SPELLING WORDS WITH CONSONANT BLENDS** Have children name the letters for each sound in *spent.* Write the letters as children write them in the air. Continue with *stamp, grand, scold,* and *smart.*

✓ **CHARACTER AND SETTING** To help children identify character and setting, ask: Do you remember *Iris and Walter?* Who were two characters in that story? When and where did the story take place?

LET'S TALK ABOUT IT Review what we can discover by exploring nature. Display Graphic Organizer 15 and add responses.

 HOMEWORK Send home this week's Family Times newsletter.

PREVIEW Day 2

Tell children that tomorrow they will read about a family that explores nature by going camping.

Day 2
AT A GLANCE

Share Literature
In the Forest

Phonics and Spelling
 Consonant Blends

Spelling: Words with Consonant Blends

Comprehension
Skill Character and Setting
Strategy Monitor and Fix Up

Build Background
Camping and Hiking Equipment

High-Frequency Words

couldn't	love	**Word Wall**
build	mother	
bear	father	straight

Vocabulary
Selection Words

shivered	lanterns
snuggled	drooled

Read Apply Phonics

(**Group Time**) < Differentiated Instruction

Henry and Mudge and the Starry Night

Interactive Writing
Letter

Grammar
Predicates

Materials

- *Sing with Me Big Book*
- Big Book *In the Forest*
- Phonics Songs and Rhymes Chart 3
- Background Building Audio
- Graphic Organizer 14
- Vocabulary Transparency 3
- Student Edition 70–87
- Tested Word Cards

Morning Warm~Up!

Today we will read about a boy and his dog who explore nature on a camping trip. What do people do when they camp?

QUESTION OF THE DAY Encourage children to sing "Tranquil Nights" from the *Sing with Me Big Book* as you gather. Write and read the message and discuss the question.

REVIEW CONSONANT BLENDS

- Read the message aloud, indicating each word as you do so.
- Have children raise their hands when they hear a word with a consonant blend at the beginning *(trip)* or end *(camp)*.

Build Background Use the Day 2 instruction on ELL Poster 3 to preview high-frequency words.

ELL Poster 3

Share Literature

BUILD CONCEPTS

NONFICTION Have children read the title *Into the Forest*. Identify the author. Review that books about real people doing real things are nonfiction. Nonfiction books often have photographs as this book does.

BUILD ORAL VOCABULARY Recall with children that animals and plants that live in the forest can be called wildlife. Sometimes you need to look **underneath,** or below the surface, to discover facts about plant life. Suggest that as you reread the book, children listen to find out what kinds of wildlife and plants are in the forest.

Big Book

MONITOR LISTENING COMPREHENSION

- What time of year do you think the antlers of the bull moose fall off? What makes you think so? (They probably fall off in late fall or winter because we know they come off after the velvet falls off, which is in fall, and the new antlers grow in the spring.)

- How do some new ferns grow? (The "spore cases" underneath their leafy parts fly away with the wind, land, and grow.)

- Why do you think the ermine changes its coat from dark in the summer to white in the winter? (so it can't be seen in the white snow in the winter)

- What is one thing the bark of a birch tree has been used for? (to make canoes by some Native Americans)

OBJECTIVES

- Discuss characteristics of nonfiction.
- Set purpose for listening.
- Build oral vocabulary.

Amazing Words to build oral vocabulary

	MONITOR PROGRESS
galaxy tranquil wildlife **underneath** identify detective fascinating slimy	**If...** children lack oral vocabulary experiences about the concept Exploration, **then...** use the Oral Vocabulary Routine. See p. DI·5 to teach *underneath*.

Build Concepts Point out to children the Look Once/Look Again format of the book. Make sure they understand that the Look Once shows something very close up and the Look Again part shows the way the same thing looks from farther away.

Consonant Blends

TEACH/MODEL

Fluent Word Reading
ROUTINE

1 **Connect** Write *mask.* You can read this word because you know how to read words with consonant blends. What sounds do the letters *sk* stand for in this word? (/sk/) What's the word? *(mask)*

2 **Model** When you come to a new word, look at the letters from left to right and think about the sounds. Say the sounds in the word to yourself and then read the word. Model reading *twin, strict, pest, crept, brisk* using onset and rime. When you come to a new word, what are you going to do?

3 **Group Practice** Write *plant, close, stress, plump, crust, space, splint.* Read these words. Look at the letters, think about the vowel sounds, say the sounds to yourself, and then read the word aloud together. Allow 2–3 seconds previewing time.

WORD READING

PHONICS SONGS AND RHYMES CHART 3 Frame each of the following words on Phonics Songs and Rhymes Chart 3. Call on individuals to read them. Guide children in previewing.

creatures	flock	crows	black
bluebird	screeching	gray	croaking
frogs	snakes	stretched	

Sing "Nature's Creatures" to the tune of "Pop Goes the Weasel," or play the CD. Have children follow along on the chart as they sing. Identify *creatures, screeching,* and *crows* if necessary. Then have individuals take turns circling and reading words with consonant blends on the chart.

 **Phonics Songs and Rhymes Audio**

Nature's Creatures

What can we discover outdoors?
What creatures can we see?
A flock of crows, a little black ant—
They interest me.

A bluebird nest, a screeching gray owl,
A pond with croaking frogs.
Snakes that like to sun themselves,
Stretched out on logs.

Phonics Songs and Rhymes Chart 3

SORT WORDS

INDIVIDUALS BUILD WORDS WITH CONSONANT BLENDS Write *-and, -ump, -ace,* and *-ide* as headings. Distribute cards for these consonant blends: *br, gr, pl, sl, sp, st, tr, str.* Have children match their blends to the phonograms and identify what words can be formed. List words. Some possible answers are shown. Have completed lists read.

-and	-ump	-ace	-ide
stand	plump	grace	bride
brand	slump	space	slide
strand	stump	trace	stride

Spelling

PRACTICE Consonant Blends

WRITE DICTATION SENTENCES Have children write these sentences. Repeat words slowly, allowing children to hear each sound. Children may use the Word Wall to help with spelling high-frequency words. **Word Wall**

Did you stop to ask about the state?

The breeze blew the nest into the stream.

Which twin put on the mask?

HOMEWORK Spelling Practice Book, p. 10

Spelling Words

Consonant Blends

1. **stop**		7. **clip**	
2. **strap***		8. **stream***	
3. **nest**		9. **mask**	
4. **hand***		10. **twin**	
5. **brave**		11. **breeze**	
6. **ask**		12. **state**	

Challenge Words

13. **browse**   15. **skeleton**
14. **straight**

* Words from the Selection

Consonant Blends

Spelling Words

stop	strap	nest	hand	brave	ask
clip	stream	mask	twin	breeze	state

Write a list word to complete each comparison.

1. Green means go. Red means __stop__.
2. One of three is a triplet. One of two is a __twin__.
3. A foot is on a leg. A __hand__ is on an arm.
4. A bee lives in a hive. A bird lives in a __nest__.
5. A mitt goes on the hand. A __mask__ goes on the face.
6. Statements tell things. Questions __ask__ things.

Write the list word that means the same as the phrase.

7. cut off __clip__   8. full of courage __brave__
9. soft wind __breeze__   10. leather strip __strap__
11. small river __stream__ 12. part of U.S.A. __state__

School + Home Home Activity Your child wrote words that contain consonant blends. Ask your child to circle each blend (st, str, nd, br, sk, cl, tw) and say its sound.

▲ **Spelling Practice Book** p. 10

Comprehension

OBJECTIVES

- Recognize character and setting.
- Monitor and fix up.
- Build background.

Read each story.
Underline the sentence that tells where the story takes place.
Draw a picture that shows where the story takes place.

1. My dad and I went camping in the desert. We set up our tent by some big rocks. We cooked our dinner over the fire. Then we took our sleeping bags out of the tent. We wanted to sleep under the stars.

2. Children's artwork should include a desert setting, tent, campfire, and stars.

3. Grandma showed me how to dig for clams at the beach. It was a windy day. The waves were crashing. We had our pails and toys. We found some wet sand. Grandma dug into the sand. She found a clam. I tried it too. Soon we had a whole pail of clams!

4. Children's artwork should include a beach setting, waves, Grandma, and clams.

Write the name of a story you have read. Draw a picture that shows where the story takes place.

5. Children's artwork should reflect the topic of the book.

Home Activity Your child identified the setting of a story. Together, write the setting of a place you would like to visit. Ask your child to describe the physical characteristics of that setting. You can fill in unknown details for him or her.

▲ **Practice Book 2.1** p. 25, Character and Setting

SKILL Character and Setting

RECOGNIZE CHARACTER AND SETTING Review with children that characters are the people or animals in a story. Authors describe the characters and tell how they look, how they act, and what kind of people they are. Setting is when and where the story takes place. Invite children to describe the characters and identify the setting of several stories they have recently read.

CONNECT TO READING

- As you read, ask yourself who the characters in the story are and where and when the story takes place. Also think about ways in which the writer tells the reader how the characters think about things.

- Pay attention to clues both in the story and in the illustrations that tell you where and when the story takes place.

STRATEGY Monitor and Fix Up

INTRODUCE THE STRATEGY Explain to children that sometimes they may have questions while they are reading. When that happens, they should keep reading to see if they discover the answers.

Think Aloud

MODEL When I read a story, sometimes I don't understand what is happening, or sometimes I don't understand what a word means. If this happens, I know that if I keep reading, I can usually find the answers to those questions.

CONNECT TO READING Encourage children to ask themselves these questions as they read *Henry and Mudge and the Starry Night*.

- When I can't figure out what is happening in the story, do I read on to understand?

- When I don't understand a word, do I read on to find clues to help me figure it out?

Build Background

DISCUSS CAMPING AND HIKING EQUIPMENT Display pictures of camping and hiking equipment such as lanterns, tents, backpacks, cooking equipment, and hiking shoes, or have children look up some of these items in a picture dictionary. Invite children to tell what they know about camping and hiking and what kind of equipment they would need.

- What do people do when they go camping or hiking?
- What do they need to sleep and eat outdoors?
- What might campers discover as they explore the outdoors?

BACKGROUND BUILDING AUDIO Have children listen to the audio and share the new information they learned about camping or hiking equipment.

 **Sing with Me/ Background Building Audio**

COMPLETE A WEB Draw a web or display Graphic Organizer 14. Write *camping and hiking equipment* in the center. Work with children to brainstorm things they might need when they go camping or hiking.

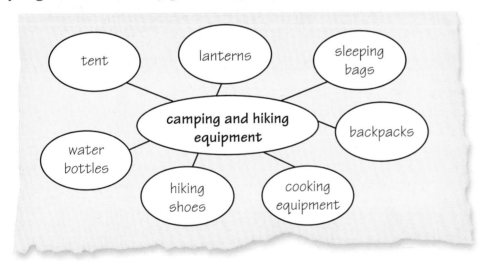

▲ **Graphic Organizer 14**

CONNECT TO SELECTION Connect background information to *Henry and Mudge and the Starry Night*.

In the story we are about to read, a boy named Henry and his dog, Mudge, go camping with Henry's parents. We'll find out what they take when they go camping on a tranquil night underneath the stars.

Activate Prior Knowledge Invite children to tell what they know about the equipment listed on the web. Ask what each item is called in their home language and have them tell how it is used.

Words to Read

love
mother
father
straight
bear
couldn't
build

Read the Words

We all love camping. My mother and father take us camping every year. We go straight to the woods when we get there. Something new always happens on these trips. Last year, we saw a bear! I couldn't believe it. This year, my dad promised to teach us how to build a campfire. I can't wait!

Genre: Realistic Fiction Realistic fiction means that a story could happen. Next read about Henry and his dog, Mudge, and, their camping trip.

70

71

High-Frequency Words

Nondecodable Words

ROUTINE

1 **Say and Spell** Look at the words on page 70. You cannot blend the sounds in these words. We will spell the words and use letter-sounds we know to learn them. Point to the first word. This word is *love, l-o-v-e, love.* What is this word? What are the letters in this word?

2 **Identify Familiar Letter-Sounds** Point to the first letter in *love.* What is this letter? What is the sound for this letter? (*l*/*l*/)

3 **Demonstrate Meaning** Tell me a sentence using this word.

Repeat the routine with the other Words to Read. Have children identify these familiar letter-sounds: *mother* (*m*/m/), *father* (*f*/f/), *straight* (*str*/str/), *bear* (*b*/b/), *couldn't* (*c*/k/), *build* (*b*/b/).

Have children read aloud the sentences on p. 71 and point to the Words to Read. Add the words to the Word Wall. **Word Wall**

Use Vocabulary Transparency 3 to review this week's words.

- Point to a word. Say and spell it.
- Have children say and spell the word.
- Ask children to identify familiar letter-sounds.

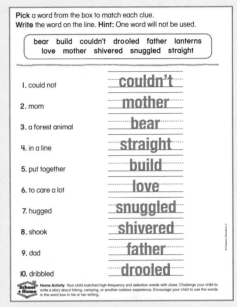

Pick a word from the box to match each clue.
Write the word on the line. **Hint:** One word will not be used.

> bear build couldn't drooled father lanterns
> love mother shivered snuggled straight

1. could not	couldn't
2. mom	mother
3. a forest animal	bear
4. in a line	straight
5. put together	build
6. to care a lot	love
7. hugged	snuggled
8. shook	shivered
9. dad	father
10. dribbled	drooled

School + Home Home Activity Your child matched high-frequency and selection words with clues. Challenge your child to write a story about hiking, camping, or another outdoor experience. Encourage your child to use the words in the word box in his or her writing.

▲ **Practice Book 2.1** p. 26, High-Frequency Words and Selection Words

---

Monitor Progress | **Check High-Frequency Words**

Point to the following words on the Word Wall and have individuals read them.

| about | bear | beautiful | build | couldn't | father | good |
| green | home | love | mother | pulling | saw | straight |

If . . . children cannot read these words,

then . . . have them practice in pairs with word cards before reading the selection. Monitor their fluency with these words during reading, and provide additional practice opportunities before the Day 5 Assessment.

SUCCESS PREDICTOR

Spiral REVIEW

- Reviews previously taught high-frequency words.

| **Day 1** Check Word Reading | ▶ **Day 2 Check High-Frequency Words** | **Day 3** Check Retelling | **Day 4** Check Fluency | **Day 5** Assess Progress |

High-Frequency Words

SUCCESS PREDICTOR

Sleeping Outside

1. When my friend and I slept in my backyard, I got so cold I shivered.

2. I snuggled with my dog Ben to keep warm.

3. He drooled on me, but I didn't care.

4. I was glad we both had lanterns so it wasn't as dark.

Words to Read			
bear	build	couldn't	father
love	mother	straight	

Unit 1 Henry and Mudge   Vocabulary **3**

▲ **Vocabulary Transparency 3**

Vocabulary

SELECTION WORDS

Use Vocabulary Transparency 3 to introduce the selection words.

- Read each sentence as you track the print.
- Frame each underlined word. Explain the word's meaning.

  shivered shook with fear

  drooled let saliva run from the mouth

  lanterns lights inside containers that can be carried

  snuggled cuddled together

- Ask children to identify familiar letter-sounds and word parts: *shivered* (*sh*/sh/), *lanterns* (/l/l/, a/a/), *snuggled* (*sn*/sn/), *drooled* (*dr*/dr/).
- Have children read each sentence aloud with you.
- To encourage discussion using the selection words, ask children to tell about a time when they or someone they know shivered, snuggled, or drooled. Then have them describe situations when they might use a lantern.

Group Time

DAY 2

On-Level	Strategic Intervention	Advanced
Read *Henry and Mudge.*	**Read** SI Decodable Reader 3.	**Read** *Henry and Mudge.*
• Use pp. 72–87.	• Read or listen to *Henry and Mudge.*	• Use the **Routine** on p. DI·37.
	• Use the **Routine** on p. DI·36.	

 Place English language learners in the groups that correspond to their reading abilities in English.

ⓘ Independent Activities

Independent Reading See p. 68j for Reading/Library activities and suggestions.

Journal Writing Write about what you might see and feel camping outside overnight. Share your writing.

Literacy Centers To provide experiences with *Henry and Mudge,* you may use the Listening Center on p. 68j.

Practice Book 2.1 Character and Settings, p. 25; High-Frequency Words and Selection Words, p. 26; Realism and Fantasy, p. 27

ELL

Access Content Use the vocabulary strategies and word cards in the ELL Teaching Guide, pp. 17–18.

Break into small groups after Vocabulary and before Writing.

Henry and Mudge
and the Starry Night

by Cynthia Rylant
illustrated by Suçie Stevenson

What will Henry and Mudge
find on a starry night?

72   73

Read
Prereading Strategies

PREVIEW AND PREDICT Have children read the title with you, decoding words
as they can. Identify the author and illustrator. Have children do a picture walk
through the first several pages of the selection and speculate what it is about.

DISCUSS REALISTIC FICTION Read the definition of realistic fiction on p. 71
aloud to children. Encourage discussion of Henry and Mudge and what they
might do on a camping trip.

SET PURPOSE Read aloud the question on p. 72. Ask children what they think
the story will be about.

ELL

Access Content Before reading,
review the story summary in English
and/or the home language. See the ELL
Teaching Guide, pp. 19–21.

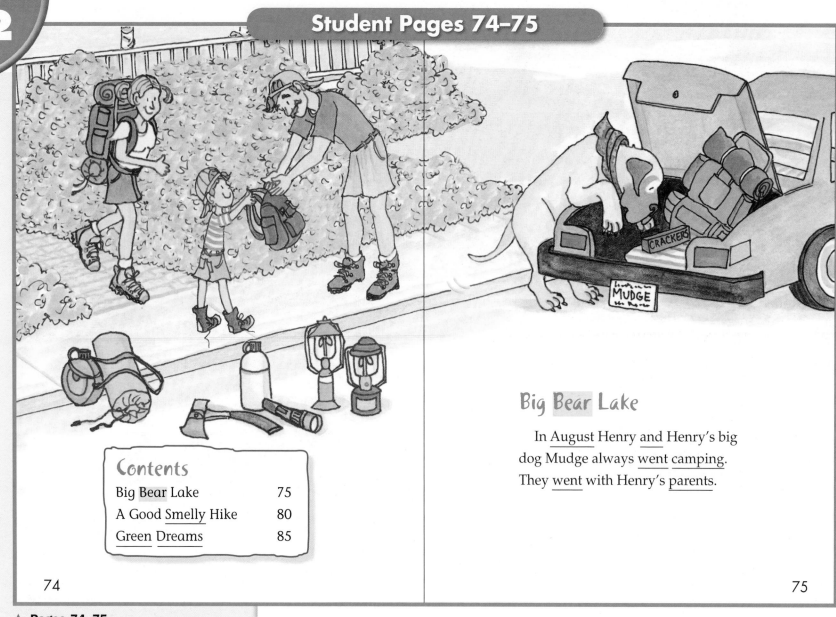

Contents

74

Big Bear Lake

In August Henry and Henry's big dog Mudge always went camping. They went with Henry's parents.

75

▲ **Pages 74–75**
Have children read and look at the pictures to find what everyone is doing to get ready to go on the camping trip.

EXTEND SKILLS

Text Features: Table of Contents, Chapter Titles

For instruction in table of contents and chapter titles, discuss the following:

• The author put a little table of contents on p. 74 to show us where chapters start. Chapters are separate parts of a story.

• Read the chapter titles. What do they tell you about what might happen in the story?

Assess Have children check their predictions as they read each page with a chapter title on it.

Guiding Comprehension

Predict • Inferential

• **What do you think will happen in this chapter of the story?**
Possible answer: I think Henry and his family will go in the car to Big Bear Lake. They will camp there.

Draw Conclusions • Inferential

• **Do you think that Henry and Mudge know what to expect when they go camping? Why?**
Possible response: They probably do because they go camping every August. They've done it before.

Character • Critical

• **Do you think Henry and Mudge enjoy camping at Bear Lake? Why?**
Possible response: Yes, because they both look like they have smiles on their faces in the picture where they are camping near a lake under the stars.

_____ Consonant Blends   high-frequency/tested vocabulary

Henry's mother had been a Camp Fire Girl, so she knew all about camping.

She knew how to build a campfire. She knew how to cook camp food.

She knew how to set up a tent.

Henry's dad didn't know anything about camping. He just came with a guitar and a smile.

76

77

Guiding Comprehension

Draw Conclusions • Critical

- **Why do you think being a Camp Fire Girl helped Henry's mother know so much about camping?**
Possible response: She must have gone camping with the Camp Fire Girls. Because of their name, it sounds as if they do a lot of camping.

Character • Critical

- ***Text to Self*** **If you went camping, would you be more like Henry's mother or his father? Why?**
Children who have been camping before might say that they are more like his mother. Others might say that they are more like his father.

▲ **Pages 76–77**
Have children read to find out about Henry's parents.

Monitor Progress	
Decoding	
If… children come to a word they don't know,	**then…** remind them to: 1. Blend the word. 2. Decide if the word makes sense. 3. Look in a dictionary for more help.

Henry and Mudge loved camping. This year they were going to Big Bear Lake, and Henry couldn't wait.

"We'll see deer, Mudge," Henry said.
Mudge wagged.

"We'll see raccoons," said Henry.
Mudge shook Henry's hand.

"We might even see a *bear*," Henry said. Henry was not so sure he wanted to see a bear. He shivered and put an arm around Mudge.

Mudge gave a big, slow, *loud* yawn. He drooled on Henry's foot.
Henry giggled. "No bear will get *us*, Mudge," Henry said. "We're too *slippery!*"

78

79

▲ **Pages 78–79**
Have children read to find out what Henry and Mudge are probably going to see when they are camping.

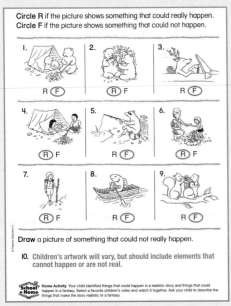

Circle R if the picture shows something that could really happen.
Circle F if the picture shows something that could not happen.

Draw a picture of something that could not really happen.

10. Children's artwork will vary, but should include elements that cannot happen or are not real.

 Home Activity Your child identified things that could happen in a realistic story and things that could happen in a fantasy. Select a favorite children's video and watch it together. Ask your child to describe the things that make the story realistic or a fantasy.

▲ **Practice Book 2.1** p. 27, Realism and Fantasy

Skills in Context

REVIEW **REALISM AND FANTASY**

- **Are Henry and Mudge really seeing deer, raccoons, and a bear? How do you know?**
No, they are not seeing these animals right now. They are thinking about the wildlife they have seen on other camping trips. Also, Henry is worried about maybe seeing a bear.

Monitor Progress	**Realism and Fantasy**
If... children have difficulty differentiating between realism and fantasy,	**then...** model how to use the text and pictures to tell the difference.

Think Aloud **MODEL** Henry and Mudge are still getting ready to leave on their camping trip, so I know they're not really seeing these animals. And I know that artists sometimes put those bubbly lines around pictures to show what people are thinking.

ASSESS Have children identify elements in the story that are realistic. (Possible response: Henry helps his parents pack for their camping trip.)

_____ Consonant Blends   high-frequency/tested vocabulary

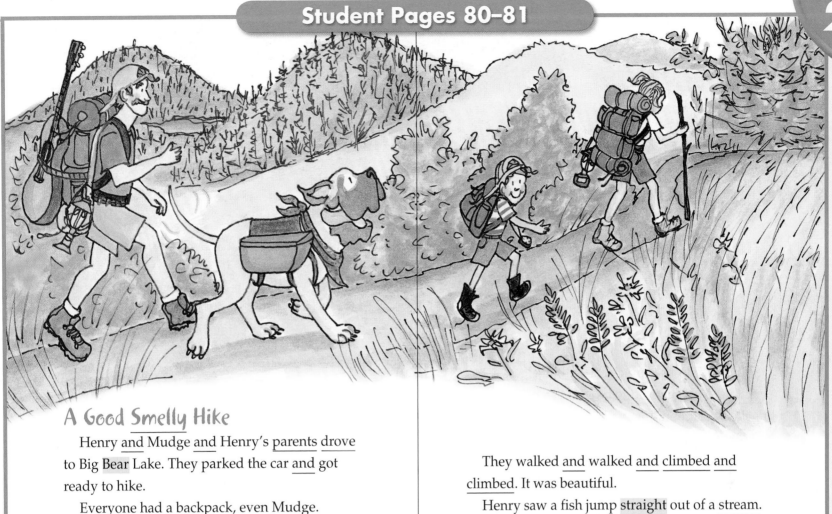

A Good Smelly Hike

Henry and Mudge and Henry's parents drove
to Big Bear Lake. They parked the car and got
ready to hike.

Everyone had a backpack, even Mudge.
(His had lots of crackers.) Henry's mother said,
"Let's go!" And off they went.

80

They walked and walked and climbed and
climbed. It was beautiful.

Henry saw a fish jump straight out of a stream.
He saw a doe and her fawn. He saw waterfalls
and a rainbow.

81

Strategies in Context

🎯 MONITOR AND FIX UP

- **Why don't Henry and Mudge and Henry's parents set up the camp right away?**
Apparently, they want to go for a long hike before they put up their tent and camp. Maybe they're looking for a good place to set up their tent.

Monitor Progress	**Monitor and Fix Up**
If... children have difficulty figuring out why they aren't setting up camp,	**then...** model how to read on to confirm understanding.

Think Aloud

MODEL I know the family is going camping. They packed all their stuff, but now they're not camping. They're hiking instead. I guess if I read some more I will probably find out what's happening.

ASSESS Have children read on to find out why the family goes on a hike first.
(to find a good place to camp)

▲ **Pages 80–81**
Have children read to find out what Mudge and the family do first.

Monitor Progress	
High-Frequency Words	
If... children have a problem reading a new high-frequency word,	**then...** use the High-Frequency Routine on p. 71a to reteach the problematic word.

Mudge didn't see much of anything. He was smelling. Mudge loved to hike and smell. He smelled a raccoon from yesterday. He smelled a deer from last night.

He smelled an oatmeal cookie from Henry's back pocket. "Mudge!" Henry laughed, giving Mudge the cookie.

Finally Henry's mother picked a good place to camp.

82

Henry's parents set up the tent. Henry unpacked the food and pans and lanterns. Mudge unpacked a ham sandwich. Finally the camp was almost ready. It needed just one more thing: "Who knows the words to 'Love Me Tender'?" said Henry's father with a smile, pulling out his guitar. Henry looked at Mudge and groaned.

83

▲ **Pages 82–83**
Have children read to find out what the characters in the story are doing.

Forest Animals

Deer and raccoons often live in the woods. Both need to be near water. Bears sometimes live in forests too, but there aren't too many of them. Sometimes raccoons and even deer show up where people camp or live. Raccoons sometimes get into people's trash. Have you ever heard raccoons in the garbage at night?

Access Content Explain that the song "Love Me Tender" was popular many years ago, and Henry is tired of hearing it.

Skills in Context

⊙ CHARACTER AND SETTING

• **Who are the characters in this story? When and where does it take place? How do you know?**
The characters include Henry, his dog Mudge, and Henry's mother and father. The story takes place in August, which is when the family always goes camping. They are near Big Bear Lake.

Monitor Progress	**Character and Setting**
If… children have difficulty identifying the characters and setting,	**then…** model how to use the text and pictures to confirm understanding.

Think Aloud **MODEL** Both people and animals can be characters in a story, so I think Mudge is a character along with Henry and his parents. The story says they go camping every August and that they drive to Big Bear Lake.

ASSESS Have children identify other clues about setting as they read. (Henry sees a stream and waterfalls.)

_____ Consonant Blends   high-frequency/tested vocabulary

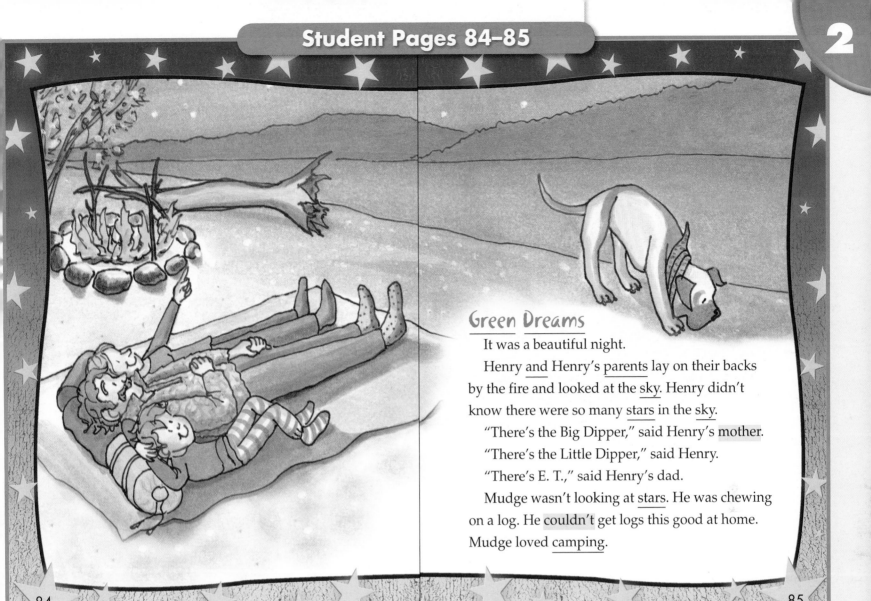

Green Dreams

It was a beautiful night.

Henry and Henry's parents lay on their backs by the fire and looked at the sky. Henry didn't know there were so many stars in the sky.

"There's the Big Dipper," said Henry's mother.

"There's the Little Dipper," said Henry.

"There's E. T.," said Henry's dad.

Mudge wasn't looking at stars. He was chewing on a log. He couldn't get logs this good at home. Mudge loved camping.

84   85

Guiding Comprehension

REVIEW Realism and Fantasy • Critical

- **Do Henry and his parents really see a Big Dipper, Little Dipper, and E.T.? How do you know?**

No, those are just outline shapes that some groups of stars seem to make in the sky, so they name the shapes.

Summarize • Inferential

- **What has happened in the story so far?**

Henry and Mudge and Henry's parents get ready to go camping. Henry and Mudge think about the wildlife they might see. They all take a long hike and then they set up their tent to camp. That night, the family looks at the stars, and Mudge chews on a log.

▲ **Pages 84–85**
Have children read to find out what the family sees in the sky.

Strategy Self-Check

Have children ask themselves these questions to check their reading.

Decoding Words

- Do I use context clues to help read a new word?
- Do I self-correct when a word doesn't fit the letters in the word?

Monitor and Fix Up: Read On

- When I can't figure out what is happening in the story, do I read on?
- If I don't understand a new word, do I read on to find clues?

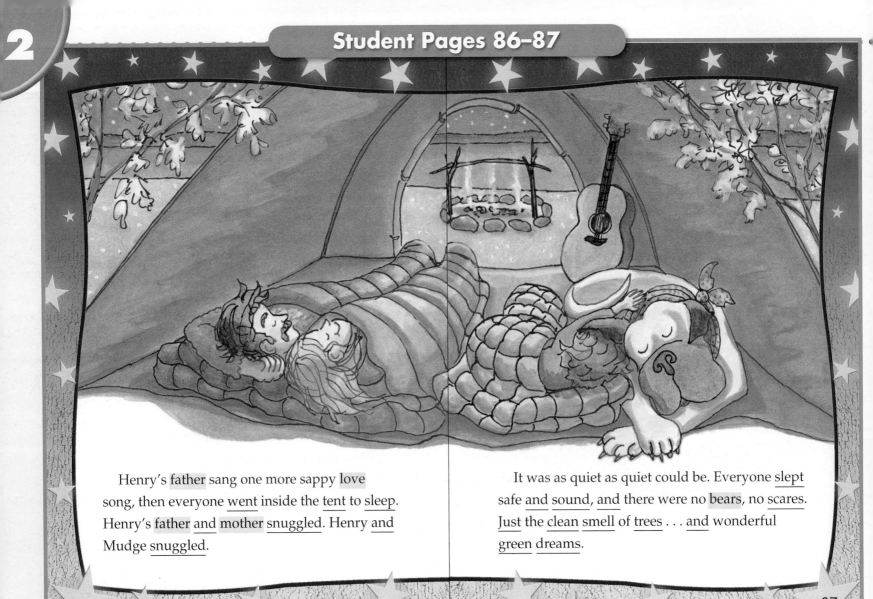

Henry's father sang one more sappy love song, then everyone went inside the tent to sleep. Henry's father and mother snuggled. Henry and Mudge snuggled.

It was as quiet as quiet could be. Everyone slept safe and sound, and there were no bears, no scares. Just the clean smell of trees . . . and wonderful green dreams.

86

87

▲ **Pages 86-87**
Have children read to find out what sleeping in the tent was like.

_____ Consonant Blends   high-frequency/tested vocabulary

Guiding Comprehension

Compare and Contrast • Critical

- *Text to World* **How is sleeping in a tent different from sleeping when you're at home? How is it the same?**
When you're camping, it is very silent, you're out in the fresh air, and lots of stars are out. When you're home, there is more noise from other people and traffic. You're inside a room, and you usually can't see many stars. In both places, it's important to be warm and comfortable.

Author's Purpose • Inferential

- *Question the Author* **Why do you think the author put those three little dots in the last sentence?**
Probably to make us slow down at that place in the sentence.

Draw Conclusions • Critical

- *Text to Self* **Would you like to go camping like Henry, Mudge, and Henry's parents did? Why or why not?**
Possible responses: Yes, because it seems like a lot of fun. No, because I might be scared of the wild animals.

Character and Setting • Critical

- **If Henry and Mudge camped in the desert, how would the story change?**
Possible response: They most likely would not be camping by a lake. Also, the types of animals they might see in the desert would be different from what they would see if they were camping in a forest by a lake.

Fluency

REREAD FOR FLUENCY

Paired Rereading

ROUTINE

1 **Reader 1 Begins** Children read the entire book, switching readers at the end of each page.

2 **Reader 2 Begins** Have partners reread; now the other partner begins.

3 **Reread** For optimal fluency, children should reread three or four times.

4 **Provide Feedback** Listen to children read and provide corrective feedback regarding their oral reading and their use of the blending strategy.

Interactive Writing

WRITE Letter

MAKE A WEB Tell children that Henry wants to write a letter to his best friend Tom about his camping trip. Make a web on the board or provide Graphic Organizer 15. In the center oval, write *About Henry's Camping Trip.* Let children fill in items in the outside ovals that Henry might want to tell Tom in his letter.

SHARE THE PEN Have children refer to their web as they participate in writing Henry's letter to his friend Tom. To begin, write *Dear Tom* as the start of the letter format. Ask questions such as:

- What kind of letter should we use at the beginning of *Dear* and *Tom?* (a capital letter)

Then discuss with children how to begin the first paragraph of the letter (indented) and what to say in the first sentence. Write the sentence, inviting individuals to write familiar letter-sounds, word parts, and high-frequency words.

- How do we begin and end the first sentence? (with a capital letter, with a period)

Continue to have children make contributions. Frequently reread what has been written while tracking the print.

READ THE LETTER Read the completed letter aloud, having children echo you.

> **Dear Tom,**
>
> **Mudge and I went camping with my mother and father. We had a great time. Mudge liked the smells. We saw lots of stars.**
>
> **Your friend,**
>
> **Henry**

INDEPENDENT WRITING

WRITE A LETTER Have children write their own friendly letter to Tom from Henry. Remind them to capitalize the salutation and closing of the letter. Let children illustrate their writing.

Strategic Intervention

Discuss with children one thing that Henry might want to tell his friend about his camping trip. Work through the letter format with children and help them write one sentence that tells about that thing.

Advanced

Invite children to write a letter to their own best friend about an adventure they have had.

Support Writing Before writing, read aloud the class letter again, pointing out the elements of the letter format.

Beginning Give children a word bank that they might use in their own letter from Henry to Tom: *Mudge, camping, liked, smells, stars.*

Intermediate You might teach children a simple declarative sentence format with subject and predicate to use in their letters, such as *We went, We saw, We liked.*

Advanced Review children's letters. Show each child where he or she might add details to make the letter more interesting to Tom.

Support Grammar In some languages, the predicates are not routinely at the end of sentences as is typical in English. Help children practice by reading sentences from the selection aloud and identifying the predicates. See the Grammar Transition lessons in the ELL and Transition Handbook.

Grammar

DEVELOP THE CONCEPT Predicates

IDENTIFY PREDICATES Write *Henry and Mudge went camping.* Point to each word as you read the sentence aloud. Discuss whether this is a sentence.

The predicate of a sentence tells what the subject does or is. What is the predicate of this sentence? (went camping) What is the subject of the sentence? (Henry and Mudge)

PRACTICE

WRITE PREDICATES Display two pictures of children doing something active. Write sentence beginnings such as *The girl* or *The two boys.* Model writing a predicate to complete each sentence about the pictures.

Think Aloud **MODEL** To write a sentence about the first picture, I have to add a predicate to *The girl.* Write *rides her bike. The girl rides her bike.* Now I have a complete sentence. To write a sentence about the second picture, I have to add a predicate to *The two boys.* I will write *play catch,* so this sentence says *The two boys play catch.*

Have children write other predicates for sentences about the pictures.

Predicates
The predicate tells what the subject of a sentence does or is.

We **drive** to the woods.
The family **hikes.**

Write the predicate of each sentence.

1. My family makes a camp.
makes a camp

2. Dad and I set up the tent.
set up the tent

3. The tent falls down.
falls down

4. The rain pours.
pours

5. We sleep in the car.
sleep in the car

▲ **Grammar and Writing Practice Book** p. 9

 # Wrap Up Your Day!

**PREVIEW Day 3**

 HIGH-FREQUENCY WORDS Write *My mother and father took me camping. I was afraid we would see a bear. I couldn't believe that my mom could build a fire. We went straight home after we camped.* Ask children to read the sentences and identify the high-frequency words *mother, father, bear, couldn't, build, straight.*

MONITOR AND FIX UP Review with children that when they have problems understanding a word or what's happening in a story, sometimes they can help themselves figure it out by reading on.

LET'S TALK ABOUT IT Discuss with children some things that Henry and Mudge discovered on their camping trip. Review the web about *Exploring Nature* and add responses.

Tell children that tomorrow they will hear about forest animals.

Share Literature
In the Forest

Phonics and Spelling
REVIEW Long Vowels CVC*e*

Spelling: Words with Consonant Blends

High-Frequency Words

couldn't	love	build	**Word Wall**
mother	bear	father	
straight			

Vocabulary
Synonyms

Fluency
Read with Accuracy and Appropriate Pace/Rate

Writing Trait
Word Choice

Grammar
Predicates

Materials

- *Sing with Me Big Book*
- Big Book *In the Forest*
- Student Edition 88–89

Morning Warm~Up!

There are many things to learn about the forest.
Some animals and plants look different close-up and far away.
What else can we discover by exploring nature in the forest?

QUESTION OF THE DAY Encourage children to sing "Tranquil Nights" from the *Sing with Me Big Book* as you gather. Write and read the message and discuss the question.

REVIEW PREDICATES

- Point to the second sentence in the message. What is the predicate in this sentence? *(look different close-up and far away)*

Build Background Use the Day 3 instruction on ELL Poster 3 to support children's use of English to communicate about lesson concepts.

ELL Poster 3

ORAL LANGUAGE

3

Share Literature

LISTEN AND RESPOND

GLOSSARY Ask children to look at the glossary in *Into the Forest.* Remind children that they can find definitions of words here. The words are written in alphabetical order.

BUILD ORAL VOCABULARY Remind children that they listened to *Into the Forest* earlier to find out about plants and animals that live there. Ask children if they can **identify,** or recognize, any of the animals in the pictures. Invite children to discuss what else they would like to listen for to learn new facts about animals and plants in the forest.

MONITOR LISTENING COMPREHENSION

• How could you identify a bull moose? (Possible response: by its antlers)

• How can a male moth identify a female moth? (by using its antenna like a nose to smell)

• What else do you think you might learn by exploring nature in the forest? (Possible answer: We could learn about the rivers and what the rain and snow do to the forest.)

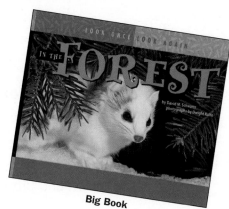

Big Book

OBJECTIVES

● Discuss the glossary.
● Set purpose for listening.
● Build oral vocabulary.

Amazing Words to build oral vocabulary

	MONITOR PROGRESS
galaxy **tranquil** **wildlife** **underneath** **identify** **detective** **fascinating** **slimy**	**If...** children lack oral vocabulary experiences about the concept Exploration, **then...** use the Oral Vocabulary Routine. See p. DI·5 to teach *identify*.

Listen and Respond Explain to children that forests like the one shown in the book do not exist everywhere in the United States. Help children realize whether forests are in your area of the country. If not, tell them where forests might be found, for example, in the mountains of the Southwest or Southeast.

Henry and Mudge **88b**

OBJECTIVES

- Review long vowel words with the CVCe spelling pattern.
- Build, blend, and read long vowel CVCe words.
- Recognize high-frequency words.
- Spell long vowel words.

▲ **Practice Book 2.1** p. 28, Long Vowels CVCe

Review Phonics

REVIEW LONG VOWELS CVCe

READ LONG VOWEL CVCe WORDS Write *late*. Look at this word. You can read this word because you know the vowel sound when you see a-consonant-e. What is the vowel sound in this word? (/ā/) What is the word?

BUILD WORDS Have children spell *mine* with letter tiles. Monitor work and provide feedback.

- Change the *i* to *a*.
  What is the new word?

  m a n e

- Change the *m* to *l*.
  What is the new word?

  l a n e

- Change the *a* to *o*.
  What is the new word?

  l o n e

- Change the *l* to *t*.
  What is the new word?

  t o n e

- Change the *o* to *u*.
  What is the new word?

  t u n e

- Change the *tu* to *fi*.
  What is the new word?

  f i n e

High-Frequency Words

PRACTICE

STORY CLUES Read the following story to children. Have children find the word on the Word Wall that fits each blank in the story. **Word Wall**

One day a baby _____ (bear) cub wanted to climb a tree. "I'd _____ (love) to climb up, but I'm afraid I'll slip and fall," said the cub. His _____ (mother) said she had a great idea. "Why don't you ask your _____ (father) to make a ladder?" she said. "You can even help him _____ (build) it. Then you can climb _____ (straight) up the tree in no time!"

"No, I _____ ," (couldn't) cried the cub. "I will get hurt."

"You will never know what you can do until you try," mother bear said gently.

Spelling

PRACTICE Consonant Blends

RHYMING CLUES Have children practice by writing the spelling words that

- rhyme with *best*, with *lap*, with *team* (nest; strap; stream)
- rhyme with *hop*, with *sneeze*, with *task* (stop; breeze; ask, mask)
- rhyme with *date*, with *save* (state; brave)
- rhyme with *band*, with *dip*, with *fin* (hand; clip; twin)

HOMEWORK Spelling Practice Book, p. 11

Pick a word from the box to finish each sentence. **Write** the word on the line.

bear	build	couldn't	father	love	mother	straight

1. The **bear** family lived in a cave.
2. They **couldn't** live in a town.
3. The family had to **build** a den in the woods.
4. The **mother** bear took care of her cubs.
5. The cubs' **father** hunted for food for his family.
6. When it got cold, they went **straight** into their den.
7. The bear family has a lot of **love**.

Home Activity Your child learned to read the words *bear, build, couldn't, father, love, mother,* and *straight.* Write each word on an index card or slip of paper. Then have your child pick a card, read the word, and use it in a sentence.

▲ **Practice Book** p. 29, High-Frequency Words

Spelling Words

Consonant Blends

1.	stop	7.	clip
2.	strap*	8.	stream*
3.	nest	9.	mask
4.	hand*	10.	twin
5.	brave	11.	breeze
6.	ask	12.	state

Challenge Words

13.	browse	15.	skeleton
14.	straight		

* Words from the Selection

Consonant Blends

Read the notice about the new ducklings. Find three spelling mistakes. Write the words correctly. Then write the first sentence with the missing end mark.

Spelling Words	
stop	clip
strap	stream
nest	mask
hand	twin
brave	breeze
ask	state

Have you seen the ducklings? Take the path an stop at the sream You can see the nest in the grass near the twine pine trees.

1. **and** 2. **stream** 3. **twin**

Frequently Misspelled Words
brother
and
went

4. **Take the path and stop at the stream.**

Fill in the circle to show the correct spelling. **Write** the word.

5. ● brave ○ brav ○ bave **brave**
6. ○ stat ● state ○ tate **state**
7. ● strap ○ strape ○ stap **strap**
8. ○ klip ○ clipe ● clip **clip**

Home Activity Your child identified misspelled words with the consonant blends *st, str, nd, br, sk, cl,* and *tw.* Take turns thinking of other words with these blends.

▲ **Spelling Practice Book** p. 11

- Discuss synonyms.
- Write sentences with synonyms.

Strategic Intervention

Write the words *large* and *big* on the board and discuss with children that these words mean close to the same thing. List on the board scrambled word pairs of synonyms and help children match them. Use word pairs such as *end, finish; turn, twist; answer, reply; find, locate; high, tall.*

Advanced

Give children a list of words and ask them to find as many synonyms for each word as they can. Let them use dictionaries and other resources. Begin with words such as *add, food, below, country, start, city.*

Extend Language Write on the board the sentence *He called across the playground to his friend.* Circle the word *called* and ask children to think of another word they could use for *called* in this sentence. Possibilities include *shouted, yelled,* and so on. Write their suggestions as they name them and have them read the sentence frame with each word in the place of *called.* Point out that all the words they named are synonyms of *called,* which means the words have the same or almost the same meaning.

Access Content Use the vocabulary strategies and word cards in the ELL Teaching Guide, pp. 17–18.

Vocabulary

SYNONYMS

DISCUSS SYNONYMS Explain to children that synonyms are words that have the same or almost the same meaning. Write on the board the words *little* and *small* as examples. Have children find the words *loud* and *giggled* on p. 79. Brainstorm with children possible synonyms for each word (*loud: noisy; giggled: laughed*). You might also have them think of synonyms for *beautiful* on p. 81 (*pretty*) and *quiet* on p. 87 (*silent*).

EXPAND SELECTION VOCABULARY Brainstorm with children synonyms for selection vocabulary words *shivered* (p. 79), *lanterns* (p. 83), and *snuggled* (p. 86). Have children test their synonyms by reading the sentences aloud with the new word in place of the old one.

He *shook* and put an arm around Mudge. *(shivered)*

Henry unpacked the food and pans and *lights*. *(lanterns)*

Henry's father and mother *cuddled*. *(snuggled)*

Group Time

On-Level	Strategic Intervention	Advanced
Read *Henry and Mudge.* • Use pp. 72–87.	**Read** or listen to *Henry and Mudge.* • Use the **Routine** on p. DI·38.	**Read** Self-Selected Reading. • Use the **Routine** on p. DI·39.

Place English language learners in the groups that correspond to their reading abilities in English.

(i) Independent Activities

Independent Reading See p. 68j for Reading/Library activities and suggestions.

Journal Writing Use synonyms in pairs of sentences about going camping. Share your writing.

Literacy Centers To provide experiences with *Henry and Mudge,* you may use the Writing Center on p. 68k.

Practice Book 2.1 Long Vowels CVCe, p. 28; High-Frequency Words, p. 29

Break into small groups after Vocabulary and before Writing.

Fluency

READ WITH ACCURACY/APPROPRIATE PACE

MODEL READING WITH ACCURACY AND APPROPRIATE PACE AND RATE
Use *Henry and Mudge and the Starry Night*.

- Have children turn to p. 75. You have learned to change how fast you read depending on how easy the selection is. Remember that you have also learned to read words accurately so that you read what is really on the page, not what you think is there.

- Ask children to follow along as you read aloud pp. 75–77.

- Have children read the pages after you. Remind them to adjust their speed and to read accurately. Continue in the same way with p. 78.

REREAD FOR FLUENCY

Choral Reading

ROUTINE

1 **Select a Passage** For *Henry and Mudge and the Starry Night,* use pp. 79–82.

2 **Divide into Groups** Assign each group a part to read. For this story, assign one page to each of four groups.

3 **Model** Have children track the print as you read.

4 **Read Together** Have children read along with you.

5 **Independent Readings** Have the groups read aloud without you. Monitor progress and provide feedback. For optimal fluency, children should reread three to four times.

Monitor Progress	Fluency
If... children have difficulty reading with accuracy and appropriate pace/rate,	**then...** pair them with good readers or with yourself and have them practice one paragraph at a time.
If... the class cannot read fluently without you,	**then...** continue to have them read along with you.

Options for Oral Reading

Use *Henry and Mudge and the Starry Night* or one of the following Leveled Readers.

On-Level
Let's Camp at Crescent Lake

Strategic Intervention
Pup Camps Out

Advanced
A Home in the Wilderness

Use *I Spy Fun* or *Henry and Mudge and the Starry Night*. Recall with children that they have previously practiced changing how fast they read depending on the material, and that they also have practiced reading carefully so that each word is correct. Model reading p. 77 of *Henry and Mudge* aloud with accuracy and at an appropriate rate of speed. Have children reread the paragraphs at the same rate of speed. Give help with accuracy as necessary.

To develop fluent readers, use Fluency Coach.

Think and Share

Retelling Plan

Retelling Plan

☑ Week 1 assess Strategic Intervention students.

☑ Week 2 assess Advanced students.

☑ **This week assess Strategic Intervention students.**

☐ Week 4 assess On-Level students.

☐ Week 5 assess any students you have not yet checked during this unit.

Look Back and Write
For test practice, assign a 10–15 minute time limit. For informal or formal assessment, see the Scoring Rubric below.

TALK ABOUT IT Model a response. I liked seeing all the trees and animals. I loved being free to follow the smells of animals in the woods. I thought the best smells were the deer and raccoon and Henry's mom's cooking.

1. **RETELL** Have children use the retelling strip in the Student Edition to retell the story using supportive facts and details.

Monitor Progress | **Check Retelling**

If... children have difficulty retelling the story,

then... use the Retelling Cards and the Scoring Rubric for Retelling on p. 88–89 to help them move toward fluent retelling.

SUCCESS PREDICTOR

Day 1 Check Word Reading
Day 2 Check High-Frequency Words
▶**Day 3 Check Retelling**
Day 4 Check Fluency
Day 5 Assess Progress

2. **CHARACTER AND SETTING** The characters are Henry, his parents, and his dog Mudge. The story takes place in August near Big Bear Lake.

3. **MONITOR AND FIX UP** Model a response. I was a little confused at the beginning when the story said they were going camping but then they went hiking. But I just continued to read and found out they were looking for a place to camp.

LOOK BACK AND WRITE Read the writing prompt on p. 88 and model your thinking. I'll look back at pages 76 and 77 and read that part of the selection again. I'll think about who knew all about camping and what that person did to help with the camping trip. Then I'll write my response. Have children write their responses.

Scoring Rubric | **Look Back and Write**

Top-Score Response A top-score response will use details from p. 76 and other parts of the selection to tell who knew about camping and what she did to help with the camping trip.
Example of a Top-Score Response Henry's mother knew all about camping. She picked the place to camp and set up the tent. She built a campfire and cooked their camp food.

For additional rubrics, see p. WA10.

Think and Share

Talk About It Pretend you are Mudge. What were the best sights and smells on the camping trip?

1. Look at the pictures below. They are in the wrong order. Reorder them, then retell the story. **Retell**

2. Who are the characters in this story? Describe the setting. **Character/Setting**

3. Did anything in this story confuse you? What did you do about it? **Monitor and Fix Up**

Look Back and Write Look at pages 76 and 77. Who knew all about camping? What did that person do to help with the camping trip? Use details from the story.

Meet the Author and the Illustrator

Cynthia Rylant

Cynthia Rylant never read many books when she was young. There was no library in her town.

After college, Ms. Rylant worked in a library. "Within a few weeks, I fell in love with children's books," she says. She has written over 60 books!

Read more books by Cynthia Rylant.

Suçie Stevenson

Suçie Stevenson has drawn pictures for most of the Henry and Mudge books. Her brother's Great Dane, Jake, was her inspiration for Mudge.

Retelling Strip

88

89

Scoring Rubric — Narrative Retelling

Rubric 4 3 2 1	4	3	2	1
Connections	Makes connections and generalizes beyond the text	Makes connections to other events, stories, or experiences	Makes a limited connection to another event, story, or experience	Makes no connection to another event, story, or experience
Author's Purpose	Elaborates on author's purpose	Tells author's purpose with some clarity	Makes some connection to author's purpose	Makes no connection to author's purpose
Characters	Describes the main character(s) and any character development	Identifies the main character(s) and gives some information about them	Inaccurately identifies some characters or gives little information about them	Inaccurately identifies the characters or gives no information about them
Setting	Describes the time and location	Identifies the time and location	Omits details of time or location	Is unable to identify time or location
Plot	Describes the events in sequence, using rich detail	Tells the plot with some errors in sequence that do not affect meaning	Tells parts of plot with gaps that affect meaning	Retelling has no sense of story

Use the Retelling Chart on p. TR20 to record retelling.

Selection Test To assess with *Henry and Mudge*, use Selection Tests, pp. 9–12.

Fresh Reads for Differentiated Test Practice For weekly leveled practice, use pp. 13–18.

Retelling

SUCCESS PREDICTOR

OBJECTIVE

● Recognize and use good word choice in writing.

DAILY FIX-IT

5. The stap on my backpack.
The <u>strap</u> on my backpack <u>broke</u>.

6. That stem of water
That <u>stream</u> of water <u>was cold.</u>

Connect to Unit Writing

Writing Trait

Have children use strategies for developing **word choice** when they write a personal narrative in the Unit Writing Workshop, pp. WA2–WA9.

Writing Trait of the Week

INTRODUCE Word Choice

TALK ABOUT WORD CHOICE Explain to children that they should choose words carefully to add style to their writing. Using exact nouns, strong verbs, and exciting adjectives will make their work clear and lively. Ask children to think about words the author of *Henry and Mudge and the Starry Night* uses to create vivid word pictures. Then model your thinking.

 MODEL When I read about Henry and Mudge's camping trip, I get a good picture of what it looked like and felt like. For example, on page 79, it says, "Mudge gave a big, slow, loud, yawn. He drooled on Henry's foot." What are some words that help you picture exactly how Mudge yawned? *(big, slow, loud)* Which vivid action verb helps you picture what Mudge did besides yawning? *(drooled)*

Everyone slept safe and sound, and there were no bears, no scares. Just the clean smell of trees . . . and wonderful green dreams.

What vivid words give readers pictures in this passage? *(bears, scares, clean, smell, trees, green, dreams)*

STRATEGY FOR DEVELOPING WORD CHOICE On the board, write the following sentences. Ask children to fill in the blanks with vivid words.

> **They fished in a _____ lake.** *(clear, blue)*
>
> **We saw _____ wildflowers.** *(bright, yellow)*
>
> **I _____ down the path.** *(hiked, jogged)*
>
> **Pam _____ at the sky.** *(gazed, squinted)*

PRACTICE

APPLY THE STRATEGY Ask children to think about a time they enjoyed the outdoors. Have them brainstorm phrases that vividly describe what they saw or felt. *(orange and red autumn leaves, sparkling white snow)* Have children use their phrases to write a paragraph that describes a vivid outdoor scene.

ELL

Word Choice To help children use exact words rather than vague ones, develop a web with a word such as *nice* in the center and around it strong words that can replace it. *(friendly, helpful, kind, polite, generous)* Pronounce each word and help children understand its meaning.

Grammar

APPLY TO WRITING Predicates

IMPROVE WRITING WITH PREDICATES Point out to children that sentences without predicates are not complete thoughts and do not make sense. Remind children to use predicates correctly in their writing.

Suggest that children write two or three sentences about something they discovered by exploring nature. Tell them to make sure all their sentences include predicates.

One day I found a baby bird on the sidewalk.
I looked up and saw the bird's nest in a tree.
The baby must have fallen out of the nest.

PRACTICE

WRITE WITH PREDICATES Have children add two or three sentences that tell something else they discovered about nature. Remind them to be sure every sentence has a predicate.

Predicates

Tell about a time when you went on a hike or a walk.
Circle the predicates in your sentences.

Possible answer:

I hiked with my mom and dad.

We walked for a long time.

I was tired. We came home.

I went to sleep.

Home Activity Your child learned how to use the predicates of sentences in writing. Have your child write you a note and ask him or her to circle the predicate in each sentence.

▲ **Grammar and Writing Practice Book** p. 10

Wrap Up Your Day!

✓ **CHARACTER AND SETTING** Ask children to recall who the characters in the story were. (Henry, Mudge, Henry's father and mother) What is the setting of the story? (It takes place in August near Big Bear Lake.)

✓ **READ WITH ACCURACY AND APPROPRIATE PACE/RATE** Review with children that they should read every word correctly and change the speed of their reading to match the difficulty of the material. Have children take turns reading the second paragraph on p. 80 accurately and with appropriate pace and rate.

LET'S TALK ABOUT IT Discuss with children what Henry and Mudge discovered by exploring nature. Display the web from Day 1 and have children add ovals to tell what Henry and Mudge discovered as they were exploring nature.

PREVIEW Day 4

Tell children that tomorrow they will read about some people who think stars make pictures in the night sky.

Share Literature
Insects Are My Life

Phonics and Spelling

Consonant Blends

Spelling: Words with Consonant Blends

Read

Group Time < Differentiated Instruction

"Star Pictures in the Sky"

Fluency
Read with Accuracy and Appropriate Pace/Rate

Writing Across the Curriculum
Captioned Drawing

Grammar
Predicates

Speaking and Listening
Be a Good Speaker

Materials

- *Sing with Me Big Book*
- *Read Aloud Anthology*
- Student Edition 90–93

Morning Warm~Up!

How do stars make pictures in the sky? You can see some star pictures during autumn and some others before the fall season.

QUESTION OF THE DAY Encourage children to sing "Tranquil Nights" from the *Sing with Me Big Book* as you gather. Write and read the message and discuss the question.

REVIEW SYNONYMS

- Ask children to identify the words they see in the message that are synonyms. *(autumn, fall)*

- Have children read the synonyms aloud, giving help as necessary.

ELL

Extend Language Use the Day 4 instruction on ELL Poster 3 to extend and enrich language.

ELL Poster 3

Share Literature

CONNECT CONCEPTS

ACTIVATE PRIOR KNOWLEDGE Recall with children the story of Henry and Mudge. Discuss ways in which Henry and Mudge explored nature. Explain that the class will hear another story about a girl who likes to explore, but this girl explores bugs.

Read Aloud Anthology
Insects Are My Life

BUILD ORAL VOCABULARY Explain to children that today you will read a story about a girl who is very interested in exploring one part of nature— insects. Tell children that Amanda likes to be a **detective** about insects. That means she wants to find out as much as she can about them. She finds insects **fascinating,** or very, very interesting, even the **slimy** ones like snails. Have children listen to the story to find out what Amanda does that shows she finds insects fascinating.

REVIEW ORAL VOCABULARY After reading, review all the Amazing Words for the week. Have children take turns using them in sentences that tell about the concept for the week. Then talk about Amazing Words they learned in other weeks and connect them to the concept, as well. For example, ask:

- If you could take a **journey** anywhere to explore nature, where would you go?
- What kind of wildlife likes to **dart** around or **investigate** everything?
- What is the most **enormous creature** you have ever seen with your own eyes?

MONITOR LISTENING COMPREHENSION

- Amanda used a detective kit to look closely at bugs. What do you think might be in a detective kit? Why do you think so? (**Possible answer: a magnifying glass**) Why might a magnifying glass be in a detective kit? (**because it helps you see things up close**)

- What did Amanda mean when she said, "Insects are fascinating?" (**She meant that she liked them a lot and thought about them a lot.**)

- What makes you think that both Amanda and her brother want to discover things by exploring nature? (**Amanda wants to know everything she can about insects. Her brother Andrew wants to know everything he can about dinosaurs.**)

OBJECTIVES

- Set purpose for listening.
- Build oral vocabulary.

Amazing Words to build oral vocabulary

Amazing Words	**MONITOR PROGRESS**
galaxy tranquil wildlife underneath identify detective fascinating slimy	**If…** children lack oral vocabulary experiences about the concept Exploration, **then…** use the Oral Vocabulary Routine. See p. DI·5 to teach *detective, fascinating,* and *slimy.*

Connect Concepts Explain to children that Amanda is a girl who is especially interested in insects. She loves looking at them and finding out about them. She likes them so much that she tries to protect and take care of them.

OBJECTIVES

- Reviews short vowels CVC, CVCC, and short *e: ea*
- Reviews long vowels CVC*e*.
- Reviews high-frequency words *everywhere, live, machines, move, woman, work, world.*

Sentence Reading

REVIEW WORDS IN CONTEXT

READ DECODABLE AND HIGH-FREQUENCY WORDS IN CONTEXT Write these sentences. Call on individuals to read a sentence. Then randomly point to words and have them read. To help you monitor word reading, high-frequency words are underlined and decodable words are circled.

The (strap) on the (backpack) (broke) and books (went) everywhere.

Who was (brave) enough to live and work in the (wide) open (West)?

Machines (help) (dump) and (spread) (piles) of (rocks).

We (will) (bake) (bread) for our (snack).

The (wind) was (strong) enough to (make) the (kite) move.

The (wise) woman (just) (went) on a (trip) around the world.

Monitor Progress	Word Reading
If... children are unable to read an underlined word,	**then...** read the word for them and spell it, having them echo you.
If... children are unable to read a circled word,	**then...** have them use the blending strategy they have learned for that word type.

Support Phonics For additional review, see the phonics activities in the ELL and Transition Handbook.

Spelling

PARTNER REVIEW Consonant Blends

READ AND WRITE Supply pairs of children with index cards on which the spelling words have been written. Have one child read a word while the other writes it. Then have children switch roles. Have them use the cards to check their spelling.

HOMEWORK Spelling Practice Book, p. 12

OBJECTIVE

● Spell words with consonant blends.

Spelling Words

Consonant Blends

1.	stop	7.	clip
2.	strap*	8.	stream*
3.	nest	9.	mask
4.	hand*	10.	twin
5.	brave	11.	breeze
6.	ask	12.	state

Challenge Words

13.	browse	15.	skeleton
14.	straight		

* Words from the Selection

Group Time

On-Level

Read "Star Pictures in the Sky."

• Use pp. 90–93.

Strategic Intervention

Read or listen to "Star Pictures in the Sky."

• Use the **Routine** on p. DI·40.

Advanced

Read "Star Pictures in the Sky."

• Use the **Routine** on p. DI·41.

ELL Place English language learners in the groups that correspond to their reading abilities in English.

DAY 4

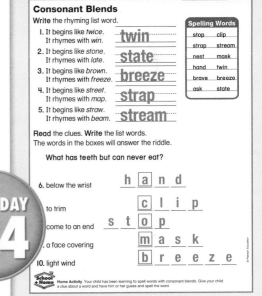

▲ **Spelling Practice Book** p. 12

(i) Independent Activities

Fluency Reading Pair children to reread *Henry and Mudge and the Starry Night.*

Journal Writing List wildlife you might find in a park or in your backyard. Share writing.

Spelling Partner Review

Independent Reading See p. 68j for Reading/Library activities and suggestions.

Literacy Centers To provide listening opportunities, you may use the Listening Center on p. 68j. To extend science concepts, you may use the Science Center on p. 68k.

Break into small groups after Spelling and before Fluency.

Star Pictures in the Sky
by Lorraine McCombs

Have you ever connected the dots to make a picture? Think about the stars in the sky. A long time ago, people saw the stars as dots in the night sky. They imagined lines going from star to star. They called these star pictures *constellations*.

On a very dark night away from the city, we can see hundreds of stars in the sky. We can even see the same constellations that people saw long ago. Here are a few of them.

90   91

AudioText

OBJECTIVE

● Recognize text structure: nonfiction.

TIME FOR Science

Stars

Stars are always in the sky. However, during daytime, the light from the sun makes it impossible for people to see the stars. At night, clouds and nearby light can also make it impossible for people to see stars.

Read Science in Reading

PREVIEW AND PREDICT Read the title and author's name on p. 90. Have children preview the article, looking at the illustrations and reading their captions. Provide help as necessary with the captions. Then ask children to predict what they think they might find out when they read the selection. Have children read to learn what they might discover by exploring the stars.

INFORMATIONAL TEXT Remind children that nonfiction tells facts about real things. Explain that the pictures in this article show how stars really appear in the sky, although the outlines of the pictures don't really exist; they are there to show them the pictures that some people see in that group of stars.

VOCABULARY/SYNONYMS Review with children that synonyms are words that have the same or almost the same meaning. Have children locate *imagined* and *few* on p. 91. What are synonyms for these words? (*thought; some*)

This star picture, or constellation, is called Orion. It is named after a famous hunter in Greek stories. We see Orion best in the winter sky. This constellation has three stars in a row. They are thought of as Orion's belt.

The Big Dipper is a star picture in the constellation called Big Bear. We can see the Big Dipper any time of the year, but it is best seen between January and October. Two stars in the Big Dipper point toward the very bright North Star.

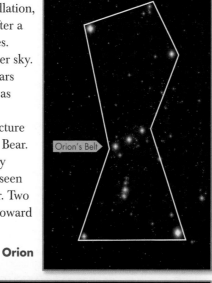

Orion

Big Dipper

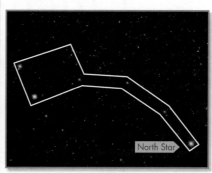

Little Dipper

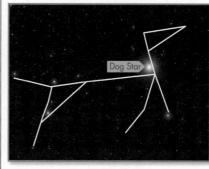

Big Dog

Another star picture is the Little Dipper. You can see the Little Dipper all year. Notice the handle. The brightest star in the handle is the North Star. It never moves. For hundreds of years, people have used the North Star to find their way.

Canis was a dog in Greek stories. *Canis* means "dog," and this constellation is known as the Big Dog. The very bright star is called the Dog Star. It is the brightest star in our whole nighttime sky. You can usually find this constellation in the summer sky between July and September.

The next time you look up at a dark, starry sky, think about these constellations. Connect the dots as people did long ago. What star pictures do you see?

92   93

BUILD CONCEPTS

Compare and Contrast • Critical

- **How are the Big Dipper and the Little Dipper alike? How are they different?**
  The Dippers both look like dippers, or ladles. However, the Little Dipper seems upside down and shaped differently.

Graphic Sources • Inferential

- **How do the outlines on the stars help you see the shapes of and identify the constellations?**
  They show exactly where the connections are between the stars so we can figure out and identify the pictures.

CONNECT TEXT TO TEXT

Do you think Henry and his parents saw some of these constellations when they were looking at stars that night? Why or why not?

Possible answer: Yes, especially the Big Dog and the Big Dipper and Little Dipper.

Access Content Explain that the stars always appear in the same positions to each other, although not all are visible every night. The word *constellation* means a group of stars that seems to make the outline of a picture.

OBJECTIVE

● Read aloud with accuracy and appropriate pace.

Options for Oral Reading

Use *Henry and Mudge* or one of the following Leveled Readers.

On-Level

Let's Camp at Crescent Lake

Strategic Intervention

Pup Camps Out

Advanced

A Home in the Wilderness

Use *I Spy Fun* or "Star Pictures in the Sky." Provide opportunities for children to read one-on-one with an aide or parent volunteer, if possible. The adult models by reading first, and then the child reads and rereads the same text, with adult guidance. Allow extra repetitions for English language learners, to improve their fluency.

To develop fluent readers, use Fluency Coach.

Fluency

READ WITH ACCURACY/APPROPRIATE PACE

MODEL READING WITH ACCURACY AND APPROPRIATE PACE Use *Henry and Mudge.*

- Have children turn to p. 83. Remind them that they may have to change their reading speed to understand what they read. Tell them to read each word exactly the way it is written so they don't make mistakes.

- Ask children to follow along as you read p. 83 aloud.

- Have children read the page after you. Encourage them to adjust their speed as necessary and to read every word accurately. Continue in the same way with pp. 86–87.

REREAD FOR FLUENCY

Paired Reading

ROUTINE

1 **Select a Passage** For *Henry and Mudge,* use pp. 75–83.

2 **Reader 1 Begins** Have children read, switching readers at the end of each page.

3 **Reader 2 Begins** Have partners reread; now the other partner begins.

Reread For optimal fluency, children should reread three or four times with attention to accuracy, pace, and expression.

4 **Provide Feedback** Listen as children read and provide corrective feedback regarding their oral reading and their use of the blending strategy.

Monitor Progress | Check Fluency WCPM

As children reread, monitor their progress toward their individual fluency goals. Current Goal: 50–60 words correct per minute. End-of-Year Goal: 90 words correct per minute.

If... children cannot read fluently at a rate of 50–60 words correct per minute,

then... make sure children practice with text at their independent level. Provide additional fluency practice, pairing nonfluent readers with fluent readers.

If... children already read fluently at 90 words correct per minute,

then... they do not need to reread three to four times.

SUCCESS PREDICTOR

Day 1 Check Word Reading

Day 2 Check High-Frequency Words

Day 3 Check Retelling

▶ **Day 4 Check Fluency**

Day 5 Assess Progress

Writing Across the Curriculum

WRITE Captioned Drawing

LOOK AT Have children look again at the illustrations on pp. 92–93. Review with them what they learned about constellations.

SHARE THE PEN Have groups of children draw several dots on a piece of paper. Ask children to make a list of different things the constellation could be. Write items from the list on the board, inviting individuals to help spell the words. Ask questions, such as the following:

- What is the first sound you hear in *the?* (/th/)
- What letters stand for that sound? *(th)* Have a volunteer write *th*.

Continue having individuals contribute to the list. Children can connect the dots to demonstrate how they found the items in the dots.

OBJECTIVE

- Create a captioned drawing.

Advanced

Encourage children to create their own constellation and write a caption for it.

E L L

Support Writing Point out that the caption for children's constellation drawings might always begin "The name of our constellation is…" Invite children to practice a similar pattern orally, saying, for example, "The name of our teacher is…" or "The name of our school is…"

4

OBJECTIVE

● Identify predicates.

DAILY FIX-IT

7. Jen's bike

Jen's bike <u>had a flat tire.</u>

8. she and Jim

She and Jim <u>walked home.</u>

Predicates

Mark the letter of the predicate that completes each sentence.

1. We ___
   - ⊗ A hiked.
   - ○ B in the woods.
   - ○ C Mom and I.

2. My dad and I ___
   - ○ A good food.
   - ⊗ B saw a snake.
   - ○ C my sister.

3. A campfire ___
   - ○ A his friend.
   - ⊗ B is fun.
   - ○ C and loud.

4. The stew ___
   - ⊗ A tastes good.
   - ○ B cold rain.
   - ○ C tired.

5. The lake ___
   - ○ A cats and dogs.
   - ○ B that time.
   - ⊗ C has many fish.

6. Dad ___
   - ○ A on the trail.
   - ⊗ B catches a fish.
   - ○ C a hot pan.

 Home Activity Your child prepared for taking tests on predicates of sentences. Have your child write several sentences about something your family did together. Ask your child to underline the predicate in each sentence.

▲ **Grammar and Writing Practice Book** p. 11

Grammar

REVIEW Predicates

DEFINE PREDICATES

- What is the predicate of a sentence? (the part that tells what the subject does or is)
- What part of a sentence tells what the subject does or is? (the predicate)

PRACTICE

IDENTIFY PREDICATES Write the following sentences, omitting the underlines. Have children work as a group to underline the predicate in each one.

Jim and Jen <u>liked to ride their bikes.</u>

They <u>wanted to explore nature.</u>

They <u>rode their bikes to the park.</u>

Both of them <u>looked for living things.</u>

They <u>found trees, insects, and birds.</u>

Speaking and Listening

BE A GOOD SPEAKER

DEMONSTRATE SPEAKING Explain to children that a good speaker does several things as he or she contributes to a classroom discussion. Write the following chart on the board and work through each direction, explaining and demonstrating it as you do so. Emphasize adjusting your speaking tone and volume to suit the setting.

Classroom Speakers

- **Speak slowly and carefully.**
- **Stand or sit up straight.**
- **Raise your hand and ask to speak.**
- **Speak loudly enough to be heard.**
- **Take turns.**

MAKE A WEB Use Graphic Organizer 15 or make a web on the board. Write in the center oval *What have we discovered by exploring nature?* Ask children to follow the rules for speakers as they brainstorm answers to add to the web.

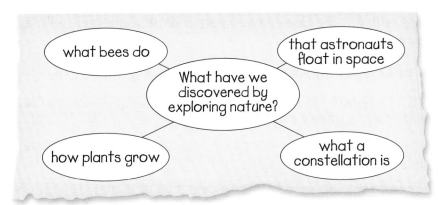

▲ **Graphic Organizer 15**

Wrap Up Your Day!

✓ *Text to Text* Review with children the story of Henry and Mudge going camping and the article about constellations. How does the article about constellations help you understand what Henry and his parents saw on the starry night?

LET'S TALK ABOUT IT Remind children that *nature* means anything that people did not make. Henry and his parents saw stars when they went camping. Are stars part of nature? How do you know? Provide the web that children worked with previously. Have them add what they learned about constellations.

PREVIEW Day 5

Remind children that they heard a story about a girl who loves bugs. Tell them that tomorrow they will hear about Amanda Frankenstein again.

Day 5
AT A GLANCE

Share Literature
Insects Are My Life

Phonics and Spelling
 Review Consonant Blends

High-Frequency Words
couldn't	love	**Word Wall**
build	mother	
bear	father	straight

Monitor Progress
Spelling Test: Words with Consonant Blends

Group Time < Differentiated Assessment

Writing and Grammar
Trait: Word Choice

Predicates

Research and Study Skills
Parts of a Book

Materials

- *Sing with Me Big Book*
- *Read Aloud Anthology*
- Reproducible Pages TE 94f–94g
- Student Edition 94–95

Morning Warm~Up!

This week we read about
exploring nature.
Henry and Mudge found wildlife
and a galaxy of stars.
If they looked underneath rocks,
could they identify fascinating insects?

QUESTION OF THE DAY Encourage children to sing "Tranquil Nights" from the *Sing with Me Big Book* as you gather. Write and read the message and discuss the question.

REVIEW ORAL VOCABULARY Discuss the message with children.

- What might you see in the sky on a tranquil night when you were on a camping trip? (a galaxy of stars)

- What might you see in the woods on a camping trip? (wildlife, fascinating birds and insects)

- If you were a wildlife detective, how would you identify slimy worms you found underneath rocks? (Possible answer: by using a magnifying glass and finding pictures of them in books that identify them)

Assess Vocabulary Use the Day 5 instruction on ELL Poster 3 to monitor children's progress with oral vocabulary.

ELL Poster 3

Share Literature

LISTEN AND RESPOND

USE PRIOR KNOWLEDGE Review with children that they listened to the story "Insects Are My Life" to find out what Amanda does that shows she finds insects fascinating. Suggest that children listen to the story again to find out what Amanda is discovering by exploring nature.

MONITOR LISTENING COMPREHENSION

- What was Amanda discovering by exploring nature? (She was finding out how fascinating insects are.)

- Amanda and her brother Andrew are two characters in the story who have different points of view about insects. What was Amanda's? (She loved insects.) What was Andrew's? (He hated insects and called them slimy.) Why do you suppose they had such different points of view? (Possible answer: They were both interested in wildlife. Andrew was interested in dinosaurs and just didn't care about insects; Amanda found them fascinating and liked to identify them.)

Read Aloud Anthology
Insects Are My Life

BUILD ORAL VOCABULARY

GENERATE DISCUSSION Recall how much Amanda loves studying insects. She even plans to make a career out of studying insects by becoming an entomologist when she grows up. Have children discuss what they love to do and how they could turn that into a career. Have them use some of this week's Amazing Words as they share their ideas.

Monitor Progress | **Check Oral Vocabulary**

Display pp. 68–69 in the Student Edition and remind children of the unit concept—Exploration. Ask them to tell you about the photographs using some of this week's Amazing Words: *galaxy, tranquil, wildlife, underneath, identify, detective, fascinating,* and *slimy.*

If... children have difficulty using the Amazing Words,

then... ask questions about the photographs using the Amazing Words. Note which questions children can respond to. Reteach unknown words using the Oral Vocabulary Routine on p. DI·1.

 SUCCESS PREDICTOR

Day 1 Check Word Reading

Day 2 Check High-Frequency Words

Day 3 Check Retelling

Day 4 Check Fluency

▶ **Day 5** Check Oral Vocabulary/ Assess Progress

OBJECTIVES

- Set purpose for listening.
- Build oral vocabulary.

 **Amazing Words** to build oral vocabulary

galaxy	identify
tranquil	detective
wildlife	fascinating
underneath	slimy

ELL

Extend Language Remind children that synonyms are words that mean the same or almost the same thing. Invite them to provide several examples from their home language. Then help them use what they know about English to name synonyms for *hot (warm), cold (chilly), bad (awful),* and *good (nice).*

Oral Vocabulary

SUCCESS PREDICTOR

◉ Consonant Blends

REVIEW

IDENTIFY CONSONANT BLEND WORDS Write these sentences. Have children read each one aloud. Call on individuals to name and underline the words with consonant blends.

The <u>green</u> <u>frog</u> is <u>small</u>.
Did you <u>slip</u> on the <u>stone</u> <u>step</u>?
We will <u>fly</u> to the <u>state</u> of <u>Florida</u>.
This <u>tree</u> is the <u>last</u> one we will <u>plant</u>.

High-Frequency Words

REVIEW

COMPLETE THE RHYME Read the following rhyme aloud. Have children write a word from Words to Know on p. 70 for each blank. Then read the completed rhyme aloud to check answers.

My _____ is the greatest dad. **(father)**
I _____ him with all my heart. **(love)**
My _____ is the greatest mom. **(mother)**
We will never be apart.

I _____ ask for better folks **(couldn't)**
To help me _____ or bake or sew. **(build)**
They help me keep my bedroom _____, **(straight)**
And give me a big _____ hug, you know! **(bear)**

ELL

Access Content For additional practice with the high-frequency words, use the vocabulary strategies and word cards in the ELL Teaching Guide, pp. 17–18.

SPELLING TEST Consonant Blends

DICTATION SENTENCES Use these sentences to assess this week's spelling words.

1. There was a <u>breeze</u> at the lake.
2. I have a cut on my <u>hand</u>.
3. His <u>twin</u> brother is at my house.
4. I see a <u>nest</u> in that tree.
5. Did you <u>stop</u> at the school?
6. I will <u>ask</u> Mom if you can visit.
7. She will fix the <u>strap</u> for you.
8. Ann will <u>clip</u> her papers together.
9. He won't put on the <u>mask</u>.
10. The girl was very <u>brave</u>.
11. Dad said not to jump over the <u>stream</u>.
12. Uncle Jim lives in another <u>state</u>.

CHALLENGE WORDS

13. I like to <u>browse</u> in the hat shop.
14. Mom said to make a <u>straight</u> line.
15. Did you see my picture of a <u>skeleton</u>?

ASSESS

● Spell words with consonant blends.

Spelling Words

Consonant Blends

1. stop	7. clip
2. strap*	8. stream*
3. nest	9. mask
4. hand*	10. twin
5. brave	11. breeze
6. ask	12. state

Challenge Words

13. browse 15. skeleton
14. straight

* Words from the Selection

Group Time

On-Level	Strategic Intervention	Advanced
Read Set B Sentences and the Story.	**Read** Set A Sentences.	**Read** Set C Sentences.
• Use pp. 94e–94g.	• Use pp. 94e–94g.	• Use pp. 94e–94g.
	• Use the **Routine** on p. DI·42.	• Use the **Routine** on p. DI·43.

DAY 5

ELL Place English language learners in the groups that correspond to their reading abilities in English.

(i) Independent Activities

Fluency Reading Children reread selections at their independent level.

Journal Writing Write about what it might be like to travel through the galaxy. Share writing.

Independent Reading See p. 68j for Reading/Library activities and suggestions.

Literacy Centers You may use the Technology Center on p. 68k to support this week's concepts and reading.

Practice Book 2.1 Parts of a Book, p. 30

Break into small groups after Spelling and before Grammar and Writing.

ASSESS

- Decode words with consonant blends.
- Read high-frequency words.
- Read aloud with appropriate speed and accuracy.
- Identify characters and setting.
- Retell a story.

Differentiated Assessment

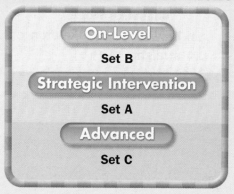

On-Level

Set B

Strategic Intervention

Set A

Advanced

Set C

Fluency Assessment Plan

- ☑ Week 1 assess Advanced students.
- ☑ Week 2 assess Strategic Intervention students.
- ☑ **This week assess On-Level students.**
- ☐ Week 4 assess Strategic Intervention students.
- ☐ Week 5 assess any students you have not yet checked during this unit.

Set individual fluency goals for children to enable them to reach the end-of-year goal.

- Current Goal: 50–60 wcpm
- End-of-Year Goal: 90 wcpm
- **ELL** Oral fluency depends not only on reading without halting but also on word recognition. After children read passages aloud for assessment, help them recognize unfamiliar English words and their meanings. Focus on each child's progress.

SENTENCE READING

ASSESS CONSONANT BLENDS AND HIGH-FREQUENCY WORDS Use one of the reproducible lists on p. 94f to assess children's ability to read words with consonant blends and high-frequency words. Call on individuals to read two sentences aloud. Have each child in the group read different sentences. Start over with sentence one if necessary.

RECORD SCORES Use the Sentence Reading Chart for this unit on p. WA19.

Monitor Progress Consonant Blends	
If... children have trouble reading words with consonant blends,	**then...** use the Reteach Lesson on p. DI·66.
High-Frequency Words	
If... children cannot read a high-frequency word,	**then...** mark the missed word on a high-frequency word list and send the list home for additional word reading practice, or have the child practice with a fluent reader.

FLUENCY AND COMPREHENSION

ASSESS FLUENCY Take a one-minute sample of children's oral reading. See Monitoring Fluency, p. WA17. Have children read "A World in the City," the on-level fluency passage on p. 94g.

RECORD SCORES Record the number of words read correctly in one minute on the child's Fluency Progress Chart.

ASSESS COMPREHENSION Have the child read to the end of the passage. (If the child had difficulty with the passage, you may read it aloud.) Ask who are the characters in the story and what the setting is. Have the child retell the passage. Use the Retelling Rubric on p. 88–89 to evaluate the child's retelling.

Monitor Progress Fluency	
If... a child does not achieve the fluency goal on the timed reading,	**then...** copy the passage and send it home with the child for additional fluency practice, or have the child practice with a fluent reader.
Character and Setting	
If... a child cannot identify the characters and setting,	**then...** use the Reteach Lesson on p. DI·66.

READ THE SENTENCES

Set A

1. The old black bear couldn't run very fast.
2. I love to ride over the bump on that bridge.
3. Let's build a tree house near the nest.
4. My mother told me to drink my milk.
5. Does your father have flowers in the yard?
6. Trot straight down that street.

Set B

1. He couldn't write with the blue ink.
2. Tom loves to swim and jump in the water.
3. Brad will help build a green doghouse.
4. My mother drives a big truck.
5. My father got a blue shirt from my mother.
6. The bear went straight to the big tree.

Set C

1. Kent couldn't stop himself as he coasted down the hill.
2. I love spring when the flowers bloom and look fresh and perfect.
3. It wasn't my dad's fault that he couldn't start to build my tree house that day.
4. My mother kept all my drawings from first grade.
5. Your father has my grandfather's old belt tied around his waist.
6. To get to Big Bear Camp, head straight down Spring Street.

Monitor Progress   **Consonant Blends**
High-Frequency Words

SUCCESS PREDICTOR

A World in the City

Grace and Trent were twins who lived in a	9
skyscraper in a huge city. One day their mother's	18
sister Chris came over to visit.	24
"How is school going?" she asked.	30
"We're reading about exploring the world,"	36
Grace said. "We found out about stars."	43
"But Grace and I can't explore the world," Trent	52
said. "We have to stay right here in this place."	62
Chris said, "Well, you have trees in the city.	71
We have birds, and we have the sky. We also	81
have flowers growing in the front yard. And most	90
of all, we have the lake!"	96
She went over to the big window. "Tell me what	106
you see from here."	110
"I see the sun and waves and the beach, and I	121
also see some small clouds," said Grace.	128
"Oh, I get it!" Trent said. "We can explore the	138
world right outside our window!"	143

See also Assessment Handbook, p. 306 • REPRODUCIBLE PAGE

Monitor Progress | Fluency Passage

94g

SUCCESS PREDICTOR

Write Now
Writing and Grammar

Story

Prompt

In *Henry and Mudge*, a family camps in the woods.
Think about a fun outdoor place. Now write a story that tells about something that happens at this place.

Writing Trait

Vivid **word choice** makes a picture for your readers.

Student Model

Topic is named in first sentence.

> Luke goes to the beach on hot summer days. He splashes in the cool water. He digs in the warm sand. He finds smooth rocks and pretty seashells for a sand castle. Luke throws bread to the noisy gulls. They always want more.

Details tell about things Luke does.

Writer chooses strong, vivid words.

94

Writer's Checklist

- **Focus** Do all sentences tell about an outdoor place?
- **Organization** Are ideas in an order that makes sense?
- **Support** Does each detail add more information?
- **Conventions** Are punctuation and spelling correct?

Grammar

Predicates

The **predicate** tells what the subject of a sentence does or is.

Henry and Mudge **walked down the trail.**

The words **walked down the trail** tell what Henry and Mudge did.

Look at the sentences in the beach story. Write the predicates of the first three sentences.

95

Writing and Grammar

LOOK AT THE PROMPT Read p. 94 aloud. Have children select and discuss key words or phrases in the prompt. *(fun outdoor place, story, something that happens at this place)*

STRATEGIES TO DEVELOP WORD CHOICE Have children

- picture the place in their minds and write details about what they "see."
- make a word web with words that tell what they see, hear, smell, taste, and feel in the place.
- look for places in their story where they can add more descriptive words.

See Scoring Rubric on p. WA11. **Rubric** 4 3 2 1

HINTS FOR BETTER WRITING Read p. 95 aloud. Use the checklist to help children revise their stories. Discuss the grammar lesson. (Answers: *goes to the beach on hot summer days, splashes in the cool water, digs in the warm sand*) Have children make sure that the sentences in their stories have predicates.

DAILY FIX-IT

9. Henry and Mudge
Henry and Mudge <u>went</u> <u>camping.</u>

10. the cooking does Henry's mother
Henry's mother <u>does</u> <u>the</u> <u>cooking.</u>

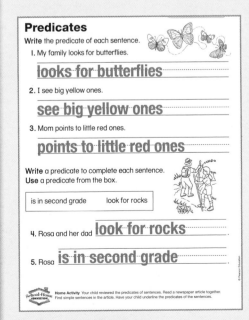

Predicates

Write the predicate of each sentence.

1. My family looks for butterflies.

<u>looks for butterflies</u>

2. I see big yellow ones.

<u>see big yellow ones</u>

3. Mom points to little red ones.

<u>points to little red ones</u>

Write a predicate to complete each sentence. Use a predicate from the box.

| is in second grade | look for rocks |

4. Rosa and her dad <u>look for rocks</u>

5. Rosa <u>is in second grade</u>

Home Activity Your child reviewed the predicates of sentences. Read a newspaper article together. Find simple sentences in the article. Have your child underline the predicates of the sentences.

▲ **Grammar and Writing Practice Book** p. 12

Look at the table of contents and the index from a book.
Write the answer to each question.

Table of Contents	Index
Nature Around Us	reptiles, 17–19
Chapter 1	lizards, 18
Plants 3	snakes, 19
Chapter 2	rocks, 30
Animals. 15	seasons, 6
Chapter 3	trees, 4–5
Land 25	water, 4, 16, 28

1. How many chapters are in this book? __3__

2. In which chapter would you look to find out about cows?

__Chapter 2: Animals__

3. On which page does Chapter 3 begin? __25__

4. On which page is there information about rocks? __30__

5. Which reptiles does the book discuss?

__lizards, snakes__

Home Activity Your child learned about parts of a book, including how to use the table of contents at the front of the book and the index in the back. With your child, look at a nonfiction book. Ask your child to find the title and author's name on the cover. Look at the table of contents together. Take turns using the index to find the location of specific topics in the book.

▲ **Practice Book 2.1** p. 30,
Parts of a Book

Access Content You may want to explain to children that not all books have all the parts discussed. Most fictional books, for example, do not have headings other than chapter titles and rarely have glossaries and indexes. Use nonfiction books or textbooks instead. ELL children may especially benefit from glossaries and indexes.

Research/Study Skills

TEACH/MODEL *Parts of a Book*

MODEL USING PARTS OF A BOOK Locate one or more books that include these features: cover; title page with title, author, and illustrator; table of contents with page numbers; chapter titles; headings; glossary; and index. If possible, find at least one book about astronomy. Explain to children that many parts of books can be very helpful to them as they read.

Model how to use a table of contents and index.

Think Aloud **MODEL** Let's say I need to locate information about constellations for a report. Here is a book about stars. Let's look in the table of contents to find out what the book is generally about. I'll read through the chapter titles to see which chapter I might like to look at and to find what page it begins on. Here's a chapter about constellations. I want to read more about those. If I want to find out whether this book talks about the Big Dipper, I can look in the index at the back of the book. I know an index lists topics in alphabetical order, so I'll look in the *B*'s for *Big Dipper*. Here it is. It's mentioned on page 24. Now I know exactly where to find it in this book.

LOCATE PARTS OF A BOOK Let pairs or small groups of children work together with nonfiction books that include the features listed above. Have them practice locating and identifying the title page with the book title and author's and illustrator's names; the table of contents with page numbers of each chapter or section; chapter titles and headings within the chapters; the glossary; and the index.

PRACTICE

USE PARTS OF A BOOK Divide children into five groups—one for each of these parts of a book: cover and title page, table of contents, chapter titles and headings, glossary, and index. Give each group a copy of the chart below. Have them list their assigned part of a book in the first column and work together to fill in the second and third columns. Finally, have each group present to the rest of the class what they discovered.

Part of a book	Where is it in the book?	How do we use it?

Wrap Up Your Week!

LET'S TALK ABOUT Exploration

QUESTION OF THE WEEK Recall this week's question.

• What can we discover by exploring nature?

Display the web that children began on Day 1 of this week. Review what they have written in the outside ovals about what they might discover by exploring nature. Add other ovals so that children can add other things they have discovered throughout the week.

CONNECT Use questions such as these to prompt a discussion:

• Henry and Mudge discovered many things about nature when they were camping. What kinds of wildlife do you suppose they might have discovered if they had camped in the desert instead of the woods near a lake?

• If Henry and Mudge had camped in the desert on a tranquil night, could they have seen stars and galaxies? Why do you think as you do?

• What might they identify in the desert if they looked underneath a rock?

Build Background Use ELL Poster 4 to support the Preview activity.

You've learned	You've learned
008 Amazing Words **this week!**	**024** Amazing Words **so far this year!**

PREVIEW Tell children that next week they will read about what they might learn by exploring the desert.

PREVIEW Next Week

Assessment Checkpoints *for the Week*

Selection Assessment

Use pp. 9–12 of Selection Tests **to check:**

 Selection Understanding

 Comprehension Skill *Character and Setting*

 High–Frequency Words

bear	love
build	mother
couldn't	straight
father	

ASSESSMENT

Scott Foresman
Selection Tests
Teacher's Manual

• Assess comprehension of weekly selections
• Assess understanding of weekly comprehension skills
• Assess knowledge of high-frequency words and selection vocabulary

Reading STREET Grade 2

Selection Tests

Leveled Assessment

On-Level

Strategic Intervention

Advanced

Use pp. 13–18 of Fresh Reads for Differentiated Test Practice **to check:**

 Comprehension Skill *Character and Setting*

 REVIEW **Comprehension Skill** *Realism and Fantasy*

 Fluency *Words Correct Per Minute*

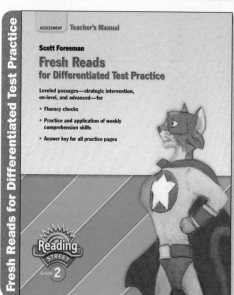

ASSESSMENT   Teacher's Manual

Scott Foresman
Fresh Reads
for Differentiated Test Practice

Leveled passages—strategic intervention, on-level, and advanced—for
• Fluency checks
• Practice and application of weekly comprehension skills
• Answer key for all practice pages

Reading STREET Grade 2

Fresh Reads for Differentiated Test Practice

Managing Assessment

Use Assessment Handbook **for:**

 Weekly Assessment Blackline Masters for Monitoring Progress

 Observation Checklists

 Record-Keeping Forms

 Portfolio Assessment

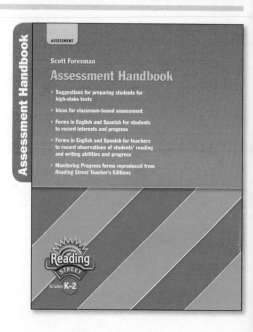

ASSESSMENT

Scott Foresman
Assessment Handbook

• Suggestions for preparing students for high-stake tests
• Ideas for classroom-based assessment
• Forms in English and Spanish for students to record interests and progress
• Forms in English and Spanish for teachers to record observations of students' reading and writing abilities and progress
• Monitoring Progress forms reproduced from *Reading Street* Teacher's Editions

Reading STREET Grades K–2

Assessment Handbook

Unit 1
Exploration

EXPAND THE CONCEPT

What can we learn by exploring the desert?

CONCEPT QUESTION

What can we learn from exploring new places and things?

CONNECT THE CONCEPT

▶ **Build Background**

arid	forbidding	ledge
discovery	haven	precipitation
dunes	landform	

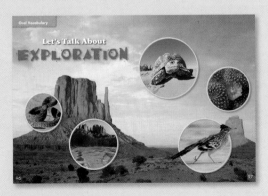

▶ **Science Content**
Earth Science: Desert; Energy: Light, Heat; Climate; Adaptation; Habitats; Interdependence

▶ **Writing**
A Report

Preview Your Week

What can we learn by exploring the desert?

A Walk in the Desert
by Caroline Arnold

100

What can you find on a walk in the desert?

101

Audio CD

Student Edition pages 100–121

Genre	Expository Nonfiction
Phonics	Inflected Endings
Comprehension Skill	Main Idea and Details
Comprehension Strategy	Text Structure

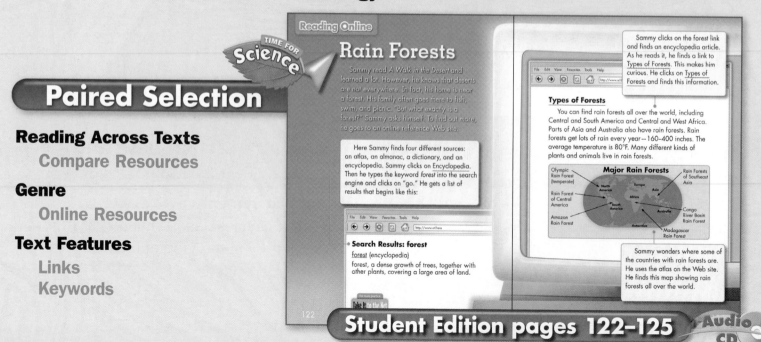

Reading Online

TIME FOR Science

Paired Selection

Reading Across Texts
Compare Resources

Genre
Online Resources

Text Features
Links
Keywords

Rain Forests

Sammy read *A Walk in the Desert* and learned a lot. However, he knows that deserts are not everywhere. In fact, his home is near a forest. His family often goes there to fish, swim, and picnic. "But what exactly is a forest?" Sammy asks himself. To find out more, he goes to an online reference Web site.

Here Sammy finds four different sources: an atlas, an almanac, a dictionary, and an encyclopedia. Sammy clicks on Encyclopedia. Then he types the keyword *forest* into the search engine and clicks on "go." He gets a list of results that begins like this:

File Edit View Favorites Tools Help
http://www.af.here

Search Results: forest

forest (encyclopedia)
forest, a dense growth of trees, together with other plants, covering a large area of land.

Take It to the Net

122

Sammy clicks on the forest link and finds an encyclopedia article. As he reads it, he finds a link to Types of Forests. This makes him curious. He clicks on Types of Forests and finds this information.

File Edit View Favorites Tools Help
http://www.af

Types of Forests

You can find rain forests all over the world, including Central and South America and Central and West Africa. Parts of Asia and Australia also have rain forests. Rain forests get lots of rain every year—160–400 inches. The average temperature is 80°F. Many different kinds of plants and animals live in rain forests.

Major Rain Forests

Olympic Rain Forest (temperate)
Rain Forest of Central America
Amazon Rain Forest
Rain Forests of Southeast Asia
Congo River Basin Rain Forest
Madagascar Rain Forest

Sammy wonders where some of the countries with rain forests are. He uses the atlas on the Web site. He finds this map showing rain forests all over the world.

Student Edition pages 122–125

Audio CD

Read It
ONLINE
PearsonSuccessNet.com
- Student Edition
- Leveled Readers
- Decodable Reader

Leveled Readers

🎯 **Skill** Main Idea and Details

🎯 **Strategy** Text Structure

Lesson Vocabulary

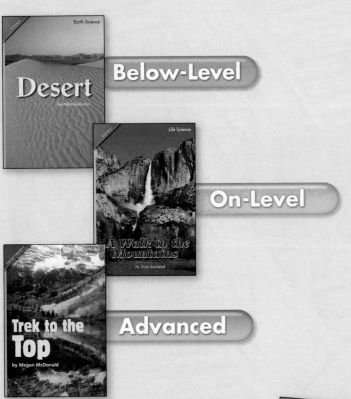

Earth Science
Desert
by Abby Seaborne
Below-Level

Life Science
A Walk in the Mountains
by Kim Borland
On-Level

Trek to the Top
by Megan McDonald
Advanced

ELL Reader
- Concept Vocabulary
- Text Support
- Language Enrichment

The Saguaro Cactus
by J. Hernandez

Decodable Readers

Apply Phonics
- *Clive's Big Box*

Decodable Reader 4
Clive's Big Box
Written by Paula Alvarez
Illustrated by Barbara Johnson

Phonics Skill
Adding -s, -ed, -ing

TIME FOR Science

Integrate Science Standards

- Earth Science: Desert
- Energy: Light, Heat
- Climate
- Adaptation
- Habitats
- Interdependence

**Read**

A Walk in the Desert
pp. 100–121

"Rain Forests" pp. 122–125

**Read**

Leveled Readers

Below-Level	On-Level	Advanced
• Support Concepts	• Develop Concepts	• Extend Concepts
		• Science Extension Activity

**Read**

ELL Reader

Build Concept Vocabulary
Exploration, pp. 96r, 96–97

Teach Science Concepts
Rainfall, p. 112–113
Adapting to Nature,
p. 116–117

Explore Science Center
Neighborhood Walk, p. 96k

A Walk in the Desert

Weekly Plan

READING

90-120 minutes

TARGET SKILLS OF THE WEEK

Phonics
Inflected Endings -s, -ed, -ing

Comprehension Skill
Main Idea and Details

Comprehension Strategy
Text Structure

DAY 1 — PAGES 96l-97d

Oral Language

QUESTION OF THE WEEK, 96l
What can we learn by exploring the desert?

Oral Vocabulary/Share Literature, 96m
Sing with Me Big Book, Song 4
Amazing Words *arid, landform, precipitation*

Word Work

Phonics, 96n–96o
Inflected Endings -s, -ed, -ing **T**

Spelling, 96p
Pretest

Comprehension/Vocabulary/Fluency

Read Decodable Reader 4

Grouping Options 96f–96g

Review High-Frequency Words
Check Comprehension
Reread for Fluency

Build Background, 96r–97
Exploration

Listening Comprehension, 97a–97b
Main Idea and Details **T**

DAY 2 — PAGES 98a-119c

Oral Language

QUESTION OF THE DAY, 98a
What will we see and hear and feel in the desert?

Oral Vocabulary/Share Literature, 98b
Read Aloud Anthology "Around One Cactus"
Amazing Words *dunes, ledge*

Word Work

Phonics, 98c–98d
Review Inflected Endings -s, -ed, -ing **T**

Spelling, 98d
Dictation

Comprehension/Vocabulary/Fluency

Read *A Walk in the Desert,* 98e–119a

Grouping Options
96f–96g

Introduce High-Frequency
Words *animals, early, eyes,
full, warm, water* **T**

Introduce Selection Words
*cactus, climate, coyote,
desert, harsh*

Main Idea and
Details **T**
Text Structure
REVIEW Compare and
Contrast **T**

Reread for Fluency

LANGUAGE ARTS

20-30 minutes

Trait of the Week

Conventions

Shared Writing, 97c
Report

Grammar, 97d
Introduce Statements and Questions **T**

Interactive Writing, 119b
Ad

Grammar, 119c
Practice Statements and Questions **T**

DAILY JOURNAL WRITING

Day 1 *List different types of landforms.*

Day 2 *Write about a desert and what it is like there.*

DAILY SCIENCE CONNECTIONS

Day 1 Exploring the Desert Concept Chart, 96r–97

Day 2 Time for Science: Rainfall, 112–113;
Adapting to Nature, 116–117

DAILY SUCCESS PREDICTORS
for Adequate Yearly Progress

Monitor Progress and Corrective Feedback

Phonics
Check Word Reading, 96o
Spiral REVIEW Phonics

Fluency
Check High-Frequency Words, 99a
Spiral REVIEW High-Frequency Words

RESOURCES FOR THE WEEK

- Practice Book 2.1, *pp. 31–40*
- Phonics and Spelling Practice Book, *pp. 13–16*
- Grammar and Writing Practice Book, *pp. 13–16*
- Selection Test, *pp. 13–16*

- Fresh Reads for Differentiated Test Practice, *pp. 19–24*
- Phonics Songs and Rhymes Chart 4
- The Grammar and Writing Book, *pp. 68–73*

Grouping Options for Differentiated Instruction

Turn the page for the small group lesson plan.

DAY 3 PAGES 120a–121b

Oral Language

QUESTION OF THE DAY, 120a
What else can we learn about animals by exploring the desert?

Oral Vocabulary/Share Literature, 120b
Read Aloud Anthology "Around One Cactus"
Amazing Word *haven*

Word Work

Phonics, 120c
REVIEW Consonant Blends **T**

High-Frequency Words, 120d
Practice *water, full, animals, early, warm, eyes* **T**

Spelling, 120d
Practice

Comprehension/Vocabulary/Fluency

Vocabulary, 120e
Descriptive Words

Read *A Walk in the Desert,* 100–121

Grouping Options
96f–96g

Fluency, 120f
Attend to Punctuation

Think and Share, 120g

Trait of the Week, 121a
Introduce Conventions

Grammar, 121b
Write with Statements and Questions **T**

Day 3 *Use descriptive words in sentences about the desert.*

Day 3 Exploring the Desert Concept Chart, 121b

DAY 4 PAGES 122a–125d

Oral Language

QUESTION OF THE DAY, 122a
Where could you find out more about the desert?

Oral Vocabulary/Share Literature, 122b
Read Aloud Anthology "Exploring the Sahara"
Amazing Words *discovery, forbidding*

Word Work

Phonics, 122c
REVIEW Sentence Reading **T**

Spelling, 122d
Partner Review

Comprehension/Vocabulary/Fluency

Read "Rain Forests," 122–125
Leveled Readers

Grouping Options
96f–96g

Descriptive Words
Reading Across Texts

Fluency, 125a
Attend to Punctuation

Writing Across the Curriculum, 125b
Web

Grammar, 125c
Review Statements and Questions **T**

Speaking and Listening, 125d
Be a Polite Listener

Day 4 *Write a story about a dry desert.*

Day 4 Time for Science: A Walk Where You Are, 96k

DAY 5 PAGES 126a–127b

Oral Language

QUESTION OF THE DAY, 126a
Can a cactus be a haven for animals?

Oral Vocabulary/Share Literature, 126b
Read Aloud Anthology "Exploring the Sahara"
Amazing Words Review

Word Work

Phonics, 126c
⊙ Review Inflected Endings *-s, -ed, -ing* **T**

High-Frequency Words, 126c
Review *animals, early, eyes, full, warm, water* **T**

Spelling, 126d
Test

Comprehension/Vocabulary/Fluency

Read Leveled Readers

Grouping Options 96f–96g

Monitor Progress, 126e–126g
Read the Sentences
Read the Story

Writing and Grammar, 126–127
Develop Conventions
Use Statements and Questions **T**

Research/Study Skills, 127a
Online Reference Sources

Day 5 *List things you can find in a desert.*

Day 5 Revisit the Exploring the Desert Concept Chart, 127b

KEY ⊙ = Target Skill **T** = Tested Skill

Comprehension Check Retelling, *120g*

Fluency Check Fluency WCPM, *125a*
Spiral REVIEW Phonics, High-Frequency Words

Oral Vocabulary Check Oral Vocabulary, *126b*
Assess Phonics, High-Frequency Words, Fluency, Comprehension, *126e*

SUCCESS PREDICTOR

Small Group Plan *for Differentiated Instruction*

Daily Plan
AT A GLANCE

Reading
Whole Group
- Oral Language
- Word Work
- Comprehension/Vocabulary

Group Time

Meet with small groups to provide:
- Skill Support
- Reading Support
- Fluency Practice

Read

This week's lessons for daily group time can be found behind the Differentiated Instruction (DI) tab on pp. DI·46–DI·53.

Whole Group
- Comprehension/Vocabulary
- Fluency

Language Arts
- Writing
- Grammar
- Speaking/Listening/Viewing
- Research/Study Skills

Use *My Sidewalks on Reading Street* for Tier III intensive reading intervention.

DAY 1

On-Level
Teacher-Led
Page 96q
- **Read** Decodable Reader 4
- **Reread** for Fluency

Strategic Intervention
Teacher-Led
Page DI·44
- Blend Words with Inflected Endings
- **Read** Decodable Reader 4
- **Reread** for Fluency

Advanced
Teacher-Led
Page DI·45
- Extend Word Reading
- **Read** Advanced Selection 4
- Introduce Concept Inquiry

(i) **Independent Activities**

While you meet with small groups, have the rest of the class...
- Reread for fluency
- Write in their journals
- Read self-selected reading
- Visit the Word Work Center
- Complete Practice Book 2.1, pp. 33–34

DAY 2

On-Level
Teacher-Led
Pages 100–119
- **Read** *A Walk in the Desert*
- **Reread** for Fluency

Strategic Intervention
Teacher-Led
Page DI·46
- Blend Words with Inflected Endings
- **Read** SI Decodable Reader 4
- **Read** or Listen to *A Walk in the Desert*

Advanced
Teacher-Led
Page DI·47
- **Read** *A Walk in the Desert*
- Continue Concept Inquiry

(i) **Independent Activities**

While you meet with small groups, have the rest of the class...
- Read self-selected reading
- Write in their journals
- Visit the Listening Center
- Complete Practice Book 2.1, pp. 35–37

DAY 3

On-Level
Teacher-Led
Pages 100–121
- **Reread** *A Walk in the Desert*

Strategic Intervention
Teacher-Led
Page DI·48
- **Reread** *A Walk in the Desert*
- Read Words and Sentences
- Review Main Idea and Details and Text Structure
- **Reread** for Fluency

Advanced
Teacher-Led
Page DI·49
- Self-Selected Reading
- Continue Concept Inquiry

(i) **Independent Activities**

While you meet with small groups, have the rest of the class...
- Read self-selected reading
- Write in their journals
- Visit the Writing Center
- Complete Practice Book 2.1, pp. 38–39

① Begin with whole class skill and strategy instruction.

② Meet with small groups to provide differentiated instruction.

③ Gather the whole class back together for fluency and language arts.

DAY 4

On-Level

Teacher-Led
Pages 122–125, LR31–LR33

• **Read** "Rain Forests"
• Practice with On-Level Reader *A Walk in the Mountains*

Strategic Intervention

Teacher-Led
Pages DI·50, LR28–LR30

• **Read** or Listen to "Rain Forests"
• **Reread** for Fluency
• Build Concepts
• Practice with Below-Level Reader *Desert*

Advanced

Teacher-Led
Pages DI·51, LR34–LR36

• **Read** "Rain Forests"
• Extend Vocabulary
• Continue Concept Inquiry
• Practice with Advanced Reader *Trek to the Top*

ⓘ Independent Activities

While you meet with small groups, have the rest of the class...

• Reread for fluency
• Write in their journals
• Read self-selected reading

• Review spelling words with a partner
• Visit the Listening and Science Centers

DAY 5

On-Level

Teacher-Led
Pages 126e–126g, LR31–LR33

• Sentence Reading, Set B
• Monitor Comprehension
• Practice with On-Level Reader *A Walk in the Mountains*

Strategic Intervention

Teacher-Led
Pages DI·52, LR28–LR30

• Practice Word Reading
• Sentence Reading, Set A
• Monitor Fluency and Comprehension
• Practice with Below-Level Reader *Desert*

Advanced

Teacher-Led
Pages DI·53, LR34–LR36

• Sentence Reading, Set C
• Monitor Comprehension
• Share Concept Inquiry
• Practice with Advanced Reader *Trek to the Top*

ⓘ Independent Activities

While you meet with small groups, have the rest of the class...

• Reread for fluency
• Write in their journals
• Read self-selected reading

• Visit the Technology Center
• Complete Practice Book 2.1, p. 40

Grouping Place English language learners in the groups that correspond to their reading abilities in English.

Use the appropriate Leveled Reader or other text at children's instructional level.

TIP Send home the appropriate Multilingual Summary of the main selection on Day 1.

Take It to the NET™ ONLINE
PearsonSuccessNet.com

Deborah Simmons and Edward Kame'enui
For research on literacy assessment, see the article "The Importance and Decision-Making Utility of a Continuum of Fluency-Based Indicators . . ." by Scott Foresman authors D. Simmons and E. Kame'enui, and by R. H. Good.

TEACHER TALK

A **base word** is a word that can stand alone or take endings and affixes, such as *walk*.

Looking Ahead

Be sure to schedule time for children to work on the unit inquiry project "Take a Trip." This week children should make predictions about what they think they will find or accomplish on their exploration.

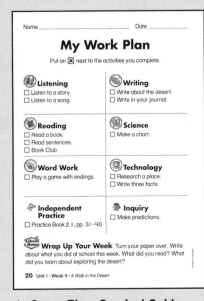

▲ **Group-Time Survival Guide**
p. 20, Weekly Contract

☑ Customize Your Plan *by Strand*

ORAL LANGUAGE

Concept Development

What can we learn by exploring the desert?

 to build oral vocabulary

| arid | discovery | dunes | forbidding |
| haven | landform | ledge | precipitation |

BUILD

❑ **Question of the Week** Use the Morning Warm-Up! to introduce and discuss the question of the week. This week children will talk, sing, read, and write about what can we learn about exploring the desert. **DAY 1** *96l*

❑ **Sing with Me Big Book** Sing a song about the desert. Ask children to listen for the concept-related Amazing Words *arid, landform, precipitation.* **DAY 1** *96m*

Sing with Me Big Book

❑ **Let's Talk About Exploration** Use the Let's Talk About It lesson in the Student Edition to build background, vocabulary, and concepts. Then create a concept chart for children to add to throughout the week. **DAY 1** *96r–97*

Let's Talk About It

DEVELOP

❑ **Question of the Day** Use the questions in the Morning Warm-Ups! to discuss lesson concepts and how they relate to the unit theme, Exploration. **DAY 2** *98a,* **DAY 3** *120a,* **DAY 4** *122a,* **DAY 5** *126a*

❑ **Share Literature** Read big books and read aloud selections that develop concepts, language, and vocabulary related to the lesson concept and the unit theme. Continue to develop this week's Amazing Words. **DAY 2** *98b,* **DAY 3** *120b,* **DAY 4** *122b,* **DAY 5** *126b*

CONNECT

❑ **Wrap Up Your Week!** Revisit the Question of the Week. Then connect concepts and vocabulary to next week's lesson. **DAY 5** *127b*

CHECK

❑ **Check Oral Vocabulary** To informally assess children's oral vocabulary, ask individuals to use some of this week's Amazing Words to tell you about the photographs on Student Edition pp. 96–97. **DAY 5** *126b*

PHONICS

⟳ **INFLECTED ENDINGS -S, -ED, -ING** For many words, adding the ending –s changes the word to be present tense. For words that end in consonant-vowel-consonant, the last consonant is doubled before the endings –ed or –ing are added. For words that end with an e, the e is dropped before adding –ed or –ing.

TEACH

❑ **Inflected Endings -s, -ed, -ing** Introduce the blending strategy for words with inflected endings -s, -ed, -ing. Then have children blend and build words and tell if the spelling changed when inflected endings –s, -ed, and –ing were added. **DAY 1** *96n–96o*

❑ **Fluent Word Reading** Use the Fluent Word Reading Routine to develop children's word reading fluency. Use the Phonics Songs and Rhymes Chart for additional word reading practice. **DAY 2** *98c–98d*

Phonics Songs and Rhymes Chart 4

PRACTICE/APPLY

❑ **Decodable Reader 4** Practice reading words with inflected endings -s, -ed, -ing in context. **DAY 1** *96q*

❑ **A Walk in the Desert** Practice decoding words in context. **DAY 2** *100–119*

Decodable Reader 4

❑ **Homework** Practice Book 2.1 p. 33. **DAY 1** *96o*

❑ **Word Work Center** Practice inflected endings -s, -ed, -ing. **ANY DAY** *96j*

Main Selection—Nonfiction

RETEACH/REVIEW

❑ **Review** Review words with this week's phonics skills. **DAY 5** *126c*

❑ **Reteach Lessons** If necessary, reteach inflected endings -s, -ed, -ing. **DAY 5** *DI·67*

❑ **Spiral REVIEW** Review previously taught phonics skills. **DAY 1** *96o,* **DAY 4** *122c*

ASSESS

❑ **Sentence Reading** Assess children's ability to read words with inflected endings -s, -ed, -ing. **DAY 5** *126e–126f*

① Use assessment data to determine your instructional focus.

② Preview this week's instruction by strand.

③ Choose instructional activities that meet the needs of your classroom.

SPELLING

INFLECTED ENDINGS For words that end in consonant-vowel-consonant, the last consonant is doubled before the endings *–ed* or *–ing* are added. For words that end with an *e*, the *e* is dropped before adding *–ed* or *–ing*.

TEACH

☐ **Pretest** Before administering the pretest, model how to segment words with inflected endings to spell them. Dictate the spelling words, segmenting them if necessary. Then have children check their pretests and correct misspelled words. **DAY 1** *96p*

PRACTICE/APPLY

☐ **Dictation** Have children write dictation sentences to practice spelling words. **DAY 2** *98d*

☐ **Write Words** Have children practice writing the spelling words by using clues. **DAY 3** *120d*

☐ **Homework** Phonics and Spelling Practice Book pp. 13–16.
DAY 1 *96p*, **DAY 2** *98d*, **DAY 3** *120d*, **DAY 4** *122d*

RETEACH/REVIEW

☐ **Partner Review** Have pairs work together to read and write the spelling words. **DAY 4** *122d*

ASSESS

☐ **Posttest** Use dictation sentences to give the posttest for words with inflected endings. **DAY 5** *126d*

Spelling Words

Inflected Endings -ed, -ing

1. talked	7. lifted
2. talking	8. lifting
3. dropped	9. hugged
4. dropping	10. hugging
5. excited	11. smiled
6. exciting*	12. smiling

Challenge Words

13. dragging	15. danced
14. amazed	

* Words from the Selection

HIGH-FREQUENCY WORDS

WORDS TO READ

animals	*early*	*eyes*	*full*
warm	*water*		

TEACH

☐ **Words to Read** Introduce this week's high-frequency words and add them to the Word Wall. **DAY 2** *98-99a*

High-Frequency Words

PRACTICE/APPLY

☐ **Words in Context** Read high-frequency words in the context of *A Walk in the Desert*. **DAY 2** *100-119*

☐ **Word Wall** Use the Word Wall to review and practice high-frequency words throughout the week. **DAY 3** *120d*, **DAY 5** *126c*

Main Selection—Nonfiction

☐ **Leveled Text** Practice this week's high-frequency words in the context of leveled text. **DAY 4** *LR28-LR36*, **DAY 5** *LR28-LR36*

☐ **Homework** Practice Book 2.1 pp. 36, 39. **DAY 2** *99a*, **DAY 3** *120d*

Leveled Readers

RETEACH/REVIEW

☐ **Spiral REVIEW** Review previously taught high-frequency words. **DAY 2** *99a*, **DAY 4** *122c*

ASSESS

☐ **Sentence Reading** Assess children's ability to read this week's high-frequency words. **DAY 5** *126e-126f*

VOCABULARY

TEACH

☐ **Vocabulary Transparency 4** Use Vocabulary Transparency 4 to introduce the selection words from *A Walk in the Desert*. Children will read these words but will not be tested on them. **DAY 2** *100a*

☐ **Descriptive Words** Have children use the selection descriptive words to tell about the desert. **DAY 3** *120e*

☑ Customize Your Plan *by Strand*

COMPREHENSION

🎯 SKILL MAIN IDEA AND DETAILS The main idea is the most important idea or what the story is mostly about. Details are the small pieces of information that tell more about the main idea.

🎯 STRATEGY TEXT STRUCTURE Text structure is how an author organizes information. Authors often use headings to help readers know what they are going to read about next.

TEACH

❏ **Listening Comprehension** Read "Saguaro Cactus" and model how to identify the *main idea and details.* DAY 1 *97a–97b*

❏ **Skill/Strategy Lesson** Review how to identify the *main idea and details.* Then introduce this week's strategy, *text structure.* DAY 2 *98e*

PRACTICE/APPLY

❏ **Skills and Strategies in Context** Read *A Walk in the Desert,* using the Guiding Comprehension questions to apply *main idea and details* and *text structure.* DAY 2 *100–119a*

Main Selection—Nonfiction

❏ **Think and Share** Use the questions on Student Edition p. 120 to discuss the selection. DAY 3 *120g–121*

❏ **Skills and Strategies in Context** Read "Rain Forests," guiding children as they apply skills and strategies. After reading have children make connections across texts. DAY 4 *122–124*

Paired Selection— Nonfiction

❏ **Leveled Text** Apply *main idea and details* and *text structure* to read leveled text. DAY 4 *LR28–LR36,* DAY 5 *LR28–LR36*

Leveled Readers

❏ **Homework** Practice Book 2.1 p. 34. DAY 1 *97a*

ASSESS

❏ **Selection Test** Determine children's understanding of the main selection and assess their ability to identify *main idea and details.* DAY 3

❏ **Story Reading** Have children read the passage "A Walk in the Woods." Ask what the *main idea and details* of the story are and have them retell. DAY 5 *126e–126g*

RETEACH/REVIEW

❏ **Reteach Lesson** If necessary, reteach *main idea and details.* DAY 5 *DI·67*

FLUENCY

SKILL ATTENDING TO PUNCTUATION When you read, watch for marks at the end of sentences. Stop when you come to a question mark and have your voice go up like you are asking a question.

REREAD FOR FLUENCY

❏ **Oral Rereading** Have children read orally from Decodable Reader 4 or another text at their independent reading level. Listen as children read and provide corrective feedback regarding their oral reading and their use of the blending strategy. DAY 1 *96q*

❏ **Paired Reading** Have pairs of children read orally from the main selection or another text at their independent reading level and apply their knowledge of attending to punctuation when reading. Listen as children read and provide corrective feedback regarding oral reading and their use of the blending strategy. DAY 2 *119a*

TEACH

❏ **Model** Use passages from *A Walk in the Desert* to model attending to punctuation. DAY 3 *120f,* DAY 4 *125a*

PRACTICE/APPLY

❏ **Choral Reading** Choral read passages from *A Walk in the Desert.* Monitor progress and provide feedback regarding children's attending to punctuation. DAY 3 *120f,* DAY 4 *125a*

❏ **Listening Center** Have children follow along with the AudioText for this week's selections. ANY DAY *96j*

❏ **Reading/Library Center** Have children build fluency by rereading Leveled Readers, Decodable Readers, or other text at their independent level. ANY DAY *96j*

❏ **Fluency Coach** Have children use Fluency Coach to listen to fluent reading or to practice reading on their own. ANY DAY

ASSESS

❏ **Story Reading** Take a one-minute timed sample of children's oral reading. Use the passage "A Walk in the Woods." DAY 5 *126e–126g*

❶ Use assessment data to determine your instructional focus.

❷ Preview this week's instruction by strand.

❸ Choose instructional activities that meet the needs of your classroom.

WRITING

Trait of the Week

CONVENTIONS Conventions are the rules for writing such as beginning with a capital letter and ending with a punctuation mark.

TEACH

☐ **Write Together** Engage children in writing activities that develop language, grammar, and writing skills. Include independent writing as an extension of group writing activities.

> **Shared Writing** DAY 1 *97c*
> **Interactive Writing** DAY 2 *119b*
> **Writing Across the Curriculum** DAY 4 *125b*

☐ **Trait of the Week** Introduce and model the Trait of the Week, *conventions.* DAY 3 *121a*

PRACTICE/APPLY

☐ **Write Now** Examine the model on Student Edition pp. 126–127. Then have children write reports. DAY 5 *126–127*

> **Prompt** *A Walk in the Desert* tells about plants and animals in the desert. Think about your neighborhood. Now write a report about who and what live there.

Write Now

☐ **Daily Journal Writing** Have children write about concepts and literature in their journals. **EVERY DAY** *96d–96e*

☐ **Writing Center** Have children write about what they see as they pretend to walk in the desert. **ANY DAY** *96k*

ASSESS

☐ **Scoring Rubric** Use a rubric to evaluate children's reports. DAY 5 *126–127*

RETEACH/REVIEW

☐ **The Grammar and Writing Book** Use pp. 68–73 of The Grammar and Writing Book to extend instruction. **ANY DAY**

The Grammar and Writing Book

SPEAKING AND LISTENING

TEACH

☐ **Be a Polite Listener** Discuss polite listening. Then have children listen politely as you talk about coyotes. DAY 4 *125d*

GRAMMAR

SKILL STATEMENTS AND QUESTIONS A statement is a sentence that tells something. A statement ends with a period (.). A question is a sentence that asks something. A question ends with a question mark (?).

TEACH

☐ **Grammar Transparency 4** Use Grammar Transparency 4 to teach *statements and questions.* DAY 1 *97d*

Grammar Transparency 4

PRACTICE/APPLY

☐ **Develop the Concept** Review the concept of *statements and questions* and provide guided practice. DAY 2 *119c*

☐ **Apply to Writing** Have children use statements and questions in writing. DAY 3 *121b*

☐ **Define/Practice** Review the definition of *statements and questions.* Then have children identify statements and questions. DAY 4 *125c*

☐ **Write Now** Discuss the grammar lesson on Student Edition p. 127. Have children use statements and questions in their own report. DAY 5 *126–127*

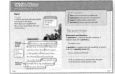
Write Now

☐ **Daily Fix-It** Have children find and correct errors in grammar, spelling, and punctuation. DAY 1 *97d*, DAY 2 *119c*, DAY 3 *121b*, DAY 4 *125c*, DAY 5 *126–127*

☐ **Homework** The Grammar and Writing Practice Book pp. 13–16. DAY 2 *119c*, DAY 3 *121b*, DAY 4 *125c*, DAY 5 *126–127*

RETEACH/REVIEW

☐ **The Grammar and Writing Book** Use pp. 68–71 of The Grammar and Writing Book to extend instruction. **ANY DAY**

The Grammar and Writing Book

RESEARCH/INQUIRY

TEACH

☐ **Online Reference Sources** Model using online reference sources. Then have children use the Internet as an online reference source to find additional information about their topics. DAY 5 *127a*

☐ **Unit Inquiry Project** Allow time for children to make predictions about what they think they will find or accomplish on their exploration. **ANY DAY** *11*

Resources for
Differentiated Instruction

LEVELED READERS

▶ **Comprehension**
  ◎ **Skill** Main Idea/Details
  ◎ **Strategy** Text Structure

▶ **Lesson Vocabulary**

High-Frequency Words

water
eyes
early
animals
full
warm

▶ **Science Standards**
  • Earth Science: Desert
  • Energy: Light, Heat
  • Climate
  • Adaptation
  • Habitats
  • Interdependence

Leveled Reader Database ONLINE

PearsonSuccessNet.com

Use the Online Database of over 600 books to

• Download and print additional copies of this week's leveled readers

• Listen to the readers being read online

• Search for more titles focused on this week's skills, topic, and content

---

On-Level

Science — Life Science

A Walk in the Mountains

by Kim Borland

On-Level Reader

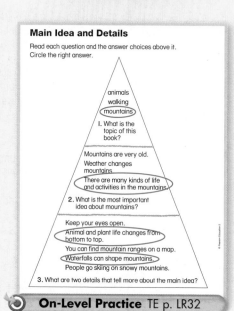

Main Idea and Details

Read each question and the answer choices above it. Circle the right answer.

animals
walking
(mountains)

1. What is the topic of this book?

Mountains are very old.
Weather changes mountains.
(There are many kinds of life and activities in the mountains.)

2. What is the most important idea about mountains?

Keep your eyes open.
(Animal and plant life changes from bottom to top.)
You can find mountain ranges on a map.
(Waterfalls can shape mountains.)
People go skiing on snowy mountains.

3. What are two details that tell more about the main idea?

◎ **On-Level Practice** TE p. LR32

Vocabulary

Write a word from the box to complete each sentence.

Words to Know		
animals	early	eyes
full	warm	water

1. Open your **eyes** to see trees and flowers and plants.

2. If you go **early** to the mountains, you might see the eagle.

3. Fill your basket **full** of flowers.

4. At the bottom of the mountain it will feel **warm**

5. Cool **water** rushes down the mountain.

6. A hare is just one of the **animals** you see on a mountain.

7. Write a sentence about things you could see or hear on a walk in the mountains. Use a word from the box. Possible response given.
You could see animals.

On-Level Practice TE p. LR33

Strategic Intervention

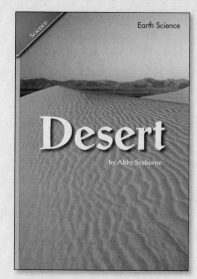

Science — Earth Science

Desert

by Abby Seaborne

Below-Level Reader

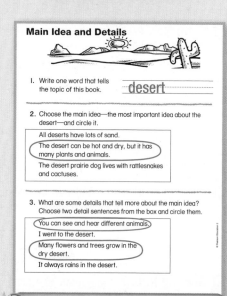

Main Idea and Details

1. Write one word that tells the topic of this book. **desert**

2. Choose the main idea—the most important idea about the desert—and circle it.

All deserts have lots of sand.
(The desert can be hot and dry, but it has many plants and animals.)
The desert prairie dog lives with rattlesnakes and cactuses.

3. What are some details that tell more about the main idea? Choose two detail sentences from the box and circle them.

(You can see and hear different animals.)
I went to the desert.
(Many flowers and trees grow in the dry desert.)
It always rains in the desert.

◎ **Below-Level Practice** TE p. LR29

Vocabulary

Circle the letter that begins each word. Write the letter on the line.

Words to Know		
animals	early	eyes
full	warm	water

1. **a** nimals
2. **e** ye
3. **e** arly
4. **w** arm
5. **w** ater
6. **f** ull

7. Write a sentence about the desert using one or more words from the box. Possible response given.
The desert is full of animals.

Below-Level Practice TE p. LR30

Advanced

Advanced Reader

Main Idea and Details
Read the selection.
Write the main idea and three supporting details.

Mountains
Mountains are important landforms. Mountains are made up of rocky land. They have steep sides and a pointed or a rounded top. Mountains are the tallest parts of Earth. They can form when Earth's crust moves or lava breaks through the crust.

Main Idea
Mountains are important landforms.

Supporting Details
rocky land
tallest parts of Earth
can form from lava

Advanced Practice TE p. LR35

Vocabulary
Draw a line from each word on the left to its definition.

Words to Know		
arid	canyons	landform
moisture	precipitation	

1. arid — a. a feature on Earth's surface, such as a mountain or valley
2. canyons — b. rain or snow that falls to Earth's surface
3. landform — c. very dry
4. moisture — d. deep, narrow valleys with steep sides
5. precipitation — e. wetness

Possible response given.
6. Choose one vocabulary word and use it in a sentence.

The desert is an arid place.

Advanced Practice TE p. LR36

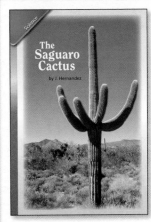

ELL Reader

ELL Poster 4

Teacher's Edition Notes
ELL notes throughout this lesson support instruction and reference additional resources at point of use.

ELL Teaching Guide pp. 22–28, 218–219
- Multilingual summaries of the main selection
- Comprehension lesson
- Vocabulary strategies and word cards
- ELL Reader 4 lesson

ELL and Transition Handbook

Ten Important Sentences
- Key ideas from every selection in the Student Edition
- Activities to build sentence power

More Reading

Readers' Theater Anthology
- Fluency practice
- Five scripts to build fluency
- Poetry for oral interpretation

Leveled Trade Books

- Extend reading tied to the unit concept
- Lessons in Trade Book Library Teaching Guide

Homework
- Family Times Newsletter
- ELL Multilingual Selection Summaries

Take-Home Books
- Decodable Readers
- Leveled Readers

Literacy Centers

 Listening

Let's Read
Along

MATERIALS `SINGLES`
CD player, headphones, print copies of recorded pieces

LISTEN TO LITERATURE As children listen to the following recordings, have them follow along or read along in the print version.

AudioText
A Walk in the Desert
"Rain Forests"

Sing with Me/Background Building Audio
"The Arid Desert"

Phonics Songs and Rhymes Audio
"Exploring the Desert"

Exploring the Desert

We hiked in the desert;
   the sun was so bright.
We looked all around at
   each wonderful sight.
A hawk that was soaring,
   each wing like a sail.
A rattlesnake sunning
   and shaking its tail.
A big old jackrabbit
   hopped over the ground.
A huge tortoise moved
   without making a sound.
A desert seems empty,
   but open your eyes.
Each sand dune you come to
   has a surprise.

Audio CD **Phonics Songs and Rhymes Chart 4**

 Reading/Library

Read It
Again!

MATERIALS `SINGLES` `PAIRS` `GROUPS`
collection of books for self-selected reading, reading logs

REREAD BOOKS Have children select previously read books from the appropriate book box and record titles of books they read in their logs. Use these previously read books:

- Decodable Readers
- Leveled Readers
- ELL Readers
- Stories written by classmates
- Books from the library

TEN IMPORTANT SENTENCES Have children read the Ten Important Sentences for *A Walk in the Desert* and locate the sentences in the Student Edition.

BOOK CLUB Encourage a group to discuss *A Walk in the Desert*. What did they learn about the plants and animals in a desert? Would they recommend this book to others? Why or why not?

 Word Work

How Does It
End?

MATERIALS `PAIRS`
15 base word cards, 3 word cards with endings, pencils, copies of three-column chart or Graphic Organizer 26

BASE WORDS AND ENDINGS -s, -ed, -ing Pairs complete a chart of base words and endings.

1. On fifteen index cards write base words. On three cards write endings -s, -ed, -ing. Place each pile face-down.
2. Label a three-column chart: No Change, Doubled Consonant, Dropped *e*.
3. Pairs take turns choosing a card from the base card pile and the ending card pile and putting them together.
4. Children read the new word and write it in the correct column of the chart.
5. Children then place the ending card on the bottom of the ending pile.
6. Play continues until all base cards are used.

 Phonics Activities CD This interactive CD provides additional practice.

No Change	Doubled Consonant	Dropped e
lifted	hugged	skating
jumped	jogging	raking
sits	stopped	

Scott Foresman Reading Street Centers Survival Kit

Use the *A Walk in the Desert* materials from the Reading Street
Centers Survival Kit to organize this week's centers.

Writing

What's in the Desert?

MATERIALS `SINGLES`
paper, pencils, crayons, markers

WRITE A STORY Review with children what they learned about the desert.

1. Children pretend they're walking through the desert.
2. Have them write several sentences about what they see there.
3. Children then illustrate their writing.

LEVELED WRITING Encourage children to write at their own ability level. Some may have limited word choice. Others will have more varied word choice. Your best writers will demonstrate varied, precise word choice.

In the desert I see a big, spiky cactus. I see a woodpecker making a nest in a cactus. I see a lizard lying on a rock.

Science

A Walk Where You Are

MATERIALS `SINGLES`
copies of a five-column chart, pencils

NEIGHBORHOOD WALK Briefly review *A Walk in the Desert* with children and discuss what they might find on a walk through their own neighborhood.

1. Make a chart like the one below with the headings See, Hear, Taste, Smell, Touch.
2. Tell children to imagine they are taking a walk through their own neighborhood.
3. Ask them to list in the appropriate column things they might see, hear, taste, smell, and touch on their walk.

See	big buildings stores houses
Hear	trucks birds
Taste	ice cream
Smell	grass buses
Touch	fence tree bark

Technology

Animals on Location

MATERIALS `SINGLES` `PAIRS`
computer with Internet access, printer, paper, pencil or pen

USE AN ONLINE REFERENCE SOURCE Have individuals or pairs of children learn about various landforms.

1. Have children or pairs of children choose a place to research. They can learn about animals that live in deserts, forests, mountains, or oceans.
2. Ask children to turn on the computer and access an online reference source.
3. Have children use the reference source to research animals in their location.
4. Ask children to write three facts they learned.

Search Engine

Mountain animals
1. Mountain goats can climb in rocky areas.
2. Gorillas live in the mountains in Africa.
3. Yaks can carry things for people in the mountains.

ALL CENTERS

Oral Vocabulary
"The Arid Desert" 4

Phonics and Spelling
Inflected Endings
Spelling Pretest:
  Adding -ed and -ing

Read Apply Phonics **Word Wall**

Group Time < Differentiated Instruction

Build Background
Let's Talk About Exploration

Listening Comprehension
Skill Main Idea and Details

Shared Writing
Report

Grammar
Statements and Questions

Materials
- *Sing with Me Big Book*
- Letter Tiles
- Decodable Reader 4
- Student Edition 96–97
- Graphic Organizer 3
- Writing Transparency 4
- Grammar Transparency 4

Take It to the NET
ONLINE

Professional Development
To learn more about oral language, go to PearsonSuccessNet.com and read "Oral Comprehension..." by A. Biemiller.

Morning Warm-Up!
Your mother and father might take you to a desert to see things that you couldn't see in a forest. What can we learn by exploring the desert?

QUESTION OF THE WEEK Tell children they will talk, sing, read, and write about what we can learn by exploring the desert. Write and read the message and discuss the question.

CONNECT CONCEPTS Ask questions to connect to the previous Unit 1 selections.

- Iris and Walter weren't in the desert, but they did learn things on a walk where they lived. What were some of the things they learned?
- What do you think astronauts might have learned on a walk in space?
- What did Henry and Mudge discover on a walk when they were camping?
- What might we learn by exploring the desert?

REVIEW HIGH-FREQUENCY WORDS

- Circle the high-frequency words *mother, father,* and *couldn't* in the message.
- Have children say and spell each word as they write it.

ELL

Build Background Use the Day 1 instruction on ELL Poster 4 to assess knowledge and develop concepts.

ELL Poster 4

Oral Vocabulary

SHARE LITERATURE Display p. 4 of the *Sing with Me Big Book.* Tell children that the class is going to sing a song about the desert. Read the title. Ask children to listen for the Amazing Words **arid, landform,** and **precipitation** as you sing. Sing the song again and encourage children to sing along. Then speak the second verse, emphasizing the Amazing Words *arid, landform,* and *precipitation.* In discussion, make sure children understand that *arid* means "very dry," *landform* means "a special kind of land," and *precipitation* means "rain or snow."

Sing with Me/
Background Building Audio

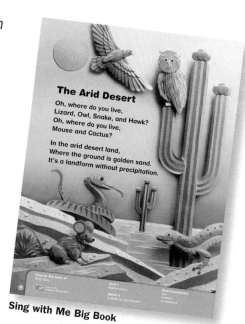

The Arid Desert

Oh, where do you live,
Lizard, Owl, Snake, and Hawk?
Oh, where do you live,
Mouse and Cactus?

In the arid desert land,
Where the ground is golden sand.
It's a landform without precipitation.

Sing with Me Big Book

OBJECTIVE
● Build oral vocabulary.

to build oral vocabulary

MONITOR PROGRESS

arid	**If...** children lack oral vocabulary experiences about the concept Exploration,
landform	
precipitation	
dunes	
ledge	**then...** use the Oral Vocabulary Routine below to teach *arid.*
haven	
discovery	
forbidding	

Oral Vocabulary ROUTINE

1 **Introduce the Word** Relate the word *arid* to the song. Supply a child-friendly definition. Have children say the word. Example: An area or location that is *arid* is very, very dry.

2 **Demonstrate** Provide an example to show meaning. Deserts are *arid* because they don't get much rain.

3 **Apply** Have children demonstrate their understanding. Which of these things is *arid*—a swimming pool or a clump of dried up dirt?

4 **Display the Word/Letter-Sounds** Write the word on a card. Display it. Identify the letter-sounds for *ar*/ar/ and *d*/d/. See p. DI·6 to teach *landform* and *precipitation.*

Build Oral Vocabulary Help children understand that *lizard, owl, snake, hawk,* and *mouse* are names of animals that live in the desert and that *cactus* is a special kind of plant that grows only in deserts. You may want to provide pictures of the animals and of cactus to help children identify them.

OBJECTIVES

- Use structural cues to decode inflected endings with spelling changes.
- Blend, read, and build inflected endings -s, -ed, -ing.

Skills Trace

⊙ Inflected Endings

Introduce/Teach	TE: 2.1 96n–o, 98c–d; 2.2 252n–o, 254c–d; 2.3 426n–o, 428c–d; 2.6 322n–o, 324c–d
Practice	TE: 2.1 96q; 2.2 252q; 2.3 426q; 2.6 322q; PB: 2.1 33, 48, 83, 98, 143; 2.2 8, 113, 128; DR4, DR9, DR15, DR27
Reteach/Review	TE: 2.1 126c, 150c, DI·67; 2.2 288c–d, 303c, DI·76; 2.2 458c, DI·68; 2.4 31c; 2.6 348c, 368c, DI·65
Assess/Test	TE: 2.1 126e–g; 2.2 280e–g; 2.3 458e–g; 2.6 348e–g; Benchmark Test: Units 1, 6

Strategic Intervention

Use **Monitor Progress,** p. 96o, during Group Time after children have had more practice with inflected endings -s, -ed, -ing.

Advanced

Use **Monitor Progress,** p. 96o, as a preassessment to determine whether this group of children would benefit from this instruction on inflected endings.

Support Phonics Languages such as Chinese, Hmong, and Vietnamese do not use inflected endings to form verb tenses. Help children understand that adding -ed to a verb indicates that the action happened in the past.

Children of various language backgrounds may not hear the difference between -ing and -in, so they may say walkin and jumpin instead of walking and jumping. Help children practice saying words that end with -ing: talk/talking; lift/lifting; hug/hugging.

⊙ Inflected Endings

TEACH/MODEL

Blending Strategy

ROUTINE

① **Connect** Write *rained* and *raining.* What do you know about reading these words? (Both have a base word and an ending. Read the base word; read the ending; then blend the two parts.) Read the words together. Today you'll learn about words whose spelling changes before an ending is added.

② **Model** Write *shop, shopped, shopping.* The last consonant in *shop, p,* was doubled before the endings were added. This happens in short-vowel words such as *shop* that end in just one consonant. This is how I blend these words. Cover the added consonant and ending to read the base word; uncover and read the ending. Blend the two parts. Let's blend these words together: *shop, ped, shopped; shop, ping, shopping.*

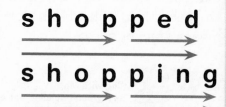

Write *like, liked, liking.* The *e* was dropped before these endings were added. This happens if a base word ends with *e,* and the ending starts with a vowel. Model blending the words; then have children blend with you.

③ **Group Practice** First, see if the base word had a spelling change. Then read the base word, read the ending, and blend the two together. Continue with *plans, planned, planning; trades, traded, trading.*

④ **Review** What do you know about reading base words with endings? See if the base word had a spelling change. Read the base word, read the ending, and then blend the two parts.

BLEND WORDS

INDIVIDUALS BLEND WORDS Call on individuals to blend *thanks, quacked, swinging, closes, plugged, swimming, smiled, shining.* Have them tell what they know about each word before reading it. (Read the base word and then blend the base word and ending to read the whole word.) For feedback, refer to step four of the Blending Strategy Routine.

BUILD WORDS

READ LONGER WORDS Write *base word, -s, -ed,* and *-ing* as headings for a four-column chart. Write several base words in the first column. Have children add the *-s, -ed,* and *-ing* endings to each base word, read the new word, and tell if the spelling changed when the endings were added and how it changed.

base word	-s	-ed	-ing
grab	grabs	grabbed	grabbing
excite	excites	excited	exciting
face	faces	faced	facing
talk	talks	talked	talking

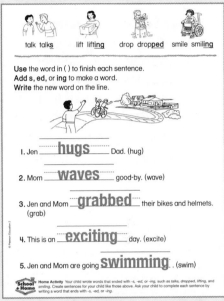

▲ **Practice Book 2.1** p. 33, Inflected Endings

Monitor Progress | **Check Word Reading** Inflected Endings

Write the following words and have individuals read them.

bringing	stacking	stinks	plunked	blocked
running	skipped	spotted	slamming	spreads
pages	traced	wiping	closed	gliding

If... children cannot blend inflected endings at this point,

then... continue to monitor their progress using other instructional opportunities during the week so that they can be successful with the Day 5 Assessment. See the Skills Trace on p. 96n.

 SUCCESS PREDICTOR

- Rows 1 and 2 review short vowels.
- Row 1 reviews consonant blends and final *ck, ng, nk.*

▶ **Day 1 Check** Word Reading | **Day 2 Check** High-Frequency Words | **Day 3 Check** Retelling | **Day 4 Check** Fluency | **Day 5 Assess** Progress

Word Reading

SUCCESS PREDICTOR

OBJECTIVES

- Segment sounds and word parts to spell words.
- Spell base words with endings *-ed, -ing*.

Spelling Words

Inflected Endings -*ed*, -*ing*

1.	**talked**	7.	**lifted**
2.	**talking**	8.	**lifting**
3.	**dropped**	9.	**hugged**
4.	**dropping**	10.	**hugging**
5.	**excited**	11.	**smiled**
6.	**exciting***	12.	**smiling**

Challenge Words

13.	**dragging**	15.	**danced**
14.	**amazed**		

* Word from the Selection

Adding -*ed* and -*ing*

Generalization Some base words do not change when -*ed* or -*ing* is added: **talked, lifting.** Others do change: **dropped, smiling.**

Sort the list words by type of ending.

-*ed* with no base word change	-*ing* with no base word change	Spelling Words
1. talked	7. talking	1. talked
2. lifted	8. lifting	2. talking
-*ed* with base word change	**-*ing* with base word change**	3. dropped
3. dropped	9. dropping	4. dropping
4. excited	10. exciting	5. excited
5. hugged	11. hugging	6. exciting
6. smiled	12. smiling	7. lifted
Challenge Words		8. lifting
-*ed* with base word change	**-*ing* with base word change**	9. hugged
13. amazed	14. dragging	10. hugging
	15. bouncing	11. smiled
		12. smiling
		Challenge Words
		13. dragging
		14. amazed
		15. bouncing

Home Activity Your child is learning to spell words with *-ed* and *-ing*. To practice at home, have your child study the word, noting the ending, and then spell the word with eyes closed.

▲ **Spelling Practice Book** p. 13

Support Spelling Before giving the spelling pretest, clarify the meaning of each spelling word with examples, such as saying *bouncing* is something you do to a ball and pointing to your smile to illustrate *smiling*.

Spelling

PRETEST Inflected Endings

MODEL WRITING FOR WORD PARTS Each spelling word has the ending *-ed* or *-ing*. Before administering the spelling pretest, model how to segment inflected endings to spell them.

- You can spell these words by thinking about the inflected endings. What base word and ending make up *stopping*? (*stop* and *-ing*)
- Start with the sounds in the base word: *stop*. What letters spell /stop/? Write *stop*.
- Now double the consonant *p* and add *-ing*. Add *ping*.
- Now spell *stopping*.
- Repeat with *stopped, dine, dined, dining*.

PRETEST Dictate the spelling words. Segment the words for children if necessary. Have children check their pretests and correct misspelled words.

HOMEWORK Spelling Practice Book, p. 13

Group Time

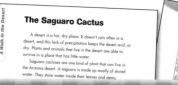

On-Level	Strategic Intervention	Advanced
Read Decodable Reader 4.	**Read** Decodable Reader 4.	**Read** Advanced Selection 4.
• Use p. 96q.	• Use the **Routine** on p. DI·44.	• Use the **Routine** on p. DI·45.

 Place English language learners in the groups that correspond to their reading abilities in English.

(i) Independent Activities

Fluency Reading Pair children to reread Leveled Readers or the ELL Reader from the previous week or other text at children's independent level.

Journal Writing List different types of landforms. Share writing.

Independent Reading See p. 96j for Reading/Library activities and suggestions.

Literacy Centers To practice Inflected Endings -*s, -ed, -ing*, you may use Word Work, p. 96j.

Practice Book 2.1 Inflected Endings, p. 33; Main Idea and Details, p. 34

Break into small groups after Spelling and before Build Background.

Apply Phonics

⊙ PRACTICE Inflected Endings

Decodable Reader 4

Clive's Big Box
Written by Paula Alvarez
Illustrated by Barbra Johnson

Phonics Skill
Adding -s, -ed, -ing

HIGH-FREQUENCY WORDS Review *every, said,* and *two* on the Word Wall. **Word Wall**

QUOTATION MARKS Point out the quotation marks on p. 27 and explain that they show that someone is talking. Have children watch for quotation marks.

READ DECODABLE READER 4

- Pages 26–27 Read aloud quietly with the group.
- Pages 28–29 Have the group read aloud without you.
- Pages 30–32 Select individuals to read aloud.

CHECK COMPREHENSION AND DECODING Have children retell the story to include characters, setting, and events. Then have children locate inflected endings *-s, -ed,* and *-ing* in the story. Review spelling changes: double final consonants, drop *e*. Sort words according to their spelling changes.

No change	Double final consonant	Drop e
makes	dropped	smiled
added	grabbed	wiped
lifted		smiling
rested		
yelled		
lifting		

HOMEWORK Take-Home Decodable Reader 4

REREAD FOR FLUENCY

Oral Rereading

ROUTINE

1 **Reader 1 Begins** Children read the entire selection, switching readers at the end of each page.

2 **Reader 2 Begins** Have partners reread; now the other partner begins.

3 **Reread** For optimal fluency, children should reread three or four times.

4 **Provide Feedback** Listen to children read and provide corrective feedback regarding their oral reading and their use of the blending strategy.

OBJECTIVES

- Apply knowledge of letter-sounds and word parts to decode unknown words when reading.
- Use context with letter-sounds and word parts to confirm the identification of unknown words.
- Practice fluency in paired reading.

Monitor Progress

Decoding

If... children have difficulty decoding a word,	then... prompt them to blend the word.
	• What is the new word?
	• Is the new word a word you know?
	• Does it make sense in the story?

Access Content

Beginning Preview the book *Clive's Big Box,* identifying *dropped* and *grabbed* in the pictures and print. Have children repeat the words and use gestures to show meaning.

Intermediate Preview *Clive's Big Box,* providing synonyms for unfamiliar words, such as *very* for *quite,* and *strange* for *odd.*

Advanced After reading *Clive's Big Box,* have partners take turns retelling the first few pages of the story.

Build Background

LET'S TALK ABOUT Exploration

DEVELOP ORAL LANGUAGE Read the title and have children view the photographs. Ask them to tell you what they see. Allow ample time for children to respond. Remind children that good listeners sit quietly and make eye contact with the speaker. If children are reluctant to talk, use open-ended prompts to model language use and to encourage conversation. For example:

Tell me about what you see here. Yes, that's right, animals, a plant, and what looks like a giant rock rising from the earth. What do you think these animals have in common? That's right, they all live in the desert. Have you ever explored in a desert? What was it like?

BUILD ORAL VOCABULARY As you continue the discussion, encourage children to use today's Amazing Words: *arid, landform, precipitation*.

- Tell me what you know about the weather in the desert. Use the word *precipitation* in your answer.
- What kind of landforms do you see in the photographs?
- How can you tell that the locations in the photographs are arid?

DEVELOP CONCEPTS

CONCEPT CHART Remind children of the question of the week.

- What can we learn by exploring the desert?

Display Graphic Organizer 3 or draw a K-W-L chart. Write *Exploring the Desert* on the topic line. Draw children's attention to the first two columns, inviting them to brainstorm answers to the following questions. Write their answers in the appropriate column. Display the K-W-L chart for use during the week.

- What do you already know about the desert?
- What do you want to know? What do you think we can learn by exploring the desert?

Explain to children that they will be able to list what they have learned about exploring the desert in the third column as they read this week's selection.

CONNECT TO READING Point out the illustration at the bottom of p. 97 in the Student Edition. Tell children that this is a roadrunner. Explain that this week they will take a reading tour through the desert, where they will learn about many animals, including the roadrunner.

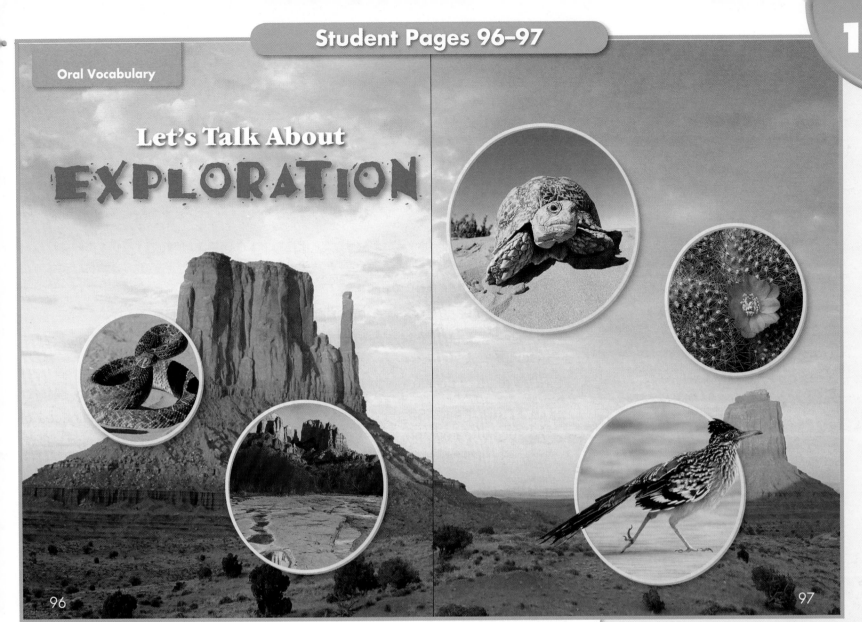

Let's Talk About
EXPLORATION

96

97

Topic Exploring the Desert

What We Know	What We Want to Know	What We Learned
It is hot and dry in the desert.	What kind of animals live in the desert?	
Cactus plants grow in the desert.	What kind of plants (besides cactus) grow there?	

▲ **Graphic Organizer 3**

Take It to the NET™
ONLINE

For a Web site that tells more about living in the desert, do an Internet search using the keywords *desert life.*

ELL

Access Content To prepare children for reading *A Walk in the Desert*, send home the story summary in English and/or the home language. See the ELL Teaching Guide, pp. 26–28.

A Walk in the Desert   96–97

Read the story. **Follow** the directions below.

"Don't forget your water bottle," Lisa said to Ben. "You are going to need it."

Ben looked around and shrugged. "Seems like a nice day to me," he said. "We're just going on a little hike." Ben did grab the water bottle. And it was a good thing he did. The sun got hotter and hotter. There were no trees in sight. Finally, the kids found a big rock that made some shade. Ben took a big swig of water.

"Good thing we have this," Ben said. "The desert is hot and dry." Lisa just nodded and smiled.

1. **Underline** the sentence that tells what Ben thought of the desert at first.

2. lots of water (no trees)

Circle the words that describe what the kids found in the desert.

3. **Write** a sentence that tells why Ben and Lisa got hot.

Possible answers: The sun got hot. There were no trees.

4. **Write** the sentence that tells the main idea of the story.

Possible answer: The desert is hot and dry.

5. **Write** a good title for this story.

Titles will vary. They should include some of these words: Desert, Hike, Hot, or Walk.

 **Home Activity** Your child identified the main idea in a story. Work with your child to write about an unusual area or climate. Find Web sites or books that talk about that place, and help with the writing. Encourage your child to give his or her story a title that tells the main idea.

▲ **Practice Book 2.1** p. 34, Main Idea and Details

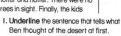

Access Content For a Picture It! lesson on main idea and details, see the ELL Teaching Guide, pp. 22–23.

Listening Comprehension

◉ TEACH/MODEL Main Idea and Details

DEFINE MAIN IDEA AND DETAILS

- The main idea is the most important idea about the topic.
- Details are small pieces of information in a selection that tell more about the main idea.
- Good readers decide which ideas are most important as they read.

READ ALOUD Read "Saguaro Cactus" and model how to identify the main idea of the second paragraph.

Think Aloud **MODEL** The second paragraph tells about things that help a saguaro cactus live in the desert. I think the main idea is that its waxy skin, protective spines, and ability to live without precipitation are all things that help the saguaro cactus survive.

PRACTICE

CLUES TO MAIN IDEA Ask children to identify the main idea of the last paragraph. What are some details in the last paragraph? (Native Americans ate fruit from saguaro cactuses. The flower of the saguaro cactus is the state flower of Arizona.) What is the main idea of this paragraph? (People have long used and liked the saguaro cactus.)

IDENTIFY MAIN IDEA Have children recall the selection *Exploring Space*.

- What were some details from *Exploring Space*? (Astronauts do experiments in space. In the space shuttle, everything floats.)
- What is the main idea of *Exploring Space*? (Astronauts do many important things while exploring space.)

CONNECT TO READING Tell children that when they read any story, they should identify the main idea and restate it in their own words.

Saguaro Cactus

If you've ever driven through the arid Sonoran Desert in California, Arizona, or Mexico, you've probably seen a saguaro cactus. This plant is easy to see—it stands out with a tall, thick stem and large arms that curve upward toward the sky.

This special cactus has several things that help it survive. A waxy, smooth skin protects it from the dry climate. Outside, spines cover it to protect the plant from animals that might want to drink the precious water inside. The saguaro can survive in the desert month after month without precipitation.

The saguaro grows only about an inch a year, but it can reach up to fifty feet! The largest saguaro plants can have more than five arms. Some plants are believed to be about two hundred years old.

People have long used and liked the saguaro cactus. Native Americans ate its juicy and tasty fruit. Today, the state of Arizona calls the creamy-white blossom of the saguaro cactus its state flower.

Shared Writing

DAILY FIX-IT

1. talked about the desert
   <u>We</u> talked about the desert<u>.</u>

2. when can we go
   <u>W</u>hen can we go<u>?</u>

This week's practice sentences appear on Daily Fix-It Transparency 4.

Strategic Intervention

Work with those children who are not able to write independently. Help them brainstorm one sentence at a time by asking them questions about your area.

Advanced

Let children think of a new column for the chart about your area, perhaps Weather or Holidays. Then have them incorporate the items they list in that column into their independent writing.

Support Writing Reread the Shared Writing report aloud to children. Let children give their own ideas about what your area is like before they write.

▲ **The Grammar and Writing Book** For more instruction and practice, use pp. 68–73.

WRITE Report

GENERATE IDEAS Ask children to think about who and what lives in their neighborhood or area. As they name plants, animals, and people, write them in the chart. Tell children they can use the chart to help them write.

WRITE A REPORT Explain that the class will first fill in a chart about who and what lives in their neighborhood and then write a report using the information.

MAIN IDEA AND DETAILS Explain that the main idea of their report—what it is really all about—will be what the area they live in is like. Tell children that the kinds of plants, animals, and people that live there are details. Those details tell more about the main idea of what the area they live in is like.

- Display Writing Transparency 4 and read the title aloud.

- Read the question at the top of the chart aloud.

- Draw children's attention to the first column and read the title aloud. Invite children to brainstorm the kinds of plants they know live in your area. List them in the column as children name them.

- Follow a similar procedure with the other two columns of the chart.

- Invite children to draft the first sentence of the report about "In Our Area," incorporating one or more items from the chart. Continue similarly to write a three- or four-sentence shared report, using some details from the chart.

HANDWRITING While writing, model the letter forms as shown on pp. TR14–TR17.

READ THE REPORT Have children read the completed report aloud as you track the print.

In Our Area

Possible answers:

What lives in our neighborhood?		
Plants	Animals	People
trees flowers	birds squirrels rabbits	children men women

Possible answers:
<u>Many things live in our neighborhood.</u>

<u>Trees and flowers live here.</u>

<u>Birds, squirrels, and rabbits live here.</u>

<u>Children, men, and women live</u>

<u>here too.</u>

Unit 1 A Walk in the Desert   Writing Model **4**

▲ **Writing Transparency 4**

INDEPENDENT WRITING

WRITE A REPORT Have children write their own report about the area they live in. Encourage them to use words from the Word Wall and the Amazing Words board. Let children illustrate their writing. You may gather children's work into a class book for self-selected reading.

ADDITIONAL PRACTICE For additional practice, use pp. 68–73 in the Grammar and Writing Book.

Grammar

TEACH/MODEL Statements and Questions

REVIEW SENTENCES Remind children that a sentence is a group of words that tells a complete idea and that the words in a sentence are in an order that makes sense. A sentence always begins with a capital letter.

IDENTIFY STATEMENTS AND QUESTIONS Display Grammar Transparency 4. Read the definitions aloud.

- Is the first sentence a statement that tells something? Or is it a question that asks something?

- This sentence asks something, so it should end with a question mark.

Continue modeling with items 2–6.

PRACTICE

SUGGEST QUESTIONS AND ANSWERS Have children provide other questions and statements. Write each one and have volunteers add the end punctuation.

- Think of a question about the weather, such as *Will the sun shine today?*

- Answer the question with a statement, such as *The sun will shine today.*

Statements and Questions

A **statement** is a sentence that tells something. A statement ends with a **period (.)**

Some places are very dry.

A **question** is a sentence that asks something. A question ends with a **question mark (?).**

What can live in a very dry place?

All statements and questions begin with capital letters.

Put a period at the end if the sentence is a statement.
Put a question mark at the end if the sentence is a question.

1. Can an oak tree live in a very dry place **?**

2. An oak tree needs plenty of water **.**

3. It cannot live in a very dry place **.**

4. Does a cactus need much water **?**

5. A cactus does not need much water **.**

6. Where does a cactus live **?**

Unit 1 A Walk in the Desert   Grammar **4**

▲ Grammar Transparency 4

Wrap Up Your Day!

 INFLECTED ENDINGS Write *He walks today. He walked yesterday. He is walking now.* Read each sentence aloud and underline *walk.* Have children identify and circle the endings.

 SPELLING INFLECTED ENDINGS Write the base words *work, stop,* and *hope.* Dictate the *-ed* and *-ing* form of each word and ask volunteers to write it on the board.

 MAIN IDEA AND DETAILS To help children distinguish between main idea and details, recall "Star Pictures in the Sky" on pp. 90–93.

- Does the title tell the main idea? How do you know?

- The selection tells about the Little Dipper. Is that the main idea of the selection or is it one detail? How do you know?

LET'S TALK ABOUT IT Display children's partially completed K-W-L chart and encourage them to add ideas to the first two columns. Is there anything else we know about the desert? What do we think we might learn by exploring a desert? What would we like to learn?

 HOMEWORK Send home this week's Family Times newsletter.

PREVIEW Day 2

Tell children that tomorrow the class will read about taking a walk in the desert.

Day 2
AT A GLANCE

Share Literature
Around One Cactus

Phonics and Spelling
Inflected Endings
Spelling: Words with Endings

Comprehension
Skill Main Idea and Details
Strategy Text Structure

Build Background
Weather in Different Climates

High-Frequency Words
water	eyes	early
animals	full	warm

Word Wall

Vocabulary
Selection Words

cactus climate coyote

harsh desert

Read Apply Phonics

Group Time < Differentiated Instruction

A Walk in the Desert

Interactive Writing
Ad

Grammar
Statements and Questions

Materials

- *Sing with Me Big Book*
- *Read Aloud Anthology*
- Phonics Songs and Rhymes Chart 4
- Background Building Audio
- Graphic Organizer 27
- Student Edition 98–119
- Tested Word Cards
- Vocabulary Transparency 4

Morning Warm-Up!

Today we will read about
walking in the desert.
What will we see and hear and feel?
What lives there?
What will we spot?

QUESTION OF THE DAY Encourage children to sing "The Arid Desert" from the *Sing with Me Big Book* as you gather. Write and read the message and discuss the questions.

REVIEW INFLECTED ENDINGS

- Read the message aloud, indicating each word as you do so.

- Draw attention to the words *walking* and *lives*. Have children write the base words and then circle the endings *-s* and *-ing*. Make sure they spell the words correctly.

Build Background Use the Day 2 instruction on ELL Poster 4 to preview high-frequency words.

ELL Poster 4

Share Literature

BUILD CONCEPTS

POETRY AND RHYME Read the title aloud, emphasizing the rhythm and rhyming words *bats* and *rats*. Discuss with children that the title sounds like a poem with rhyming words. You may want to compare it to any other familiar rhyme. Tell children this is a long poem with lots of rhyming words.

Read Aloud Anthology
Around One Cactus Owls,
Bats, and Leaping Rats

BUILD ORAL VOCABULARY Ask children whether they have ever been on a sandy beach. Explain that sometimes the wind pushes sand into big piles we call **dunes.** Discuss that sometimes beaches are down below a big shelf of rocks called a **ledge.** If possible, provide a photograph to illustrate the two words. Suggest that as you read, children listen to find out what the author says about dunes and ledges in the desert.

- What does the author say is happening to the dunes? (They are shifting, or changing or moving all the time.)
- What grows on the ledges? (bushes)

MONITOR LISTENING COMPREHENSION

- What did the boy looking at the cactus want to know? (what could be living in and around the huge cactus)
- Why couldn't he see any critters? (because he was looking in the daytime, and the critters mostly come out at night)
- What kind of animals might live in the dunes or on the ledges? (Possible answers: dunes: hyena, snake, lizard; ledge: owl, fox, antelope)

RETELL Ask children to retell the story in their own words.

Amazing Words to build oral vocabulary

	MONITOR PROGRESS
arid landform precipitation **dunes** **ledge** haven discovery forbidding	**If...** children lack oral vocabulary experiences about the concept Exploration, **then...** use the Oral Vocabulary Routine. See p. DI·6 to teach *dunes* and *ledge*.

Build Concepts Explain to children unfamiliar with desert life that many plants and animals are especially equipped to live in these hot places without much water. Point out that large cactus plants like the one shown in the book, called a saguaro, are usually home to many kind of birds and animals.

Inflected Endings

Strategic Intervention

Use **Strategic Intervention Decodable Reader 4** for more practice with inflected endings.

ELL

Support Phonics Explain that a tortoise is a turtle. Then invite children to name the animals pictured in the art for "Exploring the Desert" as you replay the Phonics Songs and Rhymes Audio CD.

TEACH/MODEL

Fluent Word Reading ROUTINE

1 **Connect** Write *chiming*. You can read this word because you know how to read base words with endings and spelling changes. What base word and ending form *chiming*? (*chime* and *-ing*) Do the same with *chimes* and *chimed*.

2 **Model** When you come to a new base word with an ending, knowing if there has been a spelling change will help you read it. Model reading *bugs, bugged, bugging, dive, dived, diving.* When you come to a new base word and ending, what are you going to do?

3 **Group Practice** Write *blames, blamed, blaming, grins, grinned, grinning.* Read these words. Look at the word, say the word to yourself, and then read the word aloud. Allow 2–3 seconds previewing time.

WORD READING

PHONICS SONGS AND RHYMES CHART 4 Frame each of the following words on Phonics Songs and Rhymes Chart 4. Call on individuals to read them. Guide children in previewing.

hiked	**seems**	**moved**	**soaring**	**looked**
sunning	**hopped**	**shaking**	**making**	**exploring**

Sing "Exploring the Desert" to the tune of "On Top of Old Smokey," or play the CD. Have children follow along on the chart as they sing. Then have individuals take turns underlining and reading words with *-s, -ed,* and *-ing* endings on the chart.

Phonics Songs and Rhymes Audio

Exploring the Desert

We hiked in the desert;
  the sun was so bright.
We looked all around at
  each wonderful sight.
A hawk that was soaring,
  each wing like a sail.
A rattlesnake sunning
  and shaking its tail.
A big old jackrabbit
  hopped over the ground.
A huge tortoise moved
  without making a sound.
A desert seems empty,
  but open your eyes.
Each sand dune you come to
  has a surprise.

Phonics Songs and Rhymes Chart 4

BUILD WORDS

INDIVIDUALS COMBINE BASE WORDS WITH ENDINGS -s, -ed, -ing Write *base word, -s, -ed,* and *-ing* as headings for a four-column chart. Write several base words in the first column. Have children add the *-s, -ed,* and *-ing* endings to each base word, read the new word, and tell how the spelling changed when the endings were added.

base word	-s	-ed	-ing
pace	paces	paced	pacing
raft	rafts	rafted	rafting
move	moves	moved	moving
spot	spots	spotted	spotting

Spelling

PRACTICE Base Words and Endings

WRITE DICTATION SENTENCES Have children write these sentences. Repeat words slowly, allowing children to hear each sound. Children may use the Word Wall to help with spelling high-frequency words. **Word Wall**

> **I was amazed that we lifted the big log.**
> **Grandma and I hugged and talked.**
> **My dog was excited when I smiled at him.**

HOMEWORK Spelling Practice Book, p. 14

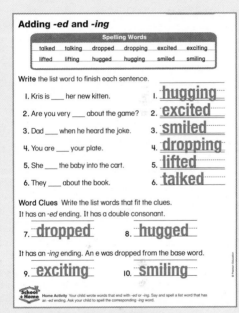

▲ **Spelling Practice Book** p. 14

Read the story.
Follow the directions below.

The trees dripped with rain. The ground felt soft under my feet. Everywhere I looked, the forest was green. The air was chilly and dark. I liked hiking in the rain forest.

1. **Write** the sentence that tells the main idea.

___I liked hiking in the rain forest.___

2. **Underline** the sentences that tell the details of the story.

I kicked up dust with my feet. The sky was open and bright. Soon the sun would set. I was glad because I knew it would cool off soon! It was hot in the desert, but it was beautiful.

3. **Write** the sentence that tells the main idea.

___It was hot in the desert, but it was beautiful.___

4. **Underline** the sentences that tell the details of the story.

Write a good title for each of these stories.

Titles will vary. They should reflect the topic of the story.
5. Possible response: A Wet Hike in the Rain Forest

6. Possible response: A Hot Walk in the Desert

School + Home **Home Activity** Your child identified the main idea in a story. Take a walk together around your neighborhood or near the school. Ask your child to describe the features of that area as you walk and to think of one sentence that describes it best.

▲ **Practice Book 2.1** p. 35, Main Idea and Details

Comprehension

SKILL Main Idea and Details

RECOGNIZE MAIN IDEA AND DETAILS Review with children that the main idea is the most important idea about the topic. Details in pictures and in the selection give smaller pieces of information that tell more about the main idea.

CONNECT TO READING

- As you read, consider what the most important idea of the selection really is. Ask yourself what all the details tell about.
- Notice details, or smaller bits of information, that tell more about the main idea.

STRATEGY Text Structure

INTRODUCE THE STRATEGY Tell children that they will understand what they are reading better if they pay attention to how the author has organized the selection. Sometimes the reader reads about things in the order they would appear during a walk with the author.

Think Aloud **MODEL** When I read, I like to pay attention to the way the author organizes the selection. Sometimes the author writes in a way that makes me feel as if I am walking along with him or her as different things are explained or pointed out.

CONNECT TO READING Encourage children to ask themselves these questions as they read *A Walk in the Desert*.

- Do I understand that the information is presented in a sequence?
- Do I find the clues that help me follow the sequence?

Build Background

DISCUSS CLIMATES AND ACTIVITIES Display pictures of regions that represent different climates, such as a desert, seashore, woods, and mountains.

- What do you think it might be like to live in each of these places?
- What outdoor activities might children do in these places?
- How is the weather where you live different from these places?

BACKGROUND BUILDING AUDIO Have children listen to the audio and share the new information they learned about activities in different climates.

 **Sing with Me/ Background Building Audio**

COMPLETE A COMPARISON CHART Draw a four-column chart or display Graphic Organizer 27. Tell children to write *Desert, Seashore, Woods,* and *Mountains* as the column headings. Brainstorm activities children could do in each climate.

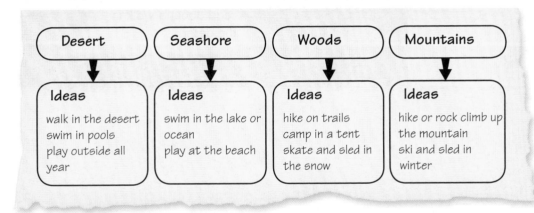

Desert	Seashore	Woods	Mountains
Ideas	**Ideas**	**Ideas**	**Ideas**
walk in the desert	swim in the lake or	hike on trails	hike or rock climb up
swim in pools	ocean	camp in a tent	the mountain
play outside all	play at the beach	skate and sled in	ski and sled in
year		the snow	winter

▲ Graphic Organizer 27

CONNECT TO SELECTION Connect background information to *A Walk in the Desert.*

In the selection we are about to read, the author takes us for a walk in the desert and shows us the special kinds of plants and animals that live there. We'll find out what the weather is like in the desert and how children play there.

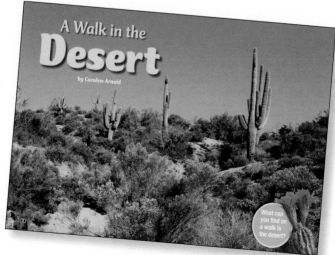

A Walk in the **Desert** by Caroline Arnold

Activate Prior Knowledge Ask children to tell what kind of climate they live in now and what activities they can do. Encourage them to tell about any other places they have lived. How was that climate different? How were their activities different?

Words to Read

water
full
animals
early
warm
eyes

Read the Words

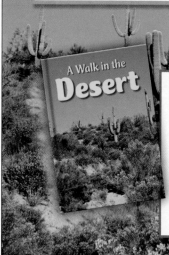

Some places on Earth have very little water. It is hot and dry, but these places are full of life. Plants and animals can live there. You can visit these places too. Go out early before the sun is too warm. Be sure to protect your eyes when you go out!

A Walk in the **Desert**

Genre: Expository Nonfiction

Expository nonfiction gives information about a topic. In the next selection, you will read about a walk in the desert.

98

99

High-Frequency Words

Nondecodable Words

ROUTINE

1 **Say and Spell** Look at the words on page 98. You cannot blend the sounds in these words. We will spell the words and use letter-sounds we know to learn them. **Point to the first word.** This word is *water, w-a-t-e-r, water.* What is this word? What are the letters in this word?

2 **Identify Familiar Letter-Sounds** Point to the first letter in *water.* What is this letter? What is the sound for this letter? (*w*/w/) Follow a similar procedure to have children identify the *t* in *water.*

3 **Demonstrate Meaning** Tell me a sentence using this word.

Repeat the routine with the other Words to Read. Have children identify these familiar letter-sounds: *full* (f/f/), *animals* (n/n/ and s/z/), *early* (l/l/), *warm* (w/w/), *eyes* (s/z/).

Have children read aloud the sentences on p. 99 and point to the Words to Read. Add the words to the Word Wall. **Word Wall**

Use Vocabulary Transparency 4 to review this week's words.

- Point to a word. Say and spell it.
- Have children say and spell the word.
- Ask children to identify familiar letter-sounds.

Write the correct word from the box to finish each sentence.

| animals early eyes full |
| harsh warm water |

1. The desert heat is **harsh** at noon in this climate.

2. The **animals** look for shade from the sun.

3. It is hard to find **water** in the desert.

4. The coyote closes his **eyes** and rests in the shade near a cactus.

5. It is cooler **early** in the morning.

6. The sky is **full** of pretty colors.

7. It will get **warm** as the sun gets higher in the sky.

School + Home **Home Activity** Your child completed sentences using high-frequency and selection words learned this week. Go to the library and check out books on desert habitats. Remind your child to look for the high-frequency or selection words in what he or she reads.

▲ **Practice Book 2.1** p. 36, High-Frequency Words and Selection Words

---

Monitor Progress | Check High-Frequency Words

Point to the following words on the Word Wall and have individuals read them.

water	world	eyes	early	woman
animals	friend	full	warm	move

If... children cannot read these words,

then... have them practice in pairs with word cards before reading the selection. Monitor their fluency with these words during reading, and provide additional practice opportunities before the Day 5 Assessment.

SUCCESS PREDICTOR

Spiral REVIEW

- Reviews previously taught high-frequency words.

High-Frequency Words

SUCCESS PREDICTOR

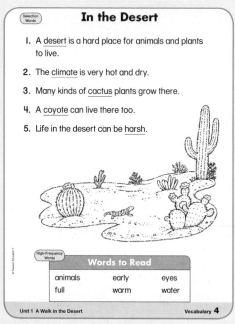

In the Desert

1. A <u>desert</u> is a hard place for animals and plants to live.

2. The <u>climate</u> is very hot and dry.

3. Many kinds of <u>cactus</u> plants grow there.

4. A <u>coyote</u> can live there too.

5. Life in the desert can be <u>harsh</u>.

Words to Read

animals	early	eyes
full	warm	water

Unit 1 A Walk in the Desert | Vocabulary **4**

▲ **Vocabulary Transparency 4**

Vocabulary

SELECTION WORDS

Use Vocabulary Transparency 4 to introduce the selection words.

- Read each sentence as you track the print.
- Frame each underlined word. Explain the word's meaning.

  desert a part of land that is sandy and without much water

  harsh very rough

  climate the kind of weather a place has

  cactus a plant with spines instead of leaves that grows in hot, dry places

  coyote a small animal like a wolf

- Ask children to identify familiar letter-sounds and word parts: *cactus* (*c*/k/), *climate* (*i*/ī/), *coyote* (can be pronounced with two syllables ending with /t/ or with three syllables ending with /ē/), *harsh* (*sh*/sh/), *desert* (*d*/d/).
- Have children read each sentence aloud with you.
- To encourage discussion using the selection words, ask children to describe a desert and tell what they might find there.

Group Time

On-Level	Strategic Intervention	Advanced
Read *A Walk in the Desert.*	**Read** SI Decodable Reader 4.	**Read** *A Walk in the Desert.*
• Use pp. 100–119.	• Read or listen to *A Walk in the Desert.*	• Use the **Routine** on p. DI•47.
	• Use the **Routine** on p. DI•46.	

 Place English language learners in the groups that correspond to their reading abilities in English.

(i) Independent Activities

Independent Reading See p. 96j for Reading/ Library activities and suggestions.

Journal Writing Write about a desert and what it is like there. Share your writing.

Literacy Centers To provide experiences with *A Walk in the Desert,* you may use the Listening Center on p. 96j.

Practice Book 2.1 Main Idea and Details, p. 35; High-Frequency Words, p. 36; Compare and Contrast, p. 37

Access Content Use the vocabulary strategies and word cards in the ELL Teaching Guide, pp. 24–25.

Break into small groups after Vocabulary and before Writing.

A Walk in the Desert
by Caroline Arnold

100

101

What can you find on a walk in the desert?

Prereading Strategies

PREVIEW AND PREDICT Read the title with children, inviting them to decode any words they can. Then read aloud the author's name. Invite children to leaf through several pages of the selection, looking at the photographs and some of the labels. Ask what children think they might learn from the selection.

DISCUSS EXPOSITORY NONFICTION Read aloud the definition of expository nonfiction on p. 99. Encourage children to discuss the kinds of information they think they may find in the selection.

SET PURPOSE Read aloud the question on p. 101. Ask children what they think it might be like to walk in the desert and what kinds of animals and plants they might see there.

Audio CD AudioText

Access Content Before reading, review the story summary in English and/or the home language. See the ELL Teaching Guide, pp. 26–28.

See the bright sun. Feel the dry air. It is hot—very hot! Where are we?

We're in the desert. Let's take a walk and see what we can find.

The ground is dry in the desert. It almost never rains. With so little water, it is hard for anything to live. But many plants and animals make their home in this harsh climate. You just have to look closely to see them.

Cactus is one kind of plant that grows in the desert. It doesn't have leaves. Instead, it has sharp spines. The spines protect the cactus from animals who might want to eat it. A cactus stores water in its stem. It uses the water when there is no rain.

Hedgehog Cactus

Teddy-Bear Cholla Cactus

Prickly Pear Cactus

Barrel Cactus

102

103

▲ **Pages 102–103**
Have children read and then look at the pictures and their labels to decide what these pages are about.

Skills in Context

MAIN IDEA AND DETAILS

- **What's the most important idea on these two pages? Are the two pages really all about cactus plants? Or are they really about the desert?**
  The two pages tell about the desert. Cactus plants are one small idea, or detail, about the desert.

Monitor Progress	Main Idea and Details
If... children are unable to identify the main idea and details,	**then...** model how to use the text and pictures to determine the main idea and details.

Think Aloud **MODEL** I think the most important idea is the desert and how arid it is. Cactus plants are one part of the desert. Since the title of this selection is *A Walk in the Desert,* I think it will be mainly about the desert.

ASSESS Have children identify the main idea and details of subsequent pages.

____ Inflected Endings *-s, -ed, -ing*   ▢ high-frequency/tested vocabulary

Look up at the tall saguaro. It is a giant among cactus plants. It took many years to grow so tall.

In late spring, white flowers bloom. Birds and insects drink the flowers' sweet nectar. After the flowers die, a red fruit <u>grows</u>.

Prickly Pear Fruit

Saguaro Cactus

Saguaro Cactus with White Flowers

104

105

Guiding Comprehension

Compare and Contrast • Critical

- *Text to World* **How is a cactus different from a tree? How is it the same?**
The cactus has spines, but most trees have leaves. Both a cactus and a tree can grow flowers or fruit. They can both grow very tall.

Author's Purpose • Inferential

- *Question the Author* **Why do you think the author included photographs of the saguaro and its flowers?**
Probably so we could see what they really look like.

▲ **Pages 104–105**
Have children read to find out about the saguaro cactus.

Monitor Progress	
Decoding	
If... children come to a word they don't know,	**then...** remind them to: 1. Blend the word. 2. Decide if the word makes sense. 3. Look in a dictionary for more help.

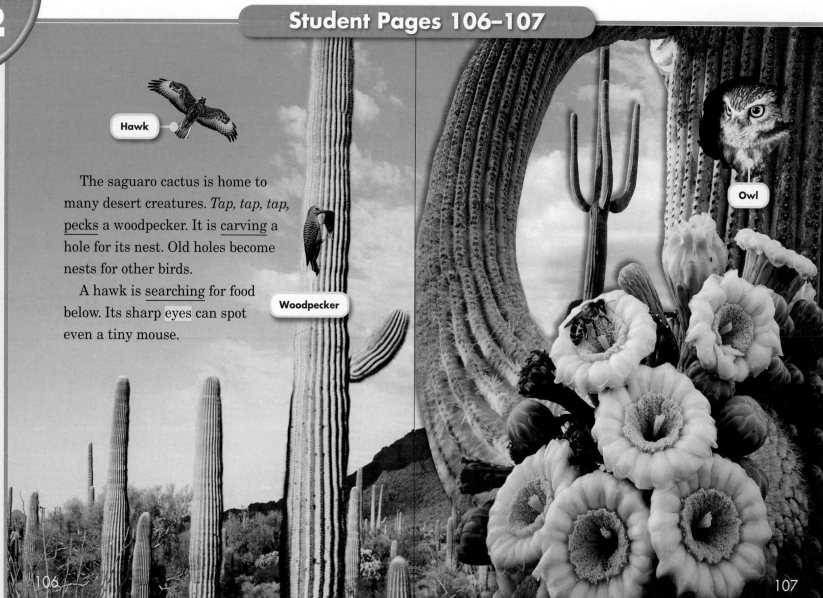

Hawk

The saguaro cactus is home to many desert creatures. *Tap, tap, tap,* pecks a woodpecker. It is carving a hole for its nest. Old holes become nests for other birds.

A hawk is searching for food below. Its sharp eyes can spot even a tiny mouse.

Woodpecker

Owl

106

107

▲ **Pages 106–107**
Have children read to find out what else they can see as they walk in the desert.

Monitor Progress

High-Frequency Words

If... children have a problem reading a new high-frequency word,	**then...** use the High-Frequency Routine on p. 99a to reteach the problematic word.

Context Clues Explain that "sharp eyes" means that the hawk has very, very good eyesight. Recall that the cactus plant has "sharp spines." The word *sharp* there means "pointed so that they can hurt."

Strategies in Context

⟳ TEXT STRUCTURE

• **As you read these pages, do you feel like you are looking around the desert as you are walking through it? What makes you feel that way?**
Yes, because we keep seeing different plants and animals in the desert just as we would if we were walking through it. And the author says things like "Look up."

Monitor Progress | Text Structure

If... children have difficulty understanding text structure,	**then...** model how to use the text and pictures to confirm understanding.

Think Aloud **MODEL** I like the way the author organized this selection. It makes me feel like I'm walking through the desert with her. First we see some cactus plants, and the author points out a big saguaro. Now I see a hawk flying overhead, a woodpecker on the saguaro, and a mouse and an owl in it.

ASSESS As children continue to read the selection, have them discuss ways in which it is like taking a walk and seeing things along the way.

___ Inflected Endings -s, -ed, -ing   high-frequency/tested vocabulary

What is that large bird? It's a roadrunner. *Coo, coo, coo,* it <u>calls</u>. The roadrunner hardly ever flies, but it can run fast. Watch it chase a lizard to eat.

Here are some other lizards. Lizards need the sun's heat to warm their scaly bodies. But when it <u>gets</u> too hot, they look for shade.

Roadrunner

Zebra-Tailed Lizard

Leopard Lizard

Short-Horned Lizard

Tree Lizard

108

109

Guiding Comprehension

🎯 **Main Idea and Details • Inferential**

- **What are these two pages mostly about? What are the details about?**
  These pages are about some wildlife in the desert. They tell some details about a roadrunner and some lizards.

Details and Facts • Literal

- **Why do lizards stay out in the sun?**
  They need to keep warm.

Categorize/Classify • Inferential

- **How are the animals on p. 109 alike? How are they different from each other?**
  They are alike because they are all lizards. They all warm themselves in the sun and need shade. They are different because they look different. The zebra-tailed lizard has a long, striped tail. The leopard lizard has spots. The short-horned lizard looks like it has horns.

▲ **Pages 108–109**
Have children read to find out about some other desert animals.

EXTEND SKILLS

Illustrations and Labels

For instruction in labels and illlustrations, discuss the following:

- The author has included some enlarged pictures with labels to provide more information.
- Look at the pictures in the circles on this page. What do the labels tell us?

Assess Have children discuss how they know the animals in the circled pictures are shown larger than the background.

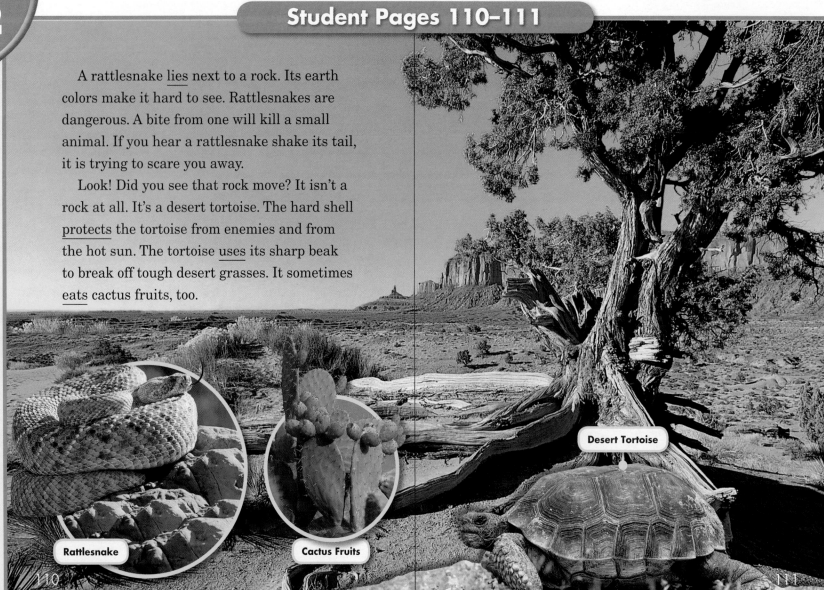

A rattlesnake lies next to a rock. Its earth colors make it hard to see. Rattlesnakes are dangerous. A bite from one will kill a small animal. If you hear a rattlesnake shake its tail, it is trying to scare you away.

Look! Did you see that rock move? It isn't a rock at all. It's a desert tortoise. The hard shell protects the tortoise from enemies and from the hot sun. The tortoise uses its sharp beak to break off tough desert grasses. It sometimes eats cactus fruits, too.

Rattlesnake

Cactus Fruits

Desert Tortoise

110

111

▲ **Pages 110–111**
Have children read to find out about some other desert animals.

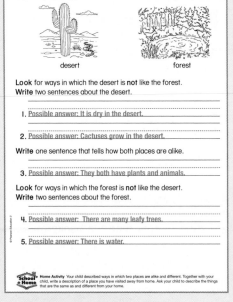

desert   forest

Look for ways in which the desert is **not** like the forest.
Write two sentences about the desert.

1. Possible answer: It is dry in the desert.

2. Possible answer: Cactuses grow in the desert.

Write one sentence that tells how both places are alike.

3. Possible answer: They both have plants and animals.

Look for ways in which the forest is **not** like the desert.
Write two sentences about the forest.

4. Possible answer: There are many leafy trees.

5. Possible answer: There is water.

 Home Activity Your child described ways in which two places are alike and different. Together with your child, write a description of a place you have visited away from home. Ask your child to describe the things that are the same as and different from your home.

▲ **Practice Book 2.1** p. 37,
Compare and Contrast

Skills in Context

(REVIEW) COMPARE AND CONTRAST

- **We read an article about astronauts in space. How is being in the desert different from being in space?**
  You float in space, but you walk in the desert. In the desert, you can see wild-life, but there isn't any in space.

Monitor Progress	**Compare and Contrast**
If... children are unable to compare and contrast,	**then...** model how to use the text and illustrations to compare and contrast.

Think Aloud **MODEL** I remember that astronauts float in space, but we walk in the desert. As we walk, we see lots of plants and animals in the desert, but I know there isn't any wildlife in space. So I know some differences between the desert and outer space.

ASSESS Have children compare what they see in the desert with what Henry and Mudge saw on their camping trip.

_____ Inflected Endings -s, -ed, -ing   high-frequency/tested vocabulary

The jack rabbit is also a plant eater. Watch it sniff the early evening air. It is alert to the sounds and smells of the desert. When danger is near, the jack rabbit's long legs help it to escape quickly.

Jack Rabbits

112

113

▲ **Pages 112–113**
Have children read to find out about jackrabbits.

Guiding Comprehension

Draw Conclusions • Critical
* *Text to World* **Why do you suppose a jackrabbit has such long ears?**
They probably help it hear better.

Author's Purpose • Inferential
* *Question the Author* **Why do you think the author wrote this article? Was she trying to tell us what the desert was like? Or was she trying to entertain us? What makes you think so?**
She is trying to tell us what the desert is like. She gives us lots of facts about the plants and animals in the desert, and shows us pictures so that we will know what everything looks like.

Compare and Contrast • Critical
* *Text to Self* **How is walking in the desert like walking in your neighborhood? How is it different?**
Possible response: We don't have cacti or lizards, but we can see plants and animals in our neighborhood. Children who live in desert regions might mention that their neighborhood has similar plants to those in the selection, but that they see houses and roads as well.

Rainfall *TIME FOR Science*
In the American desert, only 6 to 12 inches of rain fall every year. In the central and eastern regions of the country, 20 to 45 inches fall per year. Areas with the most rain include the coasts of the far northwest and southeast.

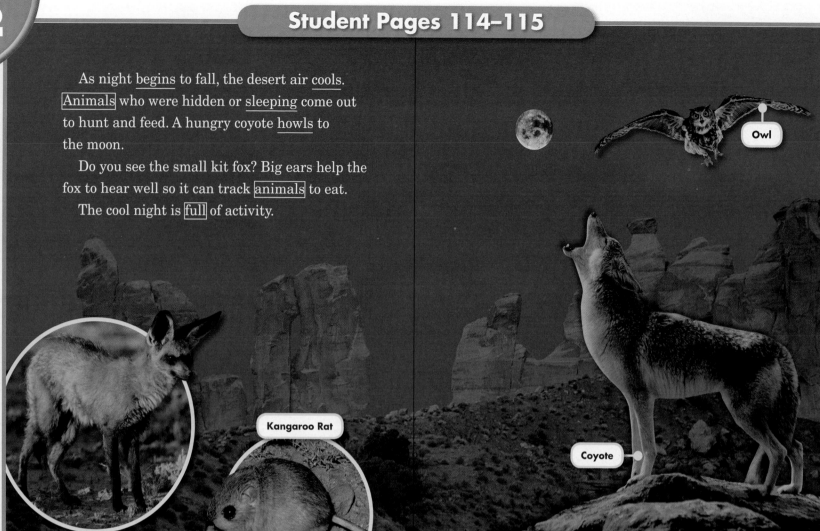

As night begins to fall, the desert air cools. Animals who were hidden or sleeping come out to hunt and feed. A hungry coyote howls to the moon.

Do you see the small kit fox? Big ears help the fox to hear well so it can track animals to eat.

The cool night is full of activity.

Owl

Kangaroo Rat

Coyote

Small Kit Fox

114

115

▲ **Pages 114–115**
Have children read to find out what the desert is like at night.

Strategy Self-Check

Have children ask themselves these questions to check their reading.

Decoding Words
- Do I use what I know about syllables to figure out new words?
- Do I compare a new word to one I already know?

Text Structure
- Do I understand that the information is presented in a sequence?
- Do I find the clues that help me follow the sequence?

Guiding Comprehension

Compare and Contrast • Inferential
- **How is night in the desert different from day?**
  Different animals, like the kit fox and the coyote, come out in the night.

Draw Conclusions • Inferential
- **Why do you think there is so much activity in the desert at night?**
  Probably because it is so much cooler and more comfortable. Some of those animals that come out at night must be able to really see and hear well in the dark.

Summarize • Inferential
- **What have we found out about the desert so far?**
  We learned some things about desert plants called cacti. They have spines instead of leaves. Lots of different animals live in the big saguaro cactus. We also learned about some desert animals—lizards, rattlesnakes, desert tortoises, and coyotes. Also, the desert is arid, without much precipitation.

_____ Inflected Endings -s, -ed, -ing   high-frequency/tested vocabulary

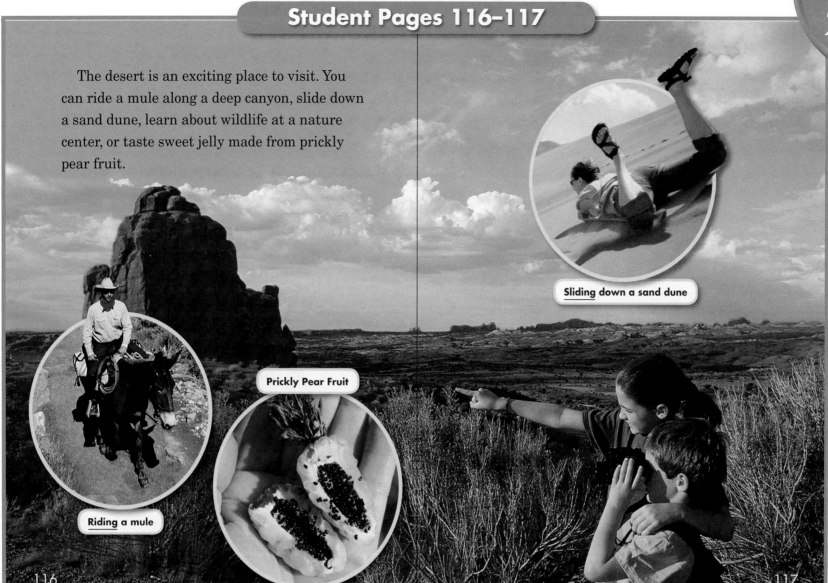

The desert is an exciting place to visit. You can ride a mule along a deep canyon, slide down a sand dune, learn about wildlife at a nature center, or taste sweet jelly made from prickly pear fruit.

Sliding down a sand dune

Prickly Pear Fruit

Riding a mule

116

117

Guiding Comprehension

Details and Facts • Inferential

- **What can you do in the desert besides walk?**
  You can ride a mule along a canyon, slide down a sand dune, learn about wildlife, and eat prickly pear jelly.

Main Idea and Details • Critical

- **Do you think this selection is mostly about what you can do in the desert, or is that one smaller idea? What do you think it is mostly about?**
  The selection is mostly about the desert. What people can do in the desert is one smaller idea.

▲ **Pages 116–117**
Have children read to find out some things they could do in the desert.

Adapting to Nature

Many living things adapt, or change over time, to fit into their surroundings. Since cacti must survive with little water, they have thick stems to store water, and their spines do not lose water as leaves do. Their roots are very thin and shallow. That helps them take in as much rainwater as possible. The tall saguaro cactus has a tap root that goes down only about 3 feet, but its network of smaller roots goes out as far as the saguaro is tall. Some of the small roots wrap around rocks to keep the saguaro anchored in wind.

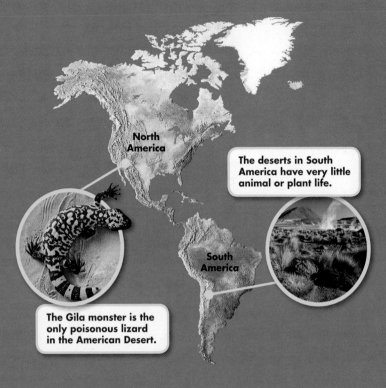

You can find deserts all over the world. Not all deserts are alike. Some are hot. Others are cold. But in all deserts there is little rain.

North America

The deserts in South America have very little animal or plant life.

South America

The Gila monster is the only poisonous lizard in the American Desert.

118

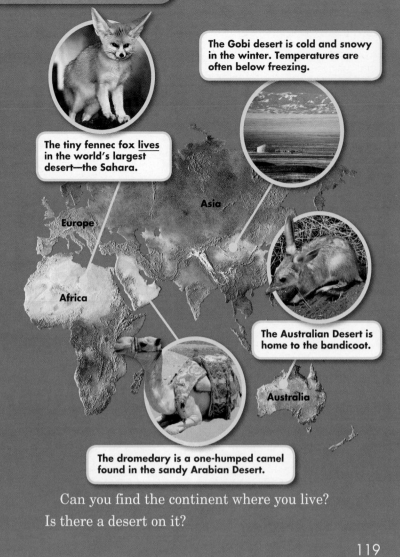

The tiny fennec fox <u>lives</u> in the world's largest desert—the Sahara.

The Gobi desert is cold and snowy in the winter. Temperatures are often below freezing.

Asia

Europe

Africa

The Australian Desert is home to the bandicoot.

Australia

The dromedary is a one-humped camel found in the sandy Arabian Desert.

Can you find the continent where you live?
Is there a desert on it?

119

Pages 118–119
Have children read to find out about deserts around the world.

____ Inflected Endings *-s, -ed, -ing*   high-frequency/tested vocabulary

Guiding Comprehension

Graphic Sources • Inferential

- **Where on this map of the world do we live? This selection is about the American Desert. Where is the American Desert?**
  We live in North America, shown on p. 118. The American Desert is in the southwestern part of our country.

Author's Purpose • Critical

- *Question the Author* **Why do you think the author included this map of the world?**
  She probably wanted us to know that there are different kinds of deserts all around the world.

REREAD FOR FLUENCY

Paired Reading

ROUTINE

1 **Reader 1 Begins** Children read the entire book, switching readers at the end of each page.

2 **Reader 2 Begins** Have partners reread; now the other partner begins.

3 **Reread** For optimal fluency, children should reread three or four times.

4 **Provide Feedback** Listen to children read and provide corrective feedback regarding their oral reading and their use of the blending strategy.

Strategic Intervention

Make sure children understand that the purpose of an ad is to interest people and persuade them to do something. Help them describe the desert in exciting terms for their own ad.

Advanced

Let children work together to develop and act out an ad for TV.

Support Writing Before writing, explain to children that the purpose of the ad is to get other people to be interested in seeing the desert.

Beginning Have children draw a picture of the desert for their ad. Then have them label the picture or dictate a sentence about the desert as their ad.

Intermediate Have children create a list of words that make the desert seem exciting and interesting. They can use some or all of the words in their own ad.

Advanced Let pairs brainstorm what to put in their ads before they write them.

Support Grammar In some languages, the markers for questions are different from the word order and end question mark in English. Let children dictate questions and statements. Write them, showing the appropriate English word order and punctuation. See the Grammar Transition lessons in the ELL and Transition Handbook.

Interactive Writing

WRITE Ad

BRAINSTORM Talk with children about ads they see on TV or in magazines or newspapers. Explain that they can develop a newspaper ad for the desert in the form of a poster. Invite them to think of what they might say in an ad that would make people want to come visit the desert.

SHARE THE PEN Have children begin to draft a headline for the ad. Point out that a headline does not have to be a complete sentence and that in a headline every important word is capitalized. Have the class agree on a headline. Write it on the board. Ask questions such as:

- What kind of letter should begin the headline? (a capital letter)

Then discuss with children what to say in the first sentence after the headline. Write the sentence, inviting individuals to write familiar letter-sounds, word parts, and high-frequency words.

- How do we begin and end the first sentence? (with a capital letter and end punctuation)

Continue to have children make contributions. Frequently reread what has been written while tracking the print.

READ THE AD Read the completed ad aloud, having children echo you.

Visit the Desert

You can see cactus plants.

You can see a roadrunner or a lizard or a rattlesnake.

You can ride a mule or slide down a sand dune.

INDEPENDENT WRITING

WRITE AN AD Have children write their own ad about the desert. Let children illustrate their writing.

Grammar

DEVELOP THE CONCEPT
Statements and Questions

IDENTIFY STATEMENTS AND QUESTIONS Write on the board *We are going for a walk in the desert. What will we see there?* Point to each word as you read the sentences aloud.

Each of these is a sentence. The first one tells something, and it ends in a period. The second sentence asks something, and it ends with a question mark. Circle each punctuation mark as you mention it. We can make the statement into a question by putting the words in a different order. Write *Are we going for a walk in the desert.* What mark should we put at the end? (a question mark)

PRACTICE

Question	Statement

WRITE QUESTIONS AND STATEMENTS Display the chart. Invite children to write a question in the first column and to answer the question with a statement in the second column.

 Think Aloud

MODEL Let me think of a question to write. I'll ask *Is it hot in the desert?* and I'll write it in the first column. I need to remember to write a question mark at the end of the question. Now let me think of a statement that answers the question. *It is hot in the desert.* I'll write that statement and remember to add a period at the end.

Have children write other questions and statements in the chart.

PREVIEW Day 3

Tell children that tomorrow the class will hear about other desert creatures.

Wrap Up Your Day!

 HIGH-FREQUENCY WORDS Write the following sentences. *It was a warm day when we went to the desert. We took water bottles and got there early. We were surprised that it was full of animals. We couldn't believe our eyes.* Read the sentences with children and have them identify the high-frequency words *warm, water, early, full, animals, eyes.*

TEXT STRUCTURE Review with children that the way an article is organized can help them understand it better. Recall that the selection *A Walk in the Desert* was organized as if the author were really walking in the desert.

LET'S TALK ABOUT IT Have children complete the K-W-L chart using what they've learned.

DAILY FIX-IT

3. did you enjoy the desert
<u>D</u>id you enjoy the desert<u>?</u>

4. I was really exited?
I was really <u>excited!</u>

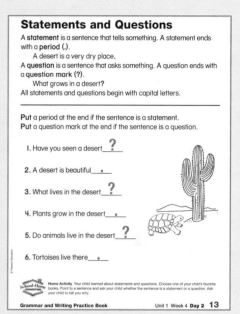

Statements and Questions

A **statement** is a sentence that tells something. A statement ends with a **period** (.).
   A desert is a very dry place.
A **question** is a sentence that asks something. A question ends with a **question mark** (?).
   What grows in a desert?
All statements and questions begin with capital letters.

Put a period at the end if the sentence is a statement.
Put a question mark at the end if the sentence is a question.

1. Have you seen a desert___?

2. A desert is beautiful___.

3. What lives in the desert___?

4. Plants grow in the desert___.

5. Do animals live in the desert___?

6. Tortoises live there___.

Home Activity Your child learned about statements and questions. Choose one of your child's favorite books. Point to a sentence and ask your child whether the sentence is a statement or a question. Ask your child to tell you why.

Grammar and Writing Practice Book   Unit 1 Week 4 **Day 2** 13

▲ **Grammar and Writing Practice Book** p. 13

Day 3
AT A GLANCE

Materials

- *Sing with Me Big Book*
- *Read Aloud Anthology*
- Letter Tiles
- Student Edition 116–117

Morning Warm-Up!

Many animals that live in the
desert sleep in the heat of the day.
They come out at night to find food.
What else can we learn about
animals by exploring the desert?

QUESTION OF THE DAY Encourage children to sing "The Arid Desert" from the *Sing with Me Big Book* as you gather. Write and read the message and discuss the question.

REVIEW STATEMENTS AND QUESTIONS

- Indicate the first sentence in the message. Is this a statement or a question? How do you know? (a statement because it tells something and ends with a period)

- Indicate the third sentence in the message. Is this a statement or a question? How do you know? (a question because it asks something and ends with a question mark)

Build Background Use the Day 3 instruction on ELL Poster 4 to support children's use of English to communicate about lesson concepts.

ELL Poster 4

Share Literature

LISTEN AND RESPOND

COMPARE POEMS Children who are familiar with "This Is the House That Jack Built" will enjoy comparing it to this selection. Read that poem aloud to children and discuss with them how it sounds like *Around One Cactus.*

BUILD ORAL VOCABULARY Recall with children that they listened for the words *dunes* and *ledge* the last time you read this selection. Ask children to explain the meanings of those two words either orally or by drawing a picture that shows both. Suggest that this time they listen for the word **haven.** Explain that a **haven** is "a place where someone or something is safe and protected."

Read Aloud Anthology
Around One Cactus

MONITOR LISTENING COMPREHENSION

- Do you think the big cactus lives on a sand dune or on a ledge? Why do you think so? (Possible answer: a dune because a ledge is rocky)

- In this selection, what is a haven for creatures? (the big cactus)

- How is this book like "This Is the House That Jack Built"? How is it different? (This book has the same repetition of previous verses included in each verse, but it is about a very different topic.)

OBJECTIVES

- Compare poems.
- Set purpose for listening.
- Build oral vocabulary.

Amazing Words to build oral vocabulary

	MONITOR PROGRESS
arid landform precipitation dunes ledge haven discovery forbidding	**If…** children lack oral vocabulary experiences about the concept Exploration, **then…** use the Oral Vocabulary Routine. See p. DI·6 to teach *haven.*

Listen and Respond Ask children to work together to draw a large poster or mural of the big cactus with the birds and animals in and around it. Have them write the label *cactus* and then label the animals, such as *rat, owl, bat, snake,* and *fox.*

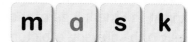

Review Phonics

REVIEW CONSONANT BLENDS

READ CONSONANT BLEND WORDS Write *twin* and *rust.* You can read these words because you know how to read consonant blends. What sounds can *tw* and *st* stand for? (They can stand for the sounds /tw/ and /st/.) What are the words?

a c i k l m p r s t

BUILD WORDS Have children spell *mask* with letter tiles. Monitor work and provide feedback.

m a s k

- Change the *k* in *mask* to *t.*
  What is the new word?

m a s t

- Change the *m* in *mast* to *p.*
  What is the new word?

p a s t

- Change the *st* in *past* to *ck.*
  What is the new word?

p a c k

- Change the *p* in *pack* to *sl.*
  What is the new word?

s l a c k

- Change the *ck* in *slack* to *p.*
  What is the new word?

s l a p

- Change the *sl* in *slap* to *str.*
  What is the new word?

s t r a p

- Change the *a* in *strap* to *i.*
  What is the new word?

s t r i p

- Take the *s* away from *strip.*
  What is the new word?

t r i p

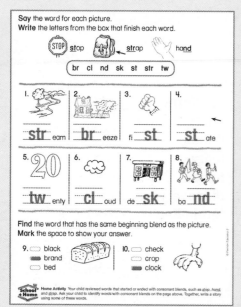

OBJECTIVES

- Review consonant blends.
- Build, blend, and read words with consonant blends.
- Recognize high-frequency words.
- Spell base words and endings *-ed, -ing.*

▲ **Practice Book 2.1** p. 38, Consonant Blends

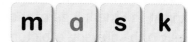

High-Frequency Words

PRACTICE

STORY CLUES Provide clues such as the following. Have children find, read, and spell the word on the Word Wall that fits each clue. **Word Wall**

- You have two of these to see with. What are they? **(eyes)**
- You drink it, cook with it, and bathe in it. What is it? **(water)**
- The word is the opposite of *late*. What is it? **(early)**
- The word is the opposite of *empty*. What is it? **(full)**
- The word is the opposite of *cool*. What is it? **(warm)**
- Cats, dogs, birds, and raccoons are examples of these. What are they? **(animals)**

Spelling

PRACTICE Inflected Endings

GIVE CLUES Have children practice by writing the spelling words that

- are things you do with your mouth *(talked, talking; smiled; smiling)*
- are things you do with your arms *(hugged, hugging; lifted, lifting; dropped, dropping; dragging)*
- are ways you can feel *(excited, exciting; amazed)*

HOMEWORK Spelling Practice Book, p. 15

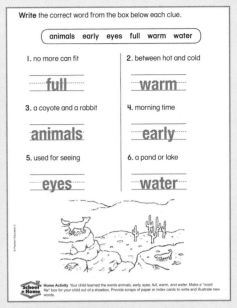

▲ **Practice Book 2.1** p. 39, High-Frequency Words

Spelling Words

Inflected Endings -ed, -ing

1. **talked**	7. **lifted**
2. **talking**	8. **lifting**
3. **dropped**	9. **hugged**
4. **dropping**	10. **hugging**
5. **excited**	11. **smiled**
6. **exciting***	12. **smiling**

Challenge Words

13. **dragging**	15. **danced**
14. **amazed**	

* Word from the Selection

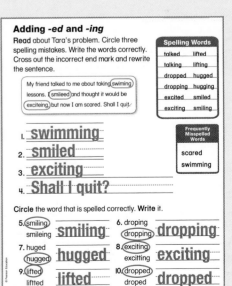

▲ **Spelling Practice Book** p. 15

A Walk in the Desert   **120d**

Strategic Intervention

Have children illustrate descriptions about the desert, such as a bright sun or a cactus with sharp spines.

Advanced

Have children write a story about the desert. Tell them they must include descriptive words.

Access Content Use the vocabulary strategies and word cards in the ELL Teaching Guide, pp. 24–25.

Vocabulary

DESCRIPTIVE WORDS

DISCUSS DESCRIPTIVE WORDS Explain to children that descriptive words tell how things look, sound, taste, feel, and smell. For example, you could describe the desert as having a bright sun and dry air, and a cactus as having sharp spines. *Bright* tells how something looks, *dry* and *sharp* tell how something feels. Invite children to think of other descriptive words that tell how things in the desert sound, taste, smell, feel, and look.

EXPAND VOCABULARY Brainstorm with children ways to use the selection descriptive word *harsh* with other selection words such as *climate, cactus,* and *desert* to tell about the desert.

Group Time

DAY 3

On-Level	Strategic Intervention	Advanced
Read *A Walk in the Desert.* • Use pp. 100–119.	**Read** or listen to *A Walk in the Desert.* • Use the **Routine** on p. DI•48.	**Read** Self-Selected Reading. • Use the **Routine** on p. DI•49.

ELL Place English language learners in the groups that correspond to their reading abilities in English.

ⓘ Independent Activities

Independent Reading See p. 96j for Reading/Library activities and suggestions.

Journal Writing Use descriptive words in sentences about the desert. Share your writing.

Literacy Centers To provide experiences with *A Walk in the Desert,* you may use the Writing Center on p. 96k.

Practice Book 2.1 Consonant Blends, p. 38; High-Frequency Words, p. 39

Break into small groups after Vocabulary and before Fluency.

Fluency

ATTEND TO PUNCTUATION

MODEL ATTENDING TO PUNCTUATION Use *A Walk in the Desert.*

- Point to the question mark on p. 101. Remember that a question mark means the sentence asks something. When we read, we need to make sure we check the punctuation marks at the ends of sentences so we understand them. If we are reading aloud, we use our voices a little differently with questions.

- Have children follow along as you read aloud p. 101.

- Ask children to read the page after you. Remind them to pay attention to the punctuation mark. Continue in the same way with p. 102.

REREAD FOR FLUENCY

Choral Reading

ROUTINE

① **Select a Passage** For *A Walk in the Desert,* use pp. 108–110.

② **Divide into Groups** Assign each group a part to read. For this selection, assign one paragraph to each of four groups.

③ **Model** Have children track the print as you read.

④ **Read Together** Have children read along with you.

⑤ **Independent Readings** Have the groups read aloud without you. Monitor progress and provide feedback. For optimal fluency, children should reread three to four times.

Monitor Progress	Fluency
If... children have difficulty attending to punctuation,	**then...** put sticky notes with large periods and question marks near one sentence at a time and have them read the sentence with you.
If... the class cannot read fluently without you,	**then...** continue to have them read along with you.

OBJECTIVE

- Read aloud fluently, while attending to punctuation.

Options for Oral Reading

Use *A Walk in the Desert* or one of the following Leveled Readers.

On-Level

A Walk in the Mountains

Strategic Intervention

Desert

Advanced

Trek to the Top

Model reading p. 108 of *A Walk in the Desert.* Point out the question mark and periods at the end of the sentences. Model correct intonation for English language learners by letting your voice go up at the end of the question and down at the end of the statements. Have children echo you.

To develop fluent readers, use Fluency Coach.

Retelling Plan

- ☑ Week 1 assess Strategic Intervention students.
- ☑ Week 2 assess Advanced students.
- ☑ Week 3 assess Strategic Intervention students.
- ☑ **This week assess On-Level students.**
- ☐ Week 5 assess any students you have not yet checked during this unit.

Look Back and Write For test practice, assign a 10–15 minute time limit. For informal or formal assessment, see the Scoring Rubric below.

Assessment Before retelling, help children name the characters and items shown. For more ideas on assessing comprehension, see the ELL and Transition Handbook.

Think and Share

TALK ABOUT IT Model a response. Watch out for rattlesnakes! But look at the cactus plants. Be careful not to touch them because their spines are sharp. Look for lizards sunning themselves on rocks.

1. RETELL Have children use the retelling strip in the Student Edition to retell what they learned from the selection.

Monitor Progress | **Check Retelling**

If... children have difficulty retelling the story,

then... use the Retelling Cards and Scoring Rubric for Retelling on p. 120–121 to help them move toward fluent retelling.

SUCCESS PREDICTOR

Day 1 Check Word Reading ⋮ **Day 2** Check High-Frequency Words ⋮ ▶**Day 3 Check Retelling** ⋮ **Day 4** Check Fluency ⋮ **Day 5** Assess Progress

2. 🔍 **MAIN IDEA AND DETAILS** Model a response. Cactus plants have spines and flowers. Many animals live in a saguaro cactus. Rattlesnakes shake and rattle their tails.

3. 🔍 **TEXT STRUCTURE** Model a response. At the beginning, the author asks, "Where are we?" Later she asks, "Do you see the small kit fox?" That made me feel like someone was walking with me and pointing things out. It helped me notice things.

 LOOK BACK AND WRITE Read the writing prompt on p. 120 and model your thinking. I'll look back at pages 116 and 117 and read that part of the selection again. I'll look for things the author says people can do in the desert. Then I'll write my response. Have children write their responses.

Scoring Rubric | **Look Back and Write**

Top-Score Response A top-score response will use details from pp. 116–117 of the selection to describe other things you can do in the desert.

Example of a Top-Score Response You can ride a mule. You can slide down a sand dune. You can learn about wildlife at a nature center or taste prickly pear jelly.

For additional rubrics, see p. WA10.

Think and Share

Talk About It You and some friends go walking in the desert. Tell your friends what to look at and listen for.

1. Use the pictures below to summarize what you learned. **Retell**

2. Look back at the story to find details that tell about desert plants and animals. **Main Idea and Details**

3. The author wrote about the desert as if she were taking you for a walk. Find examples of that in the selection. How did that help you as you read? **Text Structure**

Look Back and Write Look at pages 116–117. What other things can you do in the desert?

Meet the Author

Caroline Arnold

Caroline Arnold has walked in several deserts in the southwestern United States. After she moved to California, she says, "I grew to love the desert."

Read two other books by Caroline Arnold.

Ms. Arnold is fascinated by the way living things adapt to the extreme heat and cold and the lack of water in the desert. "I get a thrill out of watching birds, squirrels, rabbits, coyotes, peccaries, lizards, and other desert animals when I spend time in the desert," she says.

Retelling Strip

120

121

Scoring Rubric — Expository Retelling

Rubric 4 3 2 1	4	3	2	1
Connections	Makes connections and generalizes beyond the text	Makes connections to other events, texts, or experiences	Makes a limited connection to another event, text, or experience	Makes no connection to another event, text, or experience
Author's Purpose	Elaborates on author's purpose	Tells author's purpose with some clarity	Makes some connection to author's purpose	Makes no connection to author's purpose
Topic	Describes the main topic	Identifies the main topic with some details early in retelling	Identifies the main topic	Retelling has no sense of topic
Important Ideas	Gives accurate information about ideas using key vocabulary	Gives accurate information about ideas with some key vocabulary	Gives limited or inaccurate information about ideas	Gives no information about ideas
Conclusions	Draws conclusions and makes inferences to generalize beyond the text	Draws conclusions about the text	Is able to draw some conclusions about the text	Is unable to draw conclusions or make inferences about the text

Use the Retelling Chart on p. TR21 to record retelling.

Selection Test To assess with *A Walk in the Desert*, use Selection Tests, pp. 13–16.

Fresh Reads for Differentiated Test Practice For weekly leveled practice, use pp. 19–24.

Retelling

SUCCESS PREDICTOR

3

D A I L Y   F I X - I T

5. smiled at the mule
<u>He</u> smiled at the mule<u>.</u>

6. did you find some cactus jelly
<u>Did</u> you find some cactus jelly<u>?</u>

Connect to Unit Writing

Writing Trait

Have children use strategies for developing **conventions** when they write a personal narrative in the Unit Writing Workshop, pp. WA2–WA9.

Writing Trait of the Week

INTRODUCE Conventions

TALK ABOUT CONVENTIONS Explain to children that conventions are the rules for writing, including capitalization, spelling, and punctuation. Ask them to think about how the author's use of conventions helps readers understand *A Walk in the Desert*.

Think Aloud **MODEL** The author of *A Walk in the Desert* gives many facts about desert plants and animals. I can read and learn new facts easily because the author uses conventions correctly. She spells all the words correctly. She begins sentences with capital letters and ends them with punctuation marks. Let me read some sentences from the article.

Look! Did you see that rock move? It isn't a rock at all. It's a desert tortoise.

All the sentences begin with a capital letter and end with a punctuation mark. The first three sentences end with different marks. The first one shows me that the author is excited. The second one asks a question. The last two make statements. The author also spells words correctly. I could find the word *tortoise* in a dictionary to check its spelling. These are conventions that help us understand the facts.

STRATEGY FOR DEVELOPING CONVENTIONS Write the following sentences on the board. Ask children to identify incorrect use of conventions in each. Together, revise each sentence.

The dessert gets cool at night. *(The desert gets cool at night.)*

A desert fox has big ears *(A desert fox has big ears.)*

a snake shakes its tail. *(A snake shakes its tail.)*

Did you see that owl. *(Did you see that owl?)*

PRACTICE

APPLY THE STRATEGY On the board, write a class list of desert plants and animals described in the article. Ask children to write a question, an exclamation, and a statement using names from the list. Have them exchange sentences and check for correct capitalization, spelling, and end punctuation.

Grammar

APPLY TO WRITING Statements and Questions

IMPROVE WRITING WITH STATEMENTS AND QUESTIONS Explain to children that sometimes they can include questions in their writing, even though most of the time they will write statements. Point out that this can make their writing seem more interesting. Remind children to use statements and questions correctly in their own writing.

Suggest that children write a question about what someone could discover on a walk in their neighborhood and then write several statements to answer the question.

What could you find in a walk on Oak Street? You would see kids in the park. You could buy ice cream from the man with the cart. You could jump rope with the kids at the corner.

PRACTICE

WRITE WITH STATEMENTS AND QUESTIONS Have children add another question and two or three statements about a walk in their neighborhood.

OBJECTIVE

● Use statements and questions in writing.

Statements and Questions

Write two statements and two questions about this picture.

Possible answer: The desert is quiet at night. It is dark. Is that a cactus? Where are the animals?

Home Activity Your child learned how to use statements and questions in writing. Tell your child to imagine that you are going on a trip to the desert. Ask your child to write a statement and a question about the trip.

▲ **Grammar and Writing Practice Book** p. 14

Wrap Up Your Day!

MAIN IDEA AND DETAILS Help children recall the main idea of *A Walk in the Desert*. (We can see many special plants and animals in the desert.) Have them name one or two details from the selection.

ATTEND TO PUNCTUATION Remind children that when they read they need to pay special attention to periods and question marks so they know whether they are reading a statement or a question.

LET'S TALK ABOUT IT Display the KWL chart from Day 1 and review it with children. Ask them what they learned by exploring the desert during the reading of *A Walk in the Desert*. Encourage them to add to the list in the third column of What We Learned.

PREVIEW Day 4

Tell children that tomorrow they will read about using a computer and the Internet to find the answers to some questions.

Share Literature
Exploring the Sahara

Phonics and Spelling

Inflected Endings
Spelling: Words with Endings

Read Apply Phonics
Group Time < Differentiated
Instruction

"Rain Forests"

Fluency
Attend to Punctuation

Writing Across the Curriculum
Web

Grammar
Statements and Questions

Speaking and Listening
Be a Polite Listener

Materials

- *Sing with Me Big Book*
- *Read Aloud Anthology*
- Student Edition 120–121
- Graphic Organizer 15

Morning Warm-Up!

**Where could you find out more about the desert?
What could tell you that
the inside of a cactus feels slippery
or that cactus candy is sweet?**

QUESTION OF THE DAY Encourage children to sing "The Arid Desert" from the *Sing with Me Big Book* as you gather. Write and read the message and discuss the questions.

REVIEW DESCRIPTIVE WORDS

- Point out the words *slippery* and *sweet*. What kinds of words are these? (descriptive words)

- What do the words describe? (how the cactus feels and how the cactus candy tastes)

Extend Language Use the Day 4 instruction on ELL Poster 4 to extend and enrich language.

ELL Poster 4

Share Literature

CONNECT CONCEPTS

ACTIVATE PRIOR KNOWLEDGE Recall with children what they have read and heard about exploring the desert. Ask children to briefly tell some things they have learned about the desert.

Read Aloud Anthology
Exploring the Sahara

BUILD ORAL VOCABULARY Write the word *explore* on the board and discuss with children that it means "to travel where you haven't been before in order to find out new things." Explain that sometimes when people explore, they make a **discovery,** or learn something for the first time. Tell children that the desert is often a **forbidding** place because it is hard for many forms of life to live there. Ask children to listen to learn about some exciting discoveries made in a new way, including why the desert was not always such a forbidding place.

REVIEW ORAL VOCABULARY After reading, review all the Amazing Words for the week. Have children take turns using them in sentences that tell about the concept for the week. Then talk about Amazing Words they learned in other weeks and connect them to the concept, as well. For example, ask:

• What is the most **fascinating wildlife** in the desert you've learned about?

• Which desert animals do you think you could **identify?**

• Do you think there are any **slimy** animals hiding **underneath** rocks in the desert? Why or why not?

MONITOR LISTENING COMPREHENSION

• What was an exciting discovery about the Sahara desert made by the satellite? (Possible answer: The Sahara was not always a desert.)

• Why was this an exciting discovery? (Possible answer: because it tells us more about the history of the Sahara and about ancient life)

• Was the desert always a forbidding place? (No, long ago both animals and people lived there, and there were forests and grasslands.)

to build oral vocabulary

Amazing Words	**MONITOR PROGRESS**
arid landform precipitation dunes ledge haven discovery forbidding	**If…** children lack oral vocabulary experiences about the concept Exploration, **then…** use the Oral Vocabulary Routine. See p. DI·6 to teach *discovery* and *forbidding*.

Connect Concepts Explain to children that satellites are large machines that circle the Earth, sending and receiving pictures and sounds. Some receive TV pictures from one part of the Earth and send them to other parts of the Earth. That is how we sometimes see news pictures from other countries on our television sets.

Spiral REVIEW

- Reviews long vowels CVCe.
- Reviews short vowels.
- Reviews high-frequency words *bear, build, couldn't, father, love, mother, straight.*

Sentence Reading

REVIEW WORDS IN CONTEXT

READ DECODABLE AND HIGH-FREQUENCY WORDS IN CONTEXT Write these sentences. Call on individuals to read a sentence. Then randomly point to review words and have children read them. To help you monitor word reading, high-frequency words are underlined and decodable words are circled.

My mother and father jogged home without stopping.

A bear can make such a mess.

Dad will build a nice desk.

He couldn't stand running late so he waved for a cab.

I love the drums in the rock band.

We hummed tunes as we walked straight home.

Monitor Progress	Word Reading
If... children are unable to read an underlined word,	**then...** read the word for them and spell it, having them echo you.
If... children are unable to read a circled word,	**then...** have them use the blending strategy they have learned for that word type.

Support Phonics For additional review, see the phonics activities in the ELL and Transition Handbook.

Spelling

PARTNER REVIEW Inflected Endings

READ AND WRITE Supply pairs of children with index cards on which the spelling words have been written. Have one child read a word while the other writes it. Then have children switch roles. Have them use the cards to check their spelling.

HOMEWORK Spelling Practice Book, p. 16

OBJECTIVE

● Spell base words with endings -ed, -ing.

Spelling Words

Inflected Endings -ed, -ing

1. talked		7. lifted	
2. talking		8. lifting	
3. dropped		9. hugged	
4. dropping		10. hugging	
5. excited		11. smiled	
6. exciting*		12. smiling	

Challenge Words

13. dragging	15. danced
14. amazed	

* Word from the Selection

Group Time

On-Level	Strategic Intervention	Advanced
Read "Rain Forests." • Use pp. 122–125.	**Read** or listen to "Rain Forests." • Use the **Routine** on p. DI·50.	**Read** "Rain Forests." • Use the **Routine** on p. DI·51.

 Place English language learners in the groups that correspond to their reading abilities in English.

DAY 4

(i) Independent Activities

Fluency Reading Pair children to reread *A Walk in the Desert.*

Journal Writing Write a story about a dry desert. Share writing.

Spelling Partner Review

Independent Reading See p. 96j for Reading/ Library activities and suggestions.

Literacy Centers To provide listening opportunities, you may use the Listening Center on p. 96j. To extend science concepts, you may use the Science Center on p. 96k.

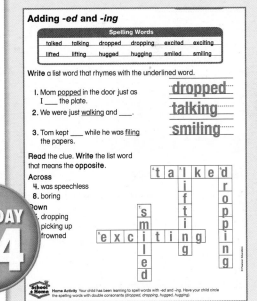

Adding -ed and -ing

▲ **Spelling Practice Book** p. 16

Break into small groups after Spelling and before Fluency.

Reading Online

Rain Forests

Sammy read *A Walk in the Desert* and learned a lot. However, he knows that deserts are not everywhere. In fact, his home is near a forest. His family often goes there to fish, swim, and picnic. "But what exactly is a forest?" Sammy asks himself. To find out more, he goes to an online reference Web site.

Here Sammy finds four different sources: an atlas, an almanac, a dictionary, and an encyclopedia. Sammy clicks on Encyclopedia. Then he types the keyword *forest* into the search engine and clicks on "go." He gets a list of results that begins like this:

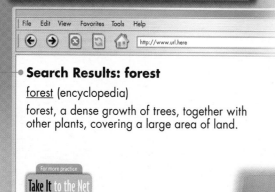

File Edit View Favorites Tools Help

http://www.url.here

Search Results: forest

forest (encyclopedia)

forest, a dense growth of trees, together with other plants, covering a large area of land.

For more practice

Take It to the Net

PearsonSuccessNet.com

122

Sammy clicks on the forest link and finds an encyclopedia article. As he reads it, he finds a link to Types of Forests. This makes him curious. He clicks on Types of Forests and finds this information.

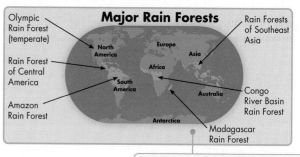

File Edit View Favorites Tools Help

http://www.url.h

Types of Forests

You can find rain forests all over the world, including Central and South America and Central and West Africa. Parts of Asia and Australia also have rain forests. Rain forests get lots of rain every year—160–400 inches. The average temperature is 80°F. Many different kinds of plants and animals live in rain forests.

Major Rain Forests

Olympic Rain Forest (temperate)

Rain Forest of Central America

Amazon Rain Forest

North America

Europe

Asia

Africa

South America

Australia

Antarctica

Rain Forests of Southeast Asia

Congo River Basin Rain Forest

Madagascar Rain Forest

Sammy wonders where some of the countries with rain forests are. He uses the atlas on the Web site. He finds this map showing rain forests all over the world.

123

OBJECTIVE

● Recognize text structure: nonfiction.

EXTEND SKILLS

Using Technology

For instruction in using technology, discuss the following:

● The Internet is a great source of information. Not only can you gain access to online dictionaries and encyclopedias, you can also find books and magazines.

● Who has used computer card catalogs at the media center? Some libraries let you search for books online through their Web sites.

Assess Have children go online to locate a book in the school's media center or the local library. After they read the book, have children compose a book summary on the computer.

Read

Reading Online

PREVIEW AND PREDICT Read the title on p. 122. Have children look through pp. 122–125 to preview the article. Point out that it will tell them how to use a computer and the Internet to find the answers to some questions. Have children read to discover how using online reference sources can help them find out more about exploring other landforms in the world.

INFORMATIONAL TEXT Explain that this selection tells and shows children how to locate information on the Internet. Make sure children understand that the illustrations show them some of the things they would see on the screen of their computer as they explored. For example, children can read the map on p. 123 to learn where rain forests are located around the world.

VOCABULARY/DESCRIPTIVE WORDS Review with children that descriptive words sometimes tell how something looks, sounds, smells, tastes, or feels. Have children locate *large* at the bottom of p. 122 and *curious* on p. 123. Help them understand that a *large* area of land describes what the land looks like and that *curious* describes how Sammy feels.

So far, Sammy has read part of an encyclopedia article and looked at a map. Sammy now goes back to the online reference Web site. He wants to find pictures of animals that live in rain forests. Sammy follows the steps and does another search. He finds these pictures on the Web site of a large university.

Trees are the foundation of the rain forest. This tree is *Pterocarpus*. Its roots grow above the ground.

Toucans live in South and Central America. Toucans are among the prettiest birds in a rain forest.

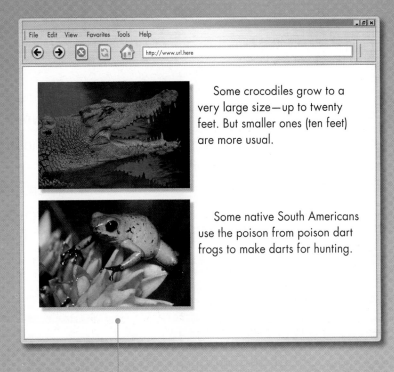

Some crocodiles grow to a very large size—up to twenty feet. But smaller ones (ten feet) are more usual.

Some native South Americans use the poison from poison dart frogs to make darts for hunting.

Sammy is so interested that he continues searching until he finds out all he needs to know about rain forests.

124

125

BUILD CONCEPTS

Draw Conclusions • Critical

- **When you are looking for information online, you need to use keywords. What do you think a keyword is?**

Possible response: A keyword names the idea you are looking for. Sammy asked the question "What exactly is a forest?" In that question, *forest* is the keyword because it names what he wants to know.

Draw Conclusions • Critical

- **What are some things you must do before you can find the answer to a question online?**

Possible response: You must have a computer, get access to the Internet, and type in the correct Internet address of a research site.

CONNECT TEXT TO TEXT

Could you find more information about deserts online? What makes you think so?

Yes, because the online encyclopedia and other reference sources will have information about many things.

Build Background Make sure children understand enough about using computers and getting on the Internet to grasp the meaning of the terms *online, keyword, type, search engine,* "go," and *link.*

Options for Oral Reading

Use *A Walk in the Desert* or one of the following Leveled Readers.

On-Level

A Walk in the Mountains

Strategic Intervention

Desert

Advanced

Trek to the Top

Use *The Saguaro Cactus* or "Rain Forests." For English language learners, emphasize repeated readings to build fluency with enjoyable passages in English, with as much teacher guidance as feasible.

To develop fluent readers, use Fluency Coach.

Fluency

ATTEND TO PUNCTUATION

MODEL ATTENDING TO PUNCTUATION Use *A Walk in the Desert.*

- Remind children to pay attention to periods and question marks when they read.
- Ask children to follow along as you read p. 114 aloud.
- Have children read the page after you. Remind them to pay attention to punctuation marks. Continue in the same way with pp. 115–119.

REREAD FOR FLUENCY

Choral Reading

ROUTINE

1 **Select a Passage** For *A Walk in the Desert,* reread pp. 103–109.

2 **Divide into Groups** Assign each group a part to read. For this selection, have each group read one page.

3 **Model** Have children track the print as you read.

4 **Read Together** Have children read along with you.

5 **Independent Readings** Have the groups read aloud without you. Monitor progress and provide feedback. For optimal fluency, children should reread three to four times.

Monitor Progress | Check Fluency WCPM

As children reread, monitor their progress toward their individual fluency goals. Current Goal: 50–60 words correct per minute. End-of-Year Goal: 90 words correct per minute.

If... children cannot read fluently at a rate of 50–60 words correct per minute,

then... make sure children practice with text at their independent level. Provide additional fluency practice, pairing nonfluent readers with fluent readers.

If... children already read at 90 words correct per minute,

then... they do not need to reread three to four times.

SUCCESS PREDICTOR

Day 1 Check Word Reading | Day 2 Check High-Frequency Words | Day 3 Check Retelling | ▶ Day 4 Check **Fluency** | Day 5 Assess Progress

Writing Across the Curriculum

WRITE Web

DISCUSS Discuss with children what they learned about life in the desert. Explain that when people explore the desert, they must be very careful to take care of themselves in the heat. Encourage children to use the oral vocabulary words *arid, landform,* and *precipitation* as they discuss the desert.

SHARE THE PEN Have children help design a web. Begin by drawing a simple web on the board or use Graphic Organizer 15. In the center circle, write *Taking Care of Yourself in the Desert.* Call on a volunteer to name one thing people should do to take care of themselves in the desert. Write it in one of the outer circles of the web. For example, one of the most important things children might mention is *Take lots of water to drink.* As you write this, invite individuals to help spell the words by writing familiar letter-sounds. Ask questions such as the following:

- What is the first sound you hear in *take?* (/t/)
- What letter stands for that sound? *(t)* Have a volunteer write *t.*
- What is the second consonant sound in *take?* (/k/)
- What is the vowel sound in *take?* (long *a*)

Continue having individuals contribute to writing a phrase in each outer circle. Add more circles as necessary. Reread the items frequently.

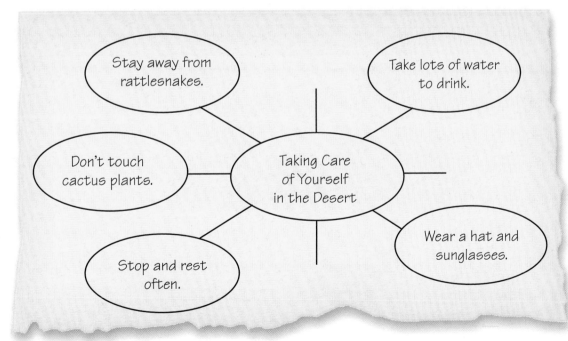

▲ **Graphic Organizer 15**

OBJECTIVE
- Create a web.

Advanced

Have children make similar webs titled *Taking Care of Yourself ___.* Ask them to choose a topic they know, such as going camping in the woods or riding bikes on the sidewalks.

ELL

Support Writing If children offer phrases that do not reflect conventional English, respond positively and restate them in conventional English as you record them on the web.

Grammar

REVIEW STATEMENTS AND QUESTIONS

DAILY FIX-IT

7. wear did you drop it.
<u>W</u>here did you drop it<u>?</u>

8. I lost it in the dessert?
I lost it in the <u>desert.</u>

Statements and Questions

Mark the correct sentence in each group.

1. ○ A lizards like the heat?
   ○ B lizards like the heat.
   ⊗ C Lizards like the heat.

2. ○ A most cactuses grow flowers.
   ⊗ B Most cactuses grow flowers.
   ○ C most cactuses grow flowers?

3. ⊗ A Do zebras live in the desert?
   ○ B do zebras live in the desert?
   ○ C Do zebras live in the desert.

4. ○ A a jack rabbit has long legs?
   ○ B a jack rabbit has long legs.
   ⊗ C A jack rabbit has long legs.

5. ○ A does it rain in the desert.
   ⊗ B Does it rain in the desert?
   ○ C Does it rain in the desert.

6. ○ A Can a desert be cold.
   ○ B can a desert be cold?
   ⊗ C Can a desert be cold?

Home Activity Your child prepared for taking tests on statements and questions. As you watch television with your child, have him or her point out statements and questions that occur in dialogue.

▲ **Grammar and Writing Practice Book** p. 15

DEFINE STATEMENTS AND QUESTIONS

- What is a statement? (a sentence that tells something) How does a written statement end? (with a period)
- What is a question? (a sentence that asks something) How does a written question end? (with a question mark)

PRACTICE

IDENTIFY STATEMENTS AND QUESTIONS Read the following sentences. Have children identify each sentence as a statement or a question and suggest the proper end punctuation.

We went for a walk in the desert.

Was it hot there?

We were careful.

Did you take water with you?

Speaking and Listening

BE A POLITE LISTENER

OBJECTIVES

● Speak to communicate information.

● Listen to be a polite listener.

MODEL LISTENING Explain to children that a good, active listener does several things when someone is speaking. Write the following chart on the board and read each direction, explaining and demonstrating it as you do so.

Listeners

- **Be polite.**
- **Pay attention to the speaker.**
- **Sit quietly.**
- **Face the speaker.**
- **Make eye contact.**

PRACTICE LISTENING Tell children to follow the rules for being a polite listener as you tell them about coyotes in the desert.

Some people call coyotes prairie wolves because they look like wolves. People often don't like coyotes because coyotes hunt small animals like pet dogs and cats or lambs and calves. A coyote can run fast enough to catch a jack rabbit. Most coyotes live in the western part of North America.

Wrap Up Your Day!

✓ **MAKING CONNECTIONS:** *Text to World* Review with children what they have read about taking a walk in the desert and finding information on the Web. If you want to find out more about rattlesnakes, the desert, or something near where we live, you could probably find the information you want on the Web. What are some other things you think people use the Web for?

LET'S TALK ABOUT IT Discuss with children what more they might learn about the desert by exploring online, the way Sammy did to find out more about rain forests.

PREVIEW Day 5

Tell children tomorrow they will hear about one of the biggest deserts in the world.

Day 5
AT A GLANCE

Share Literature
Exploring the Sahara

Phonics and Spelling
REVIEW Inflected Endings
Spelling: Words with Endings

High-Frequency Words
water   eyes   early   **Word Wall**
animals full   warm

Monitor Progress
Spelling Test

Group Time < Differentiated Assessment

Writing and Grammar
Trait: Conventions
Statements and Questions

Research and Study Skills
Technology: Using Online Reference Sources

Materials

- *Sing with Me Big Book*
- *Read Aloud Anthology*
- Reproducible Pages 126f–126g
- Student Edition 122–123

Morning Warm-Up!

This week we made many
discoveries about the arid desert.
We found out that the desert
is a landform without much precipitation.
Some deserts have sand dunes.
Can a cactus be a haven for animals?

QUESTION OF THE DAY Encourage children to sing "The Arid Desert" from the *Sing with Me Big Book* as you gather. Write and read the message and discuss the question.

REVIEW ORAL VOCABULARY Indicate the vocabulary words *discoveries*, *arid*, *landform*, *precipitation*, *dunes*, and *haven* in the message. Have children

- name several *discoveries* they made about the desert
- tell what *precipitation* is and why it is important in *arid* land
- describe a sand *dune*
- list several animals that find a *haven* in a large desert cactus

Assess Vocabulary Use the Day 5 instruction on ELL Poster 4 to monitor children's progress with oral vocabulary.

ELL Poster 4

Share Literature

LISTEN AND RESPOND

USE PRIOR KNOWLEDGE Review the exciting discoveries the satellites have made about the Sahara and how the desert was not always such a forbidding place. Ask children to listen this time to find out what else people learned from the satellites as they explored the desert.

MONITOR LISTENING COMPREHENSION

Read Aloud Anthology
Exploring the Sahara

- What discoveries have people made by exploring the desert with satellites? (Possible answer: They have learned about the history of the desert, including that there used to be lakes, mountains, and valleys where the Sahara is now. People lived there and so did dinosaurs. Later there were other animals and people who farmed there.)

- Why is the Sahara a forbidding desert today? (The land is dry and doesn't support much plant or animal life.)

- What do you think is the main idea of this selection—what is it really all about? (The main idea is that satellites help us learn that the history of the desert includes different landforms and animals.)

BUILD ORAL VOCABULARY

GENERATE DISCUSSION Remind children that, according to the Read Aloud selection, the Sahara was not always an arid climate. There were once rivers and lakes there, and animals and people thrived. Invite children to predict what Earth will be like thousands of years in the future. Have them use some of this week's Amazing Words as they share their predictions.

Monitor Progress | Check Oral Vocabulary

Display pp. 96–97 in the Student Edition and remind children of the unit concept—Exploration. Ask them to tell you about the photographs using some of this week's Amazing Words: *arid, landform, precipitation, dunes, ledge, haven, discovery,* and *forbidding.*

If... children have difficulty using the Amazing Words,

then... ask questions about the photographs using the Amazing Words. Note which questions children can respond to. Reteach unknown words using the Oral Vocabulary Routine on p. DI·1.

SUCCESS PREDICTOR

Day 1 Check
Word Reading

Day 2 Check
High-Frequency
Words

Day 3 Check
Retelling

Day 4 Check
Fluency

▶ **Day 5** Check
Oral Vocabulary/
Assess Progress

Amazing Words to build oral vocabulary

arid	ledge
landform	haven
precipitation	discovery
dunes	forbidding

ELL

Extend Language Give children the names of some things from the selection, such as *dinosaur, forest, plant.* Brainstorm with them to think of describing words that tell how these things look, sound, feel, or smell. For example, *a huge dinosaur* (look), *a damp forest* (feel), *a bitter plant* (taste).

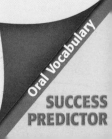

Oral Vocabulary

SUCCESS PREDICTOR

OBJECTIVES

- Review base words with endings *-ed, -ing.*
- Review high-frequency words.

Inflected Endings

REVIEW

IDENTIFY BASE WORDS WITH ENDINGS Write these sentences. Have children read each one aloud. Call on individuals to underline the base words with *-ed* and *-ing* endings and identify any spelling changes.

We are <u>hoping</u> we can begin <u>baking</u> the cakes and <u>tasting</u> them!

They <u>walked</u> in the room and <u>kissed</u> and <u>hugged</u> Grandpa.

I am <u>relying</u> on my <u>studying</u> to keep me from <u>missing</u> anything on the test.

I <u>grabbed</u> a coat, <u>chatted</u> with my dad, and <u>rushed</u> outside.

High-Frequency Words

REVIEW

COMPLETE THE RHYME Read the rhyme, leaving blanks for missing words. Ask children to complete each line with one of the review words from p. 98. Then read the rhyme together.

The sun is up _____ today. **(early)**

I ate so I am _____ all the way. **(full)**

I walk on the _____ desert sand. **(warm)**

Can I find _____ in this dry land? **(water)**

I rub my _____ and spot **(eyes)**

_____ drinking a lot! **(Animals)**

Vocabulary For additional practice with the high-frequency words, use the vocabulary strategies and word cards in the ELL Teaching Guide, pp. 24–25.

SPELLING TEST Inflected Endings

DICTATION SENTENCES Use these sentences to assess this week's spelling words.

1. Mom hugged Dad.
2. Is Mom dropping me off at home?
3. We lifted the big box.
4. She talked on the phone all day!
5. I like hugging my dog.
6. That man was lifting the wood.
7. Dad was talking to Bob.
8. Ann was smiling at me.
9. I was excited to see the cat.
10. I dropped the rag.
11. We had an exciting time!
12. I smiled at my sister.

CHALLENGE WORDS

13. They sang and danced in the play.
14. We were dragging the sack.
15. The animals amazed me!

ASSESS

- Spell base words with endings -ed, -ing.

Spelling Words

Inflected Endings -ed, -ing

1. talked
2. talking
3. dropped
4. dropping
5. excited
6. exciting*
7. lifted
8. lifting
9. hugged
10. hugging
11. smiled
12. smiling

Challenge Words

13. dragging
14. amazed
15. danced

* Word from the Selection

Group Time

On-Level	Strategic Intervention	Advanced
Read Set B Sentences.	**Read** Set A Sentences and the Story.	**Read** Set C Sentences.
• Use pp. 126e–126g.	• Use pp. 126e–126g.	• Use pp. 126e–126g.
	• Use the **Routine** on p. DI·52.	• Use the **Routine** on p. DI·53.

ELL Place English language learners in the groups that correspond to their reading abilities in English.

(i) Independent Activities

Fluency Reading Children reread selections at their independent level.

Journal Writing List things you can find in a desert. Share writing.

Independent Reading See p. 96j for Reading/ Library activities and suggestions.

Literacy Centers You may use the Technology Center on p. 96k to support this week's concepts and reading.

Practice Book 2.1 Online Reference Sources, p. 40

Break into small groups after Spelling and before Grammar and Writing.

DAY 5

Differentiated Assessment

On-Level

Set B

Strategic Intervention

Set A

Advanced

Set C

Fluency Assessment Plan

☑ Week 1 assess Advanced students.

☑ Week 2 assess Strategic Intervention students.

☑ Week 3 assess On-Level students.

☑ **This week assess Strategic Intervention students.**

☐ Week 5 assess any students you have not yet checked during this unit.

Set individual fluency goals for children to enable them to reach the end-of-year goal.

- Current Goal: 58–68 wcpm
- End-of-Year Goal: 90 wcpm
- **ELL** Fluency, particularly for English learners reading text in English, develops gradually, and through much practice. Focus on each child's improvement rather than solely monitoring the number of words correct per minute.

SENTENCE READING

ASSESS INFLECTED ENDINGS AND HIGH-FREQUENCY WORDS Use one of the reproducible lists on p. 126f to assess children's ability to read words with inflected endings and high-frequency words. Call on individuals to read two sentences aloud. Have each child in the group read different sentences. Start over with sentence one if necessary.

RECORD SCORES Use the Sentence Reading Chart for this unit on p. WA19.

Monitor Progress	Inflected Endings
If... children have trouble reading words with inflected endings,	**then...** use the Reteach Lessons on p. DI·52.
High-Frequency Words	
If... children cannot read a high-frequency word,	**then...** mark the missed words on a high-frequency word list and send the list home for additional word reading practice, or have each child practice with a fluent reader.

FLUENCY AND COMPREHENSION

ASSESS FLUENCY Take a one-minute sample of children's oral reading. See Monitoring Fluency, p. WA17. Have children read "A Walk in the Woods," the on-level fluency passage on p. 126g.

RECORD SCORES Record the number of words read correctly in one minute on the child's Fluency Progress Chart.

ASSESS COMPREHENSION Have the child read to the end of the passage. (If the child had difficulty with the passage, you may read it aloud.) Ask the child to identify the main idea and details. Have the child retell the passage. Use the Retelling Rubric on p. 88–89 to evaluate the child's retelling.

Monitor Progress	Fluency
If... children do not achieve the fluency goal on the timed reading,	**then...** copy the passage and send it home for additional practice, or have each child practice with a fluent reader.
Main Idea and Details	
If... children cannot identify the main idea and details,	**then...** use Reteach Lesson on p. DI·67.

READ THE SENTENCES

Set A

1. The water in the lake looks beautiful.
2. I shaded my eyes from the sun.
3. My dad and I will go visiting early.
4. We petted some animals at the farm.
5. We showed Mom the pail that is full of nuts.
6. I wanted a warm coat.

Set B

1. Are you getting a glass of water?
2. He was rubbing his eyes.
3. He likes to get up early.
4. Animals are living in that tree.
5. We are getting a box that is full of paper.
6. It was warm when we were walking.

Set C

1. Please water the flowers if they are drooping or dropping.
2. My sister closes her eyes when she sneezes.
3. Getting to school early leaves us time to play.
4. Tim loves animals and takes good care of them.
5. The teacher stopped and jumped on the bus that was full of kids.
6. A warm day makes people everywhere think of going outside and taking it easy.

A Walk in the Woods

Early this morning, my mom, dad, and I went for   10
a walk in the woods. Everywhere we walked, we   19
liked what we saw.   23

It had rained the night before. Water hung on the   33
tree leaves. Little showers sprinkled us when we   41
brushed by them.   44

Suddenly I saw something out of the corner of my   54
eye. I jumped back in surprise. Dad poked the grass   64
with a stick. It was a little green snake.   73

"You don't need to be afraid of this little thing,"   83
Dad said. He picked it up and showed it to me. I   95
though it was cute.   99

"Can we take it home?" I asked.   106

"No, it won't make a good pet," Mom said.   115

I couldn't take the snake home, but I did take   125
home some red leaves. When I look at them, I will   136
think about that beautiful warm day and our walk in   146
the woods.   148

See also Assessment Handbook, p. 308 · REPRODUCIBLE PAGE

Monitor Progress | Fluency Passage

126g

SUCCESS PREDICTOR

Write Now
Writing and Grammar

Report

Prompt

A Walk in the Desert tells about plants and animals in the desert.
Think about your neighborhood.
Now write a report about who and what live there.

Writing Trait

Conventions are rules for writing.

Student Model

Writer uses a question to create interest.

> Who lives in my neighborhood?
> People live in homes. Pet dogs and
> cats live there too. Flowers grow
> in the gardens. Trees grow near
> the streets. Squirrels and birds
> live in the trees. Many people and
> animals live in my neighborhood.
> Plants grow there too.

Writer follows conventions for sentences.

Ending states main idea.

126

Writer's Checklist

- **Focus** Do all sentences tell about my neighborhood?
- **Organization** Does the report have a strong beginning?
- **Support** Do details describe my neighborhood?
- **Conventions** Do sentences have correct end marks?

Grammar

Statements and Questions

A **statement** is a sentence that tells something. A statement ends with a **period (.)**.

The desert is dry**.**

A **question** is a sentence that asks something. A question ends with a **question mark (?)**.

Do you see the small kit fox**?**

. . . .

Write a statement and a question from the report.
Circle the period and the question mark.

127

Writing and Grammar

LOOK AT THE PROMPT Read p. 126 aloud. Have children select and discuss key words or phrases in the prompt. *(your neighborhood, report about who and what live there)*

STRATEGIES TO DEVELOP CONVENTIONS Have children

- practice adding capital letters and punctuation to sentences you write on the board or chart paper.
- read their sentences aloud to see whether each tells a complete idea and makes sense.
- exchange papers with a partner and check each other's sentences for correct capitalization and punctuation.

See Scoring Rubric on p. WA12. **Rubric 4 3 2 1**

HINTS FOR BETTER WRITING Read p. 127 aloud. Use the checklist to help children revise their reports. Discuss the grammar lesson. (Answers: *Sentence 1 is a question; the remaining sentences are statements. Children should circle the periods and the question mark.*) Have children make sure they wrote and correctly punctuated statements and questions in their reports.

DAILY FIX-IT

9. The desert
The desert is hot and dry.

10. did you enjoy your walk
Did you enjoy your walk?

Statements and Questions
Write each sentence correctly.

1. i talked to a gardener named Billy
I talked to a gardener named Billy.

2. will you plant me a lily
Will you plant me a lily?

3. can you grow it tonight
Can you grow it tonight?

4. i must catch a flight
I must catch a flight.

5. the desert can often be chilly
The desert can often be chilly.

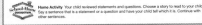

Home Activity Your child reviewed statements and questions. Choose a story to read to your child. Say a sentence that is a statement or a question and have your child tell which it is. Continue with other sentences.

▲ **Grammar and Writing Practice Book** p. 16

A Walk in the Desert **126–127**

Look at the three online reference sources below.
Write the answer to each question.

online encyclopedia | online dictionary | Internet

Encyclopedia Search | Dictionary Search | Internet Search

Go! | Go! | Go!

1. Jill wants to know how to say the word *desert* and divide it into syllables. Which online reference should she check?

dictionary

2. Dan wants facts about desert climates. Which online reference should he check first? **encyclopedia**

3. Tina wants to find many sources of information about deserts.

Where should she look? **Internet**

4. Which is the better place to learn what types of animals live in the desert—an online dictionary or an online encyclopedia? Why?

encyclopedia; you need the names of specific animals to find
out about them in the dictionary.

School + Home **Home Activity** Your child identified when to use different types of online reference sources. Discuss each type of reference source shown above. Ask your child to identify other desert-related topics of interest. Discuss which reference sources could be used to learn more about each topic.

▲ **Practice Book 2.1** p. 40,
Online Reference Sources

Access Content You may want to explore with children whether there are Internet sites in their home language that they can access for research information. Help them apply the steps to those sites.

Research/Study Skills

TEACH/MODEL Online Reference Sources

MODEL USING ONLINE REFERENCE SOURCES Recall with children what they learned earlier this week when they read "Rain Forests" on pp. 122–125. Review that they can find information online in dictionaries, encyclopedias, and other Internet sources.

Model how to use online reference sources.

Think Aloud

MODEL First I will turn the computer on, and then I'll connect to the Internet. I think I will look for more information about the saguaro cactus plant. I'll go to an online encyclopedia. I'll type *saguaro* in the search box and press Go. Here's the encyclopedia entry for *saguaro*. If I just want to know how to pronounce the word, I might go to the online dictionary instead and follow the same steps.

USE THE INTERNET Suggest topics to children, such as coyotes or Gila monsters, or let them choose their own. Help them use online reference sources to find additional information about their topics, including how to pronounce the words.

PRACTICE

USE ONLINE REFERENCE SOURCES Let children work in pairs and choose a topic to research. Provide each pair with a copy of the chart below. Ask them to write their topic in the first column. As they check the topic in an online dictionary and encyclopedia, ask them to write in the appropriate columns the information they find.

My Topic	Dictionary	Encyclopedia	Research Site

Wrap Up Your Week!

LET'S TALK ABOUT Exploration

QUESTION OF THE WEEK Recall this week's question.

• What can we learn by exploring the desert?

Display the K-W-L chart that children began on Day 1. Review with children what they have already completed of the chart. Encourage them to brainstorm what to put into the What We **L**earned column. They might also want to add new questions to the What We **W**ant to Know column. Explain that they can use these questions when they read other books about the desert.

What We **K**now	What We **W**ant to Know	What We **L**earned
It is hot and dry in the desert. Cactus plants grow in the desert.	What kind of animals live in the desert? What kind of plants besides cactus grow there? Why do jackrabbits have long ears? Where is the American Desert?	Many different kinds of plants and animals live in the desert, like rattlesnakes and cactus. Lots of animals and birds live in saguaro cactus plants. A moving rock might be a desert tortoise!

CONNECT Use questions such as these to prompt a discussion:

• Suppose you wanted to know more about landforms. Whom could you ask?

• Why do you think arid lands, such as the desert, have such little precipitation? Whom could you ask to find out?

• If you want to find out what new discoveries have been made about something that interests you, whom could you ask?

Build Background Use ELL Poster 5 to support the Preview activity.

You've learned **008** Amazing Words this week!

You've learned **032** Amazing Words so far this year!

PREVIEW Tell children that next week they will read about an ant who explores to search for an answer to a question.

PREVIEW Next Week

Assessment Checkpoints *for the Week*

Selection Assessment

Use pp. 13–16 of Selection Tests to check:

 Selection Understanding

 Comprehension Skill *Main Idea and Details*

 High–Frequency Words

animals	full
early	warm
eyes	water

Leveled Assessment

- On-Level
- Strategic Intervention
- Advanced

Use pp. 19–24 of Fresh Reads for Differentiated Test Practice to check:

 Comprehension Skill *Main Idea and Details*

 REVIEW Comprehension Skill *Compare and Contrast*

 Fluency *Words Correct Per Minute*

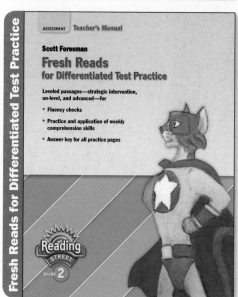

Managing Assessment

Use Assessment Handbook for:

 Weekly Assessment Blackline Masters for Monitoring Progress

 Observation Checklists

 Record-Keeping Forms

 Portfolio Assessment

Unit 1
Exploration

Week 5

EXPAND THE CONCEPT
When we are searching for answers, whom can we ask?

CONCEPT QUESTION

What can we learn from exploring new places and things?

CONNECT THE CONCEPT

▶ **Build Background**

delicate	inquire	stun
exhibit	resist	sturdy
genius	satisfaction	

▶ **Social Studies Content**
Native American Cultures/Beliefs, Exploration, Concept of Place, Oral Tradition, Geography

▶ **Writing**
A Report

Preview Your Week

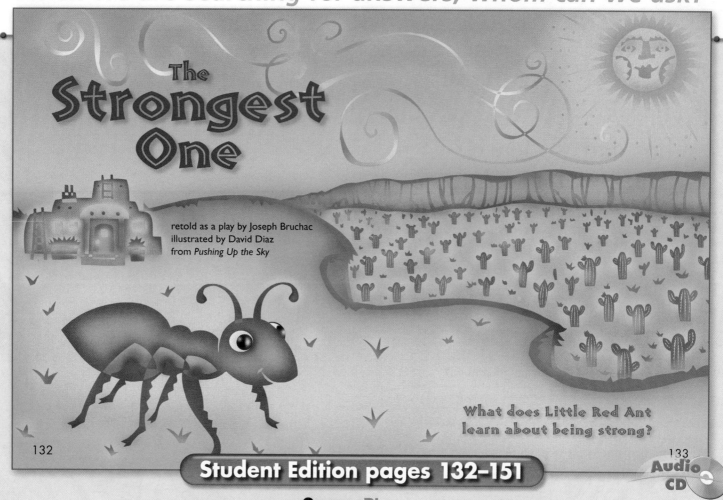

The Strongest One

retold as a play by Joseph Bruchac
illustrated by David Diaz
from *Pushing Up the Sky*

What does Little Red Ant learn about being strong?

132

133

Audio CD

Student Edition pages 132–151

Genre	Play
Phonics	Consonant Digraphs
Comprehension Skill	Realism and Fantasy
Comprehension Strategy	Monitor and Fix Up

Time for SOCIAL STUDIES

Science in Reading

ANTEATERS
by John Jacobs

Central America

South America

Where do they live?

Anteaters live mostly in South and Central America where there are lots of grasses, swamps, and rain forests. These are the kind of places where many ants live. Anteaters explore these grasses, swamps, and rain forests all day looking for ants to eat.

Have you ever heard of an anteater? Have you ever seen one? Let's learn more about them.

152

Paired Selection

Reading Across Texts

Draw Conclusions About Anteaters

Genre

Expository Nonfiction

Text Features

Questions
Subheadings

Student Edition pages 152–155

Audio CD

Read It ONLINE
PearsonSuccessNet.com
- Student Edition
- Leveled Readers
- Decodable Readers

Leveled Readers

🎯 **Skill** Realism and Fantasy

🎯 **Strategy** Monitor and Fix Up

Lesson Vocabulary

Below-Level

The Case of the Missing Fish
by Abby Seaborne
Illustrated by George Hamblin

On-Level

The Bear Man
A Native American Folk Tale
by Christine Wolf
illustrated by Sheila Bailey

Advanced

Sue's Hummingbird
by Christian Downey
illustrated by Durga Bernhard

ELL Reader
· Concept Vocabulary
· Text Support
· Language Enrichment

Rabbit and Coyote
by Cordayne Aragon

Decodable Readers

Apply Phonics

· *Will the Whale*

Decodable Reader 5
Will the Whale
Written by Allison Fisher
Illustrated by Brian Gilbert

Phonics Skill
Consonant Digraphs ch, tch, sh, th, wh

SOCIAL STUDIES

Integrate Social Studies Standards
- Native American Cultures/Beliefs
- Exploration, Geography
- Concept of Place
- Oral Tradition

✓ **Read**

The Strongest One pp. 132–151

"Anteaters" pp. 152–155

✓ **Read**

Leveled Readers

Below-Level	On-Level	Advanced
• Support Concepts	• Develop Concepts	• Extend Concepts
		• Social Studies Extension Activity

✓ **Read**

ELL Reader

Rabbit and Coyote

✓ **Build Concept Vocabulary**
Exploration, pp. 128r, 128–129

✓ **Teach Social Studies Concepts**
Information, p. 146–147
Geography, p. 152–153

✓ **Explore Social Studies Center**
Use Reference Materials,
p. 128k

The Strongest One **128c**

Weekly Plan

READING

90–120 minutes

TARGET SKILLS OF THE WEEK

- **Phonics**
  Consonant Digraphs
- **Comprehension Skill**
  Realism and Fantasy
- **Comprehension Strategy**
  Monitor and Fix Up

DAY 1   PAGES 128l–129d

Oral Language

QUESTION OF THE WEEK, 128l
When we are searching for answers, whom can we ask?

Oral Vocabulary/Share Literature, 128m
Sing with Me Big Book, Song 5
Amazing Words *delicate, inquire, sturdy*

Word Work

Phonics, 128n–128o
Introduce Consonant Digraphs **T**

Spelling, 128p
Pretest

Comprehension/Vocabulary/Fluency

Read Decodable Reader 5

Grouping Options 128f–128g

Review High-Frequency Words
Check Comprehension
Reread for Fluency

Build Background, 128r–129
Exploration

Listening Comprehension, 129a–129b
Realism and Fantasy **T**

DAY 2   PAGES 130a–149b

Oral Language

QUESTION OF THE DAY, 130a
Whom does the ant check with to find the answer?

Oral Vocabulary/Share Literature, 130b
Read Aloud Anthology "All Alone in Dinosaur Hall"
Amazing Words *exhibit, resist*

Word Work

Phonics, 130c–130d
Review Consonant Digraphs **T**

Spelling, 130d
Dictation

Comprehension/Vocabulary/Fluency

Read *The Strongest One,* 130e–149

Grouping Options
128f–128g

Introduce High-Frequency
Words *gone, learn, often,
pieces, though, together,
very* **T**

Introduce Selection Words
*dangerous, gnaws, narrator,
relatives*

Reread for Fluency

- Realism and
  Fantasy **T**
- Monitor and Fix Up
  REVIEW Character and
  Setting **T**

LANGUAGE ARTS

20–30 minutes

Trait of the Week

Sentences

Shared Writing, 129c
News Bulletin

Grammar, 129d
Introduce Commands and Exclamations **T**

Interactive Writing, 149a
Creative Story

Grammar, 149b
Practice Commands and Exclamations **T**

DAILY JOURNAL WRITING

Day 1 *List things you would like to inquire about.*

Day 2 *Write about a person or animal who is
strongest of all.*

DAILY SOCIAL STUDIES CONNECTIONS

Day 1 Whom Can We Ask? Concept Web,
128r–129

Day 2 Time for Social Studies: Information,
146–147

DAILY SUCCESS PREDICTORS

for Adequate Yearly Progress

Monitor Progress and Corrective Feedback

Phonics
Check Word Reading, *128o*
Spiral REVIEW Phonics

Fluency
Check High-Frequency Words, *131a*
Spiral REVIEW High-Frequency Words

Grouping Options for Differentiated Instruction

Turn the page for the small group lesson plan.

DAY 3 PAGES 150a–151b

Oral Language

QUESTION OF THE DAY, 150a
Did that really happen?

Oral Vocabulary/Share Literature, 150b
Read Aloud Anthology "All Alone in Dinosaur Hall"
Amazing Word *stun*

Word Work

Phonics, 150c
REVIEW Inflected Endings -s, -ed, -ing **T**

High-Frequency Words, 150d
Practice *gone, learn, often, pieces, though, together, very* **T**

Spelling, 150d
Practice

Comprehension/Vocabulary/Fluency

Vocabulary, 150e
Synonyms

Read The Strongest One, 132–151

Grouping Options
128f–128g

Fluency, 150f
Read with Expression and Intonation

Think and Share, 150g

Trait of the Week, 151a
Introduce Sentences

Grammar, 151b
Write with Commands and Exclamations **T**

Day 3 Use synonyms in sentences about being the strongest one.

Day 3 Whom Can We Ask? Concept Web, 151b

DAY 4 PAGES 152a–155d

Oral Language

QUESTION OF THE DAY, 152a
How do you think anteaters search?

Oral Vocabulary/Share Literature, 152b
Read Aloud Anthology "Can Hens Give Milk?"
Amazing Words *genius, satisfaction*

Word Work

Phonics, 152c
REVIEW Sentence Reading **T**

Spelling, 152d
Partner Review

Comprehension/Vocabulary/Fluency

Read "Anteaters," 152–155
Leveled Readers

Grouping Options
128f–128g

Synonyms
Reading Across Texts

Fluency, 155a
Read with Expression and
Intonation

Writing Across the Curriculum, 155b
Labels

Grammar, 155c
Review Commands and Exclamations **T**

Speaking and Listening, 155d
Ask and Answer Questions

Day 4 Write about having fun in a sturdy tree house.

Day 4 Time for Social Studies: Geography, 152–153

DAY 5 PAGES 156a–157b

Oral Language

QUESTION OF THE DAY, 156a
What did we find out about whom we can ask when we are looking for answers?

Oral Vocabulary/Share Literature, 126b
Read Aloud Anthology "Can Hens Give Milk?"
Amazing Words Review

Word Work

Phonics, 156c
REVIEW Consonant Digraphs **T**

High-Frequency Words, 156c
gone, learn, often, pieces, though, together, very **T**

Spelling, 156d
Test

Comprehension/Vocabulary/Fluency

Read Leveled Readers

Grouping Options 128f–128g

Monitor Progress, 156e–156g
Read the Sentences
Read the Story

Writing and Grammar, 156–157
Develop Sentences
Use Commands and Exclamations **T**

Research/Study Skills, 157a
Maps

Day 5 Write about something delicate that becomes sturdy.

Day 5 Revisit the Whom Can We Ask? Concept Web, 157b

KEY ◎ = Target Skill **T** = Tested Skill

Comprehension Check Retelling, *150g*

Fluency Check Fluency WCPM, *155a*
Spiral REVIEW Phonics,
High-Frequency Words

Oral Vocabulary Check Oral Vocabulary, *156b*
Assess Phonics,
High-Frequency Words, Fluency,
Comprehension, *156e*

SUCCESS PREDICTOR

Small Group Plan for Differentiated Instruction

Daily Plan
AT A GLANCE

Reading
Whole Group
- Oral Language
- Word Work
- Comprehension/Vocabulary

Group Time

Meet with small groups to provide:
- Skill Support
- Reading Support
- Fluency Practice

Read

This week's lessons for daily group time can be found behind the Differentiated Instruction (DI) tab on pp. DI·54–DI·63.

Whole Group
- Comprehension/Vocabulary
- Fluency

Language Arts
- Writing
- Grammar
- Speaking/Listening/Viewing
- Research/Study Skills

Use *My Sidewalks on Reading Street* for Tier III intensive reading intervention.

DAY 1

On-Level
Teacher-Led
Page 128q
- **Read** Decodable Reader 5
- **Reread** for Fluency

Strategic Intervention
Teacher-Led
Page DI·54
- Blend Words with Consonant Digraphs
- **Read** Decodable Reader 5
- **Reread** for Fluency

Advanced
Teacher-Led
Page DI·55
- Extend Word Reading
- **Read** Advanced Selection 5
- Introduce Concept Inquiry

i **Independent Activities**
While you meet with small groups, have the rest of the class...
- Reread for fluency
- Write in their journals
- Read self-selected reading
- Visit the Word Work Center
- Complete Practice Book 2.1, pp. 43–44

DAY 2

On-Level
Teacher-Led
Pages 132–149
- **Read** The Strongest One
- **Reread** for Fluency

Strategic Intervention
Teacher-Led
Page DI·56
- Blend Words with Consonant Digraphs
- **Read** SI Decodable Reader 5
- **Read** or Listen to The Strongest One

Advanced
Teacher-Led
Page DI·57
- **Read** The Strongest One
- Continue Concept Inquiry

i **Independent Activities**
While you meet with small groups, have the rest of the class...
- Read self-selected reading
- Write in their journals
- Visit the Listening Center
- Complete Practice Book 2.1, pp. 45–47

DAY 3

On-Level
Teacher-Led
Pages 132–151
- **Reread** The Strongest One

Strategic Intervention
Teacher-Led
Page DI·58
- **Reread** The Strongest One
- Read Words and Sentences
- Review Realism and Fantasy and Monitor and Fix Up
- **Reread** for Fluency

Advanced
Teacher-Led
Page DI·59
- Self-Selected Reading
- Continue Concept Inquiry

i **Independent Activities**
While you meet with small groups, have the rest of the class...
- Read self-selected reading
- Write in their journals
- Visit the Writing Center
- Complete Practice Book 2.1, pp. 48–49

① Begin with whole class skill and strategy instruction.

② Meet with small groups to provide differentiated instruction.

③ Gather the whole class back together for fluency and language arts.

DAY 4

On-Level
Teacher-Led
Pages 152–155, LR40–LR42
- **Read** "Anteaters"
- Practice with On-Level Reader *The Bear Man*

Strategic Intervention
Teacher-Led
Pages DI·60, LR37–LR39
- **Read** or Listen to "Anteaters"
- **Reread** for Fluency
- Build Concepts
- Practice with Below-Level Reader *The Case of the Missing Fish*

Advanced
Teacher-Led
Pages DI·61, LR43–LR45
- **Read** "Anteaters"
- Extend Vocabulary
- Continue Concept Inquiry
- Practice with Advanced Reader *Sue's Hummingbird*

ⓘ Independent Activities

While you meet with small groups, have the rest of the class...

- Reread for fluency
- Write in their journals
- Read self-selected reading
- Review spelling words with a partner
- Visit the Listening and Social Studies Centers

DAY 5

On-Level
Teacher-Led
Pages 156e–156g, LR40–LR42
- Sentence Reading, Set B
- Monitor Fluency and Comprehension
- Practice with On-Level Reader *The Bear Man*

Strategic Intervention
Teacher-Led
Pages DI·62, LR37–LR39
- Practice Word Reading
- Sentence Reading, Set A
- Monitor Fluency and Comprehension
- Practice with Below-Level Reader *The Case of the Missing Fish*

Advanced
Teacher-Led
Pages DI·63, LR43–LR45
- Sentence Reading, Set C
- Share Concept Inquiry
- Monitor Fluency and Comprehension
- Practice with Advanced Reader *Sue's Hummingbird*

ⓘ Independent Activities

While you meet with small groups, have the rest of the class...

- Reread for fluency
- Write in their journals
- Read self-selected reading
- Visit the Technology Center
- Complete Practice Book 2.1, p. 50

Grouping Place English language learners in the groups that correspond to their reading abilities in English.

Use the appropriate Leveled Reader or other text at children's instructional level.

TIP Send home the appropriate Multilingual Summary of the main selection on Day 1.

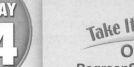

Take It to the NET™ ONLINE
PearsonSuccessNet.com

Jeanne Paratore
For ideas for successful home-school programs, see the article "Home and School Together" by Scott Foresman author Jeanne Paratore.

TEACHER TALK

A **consonant digraph** is a single sound represented by two letters, such as the *sh* in *ship* or the *th* in *this*.

 Looking Ahead

Be sure to schedule time for children to work on the unit inquiry project "Take a Trip." This week children should present their exploration plans to the class.

Name _____ Date _____

My Work Plan

Put an ☒ next to the activities you complete.

Listening
☐ Listen to a story.
☐ Listen to a song.

Writing
☐ Write questions about nature.
☐ Write in your journal.

Reading
☐ Read a book.
☐ Read sentences.
☐ Book Club

Social Studies
☐ Research ants.
☐ Answer questions.

Word Work
☐ Play a game using words with *ch, tch, sh, th, wh*.

Technology
☐ Complete a phonics activity.

Independent Practice
☐ Practice Book 2.1, pp. 41–50

Inquiry
☐ Present an exploration plan.

Wrap Up Your Week Turn your paper over. Write about what you did at school this week. What did you read? What did you learn about searching for answers?

Unit 1 • Week 5 • *The Strongest One* 21

▲ **Group-Time Survival Guide** p. 21, Weekly Contract

The Strongest One **128g**

Customize Your Plan *by Strand*

ORAL LANGUAGE

 SOCIAL STUDIES

Concept Development

When we are searching for answers, whom can we ask?

 to build oral vocabulary

delicate *exhibit* *genius* *inquire*
resist *satisfaction* *stun* *sturdy*

BUILD

☐ **Question of the Week** Use the Morning Warm-Up! to introduce and discuss the question of the week. This week children will talk, sing, read, and write about whom we can ask when we look for answers. DAY 1 *128l*

☐ **Sing with Me Big Book** Sing a song about about how to find answers to questions. Ask children to listen for the concept-related Amazing Words *delicate, inquire, sturdy*. DAY 1 *128m*

Sing with Me Big Book

☐ **Let's Talk About Exploration** Use the Let's Talk About It lesson in the Student Edition to build background, vocabulary, and concepts. Then create a concept chart for children to add to throughout the week. DAY 1 *128r–129*

Let's Talk About It

DEVELOP

☐ **Question of the Day** Use the questions in the Morning Warm-Ups! to discuss lesson concepts and how they relate to the unit theme, Exploration. DAY 2 *130a*, DAY 3 *150a*, DAY 4 *152a*, DAY 5 *156a*

☐ **Share Literature** Read big books and read aloud selections that develop concepts, language, and vocabulary related to the lesson concept and the unit theme. Continue to develop this week's Amazing Words. DAY 2 *130b*, DAY 3 *150b*, DAY 4 *152b*, DAY 5 *156b*

CONNECT

☐ **Wrap Up Your Week!** Revisit the Question of the Week. DAY 5 *157b*

CHECK

☐ **Check Oral Vocabulary** To informally assess children's oral vocabulary, ask individuals to use some of this week's Amazing Words to tell you about the illustration and photographs on Student Edition pp. 128–129. DAY 5 *156b*

PHONICS

 CONSONANT DIGRAPHS Consonant digraphs consist of two or three consonants that stand for a single sound.

TEACH

☐ **Consonant Digraphs** Introduce the blending strategy for words with consonant digraphs. Then have children sort and read words with consonant digraphs. DAY 1 *128n-128o*

☐ **Fluent Word Reading** Use the Fluent Word Reading Routine to develop children's word reading fluency. Use the Phonics Songs and Rhymes Chart for additional word reading practice. DAY 2 *130c-130d*

Phonics Songs and Rhymes Chart 5

PRACTICE/APPLY

☐ **Decodable Reader 5** Practice reading words with consonant digraphs in context. DAY 1 *128q*

☐ **The Strongest One** Practice decoding words in context. DAY 2 *132-149*

Decodable Reader 5

☐ **Homework** Practice Book 2.1 p. 43. DAY 1 *128o*

☐ **Word Work Center** Practice consonant digraphs. **ANY DAY** *128j*

Main Selection—Play

RETEACH/REVIEW

☐ **Review** Review words with this week's phonics skills. DAY 5 *156c*

☐ **Reteach Lessons** If necessary, reteach consonant digraphs. DAY 5 *DI-68*

☐ **Spiral REVIEW** Review previously taught phonics skills. DAY 1 *128o*, DAY 3 *150c* DAY 4 *152c*

ASSESS

☐ **Sentence Reading** Assess children's ability to read words with consonant digraphs. DAY 5 *156e-156f*

SPELLING

CONSONANT DIGRAPHS   Consonant digraphs consist of two or three consonants that stand for a single sound.

TEACH

☐ **Pretest** Before administering the pretest, model how to segment words with consonant digraphs to spell them. Dictate the spelling words, segmenting them if necessary. Then have children check their pretests and correct misspelled words. DAY 1 *128p*

PRACTICE/APPLY

☐ **Dictation** Have children write dictation sentences to practice spelling words. DAY 2 *130d*

☐ **Write Words** Have children practice writing the spelling words by using rhyming clues. DAY 3 *150d*

☐ **Homework** Phonics and Spelling Practice Book pp. 17–20. DAY 1 *128p*, DAY 2 *130d*, DAY 3 *150d*, DAY 4 *152d*

RETEACH/REVIEW

☐ **Partner Review** Have pairs work together to read and write the spelling words. DAY 4 *152d*

ASSESS

☐ **Posttest** Use dictation sentences to give the posttest for words with consonant digraphs. DAY 5 *156d*

Spelling Words

Consonant Digraphs

1. bunch
2. that*
3. wish
4. patch
5. when*
6. what*
7. math
8. them
9. shape
10. whale
11. itch
12. chase*

Challenge Words

13. whiskers
14. switch
15. shrimp

* Words from the Selection

HIGH-FREQUENCY WORDS

WORDS TO READ

gone   learn   often   pieces
though   together   very

TEACH

☐ **Words to Read** Introduce this week's high-frequency words and add them to the Word Wall. DAY 2 *130-131*

High-Frequency Words

PRACTICE/APPLY

☐ **Words in Context** Read high-frequency words in the context of *The Strongest One.* DAY 2 *132-149*

☐ **Word Wall** Use the Word Wall to review and practice high-frequency words throughout the week. DAY 3 *150d*, DAY 5 *156c*

Main Selection—Play

☐ **Leveled Text** Practice this week's high-frequency words in the context of leveled text. DAY 4 *LR37–LR45*, DAY 5 *LR37–LR45*

☐ **Homework** Practice Book 2.1 pp. 46, 49. DAY 2 *131a*, DAY 3 *150d*

Leveled Readers

RETEACH/REVIEW

☐ **Spiral REVIEW** Review previously taught high-frequency words. DAY 2 *131a*, DAY 4 *152c*

ASSESS

☐ **Sentence Reading** Assess children's ability to read this week's high-frequency words. DAY 5 *156e–156f*

VOCABULARY

TEACH

☐ **Vocabulary Transparency 5** Use Vocabulary Transparency 5 to introduce the selection words from *The Strongest One.* Children will read these words but will not be tested on them. DAY 2 *132a*

☐ **Synonyms** Have children expand selection words by thinking of synonyms for *dangerous.* DAY 3 *150e*

Customize Your Plan *by Strand*

COMPREHENSION

SKILL REALISM AND FANTASY A realistic story tells about something that could happen in real life. A fantasy is a story that could not happen in real life.

STRATEGY MONITOR AND FIX UP Paying attention to illustrations and to which character is talking are two ways to help you understand what you are reading.

TEACH

❏ **Listening Comprehension** Read "A Nice Place to Sleep" and model how to distinguish between *realism and fantasy*. **DAY 1** *129a-129b*

❏ **Skill/Strategy Lesson** Review how to distinguish between *realism and fantasy*. Then introduce this week's strategy, *monitor and fix up*. **DAY 2** *130e*

PRACTICE/APPLY

❏ **Skills and Strategies in Context** Read *The Strongest One*, using the Guiding Comprehension questions to apply *realism and fantasy* and *monitor and fix up*. **DAY 2** *132-149*

Main Selection—Play

❏ **Think and Share** Use the questions on Student Edition p. 150 to discuss the selection. **DAY 3** *150g-151*

❏ **Skills and Strategies in Context** Read "Anteaters," guiding children as they apply skills and strategies. After reading have children make connections across texts. **DAY 4** *152-155*

Paired Selection— Nonfiction

❏ **Leveled Text** Apply *realism and fantasy* and *monitor and fix up* to read leveled text. **DAY 4** *LR37-LR45*, **DAY 5** *LR37-LR45*

❏ **Homework** Practice Book 2.1 p. 44. **DAY 1** *129a*

Leveled Readers

ASSESS

❏ **Selection Test** Determine children's understanding of the main selection and assess their ability to identify *realism and fantasy*. **DAY 3**

❏ **Story Reading** Have children read the passage "Little Bear." Ask what the *realism and fantasy* of the story is and have them retell. **DAY 5** *156e-156g*

RETEACH/REVIEW

❏ **Reteach Lesson** If necessary, reteach *realism and fantasy*. **DAY 5** *DI-68*

FLUENCY

SKILL READ WITH EXPRESSION AND INTONATION When you read, try to use your voice to read the words the way each character would say them.

REREAD FOR FLUENCY

❏ **Oral Rereading** Have children read orally from Decodable Reader 5 or another text at their independent reading level. Listen as children read and provide corrective feedback regarding their oral reading and their use of the blending strategy. **DAY 1** *128q*

❏ **Paired Reading** Have pairs of children read orally from the main selection or another text at their independent reading level and apply their knowledge of reading with expression and intonation. Listen as children read and provide corrective feedback regarding oral reading and their use of the blending strategy. **DAY 2** *148-149*

TEACH

❏ **Model** Use passages from *The Strongest One* to model reading with expression and intonation. **DAY 3** *150f*, **DAY 4** *155a*

PRACTICE/APPLY

❏ **Readers' Theater** Have children read aloud assigned parts from *The Strongest One*, along with you. Monitor progress and provide feedback regarding children's reading with expression and intonation. **DAY 3** *150f*

❏ **Choral Reading** Choral read passages from *The Strongest One*. Monitor progress and provide feedback regarding children's reading with expression and intonation. **DAY 4** *155a*

❏ **Listening Center** Have children follow along with the AudioText for this week's selections. **ANY DAY** *128j*

❏ **Reading/Library Center** Have children build fluency by rereading Leveled Readers, Decodable Readers, or other text at their independent level. **ANY DAY** *128j*

❏ **Fluency Coach** Have children use Fluency Coach to listen to fluent reading or to practice reading on their own. **ANY DAY**

ASSESS

❏ **Story Reading** Take a one-minute timed sample of children's oral reading. Use the passage "Little Bear." **DAY 5** *156e-156g*

WRITING

Trait of the Week

SENTENCES Sentences should make sense. A mix of short and longer sentences lets writing have rhythm and style.

TEACH

☐ **Write Together** Engage children in writing activities that develop language, grammar, and writing skills. Include independent writing as an extension of group writing activities.

> **Shared Writing** DAY 1 *129c*
> **Interactive Writing** DAY 2 *149a*
> **Writing Across the Curriculum** DAY 4 *155b*

☐ **Trait of the Week** Introduce and model the Trait of the Week, *sentences*. DAY 3 *151a*

PRACTICE/APPLY

☐ **Write Now** Examine the model on Student Edition pp. 156–157. Then have children write news reports. DAY 5 *156–157*

> **Prompt** *The Strongest One* is a play with animals that talk. Think about what it would be like to discover a talking animal. Now write a news report about it.

Write Now

☐ **Daily Journal Writing** Have children write about concepts and literature in their journals. **EVERY DAY** *128d–128e*

☐ **Writing Center** Have children write three questions they would like to ask about nature. **ANY DAY** *128k*

ASSESS

☐ **Scoring Rubric** Use a rubric to evaluate children's news reports. DAY 5 *156–157*

RETEACH/REVIEW

☐ **The Grammar and Writing Book** Use pp. 74–79 of The Grammar and Writing Book to extend instruction. **ANY DAY**

The Grammar and Writing Book

SPEAKING AND LISTENING

TEACH

☐ **Ask and Answer Questions** Model how to say, ask, and answer questions. Then have partners ask and answer questions. DAY 4 *155d*

GRAMMAR

SKILL COMMANDS AND EXCLAMATIONS A command is a sentence that tells someone to do something and ends with a period (.) An exclamation shows surprise or strong feelings and ends with an exclamation mark (!).

TEACH

☐ **Grammar Transparency 5** Use Grammar Transparency 5 to teach commands and exclamations. DAY 1 *129d*

Grammar Transparency 5

PRACTICE/APPLY

☐ **Develop the Concept** Review the concept of *commands and exclamations* and provide guided practice. DAY 2 *149b*

☐ **Apply to Writing** Have children use commands and exclamations in writing. DAY 3 *151b*

☐ **Define/Practice** Review the definition of *commands and exclamations*. Then have children identify commands and exclamations. DAY 4 *155c*

☐ **Write Now** Discuss the grammar lesson on Student Edition p. 157. Have children use commands and exclamations in their own news report about a talking animal. DAY 5 *156–157*

Write Now

☐ **Daily Fix-It** Have children find and correct errors in grammar, spelling, and punctuation. DAY 1 *129d*, DAY 2 *149b*, DAY 3 *151b*, DAY 4 *155c*, DAY 5 *156–157*

☐ **Homework** The Grammar and Writing Practice Book pp. 17–20. DAY 2 *149b*, DAY 3 *151b*, DAY 4 *155c*, DAY 5 *156–157*

RETEACH/REVIEW

☐ **The Grammar and Writing Book** Use pp. 74–77 of The Grammar and Writing Book to extend instruction. **ANY DAY**

The Grammar and Writing Book

RESEARCH/INQUIRY

TEACH

☐ **Maps** Model using maps. Then have children draw a map that shows how to get to school from where they live. DAY 5 *157a*

☐ **Unit Inquiry Project** Allow time for children to present their exploration plans to the class. **ANY DAY** *11*

Resources for Differentiated Instruction

LEVELED READERS

▶ **Comprehension**

◎ **Skill** Realism and Fantasy

◎ **Strategy** Monitor/Fix Up

▶ **Lesson Vocabulary**

High-Frequency Words

together

often

learn

very

gone

though

pieces

▶ **Social Studies Standards**

- **Native American Cultures/ Beliefs**
- **Exploration, Geography**
- **Concept of Place**
- **Oral Tradition**

Leveled Reader Database ONLINE

PearsonSuccessNet.com

Use the Online Database of over 600 books to

- Download and print additional copies of this week's leveled readers
- Listen to the readers being read online
- Search for more titles focused on this week's skills, topic, and content

---

On-Level

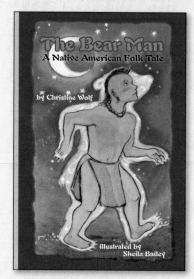

The Bear Man
A Native American Folk Tale
by Christine Wolf
illustrated by Sheila Bailey

On-Level Reader

Realism and Fantasy

A **fantasy** is a story about something that could not happen. A **realistic story** tells about something that could happen.

Read paragraph A and paragraph B. Circle **realistic story** or **fantasy** for each paragraph and write why you think as you do.

A. "If my son is ever hurt," he told the bear cub, "I hope he will be taken care of too." The man returned home and told his wife about the cub. One day much later, the man's son was hurt. Two bears found him and said, "We must take care of him."

B. A Pawnee family lives near Lincoln, Nebraska. Students have been asking the daughter Lily and her brother Thomas to do their traditional drum dance. They have practiced with their mother, and they are ready. Lily is excited.

Possible responses given.

1. Paragraph A is a   realistic story   (fantasy)

because **bears do not talk.**

2. Paragraph B is a   (realistic story)   fantasy

because **children could do a Native American dance.**

On-Level Practice TE p. LR41

Vocabulary

Circle the vocabulary words in the puzzle. All words can be read from left to right.

Words to Know

gone	learn	often	pieces
though	together	very	

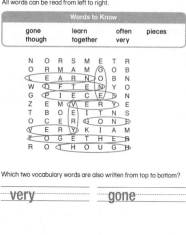

```
N O R S M E T R
O R M A M G O B
W E A R N O B N
W Q F T E N Y O
G P I E C E S N
Z E M V E R Y E
T B O E I T N S
O C E R G O N D
V E R V K I A M
T O G E T H E R
R O T H O U G H
```

Which two vocabulary words are also written from top to bottom?

very   **gone**

On-Level Practice TE p. LR42

Strategic Intervention

Social Studies

The Case of the Missing Fish

by Abby Seaborne
illustrated by George Hamblin

Below-Level Reader

Realism and Fantasy

A **fantasy** is a story about something that could not happen. A **realistic story** tells about something that could happen.

Read the sentences.
Write R on the line if the sentences begin a realistic story or F if they begin a fantasy.

F 1. Once upon a time there lived three little pigs. One wanted to build a house out of straw.

F 2. Fish said to Bird, "I often take a bath on Tuesday."

R 3. Tom never wanted to hunt bears. He always loved bears. So he asked his dad to stop hunting bears.

F 4. Long ago, in a faraway land, lived a girl with a red coat and hood. Her mother asked her to visit her grandmother. On the way, a wolf asked her where she was going.

R 5. A long, long time ago dinosaurs walked all over Earth. Some people have found huge footprints left by dinosaurs.

Below-Level Practice TE p. LR38

Vocabulary

Read each sentence. Choose the best word to finish the sentence and circle it.

Words to Know

gone	learn	often	pieces
though	together	very	

1. Sam had many ____ of paper.
   stack   (pieces)

2. LaToya could ____ well from this tutor.
   teach   (learn)

3. Sherry wanted to go out, even ____ it was raining.
   through   (though)

4. Sandy went to the park ____ with her friends.
   (together)   alone

5. Nancy ____ goes to the store for her mom.
   cannot   (often)

6. All the students except Hank had ____ home.
   (gone)   mine

7. Elephant said he loved playing ball ____ much.
   not   (very)

8. Write a sentence that Fish might say to Bird. Use a vocabulary word in your sentence. Possible response given.

"I often take a bath on Tuesday."

Below-Level Practice TE p. LR39

Advanced

Advanced Reader

Realism and Fantasy
A **fantasy** is a story about something that could not happen.
A **realistic** story tells about something that could happen.

Look back at *Sue's Hummingbird*. Draw one part of the story that is real.

Write why it is real.

Responses should include details about Sue and Zuni life.

Draw one part of the story that is make-believe.

Write why it is make-believe.

Include details about the hummingbird folk tale.

Advanced Practice TE p. LR44

Vocabulary
Choose a word from the box to complete each sentence.
Write the word on the line.

Words to Know		
delicate	inquire	sturdy

1. Sue asked Grandma lots of questions. Sue liked to
   __inquire__ about what happened long ago.

2. The hummingbird fluttered its __delicate__
   wings and floated in the air.

3. Thick mud bricks made the walls of the pueblo
   __sturdy__

Possible response given.
4. Write a sentence using at least one vocabulary word.

The house I live in is very sturdy.

Advanced Practice TE p. LR45

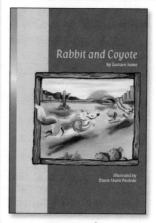

ELL Reader

ELL Poster 5

Teacher's Edition Notes
ELL notes throughout this lesson support instruction and reference additional resources at point of use.

ELL Teaching Guide pp. 29–35, 220–221
- Multilingual summaries of the main selection
- Comprehension lesson
- Vocabulary strategies and word cards
- ELL Reader 5 lesson

ELL and Transition Handbook

Ten Important Sentences
- Key ideas from every selection in the Student Edition
- Activities to build sentence power

More Reading

Readers' Theater Anthology
- Fluency practice
- Five scripts to build fluency
- Poetry for oral interpretation

Leveled Trade Books

- Extend reading tied to the unit concept
- Lessons in Trade Book Library Teaching Guide

Homework
- Family Times Newsletter
- ELL Multilingual Selection Summaries

Take-Home Books
- Decodable Readers
- Leveled Readers

Literacy Centers

Listening

Let's Read Along

MATERIALS `SINGLES`
CD player, headphones, print copies of recorded pieces

LISTEN TO LITERATURE As children listen to the following recordings, have them follow along or read along in the print version.

AudioText
The Strongest One
"Anteaters"

Sing with Me/Background Building Audio
"Where to Inquire"

Phonics Songs and Rhymes Audio
"Where Can We Turn?"

Where Can We Turn?

When we think of new things
That we wish to learn,
We must search for answers.
Where can we turn?

We can watch as people
Show us what to do.
We can check out books with facts and
Read them through and through.

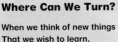
Audio CD Phonics Songs and Rhymes Chart 5

Reading/Library

Read It Again!

MATERIALS `SINGLES` `PAIRS` `GROUPS`
collection of books for self-selected reading, reading logs

REREAD BOOKS Have children select previously read books from the appropriate book box and record titles of books they read in their logs. Use these previously read books:

- **Decodable Readers**
- **Leveled Readers**
- **ELL Readers**
- **Stories written by classmates**
- **Books from the library**

TEN IMPORTANT SENTENCES Have children read the Ten Important Sentences for *The Strongest One* and locate the sentences in the Student Edition.

BOOK CLUB Have children write a letter to their penpals and tell them about *The Strongest One*.

Classroom Library

Word Work

Nature Walk

MATERIALS `GROUPS`
nature game board, number cube, game markers

DIGRAPHS *ch, tch, sh, th, wh* Have two to four children play a game using words with the above digraphs.

1. Make a nature game board that has spaces along a curved path through trees. On each space, write a word using the digraphs *ch, tch, sh, th,* or *wh*. Write some words in blue ink and others in red ink.
2. Children take turns rolling the number cube and moving the appropriate number of spaces.
3. Children read the word on their space. If the word is red, they roll again. If the word is blue, they wait for their next turn.
4. Play continues until everyone has reached the house at the end.

This interactive CD provides additional practice.

Scott Foresman Reading Street Centers Survival Kit

Use *The Strongest One* materials from the Reading Street Centers Survival Kit to organize this week's centers.

Writing

Social Studies

Technology

Nature Questions

MATERIALS `SINGLES` `GROUPS`
paper, pencils

WRITE QUESTIONS Review that Little Red Ant went outside to find an answer to his question.

1. Ask children to think of questions they have about nature.
2. Tell children to write three questions they would like to ask.
3. Groups of children can discuss possible answers to the questions.

LEVELED WRITING Encourage children to write at their own ability level. Some will show little or no control of writing conventions. Others will show fair control of writing conventions. Your best writers will show excellent control of writing conventions.

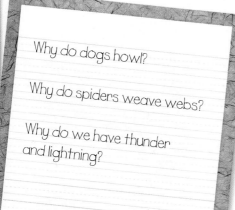

Why do dogs howl?

Why do spiders weave webs?

Why do we have thunder and lightning?

Find Out!

MATERIALS `SINGLES`
children's dictionary, trade book about ants, volume of encyclopedia with ant entry, copies of questions

ANSWER QUESTIONS Children use reference materials to find answers.

1. Provide copies of the following three questions: *What does the word colony mean? How do ants work together in a colony? What do the ants in the story do together?*
2. Tell children to use the three books to find the answers to the questions.
3. Have children write the answer to each question and which book they used to find the answer.

1. Colony means a group of people or animals that live together. (dictionary)
2. Ants work together to build their nests and get food. (encyclopedia)
3. The ants in the story work hard to get food. (trade book).

Focus on Phonics

MATERIALS `PAIRS`
computer, Phonics Practice Activities CD-ROM

USE A CD-ROM Have pairs of children use a CD-ROM.

1. Have children turn on the computer and open the Phonics Practice Activities CD-ROM.
2. Pairs complete one of the CD-ROM activities.

ALL CENTERS

Day 1
AT A GLANCE

Oral Vocabulary
"Where to Inquire"

Phonics and Spelling
Consonant Digraphs

Spelling Pretest: Words with Consonant Digraphs

Read Apply Phonics Word Wall

Group Time < Differentiated Instruction

Build Background
Let's Talk About Exploration

Listening Comprehension
Skill Realism and Fantasy

Shared Writing
News Bulletin

Grammar
Commands and Exclamations

Materials

- *Sing with Me Big Book*
- Sound-Spelling Cards 7, 32, 34, 41
- Letter Tiles
- Decodable Reader 5
- Student Edition 128–129
- Graphic Organizer 15
- Writing Transparency 5
- Grammar Transparency 5

Take It to the NET
ONLINE
Professional Development
For a review of research on effective vocabulary instruction, go to PearsonSuccessNet.com and see "Vocabulary Acquisition" by S. K. Baker and Scott Foresman authors D. Simmons and E. Kame'enui.

Morning Warm~Up!

Do you wonder about some things? Do you know why your eyes sometimes water on a warm day? When we are searching for answers, whom can we ask?

QUESTION OF THE WEEK Tell children they will talk, sing, read, and write about whom we can ask when we look for answers. Write and read the message and discuss the second question.

CONNECT CONCEPTS Ask questions to connect to Unit 1 selections.

- When Iris wanted to know who could be a friend for her, whom did she ask? (her Grandpa)

- When Henry had questions about camping, whom did he ask? (his mother and father)

- When we are searching for answers, whom can we ask? (Possible answers: our mothers, fathers, experts, and teachers)

REVIEW HIGH-FREQUENCY WORDS

- Circle the high-frequency words *eyes, water,* and *warm* in the message.

- Have children say and spell each word as they write it.

Build Background Use the Day 1 instruction on ELL Poster 5 to assess knowledge and develop concepts.

ELL Poster 5

Share Literature

BUILD ORAL VOCABULARY Display p. 5 of the *Sing with Me Big Book.* Tell children that the class is going to sing a song about how to find answers to questions. Read the title. Explain that **inquire** is another word for "ask." Ask children to listen for the Amazing Words inquire, **delicate,** and **sturdy** as you sing. Sing the song again and encourage children to sing along. Say the title and first verse, emphasizing the Amazing Words *inquire, sturdy,* and *delicate.* Talk about the title, making sure children understand that it means "where to ask" when they have questions. Discuss the verse, asking children whether they think a sturdy oak is strong or weak (strong) and whether a spider's delicate web is sturdy or easily torn (easily torn).

Where to Inquire
Everybody has questions.
Some are big; some are small.
How does a sturdy oak grow so high?
Spiders spin delicate webs. How and why?

Never be afraid to inquire.
Just ask someone who might know.
Or go look it up in a book.
Watch your smart self grow.

Sing with Me Big Book

**Sing with Me/
Background Building Audio**

Amazing Words
to build oral vocabulary

	MONITOR PROGRESS
delicate **inquire** **sturdy** **exhibit** **resist** **stun** **genius** **satisfaction**	**If…** children lack oral vocabulary experiences about the concept Exploration, **then…** use the Oral Vocabulary Routine below to teach *delicate.*

Oral Vocabulary ROUTINE

① **Introduce the Word** Relate the word *delicate* to the song. Supply a child-friendly definition. Have children say the word. Example: Something that is *delicate* is thin and easily broken.

② **Demonstrate** Provide an example to show meaning. Her mother said to be careful with the old vase because it is very *delicate*.

③ **Apply** Have children demonstrate their understanding. Which of these things is *delicate*—a model boat made of glass or your winter boots?

④ **Display the Word/Letter-Sounds** Write the word on a card. Display it. Point out the *c/k/* and *t/t/*. See p. DI·7 to teach *inquire* and *sturdy.*

Build Oral Vocabulary If children are not familiar with *oak* trees, you may want to show them a picture of one. Make sure they understand that oak trees are often enormous.

Consonant Digraphs

TEACH/MODEL

OBJECTIVES

- Associate the consonant digraph sounds with their spelling patterns.
- Blend, read, and sort words with consonant digraphs.

Skills Trace

Consonant Digraphs

Introduce/Teach	TE: 2.1 128n–o
Practice	TE: 2.1 128q, 130c–d; PB: 2.1 43; DR5
Reteach/Review	TE: 2.1 156c, DI-68; 2.2 182c; PB: 2.1 58
Assess/Test	TE: 2.1 156e–g; Benchmark Test, Unit 1

Generalization

Consonant digraphs consist of two or three consonants that stand for a single sound.

Strategic Intervention

Use **Monitor Progress,** p. 128o, during Group Time after children have had more practice with consonant digraphs.

Advanced

Use **Monitor Progress,** p. 128o, as a preassessment to determine whether this group of children would benefit from this instruction on digraphs.

ELL

Support Phonics Speakers of Chinese, French, Italian, Japanese, Korean, Spanish, and Urdu may have difficulty hearing and pronouncing the /th/ sound and may substitute other consonants when writing *th* words.

The sound of *ch* is the same in English and Spanish, but Spanish speakers will need to learn when to use the spelling *-tch.* Speakers of Hmong, Khmer, Korean, or Vietnamese may confuse /ch/ with /sh/ or initial *j.*

See the Phonics Transition Lessons in the ELL and Transition Handbook.

Blending Strategy

ROUTINE

1 **Connect** Write *disk* and *self.* What do you know about reading these words? (They both end with a consonant blend.) Today we'll learn about words that begin and end with two or three consonants that stand for a single sound.

2 **Use Sound-Spelling Card** Display Card 7. This is *chalk.* The sound you hear at the beginning of *chalk* is /ch/. Say it with me: /ch/.

3 **Model** Write *ditch.* The sound /ch/ can be spelled with the letters *ch* or *tch.* In the word *pitch,* the letters *tch* stand for /ch/. Listen as I blend this word. Blend the sounds continuously across the word. Let's blend this word together: /p/ /i/ /ch/, *pitch.* Repeat steps 2 and 3. Use Card 32 *shark* for *sh*/sh/, Card 34 *thermometer* for *th*/th/, Card 41 *whale* for *wh*/wh/, and model blending with *shape, thick,* and *white.* Some children may notice the difference between the sounds of *th* in *that* and *th* in *thing.* This difference will not affect children's ability to decode.

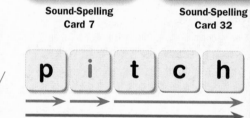

ch, -tch   **sh**

Sound-Spelling Card 7   Sound-Spelling Card 32

| p | i | t | c | h |

4 **Group Practice** Blend these words together. Continue with *which, math, those, fetch, church, bush, shy.*

5 **Review** What do you know about reading these words? They have two or three consonants that stand for a single sound.

BLEND WORDS

INDIVIDUALS BLEND CONSONANT DIGRAPH WORDS Call on individuals to blend *whip, crutch, dish, that, chip, shop.* Have them tell what they know about each word before reading it. For feedback, refer to step five of the Blending Strategy Routine.

SORT WORDS

INDIVIDUALS SORT WORDS WITH CONSONANT DIGRAPHS Write *ch, tch, sh, th,* and *wh* as headings. Then read each word in random order, and have individuals write the words under the appropriate headings and circle the letters that stand for the consonant digraph. Have all children complete the activity on paper. Ask individuals to read the words. Provide feedback as necessary.

ch	tch	sh	th	wh
such	hatch	fish	with	whether
chase	pitch	show	those	whale

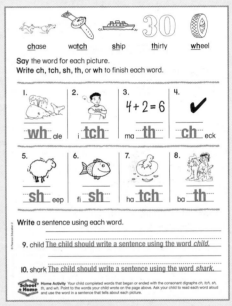

▲ **Practice Book 2.1** p. 43, Consonant Digraphs

Monitor Progress   Check Word Reading Consonant Digraphs

Write the following words and have individuals read them.

chose	with	hitch	what	shell
much	mush	bath	batch	bash
hatch	flat	sash	slip	when

If... children cannot blend words with consonant digraphs at this point,

then... continue to monitor their progress using other instructional opportunities during the week so that they can be successful with the Day 5 Assessment. See the Skills Trace on p. 128n.

SUCCESS PREDICTOR

Spiral REVIEW

● Row 3 contrasts blends and digraphs.

▶ **Day 1 Check** Word Reading   **Day 2** Check High-Frequency Words   **Day 3** Check Retelling   **Day 4** Check Fluency   **Day 5** Assess Progress

Word Reading

SUCCESS PREDICTOR

OBJECTIVES

- Segment sounds to spell words.
- Spell words with consonant digraphs.

Spelling Words

Consonant Digraphs

1. **bunch**	7. **math**
2. **that** *	8. **them**
3. **wish**	9. **shape**
4. **patch**	10. **whale**
5. **when** *	11. **itch**
6. **what** *	10. **chase** *

Challenge Words

13. **whiskers**	15. **shrimp**
14. **switch**	

* **Words from the Selection**

Digraphs ch, tch, sh, th, wh

Generalization Some words have two or three consonants together that are said as one sound: <u>th</u>at, <u>patch</u>.

Sort the list words by ch, tch, sh, th, and wh.

tch		th	
1. _patch_	7. _that_
2. _itch_	8. _math_
ch	9. _them_
3. _bunch_	**wh**
4. _chase_	10. _when_
sh	11. _what_
5. _wish_	12. _whale_
6. _shape_	

Challenge Words

tch		wh	
13. _switch_	14. _whiskers_
sh	
15. _shrimp_	

Spelling Words
1. bunch
2. that
3. wish
4. patch
5. when
6. what
7. math
8. them
9. shape
10. whale
11. itch
12. chase
Challenge Words
13. whiskers
14. switch
15. shrimp

Home Activity Your child is learning to spell words with ch, tch, sh, th, and wh. To practice at home, have your child look at the word, pronounce it, write it, and then check it.

▲ **Spelling Practice Book** p. 17

ELL

Support Spelling Before giving the spelling pretest, clarify the meaning of each spelling word with examples, such as saying a kitten has *whiskers* on its face and holding up a math book to illustrate *math*.

Spelling

PRETEST Consonant Digraphs

MODEL WRITING FOR SOUNDS Each spelling word has a consonant digraph. Before administering the spelling pretest, model how to segment words with consonant digraphs to spell them.

- What sounds do you hear in bath? (/b/ /a/ /th/)
- What is the letter for /b/? Write *b*. Continue with the *a*/a/ and *th*/th/.
- What letters stand for /th/? *(th)*

PRETEST Dictate the spelling words. Segment the words for children if necessary. Have children check their pretests and correct misspelled words.

HOMEWORK Spelling Practice Book, p. 17

Group Time

On-Level	Strategic Intervention	Advanced
Read Decodable Reader 5.	**Read** Decodable Reader 5.	**Read** Advanced Selection 5.
• Use p. 128q.	• Use the **Routine** on p. DI·54.	• Use the **Routine** on p. DI·55.

ELL Place English language learners in the groups that correspond to their reading abilities in English.

(*i*) Independent Activities

Fluency Reading Pair children to reread Leveled Readers or the ELL Reader from the previous week or other text at children's independent level.

Journal Writing List things you would like to inquire about. Share writing.

Independent Reading See p. 128j for Reading/Library activities and suggestions.

Literacy Centers To practice consonant digraphs you may use Word Work, p. 128j.

Practice Book 2.1 Consonant Digraphs, p. 43; Realism and Fantasy, p. 44

Break into small groups after Spelling and before Build Background.

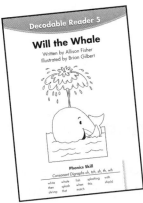

Decodable Reader 5

Will the Whale
Written by Allison Fisher
Illustrated by Brian Gilbert

Phonics Skill
Consonant Digraphs ch, tch, sh, th, wh

Apply Phonics

⏺ PRACTICE Consonant Digraphs

HIGH-FREQUENCY WORDS Review *about, friend, little,* and *pulled* on the Word Wall. **Word Wall**

READ DECODABLE READER 5

- Pages 34–35 Read aloud quietly with the group.
- Pages 36–37 Have the group read aloud without you.
- Pages 38–40 Select individuals to read aloud.

CHECK COMPREHENSION AND DECODING Ask children the following questions about *Will the Whale:*

- Who are the characters in the story? (Will, Sid, El)
- How does Will help the ship that is stuck? (He pulled it to the dock.)
- How does Will help keep Sid safe? (He hides Sid from big hunting fish.)

Then have children locate digraphs *tch, sh, th,* and *wh* in the story. Review *tch, sh, th,* and *wh* spelling patterns. Sort words according to their spelling patterns.

tch	sh	th	wh
match	fish	that	whale
	ship(s)	them	when
	shrimp	then	white
	splash	this	
	splashing	with	

HOMEWORK Take-Home Decodable Reader 5

REREAD FOR FLUENCY

Oral Rereading

ROUTINE

1 **Read** Have children read the entire story orally.

2 **Reread** To achieve optimal fluency, children should reread the text three or four times.

3 **Provide Feedback** Listen as children read and provide corrective feedback regarding their oral reading and their use of the blending strategy.

OBJECTIVES

- Apply knowledge of letter-sounds to decode unknown words when reading.
- Use context with letter-sounds to confirm the identification of unknown words.
- Practice fluency in paired rereading.

Monitor Progress

Decoding

If... children have difficulty decoding a word,	then... prompt them to blend the word. • What is the new word? • Is the new word a word you know? • Does it make sense in the story?

Access Content

Beginning Lead children on a picture walk through *Will the Whale* and have them act out action verbs, such as *swimming, splashing, jumping,* and *gliding.*

Intermediate Preview *Will the Whale* and discuss ways in which Will and Sid are alike and different.

Advanced After reading *Will the Whale,* have partners take turns retelling the story.

1

- Build background and oral vocabulary.
- Ask questions.

Strategic Intervention

Help children realize that they can always ask their parents or teachers for answers to questions. However, make sure they understand that they can also find answers in books or from other people who know certain information. For example, someone who works in a zoo can answer questions about animals.

Advanced

Some children may be familiar with using a computer and the Internet. Encourage them to explain to their classmates how they can find answers to questions there.

Activate Prior Knowledge
Invite children to look closely at the pictures on pp. 128–129. Encourage them to discuss what is shown in the pictures. Let them name several items with words from their home language.

Build Background

LET'S TALK ABOUT Exploration

DEVELOP ORAL LANGUAGE Read the title and have children view the photographs. Ask them to tell you what they see. Allow ample time for children to respond. Remind children that asking questions can help them to understand things better. Asking questions can help them to learn new things or to make certain of something. If children are reluctant to talk, use open-ended prompts to model language use and to encourage conversation. For example:

Tell me about what you see here. Yes, that's right, a gorilla holding a kitten, a big tree and a little tree, and a bird sitting on an elephant's head. How is each pair in the pictures alike? How are they different? Which photograph is the most unusual to you and why?

BUILD ORAL VOCABULARY As you continue the discussion, encourage children to use today's Amazing Words: *delicate, inquire, sturdy.*

- Which of the animals in these pictures would you consider *delicate?*
- Describe one of the pictures using the word *sturdy.*
- Which of these pictures would you most like to *inquire* about? Why?

DEVELOP CONCEPTS

CONCEPT CHART Remind children of the question of the week.

- When we are searching for answers, whom can we ask?

Display Graphic Organizer 15 or draw a web. Write *Whom Can We Ask?* in the central circle. Brainstorm with children some answers to the question to write in the outside ovals. For example, draw their attention to the pictures on pp. 128–129 and ask how they might find answers to questions about the pictures. Display the web for use during the week.

- Whom would you ask for answers to questions about the animals in the pictures?
- What do you want to know? Whom can you ask for an answer?

CONNECT TO READING Point out the illustration at the bottom of p. 129 in the Student Edition. Ask children what they think is happening in the picture. (An ant and a mouse are talking.) Explain that this week children will read about how an ant learns who is the strongest.

Oral Vocabulary

Let's Talk About
Exploration

128

129

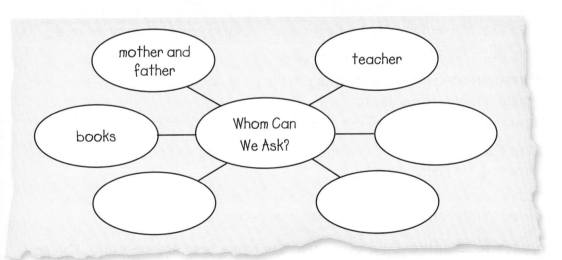

mother and father

teacher

books

Whom Can We Ask?

▲ **Graphic Organizer 15**

Tech Files ONLINE

For a Web site where you can find more stories like *The Strongest One,* do an Internet search using the keywords *Native American folk tales.*

ELL

Access Content To prepare children for reading *The Strongest One,* send home the story summary in English and/or the home language. See the ELL Teaching Guide, pp. 33–35.

Read each sentence.
Write Y if it tells something that could really happen.
Write N if it tells something that could not really happen.

Y 1. Janet lifted her bike.

N 2. Janet lifted the car.

Y 3. Janet carried her books to school.

Y 4. Janet and John ran a race.

Write a sentence about something that could not really happen.

5. Answers will vary but should be about something that

could not really happen.

School + Home Home Activity Your child identified whether a story event could really happen. Ask your child to tell two stories about events at school—one realistic (something that really happened) and one that is a fantasy (something that couldn't happen).

▲ **Practice Book 2.1** p. 44, Realism and Fantasy

Access Content For a Picture It! lesson on realism and fantasy, see the ELL Teaching Guide, pp. 29–30.

Listening Comprehension

⦿ TEACH/MODEL Realism and Fantasy

DEFINE REALISM AND FANTASY

- There are two kinds of made-up stories—those that could really happen and those that could never happen.
- A realistic story tells about something that could happen.
- A fantasy is a story about something that could not happen.
- Good readers look for clues that tell them whether a story could really happen or not.

READ ALOUD Read "A Nice Place to Sleep" and model how to distinguish between realism and fantasy.

MODEL This story is a fantasy because it is about things that could never happen. Real animals can't talk to each other about the best places to sleep. That tells me that this story is a fantasy.

PRACTICE

CLUES TO REALISM AND FANTASY Ask children what other clues tell you that this story is a fantasy. (A real deer could not build a nest from twigs or dig a hole in the ground.)

DISTINGUISH REALISM AND FANTASY Have children recall the story *Henry and Mudge and the Starry Night*.

- Do Henry and his family act like people do in real life? (yes)
- What does Henry do that reminds you of something you might do? (Possible response: He goes hiking.)
- Is this story a realistic story or a fantasy? (realistic story) Why? (because Henry, Mudge, and his family act like real people and animals do)

CONNECT TO READING Tell children that when they read any story, they should think about whether the story could or could not happen in real life.

A Nice Place to Sleep

Little Deer's mother asked him to find a nice place to spend the night. So Little Deer went into the forest and asked Bird for help.

"You need a nest," Bird said. "Here are some sticks. You can build one just like mine!"

Little Deer used the sticks to make a small, delicate nest. But when he stepped into the nest to try it out, the sticks snapped into bits. Little Deer and his mother could never sleep there. He went farther into the forest and asked Bear for help.

"Find a cave!" Bear said. "Look at mine! It's nice and cozy, just right to curl up and sleep in!"

Little Deer peered inside the cave, but it was very dark and scary. He decided to go even farther into the forest and ask Snake for help.

"You need a place to sleep?" Snake inquired. "Well, I'd dig a hole if I were you. I sleep very soundly in my snake hole."

Little Deer dug and dug in the ground, but soon he grew tired. He wasn't strong enough to dig a hole big enough for him and his mother to sleep in. Though he was sad, Little Deer went even farther into the forest to ask Squirrel for help.

Squirrel said, "See that hole high up in the tree? I sleep in a hole like that. It can keep you safe and sound."

Little Deer looked up into the tree at the small hole. Not only would he not fit, but there was no way he and his mother could climb that tree. Little Deer sighed and lay down on the ground to think about what to do next. The moss was soft and soon he was fast asleep.

Not long after, his mother found Little Deer and smiled. Her son had done a good job. He had found the perfect place for them to spend the long night.

OBJECTIVE

• Write news.

DAILY FIX-IT

1. do you really believe that story

Do you really believe that story?

2. An animal can't

An animal can't really talk.

This week's practice sentences appear on Daily Fix-It Transparency 5.

Strategic Intervention

Work with children to make sure the topic of their news bulletin is fantasy rather than realism. Let children work together to brainstorm some fantasy topics if necessary.

Advanced

Encourage interested children to extend their fantasy to include details of how the fantasy came about, what it looks like, and so on.

Support Writing Provide illustrated fairy tales or other examples of fantasy to encourage children's own imaginations as they write.

▲ **The Grammar and Writing Book**
For more instruction and practice, use pp. 74–79.

Shared Writing

WRITE News Bulletin

GENERATE IDEAS Ask children to imagine they have discovered a talking animal. Have them decide what the animal is, where they found it, what it said, as well as how they felt and what they thought when they found the animal.

NEWS BULLETIN Explain that the class will write a news bulletin telling about their discovery of a talking animal.

COMPREHENSION SKILL Explain that when a story tells about people who seem real and things that could really happen, we call it realism. When a story tells about something that could only be in someone's imagination, we call it fantasy.

- Display Writing Transparency 5 and read the title aloud.

- Read the two headings aloud.

- Read the first incomplete sentence. Discuss whether a talking animal would be realism or fantasy and why. Have children work together to brainstorm an end to the sentence.

- Continue similarly to have children dictate endings to each of the following sentences.

HANDWRITING While writing, model the letter forms as shown on pp. TR14–17.

READ NEWS BULLETIN Have children read the completed news bulletin aloud as you track the print.

In the News

An Amazing Animal!
Possible answers:

We found a talking **rabbit**!

It was in **the woods near the highway**

It said, " **Hello, my name is Roger** "

We **were so excited** .

We **wanted to tell everyone**

Unit 1 The Strongest One   Writing Model **5**

▲ **Writing Transparency 5**

INDEPENDENT WRITING

WRITE NEWS BULLETIN Have children write their own fantasy news bulletin. Encourage them to use words from the Word Wall and the Amazing Words board. Let children illustrate their writing. You may want to allow volunteers to read their news bulletins aloud as though they are television or radio newscasters.

ADDITIONAL PRACTICE For additional practice, use pp. 74–79 in the Grammar and Writing Book.

Grammar

TEACH/MODEL Commands and Exclamations

REVIEW SENTENCES Remind children that a sentence is a group of words that tells a complete idea and that the words in a sentence appear in an order that makes sense. A sentence always begins with a capital letter. Recall that some sentences are questions that end with a question mark. Other sentences are statements that end with a period.

IDENTIFY COMMANDS AND EXCLAMATIONS Display Grammar Transparency 5. Read the definitions aloud.

• Is the group of words by the number 1 a command that tells someone to do something? Or is it an exclamation that shows surprise or strong feelings?

• This sentence is a command, so it should end with a period.

Continue modeling with items 2–5.

PRACTICE

SUGGEST COMMANDS AND EXCLAMATIONS Have children say other commands and exclamations. Write each one and have volunteers add the punctuation.

• Think of a command you might give a dog.

• What might you say if you just got a new puppy?

Wrap Up Your Day!

 CONSONANT DIGRAPHS Write *My chin itches. Shut the door when the wind blows. Wash the dog in the bath.* Read each sentence aloud, underlining the consonant digraphs *ch, tch, sh, th,* and *wh*.

SPELLING WORDS WITH CONSONANT DIGRAPHS Dictate the following words and have children write them: *each, chip, watch, shed, trash, them, cloth, when*.

REALISM AND FANTASY To help children distinguish between realism and fantasy, recall *A Walk in the Desert* on pp. 100–119.

• Was this selection realism or fantasy? Why do you think so?

• Let's think about "The Three Little Pigs." Is that story realism or fantasy? Why do you think so?

LET'S TALK ABOUT IT Display children's partially completed web and suggest they add others they might ask about a fantasy animal.

School + Home **HOMEWORK** Send home this week's Family Times newsletter.

PREVIEW Day 2

Tell children that tomorrow the class will read a fantasy about an ant that wants to know who is the strongest one in the world.

Day 2
AT A GLANCE

Materials

Morning Warm-Up!

Today we will read a fantasy about an ant with a question. Whom does the ant check with to find the answer? What does he find out? Why is the ant shocked?

QUESTION OF THE DAY Encourage children to sing "Where to Inquire" from the *Sing with Me Big Book* as you gather. Write and read the message and discuss the questions.

REVIEW PHONICS

- Read the message aloud, indicating each word as you do so.

- Draw attention to the words *with, check, what, why,* and *shocked*. Write each word separately and have children circle the digraphs.

Build Background Use the Day 2 instruction on ELL Poster 5 to preview high-frequency words.

ELL Poster 5

Share Literature

BUILD CONCEPTS

REVIEW REALISM AND FANTASY Read the title and author's name aloud. Recall with children what they have learned about realism and fantasy— that realism is something that could really happen and that fantasy could never happen.

BUILD ORAL VOCABULARY Discuss with children their experiences with going to museums or other places where there are **exhibits,** or displays of information. Tell them that someone in this story tries to **resist** doing something, or fights against something. Suggest that as you read, children listen to find out what the boy in the story sees in an exhibit in a special museum and what he tries to resist.

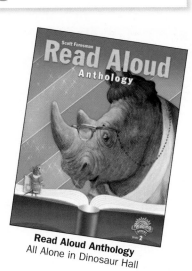

Read Aloud Anthology
All Alone in Dinosaur Hall

- Ollie was curious about an exhibit with a sign that said it was temporarily closed. What is an exhibit? (a public showing of something)

- Ollie couldn't resist going behind the sign. What does that mean? (He couldn't stop himself from doing it because it was so interesting to him.)

MONITOR LISTENING COMPREHENSION

- What did Ollie discover behind that sign? (a dinosaur exhibit that included dinosaur eggs)

- Do you think Ollie might resist exploring hidden exhibits again? Why or why not? (Possible answer: Yes, because he had a very odd experience.)

OBJECTIVES

- Discuss realism and fantasy.
- Set purpose for listening.
- Build oral vocabulary.

to build oral vocabulary

Amazing Words	MONITOR PROGRESS
delicate inquire sturdy exhibit resist stun genius satisfaction	**If...** children lack oral vocabulary experiences about the concept Exploration, **then...** use the Oral Vocabulary Routine. See p. DI·7 to teach *exhibit* and *resist*.

Build Concepts Make sure children understand that dinosaurs were real creatures who lived long, long ago. It would be impossible for their eggs to hatch now. Therefore, although dinosaur exhibits in a museum are real, the idea that their eggs would hatch is fantasy.

2

OBJECTIVES

- Review consonant digraphs.
- Sort and read words with consonant digraphs.
- Preview words before reading them.
- Spell words with consonant digraphs.

Strategic Intervention

Use **Strategic Intervention Decodable Reader 5** for more practice with consonant digraphs.

E L L

Support Phonics Explain that "through and through" means the books will be read entirely and completely. Then replay "Where Can We Turn?" on the Phonics Songs and Rhymes Audio CD.

⊙ Consonant Digraphs

TEACH/MODEL

Fluent Word Reading

ROUTINE

1 Connect Write *match.* You can read this word because you know how to read words with consonant digraphs. What sound do the letters *tch* stand for in this word? (/ch/) What's the word? *(match)* Do the same with *whim, shape, think, chat.*

2 Model When you come to a new word, look at the word parts from left to right and think about the consonant digraph sounds. Say the sounds in the word to yourself and then read the word. **Model reading** *pitch, chimp, hush, while, thud.* When you come to a new word, what are you going to do?

3 Group Practice Write *chin, shine, thick, whisk, clutch.* Read these words. Look at the word parts, say the sounds to yourself, and then read the word aloud together. **Allow 2–3 seconds previewing time.**

WORD READING

PHONICS SONGS AND RHYMES CHART 5 Frame each of the following words on Phonics Songs and Rhymes Chart 5. Call on individuals to read them. Guide children in previewing.

when	think	things	wish
search	through	where	watch
show	what	check	

Sing "Where Can We Turn?" to the tune of "Sing a Song of Sixpence," or play the CD. Have children follow along on the chart as they sing. Then have individuals take turns circling and reading words with consonant digraphs on the chart.

Phonics Songs and Rhymes Audio

Where Can We Turn?

When we think of new things
That we wish to learn,
We must search for answers.
Where can we turn?

We can watch as people
Show us what to do.
We can check out books with facts and
Read them through and through.

Phonics Songs and Rhymes Chart 5

SORT WORDS

INDIVIDUALS SORT WORDS WITH CONSONANT DIGRAPHS Write *ch, tch, sh, th,* and *wh* as headings. Have individuals write words with consonant digraphs from the Phonics Chart under the appropriate headings and circle the letters that stand for the digraph sounds. Have all children complete the activity on paper. Ask individuals to read the completed lists. Provide feedback as necessary.

ch	*tch*	*sh*	*th*	*wh*
search	watch	wish	think	when
check		show	things	where
			through	what

Spelling

PRACTICE Consonant Digraphs

WRITE DICTATION SENTENCES Have children write these sentences. Repeat words slowly, allowing children to hear each sound. Children may use the Word Wall to help with spelling high-frequency words. **Word Wall**

When will you do that math?

I wish I could chase a whale!

Tell them to pick a bunch from the patch.

HOMEWORK Spelling Practice Book, p. 18

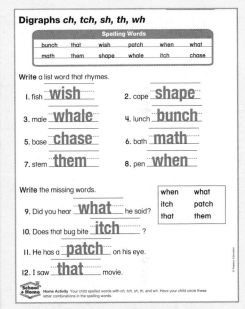

▲ **Spelling Practice Book** p. 18

Read each story. Follow the directions.

Mom and I wanted to know why the fish were dying in the creek. We filled some test tubes with creek water. The fish told us where to look. Later we will test the water. Maybe we can find out what is wrong.

1. **Underline** one sentence that tells something that could happen.
2. **Circle** the sentence that tells something that could not happen.

Terry and Jason wanted to see what was inside the old shed. They were a little scared. They crept up to the door and pushed it open. The inside of the shed was dusty and spooky. Then a hen stepped out and said, "Hello."

3. **Underline** one sentence that tells something that could happen.
4. **Circle** the sentence that tells something that could not happen.
5. **Draw** a picture of something that could not really happen at your school.
   Artwork should show something that could not really happen at school.

School + Home **Home Activity** Your child identified whether story events could really happen. Select a favorite storybook or check one out from the library. Ask your child to identify realistic events (real people doing ordinary things) and fantasies (things that cannot really happen).

▲ **Practice Book 2.1** p. 45, Realism and Fantasy

Comprehension

SKILL Realism and Fantasy

RECOGNIZE REALISM AND FANTASY Review with children that a realistic story could really happen and that a fantasy tells about something that could never really happen. Readers should look for clues in a story to tell if something could really happen or not. An animal that talks, acts, and thinks the way people do tells the reader the story is a fantasy. Have children identify several previously read stories as realism or fantasy.

CONNECT TO READING

- As you read, ask yourself if what you are reading could really happen. If it could, it is a realistic story.
- Pay attention to the characters and what they do. If they are animals that act like people, the story is fantasy.

STRATEGY Monitor and Fix Up

INTRODUCE THE STRATEGY Explain to children that they can be better readers by thinking about whether they understand what they read as they read. Point out that paying attention to the illustrations and to which character is talking are two ways they can help themselves understand what they are reading.

Think Aloud

MODEL When I read a play, I sometimes get confused about who is talking and what is happening. I look carefully at the illustrations and notice the names of the characters in front of the speaking parts in the play. That helps me figure out who is speaking and what is happening.

CONNECT TO READING Encourage children to ask themselves these questions as they read *The Strongest One*.

- Do I use the illustrations to figure out who is onstage and what is happening?
- Do I use the speakers' names to help me understand who is talking?

Build Background

DISCUSS ANT COLONIES Display pictures of ants and ant colonies or a real ant colony in a glass case. Invite children to tell what they know about ants.

- What do the ants in an ant colony do?
- What are some of the duties of different ants in a colony?
- How do ants in an ant colony work together?

BACKGROUND BUILDING AUDIO Have children listen to the audio and share the new information they learned about ant colonies and the different roles of ants.

 **Sing with Me/ Background Building Audio**

COMPLETE A MAIN IDEA/SUPPORTING DETAILS CHART Draw a chart or display Graphic Organizer 16. Write *Ant Colony* in the main idea box. Work with children to identify the different roles or duties of ants in a colony as they write the supporting details in the chart.

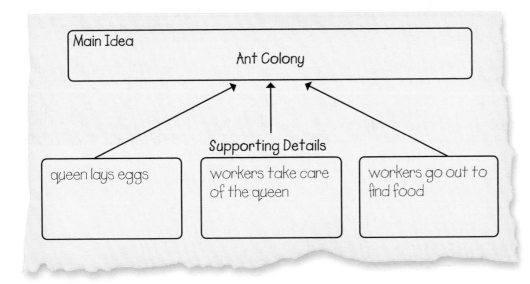

Main Idea
Ant Colony

Supporting Details

| queen lays eggs | workers take care of the queen | workers go out to find food |

▲ **Graphic Organizer** 16

CONNECT TO SELECTION Connect background information to *The Strongest One.*

Little Red Ant lives in an ant colony in a hole under the Big Rock. What do we know about ants? This ant wants to find out who is the strongest one in the world. The other ants warn him to be careful because the world can be a dangerous place, and he is very small. We'll find out what Little Red Ant learns about being strong.

Build Background Tell children that ants are insects that live in every country in the world. There are many kinds of ants, but they all live in colonies. Ask children to tell what they know about ants.

Words to Read

pieces
often
very
together
though
gone
learn

Read the Words

Chip looked at the pieces of the puzzle. He often did these things with his very best friend Mike. He and Mike couldn't work together today, though. Mike had gone to visit his uncle. Chip knew he would have to learn to do things on his own.

Genre: Play
A play is a story written to be acted out for others. Next, you will read a play about an ant who sets out to learn who is the strongest one.

130

131

_____ Consonant Digraphs   high-frequency/tested vocabulary

High-Frequency Words

Nondecodable Words

1 Say and Spell Look at the words on page 130. You cannot blend the sounds in these words. We will spell the words and use letter-sounds we know to learn them. Point to the first word. This word is *pieces, p-i-e-c-e-s, pieces*. What is this word? What are the letters in this word?

2 Identify Familiar Letter-Sounds Point to the first letter in *pieces*. What is this letter? What is the sound for this letter? (*p/p/*) Follow a similar procedure to have children identify the *c* and *s* in *pieces*.

3 Demonstrate Meaning Tell me a sentence using this word.

Repeat the routine with the other Words to Read. Have children identify these familiar letter-sounds: *often* (f/f/), *very* (v/v/ and r/r/), *together* (t/t/, g/g/, th/th/), *though* (th/th/), *gone* (g/g/), *learn* (l/l/, n/n/).

Have children read aloud the paragraphs on p. 131 and point to the Words to Read. Add the words to the Word Wall. **Word Wall**

Use Vocabulary Transparency 5 to review this week's words.

- Point to a word. Say and spell it.
- Have children say and spell the word.
- Ask children to identify familiar letter-sounds.

- Recognize high-frequency words.

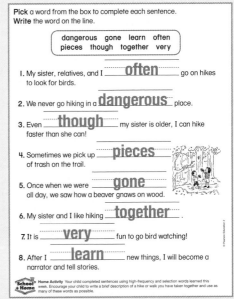

Pick a word from the box to complete each sentence. **Write** the word on the line.

> dangerous gone learn often
> pieces though together very

1. My sister, relatives, and I ____**often**____ go on hikes to look for birds.
2. We never go hiking in a ____**dangerous**____ place.
3. Even ____**though**____ my sister is older, I can hike faster than she can!
4. Sometimes we pick up ____**pieces**____ of trash on the trail.
5. Once when we were ____**gone**____ all day, we saw how a beaver gnaws on wood.
6. My sister and I like hiking ____**together**____.
7. It is ____**very**____ fun to go bird watching!
8. After I ____**learn**____ new things, I will become a narrator and tell stories.

School + Home **Home Activity** Your child completed sentences using high-frequency and selection words learned this week. Encourage your child to write a brief description of a hike or walk you have taken together and use as many of these words as possible.

▲ **Practice Book 2.1** p. 46, High-Frequency Words and Selection Words

---

Monitor Progress | Check High-Frequency Words

Point to the following words on the Word Wall and have individuals read them.

pieces	**often**	**very**	**together**	**though**	**gone**	**learn**
water	**somewhere**	**friend**	**move**	**straight**	**animals**	**full**

If... children cannot read these words,

then... have them practice in pairs with word cards before reading the selection. Monitor their fluency with these words during reading, and provide additional practice opportunities before the Day 5 Assessment.

SUCCESS PREDICTOR

 Spiral REVIEW

- Reviews previously taught high-frequency words.

Day 1 Check Word Reading ┃ ▶**Day 2 Check High-Frequency Words** ┃ **Day 3** Check Retelling ┃ **Day 4** Check Fluency ┃ **Day 5** Assess Progress

High-Frequency Words

SUCCESS PREDICTOR

The Play

Selection Words

1. Tim is the <u>narrator</u> of our class play.

2. The play is about a family with lots of <u>relatives</u>.

3. One of the boys in the family has a <u>dangerous</u> pet rat.

4. The pet rat <u>gnaws</u> the legs of tables.

High-Frequency Words

Words to Read			
gone	learn	often	pieces

▲ **Vocabulary Transparency 5**

Vocabulary

SELECTION WORDS

Use Vocabulary Transparency 5 to introduce the selection words.

• Read each sentence as you track the print.

• Frame each underlined word. Explain the word's meaning.

narrator a person who tells a story
relatives people in the same family
dangerous not safe
gnaws bites at and wears away

• Ask children to identify familiar letter-sounds and word parts: *narrator* (blend the syllables: *nar, ra, tor*), *relatives* (r/r/, s/z/), *dangerous* (a/ā/ in the first syllable).

• Have children read each sentence aloud with you.

• To encourage discussion using the selection words, ask children to use the words *dangerous* and *gnaws* to tell about something scary. Then have them pretend to be a narrator telling a story about someone's relatives.

Group Time

On-Level	Strategic Intervention	Advanced
Read *The Strongest One.*	**Read** SI Decodable Reader 5.	**Read** *The Strongest One.*
• Use pp. 132–149.	• Read or listen to *The Strongest One.*	• Use the **Routine** on p. DI·57.
	• Use the **Routine** on p. DI·56.	

 Place English language learners in the groups that correspond to their reading abilities in English.

(i) Independent Activities

Independent Reading See p. 128j for Reading/Library activities and suggestions.

Journal Writing Write about a person or animal who is strongest of all. Share your writing.

Literacy Centers To provide experiences with *The Strongest One,* you may use the Listening Center on p. 128j.

Practice Book 2.1 Realism and Fantasy, p. 45; High-Frequency Words, p. 46; Character and Setting, p. 47

ELL

Access Content Use the vocabulary strategies and word cards in the ELL Teaching Guide, pp. 31–32.

Break into small groups after Vocabulary and before Writing.

The Strongest One

retold as a play by Joseph Bruchac
illustrated by David Diaz
from *Pushing Up the Sky*

What does Little Red Ant
learn about being strong?

132

133

Prereading Strategies

PREVIEW AND PREDICT Ask children to decode the words in the title. Then read it aloud with them. Read aloud the author and illustrator names. Invite children to look through several pages of the selection and consider what it is about.

DISCUSS PLAYS Read aloud the definition of a play on p. 131. Discuss with children plays they have seen. You may want to point out that television shows and movies are often similar to plays because each character has words to say. Compare reading a play to reading a story.

SET PURPOSE Read aloud the question on p. 133. Ask children what they think they might find out as they read.

Access Content Before reading, review the story summary in English and/or the home language. See the ELL Teaching Guide, pp. 33–35.

Characters:

NARRATOR	MOUSE
LITTLE RED ANT	CAT
SECOND ANT	STICK
THIRD ANT	FIRE
FOURTH ANT	WATER
SNOW	DEER
SUN	ARROW
WIND	BIG ROCK
HOUSE	

Scene I: Inside the Ant's Hole

(On a darkened stage, the ants crouch together.)

NARRATOR: Little Red Ant lived in a hole under the Big Rock with all of its relatives. It often wondered about the world outside: Who in the world was the strongest one of all? One day in late spring Little Red Ant decided to find out.

LITTLE RED ANT: I am going to find out who is strongest. I am going to go outside and walk around.

134

SECOND ANT: Be careful! We ants are very small. Something might step on you.

THIRD ANT: Yes, we are the smallest and weakest ones of all.

FOURTH ANT: Be careful, it is dangerous out there!

LITTLE RED ANT: I will be careful. I will find out who is strongest. Maybe the strongest one can teach us how to be stronger.

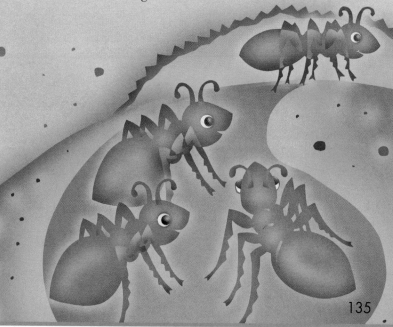

135

▲ **Pages 134–135**
Have children read to find out if this story could really happen.

Strong Animals

TIME FOR Science

Something that is strong has the power to put force on something else. Animals and people are strong in different ways. An elephant can lift much heavier loads than a person can, for example. And a big gorilla can push a heavier object than a person can.

Skills in Context

⟳ REALISM AND FANTASY

• **Does this seem like a realistic story that tells about something that could really happen? Or is it probably a fantasy that is about something that could never happen? How do you know?**
The story is probably a fantasy about something that could never happen because animals don't really talk or act like people.

Monitor Progress	**Realism and Fantasy**
If... children are unable to distinguish between realism and fantasy,	**then...** model how to use the text and pictures to tell the difference.

Think Aloud **MODEL** I can tell that this story is a fantasy that could never really happen because I know that animals like ants don't really talk to each other or go exploring to find the answer to a question.

ASSESS As they read, have children identify other clues that tell them this is a fantasy.

___ Consonant Digraphs   high-frequency/tested vocabulary

Scene II: The Mesa

(Ant walks back and forth onstage.)

NARRATOR: So Little Red Ant went outside and began to walk around. But as Little Red Ant walked, the snow began to fall.

(Snow walks onstage.)

LITTLE RED ANT: Ah, my feet are cold. This snow makes everything freeze. Snow must be the strongest. I will ask. Snow, are you the strongest of all?

136

SNOW: No, I am not the strongest.

LITTLE RED ANT: Who is stronger than you?

SNOW: Sun is stronger. When Sun shines on me, I melt away. Here it comes!

(As Sun walks onstage, Snow hurries offstage.)

LITTLE RED ANT: Ah, Sun must be the strongest. I will ask. Sun, are you the strongest of all?

SUN: No, I am not the strongest.

137

Guiding Comprehension

Realism and Fantasy • Critical
- **Is Snow a realistic character? How do you know?**
No, Snow is not realistic because snow doesn't really talk or act like a person.

Setting • Literal
- **Where are Little Red Ant and Snow? How do you know?**
They are on the mesa. The author included a description of the setting in the first line.

Predict • Critical
- **Who will Sun say is stronger?**
Maybe a storm would be stronger because the sun doesn't shine during a storm.

▲ **Pages 136–137**
Have children read to find out where Little Red Ant and Snow are.

Monitor Progress	
Decoding	
If... children come to a word they don't know,	**then**...remind them to: 1. Blend the word. 2. Decide if the word makes sense. 3. Look in a dictionary for more help.

LITTLE RED ANT: Who is stronger than you?

SUN: Wind is stronger. Wind blows the clouds across the sky and covers my face. Here it comes!

(As Wind comes onstage, Sun hurries offstage with face covered in hands.)

LITTLE RED ANT: Wind must be the strongest. I will ask. Wind, are you the strongest of all?

WIND: No, I am not the strongest.

LITTLE RED ANT: Who is stronger than you?

WIND: House is stronger. When I come to House, I cannot move it. I must go elsewhere. Here it comes!

(As House walks onstage, Wind hurries offstage.)

LITTLE RED ANT: House must be the strongest. I will ask. House, are you the strongest of all?

HOUSE: No, I am not the strongest.

LITTLE RED ANT: Who is stronger than you?

HOUSE: Mouse is stronger. Mouse comes and gnaws holes in me. Here it comes!

(As Mouse walks onstage, House hurries offstage.)

138

139

▲ **Pages 138–139**
Have children read to find out who Little Red Ant meets next.

Monitor Progress

High-Frequency Words

| If... children have a problem reading a new high-frequency word, | then... use the High-Frequency Routine on p. 131a to reteach the problematic word. |

Extend Language Explain that *stronger* means more strong than one other and *strongest* means the most strong. Invite children to offer comparative adjective forms in their own language.

Strategies in Context

MONITOR AND FIX UP

- **Whom does Little Red Ant speak to next? How do you know?**
  He talks to Wind next, then House. Each character's name appears right before the character's words. They are also in the picture.

Monitor Progress | **Monitor and Fix Up**

| If... children have difficulty determining who Little Red Ant talks to next, | then... model how to use the text and pictures to confirm understanding. |

Think Aloud

MODEL At first I was confused here. I just couldn't figure out who was saying what. Then I remembered that the name of each speaker is right before what that character says. I also looked at the illustration and saw the sun, the wind, a house, and a mouse. Ant must talk to Mouse next.

ASSESS Have children identify speakers throughout the play and explain how they know.

___ Consonant Digraphs   high-frequency/tested vocabulary

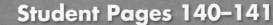
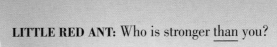

LITTLE RED ANT: Mouse must be <u>the</u> strongest. I will ask. Mouse, are you <u>the</u> strongest of all?

MOUSE: No, I am not <u>the</u> strongest.

LITTLE RED ANT: Who is stronger <u>than</u> you?

MOUSE: Cat is stronger. Cat <u>chases</u> me, and if Cat <u>catches</u> me, Cat will eat me. Here it comes!

(As Cat walks onstage, Mouse hurries offstage, squeaking.)

LITTLE RED ANT: Cat must be <u>the</u> strongest. I will ask. Cat, are you <u>the</u> strongest of all?

CAT: No, I am not <u>the</u> strongest.

140

LITTLE RED ANT: Who is stronger <u>than</u> you?

CAT: Stick is stronger. <u>When</u> Stick hits me, I run away. Here it comes!

(As Stick walks onstage, Cat hurries offstage, meowing.)

LITTLE RED ANT: Stick must be <u>the</u> strongest. I will ask. Stick, are you <u>the</u> strongest of all?

STICK: No, I am not <u>the</u> strongest.

LITTLE RED ANT: Who is stronger <u>than</u> you?

STICK: Fire is stronger. <u>When</u> I am put into Fire, Fire burns me up! Here it comes!

(As Fire walks onstage, Stick hurries offstage.)

141

Skills in Context

(REVIEW) **CHARACTER AND SETTING**

- **Who is the main character in the play so far? Where does it take place? How do you know?**
The main character is Little Red Ant. The story takes place inside Ant's hole on a mesa. We can see the ant's hole and a mesa in the illustrations. The play also tells where each scene takes place.

Monitor Progress	Character and Setting
If... children are unable to identify character and setting,	**then...** model how to use the text and illustrations to identify them.

Think Aloud

MODEL I think Little Red Ant is the main character because we follow Little Red Ant's journey in the play. I know where the play takes place because I remember to look closely at the pictures and to read the parts that tell where a scene takes place.

ASSESS Have children identify other characters and changes of setting.

▲ **Pages 140–141**
Have children read to determine who's the main character in the play.

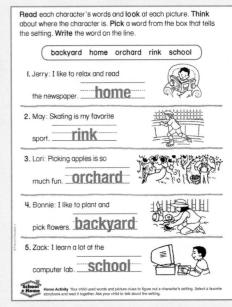

Read each character's words and look at each picture. Think about where the character is. Pick a word from the box that tells the setting. Write the word on the line.

> backyard   home   orchard   rink   school

1. Jerry: I like to relax and read the newspaper. **home**

2. May: Skating is my favorite sport. **rink**

3. Lori: Picking apples is so much fun. **orchard**

4. Bonnie: I like to plant and pick flowers. **backyard**

5. Zack: I learn a lot at the computer lab. **school**

School + Home Home Activity Your child used words and picture clues to figure out a character's setting. Select a favorite storybook and read it together. Ask your child to talk about the setting.

▲ **Practice Book 2.1** p. 47, Character and Setting

LITTLE RED ANT: Fire must be the strongest.
I will ask. Fire, are you the strongest of all?

FIRE: No, I am not the strongest.

LITTLE RED ANT: Who is stronger than you?

FIRE: Water is stronger. When Water is poured on
me, it kills me. Here it comes!

(As Water walks onstage, Fire hurries offstage.)

LITTLE RED ANT: Water must be the strongest.
I will ask. Water, are you the strongest of all?

WATER: No, I am not the strongest.

142

143

▲ **Pages 142–143**
Have children read to find out what
makes Water stronger than Fire.

Strategy Self-Check

Have children ask themselves these
questions to check their reading.

Decoding Words
• Do I blend the sounds of a new
word as I read it?
• Does the word make sense in the
sentence and in the play?

Monitor and Fix Up
Illustrations and Speakers' Names
• Do I use the illustrations to find who
is onstage and what is happening?
• Do I use the speakers' names to help
me understand who is talking?

Guiding Comprehension

Cause and Effect • Literal
• **What makes Water stronger than Fire?**
When you put water on fire, the fire goes out.

Summarize • Inferential
• **What has happened in the story so far?**
Little Red Ant wants to find out who in the world is the strongest one of all.
Ant goes to Snow, Sun, Wind, Fire, and Water and inquires about who is the
strongest. Each character says that something else is stronger than it is.

___ Consonant Digraphs   high-frequency/tested vocabulary

LITTLE RED ANT: Who is stronger than you?

WATER: Deer is stronger. When Deer comes, Deer drinks me. Here it comes!

(As Deer walks onstage, Water hurries offstage.)

LITTLE RED ANT: Deer must be the strongest. I will ask. Deer, are you the strongest of all?

DEER: No, I am not the strongest.

LITTLE RED ANT: Who is stronger than you?

DEER: Arrow is stronger. When Arrow strikes me, it can kill me. Here it comes!

(As Arrow walks onstage, Deer runs offstage with leaping bounds.)

144

145

▲ **Pages 144–145**
Have children read to find out what Deer and Arrow tell Little Red Ant.

Guiding Comprehension

Draw Conclusions • Critical

- *Text to Self* If you performed this play, how would you make a costume for the character of Water?

Possible response: The character of Water could wear something blue because water is sometimes blue. Maybe he or she could wear a piece of paper that's shaped like a raindrop or a lake.

Compare and Contrast • Critical

- *Text to Text* What other stories do you know that have animals that act like people as characters?

Recall with children other fables and fantasies that they know with animals as main characters, such as *Frog and Toad* and *The Three Little Pigs*.

EXTEND SKILLS

Genre/Play

For instruction in the genre of plays, discuss the following:

- The author shows us that this is a play by giving us the name of the character right before its words. The author also lists the characters at the beginning and tells us where scenes change.

- In parentheses and slanted type called italics, the author gives us stage directions to show us what the actors should do.

Assess Have children identify elements of plays as they find them.

The Strongest One **144–145**

LITTLE RED ANT: Arrow must be the strongest. I will ask. Arrow, are you the strongest of all?

ARROW: No, I am not the strongest.

LITTLE RED ANT: Who is stronger than you?

ARROW: Big Rock is stronger. When I am shot from the bow and I hit Big Rock, Big Rock breaks me.

LITTLE RED ANT: Do you mean the same Big Rock where the Red Ants live?

ARROW: Yes, that is Big Rock. Here it comes!

(As Big Rock walks onstage, Arrow runs offstage.)

LITTLE RED ANT: Big Rock must be the strongest. I will ask. Big Rock, are you the strongest of all?

BIG ROCK: No, I am not the strongest.

LITTLE RED ANT: Who is stronger than you?

BIG ROCK: You are stronger. Every day you and the other Red Ants come and carry little pieces of me away. Someday I will be gone.

146

147

▲ **Pages 146–147**
Have children read to find out how the next character Little Red Ant meets reminds them of where the story takes place.

Information

Time for **SOCIAL STUDIES**

We can find facts and information in many different places such as encyclopedias and other kinds of books. We can also look on the Internet. Sometimes we find information in plays or music or on TV or by talking to someone who knows. We have to be careful that the sources we use to find information can be trusted to give us the real facts.

Guiding Comprehension

Character and Setting • Inferential

• **What does the character of Big Rock tell you about the setting of the play?**
Possible response: This play must take place in a rocky area.

Draw Conclusions • Critical

• **Why does Big Rock think Red Ants are stronger? Do you think Big Rock could be right? Why or why not?**
Big Rock says Red Ants carry little pieces of rock away every day, and someday Big Rock will be all gone. He could be right, but it will take a very, very long time to know.

___ Consonant Digraphs ⬜ high-frequency/tested vocabulary

Scene III: The Ant's Hole

NARRATOR: So Little Red Ant went back home and spoke to the ant people.

(The ants crouch together on the darkened stage.)

SECOND ANT: Little Red Ant has returned.

THIRD ANT: He has come back alive!

FOURTH ANT: Tell us about what you have learned. Who is the strongest of all?

LITTLE RED ANT: I have learned that everything is stronger than something else. And even though we ants are small, in some ways we are the strongest of all.

148

149

Guiding Comprehension

Plot • Literal

- **How does the play end?**
Little Red Ant finds out that everything is stronger than something else, and in some ways sturdy ants are really the strongest of all.

Author's Purpose • Critical

- *Question the Author* **Why do you think the author told this story as a play?**
Possible response: Maybe he thought we would like to act it out. Or maybe he thought it would be easier to read as a play.

Draw Conclusions • Inferential

- *Text to Self* **What are you stronger than? Explain.**
Children may give examples of people, animals, and objects they are stronger than, such as younger siblings, pets, or pieces of paper that they can easily tear.

▲ **Pages 148–149**
Have children read to find out how the play ends.

Reread For Fluency ROUTINE

1. **Reader 1 Begins** Children read the entire book, switching readers at the end of each page.

2. **Reader 2 Begins** Have partners reread; now the other partner begins.

3. **Reread** For optimal fluency, children should reread three or four times.

4. **Provide Feedback** Listen to children read and provide corrective feedback regarding their oral reading and their use of blending.

OBJECTIVES

● Write a creative story.
● Identify commands and exclamations.

Strategic Intervention

Help children brainstorm the characters and plot of their story before they begin to write. You may want to help them with each sentence as they write it.

Advanced

Let children work together to write and present their creative story in the form of a play like *The Strongest One*.

Support Writing Before writing, point out that children can invent their own characters and what they do.

Beginning Let children draw a picture of their characters doing something. Have them dictate a sentence that tells about their picture.

Intermediate Talk with children about what they want to write in their creative stories. Restate one of their important ideas in conventional English and help them write that sentence to get them started.

Advanced Have partners think aloud with each other about what they plan to write.

Support Grammar Children with literacy skills in Spanish may be accustomed to writing an upside-down exclamation mark. Point out that in English, the exclamation mark appears only at the end. See the Grammar Transition lessons in the ELL and Transition handbook.

Interactive Writing

WRITE Creative Story

BRAINSTORM Discuss with children some of their favorite stories, including *The Strongest One*. Explain that they can write their own stories. Brainstorm with children several characters for their story and what will happen in it. You may want to suggest that they consider writing a fantasy.

SHARE THE PEN Ask children to create the first sentence of their story, inviting individuals to write familiar letter-sounds, word parts, and high-frequency words. Ask questions such as:

● What kind of letter should we begin the sentence with? (a capital letter)

Write the sentence, inviting individuals to write familiar letter-sounds, word parts, and high-frequency words.

● How do we end the first sentence? (with a period)

● If we write a sentence that shows surprise, how should we end it? (with an exclamation mark)

Continue to have children make contributions. Frequently reread what has been written while tracking the print.

READ THE STORY Read the completed story aloud, having children echo you.

> **The teddy bear walked. The doll started to dance. What happened? The toys were alive! And they were very hungry. So they ran to the kitchen. They found cookies and gobbled them up. When their girl woke up in the morning, the toys looked just the same. But they had a magic night.**

INDEPENDENT WRITING

WRITE A CREATIVE STORY Have children write their own creative story. It should be a composition of one or more paragraphs. Remind them to organize their thoughts before they begin writing. They should have one main idea for the whole story. Then they should write a beginning that makes the reader want to read more. The middle could have a part that builds excitement. The end should bring the story to a close. Let children illustrate their writing.

Grammar

DEVELOP THE CONCEPT
Commands and Exclamations

IDENTIFY COMMANDS AND EXCLAMATIONS Write *Look at that sunset. It's so beautiful!* Point to each word as you read each sentence aloud. Each of these is a sentence. The first one tells someone to do something, so it is called a command. It ends with a period. The subject of the sentence is *you*, but *you* is not shown in the sentence. The second sentence shows strong feeling or surprise. It ends with an exclamation mark. Circle each punctuation mark as you mention it. Sometimes a command can also be an exclamation. Write *Stop!* Why is this a command? Why is it an exclamation?

PRACTICE

WRITE COMMANDS AND EXCLAMATIONS Display or draw a picture of children playing soccer or baseball. Invite children to brainstorm what is happening. Model writing what the children might be saying to each other.

Think Aloud

MODEL I think this boy must be telling the girl to go get the ball. So I'll write a command that says "Get the ball." Probably one of the other kids is excited about what's happening. I'll write an exclamation to tell what she is saying. I'll write "We're winning!"

Have children write other commands and exclamations that the children in the picture might be saying.

DAILY FIX-IT

3. what time does the game start
   What time does the game start?

4. get that ball
   Get that ball!

Commands and Exclamations

A **command** is a sentence that tells someone to do something. It ends with a **period** (.).
The subject of a command is *you*, but *you* is usually not shown.
　　Find the strongest one.　　Please answer me.
An **exclamation** is a sentence that shows surprise or shows strong feelings. It ends with an **exclamation mark** (!).
　　Ouch! I tripped on that rock!　What a great idea this is!
All commands and exclamations begin with capital letters.

Write *C* if the sentence is a command.
Write *E* if it is an exclamation.

1. Get me a basket.　　　　　　　　C

2. That is a huge basket!　　　　　E

3. Put in the food.　　　　　　　　C

4. Bring the ants.　　　　　　　　 C

5. Oh, no, I dropped the food!　　 E

Home Activity Your child learned about commands and exclamations. Play the following game with your child: Set a time limit of two minutes and during that time talk to each other using only commands and exclamations.

▲ **Grammar and Writing Practice Book** p. 17

Wrap Up Your Day!

 HIGH-FREQUENCY WORDS Write: *We worked to put the puzzle pieces together. It was very hard. We often had to learn that some didn't fit even though they looked as if they would. And then we found out that some pieces were just gone!* Read the sentences with children and have them identify the high-frequency words *pieces, together, very, often, learn, though, gone.*

MONITOR AND FIX UP Recall with children that they can use the illustrations and the speakers' names to help themselves understand what is happening as they read a play.

LET'S TALK ABOUT IT Discuss with children whom they can ask when they are searching for answers. Encourage them to add to the web that they began previously.

PREVIEW Day 3

Tell children that tomorrow the class will find out more about searching for answers in "All Alone in Dinosaur Hall."

149b

Share Literature
"All Alone in Dinosaur Hall"

Phonics and Spelling
REVIEW Inflected Endings

Spelling: Words with Consonant Digraphs

High-Frequency Words
together very learn

often though gone

pieces

Vocabulary
Synonyms

Fluency
Read with Expression/Intonation

Writing Trait
Sentences

Grammar
Commands and Exclamations

Materials
- *Sing with Me Big Book*
- *Read Aloud Anthology*
- Student Edition 150–151

Morning Warm-Up!

The dinosaur eggs hatched!
Did that really happen?
Or did Ollie just think it did?
Listen again. See what you think.

QUESTION OF THE DAY Encourage children to sing "Where to Inquire" from the *Sing with Me Big Book* as you gather. Write and read the message and discuss the question.

REVIEW COMMANDS AND EXCLAMATIONS

- Indicate the first sentence in the message. Is this a command or an exclamation? How do you know? (It's an exclamation because it shows surprise or strong feeling and ends with an exclamation mark.)

- Indicate the last two sentences in the message. Are these two sentences commands or exclamations? How do you know? (They are commands because both tell someone to do something. The subject is *you* but is not shown, and both end with a period.)

Build Background Use the Day 3 instruction on ELL Poster 5 to support children's use of English to communicate about lesson concepts.

ELL Poster 5

Share Literature

LISTEN AND RESPOND

REVIEW REALISM AND FANTASY Recall with children that realism is something that could really happen, and fantasy is something that could never really happen. Discuss what children remember about "All Alone in Dinosaur Hall." Point out that many stories like this one have parts that are realism and parts that are fantasy. Most of this story could really happen. But the idea that the dinosaur eggs hatched and made noise is fantasy and could never happen.

Read Aloud Anthology
All Alone in Dinosaur Hall

BUILD ORAL VOCABULARY Recall with children that the last time they heard this story, they listened to find out what the boy in the story sees in an exhibit in a special museum and what he tries to resist. Tell children that when we are extremely surprised by something, we are **stunned**. Suggest that this time they listen to find out how Ollie felt when he took his dad back to see the hatched dinosaurs—and they weren't there!

MONITOR LISTENING COMPREHENSION

- What happened when Ollie took his dad to see the hatched dinosaur eggs? (Ollie was stunned to discover they were gone.)

- Was Ollie's dad as stunned as Ollie to discover the newly hatched dinosaurs had disappeared? Why or why not? (No, because he never saw the eggs hatch.)

- Do you think those dinosaur eggs really hatched? Or did Ollie just think they did? Why do you think as you do? (Ollie just imagined it because dinosaur eggs couldn't really hatch after millions of years.)

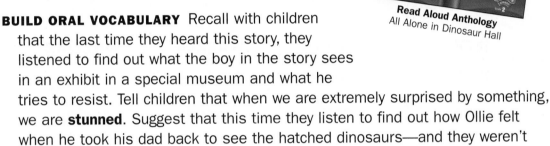

Amazing Words to build oral vocabulary

	MONITOR PROGRESS
delicate inquire sturdy exhibit resist stun genius satisfaction	**If…** children lack oral vocabulary experiences about the concept Exploration, **then…** use the Oral Vocabulary Routine. See p. DI·7 to teach *stun*.

Listen and Respond Point out that at one point after the eggs hatched, Ollie called them "baby dinos." Explain that *dino* was a short way of saying *dinosaur*. Tell children that sometimes when people talk, they shorten words in this way, such as *ad* for *advertisement*. Invite them to offer their own examples, such as *bike* for *bicycle* or *math* for *mathematics*.

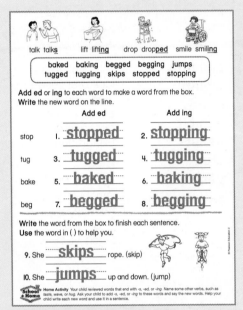

▲ **Practice Book 2.1** p. 48,
Inflected Endings

Review Phonics

REVIEW INFLECTED ENDINGS

READ -ed, -ing WORDS Write *lifted* and *lifting*. You can read these words because you know how to read base words with endings. What is the base word? (*lift*)

- Remind children that the ending *-ed* is added to show action that has happened in the past.

BUILD WORDS Write *base word, -s, -ed,* and *-ing* as headings for a four-column chart. Write several base words in the first column. Have children add the *-s, -ed,* and *-ing* endings to each base word, read the new word, and tell if/how the spelling changed when the endings were added.

base word	-s	-ed	-ing
wag	wags	wagged	wagging
look	looks	looked	looking
race	races	raced	racing
smile	smiles	smiled	smiling

High-Frequency Words

PRACTICE

CONTEXT CLUES Provide clues such as the following. Have children find the word on the Word Wall that fits each clue. **Word Wall**

- The word begins with *t* and makes sense in this sentence: I glued the two parts _____ and made one. (together)

- The word begins with *p* and makes sense in this sentence: How many _____ of pizza would you like? (pieces)

- The word begins with *l* and makes sense in this sentence: Mom plays the piano, and I want to _____ how to play too. (learn)

- The word begins with *v* and makes sense in this sentence: I am going to bed because I am _____ sleepy. (very)

- The word begins with *g* and makes sense in this sentence: Dad will have to take me to school because the bus has already _____. (gone)

- The word begins with *o* and makes sense in this sentence: I go to the library as _____ as I can. (often)

- The word begins with *t* and makes sense in this sentence: Today is a fun day even _____ it is raining. (though)

Spelling

PRACTICE Consonant Digraphs

RHYMING WORDS Have children practice by writing the spelling words that

- rhyme with *men*, with *batch* (when; patch)
- rhyme with *dish*, with *cape* (wish; shape)
- rhyme with *lunch*, with *tale* (bunch; whale)
- rhyme with *bat*, with *bath* (that; math)
- rhyme with *cut*, with *stem* (what; them)
- rhyme with *stitch*, with *vase* (itch; chase)

HOMEWORK Spelling Practice Book, p. 19

Pick a word from the box to complete each sentence. Write the word on the line.

| gone | learn | often | pieces | though | together | very |

1. Our family went rafting **together**

2. I pick up **pieces** of shell from the beach.

3. We are going to **learn** a new song tonight.

Find the word that completes the sentence. Mark the space to show your answer.

4. All of the cookies are _____ .
 - very
 - though
 - gone ●

5. That butterfly is _____ pretty.
 - very ●
 - pieces
 - though

6. I am tired, even _____ . I took a nap.
 - often
 - though ●
 - pieces

7. Brush your teeth _____ .
 - often ●
 - very
 - gone

Home Activity Your child learned the words *gone, learn, often, pieces, though, together,* and *very.* Assist your child in creating a "Helpful Words" dictionary that contains each word, a written definition, and a picture when appropriate.

▲ **Practice Book 2.1** p. 49, High-Frequency Words

Spelling Words

Consonant Digraphs

1.	**bunch**	7.	**math**
2.	**that**＊	8.	**them**
3.	**wish**	9.	**shape**
4.	**patch**	10.	**whale**
5.	**when**＊	11.	**itch**
6.	**what**＊	12.	**chase**＊

Challenge Words

13.	**whiskers**	15.	**shrimp**
14.	**switch**		

＊ **Words from the Selection**

Digraphs ch, tch, sh, th, wh

Read Mike's note. Circle three spelling mistakes. Write the words correctly. Then write the aunt's name correctly.

Spelling Words	
bunch	math
that	them
wish	shape
patch	whale
when	itch
what	chase

Dear aunt peg,
I (wish) you were here. We saw a whale. It had a white patch behind each eye. You can tell the male whale from the female whale by the (shap) of the fin. It was fun to (wach)
Love, Mike

Frequently Misspelled Words
when
watch
where

1. **wish**   2. **shape**

3. **watch**   4. **Aunt Peg**

Fill in the circle to show the correct spelling. Write the word.

5. ○ ich ● itch ○ itche   **itch**

6. ● what ○ whath ○ waht   **what**

7. ○ chas ○ shaze ● chase   **chase**

8. ○ buntch ○ bunsh ● bunch   **bunch**

Home Activity Your child identified misspelled words with ch, tch, sh, th, and wh. Have your child write a pretend postcard using some of the words.

▲ **Spelling Practice Book** p. 19

Strategic Intervention

Point out that synonyms are words that mean almost the same thing. Offer children the following word pairs and work with them to choose the pairs that are synonyms: *big, huge; small, tiny; cold, hot; up, high; in, out.*

Advanced

Ask children to write a paragraph of three or four sentences. Tell them to use, within the paragraph, at least two pairs of words that are synonyms.

Vocabulary

SYNONYMS

DISCUSS SYNONYMS Tell children that we have many words that mean almost the same thing. Remind them that they just read a story called *The Strongest One.* What are some other words that mean the same or almost the same as the word *strong?* Brainstorm with children to list synonyms for *strong* such as *tough, powerful, firm, forceful.*

EXPAND SELECTION WORDS Remind children that in the story, they read the word *dangerous.* Brainstorm with children to think of synonyms for *dangerous* such as *risky, unsafe, harmful.*

Group Time

DAY 3

On-Level	Strategic Intervention	Advanced
Read *The Strongest One.* • Use pp. 132–151.	**Read** or listen to *The Strongest One.* • Use the **Routine** on p. DI·58.	**Read** Self-Selected Reading. • Use the **Routine** on p. DI·59.

ELL Place English language learners in the groups that correspond to their reading abilities in English.

ⓘ Independent Activities

Independent Reading See p. 128j for Reading/Library activities and suggestions.

Journal Writing Use synonyms in sentences about being the strongest one. Share your writing.

Literacy Centers To provide experiences with *The Strongest One,* you may use the Writing Center on p. 128k.

Practice Book 2.1 Inflected Endings, p. 48; High-Frequency Words, p. 49

Break into small groups after Vocabulary and before Writing.

Fluency

READ WITH EXPRESSION AND INTONATION

MODEL READING WITH EXPRESSION AND INTONATION Use *The Strongest One.*

- Point to the characters' names in bold, all capital letters. These tell who is speaking in the play. Every speaker sounds different. So when we read their words aloud, we need to make our voices sound the way theirs would.

- Have children follow along as you read aloud pp. 134–135.

- Ask children to read the pages after you. Assign different children to read the parts of different characters. Continue in the same way with pp. 136–137.

REREAD FOR FLUENCY

Readers' Theater

ROUTINE

① **Select a Passage** For *The Strongest One,* begin with p. 138.

② **Divide into Character Parts** Assign one child to each character's part. Note that you may want to let more than one child take the part of Little Red Ant on different pages. Explain that children will read aloud only the lines for their character and that you will read the part of the Narrator, as well as the stage directions.

③ **Model** On p. 138, model for the child "actor" how Little Red Ant, Sun, Wind, and House sound as they speak.

④ **Read Together** Read your assigned parts as children read theirs.

⑤ **Independent Readings** Ask a volunteer to take over the part of the Narrator. Assign different children to the parts or ask for volunteers. Have children read the same pages aloud without you. Monitor progress and provide feedback. For optimal fluency, children should reread three to four times. Change the actors for the characters each time.

Monitor Progress	Fluency
If... children have difficulty reading with expression and intonation,	**then...** read each part, exaggerating somewhat the emotion in your voice to demonstrate to children how expression and intonation will change.
If... the class cannot read fluently without you,	**then...** continue to have them read along with you.

Options for Oral Reading

Use *The Strongest One* or one of the following Leveled Readers.

On-Level

The Bear Man

Strategic Intervention

The Case of the Missing Fish

Advanced

Sue's Hummingbird

Model reading p. 135 of *The Strongest One,* changing your expression and intonation with each character. Have children practice rereading the same dialogue with expression. You may want to assign the four parts to four different children, then have them change parts and read the dialogue again until each child reads each part at least once.

Retelling Plan

- ☑ Week 1 assess Strategic Intervention students.
- ☑ Week 2 assess Advanced students.
- ☑ Week 3 assess Strategic Intervention students.
- ☑ Week 4 assess On-Level students.
- ☑ **This week assess any students you have not yet checked during this unit.**

Look Back and Write
For test practice, assign a 10–15 minute time limit. For informal and formal assessment, see the Scoring Rubric below.

Think and Share

TALK ABOUT IT Model a response. I can see this as a puppet show. I see puppets made of paper bags or old socks acting out the story behind a stage made of a tall cardboard box.

1. RETELL Have children use the retelling strip in the Student Edition to retell the story.

Monitor Progress | **Check Retelling**

If... children have difficulty retelling the story,

then... use the Retelling Cards and Scoring Rubric for Retelling on p. 150–151 to help them move toward fluent retelling.

SUCCESS PREDICTOR

Day 1 Check Word Reading ┊ **Day 2** Check High-Frequency Words ┊ ▶**Day 3 Check Retelling** ┊ **Day 4** Check Fluency ┊ **Day 5** Assess Progress

2. ◉ REALISM AND FANTASY Model a response. *The Strongest One* is a fantasy because it is about animals and things that act like people, which they can't do in real life.

3. ◉ MONITOR AND FIX UP Model a response. A play is different from other stories because it just lists the characters and tells what they say. It also gives stage directions. This made me read what the characters said and imagine how they looked and felt.

LOOK BACK AND WRITE Read the writing prompt on p. 150 and model your thinking. I'll look back at page 135 and read what Little Red Ant says about why he wants to find the strongest one. I know what he says here. I can write that. Then I can write some details to explain my answer. Have children write their responses.

Scoring Rubric | **Look Back and Write**

Top-Score Response A top-score response will use details from p. 135 and other parts of the selection to tell why Little Red Ant wanted to find the strongest one.

Example of a Top-Score Response Little Red Ant hoped the strongest one would teach the ants how to be stronger. He talked to characters such as Snow, Sun, and Wind, to animals, and even to Fire, Water, and Big Rock. He found out that everything is stronger than something else. In some ways ants are the strongest of all!

For additional rubrics, see p. WA10.

Reader Response

Think and Share

Talk About It You could do this play as a dance or a puppet show. Tell how.

1. Use the pictures below to retell the story. On another piece of paper, draw more pictures to show the missing parts. **Retell**

2. Is *The Strongest One* a realistic story or a fantasy? What makes it so? **Realism and Fantasy**

3. How is a play different from other selections? How did that change the way you read it? **Monitor and Fix Up**

Look Back and Write Look back at page 135. Why does Little Red Ant want to find the strongest one? Use details from the selection in your answer.

Meet the Author
Joseph Bruchac

Read more books by Joseph Bruchac.

As a child, Joseph Bruchac loved to explore nature—the animals, birds, insects, and plants around him. His grandfather, an Abenaki Indian, taught him many things about nature.

Today, Mr. Bruchac tells traditional Native American stories. "In the Abenaki Indian tradition," he says, "there is a story connected to just about every bird, animal, and plant." One message in many of these tales is that all parts of nature are important. Even tiny ants can make a difference!

Retelling Strip

150

151

Scoring Rubric | Narrative Retelling

Rubric 4 3 2 1	4	3	2	1
Connections	Makes connections and generalizes beyond the text	Makes connections to other events, stories, or experiences	Makes a limited connection to another event, story, or experience	Makes no connection to another event, story, or experience
Author's Purpose	Elaborates on author's purpose	Tells author's purpose with some clarity	Makes some connection to author's purpose	Makes no connection to author's purpose
Characters	Describes the main character(s) and any character development	Identifies the main character(s) and gives some information about them	Inaccurately identifies some characters or gives little information about them	Inaccurately identifies the characters or gives no information about them
Setting	Describes the time and location	Identifies the time and location	Omits details of time or location	Is unable to identify time or location
Plot	Describes the events in sequence, using rich detail	Tells the plot with some errors in sequence that do not affect meaning	Tells parts of plot with gaps that affect meaning	Retelling has no sense of story

Use the Retelling Chart on p. TR20 to record retelling.

Selection Test To assess with *The Strongest One*, use Selection Tests, pp. 17–20.

Fresh Reads for Differentiated Test Practice For weekly leveled practice, use pp. 25–30.

Retelling

SUCCESS PREDICTOR

3

$\bullet\bullet\bullet\bullet\bullet\bullet\bullet\bullet\bullet\bullet\bullet\bullet\bullet\bullet\bullet\bullet\bullet\bullet$ **LANGUAGE ARTS** $\bullet\bullet\bullet\bullet\bullet\bullet\bullet\bullet\bullet\bullet$

OBJECTIVE

● Recognize and use good sentences in writing.

DAILY FIX-IT

5. Does an ant bite icth.
   Does an ant bite <u>itch</u>?

6. oh, it stings too
   <u>Oh</u>, it stings too<u>!</u>

Connect to Unit Writing

Writing Trait

Have children use strategies for developing **sentences** when they write a personal narrative in the Unit Writing Workshop, pp. WA2–WA9.

Sentences Have language learners read their sentences aloud to check rhythm, completeness, and sense. Point out opportunities to change a declarative sentence to another type or to vary sentence beginnings.

Writing Trait of the Week

INTRODUCE Sentences

TALK ABOUT SENTENCES Explain to children that good writers use different kinds of sentences to give their writing rhythm and style. A mix of short and longer sentences lets writing flow. Ask children to think about some different kinds of sentences in *The Strongest One*. Then model your thinking.

MODEL The characters in *The Strongest One* talk just like real people. When I look at the sentences said by the characters, I notice that some are short and some are longer. Some are questions, some are exclamations, and some are statements. Using different kinds of sentences makes the words the characters say sound realistic. Here are some sentences that Snow says on page 137.

Sun is stronger. When Sun shines on me, I melt away. Here it comes!

What different kinds of sentences does Snow use here? *(two statements and an exclamation)* Are the lengths of sentences the same or different? *(different; two are short and one is long)*

STRATEGY FOR DEVELOPING SENTENCES On the board, write the following two groups of ideas. Ask children to put each group of ideas together into a sentence. Point out that combining a few ideas instead of using each one in its own sentence creates sentence variety.

across the sky
the clouds
Wind blows *(Wind blows the clouds across the sky.)*

of Big Rock
Red Ants carry away
little pieces *(Red Ants carry away little pieces of Big Rock.)*

PRACTICE

APPLY THE STRATEGY Ask children to write two short sentences and two long sentences about characters in the play that are strong. Remind them to use correct capitalization and end punctuation. Have volunteers read sentences aloud.

Grammar

APPLY TO WRITING
Commands and Exclamations

IMPROVE WRITING WITH COMMANDS AND EXCLAMATIONS Explain to children that they can improve their writing by varying the kinds of sentences they use. Sometimes they can include exclamations if something is exciting. If they are writing what someone says or if they are giving someone directions, they might also include commands. Remind children to use commands and exclamations correctly in their own writing.

Have children write several sentences about something exciting that happened at a playground or park. Encourage them to include at least one command and exclamation.

"Get the balls and gloves," Tina told the other kids. "Let's have a good game!" She threw the ball to Kevin. It hit him on the arm. "Ouch!" Kevin said. "That hurt!"

PRACTICE

WRITE WITH COMMANDS AND EXCLAMATIONS Have children add to the story about Tina and Kevin, writing more commands and exclamations.

Commands and Exclamations

Imagine that you are a character in the story.
Tell why you are the strongest one.
Use a command and an exclamation.

Possible answer: Look at
how strong I am. I can move
anything! Now watch this.
I can blow that house down!
I am the strongest!

Home Activity Your child learned about how to use commands and exclamations in writing sentences. Have your child write commands and exclamations on sticky notes and post them in appropriate places, for example, a note on the refrigerator that says *I am hungry!*

▲ **Grammar and Writing Practice Book** p. 18

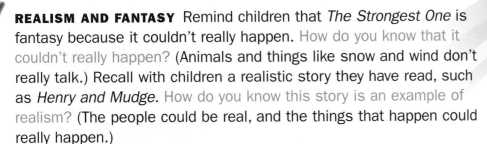

Wrap Up Your Day!

 REALISM AND FANTASY Remind children that *The Strongest One* is fantasy because it couldn't really happen. How do you know that it couldn't really happen? (Animals and things like snow and wind don't really talk.) Recall with children a realistic story they have read, such as *Henry and Mudge.* How do you know this story is an example of realism? (The people could be real, and the things that happen could really happen.)

EXPRESSION AND INTONATION Remind children that when they read what a character in a story is saying, they should make their voices sound the way that character's would.

LET'S TALK ABOUT IT Show children the web begun previously with *Whom Can We Ask?* in the center circle. Invite children to use what they've heard and read during the week to add to the web.

PREVIEW Day 4

Tell children that tomorrow they will hear more about someone searching for answers in a story called *"Can Hens Give Milk?"*

Share Literature
"Can Hens Give Milk?"

Phonics and Spelling

Consonant Digraphs

Spelling: Words with Consonant Digraphs

Read
Group Time < Differentiated Instruction

"Anteaters"

Fluency
Read with Expression/Intonation

Writing Across the Curriculum
Labels

Grammar
Commands and Exclamations

Speaking and Listening
Ask and Answer Questions

Materials

- *Sing with Me Big Book*
- *Read Aloud Anthology*
- Student Edition 152–155

Morning Warm-Up!

Some animals eat the strangest things! Today we will read about the anteater. Anteaters search for food in an unsual way. How do you think anteaters search?

QUESTION OF THE DAY Encourage children to sing "Where to Inquire" from the *Sing with Me Big Book* as you gather. Write and read the message and discuss the questions.

REVIEW SYNONYMS

- Point out the word *strangest*. What are some synonyms, or words that mean almost the same thing, for *strangest*? (Possible answers: *weirdest, most unusual, oddest*)

- Brainstorm synonyms for *unusual* as used in the message. (Possible answers: *odd, extraordinary, uncommon*)

Extend Language Use the Day 4 instruction on ELL Poster 5 to extend and enrich language.

ELL Poster 5

Share Literature

CONNECT CONCEPTS

ACTIVATE PRIOR KNOWLEDGE Review with children what they have read and learned about whom we can ask when we look for answers. Invite discussion about whom Little Red Ant asked for answers. Explain that you will read a different kind of story about finding answers.

Read Aloud Anthology
Can Hens Give Milk?

BUILD ORAL VOCABULARY Write *a smile of satisfaction* on the board and read it aloud. Discuss with children what **satisfaction** means— a feeling of being satisfied or contented and pleased. How would you smile if you were feeling pleased and happy? Invite children to demonstrate what they think a smile of satisfaction would look like. Discuss that a **genius** is someone who is very intelligent, or brilliant. Tell children to listen to the story to find out if anyone is really a genius and why someone smiles with satisfaction.

REVIEW ORAL VOCABULARY After reading, review all the Amazing Words for the week. Have children take turns using them in sentences that tell about the concept for the week. Then talk about Amazing Words they learned in other weeks and connect them to the concept, as well. For example, ask:

- What sorts of **discoveries** can you make when you ask questions?

- Do you think people will discover the secrets of the **universe?** Why or why not?

- Whom could you ask to learn more about **landforms** or **precipitation?**

MONITOR LISTENING COMPREHENSION

- Who had a smile of satisfaction? (Shlomo) Why? (because he thought he had figured out how to have the hens give milk)

- Do you think Shlomo was a genius? Why or why not? (no, because a genius would not have had such a silly idea)

- Who might have had smiles of satisfaction after the rabbi solved the problem? Why? (Possible answer: the rabbi, Shlomo, and Rivka because the rabbi had solved the problem so they all now had both eggs and milk)

OBJECTIVES

- Set purpose for listening.
- Build oral vocabulary.

to build oral vocabulary

	MONITOR PROGRESS
delicate inquire sturdy exhibit resist stun genius satisfaction	**If...** children lack oral vocabulary experiences about the concept Exploration, **then...** use the Oral Vocabulary Routine. See p. DI·7 to teach *genius* and *satisfaction*.

Connect Concepts Explain to children that this is a make-believe story about people who lived a long time ago. Make sure children understand that a rabbi is a wise leader of the Jewish people.

Spiral REVIEW

- Reviews consonant digraphs and consonant blends.
- Reviews high-frequency words *animals, early, eyes, full, warm, water.*

Sentence Reading

REVIEW WORDS IN CONTEXT

READ DECODABLE AND HIGH-FREQUENCY WORDS IN CONTEXT Write these sentences. Call on individuals to read a sentence. Then randomly point to words and have them read. To help you monitor word reading, high-frequency words are underlined and decodable words are circled.

Did Mitch catch that fish in the water by the ship?

When I get sleepy I stretch and then shut my eyes.

Check to see if these buns are fresh and warm.

The animals by the shrubs had thin legs.

I wake up early and then I brush my hair.

Each trash bin was full of cans we had to wash and crush.

Monitor Progress	Word Reading
If... children are unable to read an underlined word,	**then...** read the word for them and spell it, having them echo you.
If... children are unable to read a circled word,	**then...** have them use the blending strategy they have learned for that word type.

ELL

Support Phonics For additional review, see the phonics activities in the ELL and Transition Handbook.

Spelling

PARTNER REVIEW Consonant Digraphs

READ AND WRITE Supply pairs of children with index cards on which the spelling words have been written. Have one child read a word while the other writes it. Then have children switch roles. Have them use the cards to check their spelling.

HOMEWORK Spelling Practice Book, p. 20

OBJECTIVE

● Spell words with consonant digraphs.

Spelling Words

Consonant Digraphs

1. **bunch**
2. **that***
3. **wish**
4. **patch**
5. **when***
6. **what***
7. **math**
8. **them**
9. **shape**
10. **whale**
11. **itch**
12. **chase***

Challenge Words

13. **whiskers**
14. **switch**
15. **shrimp**

* Words from the Selection

Group Time

ANTEATERS
By John Jacobs

On-Level	Strategic Intervention	Advanced
Read "Anteaters."	**Read** or listen to "Anteaters."	**Read** "Anteaters."
• Use pp. 152–155.	• Use the **Routine** on p. DI·60.	• Use the **Routine** on p. DI·61.

 Place English language learners in the groups that correspond to their reading abilities in English.

(i) Independent Activities

Fluency Reading Pair children to reread *The Strongest One.*

Journal Writing Write about fun things that can happen inside a sturdy tree house. Share writing.

Spelling Partner Review

Independent Reading See p. 128j for Reading/Library activities and suggestions.

Literacy Centers To provide listening opportunities, you may use the Listening Center on p. 128j. To extend social studies concepts, you may use the Social Studies Center on p. 128k.

Digraphs *ch, tch, sh, th, wh*
Unscramble the letters. **Write** the word.

1. p e s a h	**shape**	
2. c a s h e	**chase**	
3. n e w h	**when**	
4. t a h m	**math**	
5. h i s w	**wish**	
6. h l e w a	**whale**	
7. c t h i	**itch**	

Spelling Words

bunch	math
that	them
wish	shape
patch	whale
when	itch
what	chase

Write list words to complete the tongue twisters.

1. Bev bought the best **bunch** of big beans.
2. Did **that** thin thief thank **them**?
3. Please **patch** pant pockets.

School + Home **Home Activity** Your child has been learning to spell words with *ch, tch, sh, th,* and *wh.* Help your child look for these letter combinations in the words on a calendar.

DAY 4

▲ **Spelling Practice Book** p. 20

4

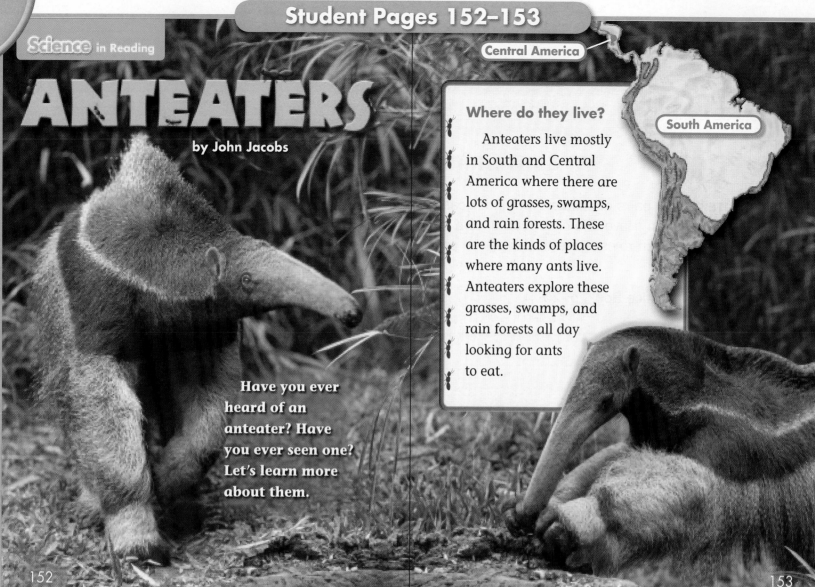

Science in Reading

ANTEATERS
by John Jacobs

Central America

South America

Where do they live?

Anteaters live mostly in South and Central America where there are lots of grasses, swamps, and rain forests. These are the kinds of places where many ants live. Anteaters explore these grasses, swamps, and rain forests all day looking for ants to eat.

Have you ever heard of an anteater? Have you ever seen one? Let's learn more about them.

152

153

 **AudioText**

Read
Science in Reading

PREVIEW AND PREDICT Read the title on p. 152. Have children look at the pictures and subheadings on pp. 152–155 to preview the article. Ask them to predict what "Anteaters" will be about. Have children read to find the answers to the questions in the subheadings.

INFORMATIONAL TEXT Explain that selections that give information, like this one, often are organized with subheadings that tell what information follows. For example, point out the first subheading on p. 153 and read it aloud. The subheading asks the question *Where do they live?* So we can expect that the section after this subheading will tell us where anteaters live.

VOCABULARY/SYNONYMS Review with children that synonyms are words with the same or almost the same meaning. On p. 154, point out the phrases *tiny mouth* and *small eyes.* Which two words are synonyms? *(tiny, small)*

OBJECTIVE
● Recognize text structure: nonfiction.

Geography *Time for SOCIAL STUDIES*

Rain forests take up only a small part of the Earth's land surface—about 6 percent—but support more than half of the world's plant and animal species. One tree in a South American rain forest can be home to more than 40 species of ants.

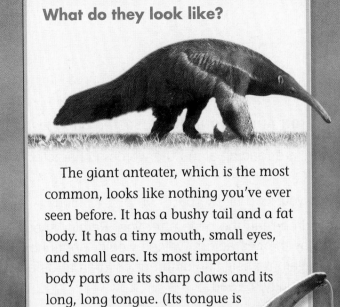

What do they look like?

The giant anteater, which is the most common, looks like nothing you've ever seen before. It has a bushy tail and a fat body. It has a tiny mouth, small eyes, and small ears. Its most important body parts are its sharp claws and its long, long tongue. (Its tongue is almost two feet long. That's as long as two rulers put together!)

154

How do they eat?

An anteater looks for ants by smelling the ground. When it finds an ants' nest, the anteater breaks it open with its sharp claws. It puts its long tongue down into the nest. Ants stick to the tongue and the anteater swallows them. The anteater does this over and over very fast until it is full. The anteater eats only a small number of ants at a time from any one nest. It does not want to run out of food! But ants, beware! It will return.

155

BUILD CONCEPTS

Draw Conclusions • Inferential

- **Why do you think an anteater's sharp claws and long tongue are so important?**
Possible response: The anteater needs sharp claws to dig for ants and a long tongue to reach them.

Cause and Effect • Critical

- **Why do you think anteaters are an important part of the rain forests?**
Possible response: Anteaters are important because they eat so many ants. If anteaters didn't eat ants, there would be too many ants.

CONNECT TEXT TO TEXT

Why do you think Little Red Ant didn't go to an anteater to inquire who was the strongest of all?
Probably because an anteater would have eaten Little Red Ant.

Activate Prior Knowledge Invite children who have lived in Central or South America to tell what they know about the rain forests.

- Read with expression and intonation.

Options for Oral Reading

Use *The Strongest One* or one of the following Leveled Readers.

On-Level

The Bear Man

Strategic Intervention

The Case of the Missing Fish

Advanced

Sue's Hummingbird

Use *Rabbit and Coyote* or "Anteaters." Provide opportunities for children to echo read, repeating a passage phrase-by-phrase as each phrase is read aloud by a teacher, aide, or another skilled reader such as a proficient student.

 To develop fluent readers, use Fluency Coach.

Fluency

READ WITH EXPRESSION AND INTONATION

MODEL READING WITH EXPRESSION AND INTONATION Use *The Strongest One.*

Remind children that when they are reading aloud the words a character is saying, they need to make their voices sound the way the character's would.

- Ask children to follow along as you read all the parts on p. 143 aloud.
- Assign the parts and have children read the page after you. Remind them to make their voices sound the way the characters' voices would. Continue in the same way with pp. 145–148, again reassigning different children to different parts to give everyone an opportunity to read.

REREAD FOR FLUENCY

Choral Reading

ROUTINE

1. **Select a Passage** For *The Strongest One,* reread pp. 136–141.

2. **Divide into Characters** Assign pairs of children to each part. You may want to have the part of Little Red Ant read by a different pair on each page.

3. **Model** Have children track the print as you read the Narrator, stage directions, and Little Red Ant on p. 136.

4. **Read Together** Have children read their parts along with you.

5. **Independent Readings** Have the pairs read aloud without you. Monitor progress and provide feedback. For optimal fluency, children should reread three to four times, so you may want to reassign pairs and characters.

Monitor Progress | Check Fluency WCPM

As children reread, monitor their progress toward their individual fluency goals. Current Goal: 50–60 words correct per minute. End-of-Year Goal: 90 words correct per minute.

If... children cannot read fluently at a rate of 50–60 words correct per minute,

then... make sure children practice with text at their independent level. Provide additional fluency practice, pairing nonfluent readers with fluent readers.

If... children already read fluently at 90 words correct per minute,

then... they do not need to reread three to four times.

SUCCESS PREDICTOR

Day 1 Check Word Reading   **Day 2** Check High-Frequency Words   **Day 3** Check Retelling   ▶ **Day 4 Check Fluency**   **Day 5** Assess Progress

Writing Across the Curriculum

WRITE Labels

LOOK AT THE PICTURES Ask children to think about what an anteater looks like. Ask how they might find the answer. Then have them look at the pictures of the anteater on pp. 152–155. Review the description of the anteater on p. 154 with them. Ask: What parts of an anteater do you think might be sturdy? What part might be delicate?

SHARE THE PEN Have children draw a picture of an anteater. Draw a simple outline on the board for them to copy. Tell children that they will work together to make labels for their drawing. Ask a volunteer to name a part of the anteater, such as its *tail*. What kind of tail does an anteater have? (a bushy tail) Write *bushy tail* as a label by the tail. As you write the label, invite individuals to help spell the words by writing familiar letter-sounds. Ask questions such as the following:

- What is the first sound you hear in *bushy*? (/b/)
- What letter stands for that sound? *(b)* Have a volunteer write *b.*
- How is /sh/ spelled? *(sh)*

Continue having individuals contribute to writing the labels as the class names parts of the anteater. Reread the items frequently.

OBJECTIVE

● Create a labeled picture.

Advanced

Help children do additional research in an encyclopedia or on the Internet to find out more about anteaters. Have them extend their drawings and labels to include the anteater's surroundings.

Support Writing Before children write the labels, review the list of body parts on p. 154 with them. You may want to have them brainstorm by making a web of lists of words that are familiar terms to them for *tail, eyes, ears,* and so on.

OBJECTIVE

• Identify commands and exclamations.

DAILY FIX-IT

7. take me to see the anteater
Take me to see the anteater.

8. It has such a strange shap
It has such a strange shape!

Commands and Exclamations

Mark the correct sentence in each group.

1. ⊗ A You are very strong!
   ○ B you are very strong.
   ○ C You are very strong

2. ○ A blow out the match.
   ⊗ B Blow out the match.
   ○ C blow out the match!

3. ○ A shoot the arrow!
   ○ B shoot the arrow.
   ⊗ C Shoot the arrow.

4. ○ A catch the cat!
   ⊗ B Catch the cat.
   ○ C catch the cat.

5. ⊗ A The wind chased me!
   ○ B the wind chased me!
   ○ C the wind chased me.

6. ○ A the rock is the strongest!
   ○ B the rock is the strongest.
   ⊗ C The rock is the strongest!

 Home Activity Your child prepared for taking tests on commands and exclamations. With your child, look through a magazine and find and mark five examples each of commands and exclamations.

▲ **Grammar and Writing Practice Book** p. 19

Grammar

REVIEW Commands and Exclamations

DEFINE COMMANDS AND EXCLAMATIONS

• What is a command? (a sentence that tells someone to do something) How does a written command end? (with a period) What is the subject of a command sentence? (*you*, but *you* is usually not shown in the sentence)

• What is an exclamation? (a sentence that shows surprise or shows strong feelings) How does a written exclamation end? (with an exclamation mark)

PRACTICE

IDENTIFY COMMANDS AND EXCLAMATIONS Write the following sentences, omitting the final punctuation. Read each sentence aloud. Have children identify each sentence as a command or exclamation and add the proper end punctuation.

Look at that anteater.

Oh, he looks so strange!

Find him some ants.

Wow, see how long his tongue is!

Speaking and Listening

ASK AND ANSWER QUESTIONS

OBJECTIVES
- Say, ask, and answer questions.
- Listen to be a polite listener.

MODEL ASKING AND ANSWERING QUESTIONS Tell children that there are many reasons for asking questions. Explain that when they ask or answer a question, they should always be polite. Model by asking a question orally and then answering it.

Asking Questions	Answering Questions
To find out something	Answer politely.
To learn something new	Look at the person speaking.
To make sure of something	

ASK AND ANSWER QUESTIONS Have children work in pairs. Tell them that one partner should start by asking the other partner this question: *When we are searching for answers, whom can we ask?* Then have the other partner answer by suggesting one person who might provide answers to our questions. Finally, have partners reverse roles.

Wrap Up Your Day!

✓ **MAKING CONNECTIONS: Text to World** Discuss with children that the anteater is an unusual animal that they have probably never seen in real life. Ask: How can you find out about animals you don't see every day? Where could you go? What could you look at?

LET'S TALK ABOUT IT Discuss how children could find out more about other animals in the world. When you are searching for answers, whom can you ask? Encourage children to add to the web they began earlier with the question *Whom Can We Ask?*

PREVIEW Day 5

Remind children that they heard a story about two foolish people who thought hens could give milk. Tell them that tomorrow they will hear about Shlomo and Rivka again.

Day 5

AT A GLANCE

Share Literature
"Can Hens Give Milk?"

Phonics and Spelling
Review Consonant Digraphs *ch, tch, sh, th, wh*

Spelling: Words with Consonant Digraphs *ch, tch, sh, th, wh*

High-Frequency Words
together   very   learn

often   though   gone

pieces

Word Wall

Monitor Progress
Spelling Test: Words with Consonant Digraphs *ch, tch, sh, th, wh*

Writing and Grammar
Trait: Sentences

Commands and Exclamations

Research and Study Skills
Maps

Materials

- *Sing with Me Big Book*
- *Read Aloud Anthology*
- Reproducible Pages TE 156f–156g
- Student Edition 156–157
- Graphic Organizer 15

Morning Warm-Up!

This week we read about asking questions.
What did we find out about whom we can ask when we are looking for answers?
Where can we inquire?

QUESTION OF THE DAY Encourage children to sing "Where to Inquire" from the *Sing with Me Big Book* as you gather. Write and read the message and discuss the questions.

REVIEW ORAL VOCABULARY

- What could be a synonym for **inquire** in the message? (ask)

- Have you ever found answers at an **exhibit?** Explain.

- When were you **stunned** by an answer?

- How could you find out whether an anteater's long tongue is **sturdy** or **delicate?**

- Might a **genius** get **satisfaction** from figuring out answers? Explain.

Assess Vocabulary Use the Day 5 instruction on ELL Poster 5 to monitor children's progress with oral vocabulary.

ELL Poster 5

Share Literature

LISTEN AND RESPOND

USE PRIOR KNOWLEDGE Recall with children that in the story "Can Hens Give Milk?" they discovered that Shlomo had a smile of satisfaction because he felt he had figured out how to make hens give milk. Suggest that children listen to the story again to find out who Rivka finally asks to figure out whether hens can give milk.

Read Aloud Anthology
Can Hens Give Milk?

MONITOR LISTENING COMPREHENSION

- Who did Rivka decide was the only one who could answer the question of whether hens can give milk? (the rabbi)

- Why did Rivka call Shlomo a genius when he told her he had figured out how to make hens give milk? (She was impressed with how smart he was to figure that out.)

- Was Rivka right when she called Shlomo a genius? How do you know? (No, because Shlomo really hadn't figured it out.)

- Do you think Rivka finally felt satisfaction after the rabbi solved the problem? Why or why not? (Yes, because they now had eggs and milk.) Do you think Shlomo felt satisfaction? Why or why not? (No, because he began to think about the goat laying eggs.)

BUILD ORAL VOCABULARY

GENERATE DISCUSSION Recall how Shlomo thought hens would be able to give milk if they ate the same food cows ate. Invite children to discuss things that they may have been sure about only to learn later that their ideas were incorrect. Have them use some of this week's Amazing Words as they share their stories.

Monitor Progress | Check Oral Vocabulary

Display pp. 128–129 in the Student Edition and remind children of the unit concept—Exploration. Ask them to tell you about the photographs using some of this week's Amazing Words: *delicate, inquire, sturdy, exhibit, resist, stun, genius,* and *satisfaction.*

If... children have difficulty using the Amazing Words,

then... ask questions about the photographs using the Amazing Words. Note which questions children can respond to. Reteach unknown words using the Oral Vocabulary Routine on p. DI·1.

SUCCESS PREDICTOR

Day 1 Check Word Reading	Day 2 Check High-Frequency Words	Day 3 Check Retelling	Day 4 Check Fluency	▶ Day 5 Check Oral Vocabulary/ Assess Progress

OBJECTIVES

- Set purpose for listening.
- Build oral vocabulary.

Amazing Words to build oral vocabulary

delicate	resist
inquire	stun
sturdy	genius
exhibit	satisfaction

ELL

Extend Language Recall that words that have the same or almost the same meaning are called *synonyms*. Let children work further with synonyms by listing the words *shout* and *said* on the board and helping them brainstorm synonyms for each word.

Oral Vocabulary

SUCCESS PREDICTOR

OBJECTIVES
- Review consonant digraphs.
- Review high-frequency words.

Consonant Digraphs

REVIEW

IDENTIFY CONSONANT BLEND WORDS Write these sentences. Have children read each one aloud. Call on individuals to name and underline the words with consonant digraphs and identify the sounds.

That bush has thick branches.

Dad gave Beth fish and chips.

Those things belong to my friend Shane.

My dog uses its mouth and teeth to catch the stick!

High-Frequency Words

REVIEW

COMPLETE THE SENTENCES Read the following sentences aloud. Have children write one of the Words to Read from p. 130 for each blank. Then read the completed sentences together.

The vase broke into many _____. (pieces)

I play with my friend Cole _____. (often)

I am strong even _____ I am small. (though)

My teacher helps me _____ my math. (learn)

The pie is all _____ now! (gone)

That dress is _____ long. (very)

You and I can work _____ on the project. (together)

ELL

Access Content For additional practice with the high-frequency words, use the vocabulary strategies and word cards in the ELL Teaching Guide, pp. 31–32.

SPELLING TEST Consonant Digraphs

DICTATION SENTENCES Use these sentences to assess this week's spelling words.

1. He stays in good <u>shape</u>.
2. Who is <u>that</u> new boy?
3. A <u>whale</u> is very big.
4. The dog likes to <u>chase</u> the cat.
5. We will pick a <u>bunch</u> of roses.
6. <u>When</u> will Dad come home today?
7. I <u>wish</u> I could fly!
8. Will you give the books to <u>them</u>?
9. I like to do <u>math</u> problems.
10. Do not scratch that <u>itch</u>!
11. Mom put a <u>patch</u> over the hole in my pants.
12. <u>What</u> will we eat for lunch?

CHALLENGE WORDS

13. The kitten has long <u>whiskers</u>.
14. Did you <u>switch</u> to another team?
15. We ate <u>shrimp</u> on Monday.

Group Time

On-Level	Strategic Intervention	Advanced
Read Set B Sentences and the Story for rechecking.	**Read** Set A Sentences and the Story for rechecking.	**Read** Set C Sentences and the Story for rechecking.
• Use pp. 156e–156g.	• Use pp. 156e–156g.	• Use pp. 156e–156g.
	• Use the **Routine** on p. DI·62.	• Use the **Routine** on p. DI·63.

DAY 5

 Place English language learners in the groups that correspond to their reading abilities in English.

(i) Independent Activities

Fluency Reading Children reread selections at their independent level.

Journal Writing Write a story about how something very delicate becomes sturdy. Share writing.

Independent Reading See p. 128j for Reading/Library activities and suggestions.

Literacy Centers You may use the Technology Center on p. 128k to support this week's concepts and reading.

Practice Book 2.1 Map, p. 50.

Break into small groups after Spelling and before Grammar and Writing.

ASSESS

- Decode words with consonant digraphs.
- Read high-frequency words.
- Read aloud with appropriate speed and accuracy.
- Distinguish between realism and fantasy
- Retell a story.

Differentiated Assessment

On-Level
Set B

Strategic Intervention
Set A

Advanced
Set C

Fluency Assessment Plan

☑ Week 1 assess Strategic Intervention students.

☑ Week 2 assess Advanced students.

☑ Week 3 assess Strategic Intervention students.

☑ Week 4 assess On-Level students.

☑ **This week assess any students you have not yet checked during this unit.**

Set individual fluency goals for children to enable them to reach the end-of-year goal.

- Current Goal: 50–60 wcpm
- End-of-Year Goal: 90 wcpm
- **ELL** Measuring a child's oral reading speed—words per minute— provides a low-stress informal assessment of fluency. Such an assessment should not take the place of more formal measures of words correct per minute.

SENTENCE READING

ASSESS CONSONANT DIGRAPHS AND HIGH-FREQUENCY WORDS Use one of the reproducible lists on p. 156f to assess children's ability to read words with consonant digraphs *ch, tch, sh, th, wh* and high-frequency words. Call on individuals to read two sentences aloud. Have each child in the group read different sentences. Start over with sentence one if necessary.

RECORD SCORES Use the Sentence Reading Chart for this unit on p. WA19.

Monitor Progress	Consonant Digraphs
If... children have trouble reading words with consonant digraphs,	**then...** use the Reteach Lesson on p. DI·68.
High-Frequency Words	
If... children cannot read a high-frequency word,	**then...** mark the missed word on a high-frequency word list and send the list home for additional word reading practice, or have the child practice with a fluent reader.

FLUENCY AND COMPREHENSION

ASSESS FLUENCY Take a one-minute sample of children's oral reading. See Monitoring Fluency, p. WA17. Have children read "Little Bear," the on-level fluency passage on p. 156g.

RECORD SCORES Record the number of words read correctly in one minute on the child's Fluency Progress Chart.

ASSESS COMPREHENSION Have the child read to the end of the passage. (If the child had difficulty with the passage, you may read it aloud.) Ask whether the story is realism or fantasy and how the child knows. Have the child retell the passage. Use the Retelling Rubric on p. 150–151 to evaluate the child's retelling.

Monitor Progress	Fluency
If... a child does not achieve the fluency goal on the timed reading,	**then...** copy the passage and send it home with the child for additional fluency practice, or have the child practice with a fluent reader.
Realism and Fantasy	
If... a child cannot distinguish between realism and fantasy,	**then...** use the Reteach Lesson on p. DI·68.

READ THE SENTENCES

Set A

1. Put the pieces of cloth together.
2. That chart is very big.
3. Garth said I can learn to fish.
4. His shirts often fit me.
5. It looks as though the wheel broke.
6. My watch is gone!

Set B

1. We can fix this thing together.
2. Look at that bunch of very big pieces.
3. I wish I could learn to play the flute.
4. The dog often wants to go with me.
5. I'll go there, though I don't want to.
6. Where have they gone?

Set C

1. Let's go to the show together.
2. I'll be very happy if you choose those pieces.
3. Can the baby learn to catch a ball?
4. Mothers often sit on that bench in the park.
5. The bag at home base should be white, though it looks pretty dirty now.
6. The chocolate chip cookies are all gone.

Monitor Progress | **Consonant Digraphs / High-Frequency Words**

SUCCESS PREDICTOR

Little Bear

Little Bear looked at the beautiful, huge tree.   8

"Mom said I can learn to go up there," she said   19

to herself. "I think I can do it if I just reach for the   33

right branch."   35

She watched a white bird fly into the tree.   44

"I wish I could fly straight up there. But I know   55

just thinking about that won't make it happen,"   63

Little Bear said.   66

"What are you waiting for?" the white bird   74

asked. "Bears everywhere in the world have gone   82

up trees. Just do it!"   87

So Little Bear started up, but then she   95

stopped. "I'm too short!" she said.   101

"No, you are not," the bird said. "You just have   111

to try, try, and try again."   117

"I'll just grit my teeth and do it," Little Bear said.   128

So she tried. And she fell. She tried and   137

she fell. She tried and she fell again. Then   146

she tried one last time.   151

And there she was, sitting on the branch.   159

"I learned to do it!" Little Bear said.   167

See also Assessment Handbook, p. 310 • REPRODUCIBLE PAGE

Monitor Progress   Fluency Passage

SUCCESS PREDICTOR

Write Now
Writing and Grammar

News Report

Prompt

The Strongest One is a play with animals that talk.
Think about what it would be like to discover a talking animal.
Now write a news report about it.

Writing Trait
Different kinds of **sentences** make writing smoother.

Student Model

Events are told in order they happened.

Exclamation shows writer's feelings.

Writer uses different kinds of sentences.

A talking raccoon appeared in my yard today. It was sitting next to a bush. It said, "Hi, my name is Rusty. Can I have a snack?" I could not believe my ears! "Wait right here, Rusty." When I came back, Rusty was gone. No other neighbors saw him.

156

Writer's Checklist

- ⏱ **Focus** Do all sentences tell about a talking animal?
- ⏱ **Organization** Are events told in order?
- ⏱ **Support** Does the report include different kinds of sentences?
- ⏱ **Conventions** Do sentences have correct end marks?

Grammar

Commands and Exclamations

A **command** is a sentence that tells someone to do something. It usually ends with a **period (.).**

Be careful out there**.**

An **exclamation** is a sentence that shows surprise or strong feeling. It ends with an **exclamation mark (!).**

I am excited**!**

Write a command and an exclamation from the news report. Circle the period and the exclamation mark.

157

Writing and Grammar

LOOK AT THE PROMPT Read p. 156 aloud. Have children select and discuss key words or phrases in the prompt. *(animals that talk, discover a talking animal, news report)*

STRATEGIES TO DEVELOP SENTENCES Have children

- try to include at least one exclamation, one command, and one question in their reports.
- look at the beginning words in their sentences and change them if they are used too often.
- count the short and long sentences and make sure they have some of both.

See Scoring Rubric on p. WA12. **Rubric** 4 3 2 1

HINTS FOR BETTER WRITING Read p. 157 aloud. Use the checklist to help children revise their reports. Discuss the grammar lesson. (Answers: Command: *"Wait right here, Rusty."* Exclamation: *I could not believe my ears!* Children should circle the period and the exclamation mark.) Have children use correct end marks for commands and exclamations in their news reports.

DAILY FIX-IT

9. look for ants near trees
   <u>L</u>ook for ants near trees<u>.</u>

10. watch out, they bite
    <u>W</u>atch out, they bite<u>!</u>

Commands and Exclamations

Write *C* if the sentence is a command.
Write *E* if it is an exclamation.

1. Knock on the door. — **C**

2. Come in the house. — **C**

3. Wow! I'm afraid of the dark! — **E**

Write each sentence correctly.

4. push the rock
   Push the rock.

5. look at Ant
   Look at Ant.

6. how strong Ant is
   How strong Ant is!

Home Activity Your child reviewed commands and exclamations. Write the commands and exclamations from this page on index cards. Hold up a card. Have your child read the sentence and tell whether it is a command or an exclamation.

▲ **Grammar and Writing Practice Book** p. 20

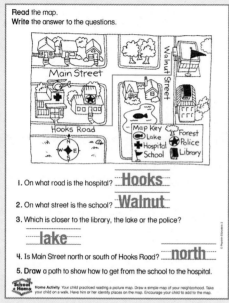

Read the map.
Write the answer to the questions.

Main Street

Walnut Street

Hooks Road

Map Key
🐟 Lake
➕ Hospital
🏫 School
🌲 Forest
★ Police
🏛 Library

1. On what road is the hospital? **Hooks**

2. On what street is the school? **Walnut**

3. Which is closer to the library, the lake or the police?
lake

4. Is Main Street north or south of Hooks Road? **north**

5. **Draw** a path to show how to get from the school to the hospital.

Home Activity Your child practiced reading a picture map. Draw a simple map of your neighborhood. Take your child on a walk. Have him or her identify places on the map. Encourage your child to add to the map.

▲ **Practice Book 2.1** p. 50, Maps

Research/Study Skills

TEACH/MODEL Maps

MODEL USING A MAP Draw and label a simple map of several blocks of the neighborhood around your school. Label street names, some familiar buildings, the school name, playground, and other familiar features. Put a star symbol at the door of the school and draw a dotted line from the star symbol to the place where children enter the schoolyard from the school bus. Put an X at that spot. In one corner of the map, make a brief legend that tells what the star symbol, dotted line, and X represent. Explain to children that a map is an outline picture of a place as if it were taken from the sky. When you are looking for a way to get somewhere, you can use a map. Help children read the labels and ask them to point out various places on the map.

Model how to trace a route between two places.

Think Aloud

MODEL I'm searching for the answer to how to get from the bus to the door of the school. I know I can use a map to figure it out. First I look at the map key that shows me which symbol stands for the bus stop and which symbol stands for the door. Then I follow the dotted line, which the map key tells me is the route to take, from the bus to the door. Now I know how to get from one place to the other.

TRACE ROUTES Call on individuals to trace other routes not already on the map, such as the way from the school to a certain street corner or to the school from another building on the map.

PRACTICE

DEMONSTRATE USING A MAP Have children draw a map that shows how to get to school from where they live. If they are not likely to know the route, provide a fictional location on the map you have provided and have them show how to get from there to the school or between two other places on the map.

Access Content As you draw and label the map, discuss each item, making sure children grasp how the label and drawing connect to actual places around school.

Wrap Up Your Week!

LET'S TALK ABOUT Exploration

QUESTION OF THE WEEK Recall this week's question.

• When we are searching for answers, whom can we ask?

Display the web that children began earlier in the week. Review how they filled out some of the circles to show whom they could ask when they search for answers. Invite them to add other circles as necessary to the web so that they can add several things Little Red Ant asked when he was searching for answers.

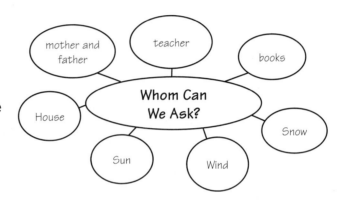

CONNECT Use questions such as these to prompt a discussion:

• Is a saguaro cactus sturdy or delicate? What makes you think so?

• Suppose you met Iris, Walter, or Henry. What would you want to inquire?

• If you went to a desert museum, what kind of exhibit would you want to see?

• What stunned you the most about exploring space with the astronauts?

• Which of the stories that we read during this unit did you enjoy the most— *Iris and Walter, Henry and Mudge,* or *The Strongest One?* Why?

Build Background Use ELL Poster 6 to support the Preview activity.

You've learned	You've learned
008 *Amazing Words*	**040** *Amazing Words*
this week!	so far this year!

PREVIEW Tell children that next week they will read about how people and animals can work together and help each other.

PREVIEW Next Week

Assessment Checkpoints *for the Week*

Selection Assessment

Use pp. 17–20 of Selection Tests **to check:**

 Selection Understanding

 Comprehension Skill *Realism and Fantasy*

 High–Frequency Words

gone	though
learn	together
often	very
pieces	

Leveled Assessment

On-Level

Strategic Intervention

Advanced

Use pp. 25–30 of Fresh Reads for Differentiated Test Practice **to check:**

 Comprehension Skill *Realism and Fantasy*

 REVIEW **Comprehension Skill** *Character and Setting*

 Fluency *Words Correct Per Minute*

Managing Assessment

Use Assessment Handbook **for:**

 Weekly Assessment Blackline Masters for Monitoring Progress

 Observation Checklists

 Record-Keeping Forms

 Portfolio Assessment

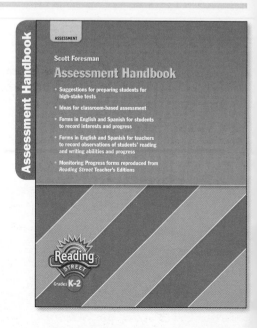

Unit 1
Concept Wrap-Up

CONCEPT QUESTION

What can we learn from exploring new places and things?

Children are ready to express their understanding of the unit concept question through discussion and wrap-up activities and to take the Unit 1 Benchmark Test.

Unit Wrap-Up

Use the Unit Wrap-Up on pp. 158–159 to discuss the unit theme, Exploration, and to have children show their understanding of the theme through cross-curricular activities.

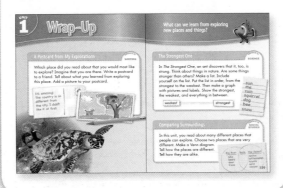

Unit Project

On p. 11 you assigned children a unit-long inquiry project, to plan a trip to explore a place where they would learn new and exciting things. Children have investigated, analyzed, and synthesized information during the course of the unit as they prepared their plans. Schedule time for children to present their projects. The project rubric can be found below.

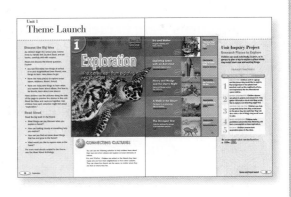

Unit Inquiry Project Rubric

4	3	2	1
• Presentation is highly detailed. Sources are relevant to inquiry question. Map is detailed and accurate. • Child has a detailed list of things to explore as well as expectations. List is complete and detailed.	• Presentation presents expectations but is not as thorough. Most sources are relevant to inquiry question. • The list of resources is useful, but not organized as well as it could be. Map is accurate but not detailed. List is complete but not too detailed.	• Presentation is vague and has little information that is relevant to inquiry question. Map has some inaccuracies. • List of resources is not always helpful and not organized. List is not complete and not well thought out.	• Presentation is not relevant to inquiry question. • List of resources is incomplete and not helpful. Map is neither complete nor accurate. List is incomplete and not useful.

Unit 1
Wrap-Up

OBJECTIVES

- Discuss the unit theme.
- Connect content across selections.
- Combine content and skills in meaningful activities that build literacy.
- Respond to unit selections through a variety of modalities.

EXPLORATION

Discuss the Big Idea

What can we learn from exploring new places and things?

Help children relate the theme question for this unit to the selections and their own experiences. Write the questions and prompt discussion with questions such as the following. Then assign the Wrap-Up activities.

- **What did the characters in these selections learn in their explorations?** (Possible answers: *Iris and Walter* Iris and Walter discover a friendship in a new place and Walter learns how to roller-skate indoors. *Exploring Space with an Astronaut* Astronauts learn about space. *Henry and Mudge and the Starry Night* Henry learns what it's like to camp outdoors. *A Walk in the Desert* Many different animals and plants can be explored in the desert. *The Strongest One* An ant learns the answer to its question.)

- **Which place from these selections would you like to explore and why?** (Possible answers: I want to explore the desert because there are so many different kinds of plants and animals that are not found elsewhere. Space would be a great place to go because it is so different from Earth and difficult to get to.)

A Postcard from My Explorations

connect

WRITIN

Which place did you read about that you would most like to explore? Imagine that you are there. Write a postcard to a friend. Tell about what you learned from exploring this place. Add a picture to your postcard.

It's amazing! The country is so different from the city. I didn't like it at first.

158

What can we learn from exploring new places and things?

The Strongest One

connect to
SCIENCE

In *The Strongest One*, an ant discovers that it, too, is strong. Think about things in nature. Are some things stronger than others? Make a list. Include yourself on the list. Put the list in order, from the strongest to the weakest. Then make a graph with pictures and labels. Show the strongest, the weakest, and everything in between.

| weakest —————— strongest |

sun
me
rain
squirrel
dog
bee
snow

Comparing Surroundings

connect to
SOCIAL STUDIES

In this unit, you read about many different places that people can explore. Choose two places that are very different. Make a Venn diagram. Tell how the places are different. Tell how they are alike.

Big Bear | Both | The Desert
lake
bears
deer
trees

cactus
rattlesnakes
coyote
sand
canyon

159

ACTIVITIES

A Postcard from My Explorations

Draw and Write Have children brainstorm places they would like to explore. Provide index cards and have them draw a picture of the place they choose on one side and write a note to a friend about what they learn as the explore on the other. Show them a model of a postcard and tell them where to write the note and the address.

The Strongest One

Make a Graph Have children make their lists first and then write numbers to show the order from strongest to weakest. Finally have them make the graph with pictures and labels.

Comparing Surroundings

Draw a Venn Diagram Have partners work together to choose two places that are very different, such as the desert and outer space. Then have them tell how the places are the same in the overlapping circles and how they are different in the right and left circles. Have partners share their results with the class.

Glossary

Aa

agriculture (ag ruh KUL cher) **Agriculture** is farming and growing crops. *NOUN*

amazing (uh MAY zing) Something that is **amazing** is very surprising: The hero made an **amazing** escape. *ADJECTIVE*

astronaut (ASS truh nawt) An **astronaut** is a person who has been trained to fly in a spacecraft. While in space, **astronauts** repair space stations and do experiments. *NOUN*

astronaut

Bb

brave (BRAYV) If you are **brave**, you are not afraid: The **brave** girl pulled her little brother away from the burning leaves. *ADJECTIVE*

buried (BAIR eed) If you have **buried** something, you have hidden or covered it up: It was so cold that she **buried** her head under the covers. *VERB*

Cc

cactus (KAK tuhss) A **cactus** is a plant with sharp parts but no leaves. Most **cactuses** grow in very hot, dry areas of North and South America. Many have bright flowers. *NOUN*

cactus

challenge (CHAL lunj) To **challenge** is to call or invite someone to a game or contest: The knight **challenged** his rival to fight a duel. *VERB*

chiles (CHIL ayz) **Chiles** are a green or red pepper with a hot taste. *NOUN*

climate (KLY mit) **Climate** is the kind of weather a place has. *NOUN*

clutched (KLUCHT) To **clutch** is to hold something tightly: I **clutched** the railing to keep from falling. *VERB*

collar (KOL er) A **collar** is a band that is put around the neck of a dog or other pet. **Collars** can be made of leather or plastic. *NOUN*

college (KOL ij) **College** is the school that you go to after high school: After I finish high school, I plan to go to **college** to become a teacher. *NOUN*

coyote (ky OH tee or KY oht) A **coyote** is a small animal that looks something like a wolf. **Coyotes** have light yellow fur and bushy tails. *NOUN*

coyote

Dd

dam (DAM) A **dam** is a wall built to hold back the water of a creek, lake, or river. *NOUN*

dangerous (DAYN jer uhss) Something that is **dangerous** is not safe: Skating on thin ice is **dangerous**. *ADJECTIVE*

delicious (di LISH uhss) When something is **delicious**, it tastes or smells very good: The cookies were **delicious**. *ADJECTIVE*

desert (DEZ ert) A **desert** is a place without water or trees but with a lot of sand. It is usually hot. *NOUN*

desert

drooled (DROOLD) To **drool** is to let saliva run from the mouth like a baby sometimes does. The dog **drooled** when it saw the bone. *VERB*

Ee

electricity (i lek TRISS uh tee) **Electricity** is a kind of energy that makes light and heat. **Electricity** also runs motors. **Electricity** makes light bulbs shine, radios and televisions play, and cars start. *NOUN*

Glossary

embarrassed (em BAIR uhst) When you feel **embarrassed**, you feel that people are thinking of you badly because of something you said or did: When I realized that I had given the wrong answer, I was **embarrassed**. *ADJECTIVE*

envelope (EN vuh lohp) An **envelope** is a folded paper cover. An **envelope** is used to mail a letter or something else that is flat. *NOUN*

excitement (ek SYT muhnt) **Excitement** happens when you have very strong, happy feelings about something that you like. *NOUN*

experiment (ek SPAIR uh muhnt) An **experiment** is a test to find out something: We do **experiments** in science class. *NOUN*

experiment

Gg

gnaws (NAWS) When an animal **gnaws**, it is biting and wearing away by biting: The brown mouse **gnaws** the cheese. *VERB*

gravity (GRAV uh tee) **Gravity** is the natural force that causes objects to move toward the center of the Earth. **Gravity** causes objects to have weight. *NOUN*

greenhouse (GREEN howss) A **greenhouse** is a building with a glass or plastic roof and sides. A **greenhouse** is kept warm and full of light for growing plants. *NOUN*

greenhouse

Hh

halfway (HAF WAY) To be **halfway** is to be in the middle: He was **halfway** through running the race. *ADJECTIVE*

harsh (HARSH) To be **harsh** is to be rough, unpleasant, and unfriendly: The **harsh** weather made us stay indoors. *ADJECTIVE*

466

467

hooves (HUVZ or HOOVZ) **Hooves** are the hard part of the feet of some animals. Horses, cattle, sheep, moose, deer, and pigs have hooves. *NOUN*

Jj

justice (JUHS tis) **Justice** happens when things are right and fair. *NOUN*

Ll

laboratory (LAB ruh tor ee) A **laboratory** is a room where scientists work and do experiments and tests. *NOUN*

ladder

ladder (LAD er) A **ladder** is a set of steps between two long pieces of wood, metal, or rope. **Ladders** are used for climbing up and down. *NOUN*

lantern

lanterns (LAN ternz) **Lanterns** are portable lamps with coverings around them to protect them from wind and rain. *NOUN*

lazy (LAY zee) If a person is **lazy**, he or she does not want to work hard or to move fast: The **lazy** cat lay on the rug all day. *ADJECTIVE*

lodge (LOJ) A **lodge** is a den of an animal: The beavers built a **lodge**. *NOUN*

luckiest (LUHK ee est) The **luckiest** person is the one who has had the best fortune. *ADJECTIVE*

lumbered (LUHM berd) To **lumber** is to move along heavily and noisily: The old truck **lumbered** down the road. *VERB*

Mm

meadow (MED oh) A **meadow** is a piece of land where grass grows: There are sheep in the **meadow**. *NOUN*

meadow

mill (MIL) A **mill** is a building in which grain is ground into flour or meal. *NOUN*

468

469

Glossary

monsters (MON sterz) **Monsters** are make-believe people or animals that are scary. In stories, some **monsters** are friendly, and others are not: Dragons are **monsters**. NOUN

musician (myoo ZISH uhn) A **musician** is a person who sings, plays, or writes music. NOUN

Nn

narrator (NAIR ayt or) A **narrator** is a person who tells a story or play. In a play, a **narrator** keeps the action moving. NOUN

Pp

persimmons (puhr SIM uhns) **Persimmons** are round, yellow and orange fruits about the size of plums. NOUN

persimmons

photograph (FOH tuh graf) A **photograph** is a picture you make with a camera. NOUN

Rr

relatives (REL uh tivs) Your **relatives** are the people who belong to the same family as you do: Your mother, sister, and cousin are all your **relatives**. NOUN

470

riverbank (RIV er bangk) A **riverbank** is the land on the side of a river or stream. NOUN

robbers (ROB ers) **Robbers** are people who rob or steal: The police chased the bank **robbers**. NOUN

robot (ROH bot or ROH BUHT) A **robot** is a machine that is run by a computer. **Robots** help people do work. **Robots** can look like people. NOUN

roller skate (ROH ler SKAYT) To **roller-skate** is to move by using **roller skates**, which are shoes that have wheels. VERB/NOUN

Ss

roller skates

shivered (SHIV erd) To **shiver** is to shake with cold, fear, or excitement: I **shivered** in the cold wind. VERB

shuttle (SHUHT uhl) A **shuttle** is a spacecraft with wings, which can orbit the earth, land like an airplane, and be used again. NOUN

471

slipped (SLIPT) When you **slip** you slide suddenly and unexpectedly: She **slipped** on the ice. VERB

smudged (SMUDJD) If something is **smudged**, it is marked with a dirty streak. ADJECTIVE

snuggled

snuggled (SNUHG uhld) To **snuggle** is to lie closely and comfortably together; cuddle: The kittens **snuggled** together in the basket. VERB

spirit (SPIR it) To have **spirit** is to have enthusiasm, courage, and loyalty: My sister has team **spirit**. NOUN

Tt

telescope (TEL uh skohp) A **telescope** is something you look through to make things far away seem nearer and larger: We looked at the moon through a **telescope**. NOUN

472

terrific (tuh RIF ik) To be **terrific** means to be very good, wonderful. She is a **terrific** tennis player. ADJECTIVE

Thanksgiving (thangks GIV ing) **Thanksgiving** is a holiday in November. NOUN

tortillas (tor TEE uhs) **Tortillas** are thin, flat, round breads usually made of cornmeal. NOUN

trash (TRASH) **Trash** is anything of no use or that is worn out. **Trash** is garbage or things to be thrown away. NOUN

trash

Ww

wad (WOD) A **wad** is a small, soft ball or chunk of something: She stepped in a **wad** of chewing gum. NOUN

weave (WEEV) To **weave** is to form threads into cloth. VERB

473

Tested Words

Unit 1

Iris and Walter

someone
somewhere
friend
country
beautiful
front

Exploring Space with an Astronaut

everywhere
live
work
woman
machines
move
world

Henry and Mudge and the Starry Night

couldn't
love
build
mother
bear
father
straight

A Walk in the Desert

water
eyes
early
animals
full
warm

The Strongest One

together
very
learn
often
though
gone
pieces

Unit 2

Tara and Tiree, Fearless Friends

family
once
pull
listen
heard
break

Ronald Morgan Goes to Bat

laugh
great
you're
either
certainly
second
worst

Turtle's Race with Beaver

enough
toward
above
ago
word
whole

474

475

The Bremen Town Musicians

people
sign
shall
bought
probably
pleasant
scared

A Turkey for Thanksgiving

door
behind
brought
minute
promise
sorry
everybody

Unit 3

Pearl and Wagner

science
shoe
won
guess
village
pretty
watch

Dear Juno

picture
school
answer
wash
parents
company
faraway

Anansi Goes Fishing

today
whatever
caught
believe
been
finally
tomorrow

Rosa and Blanca

their
many
alone
buy
half
youngest
daughters

A Weed Is a Flower

only
question
clothes
money
hours
neighbor
taught

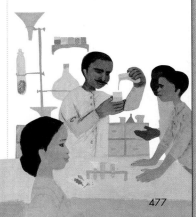

476

477

Acknowledgments

Acknowledgments

Text

Page 16: Text from *Iris And Walter*, copyright © 2000 by Elissa Haden Guest, reprinted by permission of Harcourt, Inc.

Pages 38–39: From *Poems for Small Friends* by Bobbi Katz, copyright © 1989 by Random House, Inc. Illustrations © 1989 by Gyo Fujikawa. Used by permission of Random House Children's Books, a division of Random House, Inc.

Page 46: *Exploring Space with an Astronaut* by Patricia J. Murphy, copyright © Enslow Publishers, Inc., Berkeley Heights, NJ. All rights reserved. Reprinted by permission.

Page 72: From *Henry and Mudge and the Starry Night.* Text copyright © 1998 by Cynthia Rylant. Illustrations copyright © 1998 by Suçie Stevenson. Reprinted with permission of Simon & Schuster for Young Readers, Simon & Schuster Children's Publishing Division. All rights reserved.

Page 100: From *A Walk in the Desert* by Caroline Arnold. Copyright © Alloy Entertainment and Al Jarcon. Reprinted by permission. All rights reserved.

Page 122: From www.factmonster.com from *The Columbia Electronic Encyclopedia, 6E.* Copyright © 2004 Columbia University Press. Licensed from Columbia University Press. All rights reserved. Reprinted by permission.

Page 132: "*The Strongest One* (Text)", from *Pushing Up The Sky* by Joseph Bruchac, copyright © 2000 by Joseph Bruchac, text. Used by permission of Dial Books for Young Readers, A Division of Penguin Young Readers Group, A Member of Penguin Group (USA) Inc., 345 Hudson Street, New York, NY 10014. All rights reserved.

Page 166: From *Tara and Tiree, Fearless Friends.* Text copyright © 2002 by Andrew Clements. Reprinted with permission of Simon & Schuster Books for Young Readers, Simon & Schuster Children's Publishing Division. All rights reserved.

Page 194: From *Ronald Morgan Goes to Bat* by Patricia Reilly Giff, copyright © 1988 by Patricia Reilly Giff. Used by permission of Viking Penguin, A Division of Penguin Young Readers Group, A Member of Penguin Group (USA) Inc., 345 Hudson Street, New York, NY 10014. All rights reserved.

Page 214: "Spaceball" from *Giant Children* by Brod Bagert. Copyright © 2002 by Brod Bagert, text. Copyright © 2002 by Tedd Arnold, pictures. Used by permission of Dial Books for Young Readers, A Division of Penguin Young Readers Group, A Member of Penguin Group (USA) Inc., 345 Hudson Street, New York, NY 10014. All rights reserved.

Page 222: *Turtle's Race with Beaver* by Joseph Bruchac & James Bruchac, illustrations by Jose Aruego & Ariane Dewey, Dial Books for Young Readers, 2003.

Page 246: From "The Secret Life of Ponds" by Elizabeth Schleichert, Illustrations by Frank Fretz. Reprinted from the June 2003 issue of *Ranger Rick*® magazine, with the permission of the publisher, the National Wildlife Federation®. Copyright © 2003 by the National Wildlife Federation®. Illustrations reprinted by permission of Frank Fretz © 2003.

Page 256: From *Easy-To-Read Folk and Fairy Tale Plays* by Carol Pugliano. Copyright © 1997 by Carol Pugliano. Reprinted by permission of Scholastic Inc.

Page 286: From *A Turkey for Thanksgiving* by Eve Bunting, illustrated by Diane de Groat. Text copyright © 1991 by Eve Bunting. Illustrations copyright © 1991 by Diane de Groat. Reprinted by permission of Clarion Books, a division of Houghton Mifflin Company. All rights reserved.

Page 306: *www.vispa.com*

Page 320: *Pearl and Wagner, Two Good Friends* by Kate McMullan, Illustrations by R. W. Alley, Dial Books for Young Readers, 2003.

Page 340: "Robots at Home" from *Robots* by Clive Gifford. Copyright © Kingfisher Publication Plc, 2003. Reproduced by permission of the publisher, all rights reserved.

Page 348: From *Dear Juno* by Soyung Pak, copyright © 1999 by Soyung Pak, text. Used by permission of Viking Penguin, A Division of Penguin Young Readers Group, A Member of Penguin Group (USA) Inc., 345 Hudson Street, New York, NY 10014. All rights reserved.

Page 368: From *Saying It Without Words: Signs and Symbols* by Arnulf K. & Louise A. Esterer, 1980. Reprinted by permission of Prentice Hall.

Page 376: From *Anansi Goes Fishing* by Eric A. Kimmel. Text copyright © 1992 by Eric A. Kimmel. Illustrations copyright © 1992 by Janet Stevens. All rights reserved. Reprinted by permission of Holiday House, Inc.

Page 398: "Do Spiders Stick to Their Own Webs" (text) from *Where Fish Go in Winter and Other Great Mysteries* by Amy Goldman Koss, copyright © 1987 by Amy Goldman Koss, text. Used by permission of Dial Books for Young Readers, A Division of Penguin Young Readers Group, A Member of Penguin Group (USA) Inc., 345 Hudson Street, New York, NY 10014. All rights reserved.

Page 406: From *Rosa and Blanca* by Joe Hayes, Illustrated by José Ortega, 1993. Reprinted by permission of Joe Hayes.

Page 420: From *The Crow and the Pitcher* retold by Eric Blair, Illustrated by Dianne Silverman. Copyright © 2004 by Picture Window Books. All rights reserved. Reprinted by permission.

Page 430: From *A Weed is a Flower.* Copyright © 1998 by Aliki Brandenberg. Reprinted with permission of Simon & Schuster Books for Young Readers, Simon & Schuster Children's Publishing Division. All rights reserved.

Page 454: "Products Made from Corn" from Ohio Corn Marketing Program Web site, www.ohiocorn.org. Reprinted by permission of Ohio Corn Marketing Program.

Illustrations

Cover: Scott Gustafson; **158-159, 244-245, 275, 312-313, 339, 397, 420-423, 453, 460-461** Laura Ovresat; **129-150, 160** Courtesy David Diaz; **153** Derek Grinnell; **163-181** Scott Gustafson; **246** Russell Farrell; **253-273** Jon Goodell; **314** Bill Mayer; **344-345** Gideon Kendall

Photographs

Every effort has been made to secure permission and provide appropriate credit for photographic material. The publisher deeply regrets any omission and pledges to correct errors called to its attention in subsequent editions.

Unless otherwise acknowledged, all photographs are the property of Scott Foresman, a division of Pearson Education.

Photo locators denoted as follows: Top (T), Center (C), Bottom (B), Left (L), Right (R), Background (Bkgd).

10 (Bkgd) ©A. Witte/C. Mahaney/Getty Images, (C) Digital Vision; **12** (Bkgd) ©Doug Armand/Getty Images, (CR) ©Phil Schermeister/Corbis; **13** (TR, CL) ©Ariel Skelley/Corbis; **42** (Bkgd) ©Shilo Sports/Getty Images, (BC) ©Royalty-Free/Corbis; **43** (TR) ©George Hall/Corbis, (CL) ©Museum of Flight/Corbis, (BR) ©NASA; **44** Corbis; **45** (TR, CR) ©NASA, (BR) ©Royalty-Free/Corbis, (Bkgd) Getty Images; **46** (Bkgd, T, C, B) Getty Images; **47-51** ©NASA; **52** (B) ©NASA/Roger Ressmeyer/Corbis; **53-58** ©NASA; **60** Getty Images; **62** (CC) Getty Images, (Bkdg) ©Royalty-Free/Corbis; **63** (T) Corbis, (CR, C) ©Richard T. Nowitz/Corbis, (BR) ©Joseph Sohm/ChromoSohm Inc./Corbis; **64** (B, TR) ©Richard T. Nowitz/Corbis; **65** (TR) ©Franz-Marc Frei/Corbis, (BR) ©Richard T. Nowitz/Corbis; **66** NASA; **67** ©NASA; **68** (Bkgd) ©Jim Ballard/Getty Images, (CL) ©Joe McDonald/Corbis, (BR) Digital Vision; **69** (CL) ©Nigel J. Dennis/Gallo Images/Corbis, (TR) ©Michael & Patricia Fogden/Corbis; **90** ©Gabe Palmer/Corbis; **92** (BL) Getty Images, (T, BR) ©Roger Ressmeyer/Corbis; **93** (T)© Roger Ressmeyer/Corbis, (BL) ©Bill and Sally Fletcher; **96** (Bkgd) ©George H. H. Huey/Corbis, (CL) ©Altrendo Nature/Getty Images, (BR) ©Galen Rowell/Corbis; **97** (TL) Digital Vision, (CR) Brand X Pictures, (BR) ©Steve Maslowski/Visuals Unlimited; **98** (BC) ©David A. Northcott/Corbis, (TL) ©Ralph Hopkins/Lonely Planet Images; **99** (TR) ©Tim Flach/Stone, (Bkgd) Getty Images, (BR) ©David Muench/Corbis; **100** Getty Images; **101** ©Maryellen Baker/Botanica; **102** (BL) ©Jeri Gleiter/Getty Images, (Bkgd) Getty Images, (BR) ©Marco Simoni/Robert Harding Picture Library Ltd.; **103** (CL) ©Ron Thomas/Getty Images, (B) ©Robert Van Der Hilst/Getty Images; **104** ©Paul McCormick/Getty Images; **105** (BR) ©Bates Littlehales/NGS Image Collection, (BL) ©David Muench/Corbis, (CR) ©Gary W. Carter/Corbis; **106** (CR) ©Charles C. Place/Getty Images, (TC) ©Ralph Hopkins/Lonely Planet Images, (Bkgd) Getty Images; **107** (C) ©David Maitland/Getty Images, (TR) ©David Aubrey/Getty Images, (TC, C) ©Jack Dykinga/Getty Images; **108** (BC) Getty Images, (Bkgd) ©Arthur S. Aubry/Getty Images, (C) ©Steve Maslowski/Visuals Unlimited; **109** (TR) ©George D. Lepp/Corbis, (BR) ©David A. Northcott/Corbis, (CL) ©Joe McDonald/Corbis; **110** (BL) ©Farrell Grehan/Corbis, (Bkgd) Digital Vision, (BR) ©Shai Ginott/Corbis; **111** ©Tom Bean/Corbis; **112** ©Joe McDonald/Corbis; **113** (BR) Getty Images, (BL) ©Jonathan Blair/NGS Image Collection, (CR) ©David Muench/Corbis; **114** (Bkgd, BL) Getty Images, (BR) ©Michael & Patricia Fogden/Corbis; **115** (TR) ©Mel Yates/Getty Images, (BR, TL) Getty Images; **116** (BL) ©Tom Bean/Getty Images, (Bkgd) ©Arthur Tilley/Getty Images, (BR) ©Layne Kennedy/Corbis; **117** ©Matthias Clamer/Getty Images; **118** (CL) ©Tim Flach/Stone, (CR) ©William J. Hebert/Getty Images, (Bkgd) ©Ira Rubin/Getty Images; **119** (BC) ©Ira Rubin/Getty Images, (TL) ©Royalty-Free/Corbis, (CR) ©Jean Paul Ferrero/Ardea, (TR) ©Rogier Gruys; **120** ©Steve Maslowski/Visuals Unlimited; **124** (CL) ©Gary Braasch/Corbis, (BL) ©Theo Allofs/Corbis; **125** (CL) ©Tom Brakefield/Corbis, (TL) ©Bill Varie/Corbis; **127** ©Robert Van Der Hilst/Getty Images; **129** (TL) ©Ron Watts/Corbis, (TR) ©Martin Harvey/Peter Arnold, Inc.; **152** ©Tom Brakefield/Corbis; **153** ©Tom Brakefield/Corbis; **154** (T) ©Roland Seitre/Peter Arnold, Inc., (B) ©John H. Hoffman/Bruce Coleman Inc.; **155** ©Theo Allofs/Corbis; **158** (BL) ©A. Witte/C. Mahaney/Getty Images, (BC) Digital Vision; **159** Getty Images; **162** ©Brand X Pictures/Getty Images; **163** (TL) ©Matthew Polak/Corbis, (CR) ©AFP/Getty Images, (BL) Getty Images; **183** (TL) Photo of Andrew Clements used with permission of Simon & Schuster, Inc. ©Bill Crofton, (CL) Brand X Pictures; **184** ©Tim Davis/Corbis; **185** (TL) ©Andrea Comas/Corbis, (CL) ©Jean-Bernard Vernier/Corbis, (BL) ©Tom Nebbia/Corbis; **186** (Bkgd) ©Owen Franken/Corbis, (TR) ©Vaughn Youtz/Corbis, (CR) ©Armando Arorizo/Corbis, (CL) ©Shamil Zhumatov/Corbis; **187** (TL) ©Kai Pfaffenbach/Corbis, (BR) ©Ralf-Finn Hestoft/Corbis; **190** (Bkgd) ©Royalty-Free/Corbis, (CL) ©Brand X Pictures/Getty Images, (BR) ©Julia Fishkin/Getty Images; **191** (CL) ©CLEO Freelance/Index Stock Imagery, (TR) BananaStock; **218** ©Kennan Ward/Corbis; **219** ©Royalty-Free/Corbis; **247** Getty Images; **252** ©Ariel Skelley/Corbis; **253** (CR) ©Michael Pole/Corbis, (TR) ©Paul Harris/Getty Images; **276** (Bkgd) ©Dex Image/Getty Images, (B) ©Darryl Torckler/Getty Images; **277** Getty Images; **278** (T) ©Ariadne Van Zandbergen/Lonely Planet Images, (TR) ©Eric and David Hosking/Corbis, (CL) ©Lester Lefkowitz/Getty Images, (CL) ©Cliff Beittel, (B) ©Peter Cade/Getty Images; **279** (B) ©Winifred Wisniewski/Frank Lane Picture Agency/Corbis, (CL) ©Nigel J. Dennis/Gallo Images/Corbis, (T) ©Ian Beames/Ardea; **282** (CL) ©Tom Stewart/Corbis, (BR) ©Ariel Skelley/Corbis, (Bkgd) ©Digital Vision/Getty Images; **283** (TL) ©Ariel Skelley/Corbis, (CL) ©Steve Satushek/Getty Images, (TR) ©Brooklyn Productions/Getty Images; **304** Getty Images; **305** (BR) ©Royalty-Free/Corbis, (T) Brand X Pictures; **307** (CR) ©Catherine Karnow/Corbis, (CL) ©Kevin Fleming/Corbis; **308** (BR) ©Jose Luis Pelaez, Inc/Corbis, (TR) Corbis; **309** ©Larry Williams/Corbis; **312** Getty Images; **316** (Bkgd) ©Comstock, Inc., (C) ©Jim Cummins/Getty Images; **317** (T) ©Jose Luis Pelaez, Inc/Corbis, (BL) ©Mike Timo/Getty Images; **340** (BL) ©Roger Ressmeyer/

478

479

Corbis, (TR) ©Koichi Kamoshida/Getty Images; **341** ©NEC Corporation; **368** (BCR, BR, CR) Getty Images; **369** (C) ©Ryan McVay/Getty Images, (BL, TC, TR, CC) ©Royalty-Free/Corbis, (CR) Getty Images **372-373** ©Scott Gustafson, 2003. All rights reserved. From Classic Fairy Tales, illustrated by Scott Gustafson, published by The Greenwich Workshop Press; **396** ©Davies & Starr/Getty Images; **397** ©GK Hart/Vikki Hart/Getty Images; **398** (BL) ©PBNJ Productions/Corbis, (CL) Getty Images; **399** ©Mark E. Gibson/Corbis; **402** ©Royalty-Free/Corbis; **403** (TR) ©Tom Stewart/Corbis, (CL) ©Jim Cummins/Corbis; **426** (Bkgd) Getty Images, (C) ©George Disario/Corbis; **427** (TL) ©Kevin R. Morris/Corbis, (TR) ©Peter Beck/Corbis, (BL) ©Royalty-Free/Corbis; **456** (C, B) Corbis; **457** (BR, TR, BL, CR) Getty Images; **494** Corbis; **495** ©Ron Thomas/Getty Images; **496** Getty Images; **497** ©Jose Fuste Raga/Corbis; **499** ©Jim Winkley/Corbis; **500-503** Getty Images; **504** ©Royalty- Free/Corbis; **505** Getty Images; **506** (CL) ©Tim Flach/ Stone, (BR) ©Paul McCormick/Getty Images

480

City Mouse and Country Mouse

SUMMARY Children compare life in the city to life in the country as they read a story about two mice. The characters' traits and observations drive the plot.

INTRODUCE THE BOOK

BUILD BACKGROUND Discuss other stories children have read where animals are personified. Then look at the cover illustration together. Ask: Are the mice characters in this story make-believe? How do you know?

PREVIEW/USE ILLUSTRATIONS Encourage children to look at the illustrations and think about the genre, characters, and setting. Ask: Do you think this story could really happen? Where does the story takes place?

TEACH/REVIEW VOCABULARY Write each word and its definition on separate index cards. Place them writing-side-down in rows. Have children take turns turning over two cards at a time to find a match.

ELL Play vocabulary charades. Pair children with proficient English speakers and assign each pair a different vocabulary word.

TARGET SKILL AND STRATEGY

◎ **CHARACTER AND SETTING** Explain to children that authors tell what the *characters* in the story are like. After children read page 3, pause and ask them to look at the picture and read the text to find out about the characters. Ask: What do the two main characters both like to do? What are they wearing in the picture? After reading, lead children to identify the *setting*. Explain that the setting is both the time and place of the story. Ask children to recall the two places in the story. Then ask children when the story took place.

◎ **PREDICT** Remind children that when they know the characters in a story, they can *predict* what the characters might do next. Model how to make predictions after children read page 4: We can predict that City Mouse and Country Mouse will go the city because Country Mouse says, "Maybe the city is better."

READ THE BOOK

Use the following questions to support comprehension.

PAGE 5 What is the main reason that City Mouse missed the city? *(There is a lot to do in the city.)*

PAGE 6 How does the city make Country Mouse feel? *(tired)*

PAGE 7 In what settings did Country Mouse and City Mouse have fun? *(country and city)*

TALK ABOUT THE BOOK

THINK AND SHARE
1. characters—City Mouse and Country Mouse
   setting—the city and the country
2. Answers will vary.
3. Possible response: My friend likes ice cream.
4. Possible response: Both like their own homes.

RESPONSE OPTIONS

WRITING Ask children to write two sentences about the differences between the city and the country.

CONTENT CONNECTIONS

SOCIAL STUDIES Children can learn what is special about their own communities by giving short oral reports about special places that they have visited, such as a park or zoo.

Time for SOCIAL STUDIES

Name _____

Character and Setting

Read the following paragraph from the story.
Write what you know about the setting.

> The very next day Country Mouse went to see her friend in the city. The mice went roller-skating on the sidewalk. They ate bread at a bakery. They heard someone sing at a club.

Setting:

_____ _____

_____ _____

_____ _____

_____ _____

Character:

Think about what you know about Country Mouse and City Mouse after reading the story. Match the characters to what each character likes.

Characters
1. Country Mouse

2. City Mouse

What Characters Like
a. the country best
b. the city best
c. peace and quiet
d. to do many things
e. to visit other places

© Pearson Education 2

14

Name _____

Vocabulary

Synonyms are words that have the same meaning. Draw a line to match the synonyms.

1. beautiful

2. country

3. friend

a. nation—a large group of people that share the same government

b. playmate—a child that plays with other children

c. pretty—pleasing to look at

4. Write a sentence with the word *someone*.

_____
- -
═══
- -
_____

5. Write a sentence with the word *somewhere*.

_____
- -
═══
- -
_____

© Pearson Education 2

15

🔘 **CHARACTER AND SETTING**

🔘 **PREDICT**

LESSON VOCABULARY beautiful, country, friend, someone, somewhere

The New Kid

SUMMARY While spending summer in Indonesia, Denny learns that being different can mean being special. Children explore character as they read clues about Denny's character traits.

INTRODUCE THE BOOK

BUILD BACKGROUND Elicit a discussion about moving and traveling to a new place. Ask: Where did you travel or move to? How did you feel before you left? How did you feel when you were there? Do you want to go back?

PREVIEW/USE ILLUSTRATIONS As children look through the book at the illustrations, encourage them to think about the genre, characters, and setting. Ask: Do you think this story could happen? Who is the new kid? Do the pictures give you clues about where the story takes place?

TEACH/REVIEW VOCABULARY Write each vocabulary word and its definition on separate index cards, and place the cards face down. Have children take turns looking at two cards at a time to find a match.

ELL Play vocabulary charades. Pair children with proficient English speakers and assign each pair a different vocabulary word.

TARGET SKILL AND STRATEGY

🔘 **CHARACTER AND SETTING** Explain how authors tell readers what the *characters* are like in a story. Prompt children to think about character by brainstorming a list of character traits. After children read page 3, ask them to identify information about the main character. After reading, ask children to describe the *setting*. Explain that the setting is both the time and place of the story. Ask children to recall the two places in the story. Then ask children when the story took place.

🔘 **PREDICT** Remind children that when they know about the characters in a story, they can *predict* what the characters may think or do next. As children reach page 10, have them pause. Ask: Now that Denny is back home, what do you think he will miss about Bali?

READ THE BOOK

Use the following questions to support comprehension.

PAGE 3 How do you think Denny made new friends? *(by playing soccer)*

PAGE 5 Who picked up Bali customs faster, Denny or his parents? *(Denny)*

PAGE 10 What do we learn about Denny on this page? *(Possible responses: He lives in California; he is in second grade.)*

TALK ABOUT THE BOOK

THINK AND SHARE
1. Bali and California
2. Answers will vary.
3. Possible response: page 4—*it, Mom, and, Dad, didn't, at, helped, them, lot*
4. Possible responses: the language, the food

RESPONSE OPTIONS

WRITING Have children write a short paragraph about their experiences trying something new and different.

CONTENT CONNECTIONS

SOCIAL STUDIES The puppet show that Denny saw at the temple may have used shadow puppets. Shadow puppet shows are generally about Indonesian myths. Ask your librarian to collect books with pictures of Indonesian shadow puppets and Indonesian myths. Read one of these myths to the class.

Time for **SOCIAL STUDIES**

Name _____

Character and Setting

Read the paragraphs.

Look for words that tell you about the setting. Write these words under Setting.

Then, look for words that tell you about the character, Denny. Write these words under Character.

When Dad got the job I was glad. I like traveling with my family to see new places. I like the adventure of going to different places, even if I have to be the new kid there.

Dad helps out on small farms around the world. This summer we went to the island country of Bali. Kids speak Indonesian there. They eat meals with their fingers. And best of all, they love soccer, just like at home!

Setting

_____

_____

_____

_____

_____

_____

_____

_____

_____

_____

_____

Character

_____

_____

_____

_____

_____

_____

_____

_____

_____

_____

_____

14

Vocabulary

Synonyms are words that have the same meaning. Draw lines to match the synonyms.

1. beautiful

2. country

3. friend

a. playmate—a child that plays with other children

b. pretty—pleasing to look at

c. nation—a large group of people that share the same government

4. Write a sentence with the word *someone*.

_____

- -

_____

_____

- -

_____

5. Write a sentence with the word *somewhere*.

_____

- -

_____

_____

- -

_____

15

Advanced-Level Reader

City Friends, Country Friends

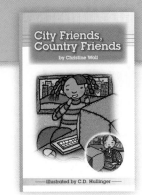

🎯 **CHARACTER AND SETTING**

🎯 **PREDICT**

LESSON VOCABULARY investigate, rural, urban

SUMMARY In this story, two e-pals use e-mail to learn how the other lives. The story extends the lesson concept of what we might find in a new neighborhood.

INTRODUCE THE BOOK

BUILD BACKGROUND Ask children to share what they know about rural living versus urban living.

ELL Invite children to share any knowledge or memories of life in their native countries.

PREVIEW/USE ILLUSTRATIONS Have children preview the pictures and one of the e-mail messages. Ask: Why are parts of the story set in slanted type? Have children preview page 16. Ask: Why did the author include this page?

TEACH/REVIEW VOCABULARY Have children make a three-column chart with the vocabulary words as headings. On the board, write: *country, explore, city, spy, study, farms, crowds, skyscrapers, cows*. Have children write each word in the column in which it best belongs.

TARGET SKILL AND STRATEGY

🎯 **CHARACTER AND SETTING** *Characters* are the people or animals in stories. Authors describe what characters look like, how they act, and what kind of people they are. As they read, have children answer questions about each character's appearance, words, thoughts, feelings, and actions. Next, tell children that the *setting* is the time and place of a story. Explain that a setting can be a real place or an imaginary one. After a few pages, have children identify the main setting. *(present day and Tasha's school)* After page 14, have children tell how the setting changes.

🎯 **PREDICT** Tell children that as they read, they should predict what might happen next. To predict, use what you have read and what you already know. During the preview, ask children to predict what will happen and have them justify their predictions.

READ THE BOOK

Use the following questions to support comprehension.

PAGE 4 Which character trait best describes Mrs. Jennings: mean, smart, or sleepy? *(smart)*

PAGE 7 Does this story take place in fewer than two days or for more than two days? How do you know? *(It is more than two days because the text says that two days had already passed.)*

PAGE 10 Why did Mrs. Jennings ask for all eyes on the board? *(She wanted the class to give her its full attention.)*

PAGE 14 What did Henry mean when he wrote that the piglets were so sweet? *(They are cute and lovable.)*

TALK ABOUT THE BOOK

THINK AND SHARE

1. Possible responses: Characters: Tasha, an urban girl; Henry, a rural boy; Mrs. Jennings, an urban teacher; Setting: present times; city; farm; children's classrooms

2. Responses will vary, but they should be based on story content.

3. Possible response: A farm is rural. A city is urban. You investigate to find something out.

4. Responses will vary, but children should discuss themselves and how they live.

RESPONSE OPTIONS

WRITING Have children compose an e-mail about themselves for an e-pal who lives far away.

CONTENT CONNECTIONS

SOCIAL STUDIES Display information about careers that might be urban-based, rural-based, or both. Have children group the jobs in a Venn diagram that corresponds to those categories.

Time for **SOCIAL STUDIES**

Name _____

Character and Setting

Read this chart from the story. Think about what the chart tells you about the story's characters and settings. Then fill in the diagram below.

5 Senses	Henry's Favorite	Tasha's Favorite
Sight	Green fields, pigs	View from apartment
Sound	Crickets, tractors	People shouting "Taxi"
Smell	Grass, mud, Mom's pie	Mom's perfume
Touch	Soft skin on piglets	Elevator buttons
Taste	Water from our well	Fresh bagels, Mom's pie

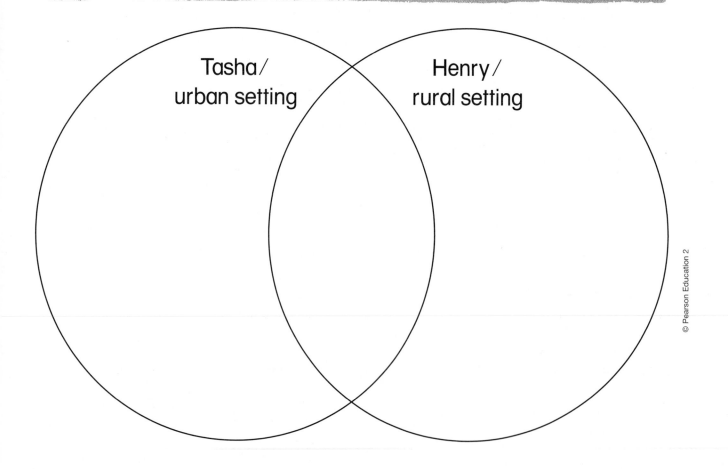

Tasha/
urban setting

Henry/
rural setting

© Pearson Education 2

14

Name _____

Vocabulary

Choose the word from the box that best completes
each sentence.

Words to Know		
investigate	rural	urban

_____
- - - - - - - - - - - - - - - - - -
1. In _____ places many people live in apartment
   buildings.

_____
- - - - - - - - - - - - - - - - - -
2. The teacher asked us to _____ the trees
   around the school.

_____
- - - - - - - - - - - - - - - - - -
3. My friend from a _____ town likes to ride the
   tractor with his father.

Antonyms are two words that mean the opposite of each other.

4. Which two words from the word box are antonyms?

   _____   _____
   - - - - - - - - - - - - - - - - -   - - - - - - - - - - - - - - - - -
   _____   _____

15

Being an Astronaut

Unit 1 Week 2

◉ **MAIN IDEA AND DETAILS**

◉ **TEXT STRUCTURE**

LESSON VOCABULARY everywhere, live, machines, move, woman, work, world

SUMMARY This book explains what you need to know to be an astronaut. It extends the lesson concept of why someone would want to explore space.

INTRODUCE THE BOOK

BUILD BACKGROUND Discuss what children know about astronauts. Ask: What does an astronaut do?

PREVIEW/TAKE A PICTURE WALK Have children preview the photographs, headings, and captions. Ask: What is special about the headings?

TEACH/REVIEW VOCABULARY Give pairs of children a set of vocabulary word cards and another set with these clues: This is all over the place. This means "to be." This is a job. A mother is this. These help people do work. When you run, you do this. The earth is this. Have pairs play a memory game by revealing each word and its clue.

ⒺⓁⓁ Help children make cards with a vocabulary word on one side and a translation in a common home language on the other side. Lay out the cards, translation side up, and have children capture cards by naming the vocabulary words.

TARGET SKILL AND STRATEGY

◉ **MAIN IDEA AND DETAILS** Tell children: A *topic* is what a paragraph or article is about. It can usually be stated in one or two words. The *main idea* is the most important idea about the topic. Usually the main idea is given in a sentence. Say: First figure out the topic. Next, figure out the main idea. Last, identify the details that support or tell more about the main idea.

◉ **TEXT STRUCTURE** Remind children that they should think about the *text structure,* or pattern, that is used in a piece of writing. Have children read the headings and identify them as questions. Guide children to see that the author used a question-and-answer text structure. Explain that each heading covers a new topic. As they read, have children fill out a graphic organizer like the one in Think and Share and use it to summarize the text.

READ THE BOOK

Use the following questions to support comprehension.

PAGE 5 What is the main idea? *(Astronauts need to wear spacesuits.)*

PAGE 7 Why don't astronauts just do their experiments on Earth? *(Possible response: They want to see if things work differently in space.)*

PAGE 8 Why is it important for an astronaut to be able to call home? *(Possible response: They miss their families and don't want them to worry.)*

TALK ABOUT THE BOOK

THINK AND SHARE
1. Astronauts live differently in space.
2. Children's webs should include the questions in the book's headings.
3. Possible responses: *astronaut, spaceship, spacesuit*
4. Possible response: Do you have to be a pilot or scientist to be an astronaut?

RESPONSE OPTIONS

WRITING Have children write a letter to an astronaut asking their questions from Think and Share.

CONTENT CONNECTIONS

SCIENCE Display information about space travel. Have children list differences between living in space and on Earth.

TIME FOR Science

Name _____

Main Idea and Details

Read the passage below.

Fill in the topic, the main idea, and two supporting details.

Where do astronauts sleep?
Some astronauts sleep in sleeping
bags. Other astronauts sleep in bunks.
Some just find a quiet spot to rest.

Topic

_____

- -

_____

Main Idea

_____

- -

_____

Supporting Details

18

© Pearson Education 2

Vocabulary

Draw a line from each word to the word that means the opposite.

l. everywhere   **a.** man

2. live   **b.** nowhere

3. move   **c.** die

4. woman   **d.** stay

Write the words from the box to best complete the sentence.

Words to Know

machines   work   world

_____

5. All around the _____, people

use _____ to help them

do their _____ .

© Pearson Education 2

19

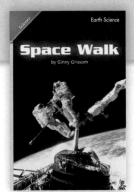

Unit 1 Week 2

Space Walk

🔊 **MAIN IDEA AND DETAILS**

🔊 **TEXT STRUCTURE**

LESSON VOCABULARY everywhere, live, machines, move, woman, work, world

SUMMARY This nonfiction book explains how astronauts use space walks to solve problems in space. It extends the lesson concept of why someone would want to explore space.

INTRODUCE THE BOOK

BUILD BACKGROUND Have children discuss survival in space. Ask: Do you need special ships or clothing to live in space? Why or why not?

PREVIEW/TAKE A PICTURE WALK Have children preview the photographs, captions, and labels. Explain that the captions tell what the photos are about.

ELL Use the photographs and captions to help children understand certain terms that are used in the book, such as *astronaut, pack, rockets, space, space station, tether,* and *space walk.*

TEACH/REVIEW VOCABULARY Give children sets of vocabulary word cards. Give clues to the words, such as "the opposite of play." Ask children to show the vocabulary word that goes with each clue.

TARGET SKILL AND STRATEGY

🔊 **MAIN IDEA AND DETAILS** Tell children: A *topic* is what a paragraph or article is about. It can usually be stated in one or two words. The *main idea* is the most important idea about the topic. Sometimes the main idea is given in a sentence; at other times you have to use your own words. Explain the process: First, figure out the topic. Next, figure out the main idea. Last, identify the *details* that support or tell more about the main idea. Encourage children to look for the main ideas as they read this book.

🔊 **TEXT STRUCTURE** Remind children that they should think about the *text structure,* or pattern, that is used in a piece of writing. Guide children to see that this author uses a problem-and-solution text structure. During reading, have children use a problem-and-solution chart to explore the text structure. Have children use the completed chart to remember basic points and to summarize the text.

READ THE BOOK

Use the following questions to support comprehension.

PAGE 3 Look at the photo. What do you think it feels like to wear a spacesuit? *(Possible response: It is hot, and it is hard to move your arms and legs.)*

PAGE 6 What is the main idea? *(A spacesuit solves many problems for astronauts in space.)*

PAGE 11 Astronauts sometimes bring objects from space back to Earth. What is a reason that astronauts might bring objects back to a spaceship? *(Possible response: to study them or to repair them)*

TALK ABOUT THE BOOK

THINK AND SHARE

1. Possible response: Scientists and astronauts have made space walks an important part of exploring space.
2. Possible responses: Problems: may be hot in space, hard to move in space, tools can float away. Solution: water-cooled spacesuits, rocket packs, tools with loops.
3. Possible response: There is no air in *space. Astronauts* wear *spacesuits.*
4. Possible response: Page 4 shows an astronaut practicing what she will do on a space walk. Page 5 shows her on the space walk.

RESPONSE OPTIONS

WRITING Have children describe what they might see or do on a space walk.

CONTENT CONNECTIONS

SCIENCE Display information about conditions in space. Have children work in pairs to make a chart that contrasts conditions in space and conditions on Earth.

TIME FOR **Science**

Name _____

Main Idea and Details

Read the passage below.
Fill in the topic, the main idea, and two supporting details.

There are problems for an astronaut on a space walk. In space, there is no air to breathe. There is no water to drink. Rocks, ice, and "space junk" can hit you.

Topic

_____
- -
_____

Main Idea

_____
- -
_____

Supporting Details

_____
- - - - - - - - - - - - - - -
_____
- - - - - - - - - - - - - - -
_____

_____
- - - - - - - - - - - - - - -
_____
- - - - - - - - - - - - - - -
_____

18

Name _____

Vocabulary

Write a word from the box to answer each riddle.

Words to Know			
everywhere	live	machines	move
woman	work	world	

1. Some people travel around this. _____

2. Your work will be easier with these to help.
   _____
   _____

3. If I am your mother, I must be this. _____

4. Food, air, and water will help you do this. _____

5. Don't do this if you want to hide. _____

6. We can't be here at the same time.
   _____
   _____

7. You must do this to do a good job. _____

19

Explore the Galaxy

Explore the Galaxy
by Eve Beck

◎ **MAIN IDEA AND DETAILS**

◎ **TEXT STRUCTURE**

LESSON VOCABULARY ascend, asteroids, descend, gravity, laboratory, orbit, satellites

---

SUMMARY *Explore the Galaxy* describes our solar system and examines scientists' efforts to learn more about it.

INTRODUCE THE BOOK

BUILD BACKGROUND Invite children to share what they know and what they would like to learn about the solar system and space exploration. List their ideas in a KWL chart.

PREVIEW/USE TEXT FEATURES Turn the pages of *Explore the Galaxy* with the children and examine the photographs, captions, headings, and other text features. Discuss the function of the Table of Contents. On pages 4 and 5, point out the chapter heading, the diagram, and the words in dark letters. Look up *asteroids* in the Glossary.

TEACH/REVIEW VOCABULARY Read page 13 and ask children what they think *ascend* and *descend* might mean. Model looking for context clues: *Ascend* and *descend* are what astronauts do in space. They go up in space and come back down. With children, look up the words in the glossary to verify their meanings. Repeat for other selection vocabulary.

ⒺⓁⓁ Write vocabulary words on word cards and spread them facedown on a table. Have children work in pairs selecting cards and acting out the words.

TARGET SKILL AND STRATEGY

◎ **MAIN IDEA AND DETAILS** Remind children that good readers think about a book's topic and its main ideas. Looking for the topic and main ideas helps readers understand what they are reading. A *topic* is a word or two that describes what a paragraph or book is about. A *main idea* is the most important idea about the topic. Turn to pages 4 and 5 and model finding the topic, main idea, and supporting details. (*Topic: our solar system; Main idea: There are nine planets that travel around the sun.*)

◎ **TEXT STRUCTURE** Point out to children that a good reader thinks about a book's text structure, or how it is organized. Understanding how a book is organized makes it easier to recognize the topic and main idea.

READ THE BOOK

Use the following questions to support comprehension.

PAGES 6–7 Which planet has the most moons? Which planets have the fewest? (*Jupiter has the most moons; Mercury and Venus have none.*)

PAGES 12–13 What is the topic of this chapter? What are the main ideas? (*The topic is the future. Possible main ideas: Scientists have many plans for the future; they are learning new things all the time.*)

PAGE 13 What does *ascend* mean? Explain in your own words. (*Possible response:* Ascend *means "to go up."*)

TALK ABOUT THE BOOK

THINK AND SHARE
1. Main idea: Scientists use spaceships, robots, and satellites to explore space. Supporting details can include any of the specific examples of space missions outlined in the chapter.
2. The book's three chapters tell what we already know, what we are learning, and what might happen in the future.
3. Responses should reflect comprehension of the word *orbit*.
4. Possible reponse: We can learn a lot from space exploration. The book describes past and future space missions.

RESPONSE OPTIONS

WRITING Suggest that children write and illustrate a short question-and-answer book about the Solar System. Have them write a question on each right-hand page and its answer on the page that follows.

CONTENT CONNECTIONS

SCIENCE Encourage each child to find out more about one of the planets in the Solar System. Suggest that they use the library and the Internet to find a few key facts about their planet.

TIME FOR Science

Name _____

Main Idea and Details

Read the paragraph below. Write the topic, the main idea, and three supporting details.

> People called astronauts travel into space. Many astronauts are also scientists. Astronauts train for many years to do their jobs. They need to be healthy. They also need to know how spaceships work.

1. Topic: _____

2. Main Idea: _____

3. Details: _____

18

© Pearson Education 2

Vocabulary

Choose a word from the box to finish each sentence.

Words to Know			
ascend	asteroids	descend	gravity
laboratory	orbit	satellites	

1. The astronauts _____ around Earth on the space shuttle.

2. The astronauts _____ back to Earth at the end of their trip.

3. When will the astronauts _____ into space again?

4. Astronauts often see rocks, or _____, orbiting the sun.

5. _____ can be used to broadcast television and radio signals.

6. Astronauts float in space, but _____ keeps us on Earth.

7. The astronauts use a _____ on the shuttle to do experiments.

19

Pup Camps Out

SUMMARY A puppy goes with his mother and father on his first camping trip. The story extends the lesson concept of what we can discover by exploring nature.

INTRODUCE THE BOOK

BUILD BACKGROUND Ask children to share what they know about camping. Ask: How is camping different from living at home?

PREVIEW/USE ILLUSTRATIONS Have children preview the pictures. Ask: Who is the story about? What is happening? Have children read the heading for the information on page 8. Discuss: What is this part of the book about?

TEACH/REVIEW VOCABULARY Give each child a set of vocabulary word cards. Write these combinations on the board: _____ or wouldn't; _____ and kisses; plan and _____; _____ and son, wolf and _____; _____ and daughter; _____ and even. Read each pair aloud, and have children show the best word to fill in each blank.

TARGET SKILL AND STRATEGY

◎ **CHARACTER AND SETTING** Tell children that *characters* are the people or animals in stories. Authors describe what the characters look like and how they act. Have children look at each character's physical appearance and what the character says, thinks, feels, and does. Next, explain that *setting* is the time and place of a story. Have children identify the main setting.

ELL Give each child three word webs. Guide them to complete the web with character traits for *Pup, Mother Dog,* and *Father Dog* as they read the story.

◎ **MONITOR AND FIX UP** Remind children that they should check as they read to make sure they understand what they are reading. One way to check understanding is to read on. Have children jot a note when they come to something they don't understand. Have them check off a note if it is cleared up later in the story.

READ THE BOOK

PAGE 3 Why do you think Pup is happy? *(Possible response: He is having fun doing something new.)*

PAGE 5 Which character trait best describes Pup— helpful, shy, or hungry? *(helpful)*

PAGE 7 Why is Pup sleepy? *(He is tired from helping his parents and playing.)*

PAGE 7 Where did they go fishing? *(by a stream)*

TALK ABOUT THE BOOK

THINK AND SHARE

1. Pup; He likes to learn new things and have fun.
2. Possible response: in the country; Pup learns about camping.
3. *place, please, stream*
4. Possible response: A child should not use fire or an ax, but a child can help an adult who uses them.

RESPONSE OPTIONS

VIEWING Have children write a sentence for each picture in the story, describing what happened.

CONTENT CONNECTIONS

SCIENCE Display information about camping. Have children list things they should do to protect camp areas, such as putting out campfires and disposing of trash.

TIME FOR Science

Character and Setting

Read each sentence below. Then circle the answer that best completes each sentence.

I. When Pup asked Father Dog to teach him, he was by the

    a. car.   b. tent.   c. house.

2. The story happened

    a. at night.   b. 100 years ago.   c. in the present day.

3. Mother Dog

    a. likes to camp.   b. stayed at home.   c. is reading a book.

4. Father Dog is

    a. wise.   b. forgetful.   c. angry.

5. Write a sentence about Pup.

_____

- -

_____

- -

_____

22

Name _____

Vocabulary

Draw a line from each word at the left to the word or words at the right that mean the same.

1. build   **a.** dad

2. father   **b.** care about

3. love   **c.** mom

4. mother   **d.** make

Complete the sentence using the words from the box.

Words to Know
bear   couldn't   straight

5. The big _____ was strong, but he _____

run in a _____ line.

23

Let's Camp at Crescent Lake

Unit 1 Week 3

◉ **CHARACTER AND SETTING**

◉ **MONITOR AND FIX UP**

LESSON VOCABULARY bear, build, couldn't, father, love, mother, straight

SUMMARY A family prepares for a camping trip. The story extends the lesson concept of what we can discover by exploring nature.

INTRODUCE THE BOOK

BUILD BACKGROUND Ask children to share what they know about camping. Ask: What kinds of things do people use when they go camping?

ELL Use maps and pictures of camping areas to help children understand what camping is all about.

PREVIEW/USE TEXT FEATURES Have children preview the pictures. Ask: What is this story about? Have children look at the heading, photograph, and caption on page 12. Ask: What is this part of the book about?

TEACH/REVIEW VOCABULARY Write this story on the board, without the underlined words, and have children use vocabulary words to complete the sentences: <u>Father</u> *will* <u>build</u> *a campfire. The boy and the girl* <u>couldn't</u> *find many* <u>straight</u> *sticks.* <u>Mother</u> *said, "Crooked ones are fine. We just need to make a big fire to keep away a* <u>bear</u> *that would* <u>love</u> *to snack on our food."*

TARGET SKILL AND STRATEGY

◉ **CHARACTER AND SETTING** *Characters* are the people or animals in stories. Authors tell what their characters look like and how they act. As they read, have children describe each character. Next, tell children that the *setting* is the time and place of a story. Explain that a setting can be a real place or an imaginary one. Have children identify the story's setting.

◉ **MONITOR AND FIX UP** Remind children that good readers know that what they read must make sense. Tell them to check as they read this book to make sure they understand what they are reading. Explain that they can read on or reread to fix up their understanding. Have children use sticky notes to mark anything they don't understand. They can pull off a note, if it is cleared up later, and get help for any remaining notes.

READ THE BOOK

PAGE 3 Which character trait best describes Jean: boy, old, happy? *(happy)*

PAGES 4–6 Who had the best idea for where to camp? Why? *(Possible response: Father; He picked a place that Jean and Richard could both enjoy.)*

PAGE 6 What is a trail? *(Possible response: a path in the forest)*

PAGE 8 Where did the family put all things they had packed? *(the kitchen)*

TALK ABOUT THE BOOK

THINK AND SHARE

1. the family's home; Crescent Lake. One is indoors; the other is outdoors.
2. Look for the speaker's name. Possible response: Richard: Let's camp high on a mountain. Jean: At the beach we could build a sand castle. Mother: Let's plan ahead. Father: I have an idea.
3. *str–:* straight, stream; *pl–:* explore, play, please, plan
4. Possible response: The answer is "Yes," since everyone seemed happy when they arrived.

RESPONSE OPTIONS

WRITING Have children describe what the family might see and do at Crescent Lake.

CONTENT CONNECTIONS

SCIENCE Display various travel brochures. Have children design brochures for a local nature destination.

Name _____

Character and Setting

Read each sentence below.

Circle the answer that best completes each sentence.

I. In the beginning of the story, Mother wants to

    a. read the newspaper.   b. plan a trip.   c. go back to bed.

2. The family camped

    a. in the desert.   b. near the beach.   c. in the forest.

3. Father was

    a. helpful.   b. sad.   c. tired.

4. In the story, Mother

    a. drove the car.   b. read the map.   c. saw a bear.

5. Write three things that Jean liked.

_____

_____

_____

_____

22

Name _____

Vocabulary

Draw a line to match each word on the left with the word or words on the right that mean the opposite.

1. build   **a.** hate

2. couldn't   **b.** mother

3. father   **c.** was able to

4. love   **d.** tear down

Write each word from the box to best complete the sentence.

Words to Know
bear   mother   straight

5. The little _____ cub walked

_____ up to Jean's

_____.

23

A Home in the Wilderness

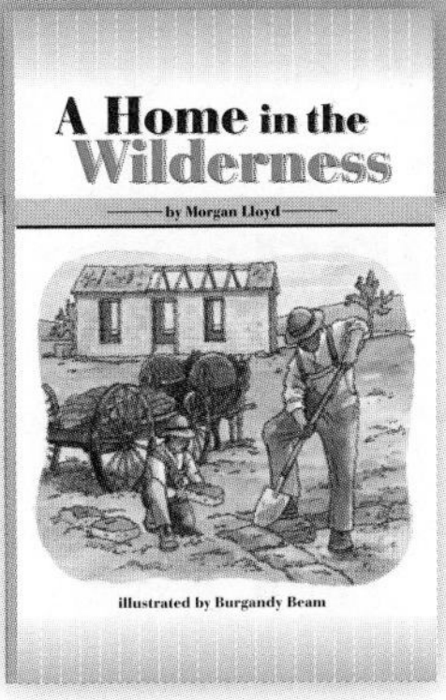

Unit 1 Week 3

CHARACTER AND SETTING

MONITOR AND FIX UP

LESSON VOCABULARY galaxy, tranquil, wildlife

SUMMARY *A Home in the Wilderness* tells the fictional story of an African American family building a homestead in the 1870s Nebraska wilderness while learning to live with and adjust to the challenges of nature.

INTRODUCE THE BOOK

BUILD BACKGROUND Have children share their thoughts when they hear the word *wilderness.* Discuss the challenges people who moved to the wilderness might have faced.

PREVIEW/USE ILLUSTRATIONS Ask children to preview the illustrations in the book. Point out the covered wagon on page 3. Point to the funnel cloud on page 8 and discuss tornadoes. Ask children to predict how the story might end. Then turn to pages 14 and 15 to see the final illustrations.

TEACH/REVIEW VOCABULARY Have children read the first paragraph on page 5. Model how to use context clues to figure out the meaning of the word *tranquil,* and explain that these clues make you think that *tranquil* means "calm." Reread the sentence to see if the word *calm* makes sense. Then look up the word in a dictionary to verify its meaning. Repeat the exercise for *galaxy* and *wilderness.*

ELL Use pictures to reinforce the meaning of the words *galaxy* and *wilderness* for students.

TARGET SKILL AND STRATEGY

CHARACTER AND SETTING Remind children that every story has *characters* (people or animals) and a *setting* (a time and place where the story happens). Knowing about characters and setting makes it easier to talk about a story. As children discuss the story, ask them to describe what Ruthie says and does. Repeat the exercise for Papa and Jeremiah. Then ask children to tell where and when the story takes place.

MONITOR AND FIX UP Remind children that if something they read is confusing, it can be helpful to keep reading. Often the answer can be found later in the story.

READ THE BOOK

Use the following questions to support comprehension.

PAGE 4 Why did the family fill their wagon with food? *(Possible response: They brought food because there wasn't much food in the wilderness.)*

PAGE 9 Why did Ruthie cry? *(Possible response: She was sad because so much damage had been done.)*

PAGE 15 What clues in the story tell us what Jeremiah is like? *(Possible response: Jeremiah helped Papa, and he found prairie chicken eggs for Ruthie. He is helpful.)*

TALK ABOUT THE BOOK

THINK AND SHARE

1. Responses will vary, but should include details about the weather, era, location, terrain, etc.
2. Mud fell down when it rained because the roof was made of mud and grass.
3. Possible responses include *quiet, calm, peaceful,* or *still.*
4. Responses will vary but should reflect children's comprehension of the hardships faced by homesteaders and the commonalities of family life.

RESPONSE OPTIONS

WRITING Ask children to pretend that they are Ruthie or Jeremiah. Suggest that they write a letter to a friend back East telling about their adventures.

CONTENT CONNECTIONS

TIME FOR Science

SCIENCE Encourage children to investigate prairie chickens by visiting the library or using the Internet. Suggest that they find out what prairie chickens look like and whether they actually are chickens.

Name _____

Character and Setting

Answer these questions about Jeremiah.

1. Where did he live?

_____

- -

_____

2. When did he live?

_____

- -

_____

- -

_____

3. What did he do? What happened to him?

_____

- -

_____

- -

_____

- -

_____

4. How did he feel about Ruthie?

_____

- -

_____

- -

_____

- -

_____

© Pearson Education 2

22

Vocabulary

Choose the best word from the box to complete each sentence.

Words to Know
galaxy   tranquil   wildlife

_____

1. Many kinds of _____, such as prairie chickens, coyotes, and rabbits, lived on the prairie.

2. On summer nights, the prairie was quiet and

_____

_____ .

_____

3. All the stars in the _____ glowed in the night sky.

Write a sentence about life on the prairie. Use a vocabulary word in your sentence.

_____

_____

_____

_____

_____

23

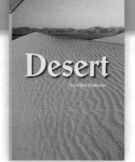

🎯 **MAIN IDEA AND DETAILS**

🎯 **TEXT STRUCTURE**

LESSON VOCABULARY animals, early, eyes, full, warm, water

Desert

SUMMARY This nonfiction book involves all the senses as it describes the climate, animals, and plants in the desert.

INTRODUCE THE BOOK

BUILD BACKGROUND If possible, have a box of sand and a cactus on hand. Invite children to feel the sand and carefully touch the cactus. Have them imagine walking for many days in sand. Ask them to tell about their "experiences."

PREVIEW/USE TEXT FEATURES As you preview the book, draw childrens' attention to the various text features, including photographs and captions. Read a caption, and explain to the children why it is interesting to you. Ask them to do the same as they go through the book.

TEACH/REVIEW VOCABULARY Post pictures representing the five senses. Divide the class into five groups— one for each sense. Have each group come up with sentences relating the vocabulary words to their sense. For example, the group for the sense of touch can say how *water* feels after many days in a dry desert.

ELL After writing each vocabulary word on an index card, have children write clue words or phrases on the back. Suggest that the clues relate to their senses.

TARGET SKILL AND STRATEGY

🎯 **MAIN IDEA AND DETAILS** Review the *main idea*—the most important idea in a story or paragraph and the *details*—information that tells more about the main idea. Help children organize information to determine the story's main idea.

🎯 **TEXT STRUCTURE** The descriptions of life in the desert form the *text structure* and can be grouped around each sense. Make a five-column chart entitled *Desert*, using each of the senses as a column heading. Ask children to tell what one can see, hear, etc., in the desert. Write each item in the proper column.

READ THE BOOK

Use the following questions to support comprehension.

PAGE 3 What is one way of finding out what the desert is like? *(You can read about life in the desert.)*

PAGES 5–6 What animals might you see in the desert? *(prairie dogs, lizards, coyotes)*

PAGE 7 Why do cactuses do well in the desert? *(They can store water.)*

PAGE 8 Why must you bring water when you go to the desert? *(It is very dry.)*

TALK ABOUT THE BOOK

THINK AND SHARE

1. Possible response: Main idea answers will vary but should note it is about the desert. Details can include: There are many things to see and hear and smell in the desert. The desert has little water.

2. The chart should include questions and answers posted on pages 3 or 4 and the answers provided throughout the book.

3. *visited, flying, digging, shaking, running, howling; visit, fly, dig, shake, run, howl*

4. barn owl, scorpion, horned lizard, prairie dog, coyote

RESPONSE OPTIONS

WORD WORK Start a list titled *Things I Like About Sand.* Write children's responses on strips of paper. Stand them in your box of sand—the "Word Desert."

CONTENT CONNECTIONS

SCIENCE Choose one animal from those shown in the book. Read about that animal and talk with a partner about how your animal lives in the desert.

Name _____

Main Idea and Details

1. Write one word that tells
   the topic of this book.

   _____
   -
   _____

2. Choose the main idea—the most important idea about the
   desert—and circle it.

   > All deserts have lots of sand.
   >
   > The desert can be hot and dry, but it has
   > many plants and animals.
   >
   > The desert prairie dog lives with rattlesnakes
   > and cactuses.

3. What are some details that tell more about the main idea?
   Choose two detail sentences from the box and circle them.

   > You can see and hear different animals.
   >
   > I went to the desert.
   >
   > Many flowers and trees grow in the
   > dry desert.
   >
   > It always rains in the desert.

26

Name _____

Vocabulary

Circle the letter that begins each word.
Write the letter on the line.

Words to Know
animals   early   eyes
full   warm   water

b   a
_____ _____
- - - - - -

1. _____ nimals

e   a
_____ _____
- - - - - -

2. _____ ye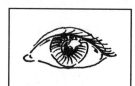

s   e
_____ _____
- - - - - -

3. _____ arly

w   t
_____ _____
- - - - - -

4. _____ arm

r   w
_____ _____
- - - - - -

5. _____ ater

f   t
_____ _____
- - - - - -

6. _____ ull

7. Write a sentence about the desert using one or more words from the box.

_____

- -

_____

27

A Walk in the Mountains

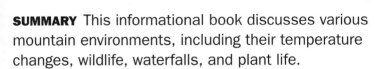

🔊 **MAIN IDEA AND DETAILS**

🔊 **TEXT STRUCTURE**

LESSON VOCABULARY animals, early, eyes, full, warm, water

SUMMARY This informational book discusses various mountain environments, including their temperature changes, wildlife, waterfalls, and plant life.

INTRODUCE THE BOOK

BUILD BACKGROUND Have children imagine how a walk in the mountains would be different from driving through or flying over mountains. Suggest that they read using all their senses to think about what mountains have to offer.

PREVIEW/USE TEXT FEATURES Allow children to leaf through the book and look at the photographs. Encourage them to stop and read captions of photos that interest them most. Ask them what part of mountain life they want to read about most.

TEACH/REVIEW VOCABULARY On the board, write the vocabulary words inside a simple sketch of a mountain. Leave space around each word. Ask volunteers to make small drawings of each word next to the printed word. Then have children write a sentence for each word using the drawings as rebus pictures.

ELL Ask students to make a picture of mountains or an animal or a plant that is familiar. Then help them write a sentence using one of the vocabulary words.

TARGET SKILL AND STRATEGY

🔊 **MAIN IDEA AND DETAILS** As they read, help children discern the *main idea* of each page or spread. Point out different details given about mountains and how the details tell more about the main idea.

🔊 **TEXT STRUCTURE** The photographs and captions in this book form a descriptive *text structure*. To help children see how the book is organized, draw a word web on the board with the word *Mountains* in the main circle. As children tell you things they've learned about mountains, write each comment in a different circle around the main idea.

READ THE BOOK

Use the following questions to support comprehension.

PAGE 3 Why would you keep both your eyes and ears open on a walk in the mountains? *(There are things to see and to hear.)*

PAGE 8 Why do animals, plants, and trees live in mountains? *(They are able to grow and thrive there.)*

PAGE 11 Where is a good place to find plants in the mountains? *(near streams)*

TALK ABOUT THE BOOK

THINK AND SHARE
1. Possible response: Main idea: Many animals and plants live in the mountains. Detail: Mountain goats are good climbers and live in the mountains. Detail: Edelweiss is a mountain flower.
2. Possible response: nonfiction; It is not a story, it gives information, and it has photos and captions.
3. Possible response: *empty, cool, late;* The eagle's nest was empty. It was cool on the mountaintop. I like to walk late in the day.
4. Possible responses: A hare's fur turns white to protect it from other animals. It can't be seen in snow.

RESPONSE OPTIONS

WORD WORK Continue the rebus sentence activity from the vocabulary review. Assign a different word to each student to use in a new rebus sentence. Hang the pictures up on a "Mountain Wall."

CONTENT CONNECTIONS

SOCIAL STUDIES Have books on hand for children to do a map study of mountains in one region of the United States. Make legends, using small drawings to show plants or animals found in certain mountains.

Time for **SOCIAL STUDIES**

Name _____

Main Idea and Details

Read each question and the answer choices above it.
Circle the right answer.

animals

walking

mountains

1. What is the topic of this book?

Mountains are very old.

Weather changes mountains.

There are many kinds of life and activities in the mountains.

2. What is the most important idea about mountains?

Keep your eyes open.

Animal and plant life changes from bottom to top.

You can find mountain ranges on a map.

Waterfalls can shape mountains.

People go skiing on snowy mountains.

3. What are two details that tell more about the main idea?

© Pearson Education 2

26

Name _____

Vocabulary

Write a word from the box to complete each sentence.

Words to Know		
animals	early	eyes
full	warm	water

1. Open your _____ to see trees and flowers and plants.

2. If you go _____ to the mountains, you might see the eagle.

3. Fill your basket _____ of flowers.

4. At the bottom of the mountain it will feel _____.

5. Cool _____ rushes down the mountain.

6. A hare is just one of the _____ you see on a mountain.

7. Write a sentence about things you could see or hear on a walk in the mountains. Use a word from the box.

_____

_____

_____

_____

27

Trek to the Top

Trek to the Top
by Megan McDonald

⟳ **MAIN IDEA AND DETAILS**

⟳ **TEXT STRUCTURE**

LESSON VOCABULARY arid, canyons, landform, moisture, precipitation

---

SUMMARY Oceans, lakes, rivers, mountains, and valleys are among the features that make up the Earth's surface. Some landforms are the result of changes deep within the Earth. Others result from the movement of wind and water.

INTRODUCE THE BOOK

BUILD BACKGROUND Brainstorm a list of Earth's features. Begin by listing a couple of examples (lakes, valleys).

PREVIEW/USE TEXT FEATURES Invite children to preview the book's illustrations, headings, and captions. On page 3, point out the word *landforms* in dark print. Look up this word in the Glossary. On page 6, read the heading and ask children discuss any lakes and ponds they have seen. Continue discussing the illustrations and captions on the remaining page.

TEACH/REVIEW VOCABULARY Point out the word *arid* on page 12. Remind children that when they see an unfamiliar word, they can sometimes figure out its meaning by noticing how it is used in a sentence. Model using context to figure out the definition: *Arid* is another word for *dry*. Repeat with other lesson vocabulary.

ELL Use photographs and illustrations to reinforce the meaning of vocabulary words for children.

TARGET SKILL AND STRATEGY

⟳ **MAIN IDEA AND DETAILS** Show how being able to identify the main ideas in a selection will help children understand what they read. Model how to identify the topic of page 4 *(oceans)*, the most important idea *(oceans cover much of the earth),* and some supporting details. *(an ocean is the largest body of water on Earth; oceans hold most of Earth's water supply)* Turn to other pages and ask: What is this paragraph about? What sentence gives the most important idea?

⟳ **TEXT STRUCTURE** Remind children that figuring out how a book is organized, or its *text structure,* can help them understand the book and find its main ideas.

READ THE BOOK

Use the following questions to support comprehension.

PAGES 4–5 How are seas like oceans? How are they different? *(Both are salt water; seas are closed in by land).*

PAGE 8 What is one way that the water cycle helps create the Earth's landforms? *(Possible answer: Rain collects in rivers that carve valleys.)*

PAGE 10 What is the main idea on this page? *(Possible response: Valleys are low places between mountains.)*

TALK ABOUT THE BOOK

THINK AND SHARE

1. Main idea: Mountains are important landforms. Details: Mountains are steep; they are the tallest landforms on Earth. Mountains are made up of rocky land.
2. The book is divided into sections that discuss Earth's features. The author first discusses bodies of water and then talks about land features.
3. Dry places, such as deserts, do not get much rain.
4. Pacific, Atlantic, Arctic, and Indian Oceans

RESPONSE OPTIONS

WORD WORK Ask children to consider why the end of a river is called a *mouth*. Point out that the beginning of a river is called the *head*.

CONTENT CONNECTIONS

SOCIAL STUDIES Suggest that children look for bodies of water and landforms on a state map. Have them list the rivers, lakes, valleys, and other features that they find and share this information with the class.

Time for **SOCIAL STUDIES**

Name _____

Main Idea and Details

Read the selection.
Write the main idea and three supporting details.

Mountains
Mountains are important landforms. Mountains are made up of rocky land. They have steep sides and a pointed or a rounded top. Mountains are the tallest parts of Earth. They can form when Earth's crust moves or lava breaks through the crust.

Main Idea

_____
- -
_____
_____
- -
_____

Supporting Details

_____
- -
_____
_____
- -
_____
_____
- -
_____

© Pearson Education 2

26

Vocabulary

Draw a line from each word on the left to its definition.

Words to Know
arid   canyons   landform
moisture   precipitation

1. arid

2. canyons

3. landform

4. moisture

5. precipitation

a. a feature on Earth's surface, such as a mountain or valley

b. rain or snow that falls to Earth's surface

c. very dry

d. deep, narrow valleys with steep sides

e. wetness

6. Choose one vocabulary word and use it in a sentence.

_____

_ _

_____

_ _

_____

The Case of the Missing Fish

The Case of the Missing Fish

by Abby Seaborne
illustrated by George Hamblin

REALISM AND FANTASY

MONITOR AND FIX UP

LESSON VOCABULARY gone, learn, often, pieces, though, together, very

---

SUMMARY This play presents a brief story of Bird's search for Fish. He asks several animals before finding Elephant, who helps him see the answer.

INTRODUCE THE BOOK

BUILD BACKGROUND Ask children about their experiences with plays and how they are different from reading stories. Discuss how the characters in a play act out a story line. Point out that the characters in the selection seem to be talking animals.

PREVIEW/USE TEXT FEATURES Help children look through the play and notice how each character's part is identified. Ask them who they think the main character is.

TEACH/REVIEW VOCABULARY Suggest that children copy the vocabulary words on paper and write a sentence using each one. Make some distinctions by asking questions such as: What is the difference in meaning between the sentences "I go to the store" and "I go to the store *often*?" How does the word *often* change the sentence?

ELL Have more proficient English speakers say a sentence frame that leaves out a vocabulary word. Then have other children complete the sentence. After all the words have been covered once, reverse the roles.

TARGET SKILL AND STRATEGY

REALISM AND FANTASY Help children distinguish between *realism* and *fantasy* by deciding whether texts are make-believe or if they could really happen. Tell a simple fishing story that could be true. Then ask children to talk about the differences between *The Case of the Missing Fish* and the story you just told. Have them write a sentence telling why the book is a fantasy.

MONITOR AND FIX UP Explain that *monitoring* reading can help us fix problems and better understand what we read. Model how children should stop, identify a problem, and reread the page or read on to clear things up.

READ THE BOOK

Use the following questions to support comprehension.

PAGE 4 Why was it important that Squirrel heard a splash? *(Bird thinks more about where Fish could be.)*

PAGE 5 Why was Bird interested in the splash and what Fish had said? *(He knew they were clues.)*

PAGE 6 What does Elephant figure out? *(Fish often takes a bath on Tuesday.)*

TALK ABOUT THE BOOK

THINK AND SHARE
1. The animals talk and act like people.
2. Squirrel and Zebra; the animals' names are in dark letters, followed by a colon, and come before their lines.
3. Responses will vary.
4. Responses will vary.

RESPONSE OPTIONS

DRAMA Children may enjoy performing this play. Some children can make costumes and simple sets, and others can be characters. The play may be performed for a younger class or children's families.

CONTENT CONNECTIONS

SOCIAL STUDIES Remind children that there are many places to look when we have questions, such as the dictionary. Ask them to suggest resources for answering questions. Write a list on the board as they respond. Tell them not to forget their own thinking skills, which Bird used, to find answers to questions.

Time for SOCIAL STUDIES

Realism and Fantasy

A **fantasy** is a story about something that could not happen.
A **realistic story** tells about something that could happen.

Read the sentences.
Write R on the line if the sentences begin a realistic story
or F if they begin a fantasy.

_____

_____ **1.** Once upon a time there lived three little pigs.
One wanted to build a house out of straw.

_____

_____ **2.** Fish said to Bird, "I often take a bath on Tuesday."

_____

_____ **3.** Tom never wanted to hunt bears. He always loved
bears. So he asked his dad to stop hunting bears.

_____

_____ **4.** Long ago, in a faraway land, lived a girl with a red
coat and hood. Her mother asked her to visit her
grandmother. On the way, a wolf asked her where
she was going.

_____

_____ **5.** A long, long time ago dinosaurs walked all over Earth.
Some people have found huge footprints left by
dinosaurs.

© Pearson Education 2

30

Name _____

Vocabulary

Read each sentence. Choose the best word to finish the sentence and circle it.

Words to Know			
gone	learn	often	pieces
though	together	very	

1. Sam had many _____ of paper.
   stack   pieces

2. LaToya could _____ well from this tutor.
   teach   learn

3. Sherry wanted to go out, even _____ it was raining.
   through   though

4. Sandy went to the park _____ with her friends.
   together   alone

5. Nancy _____ goes to the store for her mom.
   cannot   often

6. All the students except Hank had _____ home.
   gone   mine

7. Elephant said he loved playing ball _____ much.
   not   very

8. Write a sentence that Fish might say to Bird. Use a vocabulary word in your sentence.

   _____
   _____
   _____
   _____
   _____

© Pearson Education 2

31

The Bear Man

SUMMARY A Native American folk tale is retold as a simple story of how a father's love for bears is carried over to the way he and his wife raise their son.

INTRODUCE THE BOOK

BUILD BACKGROUND Talk with children about folk tales they know to set up a later discussion of realism and fantasy.

PREVIEW/USE ILLUSTRATIONS Have children look at the pictures in the book to see whom the story is about. Ask: Do you think this story is about a man or a bear? Do any pictures give you clues? What do you think will happen to the Bear Man?

ELL Ask volunteers to tell the class about a folk tale from their native culture. Point out any similar themes in other folk tales children may know.

TEACH/REVIEW VOCABULARY Write the vocabulary words on the board and ask volunteers to watch for a certain vocabulary word as they read the story. Afterward, each volunteer can tell what his or her word meant at that part of the story. Help children see how these everyday words can be used to tell a good story.

TARGET SKILL AND STRATEGY

◉ **REALISM AND FANTASY** Remind children that there are *realistic* stories that could happen and make-believe stories called *fantasy*. Ask: What happens in *The Bear Man* that makes you think you are reading a make-believe story? As children discuss talking animals, help them understand that these kinds of events in *The Bear Man* could not have happened, making the story a fantasy.

◉ **MONITOR AND FIX UP** Point out that children can try to tell the beginning, middle, and end of the story to check their understanding. If they have difficulty remembering or understanding, they can reread.

READ THE BOOK

Use the following questions to support comprehension.

PAGE 7 If a boy acts like a bear, is it make-believe or can it be real? *(Possible response: A child can act like an animal, so it is real.)*

PAGE 8 What happened when Bear Man's people went to war? *(All the warriors died except Bear Man.)*

PAGE 9 How did Bear Man get better after being badly hurt? *(The bears helped him.)*

TALK ABOUT THE BOOK

THINK AND SHARE
1. Possible response: No, bears do not talk.
2. Possible response: Kindness to animals can also help humans.
3. Responses will vary.
4. Responses will vary.

RESPONSE OPTIONS

WRITING Have children write a modern folk tale as a class. Talk about a situation in which good wins out over bad. Ask what other things they noticed were in this folk tale—for example, a hero, a challenge, a good deed.

CONTENT CONNECTIONS

SOCIAL STUDIES Have on hand several anthologies of folk tales, or take children to the library to find some. Divide children into small groups. Have each group read a folk tale from a different place around the world and find the lesson, or moral, contained in it.

Name _____

Realism and Fantasy

A **fantasy** is a story about something that could not happen.
A **realistic story** tells about something that could happen.

Read paragraph A and paragraph B. Circle **realistic story** or **fantasy** for each paragraph and write why you think as you do.

A. "If my son is ever hurt," he told the bear cub, "I hope he will be taken care of too." The man returned home and told his wife about the cub. One day much later, the man's son was hurt. Two bears found him and said, "We must take care of him."

B. A Pawnee family lives near Lincoln, Nebraska. Students have been asking the daughter Lily and her brother Thomas to do their traditional drum dance. They have practiced with their mother, and they are ready. Lily is excited.

_____

1. Paragraph A is a   realistic story   fantasy

_____

because _____

_____

2. Paragraph B is a   realistic story   fantasy

_____

because _____

_____

30

Name _____

Vocabulary

Circle the vocabulary words in the puzzle.
All words can be read from left to right.

Words to Know			
gone	learn	often	pieces
though	together	very	

```
N  O  R  S  M  E  T  R
O  R  M  A  M  G  O  B
L  E  A  R  N  O  B  N
W  O  F  T  E  N  Y  O
G  P  I  E  C  E  S  N
Z  E  M  V  E  R  Y  E
T  B  O  E  I  T  N  S
O  C  E  R  G  O  N  E
V  E  R  Y  K  I  A  M
T  O  G  E  T  H  E  R
R  O  T  H  O  U  G  H
```

Which two vocabulary words are also written from top to bottom?

_____   _____

- - - - - - - - - - - - - - - -   - - - - - - - - - - - - - - - -

_____   _____

31

Sue's Hummingbird

Sue's Hummingbird
by Christian Downey
illustrated by Durga Bernhard

Unit 1 Week 5

🔊 **REALISM AND FANTASY**

🔊 **MONITOR AND FIX UP**

LESSON VOCABULARY delicate, inquire, sturdy

SUMMARY Sue lives on a pueblo in New Mexico, where her family follows the traditions of the Zuni people. Her grandma tells the story of a magical hummingbird and surprises Sue with a special good luck charm.

INTRODUCE THE BOOK

BUILD BACKGROUND Involve children in a discussion about folk tales. Explain that *Sue's Hummingbird* is a story that contains a folk tale. Ask children to name some other folk tales they know.

PREVIEW/USE ILLUSTRATIONS Invite children to look through the book and scan the illustrations. Point out Sue in the illustration on page 3 and introduce the word *pueblo*. On page 5, ask: What might Sue be thinking? Point out the hummingbird on page 8.

TEACH/REVIEW VOCABULARY Write the word *sturdy* on the board. Ask a volunteer to find and read the sentence on page 3 that contains this word. Discuss what *sturdy* might mean, based on its use in the sentence. Ask children to brainstorm synonyms for *sturdy* and to make up sentences containing the word. Repeat the exercise for *delicate* (page 7) and *inquire* (page 10).

ELL Introduce the idiom *lives off the land* (page 4) to children. Provide a definition of this phrase and ask children to use it in a sentence.

TARGET SKILL AND STRATEGY

🔊 **REALISM AND FANTASY** Discuss examples of *realistic* stories and *fantasies* that children have already read. As children read *Sue's Hummingbird,* discuss the story events. Ask: Could this really happen? Remind children to give reasons for their answers.

🔊 **MONITOR AND FIX UP** Remind children that good readers ask themselves questions as they read to *monitor* their understanding of a story. When readers have questions about a story or are unsure whether the story is realistic or make-believe, looking at the illustrations and noticing that what the characters do or say can help answer those questions.

READ THE BOOK

Use the following questions to support comprehension.

PAGE 7 How would you describe Grandma? What did she do? *(Answers will vary, but they should relate to Grandma's characterization.)*

PAGES 8–9 Which parts of the hummingbird story are make-believe? Is Grandma's story realistic or a fantasy? *(Possible responses: the hummingbird wearing a coat and falling in love with a human; it is a fantasy.)*

PAGE 11 In your own words, describe how Sue's mother made pottery. Use the illustration to help you. *(Responses will vary but should reflect an understanding of the text and illustration.)*

TALK ABOUT THE BOOK

THINK AND SHARE
1. Real: Sue living in New Mexico, her family's crafts Make-believe: talking animals and other aspects of the hummingbird story
2. Responses should reflect comprehension of text, Sue's identity, and the meaning of the word *pueblo*.
3. *Inquire* means to ask about.
4. Responses may include apartments, condos, townhouses, and houses made of brick, wood or stucco.

RESPONSE OPTIONS

WRITING Suggest that each child write down a story that somebody in their family has told. They may need to talk with family members beforehand.

CONTENT CONNECTIONS

SOCIAL STUDIES Use a map to indicate where the Zuni people live. Have children use the library to research three facts about the Zuni people. Encourage them to share their discoveries with the class.

Time for SOCIAL STUDIES

Name _____

Realism and Fantasy

A **fantasy** is a story about something that could not happen.
A **realistic story** tells about something that could happen.

Look back at *Sue's Hummingbird*. Draw one part of the story that is real.

Write why it is real.

_____
- -
_____
- -
_____

Draw one part of the story that is make-believe.

Write why it is make-believe.

_____
- -
_____
- -
_____

30

Name _____

Vocabulary

Choose a word from the box to complete each sentence.
Write the word on the line.

Words to Know
delicate   inquire   sturdy

1. Sue asked Grandma lots of questions. Sue liked to

   _____

   _____ about what happened long ago.

2. The hummingbird fluttered its _____

   ----

   wings and floated in the air.

3. Thick mud bricks made the walls of the pueblo

   _____

   _____.

4. Write a sentence using at least one vocabulary word.

   _____

   _____

   _____

31

Answer Key for Below-Level Reader Practice

City Mouse and Country Mouse
LR1

🔄 Character and Setting, LR2
Setting: city, bakery, sidewalk, club **1.** a c e **2.** b d e

Vocabulary, LR3
1. c **2.** a **3.** b
Possible responses given. **4.** On my birthday I feel like someone special. **5.** Each winter, we take a trip somewhere warm.

Being an Astronaut
LR10

🔄 Main Idea and Details, LR11
Possible responses given.
Topic: where astronauts sleep
Main Idea: Astronauts sleep in different places.
Supporting Details: Some use sleeping bags. Some sleep in bunks.

Vocabulary, LR12
1. b **2.** c **3.** d **4.** a **5.** world, machines, work

Pup Camps Out
LR19

🔄 Character and Setting, LR20
1. b **2.** c **3.** a **4.** a **5.** Possible responses given: Pup likes to camp.

Vocabulary, LR21
1. d **2.** a **3.** b **4.** c **5.** bear, couldn't, straight

Desert
LR28

🔄 Main Idea and Details, LR29
1. desert **2.** The desert can be hot and dry, but it has many plants and animals. **3.** You can see and hear different animals. Many flowers and trees grow in the dry desert.

Vocabulary, LR30
1. a **2.** e **3.** e **4.** w **5.** w **6.** f
7. Possible response given: The desert is full of animals.

The Case of the Missing Fish
LR37

🔄 Realism and Fantasy, LR38
1. F **2.** F **3.** R **4.** F **5.** R

Vocabulary, LR39
1. pieces **2.** learn **3.** though **4.** together **5.** often **6.** gone **7.** very
8. Possible response given: "I often take a bath on Tuesday."

Answer Key for On-Level Reader Practice

The New Kid   LR4

🔄 Character and Setting, LR5

Setting: small farms, Bali, island, summer; Characters: glad, new kid, adventurous, likes soccer

Vocabulary, LR6

1. b **2.** c **3.** a

Possible responses given. **4.** Mom says someone from school can come along. **5.** I know my key is somewhere in my room.

Space Walk   LR13

🔄 Main Idea and Details, LR14

Possible responses given.
Topic: space walks
Main Idea: There are problems on a space walk.
Supporting Details: There is no air in space. Space junk can hit you.

Vocabulary, LR15

1. world **2.** machines **3.** woman **4.** live **5.** move **6.** everywhere **7.** work

Let's Camp at Crescent Lake   LR22

🔄 Character and Setting, LR23

1. b **2.** c **3.** a **4.** b **5.** Possible responses given: pancakes, the beach, building sand castles

Vocabulary, LR24

1. d **2.** c **3.** b **4.** a **5.** bear, straight, mother

A Walk in the Mountains   LR31

🔄 Main Idea and Details, LR32

1. mountains **2.** There are many kinds of life and activities in the mountains. **3.** Animal and plant life changes from bottom to top. Waterfalls can shape mountains.

Vocabulary, LR33

1. eyes **2.** early **3.** full **4.** warm **5.** water **6.** animals
7. Possible response given: You could see animals.

Bear Man   LR40

🔄 Realism and Fantasy, LR41

1. fantasy; because bears do not talk. **2.** realistic story; because children could do a Native American dance.

Vocabulary, LR42

Across: LEARN, OFTEN, PIECES, VERY, GONE, VERY, TOGETHER, THOUGH; Down: VERY, GONE.

Answer Key for Advanced-Level Reader Practice

City Friends, Country Friends   LR7

Character and Setting, LR8
Tasha/urban setting: apartment, taxis, elevator
Henry/rural setting: pigs, mud, well water, tractors
Both: Mom's pie, bagels, grass, perfume

Vocabulary, LR9
1. urban **2.** investigate **3.** rural **4.** rural, urban

Exploring the Galaxy   LR16

Main Idea and Details, LR17
Possible responses given. **1.** astronauts **2.** Astronauts need to be well trained. **3.** Many are scientists. They need to be healthy. They need to know how spaceships work.

Vocabulary, LR18
1. orbit **2.** descend **3.** ascend **4.** asteroids **5.** Satellites **6.** gravity
7. laboratory

A Home in the Wilderness   LR25

Character and Setting, LR26
Possible responses given. **1.** in the wilderness; in Nebraska **2.** back when people were moving west in wagons **3.** heard a coyote; helped Papa work; worked in garden; saw a tornado; found chicken eggs for Ruthie **4.** He cared for her; he helped take care of her when she was sick.

Vocabulary, LR27
1. wildlife **2.** tranquil **3.** galaxy **4.** Responses will vary.

Trek to the Top   LR34

Main Idea and Details, LR35
Main Idea: Mountains are important landforms.
Supporting Details: rocky land, tallest parts of Earth, can form from lava

Vocabulary, LR36
1. c. **2.** d. **3.** a. **4.** e. **5.** b.
6. Possible response given: The desert is an arid place.

Sue's Hummingbird   LR43

Realism and Fantasy, LR44
Responses should include details about Sue and Zuni life. Responses should include details about the hummingbird folk tale.

Vocabulary, LR45
1. inquire **2.** delicate **3.** sturdy
4. Possible response given: The house I live in is very sturdy.

Let's Learn Amazing Words

TEACH/MODEL

 to build oral vocabulary

ROUTINE

Oral Vocabulary

1 Introduce the Word Relate the word to the song or story in which it appears. Supply a child-friendly definition. Have children say the word. Example:
- People who live in the country live in a *rural* place. A *rural* place is peaceful and has farms and lots of open spaces. Say the word *rural* with me, *rural.*

2 Demonstrate Provide familiar examples to demonstrate meaning. When possible, use gestures to help convey meaning. Examples:
- People who live in *rural* places have lots of room to run and play, with trees to climb and sometimes horses to ride.

3 Apply Have children demonstrate understanding with a simple activity. Suggestions for step 3 activities appear on the next page. Example:
- Tell me which of these things you would be able to do in a *rural* place—ride a bike, climb a tree, ride a pony, go up in an elevator.

4 Display the Word/Letter-Sounds Write the word on a card and display it on a classroom Amazing Words board. Have children identify some familiar letter-sounds or word parts. Example:
- This word is *rural.* What consonant letter and sound is at the beginning and in the middle of *rural?*

Use the Oral Vocabulary Routine along with the definitions, examples, letter-sounds, and word parts that are provided on the following pages to introduce each Amazing Word.

ABOUT ORAL VOCABULARY A child's oral vocabulary development is a predictor of future reading success. Oral vocabulary development now boosts children's comprehension as they become fluent readers. Oral vocabulary is informally assessed.

ACTIVITIES

To allow children to demonstrate understanding of the Amazing Words, use activities such as these in step 3 of the Routine.

ANSWER QUESTIONS Would you prefer to have a *festive* day or an *ordinary* day? Why?

CREATE EXAMPLES What is something a good *citizen* might do?

MAKE CHOICES If any of the things I name can *hatch*, say *hatch*; if not, say nothing: a train, a chicken, a jar of jam, a snake, a tadpole, a horse.

PANTOMIME Show me how an eagle *soars*, a rocket, an airplane.

PERSONAL CONTEXT Some people are *fond* of fishing. Tell about something you are *fond* of. Use the word *fond* when you tell about it.

SYNONYMS AND ANTONYMS Name a word that means the opposite of *genuine*; name a word that means about the same as *genuine*.

Monitor Progress | Check Oral Vocabulary

To monitor understanding of concepts and vocabulary that have been explicitly taught each week:

• Display the week's Build Background pages in the Student Edition.

• Remind the child of the concept that the class has been talking about that week.

• Ask the child to tell you about the Build Background illustrations using some of the week's Amazing Words.

If... a child has difficulty using the Amazing Words,

then... ask questions about the illustration using the Amazing Words. Note which questions the child can respond to. Reteach unknown words using the Oral Vocabulary Routine.

SUCCESS PREDICTOR

Amazing Words

to build oral vocabulary

Definitions, examples, and **letter-sounds** to use with Oral Vocabulary Routine on p. DI·1

USE WITH

DAY 1

1 **INVESTIGATE** When you *investigate* something, you try to find out all about it.

2 **Example:** Let's *investigate* our new neighborhood. (Step 3: Have children show how they might *investigate* something inside a drawer or bag.)

4 **Word Parts:** Say the word slowly and clap with each syllable. Have children do it with you.

1 **RURAL** People who live in the country live in a *rural* place.

2 **Example:** My aunt lives on a farm in a *rural* part of the state.

4 **Letter-Sounds:** Identify the letter-sounds for r/r/. Point out final l/l/.

1 **URBAN** People who live in a city live in an *urban* place.

2 **Examples:** There is lots of traffic with cars, trucks, and buses in an *urban* place. If you live in a big apartment building, you probably live in an *urban* area.

4 **Letter-Sounds:** Identify the letter-sounds for r/r/ and b/b/. Point out final n/n/.

DAY 2

1 **CREATURE** A *creature* is an animal or person that is living.

2 **Examples:** Many *creatures* live in the forest. I heard a *creature* making noise in that bush.

4 **Letter-Sounds:** Identify the letter-sounds for cr/kr/ and the final s/z/.

DAY 3

1 **UNDERGROUND** *Underground* means under the ground you walk on.

2 **Examples:** If you dig a hole, you can find something that is *underground*. Squirrels and chipmunks bury their food in *underground* holes.

4 **Word Parts:** Children can decode and identify the words *under* and *ground* and combine them to make the compound word *underground*.

DAY 4

1 **BRITTLE** Something that is *brittle* breaks very easily.

2 **Examples:** If you drop an egg, you'll find out that its shell is *brittle*. Some *brittle* plastic toys shatter and break.

4 **Letter-Sounds:** Identify the letter-sounds for br/br/ and i/i/.

1 **DECISION** When you make up your mind to do something, you make a *decision*.

2 **Examples:** I made a *decision* to have a peanut-butter-and-jelly sandwich for lunch. You can make your own *decision* about which shirt to wear today.

4 **Letter-Sounds:** Identify the letter-sounds for d/d/ and c/s/.

1 **DART** When something *darts*, it moves very quickly from one place to another.

2 **Example:** On a windy day, clouds *dart* across the sky. (Step 3: Let children show how they would *dart* from one end of the room to the other.)

4 **Letter-Sounds:** Children can decode *dart*.

Exploring Space with an Astronaut

Definitions, examples, and letter-sounds to use with Oral Vocabulary Routine on p. DI·1

Amazing Words to build oral vocabulary

USE WITH

DAY 1

1 ASCEND When you *ascend*, you go up.

2 Examples: Astronauts *ascend* into space in their space shuttles. You *ascend* to the second floor when you walk upstairs. (Step 3: Have children show how they *ascend* stairs.)

4 Letter-Sounds: Identify the sounds for *sc*/s/ and final *nd*/nd/.

1 DESCEND When you *descend*, you go down.

2 Examples: Astronauts *descend* when they come down from space in their space shuttles. You *descend* when you walk downstairs. (Let children show how they *descend* stairs.)

4 Word Parts: Point out *de*. *De* is a word part that can mean "down." *Descend* means "to move down to a lower place."

1 ORBIT An *orbit* is the path of something like a spacecraft or planet around something in space, such as Earth or the sun.

2 Examples: Earth *orbits* the sun, and the moon *orbits* Earth.

4 Word Parts: Identify the syllables *or* and *bit*, which children can decode separately and then put together.

DAY 2

1 UNIVERSE The *universe* is made up of Earth, the sun, the moon, and all the other planets and stars in the sky.

2 Examples: Our world is a small part of the *universe*. When we look at the stars, we think how huge our *universe* must be.

4 Letter-Sounds/Word Parts: Children can identify the long *u* in the first syllable. Clap the three syllables with them.

DAY 3

1 ENORMOUS Something that is *enormous* is very big and huge.

2 Examples: An *enormous* cloud can almost cover the whole sky. An *enormous* building is so big you can't see it all at the same time.

4 Letter-Sounds: Identify the short *i* of the first syllable. Children can decode the syllable *nor*.

1 JOURNEY A *journey* is a long trip.

2 Examples: When a family drives for several days to go somewhere, they go on a *journey*. An astronaut goes on a *journey* into space.

4 Letter-Sounds: Point out *j*/j/, *r*/r/, and *n*/n/.

DAY 4

1 LAUNCH You *launch* something when you get it started or set it going.

2 Examples: We *launch* a boat or a plane when we get ready to go. A space shuttle is *launched* when it starts up and gets into the sky.

4 Letter-Sounds: Identify the *l*/l/ and the final *ch*/ch/.

1 METEORITE A *meteorite* is a piece of stone from space that hits something.

2 Examples: Spaceships sometimes are hit by *meteorites*. Some *meteorites* that hit Earth leave big dents in the ground.

4 Letter-Sounds: Children can identify *m*/m/ and *t*/t/.

Amazing Words to build oral vocabulary

Definitions, examples, and **letter-sounds** to use with Oral Vocabulary Routine on p. DI·1

USE WITH

DAY 1

1. **GALAXY** A *galaxy* is a huge group of stars. Earth and the sun are part of a big *galaxy*.

2. **Examples:** On a clear night you can see a *galaxy* of stars. Scientists say there are lots of *galaxies* besides the one we are in.

4. **Letter-Sounds:** Point out g/g/, l/l/, and x/ks/.

1. **TRANQUIL** *Tranquil* is how you feel when you are very calm and peaceful.

2. **Examples:** Looking at the stars makes me feel *tranquil*. A warm summer night seems *tranquil*. (Step 3: Have children act out feeling *tranquil*.)

4. **Letter-Sounds:** Identify the initial *tr*/tr/ and point out *qu*/kw/.

1. **WILDLIFE** Animals and plants that live wild outdoors are called *wildlife*.

2. **Examples:** There are many kinds of *wildlife* in the forest. We saw many kinds of *wildlife* when we went camping.

4. **Word Parts:** Help children to decode *wild* and *life* and combine them to make the compound word *wildlife*.

DAY 2

1. **UNDERNEATH** If you put a book under your chair, you can say the book is *underneath* your chair.

2. **Examples:** My socks are *underneath* my pajamas in the top drawer. In my lunchbox I have an apple *underneath* my sandwich. (Step 3: Have children put one thing under another and show which is *underneath*.)

4. **Word Parts:** Children can identify the word *under* in *underneath*.

DAY 3

1. **IDENTIFY** When you *identify* something, you tell what it is.

2. **Examples:** The tags on a dog's collar *identify* the dog's owner. I put my name on my lunchbox to *identify* it. (Step 3: Have children *identify* their own coats or other possessions.)

4. **Letter-Sounds:** Indicate the long *i* sound of the first syllable and *nt*/nt/ in the middle of the word.

DAY 4

1. **DETECTIVE** A *detective* is a person who tries to solve a mystery or figure out a problem.

2. **Examples:** You are a word *detective* when you figure out what a word means. A police *detective* figures out who is responsible for a crime.

4. **Word Parts:** The word *detect* means to discover or find out.

1. **FASCINATING** Something that is *fascinating* is very interesting.

2. **Examples:** We read about a girl who found insects *fascinating*. I read a *fascinating* book about elephants.

4. **Letter-Sounds:** Point out f/f/ and *sc*/s/.

1. **SLIMY** Something *slimy* feels slippery and gooey when you touch it.

2. **Examples:** Some people think snakes feel *slimy*, but they really don't. The mud at the bottom of the river felt *slimy* on my feet.

4. **Letter-Sounds:** Identify *sl*/sl/ and the long *e* sound of *y* at the end of the word.

Definitions, examples, and letter-sounds to use with Oral Vocabulary Routine on p. DI·1

Amazing Words

to build oral vocabulary

USE WITH

DAY 1

1 **ARID** (Use with Step 1): Something that is *arid* is very, very dry.

2 **Examples:** Deserts are *arid* because they don't get much rain. The air in your house in the winter might be *arid* because the heat is on all the time.

4 **Letter-Sounds:** Identify the letter-sounds for ar/ar/ and d/d/.

LANDFORM A *landform* is the shape formed on land. *Landforms* are things like hills, mountains, lakes, and deserts.

Examples: The *landforms* in Arizona include mountains and desert, as well as rivers.

Word Parts: Children can identify the word parts *land* and *form* and combine them into the compound *landform*.

PRECIPITATION *Precipitation* means any kind of rain, snow, hail, or other form of water that comes down from the clouds to the ground.

Examples: A desert area is dry because it gets very little *precipitation*. Many kinds of trees that grow in forests need a lot of *precipitation*.

Letter-Sounds/Word Parts: Children can decode the syllable *pre*. Point out the c/s/, p/p/, and the ending *-tion* /shən/ sounds.

DAY 2

1 **DUNES** A *dune* is a hill of sand in a desert. *Dunes* are formed when the wind blows the sand.

2 **Examples:** That *dune* wasn't there last time we came to this beach. The *dunes* in a desert shift and change.

4 **Letter-Sounds:** Children can decode *dune*.

LEDGE A *ledge* is a shelf.

Examples: If you are in the desert, you might see a coyote up on a *ledge*. There is a toy on the window *ledge*.

Letter-Sounds: Children can decode *ledge*.

DAY 3

1 **HAVEN** A *haven* is a safe place.

2 **Examples:** A big cactus is a *haven* for lots of animals. Your school is a *haven* for you during a big rainstorm.

4 **Letter-Sounds:** Point out the long *a* sound in the first syllable. Children can decode the second syllable.

DAY 4

1 **DISCOVERY** A *discovery* is something someone finds out for the first time.

2 **Examples:** You made a *discovery* about school the first day you came. When Iris first moved she made lots of new *discoveries* about the country.

4 **Word Parts:** Have children note the base word *cover* in discovery. Point out that the word part *dis* can mean "to undo" something. So *discover* means "uncover" or "find."

FORBIDDING Something that is *forbidding* seems dangerous and scary.

Examples: Even your familiar schoolroom can seem *forbidding* and strange at night. Many places that seem *forbidding* at night are not scary during the day.

Word Parts: Children can decode the syllables *for* and *bid*.

Amazing Words to build oral vocabulary

Definitions, examples, and **letter-sounds** to use with Oral Vocabulary Routine on p. DI·1

USE WITH

DAY 1

1 DELICATE Something that is *delicate* is thin and easily broken. *Delicate* means the opposite of sturdy.

2 Examples: My mom says to be very careful with that old vase because it's so *delicate*. Be careful not to step on the *delicate* flowers in the garden.

4 Letter-Sounds: Children can decode the syllable *del*. Point out c/k/ and t/t/.

1 INQUIRE *Inquire* means to ask questions or to try to find out something.

2 Examples: My dad *inquired* about the soccer schedule. My teacher *inquired* whether I had done all my homework.

4 Letter-Sounds: Children can decode the syllable *in*. Identify qu/kw/.

1 STURDY Something that is *sturdy* is strong and solid.

2 Examples: You can stand on that *sturdy* bench to reach the cupboard. The *sturdy* tree in the park was not affected by the big storm.

4 Letter-Sounds: Identify the letter-sounds for st/st/. Point out the long e sound of the final *y*.

DAY 2

1 EXHIBIT An *exhibit* is something set up for you to look at in a place like a museum or zoo.

2 Examples: We were amazed at the size of the dinosaur we saw in the *exhibit*. My favorite *exhibit* at the zoo is the monkey house.

4 Letter-Sounds: Point out the silent *h*. Children can decode the final syllable *bit*.

1 RESIST When you *resist* something, you work against it because you don't want it.

2 Examples: I couldn't *resist* laughing out loud at the clown. When you are healthy, your body *resists* getting sick.

4 Letter-Sounds: Point out the s/z/ at the beginning of the second syllable and the st/st/ at the end.

DAY 3

1 STUN When you are *stunned*, you are shocked and very surprised.

2 Examples: I was *stunned* when I found out my favorite teacher was leaving. My sister was *stunned* when she won the prize.

4 Letter-Sounds: Children can decode *stun*.

DAY 4

1 GENIUS Someone who is very, very smart can be called a *genius*.

2 Examples: I think it would take a *genius* to figure out this math problem. A *genius* comes up with good solutions to problems.

4 Letter-Sounds: Point out g/j/ followed by a long e sound.

1 SATISFACTION When you feel *satisfaction*, you are pleased and contented with something.

2 Examples: It gave me *satisfaction* to do so well on the spelling test. The team got great *satisfaction* from winning the game.

4 Word Parts: Clap the four syllables as you say the word aloud.

Grade 2
Oral Vocabulary Words

UNIT 1 Exploration	UNIT 2 Working Together	UNIT 3 Creative Ideas	UNIT 4 Our Changing World	UNIT 5 Responsibility	UNIT 6 Traditions

DEVELOP LANGUAGE

Exploration	Working Together	Creative Ideas	Our Changing World	Responsibility	Traditions
brittle	avalanche	construct	concentration	caretaker	athlete
creature	blustery	contraption	frown	community	challenge
dart	courageous	daydream	homeland	instrument	champion
decision	fast-paced	foolproof	patient	lug	dainty
investigate	hazard	project	preserve	operation	disguise
rural	instinct	scrap	represent	responsible	effort
underground	rescue	sidekick	tough	supplies	professional
urban	skittish	unique	valuable	teamwork	shortstop
ascend	actuate	correspond	adapt	concern	allegiance
descend	aloft	cove	ancient	fragile	frayed
enormous	compete	deaf	annual	growth	history
journey	contribute	footprint	bury	litter	independence
launch	deserve	imitate	massive	pellets	indivisible
meteorite	mope	postage	nutrients	pollute	patriotic
orbit	recreation	sign language	sprout	protection	symbol
universe	tinker	transport	undisturbed	release	unfurl
detective	coax	boast	appearance	behavior	angle
fascinating	conflict	consume	canopy	companion	brilliant
galaxy	inhabit	contentment	forage	confident	celebration
identify	ramp	cure	forepaw	consider	create
slimy	resolve	gloat	pursue	cooperate	custom
tranquil	serape	incident	restless	obedient	inspect
underneath	startle	prey	stage	properly	snapshot
wildlife	vacation	shrewd	transform	reprimand	tradition
arid		snicker	accent	advantage	buckaroo
discovery	depend		adjust	appreciate	climate
dunes	familiar	abundant	foreign	communicate	drover
forbidding	insist	assist	forlorn	defiant	lariat
haven	miserable	beam	landmark	demand	legend
landform	partnership	dismay	quiver	ferocious	livestock
ledge	solution	efficient	tease	firmly	occupation
precipitation	struggle	forever	unexpected	respect	rawhide
delicate	survival	generous			
exhibit	banquet	situation	breeze	apologize	ceremony
genius	decorate		condition	citizen	compliment
inquire	dine	accomplish	funnel	hoard	culture
resist	flare	excel	predict	interrupt	evergreen
satisfaction	glimmer	opportunity	sparkle	judgment	festival
stun	holiday	original	swirl	protest	fidget
sturdy	participate	process	terrifying	scold	multicolored
	whispery	research	whip	troublemaker	sash
		scientist			
		unusual			

REMEMBER that oral vocabulary is informally assessed.

New to the City

Joan woke to a loud thud as a garbage truck collected the trash outside her family's new apartment. She heard bottles breaking and the truck's motor as it roared down the block. She got up to fix herself a bowl of cereal and saw that her mother was already sitting at the table. "Did the garbage truck wake you up too?" Mom asked.

"I liked it better when the rooster would wake me up with his cock-a-doodle-do," Joan said, nodding. She and her family had lived on a farm in a rural area, but they moved to a large urban area so that Joan's father could take a new job. "I really miss the animals," Joan said sadly. "There are no animals in the city."

"I have an idea," said Mom. "Let's go to the park today. We'll take this bread with us."

"What will we need bread for?" asked Joan.

"You'll see," said Mom, a bit mysteriously.

After arriving at the park and seeing a sign that said it was okay to do so, Joan's mom gave her bread to feed the ducks and swans near the lake. Joan laughed delightedly as the animals flocked around her. Then they went to the zoo and saw all sorts of exotic animals, including lions and cheetahs.

"See," said Mom, pointing to a squirrel as they walked home, "there are a lot of animals in the city. You just need to know where to look."

ADVANCED SELECTION 1   VOCABULARY: rural, urban

Mae Jemison

Mae Jemison was the first African American woman astronaut. She studied science in college, and then she went to medical school. Jemison actually worked as a doctor before she became an astronaut.

Jemison went on her first space mission in 1992 for the National Aeronautics and Space Administration (NASA). She was part of the crew of the space shuttle *Endeavor*.

As a member of the *Endeavor* crew, Jemison conducted experiments as the shuttle was in orbit around Earth. Many of the experiments focused on plants and animals. What she learned helped us better understand how weightlessness affects plants and animals. This is important to understand if people want to spend more time in space and perhaps even live there.

Jemison was excited about her time in space. Going into space had been her dream. When she was only five years old, she had told her teacher that she wanted to be a scientist. Her dream had come true.

"I felt like I belonged right there in space," Jemison said.

Mae Jemison left NASA in 1993. She became a college teacher and started a company called The Jemison Group. This company helps to bring science into everyday life.

Through her dedication to science, Mae Jemison continues to be an inspiration to young people.

ADVANCED SELECTION 2   VOCABULARY: orbit

The Milky Way

Think about where you live. You live in a community, maybe a town or city, in a state, in the United States of America, on planet Earth, in our solar system, in the Milky Way galaxy.

The Milky Way galaxy is made up of stars, comets, asteroids, and planets, including Earth. It is shaped like a disk with a bulge in the middle. It is a spiral galaxy in that it spins around its center like a tornado. If you could look at it from above, the Milky Way would look like a giant, spinning pinwheel.

Our planet is close to the edge of the Milky Way galaxy. On a clear night, away from city lights, you can see the Milky Way in the night sky. It looks like a thick band of light that stretches across the dark sky.

The band of light is really billions of stars. The light from the stars blurs together. Long ago, people thought it looked like a river or road of milk. That's how it got its name, the Milky Way.

There are billions of other galaxies in space, but the Andromeda galaxy is the closest to the Milky Way. It is actually possible for people on Earth to see the Andromeda galaxy without using a telescope.

There is still a lot more to learn about our home in the universe. Remember that the next time you think about where you live.

ADVANCED SELECTION 3 **VOCABULARY:** galaxy

Advanced Selections **DI•11**

The Saguaro Cactus

A desert is a hot, dry place. It doesn't rain often in a desert, and this lack of precipitation keeps the desert arid, or dry. Plants and animals that live in the desert are able to survive in a place that has little water.

A saguaro cactus can live in the arid Arizona desert because it stores water inside its leaves and stems. When there is a heavy rain, the roots of a saguaro cactus soak up as much water as they can hold, allowing the saguaro to survive long periods of dry weather.

The saguaro, or giant cactus, can grow as tall as fifty feet high and live for more than a hundred years in the desert.

The saguaro is a source of water, food, and shelter for some desert animals. Woodpeckers make holes in the saguaro looking for food and water. Then birds and insects live in the holes made by the woodpeckers.

Many animals survive by drinking the juice and eating the seeds of the saguaro. This helps the saguaro survive because the animals spread the seeds to other parts of the desert, where new saguaros then grow.

ADVANCED SELECTION 4   VOCABULARY: arid, precipitation

America's First Dictionary

When you want to inquire about a word, where do you look? Chances are, you look in a dictionary. It might even be a Webster's dictionary, which was originally written by one man, Noah Webster.

Born in 1758, Noah Webster had an average colonial upbringing. Few people went to college then, but Webster had a love of learning, so his parents let him study at a college in New England.

After he graduated, he worked at improving the school systems. The books students used came from England, but Webster thought that they should be learning English from North American books. So in 1783 he wrote his own textbook, *A Grammatical Institute of the English Language.* It was the most popular American book of its time—even Benjamin Franklin used this book to teach his granddaughter to read.

In 1801 Webster began writing the first American dictionary. People in different parts of the country spelled, pronounced, and used words differently, but Webster thought that all Americans should speak the same way. It took him twenty-seven years to write, but in 1828 he finished his dictionary of more than 70,000 words.

When Noah Webster died in 1843, he was considered an American hero because of his big ideas.

ADVANCED SELECTION 5   VOCABULARY: inquire

Group Time

Strategic Intervention

ROUTINE

1 Word Work

PHONEMIC AWARENESS Write the word pairs below one at a time. Model segmenting and blending each word in the pair; have children repeat after you. Then have them isolate the vowel sound in each word.

   at—pat   up—cup   an—pan   in—win

SHORT VOWELS Reteach p. 12n. Additional words to blend:

   ring   bank   lick   stop   flip

Then have children spell *pick* with letter tiles. Monitor their work.

• Change the *i* in *pick* to *a*.
  What is the new word?

| p | a | c | k |

• Change the *ck* in *pack* to *t*.
  What is the new word?

| p | a | t |

• Change the *pa* in *pat* to *cu*.
  What is the new word?

| c | u | t |

SPELLING Reteach p. 12p. Model spelling *chop* and *sack*. You may wish to give children fewer words to learn.

2 Read Decodable Reader 1

BEFORE READING Review the short vowel words on p. 12q and have children blend these story words: *back, bunk, fond, hand, lick, long, rang.*

DURING READING Use p. 12q.

Monitor Progress	Word and Story Reading
If... children have difficulty with any of these words,	**then...** reteach them by modeling. Have children practice the words, with feedback from you, until they can read them independently.
If... children have difficulty reading the story individually,	**then...** read a page aloud as children follow along. Then have the group reread the page. Continue reading in this way before children read individually.

3 Reread for Fluency

Use the Oral Rereading Routine, p. 12q, and text at each child's independent reading level.

Decodable Reader 1

Gus
Written by Harriet Yi
Illustrated by Josh Bermann

Phonics Skills
Short Vowels CVC, CVCC   Consonants -ck, -ng -nk

MORE READING FOR

Group Time

Use this Leveled Reader or other text at children's instructional level.

Below-Level

Reviews
• High-frequency words *beautiful, country, friend, front, someone, somewhere*
• Character and setting

Check this database for additional titles.

Leveled Reader Database ONLINE

PearsonSuccessNet.com

Advanced

ROUTINE

DAY 1

1 Word Work

🎯 **SHORT VOWELS** Practice with longer words. If children know the words on first read, they may need no further practice. Practice items:

bread	headline	dreadful	wealth	breakfast
check	letter	flung	sling	flick
blank	shock	entrance	blink	leather

Have children write the words on cards and sort by *ea, e, ck, ng, nk*. Then have individuals choose several words to use in a sentence.

2 Read Advanced Selection 1

BEFORE READING Have children identify this oral vocabulary word: *rural*.

DURING READING Children may read silently. Provide guidance as needed.

AFTER READING Have children recall the two characters in the selection. (Joan and her mother) Ask:

- How does Joan feel about moving to the city? How do you know?
- List one trait, or characteristic, of Joan's mother. Tell about it.

On the back of the selection page have children write how they would feel about moving to a new place compared to how Joan felt.

3 Extend Concepts Through Inquiry

IDENTIFY QUESTIONS Have children choose another "neighborhood to visit." They should choose a place to learn about what is different from where they now live. During the week, they should learn more about their choice from reading, studying pictures, and talking with adults or older children. On Day 5 they will share what they learned. As students work through Unit 1, help them learn the methods that they will use to work independently. Guide children in brainstorming possible choices.

- Think about where you live now. Where would you like to visit that is different from what you have always known? Would you learn something new by going there?

New to the City

DI•9

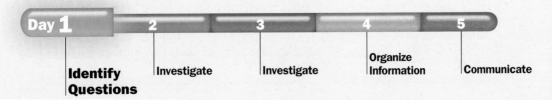

Day **1**	2	3	4	5
Identify Questions	Investigate	Investigate	**Organize Information**	Communicate

MORE READING FOR
Group Time

Use this Leveled Reader or other text at children's instructional level.

Advanced

Reviews
- Concept vocabulary
- Character and setting

Iris and Walter
Group Time

AudioText

AudioText

Strategic Intervention

ROUTINE

1 Word Work

🔊 **SHORT VOWELS** Reteach pp. 14c–14d. Additional words to blend:

head	dock	deck	truck
rib	sack	list	tub

HIGH-FREQUENCY WORDS Reteach pp. 14–15. Have individuals practice reading the words from word cards.

2 Read Strategic Intervention Decodable Reader 1

BEFORE READING Before reading, review *beautiful, country, friend, front, someone,* and *somewhere* on the Word Wall. Point out *Les* and *That* on p. 2 and explain that these words begin with capital letters because *Les* is a person's name and *That* is the first word of a sentence.

AFTER READING Check comprehension by having children retell the story, including the characters, setting, and plot.

Have children locate CVC and CVCC words in the story. List words children name. Review CVC and CVCC spelling patterns. Have children sort the words they found next to *add* and *big.*

add (CVCC): *bell, fill, hill, last, lock, pack, pink, ring, rock, sack, tell, well, will*

big (CVC): *box, can, dad, fit, got, gum, has, his, in, is, kid, Les, on, tag*

3 Read Iris and Walter

BEFORE READING Have children practice the words below—first as a group and then individually. Then use Guiding Comprehension, pp. 16–35, to monitor understanding.

country	explorers	blooming	amazing
wonderful	rolled	collection	stoop

Monitor Progress	Word and Story Reading
If... children have difficulty with any of these words,	**then...** reteach them by modeling. Have children practice the words, with feedback from you, until they can read them independently.
If... children have difficulty reading the story individually,	**then...** have them follow along in their books as they listen to the AudioText. You may also have them read pages of the selection aloud together, first with you and then without you, before reading individually.

1 **Read** *Iris and Walter*

DURING READING Have children read silently to p. 28. Provide guidance as needed. Ask:

- Do you think Iris enjoys being with Grandpa? How can you tell?
- What do you think is going to happen between Iris and Walter? What makes you think so?

Have children read silently to p. 34. Then ask:

- How do Walter and Iris differ in their feelings about country life?
- Do you think Iris and Walter will remain friends? Why?

CHARACTER AND SETTING Have children recall the three characters in the story. (Iris, Grandpa, and Walter) Discuss how their actions tell the reader what kind of people they are.

- What does Iris do that tells you what kind of person she is? Would you like Iris?
- What does Grandpa do that tells you what kind of person he is? Name one trait, or characteristic, of Grandpa.
- Name one way that Walter is different from Iris. What does he do that shows you this?

PREDICT Children can make a prediction after previewing. Draw a chart or distribute copies of Graphic Organizer 1.

RESPONSE Ask children to suppose they are tree-house designers. Have them draw an unusual tree house for Walter and write about it.

Audio CD AudioText

2 **Extend Concepts Through** **Inquiry**

INVESTIGATE Guide children in choosing material at their independent reading level to explore their topic. Some books that may be appropriate are *Neighborhood Odes*, poems about a Hispanic American neighborhood by Gary Soto; and *The City by the Bay: A Magical Journey Around San Francisco*, a nonfiction book by Tricia Brown. Show them how to use the titles of sections or table of contents and index to know what the book is about.

Help children decide how they will present their information. Children may use a graphic organizer, a written format, photographs, drawings, or models. Tell them the advantages of each for this particular project.

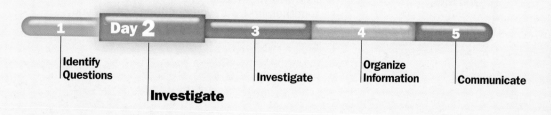

1	Day 2	3	4	5
Identify Questions	Investigate	Investigate	Organize Information	Communicate

Group Time

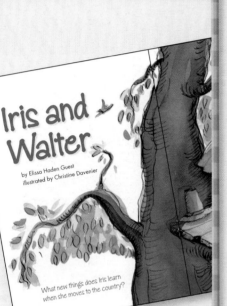

DAY 3

Audio CD AudioText

Strategic Intervention

ROUTINE

1 Word Work

REVIEW **SYLLABLE PATTERNS WITH SHORT VOWELS** Review p. 36c, using these additional words. Have children sort the words into VC/CV and VCC/V lists.

ginger	kitten	under	packet	pepper
chicken	better	socket	bucket	butter
crackers				

REVIEW **SENTENCE READING** Have individuals read these sentences to review decoding skills.

Ginger the kitten went under the fence.
I put a packet of pepper on the chicken.
Dad better put the plug in the socket.
He fills the bucket with butter, crackers, and a bottle of soda.

2 Comprehension

CHARACTER AND SETTING/PREDICT Reteach p. 14e. Have children respond to the Connect to Reading questions after completing step 3 Reread for Fluency.
- Now read the story again quietly. When you have finished, I'd like you to tell me who the story is about, where and when it takes place, and if your predictions were correct.

3 Reread for Fluency

READ WITH APPROPRIATE PACE/RATE Teach p. 36f using text at children's independent level. Reading options include Student Edition selections, Decodable Readers, Strategic Intervention Decodable Readers, and Leveled Readers.

Monitor Progress	Fluency
If… children have difficulty reading with appropriate pace and rate,	**then…** discuss with them the appropriate pace and rate to be used with each passage and provide additional modeling. Have them listen to your model and then read aloud together, first with you and then without you, before reading individually.

Advanced

1 Read Self-Selected Reading

BEFORE READING Have children select a trade book or Leveled Reader to read independently. Guide children in selecting books of appropriate difficulty.

AFTER READING When they have finished, have each child select the thing they liked best and the thing they liked least about the place they chose to "visit."

2 Extend Concepts Through Inquiry

INVESTIGATE Give children time to investigate the place they plan to "visit" and to begin preparing their information. Help children who need to find more information. Suggest other places in the library/media center for them to look. Use information that one child has found and model how to use that information to prepare a presentation in the chosen format.

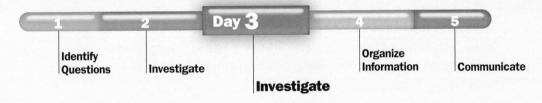

1	2	Day 3	4	5
Identify Questions	Investigate	Investigate	Organize Information	Communicate

DAY 3

Trade Books for Self-Selected Reading

NEIGHBORHOOD ODES
by Gary Soto, Harcourt Children's Books, 1992

THE CITY BY THE BAY: A MAGICAL JOURNEY AROUND SAN FRANCISCO
by Tricia Brown, Chronicle Books, 1998

MORE READING FOR

Group Time

Use this Leveled Reader or other text at children's instructional level.

Advanced

Reviews
• Concept vocabulary
• Character and setting

Group Time

DAY 4

Audio CD **AudioText**

Strategic Intervention

ROUTINE

1 Read "Morning Song"/"My Travel Tree"

BEFORE READING Have children practice the words below—first as a group and then individually. Then use Poetry in Reading, pp. 38–39.

tadpoles   rustling   adventures   perched

Monitor Progress	Word and Selection Reading
If… children have difficulty with any of these words,	**then…** have them practice in pairs reading word cards before reading the selection.
If… children have difficulty reading the selection individually,	**then…** have them follow along in their books as they listen to the AudioText. You may also have them read pages of the selection aloud together, first with you and then without you, before reading individually.

2 Reread for Fluency

Preteach p. 39a, using text at children's independent reading level. Reading options include Student Edition selections, Decodable Readers, Strategic Intervention Decodable Readers, and Leveled Readers.

3 Build Concepts

Use the Oral Vocabulary Routine, pp. DI·1–DI·3, and the Oral Vocabulary Words on p. DI·8.

MORE READING FOR
Group Time

Use this Leveled Reader or other text at children's instructional level.

Below-Level

Reviews
- High-frequency words *beautiful, country, friend, front, someone, somewhere*
- Character and setting

Advanced

1 Read Poetry

AFTER READING Ask:

• Who do you think is talking in "Morning Song"?

• Who do you think is talking in "My Travel Tree"?

• What kind of special tree would you like to have? Why?

2 Vocabulary

Extend vocabulary with questions such as these:

• Which is most likely to be *rural*, a city or a farm? Why?

• If you made a *decision* to live in a city, would you be living in a *rural* or an *urban* area? Define the area you choose.

• If you were to *investigate* an *underground* cave, would it most likely be in a *rural* location? Why or why not?

• Is a *dart* more likely to be *brittle* or strong? Why?

Encourage children to use the words in their writing.

3 Extend Concepts Through Inquiry

ORGANIZE INFORMATION Give children time to continue reading about their new "neighborhood." Remind them that tomorrow they will share their information. By now they should have begun putting the information in a presentation format. Help students who need help organizing their information into their presentation format.

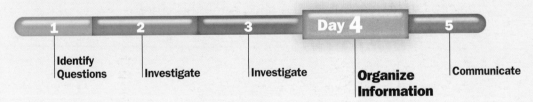

1	2	3	Day 4	5
Identify Questions	Investigate	Investigate	**Organize Information**	Communicate

My Travel Tree
by Bobbi Katz

There are oh-so-many
kinds of trees—
apple, pear, pine—
but there is just one special tree
I feel is somehow mine.
Its branches form
such cozy nooks
for dreaming dreams
and reading books.
I sail to almost anywhere,
perched among the leaves up there.
If naming things were up to me,
I'd call this one my travel tree.

39

   AudioText

MORE READING FOR

Group Time

Use this Leveled Reader or other text at children's instructional level.

Advanced

Reviews
• Concept vocabulary
• Character and setting

Iris and Walter

Group Time

DAY 5

ROUTINE

1 Word Work

SHORT VOWELS Have children read aloud as you track the print. Call on individuals to blend the underlined words.

> I saw a <u>frog</u> on the <u>back</u> of a <u>cat</u>.
> <u>Did</u> you <u>fill</u> the sack with <u>bread</u>?
> The <u>duck</u> <u>hit</u> its <u>head</u> on a rock.
> The <u>bell</u> <u>rang</u> so we <u>went</u> in.

HIGH-FREQUENCY WORDS Use pp. 14–15 to review *beautiful, country, friend, front, someone, somewhere.*

Monitor Progress	High-Frequency Words
If… children have difficulty with any of these words,	**then…** tell them the word and have them repeat it. Have children spell the word and tell what word they spelled. Have them practice in pairs with word cards.

2 Monitor Progress

SENTENCE READING SET A Use Set A on reproducible p. 40f to assess children's ability to read decodable and high-frequency words in sentences.

COMPREHENSION To assess comprehension, have each child read Strategic Intervention Decodable Reader 1 or other text at the child's independent level. Ask when and where the story takes place (setting) and have the child retell the story.

MORE READING FOR
Group Time

Use this Leveled Reader or other text at children's instructional level.

Below-Level

Reviews
- High-frequency words *beautiful, country, friend, front, someone, somewhere*
- Character and setting

Advanced

1 Monitor Progress

SENTENCE READING SET C Use Set C on reproducible p. 40f to assess children's ability to read decodable and high-frequency words in sentences. If you have any question about whether children have mastered this week's skills, have them read the Set B sentences.

COMPREHENSION Have each child read "The New Friend" on reproducible p. 40g. Ask one trait, or characteristic, of the main character, and have the child retell the passage. Use the Retelling Rubric on p. 36–37 to evaluate the child's retelling.

2 Extend Concepts Through Inquiry

COMMUNICATE Have children share their new "neighborhood."

1	2	3	4	Day 5
Identify Questions	Investigate	Investigate	Organize Information	

Communicate

MORE READING FOR
Group Time

Use this Leveled Reader or other text at children's instructional level.

Advanced

Reviews
- Concept vocabulary
- Character and setting

Exploring Space

Group Time

DAY 1

Strategic Intervention

ROUTINE

1 Word Work

PHONEMIC AWARENESS Write the word pairs below one at a time. Model segmenting and blending each word in the pair; have children repeat after you. Then have them isolate the vowel sound in each word.

mad—made   wag—wage   cub—cube   rid—ride

LONG VOWELS CVCe Reteach p. 42n. Additional words to blend:

pose   rake   rude   file   dime

Then have children spell *take* with letter tiles. Monitor their work.

- Change the *ta* in *take* to *po*. What is the new word?

p	o	k	e

- Change the *ok* in *poke* to *il*. What is the new word?

p	i	l	e

- Change the *p* in *pile* to *f*. What is the new word?

f	i	l	e

SPELLING Reteach p. 42p. Model spelling *mice* and *blaze.* You may wish to give children fewer words to learn.

2 Read Decodable Reader 2

BEFORE READING Review the CVCe words on p. 42q and have children blend these story words: *cute, game, made, poke, rose, add, quick, small.* Be sure children understand meanings of words such as *quite.*

DURING READING Use p. 42q.

Monitor Progress	Word and Story Reading
If... children have difficulty with any of these words,	**then...** reteach them by modeling. Have children practice the words, with feedback from you, until they can read them independently.
If... children have difficulty reading the story individually,	**then...** read a page aloud as children follow along. Then have the group reread the page. Continue reading in this way before children read individually.

3 Reread for Fluency

Use the Paired Reading Routine, p. 42q, and text at each child's independent reading level.

Decodable Reader 2

Ike and Ace
Written by Harry Doyle
Illustrated by Dan Vick

MORE READING FOR
Group Time

Use this Leveled Reader or other text at children's instructional level.

Below-Level

Reviews
- High-frequency words *everywhere, live, work, machines, woman, move, world*
- Main idea and details

Check this database for additional titles.

Leveled Reader
Database
ONLINE

PearsonSuccessNet.com

Advanced

ROUTINE

1 Word Work

🎯 **LONG VOWELS CVCe** Practice with longer words. If children know the words on first read, they may need no further practice. Practice items:

accuse	**admire**	**germ**	**imitate**	**celebrate**
grace	**entire**	**explode**	**citizen**	**general**
cement	**gentle**	**chosen**	**prison**	**thrive**

Have children circle the long vowel CVCe words and put a check mark above each word that has an s that sounds like z. Then have individuals choose several words to use in a sentence.

2 𝓡𝓮𝓪𝓭 Advanced Selection 2

BEFORE READING Have children identify the oral vocabulary word *orbit*.

DURING READING Children may read silently. Provide guidance as needed.

AFTER READING Have children recall the most important idea. (Mae Jemison was the first African American woman astronaut.) Ask:
- Do you think Mae's life as an astronaut helped her in the years following this experience? What makes you think so?
- Which of the following would be the best title for this selection? *The First African American Woman Astronaut, How Weightlessness Affects Plants and Animals,* or *The Importance of Doctors in Space?*

On the back of the selection page, have children write a short four-line poem about Mae Jemison.

3 Extend Concepts Through 𝙸𝙽𝚚𝚞𝚒𝚛𝚢

IDENTIFY QUESTIONS Have children work in pairs to choose another astronaut to study. During the week, they should learn more about their choice from reading, studying pictures, and talking with adults or older children. On Day 5 they will share what they learned. Guide children in brainstorming possible choices.
- Think about astronauts you may have heard about. Would you prefer to study a male or a female astronaut? Would you prefer to study one of the first astronauts or a more recent one?

Mae Jemison

Mae Jemison was the first African American woman astronaut. She studied science in college, and then she went to medical school. Jemison actually worked as a doctor before she became an astronaut.

Jemison went on her first space mission in 1992 for the National Aeronautics and Space Administration (NASA). She was part of the crew of the space shuttle *Endeavor*.

As a member of the *Endeavor* crew, Jemison conducted experiments as the shuttle was in orbit around Earth. Many of the experiments focused on plants and animals. What she learned helped us better understand how weightlessness affects plants and animals. This is important to understand if people want to spend more time in space and perhaps even live there.

Jemison was excited about her time in space. Going into space had been her dream. When she was only five years old, she told her teacher that she wanted to be a scientist. Her dream had come true.

"I felt like I belonged right there in space," Jemison said.

Mae Jemison left NASA in 1993. She became a college teacher and started a company called the Jemison Group. This company helps to bring science into everyday life. Through her dedication to science, Mae Jemison continues to be an inspiration to young people.

DI•10

MORE READING FOR

Group Time

Use this Leveled Reader or other text at children's instructional level.

Advanced

Reviews
- Concept vocabulary
- Main idea and details

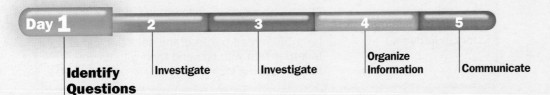

Day **1**	**2**	**3**	**4**	**5**
Identify Questions	Investigate	Investigate	**Organize Information**	Communicate

Group Time

DAY 2

Audio CD AudioText

ROUTINE

1 Word Work

LONG VOWELS CVCe Reteach p. 44c. Additional words to blend:

joke	mule	ripe	stare
tube	bone	drape	bride

HIGH-FREQUENCY WORDS Reteach pp. 44–45. Have individuals practice reading the words from word cards.

2 Read Strategic Intervention Decodable Reader 2

BEFORE READING Before reading, review *everywhere, live, work, woman, machines, move,* and *world* on the Word Wall. Preview the story with children and ask them to predict what they think it will be about.

AFTER READING Check comprehension by having children retell the main idea of the story.

Have children locate CVCe words in the story. List words children name. Review the CVCe spelling patterns. Have children sort words according to their spelling patterns.

a: age, bake, cake, Dave, game, Jane, Kate, made, make, page, race

i: fine, hike, like, nice, quite

o: home, Rose

u: huge, rule, use

3 Reread *Exploring Space with an Astronaut*

BEFORE READING Have children practice the words below—first as a group and then individually. Then use Guiding Comprehension, pp. 46–59, to monitor understanding.

pilot	sleeping	toilets	exercise
computers	scientists	universe	machines

Monitor Progress	Word and Story Reading
If... children have difficulty with any of these words,	**then...** reteach them by modeling. Have children practice the words, with feedback from you, until they can read them independently.
If... children have difficulty reading the story individually,	**then...** have them follow along in their books as they listen to the AudioText. You may also have them read pages of the selection aloud together, first with you and then without you, before reading individually.

Advanced

ROUTINE

1 Read *Exploring Space*

DURING READING Have children read silently to p. 59. Provide guidance as needed. Ask:

- From reading this selection, what do you think is the hardest part of being an astronaut in orbit? Why?
- What is different about being in space from being on Earth?

MAIN IDEA AND DETAILS Have children think about what the author is trying to tell them (what life is like on a space mission).

- Which details support the main idea? (Astronauts did experiments with plants and exercise machines; the astronauts used robot arms to move things and people outside the shuttle.)
- What would you still like to learn about space? Why?

TEXT STRUCTURE Children can work with a partner to list the headings used in the selection and then tell if this text structure was helpful to them as they read.

RESPONSE Have children write questions for an interview with Eileen Collins.

2 Extend Concepts Through Inquiry

INVESTIGATE Guide children in choosing material at their independent reading level to explore their topic. Some books that may be appropriate are *The Man Who Went to the Far Side of the Moon: The Story of Apollo 11 Astronaut Michael Collins* by Bea Schyffert and *Space Heroes: Amazing Astronauts* by James Buckley. Show students the materials they may use and continue to model how to find information in the table of contents and index. Explain the procedure for using the library/media center.

Help children decide how they will present their information. Children may use other graphic organizers, a written format, photographs, drawings, or models.

 AudioText

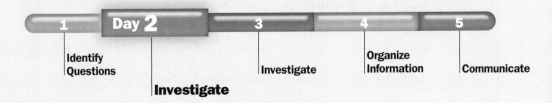

1	Day 2	3	4	5
Identify Questions	Investigate	Investigate	Organize Information	Communicate

Group Time

AudioText

DAY 3

ROUTINE

1 Word Work

REVIEW SHORT VOWELS Review p. 60c, using these additional words. Have children sort the words into CVC, CCVC, and CVCC lists.

did	cut	head	fix	crack	bank
bell	clock	rang	think	thing	read

REVIEW SENTENCE READING Have individuals read these sentences to review decoding skills.

> **Did you see the cut on her head?**
> **He can fix the crack in my bank.**
> **The bell on the clock rang.**
> **I cannot think of a thing I just read.**

2 Comprehension

MAIN IDEA AND DETAILS/TEXT STRUCTURE Reteach p. 44e. Have children respond to the Connect to Reading questions after completing step 3 Reread for Fluency.

- Now read the story again quietly and pay attention to the bold headings the author uses to help you know what you are going to read about next. When you have finished, I'd like you to tell me what the story is mainly about and some details that tell more about the main idea.

3 Reread for Fluency

READ WITH ACCURACY Teach p. 60f, using text at children's independent level. Reading options include Student Edition selections, Decodable Readers, Strategic Intervention Decodable Readers, and Leveled Readers.

Monitor Progress	Fluency
If... children have difficulty reading with accuracy,	**then...** discuss with them ways to read more difficult words and provide additional modeling. Have them listen to your model and then read aloud together, first with you and then without you, before reading individually.

MORE READING FOR
Group Time

Use this Leveled Reader or other text at children's instructional level.

Below-Level

Reviews
- High-frequency words *everywhere, live, machines, live, woman, work, world*
- Main idea and details

Advanced

ROUTINE

1 Read Self-Selected Reading

BEFORE READING Have children select a trade book or Leveled Reader to read independently. Guide children in selecting books of appropriate difficulty.

AFTER READING When they have finished, have each child select an interesting passage and read it to a partner.

2 Extend Concepts Through Inquiry

INVESTIGATE Give children time to investigate the astronaut they are studying and to begin preparing their information. Assist children who need help finding and/or organizing information.

1	2	Day **3**	4	5
Identify Questions	Investigate	**Investigate**	Organize Information	Communicate

Trade Books for Self-Selected Reading

THE MAN WHO WENT TO THE FAR SIDE OF THE MOON: THE STORY OF APOLLO 11 ASTRONAUT MICHAEL COLLINS by Bea Schyffert, Chronicle Books LLC, 2003

SPACE HEROES: AMAZING ASTRONAUTS by James Buckley, D.K. Children, 2004

MORE READING FOR
Group Time

Use this Leveled Reader or other text at children's instructional level.

Advanced

Reviews
• Concept vocabulary
• Main idea and details

Exploring Space
Group Time

Strategic Intervention

ROUTINE

1 Read "A Trip to Space Camp"

BEFORE READING Have children practice the words below—first as a group and then individually. Then use Science in Reading, pp. 62–65.

machines   astronauts   straight   missions

Monitor Progress	Word and Selection Reading
If... children have difficulty with any of these words,	**then...** have them practice in pairs, reading word cards before reading the selection.
If... children have difficulty reading the selection individually,	**then...** have them follow along in their books as they listen to the AudioText. You may also have them read pages of the selection aloud together, first with you and then without you, before reading individually.

2 Reread for Fluency

Preteach p. 65a, using text at children's independent reading level. Reading options include Student Edition selections, Decodable Readers, Strategic Intervention Decodable Readers, and Leveled Readers.

3 Build Concepts

Use the Oral Vocabulary Routine, pp. DI·1–DI·2, DI·4, and the Oral Vocabulary Words on p. DI·8.

Science in Reading

A Trip to Space Camp

by Ann Weil

What does it feel like to go into space? Would you like to find out? Then maybe Space Camp is for you!

Audio CD   **AudioText**

MORE READING FOR
Group Time

Use this Leveled Reader or other text at children's instructional level.

Below-Level

Reviews
- High-frequency words
  everywhere, live, work, woman, machines, move, world
- Main idea and details

Advanced

1 Read "A Trip to Space Camp"

AFTER READING Ask:
- Why do you think people go to space camps?
- If you were at space camp and could choose when to do the activities, which would you choose to do first? Why?
- How is "A Trip to Space Camp" similar to *Exploring Space with an Astronaut*?

2 Vocabulary

Extend vocabulary with questions such as these:
- If you are beginning your return *journey* to Earth from space, are you starting to *ascend* or *descend*? How do you know?
- If your spacecraft were in *orbit* around the moon, would you be going around the moon or ascending to it? Why?
- Would you call the *universe enormous*? Why or why not?

Encourage children to use the words in their writing.

3 Extend Concepts Through Inquiry

ORGANIZE INFORMATION Give children time to continue reading about the astronaut they are researching. Remind them that tomorrow they will share their information. By now they should have begun putting the information in a presentation format.

DAY 4

AudioText

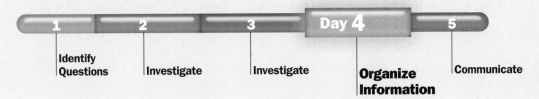

1	2	3	**Day 4**	5
Identify Questions	Investigate	Investigate	**Organize Information**	Communicate

MORE READING FOR
Group Time

Use this Leveled Reader or other text at children's instructional level.

Advanced

Reviews
- Concept vocabulary
- Main idea and details

Group Time

Strategic Intervention

ROUTINE

1 Word Work

↻ **LONG VOWELS CVCe** Have children read aloud as you track the print. Call on individuals to blend the underlined words.

I <u>chose</u> a <u>cage</u> for the <u>mice</u>.
I will <u>slice</u> some <u>cake</u> for <u>Kate</u>.
Look at the <u>size</u> of that <u>nice</u> big <u>rose</u>.
What was the <u>price</u> of that <u>white</u> <u>cape</u>?

HIGH-FREQUENCY WORDS Use pp. 44–45 to review *everywhere, live, work, woman, machines, move,* and *world*

Monitor Progress	High-Frequency Words
If... children have difficulty with any of these words,	**then...** tell them the word and have them repeat it. Have children spell the word and tell what word they spelled. Have them practice in pairs with word cards.

2 Monitor Progress

SENTENCE READING SET A Use Set A on reproducible p. 66f to assess children's ability to read decodable and high-frequency words in sentences.

COMPREHENSION To assess comprehension, have each child read Strategic Intervention Decodable Reader 2 or other text at the child's independent level. Ask about the main idea of the story and have the child retell the story.

MORE READING FOR
Group Time

Use this Leveled Reader or other text at children's instructional level.

Below-Level

Reviews
• High-frequency words *everywhere, live, machines, work, woman, move, world*
• Main idea and details

Advanced

DAY 5

1 **Monitor Progress**

SENTENCE READING SET C Use Set C on reproducible p. 66f to assess children's ability to read decodable and high-frequency words in sentences. If you have any question about whether children have mastered this week's skills, have them read the Set B sentences.

COMPREHENSION Have each child read "Going into Space" on reproducible p. 66g. Ask what the selection is mainly about, and have the child retell the passage. Use the Retelling Rubric on p. 60–61 to evaluate the child's retelling.

2 **Extend Concepts Through INQUIRY**

COMMUNICATE Have partners share the information about their astronaut.

1	2	3	4	Day 5
Identify Questions	Investigate	Investigate	Organize Information	

Communicate

MORE READING FOR
Group Time

Use this Leveled Reader or other text at children's instructional level.

Advanced

Reviews
- Concept vocabulary
- Main idea and details

Group Time

Strategic Intervention

ROUTINE

1 Word Work

PHONEMIC AWARENESS Write the word pairs below one at a time. Model segmenting and blending each word in the pair; have children repeat after you. Then have them isolate the vowel sound in each word.

tip—trip   sat—slat   log—long   pat—past

CONSONANT BLENDS Reteach p. 68n. Additional words to blend:

bust   stink   slope   twice   crest

Then have children spell *crank* with letter tiles. Monitor their work.

- Change the *r* in *crank* to *l*. What is the new word?

| c | l | a | n | k |

- Change the *c* in *clank* to *b*. What is the new word?

| b | l | a | n | k |

- Change the *nk* in *blank* to *st*. What is the new word?

| b | l | a | s | t |

SPELLING Reteach p. 68p. Model spelling *brave* and *stream*. You may wish to give children fewer words to learn.

2 Read Decodable Reader 3

BEFORE READING Review words with consonant blends on p. 68q and have children blend these story words: *act, prop, stage, strap, strong, sings, wide, mask.* Be sure children understand meanings of words such as *prop*.

DURING READING Use p. 68q.

Monitor Progress	Word and Story Reading
If... children have difficulty with any of these words,	**then...** reteach them by modeling. Have children practice the words, with feedback from you, until they can read them independently.
If... children have difficulty reading the story individually,	**then...** read a page aloud as children follow along. Then have the group reread the page. Continue reading in this way before children read individually.

3 Reread for Fluency

Use the Oral Rereading Routine, p. 68q, and text at each child's independent reading level.

Decodable Reader 3

On Stage

Written by Amy Thornton
Illustrated by Kim Grant

Phonics Skill
Consonant Blends

MORE READING FOR
Group Time

Use this Leveled Reader or other text at children's instructional level.

Below-Level

Reviews
- High-frequency words *bear, build, couldn't, father, love, mother, straight*
- Character and setting

Check this database for additional titles.

Leveled Reader Database ONLINE

PearsonSuccessNet.com

Advanced

ROUTINE

DAY 1

① Word Work

⟳ **CONSONANT BLENDS** Practice with longer words. If children know the words on first read, they may need no further practice. Practice items:

throat	scrape	shrimp	strut	product
blush	drawn	dwelling	drench	sprawl
string	sprout	square	draft	bluebird

Have children write the words on cards. Then have them sort by initial blends, final blends, and those with both. Have individuals choose two words to use in a sentence.

② Read Advanced Selection 3

BEFORE READING Have children identify the oral vocabulary word *galaxy*.

DURING READING Children may read silently. Provide guidance as needed.

AFTER READING Have children think about the characteristics of the Milky Way. Ask:

- What is the author trying to show you by listing (in the second sentence) all the places you live?
- Based on its characteristics, what could be another name for the Milky Way? Explain.

On the back of the selection page, have children draw the Milky Way based on the description in the selection. Then have them write a journal entry about the night sky.

The Milky Way

DI•11

③ Extend Concepts Through Inquiry

IDENTIFY QUESTIONS Have children work in pairs to choose two planets to compare and contrast. During the week, they should learn more about their choices from reading, studying pictures, and talking with adults or older children. On Day 5 they will share what they learned. Guide children in brainstorming.

- Think about your choices. Are they alike in some ways? Are they different in some ways?

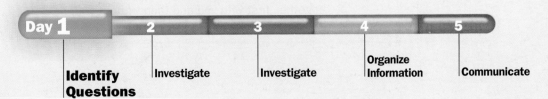

Day 1	2	3	4	5
Identify Questions	Investigate	Investigate	Organize Information	Communicate

MORE READING FOR Group Time

Use this Leveled Reader or other text at children's instructional level.

Advanced

Reviews
- Concept vocabulary
- Character and setting

Group Time

DAY 2

Strategic Intervention

① Word Work

CONSONANT BLENDS Reteach p. 70c. Additional words to blend:

stick	clap	twist	trunk
stripe	last	flake	grind

HIGH-FREQUENCY WORDS Reteach pp. 70–71. Have individuals practice reading the words from word cards.

② Read Strategic Intervention Decodable Reader 3

BEFORE READING Before reading, review *bear, build, couldn't, father, love, mother,* and *straight* on the Word Wall. Point out quotation marks on p. 2 and explain that they show someone is talking.

AFTER READING Check comprehension by having children retell the story, including the characters, setting, and plot.

Have children locate words with consonant blends in the story. List words children name. Review the consonant blend spelling patterns. Then circle the initial and final consonant blends in the story words below.

and, ask, best, blades, brave, fast, felt, Fred, glad, glide, help, must, pride, skate, skills, slide, smile, stop, strap, strong, went

③ Read Henry and Mudge and the Starry Night

BEFORE READING Have children practice the words below—first as a group and then individually. Then use Guiding Comprehension, pp. 72–87, to monitor understanding.

guitar	wagged	raccoons	giggled
slippery	yesterday	oatmeal	chewing

Monitor Progress	Word and Story Reading
If... children have difficulty with any of these words,	**then...** reteach them by modeling. Have children practice the words, with feedback from you, until they can read them independently.
If... children have difficulty reading the story individually,	**then...** have them follow along in their books as they listen to the AudioText. You may also have them read pages of the selection aloud together, first with you and then without you, before reading individually.

AudioText

Advanced

1 Read *Henry and Mudge and the Starry Night*

DURING READING Have children read silently to p. 80. Provide guidance as needed. Ask:

- If you had to rate how much each of the four characters looked forward to the camping trip, which character would be last? Explain.
- Do you think Mudge would enjoy the camping trip as much if Henry were not along? Why or why not?

Have children read silently to p. 87. Provide guidance as needed. Ask:

- Would you like the story better if Henry and Mudge had seen a bear? Why or why not?
- What does the author mean by "green dreams"?

CHARACTER AND SETTING Have children think about the characters (Henry, Mudge, Henry's mother, and Henry's father).

- Compare Henry's mother's and father's points of view about the camping trip. How are they alike? How are they different?
- Do you think Mudge has a point of view? If so, what is it?

MONITOR AND FIX UP Children can stop at p. 80 and write a question they have about the story. Then they can read on to see if their question is answered.

RESPONSE Have children rewrite the ending to the story with Henry and Mudge having seen a bear.

Audio CD   **AudioText**

2 Extend Concepts Through Inquiry

INVESTIGATE Guide children in choosing material at their independent reading level to explore their topic. Some books that may be appropriate are *The Planets* by Roy A. Gallant and *Other Worlds: A Beginner's Guide to Planets and Moons* by Terrence Dickinson. Continue to explain and model ways to research.

Help children decide how they will present their information. Children may use a Venn diagram or other graphic organizer, a written format, photographs, drawings, or models.

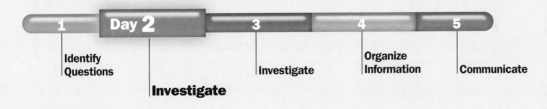

1 **Day 2** | 3 | 4 | 5

Identify Questions

Investigate

Investigate

Organize Information

Communicate

Group Time

AudioText

ROUTINE

1 Word Work

REVIEW **LONG VOWELS CVC*e*** Review p. 88c, using these additional words. Have children sort the words into *long vowel* and *not long vowel* lists.

wind	nest	cake	lane	twins	plate
shake	twigs	home	drop	snap	from

REVIEW **SENTENCE READING** Have individuals read these sentences to review decoding skills.

> **The wind made the nest rock.**
> **The twins can play at home plate.**
> **I can snap those sticks and twigs.**
> **Did you drop the cake from Grandma?**

2 Comprehension

CHARACTER AND SETTING/MONITOR AND FIX UP Reteach p. 70e. Have children respond to the Connect to Reading questions after completing step 3 Reread for Fluency.

• Now read the story again quietly. When you have finished, I'd like you to tell me who the story is about, where and when it takes place, and if all their questions were answered by the end of the story.

3 Reread for Fluency

READ WITH ACCURACY AND APPROPRIATE PACE/RATE Teach p. 88f using text at children's independent level. Reading options include Student Edition selections, Decodable Readers, Strategic Intervention Decodable Readers, and Leveled Readers.

Monitor Progress	Fluency
If… children have difficulty reading with accuracy and appropriate pace/rate,	**then…** prompt them to read more slowly, pay close attention to each word, and provide them with additional modeling. Have them listen to your model and then read aloud together, first with you and then without you, before reading individually.

MORE READING FOR
Group Time

Use this Leveled Reader or other text at children's instructional level.

Below-Level

Reviews
• High-frequency words *bear, build, couldn't, father, love, mother, straight*
• Character and setting

Advanced

① Read Self-Selected Reading

BEFORE READING Have children select a trade book or Leveled Reader to read independently. Guide children in selecting books of appropriate difficulty.

AFTER READING When they have finished, have each child choose their favorite planet and write a sentence telling why it is their favorite.

② Extend Concepts Through Inquiry

INVESTIGATE Give children time to investigate the planets they are comparing and contrasting and to begin preparing their information. Help children with their chosen methods of presentation.

1	2	Day 3	4	5
Identify Questions	Investigate	Investigate	Organize Information	Communicate

DAY 3

Trade Books for Self-Selected Reading

OTHER WORLDS: A BEGINNER'S GUIDE TO PLANETS AND MOONS by Terrence Dickinson, Firefly Books, LTD, 1995

THE PLANETS by Roy A. Gallant, Benchmark Books, 2000

MORE READING FOR
Group Time

Use this Leveled Reader or other text at children's instructional level.

Advanced

Reviews
• Concept vocabulary
• Character and setting

Group Time

DAY 4

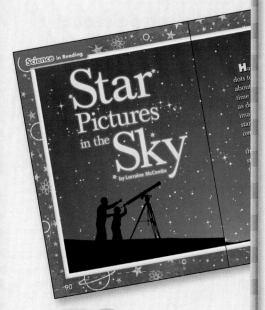

AudioText

Strategic Intervention

ROUTINE

1 **Read** "Star Pictures in the Sky"

BEFORE READING Have children practice the words below—first as a group and then individually. Then use Science in Reading, pp. 90–93.

connected   constellations   famous   nighttime

Monitor Progress	Word and Selection Reading
If… children have difficulty with any of these words,	**then…** have them practice in pairs reading word cards before reading the selection.
If… children have difficulty reading the selection individually,	**then…** have them follow along in their books as they listen to the AudioText. You may also have them read pages of the selection aloud together, first with you and then without you, before reading individually.

2 **Reread** for Fluency

Preteach p. 93a, using text at children's independent reading level. Reading options include Student Edition selections, Decodable Readers, Strategic Intervention Decodable Readers, and Leveled Readers.

3 **Build Concepts**

Use the Oral Vocabulary Routine, pp. DI·1–DI·2, DI·5, and the Oral Vocabulary Words on p. DI·8.

MORE READING FOR

Group Time

Use this Leveled Reader or other text at children's instructional level.

Below-Level

Reviews
- High-frequency words *bear, build, couldn't, father, love, mother, straight*
- Character and setting

Advanced

1 Read "Star Pictures in the Sky"

AFTER READING Ask:

- Why do you think early people needed to "draw" pictures in the sky?
- Look at the pictures of the Big and Little Dippers on pp. 92–93. How are they alike? How are they different?
- In what situations might people today need to know the location of the North Star?

2 Vocabulary

Extend vocabulary with questions such as these:

- Would you find *wildlife* in a *galaxy*? Why or why not?
- Can *wildlife* ever be *tranquil*? Explain.
- Would you someday like to explore another *galaxy*? Explain.
- Are you likely to find *wildlife* in a *rural* area? Why or why not?

Encourage children to use the words in their writing.

3 Extend Concepts Through Inquiry

ORGANIZE INFORMATION Give children time to continue reading about the planets they are researching. Remind them that tomorrow they will share their information. By now they should have begun putting the information in a presentation format. Assist anyone needing help.

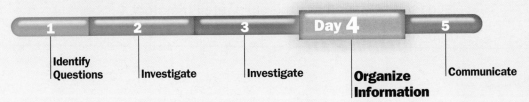

1	2	3	Day 4	5
Identify Questions	Investigate	Investigate	Organize Information	Communicate

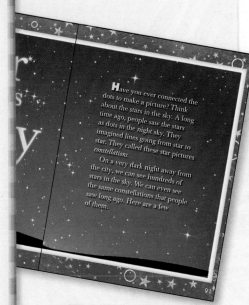

 AudioText

MORE READING FOR

Group Time

Use this Leveled Reader or other text at children's instructional level.

Advanced

Reviews
- Concept vocabulary
- Characters and setting

Group Time

ROUTINE

DAY 5

1 Word Work

CONSONANT BLENDS Have children read aloud as you track the print. Call on individuals to blend the underlined words.

> Dad will <u>bring</u> the <u>blue</u> <u>sack</u>.
> I <u>broke</u> the <u>small</u> <u>clip</u>.
> That was the <u>last</u> <u>clean</u> <u>plate</u>.
> I <u>drank</u> my <u>milk</u> and ate my <u>snack</u>.

HIGH-FREQUENCY WORDS Use pp. 70–71 to review *bear, build, couldn't, father, love, mother, straight*.

Monitor Progress	High-Frequency Words
If… children have difficulty with any of these words,	**then…** tell them the word and have them repeat it. Have children spell the word and tell what word they spelled. Have them practice in pairs with word cards.

2 Monitor Progress

SENTENCE READING SET A Use Set A on reproducible p. 94f to assess children's ability to read decodable and high-frequency words in sentences.

COMPREHENSION To assess comprehension, have each child read Strategic Intervention Reader Decodable 3 or other text at the child's independent level. Ask when and where the story takes place (setting), and have the child retell the story.

MORE READING FOR Group Time

Use this Leveled Reader or other text at children's instructional level.

Below-Level

Reviews
- High-frequency words *bear, build, couldn't, father, love, mother, straight*
- Character and setting

Advanced

DAY 5

1 Monitor Progress

SENTENCE READING SET C Use Set C on reproducible p. 94f to assess children's ability to read decodable and high-frequency words in sentences. If you have any question about whether children have mastered this week's skills, have them read the Set B sentences.

COMPREHENSION Have each child read "A World in the City" on reproducible p. 94g. Ask the child to describe the main characters and where the story takes place, and have the child retell the passage. Use the Retelling Rubric on p. 88–89 to evaluate the child's retelling.

2 Extend Concepts Through **Inquiry**

COMMUNICATE Have partners share their comparison of two planets.

1	2	3	4	Day 5
Identify Questions	Investigate	Investigate	Organize Information	

Communicate

Group Time

DAY 1

Decodable Reader 4

Clive's Big Box
Written by Paula Alvarez
Illustrated by Barbra Johnson

Strategic Intervention

1 Word Work

↻ **BASE WORDS AND ENDINGS *-s, -ed, -ing*** Reteach p. 96n.
Additional words to blend:

snapped   bakes   scaring   looked   confusing

Then have children add the *-s, -ed,* and *-ing* endings to each base word, read the new word, and tell how the spelling changed when the endings were added.

base word	-s	-ed	-ing
drag	drags	dragged	dragging
amaze	amazes	amazed	amazing
race	races	raced	racing
walk	walks	walked	walking

SPELLING Reteach p. 96p. Model spelling *dropped* and *hugging*. You may wish to give children fewer words to learn.

2 Read Decodable Reader 4

BEFORE READING Review base words with endings *-s, -ed,* and *-ing* on p. 96q and have children blend these story words: *dropped, lifting, rested, wiped, odd, yelled, quite, snug.* Be sure children understand meanings of words such as *odd.*

DURING READING Use p. 96q.

Monitor Progress	Word and Story Reading
If... children have difficulty with any of these words,	**then...** reteach them by modeling. Have children practice the words, with feedback from you, until they can read them independently.
If... children have difficulty reading the story individually,	**then...** read a page aloud as children follow along. Then have the group reread the page. Continue reading in this way before children read individually.

3 Reread for Fluency

Use the Paired Reading Routine, p. 96q, and text at each child's independent reading level.

MORE READING FOR
Group Time

Desert

(Below-Level)

Reviews
- High-frequency words *animals, early, eyes, full, warm, water*
- Main idea and details

Check this database for additional titles.

Leveled Reader Database
ONLINE

PearsonSuccessNet.com

Use this Leveled Reader or other text at children's instructional level.

Advanced

ROUTINE

1 Word Work

🔄 **BASE WORDS WITH ENDINGS -s, -ed, -ing** Practice with longer words. If children know the words on first read, they may need no further practice. Practice items:

crouches	steadied	crumbled	rehearsing	stacked
shrugged	muffles	amuses	disturbing	echoes
grinding	knitting	plugged	realized	rumbling

Have children write the words on cards. Then have them sort by endings. Have individuals choose several words to use in a sentence.

2 Read Advanced Selection 4

BEFORE READING Have children identify these oral vocabulary words: *arid, precipitation.*

DURING READING Children may read silently. Provide guidance as needed.

AFTER READING Have children recall what the author is trying to tell them. (facts about the saguaro cactus) Ask:
- Which fact do you find the most interesting? Why?
- Why is the saguaro such an important plant in the desert?

On the back of the selection page, have children write a haiku about the saguaro cactus (three lines, five syllables in the first and third lines, and seven syllables in the second line).

3 Extend Concepts Through Inquiry

IDENTIFY QUESTIONS Have children work with a partner and choose two desert plants or two desert animals to study. During the week, they should learn more about their choices from reading, studying pictures, and talking with adults or older children. On Day 5 they will share what they learned.

Guide children in brainstorming possible choices.
- Think about your choices. In which desert do they grow or live? What makes them able to live in that particular desert or deserts?

Day 1	2	3	4	5
Identify Questions	Investigate	Investigate	**Organize Information**	Communicate

The Saguaro Cactus

A desert is a hot, dry place. It doesn't rain often in a desert, and this lack of precipitation keeps the desert arid, or dry. Plants and animals that live in the desert are able to survive in a place that has little water.

A saguaro cactus can live in the arid Arizona desert because it stores water inside its leaves and stems. When there is a heavy rain, the roots of a saguaro cactus soak up as much water as they can hold, allowing the saguaro to survive long periods of dry weather.

The saguaro, or giant cactus, can grow as tall as fifty feet high and live for more than a hundred years in the desert.

The saguaro is a source of water, food, and shelter for some desert animals. Woodpeckers make holes in the saguaro looking for food and water. Then birds and insects live in the holes made by the woodpeckers.

Many animals survive by drinking the juice and eating the seeds of the saguaro. This helps the saguaro survive because the animals spread the seeds to other parts of the desert, where new saguaros then grow.

DI·12

MORE READING FOR
Group Time

Use this Leveled Reader or other text at children's instructional level.

Advanced

Reviews
- Concept vocabulary
- Main idea and details

A Walk in the Desert
Group Time

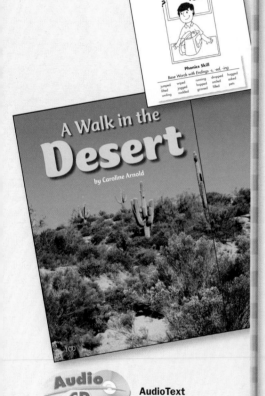

Strategic Intervention

ROUTINE

1 Word Work

BASE WORDS AND ENDINGS -s, -ed, -ing Reteach p. 98c. Additional words to blend:

gagged	saved	dining	pretends
opening	loved	happened	bugging

HIGH-FREQUENCY WORDS Reteach pp. 98–99. Have individuals practice reading the words from word cards.

2 Read Strategic Intervention Decodable Reader 4

BEFORE READING Before reading, review *animals, early, eyes, full, warm,* and *water*. Read the title and show children the cover. Have them predict what they think the story might be about.

AFTER READING Check comprehension by having children retell the story, including the characters, setting, and plot.

Have children locate base words with endings -s, -ed, and -ing in the story. List words children name. Review -s, -ed, and -ing spelling patterns. Have children sort the words they found beside *asked* and *running*.

asked: *dropped, filled, hopped, hugged, jogged, jumped, lifted, nodded, pets, smiled, wiped*

running: *smiling*

3 Read A Walk in the Desert

BEFORE READING Have children practice the words below—first as a group and then individually. Then use Guiding Comprehension, pp. 100–119, to monitor understanding.

saguaro	nectar	creatures	scaly
dangerous	tortoise	activity	canyon

Monitor Progress	Word and Selection Reading
If... children have difficulty with any of these words,	**then...** reteach them by modeling. Have children practice the words, with feedback from you, until they can read them independently.
If... children have difficulty reading the story individually,	**then...** have them follow along in their books as they listen to the AudioText. You may also have them read pages of the selection aloud together, first with you and then without you, before reading individually.

Advanced

ROUTINE

1 Read *A Walk in the Desert*

DURING READING Have children read silently to p. 110. Provide guidance as needed. Ask:

- Look at the pictures of plants on pp. 102–105. What particular kinds of plants are on these pages?
- What classifications does the author use on pp. 106–109?

Have children read silently to p. 119. Provide guidance as needed. Ask:

- Does any information in this selection about deserts surprise you? Why or why not?
- Is this an important selection for other children to read? Why or why not?

MAIN IDEA AND DETAILS Have children think about what the author is trying to tell them in this selection (what life is like in the desert). Discuss which pictures in the selection convey the main idea.

- Why do you think the author uses the pictures on pp. 118–119?
- Is the text on p. 108 telling the main idea or a supporting detail? How can you tell?

TEXT STRUCTURE Children can work with a partner to list the selection topics in order (desert plants, desert animals, desert activities, desert locations).

RESPONSE Have students pretend they are one of the animals in the desert and write a short paragraph describing one day in their life.

2 Extend Concepts Through Inquiry

INVESTIGATE Guide children in choosing material at their independent reading level to explore their topic. Some books that may be appropriate are *Life in the Deserts: Animals, People, Plants* by Lucy Baker and *America's Deserts: Guide to Plants and Animals* by Marianne D. Wallace. Continue to explain and model ways to research.

Help children decide how they will present their information. Children may use a graphic organizer, a written format, photographs, drawings, or models.

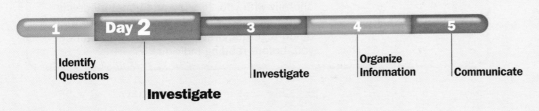

 AudioText

Group Time

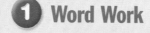

DAY **3**

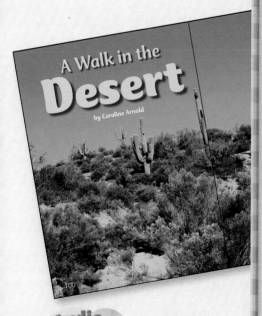

Audio CD **AudioText**

Strategic Intervention

ROUTINE

1 Word Work

REVIEW **CONSONANT BLENDS** Review p. 120c, using these additional words. Have children write the words and circle initial and final consonant blends.

drink	last	glass	milk	strike	band
brush	dust	crate	striped	snake	small

REVIEW **SENTENCE READING** Have individuals read these sentences to review decoding skills.

> Did you drink the last glass of milk?
> Dad said, "Strike up the band!"
> Can you brush the dust off the crate?
> The striped snake is small but quick.

2 Comprehension

MAIN IDEA AND DETAILS/TEXT STRUCTURE Reteach p. 98e. Have children respond to the Connect to Reading questions after completing step 3 Reread for Fluency.
- Now read the story again quietly and pay attention to the way the author organizes the selection. When you have finished, I'd like you to tell me what the selection is mostly about and details that support the main idea.

3 Reread for Fluency

ATTEND TO PUNCTUATION Teach p. 120f, using text at children's independent level. Reading options include Student Edition selections, Decodable Readers, Strategic Intervention Decodable Readers, and Leveled Readers.

Monitor Progress	Fluency
If... children have difficulty attending to punctuation,	**then...** have them put sticky notes with large periods and question marks near one sentence at a time and have them read the sentence chorally with you. Provide additional modeling. Have them listen to your model and then read aloud together, first with you and then without you, before reading individually.

Advanced

ROUTINE

1 Read Self-Selected Reading

BEFORE READING Have children select a trade book or Leveled Reader to read independently. Guide children in selecting books of appropriate difficulty.

AFTER READING When they have finished, have each child select an interesting passage to read aloud to a partner.

2 Extend Concepts Through Inquiry

INVESTIGATE Give children time to investigate the animals or plants they are studying and to begin preparing their information. Help children with their chosen methods of presentation.

| 1 | 2 | **Day 3** | 4 | 5 |

Identify Questions | Investigate | | Organize Information | Communicate

Investigate

DAY

3

Trade Books for Self-Selected Reading

AMERICA'S DESERTS: GUIDE TO PLANTS AND ANIMALS by Marianne D. Wallace, Fulcrum Publishing, 1996

LIFE IN THE DESERTS: ANIMALS, PEOPLE, PLANTS by Lucy Baker, Two-Can Publishers, 2000

MORE READING FOR
Group Time

Use this Leveled Reader or other text at children's instructional level.

Advanced

Reviews
• Concept vocabulary
• Main idea and details

Group Time

Audio CD **AudioText**

Strategic Intervention

ROUTINE

1 Read "Rain Forests"

BEFORE READING Have children practice the words below—first as a group and then individually. Then use Reading Online, pp. 122–125.

atlas	almanac	dictionary	encyclopedia
article	information	curious	university

Monitor Progress	Word and Selection Reading
If... children have difficulty with any of these words,	**then...** have them practice in pairs, reading word cards before reading the selection.
If... children have difficulty reading the selection individually,	**then...** have them follow along in their books as they listen to the AudioText. You may also have them read pages of the selection aloud together, first with you and then without you, before reading individually.

2 Reread for Fluency

Preteach p. 125a, using text at children's independent reading level. Reading options include Student Edition selections, Decodable Readers, Strategic Intervention Decodable Readers, and Leveled Readers.

3 Build Concepts

Use the Oral Vocabulary Routine, p. DI·1–DI·2, DI·6, and the Oral Vocabulary Words on p. DI·8.

MORE READING FOR
Group Time

Use this Leveled Reader or other text at children's instructional level.

Below-Level

Reviews
- High-frequency words *animals, early, eyes, full, warm, water*
- Main idea and details

Advanced

DAY **4**

1 Read "Rain Forests"

AFTER READING Ask:
- What do you think the writer is trying to teach the reader?
- You want to use online reference sources to learn more about deserts, just as Sammy did about rain forests. What would you need to do?
- Name one way in which rain forests are different from deserts and one way they are the same.

2 Vocabulary

Extend vocabulary with questions such as these:
- Do you consider a desert a *forbidding* place to visit? Why or why not?
- Would you consider sand *dunes* a *haven*? Why or why not?
- If you were in a desert, would you see much *precipitation*? Why or why not?
- Can a *landform* be *arid*? Why or why not?

Encourage children to use the words in their writing.

3 Extend Concepts Through Inquiry

ORGANIZE INFORMATION Give children time to continue reading about the plants or animals they are researching. Remind them that tomorrow they will share their information. By now they should have begun putting the information in a presentation format. Help anyone needing assistance.

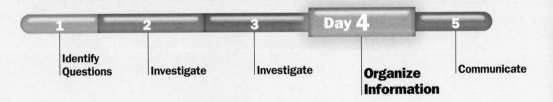

1	2	3	Day 4	5
Identify Questions	Investigate	Investigate	Organize Information	Communicate

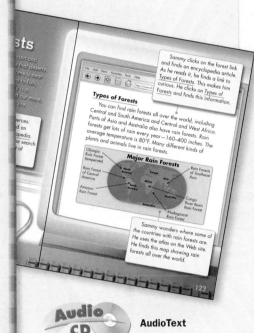

AudioText

MORE READING FOR
Group Time

Use this Leveled Reader or other text at children's instructional level.

Advanced

Reviews
- Concept vocabulary
- Main idea and details

Group Time

ROUTINE

DAY 5

1 Word Work

BASE WORDS AND ENDINGS -s, -ed, -ing Have children read aloud as you track the print. Call on individuals to blend the underlined words.

I was <u>running</u> and I <u>dropped</u> my <u>bags</u>.
Dad said <u>playing</u> is more fun than <u>winning</u> or <u>losing</u>.
I <u>hoped</u> that the <u>kittens</u> were <u>sleeping</u>!
We were <u>hiding</u>, and he <u>looked</u> for us near the <u>bushes</u>.

HIGH-FREQUENCY WORDS Use pp. 98–99 to review *animals, early, eyes, full, warm, water.*

Monitor Progress	High-Frequency Words
If... children have difficulty with any of these words,	**then...** tell them the word and have them repeat it. Have children spell the word and tell what word they spelled. Have them practice in pairs with word cards.

2 Monitor Progress

SENTENCE READING SET A Use Set A on reproducible p. 126f to assess children's ability to read decodable and high-frequency words in sentences.

COMPREHENSION To assess comprehension, have each child read Strategic Intervention Decodable Reader 4 or other text at the child's independent level. Ask when and where the story takes place (setting), and have the child retell the story.

MORE READING FOR
Group Time

Use this Leveled Reader or other text at children's instructional level.

Below-Level

Reviews
• High-frequency words *animals, early, eyes, full, warm, water*
• Main idea and details

Advanced

1 Monitor Progress

SENTENCE READING SET C Use Set C on reproducible p. 126f to assess children's ability to read decodable and high-frequency words in sentences. If you have any question about whether children have mastered this week's skills, have them read the Set B sentences.

COMPREHENSION Have each child read "A Walk in the Woods" on reproducible p. 126g. Ask what the main idea of the passage is, and have the child retell the passage. Use the Retelling Rubric on p. 120–121 to evaluate the child's retelling.

2 Extend Concepts Through **Inquiry**

COMMUNICATE Have partners share their project about two plants or animals.

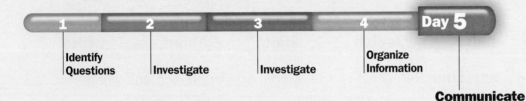

1	2	3	4	Day **5**
Identify Questions	Investigate	Investigate	Organize Information	

Communicate

MORE READING FOR

Group Time

Use this Leveled Reader or other text at children's instructional level.

Advanced

Reviews
- Concept vocabulary
- Main idea and details

Group Time

ROUTINE

DAY 1

1 Word Work

PHONEMIC AWARENESS Write the word pairs below one at a time. Model segmenting and blending each word in the pair; have children repeat after you. Then have them isolate the vowel sound in each word.

> sting—stitch   slip—ship   drop—chop   trick—thick

CONSONANT DIGRAPHS Reteach p. 128n. Additional words to blend:

> bath   when   latch   shack   lunch

Write *ch*, *tch*, *sh*, *th*, and *wh* as headings. Then read each word in random order and have children write the words under the appropriate headings and circle the letters that stand for the consonant digraph. Have all children complete the activity on paper. Ask individuals to read the words. Provide feedback as necessary.

ch	*tch*	*sh*	*th*	*wh*
bench	fetch	mash	path	when
chose	match	shake	thank	white

SPELLING Reteach p. 128p. Model spelling *bunch* and *whale*. You may wish to give children fewer words to learn.

2 Read Decodable Reader 5

BEFORE READING Review the consonant digraphs on p. 128q and have children blend these story words: *match, shrimp, splashing, whale, gliding, hunting, jumping.* Be sure children understand meanings of words such as *gliding.*

Monitor Progress	Word and Story Reading
If... children have difficulty with any of these words,	**then...** reteach them by modeling. Have children practice the words, with feedback from you, until they can read them independently.
If... children have difficulty reading the story individually,	**then...** read a page aloud as children follow along. Then have the group reread the page. Continue reading in this way before children read individually.

3 Reread for Fluency

Use the Oral Rereading Routine, p. 128q, and text at each child's independent reading level.

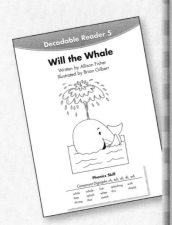

Decodable Reader 5

Will the Whale
Written by Allison Fisher
Illustrated by Brian Gilbert

Phonics Skill
Consonant Digraphs ch, tch, sh, th, wh

MORE READING FOR

Group Time

Use this Leveled Reader or other text at children's instructional level.

Below-Level

Reviews
• High-frequency words *gone, learn, often, pieces, though, together, very*
• Realism and fantasy

Check this database for additional titles.

Leveled Reader
Database
ONLINE

PearsonSuccessNet.com

Advanced

1 Word Work

⟳ **CONSONANT DIGRAPHS** Practice with longer words. If children
know the words on first read, they may need no further practice.
Practice items:

shudder	approach	whisk	sketch	chute
beneath	throughout	scratching	shrub	theater
crouch	something	together	stretch	furnish

Have children write the words on cards and sort them by digraph.
Have individuals choose several words to use in a sentence.

2 Read Advanced Selection 5

BEFORE READING Have children identify the oral vocabulary
word *inquire*.

DURING READING Children may read silently. Provide guidance
as needed.

AFTER READING Have children recall the most important idea in the
selection (Noah Webster wrote the first American dictionary). Ask:
- Why did Webster write the first American dictionary?
- How could you make this selection a fantasy?

On the back of the selection page, have children write a ballad
(a four-line poem that tells a story, in which second and fourth lines
rhyme) about Noah Webster.

America's First Dictionary

When you want to inquire about a word, where do you look? Chances are, you look in a dictionary. It might even be a Webster's dictionary, which was originally written by one man, Noah Webster.

Born in 1758, Noah Webster had an average colonial upbringing. Few people went to college then, but Webster had a love of learning, so his parents let him study at a college in New England.

After he graduated, he worked at improving the school systems. The books students used came from England, but Webster thought that they should be learning English from North American books. So in 1783 he wrote his own textbook, *A Grammatical Institute of the English Language*. It was the most popular American book of its time—even Benjamin Franklin used this book to teach his granddaughter to read.

In 1801 Webster began writing the first American dictionary. People in different parts of the country spelled, pronounced, and used words differently, but Webster thought that all Americans should speak the same way. It took him twenty-seven years to write, but in 1828 he finished his dictionary of more than 70,000 words.

When Noah Webster died in 1843, he was considered an American hero because of his big ideas.

DI • 13

3 Extend Concepts Through Inquiry

IDENTIFY QUESTIONS Have children do a genre study of fantasy,
such as animal or Native American fantasy. During the week, they
should learn more about their choices from reading, studying
pictures, and talking with adults or older children. On Day 5 they
will share what they learned.

Guide children in brainstorming possible choices.
- Think about the fantasy genre. Is it fiction or nonfiction? What
makes it different from other genres?

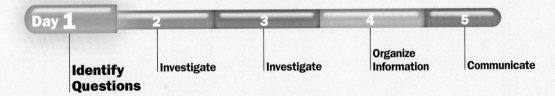

Day 1	2	3	4	5
Identify Questions	Investigate	Investigate	Organize Information	Communicate

The Strongest One
Group Time

DAY 2

Strategic Intervention Decodable Reader 5

Shane
Written by Renée McLean
Illustrated by Sam Mok

Phonics Skill
Consonant Digraphs ch, tch, sh, th, wh

AudioText

1 Word Work

CONSONANT DIGRAPHS Reteach pp. 130c–130d. Additional words to blend:

thump	white	chase	hatch
shone	chest	while	patch

HIGH-FREQUENCY WORDS Reteach pp. 130–131. Have individuals practice reading the words from word cards.

2 Read Strategic Intervention Decodable Reader 5

BEFORE READING Before reading, review *gone, learn, often, pieces, though, together,* and *very* on the Word Wall. On pp. 3–6, point out that "Shane had an itch" is repeated each time Shane has an itch on a different part of his body.

AFTER READING Check comprehension by having children retell the story, including the characters, setting, and plot.

Have children locate words with consonant digraphs and list them. Review digraph spelling patterns and have children sort the words.

ch	*tch*	*sh*	*th*	*wh*
chased	itch	Shane	that	when
chest	itching	shin		
chin	scratched	bush		

3 Reread *The Strongest One*

BEFORE READING Have children practice the words below—first as a group and then individually. Then use Guiding Comprehension, pp. 132–149, to monitor understanding.

wondered	strongest	elsewhere	offstage
poured	arrow	pieces	returned

Monitor Progress	Word and Story Reading
If... children have difficulty with any of these words,	**then...** reteach them by modeling. Have children practice the words, with feedback from you, until they can read them independently.
If... children have difficulty reading the story individually,	**then...** have them follow along in their books as they listen to the AudioText. You may also have them read pages of the selection aloud together, first with you and then without you, before reading individually.

ROUTINE

Advanced

DAY 2

1 Read *The Strongest One*

DURING READING Have children read silently to p. 140. Provide guidance as needed. Ask:

- What is the problem in this play?
- What do you think will happen in the rest of the play?

Have children read silently to p. 149. Provide guidance as needed. Ask:

- How was the problem solved?
- Do you think a person could learn anything from what Little Red Ant learned? Explain.

REALISM AND FANTASY Have children think about the characters in the play. Discuss how characters help reveal that a selection is a fantasy.

- Which characters in the selection can walk in real life and which ones cannot?
- Name something the characters do that tells you the selection is a fantasy.

TEXT STRUCTURE Children can write a sentence telling what the illustration on p. 137 shows and another sentence to tell which two characters are speaking on p. 143.

RESPONSE Have students suppose they are costume designers. Have them design a costume for Little Red Ant to wear as he goes out to find the strongest one.

2 Extend Concepts Through *Inquiry*

INVESTIGATE Guide children in choosing material at their independent reading level to explore their topic. Books that may be appropriate are *The Story of the Milky Way* by Joseph Bruchac or *Bruno the Baker* by Lars Klinting.

Help children decide how they will present their information. Children may use a graphic organizer, a written format, photographs, drawings, or models.

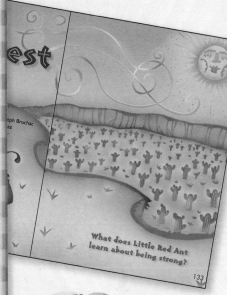

What does Little Red Ant learn about being strong?
133

AudioText

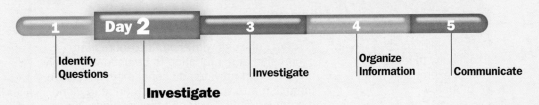

1	Day 2	3	4	5
Identify Questions	Investigate	Investigate	Organize Information	Communicate

The Strongest One

Group Time

DAY
3

retold as a play by Joseph Bruchac
illustrated by David Diaz
from Pushing Up the Sky

132

Audio CD AudioText

1 Word Work

REVIEW BASE WORDS AND ENDINGS -s, -ed, -ing Review p. 150c, using these additional words. Have children sort the words into *-s*, *-ed*, and *-ing* lists.

watched	grabbed	things	looked	placed
bins	running	jumping	tagged	pecked
chips	gobbled			

REVIEW SENTENCE READING Have individuals read these sentences to review decoding skills.

I watched while Mom grabbed our things from the shelf.
We looked for the book I placed in one of the bins.
Chris was running and jumping over the bush, but
I tagged him!
The chicken pecked at the chips and then gobbled them up.

2 Comprehension

REALISM AND FANTASY/MONITOR AND FIX UP Reteach p. 130e. Have children respond to the Connect to Reading questions after completing step 3 Reread for Fluency.
• Now read the story again quietly and think about whether you understand what you are reading. When you have finished, I'd like you to tell me whether what you read could really happen or if it is fantasy.

3 Reread for Fluency

READ WITH EXPRESSION AND INTONATION Teach p. 150f using text at children's independent level. Reading options include Student Edition selections, Decodable Readers, Strategic Intervention Decodable Readers, and Leveled Readers.

Monitor Progress	Fluency
If... children have difficulty reading with expression and intonation,	**then...** discuss with them the appropriate expression and intonation to be used with each passage and provide additional modeling. Have them listen to your model and then read aloud together, first with you and then without you, before reading individually.

MORE READING FOR
Group Time

Use this Leveled Reader or other text at children's instructional level.

Below-Level

Reviews
• High-frequency words *gone, learn, often, pieces, though, together, very*
• Realism and fantasy

Advanced

ROUTINE

① Read Self-Selected Reading

BEFORE READING Have children select a trade book or Leveled Reader to read independently. Guide children in selecting books of appropriate difficulty.

AFTER READING When they have finished, have each child choose their favorite passage and read it aloud to a partner.

② Extend Concepts Through Inquiry

INVESTIGATE Give children time to investigate their genre and begin preparing their information. Help students with their chosen methods of presentation.

1   2   **Day 3**   4   5

Identify Questions   Investigate   **Investigate**   Organize Information   Communicate

DAY 3

Trade Books for Self-Selected Reading

A LONG AND UNCERTAIN JOURNEY: THE 27,000 MILE VOYAGE OF VASCO DA GAMA by Joan Goodman, Mikaya Press, 2001

THE CALIFORNIA GOLD RUSH by Joan Blashfield, Compass Point Books, 2000

MORE READING FOR
Group Time

Use this Leveled Reader or other text at children's instructional level.

Advanced

Reviews
- Concept vocabulary
- Realism and fantasy

Group Time

DAY 4

AudioText

Strategic Intervention

ROUTINE

① Read "Anteaters"

BEFORE READING Have children practice the words below—first as a group and then individually. Then use Science in Reading, pp. 152–155.

anteater   giant   tongue   swallows

Monitor Progress	Word and Selection Reading
If… children have difficulty with any of these words,	**then…** have them practice in pairs reading word cards before reading the selection.
If… children have difficulty reading the selection individually,	**then…** have them follow along in their books as they listen to the AudioText. You may also have them read pages of the selection aloud together, first with you and then without you, before reading individually.

② Reread for Fluency

Preteach p. 155a, using text at children's independent reading level. Reading options include Student Edition selections, Decodable Readers, Strategic Intervention Decodable Readers, and Leveled Readers.

③ Build Concepts

Use the Oral Vocabulary Routine, pp. DI·1–DI·2, DI·7, and the Oral Vocabulary Words on p. DI·8.

MORE READING FOR
Group Time

Use this Leveled Reader or other text at children's instructional level.

Below-Level

Reviews
- High-frequency words *gone, learn, often, pieces, though, together, very*
- Realism and fantasy

1 Read "Anteaters"

AFTER READING Ask:
- Why do you think the anteater has such a long, thin tongue?
- In what way do you think the anteater is a helpful creature?
- Why do you think the anteater has to spend so much time each day looking for ants to eat?

2 Vocabulary

Extend vocabulary with questions such as these:
- Do you think the anteater is a *sturdy* or a *delicate* creature? Why?
- If you planned an *exhibit* about anteaters, what would you include?
- Do you think an anteater can *resist* eating ants?
- If you wanted to *inquire* about measles, would you go to the library or to the hospital? Why?

Encourage children to use the words in their writing.

3 Extend Concepts Through Inquiry

ORGANIZE INFORMATION Give children time to continue reading the fantasy genre. Remind them that tomorrow they will share their information. By now they should have begun putting the information in a presentation format.

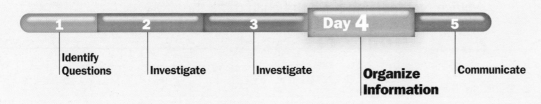

1	2	3	Day 4	5
Identify Questions	Investigate	Investigate	**Organize Information**	Communicate

Central America

Where do they live?
Anteaters live mostly in South and Central America where there are lots of grasses, swamps, and rain forests. These are the kind of places where many ants live. Anteaters explore these grasses, swamps, and rain forests all day looking for ants to eat.

South America

AudioText

MORE READING FOR
Group Time

Use this Leveled Reader or other text at children's instructional level.

Advanced

Reviews
- Concept vocabulary
- Realism and fantasy

The Strongest One

Group Time

Strategic Intervention

ROUTINE

1 Word Work

CONSONANT DIGRAPHS Have children read aloud as you track the print. Call on individuals to blend the underlined words.

Which stitch did you check?
What time does that watch say?
They made a batch of food for lunch.
I will wash the mud from the ditch off my things.

HIGH-FREQUENCY WORDS Use pp. 130–131 to review *gone, learn, often, pieces, though, together, very.*

Monitor Progress	High-Frequency Words
If... children have difficulty with any of these words,	**then...** tell them the word and have them repeat it. Have children spell the word and tell what word they spelled. Have them practice in pairs with word cards.

2 Monitor Progress

SENTENCE READING SET A Use Set A on reproducible p. 156f to assess children's ability to read decodable and high-frequency words in sentences.

COMPREHENSION To assess comprehension, have each child read Strategic Intervention Decodable Reader 5 or other text at the child's independent level. Ask when and where the story takes place (setting) and have the child retell the story.

MORE READING FOR
Group Time

Use this Leveled Reader or other text at children's instructional level.

(Below-Level)

Reviews
• High-frequency words *gone, learn, often, pieces, though, together, very*
• Realism and fantasy

Advanced

ROUTINE

DAY **5**

1 Monitor Progress

SENTENCE READING SET C Use Set C on reproducible p. 156f to assess children's ability to read decodable and high-frequency words in sentences. If you have any question about whether children have mastered this week's skills, have them read the Set B sentences.

COMPREHENSION Have each child read "Little Bear" on reproducible p. 156g. Ask what the main idea is, and have the child retell the passage. Use the Retelling Rubric on p. 150–151 to evaluate the child's retelling.

2 Extend Concepts Through **Inquiry**

COMMUNICATE Have children share their study of the fantasy genre and their example.

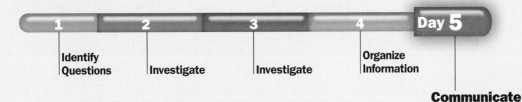

1	2	3	4	Day 5
Identify Questions	Investigate	Investigate	Organize Information	Communicate

---

MORE READING FOR
Group Time

Use this Leveled Reader or other text at children's instructional level.

Advanced

Reviews
- Concept vocabulary
- Realism and fantasy

Iris and Walter

Short Vowels; ea/e/

1 TEACH

Write *deck, sing, lock, luck, sick, man,* and *dust* on the board. Have volunteers read the words aloud and name the vowel sound in each. Help children understand that all the words have the short vowel sound.

Write *head* on the board. Frame *ea* and stretch out the sound as you say *head.* Say: The letters *ea* can sometimes spell the short *e* sound.

Write the following words on chart paper: *breath, clock, bread, thread, desk, ready, back, leather, sack, thick, tuck.* Read aloud each word. Invite a volunteer to circle the letter or letters in each word that stand for the short vowel sound.

Remind children that when they see a word with the letters *ea,* they might try using both the long *e* sound and the short *e* sound to sound out the word. They should choose the sound that makes a word and that makes sense.

2 PRACTICE AND ASSESS

Write the following words on the board. Have children read each word. If the word has a short vowel sound, the child uses it in a sentence.

weather	wheat	treat	spread
black	feather	king	drum
crib	thread	head	shock

Then write *king* on the board. Have children make new words as you give the following instructions:

Change the *k* to *br*. Read the word. (bring)
Change the *ing* to *ead*. Read the word. (bread)
Change the *d* to *th*. Read the word. (breath)
Change the *br* to *f* and add *er* at the end. Read the word. (feather)
Change the *f* to *l*. Read the word. (leather)

Iris and Walter

Character and Setting

1 TEACH

Tell children that authors show their readers what the story characters are like. They want the characters to seem like real people. Readers can see what the characters are feeling through the things they do, think, and say.

Say: At the beginning of *Iris and Walter,* Iris hates the country. After she meets Walter, her feelings about the country change. She has someone to spend time with and she appreciates the country more. The author shows what the country is like through words and pictures.

Explain that the setting is the time and place of a story. Settings can be real or imaginary. Ask students to name the setting of *Iris and Walter.* (in the country in the present)

2 PRACTICE AND ASSESS

Recall the fable *The Tortoise and the Hare.* Ask: Where does the fable take place? Would you say the tortoise was mean, fast, or steady? (The fable takes place on a country path; the tortoise is steady because he keeps going and doesn't give up.)

Read each of the descriptions below to children. Ask them to name the setting and to tell what they know about each main character.

David's class is practicing for a program. David likes to sing, but he doesn't like to sing in front of others. He doesn't like acting in plays either. David is _____. (Possible response: shy; setting—school)

Keisha's uncle took her on his boat for the first time. The wind kicked up, and Keisha's uncle needed her help to move the sail. Keisha wasn't afraid to try something new. Keisha was _____. (Possible response: brave; setting—in a boat)

Long Vowels CVC*e*

1 TEACH

Write *plan* on the board. Ask children what vowel sound they hear in *plan*. (the short *a* sound) Below *plan*, write *plane*. Say the word, and have children repeat it. Explain that *plane* has the long *a* sound. Frame the letters *ane*. Identify the letters as V/C/*e*. Tell children that when a vowel is followed by a consonant and the letter *e*, the first vowel usually has its long vowel sound and the *e* is silent.

Write *nice, rage,* and *nose* on the board. Ask children what vowel sound they hear. (long vowel sound) Review with children each ending sound.

2 PRACTICE AND ASSESS

Write these words on the board:

mad   rid   bit   hop   us

Have children read each word and identify the short vowel. Ask volunteers to come to the board and add a final *e* to each word. Have them read each new word and identify the long vowels. Review the vowel/consonant/*e* rule.

Write this sentence on the board:

The snake chose a nice hole for its home.

Have children read the sentence aloud. Ask them to identify each long vowel and tell why it has a long vowel sound.

Provide phonogram cards *ace, ake, ice, ime,* and letter cards *d, l, m, n, p,* and *t*. Have children use the cards to build words that have long vowels and end in *e*. (*dice, dime, lace, lake, lice, lime, make, mice, mime, nice, pace, take, time*)

Record words children build on the board. Invite volunteers to use each word in a sentence.

Main Idea

1 TEACH

Write the following sentences on the board and read them aloud with the class:

a.   José saw yogurt.
b.   José found cheese.
c.   José was hungry and found something to eat.

Then read aloud the following paragraph: José was hungry. He wanted to eat. He looked in the refrigerator. He saw bread. He saw meat. He saw cheese. Nothing looked good. Then he saw yogurt. He grabbed the yogurt. He gobbled it down.

Ask children to pick from the sentences on the board the one that tells the most important idea of the paragraph. (c) If necessary, reread the paragraph. Explain that c tells what the paragraph is mostly about, so c tells the main idea of the paragraph. Tell children that the other two choices are only small parts, or details, of the paragraph. Details tell more about the main idea.

2 PRACTICE AND ASSESS

Recall with children the story *Exploring Space with an Astronaut*. Reread page 55. Write the following sentences on the board and ask children to identify the sentence that best states the main idea.

a.   Astronauts use robot arms to move things and people outside the shuttle.
b.   A space shuttle is a giant toolbox!
c.   On space walks, space suits keep astronauts safe.

Guide children in recognizing that *b* is the correct answer. Help them understand that a and c tell more about the main idea. They are details.

Henry and Mudge

Consonant Blends

1 TEACH

Remind children that when two or three consonants are together in a word, they should blend their sounds together. Write _ride_ and have children read the word. Then write _bride._ Say: Listen as I blend this word. Blend the sounds of the word. Notice that you hear /b/ and /r/ blended at the beginning of the word.

Write _stump_ and read the word. Say: Notice /st/ at the beginning of the word and /mp/ at the end.

Write these words on the board. Ask volunteers to read the word and circle the beginning and/or ending blend.

| strap | clamp | slip | plug |
| smile | crust | plank | |

2 PRACTICE AND ASSESS

Display the following word cards, one at a time. Have children identify the letters that stand for the beginning and/or final consonant sounds in each word and read the words.

Have children work individually or in pairs to sort the word cards according to beginning or ending sounds. _(bride/brake; strap/string/strong; mask/ tusk; pond/send/land; flop/flute; camp/bump; lost/ dust)_ Then have children name another word that begins or ends with each consonant blend.

Henry and Mudge

Character and Setting

1 TEACH

Tell children that writers tell about the characters in their stories through what the character says, what the character does, and how others in the story act toward the character. Writers also give clues about the setting, where and when the story takes place. Settings can be real or imaginary.

Ask children to think about the setting of the story. Have them tell where and when the story takes place and what kind of person they think Henry is. Have them find sentences to support their answers.

2 PRACTICE AND ASSESS

Tell children the story that follows.

"This is great!" thought Zane as he zoomed across the moon's surface with his jet pack. Second graders were allowed to leave early for Moon School. "When we were children on Earth," his dad would always say, "we didn't have jet packs to get to school. We walked or took a bus."

Ask these questions:

What is Zane like? How do you know? (Possible response: He's daring. I know because the story tells that he loved going fast.)

Where did this story take place? How do you know? (Possible response: It happened outside on the moon. The story tells that this is the moon.)

When did this story happen—in the past, during the present, or in the future? How do you know?

Help children see that the story could not be set in the past and could not happen in the present because children cannot yet zip around the moon with jet packs. The story must be set in the future.

A Walk in the Desert

Inflected Endings -s, -ed, -ing

1 TEACH

Write the sentences below on the board.

Tom jumps.
He is jumping now.
He jumped last week too.

Have the sentences read. Underline *jump* and point out that *jump* is a base word. Adding *-s* to a base word makes a new word. Have a child circle the endings in *jumps, jumping,* and *jumped.*

Explain that if a base word ends with a vowel followed by one consonant, the consonant is doubled before an ending is added. Demonstrate this by writing *hop, hopped,* and *hopping.* Identify the base word and endings. Point out the vowel and final consonant in *hop.* Ask which consonant was doubled before an ending was added. Tell children the *p* is not doubled before adding *-s.*

Write *hike, hikes, hiked,* and *hiking.* Explain that *hike* is the base word. Tell children that the final *e* is dropped before *-es, -ed,* or *-ing* is added.

2 PRACTICE AND ASSESS

Create a chart as shown. Ask children to tell you which words will need to have the last consonant doubled before adding an ending.

	-ed	-ing
jump		
pat		
rub		
ask		

Have children take turns coming to the board and adding the endings to complete the chart. Then review the sounds of *-ed* in *jumped* (/t/), *patted* (/ed/), and *rubbed* (/d/).

A Walk in the Desert

Main Idea

1 TEACH

Remind children that the main idea is the most important idea in something that they read. The main idea usually tells what the writing is about. Children should think about the whole paragraph or story when looking for the main idea. Usually the main idea will be in one sentence. Remind children that details tell more about the main idea.

Read aloud the following paragraph. Fido was a happy dog. He ate a big meal in the morning. He went for a walk in the afternoon. He had his bath once a month. He slept in a fluffy dog bed. He was sure that no dog could be happier.

Write these sentence choices on the board. Ask children to think about Fido and the paragraph they just heard. Read each sentence aloud. Have children tell whether the sentence tells a detail or the main idea.

a. Fido ate in the morning.
b. Fido was a happy dog.
c. Fido had a bath once a month.

Guide children in identifying *a* and *c* as details and *b* as the main idea. Explain that *a* and *c* are only small parts of the paragraph, but *b* tells what the paragraph is mostly about, so it is the main idea.

2 PRACTICE AND ASSESS

Assign small groups a different page from *A Walk in the Desert.* After the group reads the page, have them decide what the main idea is and write a sentence that states the main idea. Groups can share their findings with classmates.

The Strongest One

Consonant Digraphs

1 TEACH

Say: The chick cheeped while the child changed channels. What sound is repeated? (/ch/)

Write *chalk* on the board. Circle the letters *ch*. Explain that *ch* stands for the sound /ch/. Tell children that sometimes two consonants together stand for one new sound. Touch *ch* and have children say /ch/ with you. Write the following words on the board:

ship	thin	whale	catch
with	dash	each	

Have children read the words and circle the two or three consonants in each word that stand for one sound: *sh, th, wh, ch, tch.*

2 PRACTICE AND ASSESS

Have children suggest other words that begin or end with the same sounds as the words on the board. Add their words. Ask volunteers to circle the letters that stand for the beginning or ending consonant sound in each word.

Write the following sentences. Have children circle the digraphs and say their sounds.

Charlie fed each chicken so much food.
She will wash shells as shy people fish.
Thad hit his thumb with a thick stick.
Whales whistle while water whirls.
I will watch Mom strike the match.

Provide pictures of a whistle, a chicken, a shell, the number 3, and a match. On index cards, write these words: *while, whale, when, what, thirsty, bath, think, path, shape, wish, shirt, splash, chop, pinch, check, such, latch, patch, ditch, catch.* Have children place each card below the picture whose name begins or ends with the same digraph.

The Strongest One

Realism and Fantasy

1 TEACH

Tell children that a realistic story tells about something that could really happen. A fantasy is a story about something that could not happen.

Ask children who are familiar with the rhyme to recite "Hey Diddle Diddle" with you. Then model thinking about this rhyme.

Say: When I hear "Hey Diddle Diddle, the cat and the fiddle, the cow jumped over the moon," I know that a cat can't play a fiddle. I also know there's no way a cow can jump over the moon. That tells me that this rhyme is a fantasy.

Then repeat the rhyme "Jack Be Nimble." Say: When I hear "Jack jump over the candlestick," I know that a boy really might be able to jump over a candle—even though he probably shouldn't. That tells me that this rhyme might be called realistic because what Jack does might really happen.

2 PRACTICE AND ASSESS

Have children listen as you read some sentences. They should tell you whether each one is realistic or a fantasy and why.

A cat is sleeping on a windowsill. (realistic; cats do sleep on windowsills)

A cat plans a trip to the moon. (fantasy; cats can't plan a trip)

A fish tells a fisherman that a storm is coming. (fantasy; a fish can't talk)

A bear eats berries off a bush. (realistic; bears might really eat berries)

Providing children with reading materials they can and want to read is an important step toward developing fluent readers. A running record allows you to determine each child's instructional and independent reading level. Information on how to take a running record is provided on pp. DI•71–DI•72.

Instructional Reading Level

Only approximately 1 in 10 words will be difficult when reading a selection from the Student Edition for children who are at grade level. (A typical second-grader reads approximately 90–100 words correct per minute.)

- Children reading at grade level should read regularly from the Student Edition and On-Level Leveled Readers, with teacher support as suggested in the Teacher's Editions.
- Children reading below grade level can read the Strategic Intervention Leveled Readers and the Decodable Readers. Instructional plans can be found in the Teacher's Edition and the Leveled Reader Teaching Guide.
- Children who are reading above grade level can use the Advanced Leveled Readers and the Advanced Selection in the Teacher's Edition. Instructional plans can be found in the Teacher's Edition and the Leveled Reader Teaching Guide.

Independent Reading Level

Children should read regularly in independent-level texts in which no more than approximately 1 in 20 words is difficult for the reader. Other factors that make a book easy to read include the child's interest in the topic, the amount of text on a page, how well illustrations support meaning, and the complexity and familiarity of the concepts. Suggested books for self-selected reading are provided for each lesson on p. TR18 in this Teacher's Edition.

Guide children in learning how to self-select books at their independent reading level. As you talk about a book with children, discuss the challenging concepts in it, list new words children find in sampling the book, and ask children about their familiarity with the topic. A blackline master to help children evaluate books for independent reading is provided on p. DI•70.

Self-Selected/Independent Reading

While oral reading allows you to assess children's reading level and fluency, independent reading is of crucial importance to children's futures as readers and learners. Children need to develop their ability to read independently for increasing amounts of time.

- Schedule a regular time for sustained independent reading in your classroom. During the year, gradually increase the amount of time devoted to independent reading.
- More fluent readers may choose to read silently during independent reading time. Other children might read to a partner, to a stuffed animal, or to an adult volunteer.
- Help children track the amount of time they read independently and the number of pages they read in a given amount of time. Tracking will help motivate them to gradually increase their duration and speed. Blackline masters for tracking independent reading are provided on pp. DI•70 and TR19.

Choosing a Book to Read by Yourself

These questions can help you pick a book to read.

_____ 1. Is this book about something that I like?

_____ 2. This book may be about a real person, about facts, or a made-up story. Do I like reading this kind of book?

_____ 3. Have I read other things by this author? Do I like the author?

If you say "yes" to question 1, 2, or 3, go on.

_____ 4. Were there fewer than 5 hard words on the first page?

_____ 5. Does the number of words on a page look about right to me?

If you say "yes" to questions 4 and 5, the book is right for you.

Silent Reading

Write the date, the title of the book, and the number of minutes you read.

Date	Title	Minutes

Taking a Running Record

A running record is an assessment of a child's oral reading accuracy and oral reading fluency. Reading accuracy is based on the number of words read correctly. Reading fluency is based on the reading rate (the number of words correct per minute) and the degree to which a child reads with a "natural flow."

How to Measure Reading Accuracy

1. Choose a grade-level text of about 80 to 120 words that is unfamiliar to the child.
2. Make a copy of the text for yourself. Make a copy for the child or have the child read aloud from a book.
3. Give the child the text and have the child read aloud. (You may wish to record the child's reading for later evaluation.)
4. On your copy of the text, mark any miscues or errors the child makes while reading. See the running record sample on page DI•72, which shows how to identify and mark miscues.
5. Count the total number of words in the text and the total number of errors made by the child. Note: If a child makes the same error more than once, such as mispronouncing the same word multiple times, count it as one error. Self-corrections do not count as actual errors. Use the following formula to calculate the percentage score, or accuracy rate:

$$\frac{\text{Total Number of Words} - \text{Total Number of Errors}}{\text{Total Number of Words}} \times 100 = \text{percentage score}$$

Interpreting the Results

- A child who reads **95–100%** of the words correctly is reading at an **independent level** and may need more challenging text.
- A child who reads **90–94%** of the words correctly is reading at an **instructional level** and will likely benefit from guided instruction.
- A child who reads **89%** or fewer of the words correctly is reading at a **frustrational level** and may benefit most from targeted instruction with lower-level texts and intervention.

How to Measure Reading Rate (WCPM)

1. Follow Steps 1–3 above.
2. Note the exact times when the child begins and finishes reading.
3. Use the following formula to calculate the number of words correct per minute (WCPM):

$$\frac{\text{Total Number of Words Read Correctly}}{\text{Total Number of Seconds}} \times 60 = \text{words correct per minute}$$

Interpreting the Results

An appropriate reading rate for a second-grader is 90–100 (WCPM).

Running Record Sample

Running Record Sample

Just then a fly crawled near Fred.
and
Fred's long, ˄ sticky tongue shot out in a
/ti ne/
flash and caught the tiny insect.
H
"Delicious! I'm full now," he said
loudly. He had already eaten three other
insects and a worm in the past hour.
(sc)

Frankie overheard Fred and climbed
down a few branches. He moved quickly
and easily without falling.

"What are you doing, (Fred?)" he
asked in a friendly voice.

"I was just finishing up my lunch,"
there
Fred answered. "How is life up ~~high~~
today, my friend?"

—From *Frog Friends*
On-Level Reader 2.4.3

Miscues

Insertion
The student inserts words or parts of words that are not in the text.

Mispronunciation/Misreading
The student pronounces or reads a word incorrectly.

Hesitation
The student hesitates over a word, and the teacher provides the word. Wait several seconds before telling the student what the word is.

Self-Correction
The student reads a word incorrectly but then corrects the error. Do not count self-corrections as actual errors. However, noting self-corrections will help you identify words the student finds difficult.

Omission
The student omits words or word parts.

Substitution
The student substitutes words or parts of words for the words in the text.

Running Record Results ▶ **Reading Accuracy** ▶ **Reading Rate—WCPM**

Total Number of Words: **86**

Number of Errors: **5**

$$\frac{86-5}{86} = \frac{81}{86} = .9418 = 94\%$$

$$\frac{81}{64} \times 60 = 75.9 = 76 \text{ words correct per minute}$$

Reading Time: **64 seconds**

Accuracy Percentage Score: **94%**

Reading Rate: **76 WCPM**

Unit 1
Exploration

Week 1

What might we discover in a new neighborhood?

Week 2

Why would anyone want to explore space?

Week 3

What can we discover by exploring nature?

Week 4

What can we learn by exploring the desert?

Week 5

When we are searching for answers, whom can we ask?

EXPAND THE CONCEPT
What might we discover in a new neighborhood?

Time for SOCIAL STUDIES

Iris and Walter
by Elissa Hoden Guest
illustrated by Christine Davenier

Poetry

Morning Song
by Bobbi Katz

Today is a day to catch tadpoles.
Today is a day to explore.
Today is a day to get started.
Come on! Let's not sleep anymore.

Outside the sunbeams are dancing.
The leaves sing a rustling song.
Today is a day for adventures,
and I hope that you'll come along!

My Travel Tree
by Bobbi Katz

There are oh-so-many
kinds of trees—
apple, pear, pine—
but there is just one special tree
I feel is somehow mine.
Its branches form
such cozy nooks
for dreaming dreams
and reading books.
I sail to almost anywhere,
perched among the leaves up there.
If naming things were up to me,
I'd call this one my travel tree.

CONNECT THE CONCEPT

▶ **Build Background**

brittle	decision	underground
creature	investigate	urban
dart	rural	

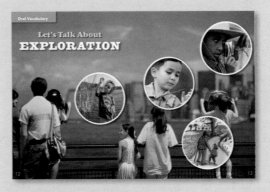

Oral Vocabulary

Let's Talk About
EXPLORATION

▶ **Social Studies Content**
Comparing Communities; Geography: Urban, Suburban, Rural; Exploration; Friendship

▶ **Writing**
A Plan

Preview Your Week

What might we discover in a new neighborhood?

Iris and Walter
by Elissa Haden Guest
illustrated by Christine Davenier

What new things does Iris learn when she moves to the country?

16

17

Student Edition pages 16–37

Audio CD

Genre Realistic Fiction

◉ **Phonics** Short Vowels

◉ **Comprehension Skill** Character and Setting

◉ **Comprehension Strategy** Predict

Time for SOCIAL STUDIES

Paired Selection

Reading Across Texts
Recite Poetry

Genre
Poetry

Text Features
Lines That Rhyme and Have Rhythm

Morning Song
by Bobbi Katz

Today is a day to catch tadpoles.
Today is a day to explore.
Today is a day to get started.
Come on! Let's not sleep anymore.

Outside the sunbeams are dancing.
The leaves sing a rustling song.
Today is a day for adventures,
and I hope that you'll come along!

My Travel Tree
by Bobbi Katz

There are oh-so-many
kinds of trees—
apple, pear, pine—
but there is just one special tree
I feel is somehow mine.
Its branches form
such cozy nooks
for dreaming dreams
and reading books.
I sail to almost anywhere,
perched among the leaves up there.
If naming things were up to me,
I'd call this one my travel tree.

Student Edition pages 38–39

Audio CD

Read It
ONLINE
PearsonSuccessNet.com

- Student Edition
- Leveled Readers
- Decodable Reader

Leveled Readers

Skill Character and Setting

Strategy Predict

Lesson Vocabulary

Below-Level

On-Level

Advanced

ELL Reader

- Concept Vocabulary
- Text Support
- Language Enrichment

Off to School We Go!
by Laura Ivy
Illustrated by Darryl Ligasan

Decodable Readers

Apply Phonics

- *Gus*

Decodable Reader 1
Gus
Written by Harriet Yi
Illustrated by Josh Bermann

Time for
SOCIAL STUDIES

Integrate Social Studies Standards

- Comparing Communities
- Geography
- Exploration
- Friendship

✓ Read

Iris and Walter pp. 16–37

"Morning Song"/"My Travel Tree" pp. 38–39

✓ Read

Below-Level · On-Level · Advanced

- Support Concepts
- Develop Concepts
- Extend Concepts
- Social Studies Extension Activity

✓ Read

ELL Reader

✓ Build **Concept Vocabulary**
Exploration, pp. 12r, 12–13

✓ Teach **Social Studies Concepts**
Cities, Suburbs, Country,
p. 22–23
Big Cities, p. 34–35

✓ Explore **Social Studies Center**
Make a Venn Diagram, p. 12k

Iris and Walter **12c**

Weekly Plan

READING

90–120 minutes

TARGET SKILLS OF THE WEEK

- **Phonics**
  Short Vowels

- **Comprehension Skill**
  Character and Setting

- **Comprehension Strategy**
  Predict

DAY 1 · PAGES 12l–13d

Oral Language

QUESTION OF THE WEEK, 12l
What might we discover in a new neighborhood?

Oral Vocabulary/Share Literature, 12m
Sing with Me Big Book, Song 1
Amazing Words *investigate, rural, urban*

Word Work

Phonics, 12n–12o
  Introduce Short Vowels; *ea/e/* **T**

Spelling, 12p
Pretest

Comprehension/Vocabulary/Fluency

Read Decodable Reader 1

Grouping Options 12f–12g

Review High-Frequency Words
Check Comprehension
Reread for Fluency

Build Background, 12r–13
Exploration

Listening Comprehension, 13a–13b
  Character and Setting **T**

DAY 2 · PAGES 14a–35c

Oral Language

QUESTION OF THE DAY, 14a
What could Iris discover that might help her?

Oral Vocabulary/Share Literature, 14b
Big Book *In the Forest*
Amazing Word *creature*

Word Work

Phonics, 14c–14d
  Review Short Vowels; *ea/e/* **T**

Spelling, 14d
Dictation

Comprehension/Vocabulary/Fluency

Read *Iris and Walter,* 14e–35a

Grouping Options
12f–12g

Introduce High-Frequency
  Words *beautiful, country,
  friend, front, someone,
  somewhere* **T**

Introduce Selection Words
  *amazing, ladder, meadow,
  roller-skate*

Reread for Fluency

  Character and
  Setting **T**
  Predict
  REVIEW Main Idea and
  Details **T**

LANGUAGE ARTS

20–30 minutes

Trait of the Week

Voice

Shared Writing, 13c
Plan

Grammar, 13d
Introduce Sentences **T**

Interactive Writing, 35b
Paragraph

Grammar, 35c
Practice Sentences **T**

DAILY JOURNAL WRITING

Day 1 *Write about whether your neighborhood is urban or rural.*

Day 2 *Write about a time you explored or investigated a rural or an urban place.*

DAILY SOCIAL STUDIES CONNECTIONS

Day 1 Urban/Rural Concept Chart, 12r–13

Day 2 Time for Social Studies: Cities, Suburbs, Country, 22–23; Big Cities, 34–35

DAILY SUCCESS PREDICTORS
for Adequate Yearly Progress

Monitor Progress and Corrective Feedback

Phonics
Check Word Reading, *12o*
Spiral REVIEW Phonics

Fluency
Check High-Frequency Words, *15a*
Spiral REVIEW High-Frequency Words